"As he has taught the Greek text of Galatians for more than thirty-five years, T. David Gordon's *Promise, Law, Faith* represents the fruit of this labor. Focusing on the meaning of the 'law' in Galatians, he attempts to give a critique of both the New Perspective and the traditional (Lutheran, Protestant) views, thus creating a middle road between them. Though one may not agree with all of Gordon's views, it cannot be denied that he has defended them well and made a very good case for this 'middle road.' Not only is this book based on outstanding exegesis and biblical-theological work, Gordon is also an engaging writer who does not lack wit. This is a significant contribution to scholarship on Galatians, and anyone teaching, writing, or preaching on Galatians needs to read it. Indeed, it is a *tour de force*. A special bonus is the approximately seventy-five-page excursus on 'the righteousness (δικαιοσύνη) of God.' I hope we will receive more works of such quality from T. David Gordon's pen."

—**G. K. Beale**
J. Gresham Machen Chair and Research Professor of New Testament
Westminster Theological Seminary, Philadelphia, Pennsylvania

"With his signature verve and vigor, T. David Gordon cuts a path between common Protestant and New Perspective readings of Paul's Epistle to the Galatian churches. While all may not agree with his case, Gordon definitely will cause readers to think, reread their Hebrew and Greek texts, and carefully weigh his arguments. Any serious student of Galatians will profit immensely from Gordon's exegetical spadework and his decades-long study of the New Testament."

—**J. V. Fesko**
Professor of Systematic and Historical Theology
Reformed Theological Seminary, Jackson, Mississippi

"T. David Gordon's exploration of Galatians in *Promise, Law, Faith* charts a distinctive course between traditional Protestant interpretations of Paul and the so-called New Perspective. His covenantal reading of the letter is compelling and merits serious consideration for every student of Pauline theology. He writes with a clarity, liveliness, and humor that are rare in academic books. I encourage seasoned scholars and students alike to read this important work."

—**Sean M. McDonough**
Professor of New Testament
Gordon-Conwell Theological Seminary, South Hamilton, Massachusetts

PROMISE,
LAW,
FAITH

PROMISE, LAW, FAITH

Covenant-Historical Reasoning in Galatians

T. DAVID GORDON

HENDRICKSON ACADEMIC

Promise, Law, Faith: Covenant-Historical Reasoning in Galatians

© 2019 T. David Gordon

Hendrickson Publishers Marketing, LLC
P. O. Box 3473
Peabody, Massachusetts 01961-3473
www.hendrickson.com

ISBN 978-1-68307-208-9

Printed in the United States of America

First Printing — August 2019

Library of Congress Control Number: 2019941945

This volume is dedicated to the memory of my doctoral advisor,
Paul J. Achtemeier, whose thorough scholarship, judicious reasoning, collegial
nature, love for family, and personal encouragements I will never forget.

"I have protracted my work till most of those whom I wished to please have sunk
into the grave, and success and miscarriage are empty sounds: I therefore dismiss
it with frigid tranquility, having little to fear or hope from censure or from praise."

Samuel Johnson, Preface to his *Dictionary*

.

Contents

Acknowledgments

Many years ago, my doctoral advisor (Paul J. Achtemeier) suggested that someone study the relation of law and covenant in Paul's thought. While I did not pursue that avenue during my doctoral studies (pursuing instead the closely related matter of Paul's understanding of the law), the thought was well planted, and I have been intrigued with the question for three decades now. In addition to Professor Achtemeier's influence, I must mention my former colleague at Gordon-Conwell Theological Seminary, the late Meredith G. Kline. Professor Kline's study of ancient Near Eastern covenant treaties, and the bearing of such on biblical studies, has stimulated the thinking of all who have known his work. He also has stimulated my interest in the relation of law and covenant, whether in the Bible generally or in Paul's letters specifically. Whether Professors Achtemeier or Kline would be satisfied or instructed with the results of my pursuing this line of questioning, I may never know; but I do know that I am grateful to them both for stimulating the pursuit.

I should also herein acknowledge my appreciation to those students at Gordon-Conwell Theological Seminary, Westminster Theological Seminary, Covenant Theological Seminary, and Grove City College who have studied Galatians and/or Paul with me since 1984. They dutifully fulfilled their assigned tasks in the scheme of things by playing "stump the teacher" with untiring, if not always equally cogent, zeal. (One student objected to my views on the ground that he couldn't find them represented in the current commentaries. I asked him if he would believe them if I wrote a commentary, and he looked even more puzzled than before.) In the process, they have caused me to modify and more carefully express a number of my thoughts about the book of Galatians. Just as importantly, not one has come even close to shaking my confidence in my fundamental perspective (regarding the problem at Galatia[1] or the nature of Paul's reasoning therein). Considering how motivated they ordinarily are to rebut the cockamamie hypotheses of their professors, their inability to shake my confidence in my position has, in fact, enhanced that confidence.

I would like to express appreciation to the Grove City College Board of Trustees and administration for granting me a sabbatical leave for the fall semester in the academic year of 2012–13, which enabled me to begin working on this project. I also wish to express my gratitude to Brian Hutchinson and Ethan Magness for a decade of conversations about Galatians, the dominant Protestant perspective on Paul, and the New Perspective on Paul. Those conversations both sharpened my viewpoints and encouraged my efforts. I am extremely grateful to my former colleague at Gordon-Conwell Theological Seminary, Gregory K. Beale, who—when I asked if he might glance at the opening and concluding chapters—read the entire manuscript carefully and offered numerous suggestions for improvement.

---

1. Cf. my "The Problem at Galatia," *Interpretation* 41 (January 1987): 32–43.

Finally, I wish to acknowledge gratitude to several editors at Hendrickson Publishers—Patricia Anders, Tirzah Frank, and Jonathan Kline—for slogging through a fairly technical manuscript that almost blinded them at some moments, and perhaps made them yearn to be blind at others. None of those who have assisted me are responsible for the many imperfections that remain in the manuscript.

Introduction

E. P. Sanders has served the field of Pauline scholarship well in recent decades.[1] Aspects of his theses have not enjoyed universal popularity, yet he has stimulated the field to reevaluate Paul in a profoundly fresh way. Whether Palestinian Judaism was precisely as Sanders described it, or perhaps more "variegated,"[2] is now somewhat irrelevant to Pauline studies. The important contribution is this: We no longer assume, prima facie, that Paul's "problem" with the law was exclusively or primarily due to an alleged meritorious abuse thereof. While Professor James Dunn, referring primarily to Sanders, may have been optimistic in referring to a *single* "New Perspective on Paul," I think it is fair to say that there are many new perspectives on Paul that have arisen from Sanders's raising the question of whether there may not be more to Paul's polemic with the law than merely meritorious legalism. Indeed, it is easy to agree with Professor I. Howard Marshall's assessment that many of the newer interpretations need not be perceived as mutually exclusive.[3]

At least in two areas, if I read the literature optimistically, consensus may be developing in the study of Galatians that undergirds much of what I am attempting to accomplish. First is the *lexical* observation that ὁ νόμος in Paul's vocabulary ordinarily refers to the Mosaic law,[4] or even more precisely to the Mosaic covenant itself (by

---

1. See especially *Paul and Palestinian Judaism: A Comparison of Patterns of Religion* (Philadelphia: Fortress, 1978). Among the early unfavorable reviews, cf. Anthony J. Saldarini, review of *Paul and Palestinian Judaism: A Comparison of Patterns of Religion*, by E. P. Sanders, *Journal of Biblical Literature* 98, no. 2 (June 1979): 299–300, 302–3; and Jacob Neusner, "Comparing Judaisms," review of *Paul and Palestinian Judaism: A Comparison of Patterns of Religion*, by E. P. Sanders, *History of Religions* 18, no. 2 (November 1978): 177–91. I am largely sympathetic with the criticisms of Saldarini and Neusner. I do not believe Sanders achieved his goal of a holistic comparison of religions; I do not believe he evaded or avoided "imposing" the systematic categories of one religion on another, and I believe his "getting in and staying in" paradigm does not work at all in describing the Sinai covenant, a covenant the Israelites resisted from the outset (see my later excursus, "Getting Out and Staying Out: Israel's Dilemma at Sinai"). Despite these defects, however, Sanders did shift the burden of proof on the question of legalism in Second Temple Judaism, and this has benefited Pauline scholarship substantially.

2. D. A. Carson, P. T. O'Brien, and Mark A. Seifrid, *Justification and Variegated Nomism*, 2 vols. (Grand Rapids: Baker, 2004).

3. I. Howard Marshall, "Salvation, Grace and Works in the Later Writings in the Pauline Corpus," *New Testament Studies* 42, no. 3 (July 1996): 356–57. Cf. also Guy Prentiss Walters, *Justification and the New Perspectives on Paul: A Review and Response* (Phillipsburg, NJ: P&R, 2004).

4. I say "refers to," because I believe the *referent* of ὁ νόμος is ordinarily the Sinai covenant. But referential meaning and semantic meaning are not the same thing; all figurative language skillfully interweaves both the referential meaning and the semantic meaning, as when Jesus called Herod a "fox" (ἀλώπηξ, Luke 13:32). In this case, the referent of "fox" was manifestly Herod, but the term "fox" does not, semantically, mean "Herod." So also, when Paul employs ὁ νόμος, the ordinary Greek term for "law" (and the ordinary LXX rendering of *Torah*), he does so skillfully, by employing the synecdoche to *refer* to a covenant characterized by law-giving.

synecdoche, since the covenant is so characterized by law-giving).[5] So Frank J. Matera suggests regarding Galatians 3:17, "The Law (*nomos*) is the Mosaic Law given to the Israelites on Mount Sinai."[6] Second is the now-common *historical* observation that Paul's difficulty with the law is motivated largely, primarily, or even exclusively by the reality that the law segregated Jews from Gentiles.

Exegetical progress sometimes results from new discoveries in archaeology, history, lexicography, text criticism, grammar, or semantics. Just as often, exegetical progress results from a different paradigm, a different way of construing the available data (as argued in Thomas Kuhn's *The Structure of Scientific Revolutions*). If exegetical progress is made from my labor, it will not be due to my discovering much new about grammar, lexicography, the transmission of the New Testament text, or any other technical matter. Rather, it will be due to my raising slightly different questions than have been raised in the past. The paradigm from which Paul (indeed, the Bible) was interpreted for many years was largely dominated by systematic theological considerations of an *ordo salutis* nature. In the twentieth century, Paul's students profited greatly by complementing such

---

5. Douglas J. Moo, "'Law,' 'Works of the Law,' and Legalism in Paul," *Westminster Theological Journal* 45 (1983): 73–100. I will develop this argument in more detail later. I do not think the full weight of this lexical observation has been manifested in Pauline studies; to the contrary, I hope this work will contribute to that very end. But at least the older conceptions of "law" as either "God's moral will" or (worse) "legalism" have lost much/most of their steam, and "law" is increasingly perceived as the Mosaic legislation in its entirety, though I do not believe this has yet become the majority position. Stephen Westerholm says that, in Galatians, it is "the Sinaitic legislation" and "the divine requirements imposed upon Israel at Mount Sinai." Westerholm, *Perspectives Old and New on Paul: The "Lutheran" Paul and His Critics* (Grand Rapids: Eerdmans, 2004), 301, 304, focuses on the stipulations of the covenant, though not the covenant itself. But to date I find no one arguing as I will throughout that νόμος is a synecdoche for the Sinai covenant in its entirety. So, while I am gratified that scholars increasingly perceive that νόμος is a Sinaitic reality, I will be even more gratified when they recognize that in Galatians it refers to that covenant in its entirety, including its stipulations, its segregating of Israel from the nations, and its threatened cursings for noncompliance. I also recognize there is ongoing discussion about what constitutes "synecdoche," compared to what constitutes "metonymy." Either term could work here, and it is even possible that synecdoche is a subcategory of metonymy. As I understand it, "synecdoche" is a proper description for, among other things, when an important part of a thing is spoken of as the thing itself (*Pars pro toto*). Certainly, Torah is at the center of the Sinai covenant and is therefore an extremely important part thereof. Further, "metonymy" can be employed merely to indicate something that is tangentially related to a thing to refer to the thing (e.g., "the Oval Office" to refer to the executive branch of government), whereas Torah is at the very center of the Sinai covenant—so central that the ark that contains the tablets is called the "ark of the covenant." Finally, it is not at all uncommon for Galatian interpreters to use "synecdoche" to describe how Paul uses πίστις in Gal. 4:4 ("when faith came"). For these imperfect (and debatable) reasons, I have chosen to employ "synecdoche" rather than "metonomy," which I will do consistently, while recognizing that the final word on the best description of these figures of speech has surely not been rendered here.

6. Frank J. Matera, *Galatians*, Sacra Pagina Series, ed. Daniel J. Harrington, no. 9 (Collegeville, MN: Liturgical Press, 2007), 127n17. Similarly, according to Heikki Räisänen, *nomos* "refers to the authoritative tradition of Israel, anchored in the revelation on Sinai, which separates the Jews from the rest of mankind." Räisänen rightly recognizes the relation to Sinai and to the revelation that segregates the Jews from Gentiles, though he does not expressly take it, as I do, to be a synecdoche for the Sinai covenant itself. Cf. Räisänen, *Paul and the Law* (Philadelphia: Fortress, 1983), 16.

studies with biblical-theological or redemptive-historical considerations of a *historia salutis* nature (Geerhardus Vos, Herman N. Ridderbos, Werner Georg Kümmel, Ernst Käsemann, et al.). Closely related to the latter, though different from it in precise detail, is what I will endeavor to encourage here: a consideration of those matters that might be called *historia testamentorum*, the history of God's various covenanting acts. This work attempts to understand Galatians as Geerhardus Vos recommended for understanding the entire Bible:

> The Bible is, as it were, conscious of its own organism; it feels, what we cannot always say of ourselves, its own anatomy. The principle of successive *Berith*-makings (Covenant-makings), as marking the introduction of new periods, plays a large role in this, and should be carefully heeded.[7]

The difference between salvation-historical/redemptive-historical categories and covenant-historical categories is this: The former (salvation/historical) narrates those particular events or deeds that are judged to be significant in the overall work of redemption, overcoming what is lost in the first Adam and restored in the last. But the latter (covenant-historical) narrates the successive covenant-administrations by which God binds himself to his people (and vice versa). Thus the Exodus is a significant salvation-historical event, but it introduces, by itself, no covenantal change. Not until the event at Mount Sinai is a covenant instituted that relates Yahweh to those he delivered from Egypt in a particular way. Similarly, the incarnation is a monumental act in salvation history—so much so, that Eastern and Western Christendom sometimes debate whether it is equal in prominence with the Passion. But the incarnation, significant enough as it is in redemptive-historical terms, does not, by itself, inaugurate any change in covenant-administration. The incarnate Christ was born "under the Law," under the Sinai covenant-administration, and he lived out his earthly existence submissive to its stipulations, teaching his followers to do the same (Matt. 5:17–21; 23:1–3). But later, a "new covenant" was inaugurated in his sacrificial death: "This cup is the new covenant in my blood" (1 Cor. 11:25; cf. Luke 22:20). Each successive covenant-administration institutes some new practices (some sacramental) and stipulations. Abraham's descendants were not expressly required to offer animal sacrifices until the Sinai covenant was administered; after that, they were. Similarly (and importantly, in Galatians), his descendants were not required to be ritually or dietarily separate from the Gentiles until the Sinai covenant was administered; after that, they were.

It is common—and helpful—for students of Galatians to be cognizant of redemptive-historical categories. Don Garlington, for instance, refers to the difficult statement that ὁ δὲ νόμος οὐκ ἔστιν ἐκ πίστεως in Galatians 3:12, and rightly says that "the law and faith belong to distinctly different historical realms: the former does not occupy the same turf in the salvation-historical continuum as the latter."[8] Similarly, Moisés Silva, also commenting on Galatians 3:12, says, "In other words, to say that 'the law' is not of faith is to claim that the Sinaitic Covenant belongs to a different redemptive-historical

---

7. Geerhardus Vos, *Biblical Theology of the Old and New Testaments* (Grand Rapids: Eerdmans, 1948), 16.

8. Don Garlington, "Role Reversal and Paul's Use of Scripture in Galatians 3.10–13," *Journal for the Study of the New Testament*, no. 65 (March 1, 1997): 101.

epoch than the gospel."[9] Such comments take us significantly beyond the more static systematic theological understanding that has characterized so much of Galatians interpretation in the past. But they do not go quite far enough in being expressly *covenant*-historical; Paul's reasoning is not merely that the Abrahamic (or new) covenant is located at a different season of salvation history than the Sinai covenant; his point is that these covenants *themselves* have different characteristics. The Abrahamic covenant is characterized by *believing* that God will fulfill several remarkable pledges; the Sinai covenant is characterized by *doing* the things the same God commanded on the tablets of the covenant. In this sense, the law is not of faith (ὁ δὲ νόμος οὐκ ἔστιν ἐκ πίστεως). The Sinai covenant is not essentially characterized in the same manner as the Abrahamic covenant; whatever its proposed benefits are, they will not arrive (as the benefits proposed to Abraham did) by believing, but by *doing* the things commanded.

In Galatians, Paul traces how three of these covenant administrations differed in their stipulations and especially in those stipulations that related Jew to Gentile. My approach greatly appreciates that of Ben Witherington III but goes further. Witherington says,

> As this commentary develops it should become clearer all the time that Paul does indeed operate with a two- or perhaps even three-covenant theology (depending on whether one sees the new covenant as the fulfillment of the Abrahamic one and therefore part of it, or as fulfillment without being part of it).[10]

My approach (disclosed in the title, *Promise, Law, Faith*) is self-consciously tri-covenantal throughout (and there is no "perhaps" in my poly-covenantalism). In Galatians, Paul does not provide a complete history of God's covenanting. He says nothing expressly about any covenant with Adam,[11] nothing about any covenants with Noah (whether antediluvian or postdiluvian), nothing about any covenant with Phinehas to be a priesthood, and nothing about a covenant with David to build God a house.[12] Paul's exclusive covenantal interest in this letter is with three covenants and how they are like and unlike one another (especially in terms of the relation of Jew and Gentile). Obviously, as a minister of the new covenant, he is interested in the new covenant. Additionally, because of the insistence of the Judaizers at Galatia on the observance of the stipulations of the Mosaic covenant, Paul wishes to discuss the relation of these two. However, he finds it expedient to do so in terms of a third covenant (though temporally prior to the other two): the Abrahamic. Indeed, Paul argues that the new covenant and the Abrahamic covenant are profoundly similar in kind; while the Sinai covenant

---

9. Moisés Silva, "Abraham, Faith, and Works: Paul's Use of Scripture in Galatians 3:6–14," *Westminster Theological Journal* 63, no. 2 (September 1, 2001): 265.

10. Ben Witherington III, *Grace in Galatia: A Commentary on Paul's Letter to the Galatians* (New York: T & T Clark, 2004), 247.

11. Though he surely does at Rom. 5:12–21 and throughout much of 1 Cor. 15.

12. This was earlier observed by Charles Talbert: "Of some of these covenants Paul makes no mention: Noah, Phinehas, Joshua, Josiah, Ezra. The covenant with David is not central to Paul's thought. . . . Three of the covenants of his Bible receive significant attention in Paul's letters: (1) the covenant with Abraham, (2) the covenant through Moses, and (3) the new covenant of Jeremiah 31." Cf. "Paul on the Covenant," *Review and Expositor* 84, no. 2 (Spring 1987): 300.

is different from these two in some important ways.[13] There are also some similarities between Abrahamic/new on the one hand and Sinai on the other, but Paul does not mention them in this letter because his concern is local, practical, and polemical. Therefore, one could derive a somewhat distorted picture of Paul's thought by reading Galatians alone; the Roman letter, being less polemical, provides an occasion in which Paul's statements about the Sinai administration are somewhat more favorable (because more comprehensive and less polemical) than they are in Galatians.

It is no part of my thesis to attempt to determine when Paul first arrived at his covenant-historical reasoning. I leave it to Hans Hübner, Seyoon Kim, Francis Watson,[14] et al., to trace the development (if any) of Paul's thinking. Whether Paul's understanding of the Abrahamic and Sinai covenants changed after Damascus or not is also no part of my thesis (though surely his understanding of the new covenant did). My thesis is concerned to demonstrate that the reasoning in the letter itself, regardless of when or where it was originally derived, was/is covenant-historical: Paul addressed issues in the new covenant community in light of the realities associated with two previous covenants—one with Abraham and one with the Israelites at Sinai.

---

13. It has become almost commonplace now for students of the Old Testament to recognize two different kinds of treaties in the ancient Near East: the land-grant treaty and the suzerainty treaty. If my understanding of Paul is correct, he also recognizes this difference and that the Abrahamic covenant is structurally more similar to the land-grant treaty, whereas the Sinai covenant is more similar to the suzerainty treaty. The new covenant, if indeed my reading of Paul is correct, constitutes the third aspect of the land-grant treaty to Abraham, the aspect in which Abraham's "seed" would become a blessing to all nations. Cf. G. E. Mendenhall, "Covenant Forms in Israelite Tradition," *The Biblical Archaeologist* 17, no. 3 (1954): 50–76; John Bright, *A History of Israel*, 2nd ed. (Philadelphia: Westminster, 1959), 146–51; John Sailhamer, *Biblical Prophecy* (Grand Rapids: Eerdmans, 1998), 35; and Meredith G. Kline, *The Structure of Biblical Authority* (Grand Rapids: Eerdmans, 1972). Some critics of both Mendenhall and Kline have argued that the ANE treaties were more fluid and that their forms permitted more than an either/or: that is, either land-grant or suzerainty. Whether this criticism is fair to Mendenhall or Kline, I could not say. For my purposes, it is enough to comment that the Abrahamic covenant is structurally more similar to the land-grant treaty, whereas the Sinai covenant is more similar to the suzerainty treaty. For my purposes, neither needs to be identical to its closest ANE counterpart; it is enough to indicate that ANE treaties were not all identical. That is, the term *berith* in OT literature (and its cognates in the surrounding ANE) is not determinative for the content of a given covenant. We know from the treaties of the nations around Israel that "treaty" can be employed for a variety of different purposes. This alone should create suspicion about any monocovenantalist assertions (more on that later). Some treaties are similar to some treaties and dissimilar to others; the fact that they are both designated as *berith* determines little or nothing about their content. That is, I do *not at all* find what John Murray claimed: "From the beginning of God's disclosures to men in terms of covenant we find a unity of conception which is to the effect that a divine covenant is a sovereign administration of grace and of promise." Murray, *The Covenant of Grace: A Biblico-Theological Study* (London: Tyndale, 1954), 19. The mere fact that God discloses himself "in terms of covenant" says nothing itself, in and of itself, about what those terms will be. A *berith* may or may not be gracious, and it may or may not be promissory. Only its particular terms, disclosed in the treaty document itself, can disclose what the particular terms are.

14. Hans Hübner, *Law in Paul's Thought*, trans. James C. G. Greig (Edinburgh: T & T Clark, 1984); Seyoon Kim, *Paul and the New Perspective: Second Thoughts on the Origin of Paul's Gospel* (Grand Rapids: Eerdmans, 2002); and Francis B. Watson, *Paul, Judaism and the Gentiles Beyond the New Perspective*, rev. ed. (Grand Rapids: Eerdmans, 2007).

In the following, building upon what others have argued recently, I will attempt to persuade the reader that Paul's argument in Galatians is not in the first place (if at all) designed to correct systematic theological errors of an *ordo salutis* nature (i.e., faith as the instrument of justification). Rather, his argument in Galatians is designed to correct implicit[15] errors of a *historia testamentorum* nature (whether Israel's Messiah has brought blessings only to the members of the Sinai covenant community or also to individuals from all nations; and what this means for observing the stipulations, especially the segregating/marking[16] stipulations, of the Sinai covenant). Paul's argument in Galatians is covenant-historical; he corrects misbehaviors (requiring observance of the Mosaic law) associated with the new covenant by describing the relation of that new covenant to two covenants that were instituted before it, the Abrahamic and the Sinaitic.[17] The error of the Galatian community resides in its (practical, if not theoretical) insistence that the Sinai covenant is everlasting, with the logical corollary that the stipulations of that covenant, including those that distinguish one ethnic group from another, are also everlasting. Effectively, Paul argues that the new covenant is not merely a new reality associated with the Sinai covenant; rather, it is a covenant in its own right that displaces the temporary, Christ-anticipating, Israel-threatening, and Gentile-excluding Sinai covenant.

Throughout this work, I will argue that Paul conceived the Sinai covenant as "temporary," which could be misunderstood by some. In employing the term "temporary," I mean that the covenant itself, made at Sinai with the Israelites, governed the children of Abraham from that time until Christ came. I do not mean that its instructive benefits were merely temporary; to the contrary, both Jews and Christians continue to find themselves instructed by the realities of that covenant. John the Baptist, for instance, could not have referred intelligibly to Jesus as "the lamb of God, who takes away the world's sins" (John 1:29) had there never been a Passover lamb or other Jewish sacrifices. The Epistle to the Hebrews largely consists of explaining the work of Christ in terms of those theological types that antedated him and created a theological matrix by which his person and work were comprehensible. We continue to benefit from what

---

15. I say "implicit" because the actual problem at Galatia may have been entirely of a practical nature, to wit: requiring Gentiles to observe the Mosaic marking ceremonies. But this practical error reflects an implicit misapprehension of the priority of the Abrahamic to the Sinai covenant, and so Paul argues covenant-historically to straighten the matter out.

16. I am appreciative of Prof. Dunn's many observations about the "marking" laws in the Sinai covenant and, for substance, I agree with what he says about them (though not with his precise discussion of ἔργα νόμου). However, I am as likely to call them "segregating" stipulations as I am "marking" stipulations, because they not only marked Israel as distinctive, but they also intentionally segregated it from the other nations. I don't believe Prof. Dunn would disagree with this at all, because this is largely what he means by "marking" ordinances.

17. As I have observed elsewhere, much confusion in Pauline studies pertains to people referring to the realities of the pre-Christian revelation as "the covenant," rather than the "covenants." The canonical Old Testament contains the record of many covenants, not a single "covenant." The failure to distinguish them, especially the failure to distinguish the Abrahamic from the Mosaic, leads to many confusions. Cf. my "Reflections on Auburn Theology," in *By Faith Alone: Answering the Challenges to the Doctrine of Justification*, ed. Gary L. W. Johnson and Guy P. Waters (Wheaton, IL: Crossway, 2006), 113–25; and my "Confusion about the Law in Paul," in *Justified: Modern Reformation Essays on the Doctrine of Justification*, ed. Ryan Glomsrud and Michael S. Horton (Escondido, CA: Modern Reformation, 2010), 33–39.

we learned from the Sinai covenant. But that covenant itself, made with the Israelites, came *after* the Abrahamic covenant and *before* the new covenant (and ended therewith). The covenant itself was therefore temporary, even though its typological instructions continue to benefit us today. Some years from now, I will pay the last payment on my house and my mortgage contract will then end, because it is a temporary contract. I will still benefit from the contract, because I will still live in the home. But I will no longer have any obligation to that covenant or its requirements; neither I nor anyone else will be obligated to it.

1. Why Not Covenant-*Theological*? Why Covenant-*Historical*?

Some may wonder why I do not describe Paul's reasoning in the Galatian letter as covenant-theological. I could do so, and if one did so, the explanation could work reasonably well. But "covenant-historical" is better suited to Galatians, because so many of Paul's statements are of a temporal nature (which I will discuss later), where he reminds them that the Abrahamic covenant antedated the Sinai covenant by 430 years and thus temporalized/relativized the Sinai administration (Gal. 3:17). In this letter, Paul conceived the Sinai covenant as a temporary, provisional covenant-administration that governed between the other two covenants; it governed *after* the Abrahamic covenant and *before* the new covenant. The temporal analogies Paul employed to describe the tutelage of the Sinai covenant ("guardians," "managers," "trustees") all point to this temporary/provisional nature of the Sinai covenant; and to understand Paul, we must adjust our thinking to his thoroughly *historical* reasoning.

It may be helpful to entertain the possibility that the problem at Galatia may have been entirely practical and not theoretical at all. That is, in practice the Galatian Judaizers required the participants in the new covenant to observe the rites and ordinances of the Mosaic covenant. We do not know what their theoretical rationale for this practice was, and perhaps it is unnecessary to speculate further. Paul considered the practice to be inconsistent with the theoretical realities of the new covenant, but it was the practice itself, not necessarily the theory (theories?) behind it, that was the problem. That is, contrary to nearly all previous interpretations of the book of Galatians, we might consider the possibility that, for Paul, some practices are wrong in themselves, regardless of the theoretical foundations behind them.[18]

Theoretical foundations are sometimes implicit rather than explicit; and it is true that the implicit foundation to the Galatian error was that, in some sense or senses, the Sinai covenant (and its stipulations) was eternal. This tendency, at an implicit level, to regard the Mosaic covenant and/or its stipulations as eternal, is still with us and enshrined in the confession of my own tradition, the Westminster Confession of Faith. In chapter 19:1, the divines at Westminster affirmed that God "gave to Adam a law." In the next section, 19:2, they said, "This law, after his fall, continued to be a perfect rule of righteousness; and, as such, was delivered by God upon Mount Sinai, in ten commandments." While not explicitly saying that the Mosaic law was eternal,

---

18. Paul corrected the sexual behavior of the individual in 1 Cor. 5 without any commentary on whatever doctrinal implications might have either informed it or resulted from it.

the Westminster Confession appears to have implied that the Mosaic law had, in some senses, been published first in the garden and that it was "perfect." So, if after sixteen centuries of the Common Era, Christian confessional literature tends to regard the Mosaic covenant as eternal, we can be patient with the fact that perhaps some first-century Jewish Christians had a similar misunderstanding.[19]

For whatever theoretical reasons, then, the practical reality was that Gentiles were being required to observe those very Mosaic practices that had been designed to exclude them and to protect the Israelites from intermarriage and corruption *by* them. Those very stipulations of the Mosaic covenant that had been designed to preserve Israel as a "peculiar people," distinct from and indeed separate from the nations of the world, were being required of members of those nations. But for Paul (though unlike the Galatians or the Westminster Assembly), the stipulations of a covenant cannot simply be lifted from their covenantal context; they are part and parcel *of* that covenant. If we still observe the Gentile-excluding stipulations of the Mosaic covenant, if we still regard the nations as unclean, then the promises to Abraham that his "Seed" would bless all the nations appears not to have been fulfilled. On the other hand, if the promise to bless the nations through Abraham's Seed *has* been fulfilled, then there is no longer any purpose for the covenant administration that excluded those nations. Far from leading them away from faith in Abraham's God, such Gentiles believe in Abraham's God also.

Paul's thinking in Galatians is also deeply *historia salutis*, as well as pervasively eschatological.[20] The reader will quickly discover my dependence upon those twentieth-century interpretations of Paul that have (rightly) disclosed the pervasively eschatological nature of his theological conceptions (including, but not limited to, his eschatological understanding of the Spirit, his eschatological conception of justification, and his eschatological understanding of Abraham's promised blessings to the nations).[21] Thus, in introducing somewhat more overtly the category of *historia testamentorum*, it is not in any way my intention to diminish the importance of *historia salutis* categories in the deeper substructure of Paul's thought. Rather, it is designed to facilitate understanding how it is that Paul reasons about the new covenant realities in light of two previous covenants: the Abrahamic and the Mosaic covenants.

---

19. And yes, I am suggesting that the problem at Galatia may have had as many analogies to my own Reformed and Protestant tradition as it did to medieval Roman Catholic practices. It is within my own tradition, for instance, that "Theonomy" has arisen—a movement among conservative Reformed communions that teaches that the civil laws of Moses are obligatory upon all, even non-theocratic nations and cultures. The tendency, therefore, to be unwilling to let go of the Sinai covenant when it is replaced by the new covenant is a tendency that has contemporary Reformed and Protestant representation, not merely medieval Catholic representation.

20. Cf. Moisés Silva, "Eschatology in Galatians," *Explorations in Exegetical Method: Galatians as a Test Case* (Grand Rapids: Baker, 1996), 169–88.

21. I recognize that "eschatological" is not, for some, as appropriate a term as "apocalyptic." For my purposes, however, the terms are essentially interchangeable, even though I acknowledge that the eschatology of the Hebrew Bible, for instance, does not always employ apocalyptic language. Apocalyptic is always eschatological, though eschatology is not always apocalyptic. The self-consciously apocalyptic readings of Paul are surely due largely to the work of J. C. Beker, *Paul the Apostle: The Triumph of God in Life and Thought* (Philadelphia: Fortress, 1980). Among recent apocalyptic approaches to Galatians, cf. J. Louis Martyn, *Galatians: A New Translation with Introduction and Commentary* (New York: Doubleday, 1997).

In a variety of ways, the new covenant is profoundly and pervasively eschatological, and it would require an additional monograph to demonstrate how eschatological the "new covenant" was conceived by Jeremiah even before Paul. While I cannot do justice to the relationship between "new covenant" and eschatology in this monograph, I mention it here because any emphasis on eschatology will eventually lead to an appreciation of covenant-historical reasoning and vice versa. Consider just the expression "the days are coming" from Jeremiah—an expression that does not merely appear in verse 31: "when I will make a new covenant with the house of Israel and the house of Judah." Consider these also:

> "Behold, the days are coming, declares the LORD, when I will raise up for David a righteous Branch, and he shall reign as king and deal wisely, and shall execute justice and righteousness in the land." (Jer. 23:5)

> "For behold, days are coming, declares the LORD, when I will restore the fortunes of my people, Israel and Judah, says the LORD, and I will bring them back to the land that I gave to their fathers, and they shall take possession of it." (Jer. 30:3)

> "Behold, the days are coming, declares the LORD, when the city shall be rebuilt for the LORD from the tower of Hananel to the Corner Gate." (Jer. 31:38)

> "Behold, the days are coming, declares the LORD, when I will fulfill the promise I made to the house of Israel and the house of Judah." (Jer. 33:14)

> "Therefore, behold, the days are coming, declares the LORD, when I will cause the battle cry to be heard against Rabbah of the Ammonites; it shall become a desolate mound, and its villages shall be burned with fire; then Israel shall dispossess those who dispossessed him, says the LORD." (Jer. 49:2)

> "Therefore, behold, the days are coming when I will punish the images of Babylon; her whole land shall be put to shame, and all her slain shall fall in the midst of her." (Jer. 51:47)

> "Therefore, behold, the days are coming, declares the LORD, when I will execute judgment upon her images, and through all her land the wounded shall groan." (Jer. 51:52)

We observe, then, that the "new covenant" long before Paul was itself deeply eschatological—an aspect of the coming days—and I therefore appreciate those various approaches to his letters that are sensitive to such. My only point here is that my covenant-historical approach does not exclude the validity of the various eschatological interpretations; it augments them.

If we permit Paul to reason covenant-historically, and if we permit ourselves to reason with Paul, using the categories of *historia testamentorum*, we will find his argumentation in Galatians to be more accessible than if we approach Galatians by other categories. Indeed, even in the helpful discussions of Paul by James D. G. Dunn, the categories are not quite right, though they are close. Dunn's approach is essentially sociological: Jews and Gentiles are united in Christ and are not, therefore, to be separated by those "works of the law" that have this tendency. While this is close to the heart of the matter, it is unsatisfactory apart from *historia testamentorum* categories. The Jews and Gentiles were not separated merely because they were ethnic or geopolitical competitors or strangers. Xenophobia was not the entire problem, and plausibly was no part of the problem at all. They were separated by the terms of the Mosaic administration *itself*, not by ethnic or geopolitical suspicions or hatreds. To the contrary, the entire history of the Israelites from the time of the conquest on was one of being too "Gentile-friendly," as it were. It was Yahweh who insisted on the Israelites being separate, and the Israelites who did not desire to be so. It was Yahweh who insisted on destroying utterly the *am ha-aretz* during the conquest, and the Israelites who did not do so. It was Yahweh who proscribed intermarriage with the *am ha-aretz*, and the Israelites who insisted on doing so. So it was not ordinary sociological differences that separated Israel from the nations; it was the Mosaic *covenant* and its stipulations.

Paul's *historia testamentorum* categories are not always overt, and he only employs διαθήκη three times explicitly in Galatians.[22] Sometimes the terminology he employs for describing these realities can be misleading to us, unless we consider that he may be using terms in a particular manner. Note, for instance, the use of νόμος and ἐπαγγελία in Galatians 3:17:

> This is what I mean: the *law*, which came 430 years afterward, does not annul [ἀκυροῖ] a covenant previously ratified [προκεκυρωμένην] by God, so as to make the *promise* void.

Note here that whatever Paul means by law/νόμος on the one hand and promise/ἐπαγγελία on the other, they are separated by 430 years. To what, then, does he refer? He refers to two covenant-administrations ("does not annul a *covenant*"), one with Abraham, and one with Moses, separated by 430 years (which Stephen, in his speech, "rounded off" to 400 years). So Paul's actual reasoning in this verse, if I may paraphrase, is:

> This is what I mean: the Sinai covenant, which came 430 years afterward, does not annul a covenant previously ratified by God, so as to make the Abrahamic promissory covenant void.

That is, for Paul in Galatians, "law" is ordinarily a synecdoche for the Sinai covenant-administration, an administration characterized by law-giving.[23] And "promise" in the

---

22. The scarcity of διαθήκη in the NT is somewhat surprising. If we compare "covenant" to "law," for instance, we find in the Hebrew Bible 223 uses of תורה, but 289 uses of ברית. By the time of the Pseudepigrapha and the Greek New Testament, the vocabulary usage is quite different. In the Pseudepigrapha, there are 147 uses of νόμος and only 34 of διαθήκη. Similarly, in the NT there are 194 uses of νόμος and only 33 uses of διαθήκη. At first glance, some might suggest this means that covenantal thinking recedes from these bodies of literature. I suggest, by contrast, that covenantal thinking is so woven into the fabric of Jewish life by this point that it exists even where it is implicit. Further, sometimes this later literature uses νόμος as a synecdoche *for* the Sinai covenant, so covenantal thinking is present even where διαθήκη is not.

23. νόμος is not the only synecdoche Paul employs for the Sinai covenant-administration. In 2 Cor. 3, he employs τὸ γράμμα, because his controlling metaphor throughout that passage is that of "writing"—a figure he had himself derived from Jeremiah's referring to the new covenant as consisting of God writing the law on their hearts: ἐπιστολῶν . . . ἡ ἐπιστολὴ . . . ἐγγεγραμμένη . . . ἀναγινωσκομένη . . . ἐπιστολή . . . ἐν πλαξὶν λιθίναις . . . γράμματος . . . τὸ γὰρ γράμμα . . . ἐν γράμμασιν . . . τῇ ἀναγνώσει τῆς παλαιᾶς . . . ἡνίκα ἂν ἀναγινώσκηται Μωϋσῆς. And there, he also refers to the Sinai covenant-administration in its entirety: "Who has made us competent to be ministers of a new covenant, not of the letter but of the Spirit. . . . Now if the ministry of death [ἡ διακονία τοῦ θανάτου] . . . the ministry of the Spirit [ἡ διακονία τοῦ πνεύματος]. . . . For to this day, when they read the old covenant [ἐπὶ τῇ ἀναγνώσει τῆς παλαιᾶς διαθήκης] . . ."

same letter is ordinarily a synecdoche for the Abrahamic covenant-administration, a covenant characterized by promise-giving.[24]

In Galatians 3:17, this way of reading the matter is not difficult, and most people find it fairly straightforward, because of the temporal language of 430 years. But in other Galatians passages, Paul's reasoning is the same; yet to some minds it is less obviously so. "Law" still sounds to some like God's moral will (or legalism), and "promise" sounds to some like a vague theological category.[25] As I will argue in the appropriate places, the matter is even more complex, because Paul often uses a third synecdoche, "faith," to refer to the new covenant. He does so because it is a covenant characterized by faith in the dying-and-rising Christ. But this synecdoche evades us also, because to our minds "faith" is a reference to the human/existential act of trust (and indeed, Paul sometimes uses πίστις to refer to such in Galatians). So, then, ordinarily when Paul speaks in Galatians of promise, law, and faith, he means the Abrahamic covenant (characterized by promise-giving), the Sinai covenant (characterized by law-giving), and the new covenant (characterized by faith in the dying-and-rising Christ); but we (mistakenly) *hear* him speaking of general theological categories/realities of God's pledges, God's moral demands, and our faith in such a God.

That is, for Paul in Galatians, "law" is ordinarily, if not regularly, a synecdoche for the Sinai covenant-administration, an administration characterized by law-giving. And "promise" in the same letter is ordinarily a synecdoche for the Abrahamic covenant-administration, a covenant characterized by promise-giving. If this is so, then Paul's reasoning is much more covenantal than we may think at first blush, because the three uses of διαθήκη are not the only instances of his reasoning covenantally. The thirty-two uses of νόμος and the ten uses of ἐπαγγελία (ordinarily) are also covenantal in substance. And, if this is so, when discussing who "inherits" the promises of the Abrahamic covenant (employing κληρονομέω, κληρονομία, or κληρονόμος), we find six more occasions of covenantal reasoning, which is also the case when "ratify/annul" (κυρόω, ἀκυρόω, or προκυρόω) language is employed. Similarly, a statement such as Ὅσοι γὰρ ἐξ ἔργων νόμου εἰσίν, ὑπὸ κατάραν εἰσίν· ("all who are of works of the law are under a curse," Gal. 3:10) does not employ the lexical stock of διαθήκη, but the reasoning is covenantal: all who are parties to the Sinai covenant fall under its

---

So, when his purposes dictate, he is flexible enough to employ other synecdoches for the Sinai covenant-administration.

24. So Stephen Westerholm: "Paul proceeds by sharply distinguishing the promise God gave Abraham from the law delivered at Sinai"; and in a footnote to the word *promise*, Westerholm says, "Or 'covenant.'" *Perspectives Old and New on Paul*, 377.

25. Made even vaguer, as I suggested above, by those various interpreters who consistently and confusingly persist in referring to the pre-Christian covenants by the singular form, "the covenant." N. T. Wright, for instance, routinely refers to the realities of the pre-Christian era as "the covenant." An early work was titled *The Climax of the Covenant: Christ and the Law in Pauline Theology* (Philadelphia: Fortress, 1991), wherein Wright routinely speaks of God's δικαιοσύνη as "God's faithfulness to his covenant with Israel"; cf. *What Saint Paul Really Said: Was Paul of Tarsus the Real Founder of Christianity?* (Grand Rapids: Eerdmans, 1997), 97. Such language suggests that God made only one covenant with Israel, whereas Paul speaks of Israel's "covenants" in the plural at Rom. 9:4 and Gal. 4:24, or at Eph. 2:12. Wright is surely (and helpfully) correct in calling attention to the covenantal nature of the revelation in the Hebrew Bible; I merely wish he were more explicit about that revelation being *poly*-covenantal, which is a truth that he does not deny.

threatened curse sanctions (as the following quote in Galatians 3:10 from Deuteronomy 27:26 demonstrates, γέγραπται γὰρ ὅτι ἐπικατάρατος πᾶς ὃς οὐκ ἐμμένει πᾶσιν τοῖς γεγραμμένοις ἐν τῷ βιβλίῳ τοῦ νόμου τοῦ ποιῆσαι αὐτά).

A good example of this use of synecdoche for covenant-administrations is found in Gal. 3:23–25:

> Now before faith came [Πρὸ τοῦ δὲ ἐλθεῖν τὴν πίστιν],
>   we were held captive under the law [ὑπὸ νόμον],
>   imprisoned until the coming faith would be revealed.
> So then, the law was our guardian until Christ came [εἰς Χριστόν],
>   in order that we might be justified by faith.
> But now that faith has come [ἐλθούσης δὲ τῆς πίστεως],
>   we are no longer under a guardian.

Note here the contrast between the two temporal clauses: "before faith came" and "now that faith has come." At first, it may appear that Paul was employing ἡ πίστις to refer to the human, existential capacity to exercise trust. However, in 3:6–9, Paul had made it abundantly clear not only that Abraham had faith, but that he was therefore the father of all who also had faith:

> Just as Abraham "believed [ἐπίστευσεν] God, and it was counted to him as righteousness. . . ." Know then that it is those of faith [οἱ ἐκ πίστεως] who are the sons of Abraham. . . . So then, those who are of faith [οἱ ἐκ πίστεως] are blessed along with Abraham, the man of faith [τῷ πιστῷ Ἀβραάμ].

For Paul, faith, as an existential human capacity, even faith as the instrument of justification, had been here since Abraham. Therefore, when Paul in the same chapter says that "before faith came, we were . . . under the law," he must be using "faith" as a reference to the new covenant, so that "before faith came" and "before Christ came" have virtually the same meaning. Indeed, many commentators have routinely recognized that "before faith came" in this passage refers to the new covenant realities, and that "faith" here is a synecdoche for the new covenant or realities associated with it.[26] What they less frequently recognize, at least explicitly, is that ὁ νόμος here is a synecdochal reference to the Sinai covenant-administration, a point I will attempt to argue throughout.

Static systematic-theological categories are incapable of processing the deeply historical/temporal (and covenantal) reasoning in Galatians. Paul understands God to

---

26. E.g., J. B. Lightfoot, "Before the Dispensation of Faith Came," *The Epistle of St. Paul to the Galatians: With Introductions, Notes and Dissertations* (1865; repr., Zondervan, 1981), 148; Hans Dieter Betz, "Two Mythico-Historical Periods Are to Be Distinguished," *A Commentary on Paul's Letter to the Churches in Galatia*, Hermeneia—A Critical and Historical Commentary on the Bible (Philadelphia: Fortress, 1979), 175; F. F. Bruce, "The 'coming of faith' . . . may be understood both on the plane of salvation-history and in the personal experience of believers," *The Epistle to the Galatians: A Commentary on the Greek Text*, The New International Greek Text Commentary (Grand Rapids: Eerdmans, 1982), 181; Richard N. Longenecker, "The Christian Gospel as the Culmination of the Purposes of the Law," *Galatians*, Word Biblical Commentary, vol. 41 (Dallas: Word Books, 1990), 145; and J. Louis Martyn, "That multifaceted advent that has brought to a close the parenthetical period of the Law," *Galatians: A New Translation with Introduction and Commentary*, The Anchor Bible (New Haven, CT: Yale University Press, 2004), 362.

have unfolded his redemptive purposes in a series of covenants over time, and Paul's reasoning is therefore profoundly temporal. Notice, even in the stretch from 3:17 to 4:4, the frequency of temporal language (indicated in the following by added italics):

> This is what I mean: the law, which came 430 years *afterward*, does not annul a covenant *previously* ratified by God, so as to make the promise void. . . . Why then the law? It was *added* because of transgressions, *until* the offspring should come to whom the promise had been made. . . . Now *before* faith came, we were held captive under the law, imprisoned until the *coming* faith would be revealed. So then, the law was our guardian *until* Christ came, in order that we might be justified by faith. But *now* that faith has come, we are *no longer* under a guardian. . . . I mean that the heir, *as long as he is a child*, is no different from a slave, though he is the owner of everything, but he is under guardians and managers *until the date* set by his father. In the same way we also, *when* we were children, were enslaved to the elementary principles of the world. But *when* the fullness of time had come, God sent forth his Son.

Paul reasons here that things change with the introduction of each distinctive covenant and that, especially, the Sinai covenant was temporary. It had a beginning, 430 years after the Abrahamic, and an end, with the arrival of what was pledged to Abraham in the coming Christ/Seed and his new covenant. The problem, therefore, was neither with the Sinai covenant nor some alleged abuse thereof; the problem resided in regarding a temporary covenant (and/or its Gentile-excluding stipulations) as permanent.

I therefore understand why Paul's interpreters have not yet, in my judgment, correctly understood the Galatian letter. The purpose of this work is to promote the category of *historia testamentorum* to Paul's interpreters (I don't recall Vos using that exact expression), and to suggest that reading Paul's letter by means of such a category provides a more satisfactory reading. But sociological categories won't work, and the traditional systematic-theological categories won't work. They are not Paul's categories in Galatians, and his thought can no more fit into such categories than can square pegs fit into round holes.

If we return to a confessional standard that informed what Sanders called the "dominant Protestant" approach, consider again our earlier citation of portions of chapter 19 of the Westminster Confession of Faith. In 19:1, the Westminster Confession affirmed that God "gave to Adam a law, as a covenant of works, by which he bound him and all his posterity to personal, entire, exact, and perpetual obedience." In the next section, 19:2, it said: "This law, after his fall, continued to be a perfect rule of righteousness; and, as such, was delivered by God upon Mount Sinai, in ten commandments." Note, then, that Westminster 19 tended (and intended) to do with "law" the precise opposite of what Paul tended (and intended) to do with ὁ νόμος in the Galatian letter: Westminster 19 *eternalized* "law"; Paul *temporalized* ὁ νόμος. Westminster 19 thereby *absolutized* "law"; Paul *relativized* ὁ νόμος. Westminster 19 *universalized* "law"; Paul *localized* ὁ νόμος (as a covenant that excluded all nations but Israel). Paul not only did not drive ὁ νόμος back into Eden; he expressly argued that sin (Gen. 3) was in the world *before* ὁ νόμος (Rom. 5:13). And in Galatians, he argued that ὁ νόμος was relativized even by the Abrahamic administration, which antedated it by at least 430 years. Westminster 19 made "law" a universal reality, "by which he bound him [Adam] and *all his posterity* to personal, entire, exact, and perpetual obedience";[27] whereas Paul understood ὁ νόμος to be a covenant that excluded all but the Israelites.

Alongside this tendency in Westminster chapter 19, however, there was another use of "law" in the Westminster standards that comports closely with Paul's usage, as at WCF 25:2: "The visible church, which is also catholic or universal *under the gospel* (not confined to one nation, as before *under the law*), consists of all those throughout the world that profess the true religion; and of their children: and is the kingdom of the Lord Jesus Christ, the house and family of God, out of which there is no ordinary possibility of salvation" (parentheses theirs; emphases mine). This appears to be the same usage at WCF 7:5:

> This covenant was differently administered in the time of the law, and in the time of the gospel: *under the law*, it was administered by promises, prophecies, sacrifices, circumcision, the paschal lamb, and other types and ordinances delivered to the people of the Jews, all foresignifying Christ to come.

In passages that contain "under the law," "law" is a synecdoche by which that covenant-administration so characterized by law-giving is referred to by its central feature.[28] However, apart from the almost technical phrase "under the law" elsewhere in the Westminster Confession (and many Protestant confessions), "law," unless qualified in some other way, means God's moral will.

It is not surprising, then, that the "dominant Protestant" approach has had difficulty making good sense of Galatians.[29] It has been forced, as I say, to "read between the lines" of Galatians rather than read the lines themselves. It has been forced to invent a problem never expressly mentioned in the letter, and contrary to much/most of what the reliably dated and pertinent sources actually say. Not only has that approach mis-understood late Second Temple Judaism, it has sometimes projected its own use and understanding of "law" onto Paul's use of ὁ νόμος, which makes of the Galatian letter an utterly inexplicable puzzle. Until and unless interpreters grasp that in Galatians[30] ὁ

---

27. Westminster 19 also identified "the law" with what it called "the moral law," which "doth forever bind all" (WCF 19:5); whereas Paul argues throughout that ὁ νόμος did not oblige Father Abraham, who never knew of a reality that came 430 years later, that ὁ νόμος did not oblige the Galatians, that Peter's observance of its requirements was cowardly and hypocritical, and that "we are no longer under" the tutelage of ὁ νόμος (Gal. 3:25).

28. WCF 7:5; 8:4; 19:6 (twice); 20:1; 25:2, and Westminster Shorter Catechism 27.

29. As my citation of the Westminster Confession indicates, the "dominant approach" is not equal to the "Lutheran Paul" of which so many today complain. My Reformed confessional tradition is scarcely better than or different from the Lutheran confessional tradition on this point. Each employs "law" in a different way than Paul employed ὁ νόμος. I employ "dominant Protestant" approach as I believe E. P. Sanders did: *not* to describe any particular *confessional* tradition, but rather to describe a tendency, common among Protestants, to regard Palestinian Judaism as teaching a Pelagian soteriology. The various Protestant confessions render no opinion on first-century Judaism, so nothing confessional is at stake in the conversation (the term "Judaism" does not appear in the Westminster Confession, nor do the terms "legalistic" or "legalism"). To be sure, while N. T. Wright often makes sweeping statements of a condemnatory nature about the Protestant confessional tradition (though without ever citing particulars), E. P. Sanders did not.

30. And, in my judgment, elsewhere in his letters as well.

νόμος is ordinarily employed as a synecdoche for the particular and temporary treaty Yahweh made with the Israelites at Sinai 430 years after making unconditional pledges to Abraham, the Galatian letter will remain to us what the Soviet Union remained to Prime Minister Churchill: "a riddle, wrapped in a mystery, inside an enigma."[31]

I expect to encounter some objections to the thesis. I also anticipate, however, that they will not be due to my making idiosyncratic or risky conclusions of a grammatical, lexical, or historical nature. Rather, they will be due, largely, to other considerations arising from three entirely different directions. First, the post-Holocaust study of Paul's relation to the Jews and their covenant(s) is profoundly intent on discovering that Paul does not perceive Judaism and Christianity as being, in any significant way, different from each other.[32] In such an environment, it would be preferable for Paul to conclude that God has made in history only one covenant—one that embraces Jew and Gentile alike. Regrettably, such a conclusion is not possible (though the Abrahamic covenant pledged blessings *to* all the tribes of the earth). It will not arise from the available literature, and it will not fit well if imposed upon it. The Jews themselves had several covenants, not one, as Paul himself observed: "They are Israelites, and to them belong the adoption, the glory, *the covenants*" (αἱ διαθῆκαι, Rom. 9:4).

Second, some North American covenant theologians of the twentieth century (with a little help from the seventeenth-century's nomenclature of a single "covenant of grace") in their debates with dispensational theologians have adopted a biblical theology that is also (implicitly if not explicitly) monocovenantal, in their desire to avoid what they perceive to be the errors of American Dispensationalism.[33] Such, I would

---

31. Indeed, the element of truth in Heikki Räisänen's claim that Paul is simply inconsistent resides in the reality that neither the dominant Protestant approach nor the New Perspectives approach can make good sense of Paul's reasoning. Where I differ with Räisänen is that I believe a covenant-historical approach can relieve what he regards as an irreconcilable contradiction. Cf. his *Paul and the Law, Wissenschaftliche Untersuchungen zum Neuen Testament* 29 (Tübingen: Mohr-Siebeck, 1983).

32. Of the two things we must understand in order to perceive the New Perspective correctly, according to Peter Stuhlmacher, one is the attempt to address the Jewish-Christian dialogue in a manner that is fair to the Jewish party to the discussion: "We must also keep in mind the apparent goal of these authors to make a new beginning in Pauline interpretation, so as to free Jewish-Christian dialogue from improper accusations against the Jewish conversation partners." Cf. Peter Stuhlmacher, *Revisiting Paul's Doctrine of Justification: A Challenge to the New Perspective; With an Essay by Donald A. Hagner* (Downers Grove, IL: IVP Academic, 2001), 34. Stuhlmacher puts the matter mildly. Post-Holocaust, the motivation is not merely to be fair-minded; the motivation appears to be anti-anti-Semitic (not a typo; a neologism). Similarly, Francis Watson has said, "After Auschwitz, new language and new conceptualities would have to be found." *Paul, Judaism, and the Gentiles: Beyond the New Perspective*, rev. ed. (Grand Rapids: Eerdmans, 2007), 2. That is, especially in Europe and even more especially in Germany, Protestant interpreters are at understandable pains to say nothing that might give the appearance of anti-Semitism. And undoubtedly, Luther's strong law-gospel contrast appears to many to suggest a fundamental difference in *kind* between the religion of the Hebrew Bible and the religion of the New Testament—a difference in kind that might lead many to the belief that the first is inferior to the second. I intend to address this later in some concluding thoughts, but for now I simply wish to alert readers to how the post-Holocaust situation influences our interpretation of Paul.

33. Cf. esp. "John Murray's Mono-covenantalism," 118–24, in my "Reflections on Auburn Theology," in *By Faith Alone*, 113–25.

argue elsewhere, is contrary to the majority report of historic covenant theology, and it is surely contrary to Paul. "These are *two* covenants" (αὖται γάρ εἰσιν δύο διαθῆκαι, 4:24) cannot responsibly be construed to mean, "These are *one* covenant." If Paul's reasoning in Galatians addresses three specific covenants in terms of their distinctive features, then we will not be able to assess well his reasoning if we refer to all three, or even two of the three, as "the covenant."

Third, in the ongoing "faith-works" discussion (a discussion that has, in dogmatic history, both a Lutheran and an evangelical host), there are those for whom the categories of "faith" and "works" have never been covenantal, but theological and/or existential. It will quickly be evident that I think they use Pauline *terms* in a way that Paul himself did not. They tend to use "faith" and "works" abstractly, whereas Paul contrasts specifically "faith *in Christ*" with "works *of the Law*." Whether the *conclusions* they reach theologically, with their redefined terms, are true or Pauline is not a matter in which I have much publication interest; but I expect to encounter some resistance from them for my arguing for what I perceive to be a different definition of those terms.

To the reader, then, I offer a "covenant-historical" model for reading Galatians. I do not offer it on the ground that such a model solves all of the interpretive difficulties in the letter.[34] I merely offer it on the twofold premise that it solves difficulties that other models do not solve, and that it provides a method for reading the entire book without major difficulty or inconsistency. I assume that the test of any model is its comparative adequacy: Does it account for more of the available evidence and data than alternative models? If it does, it is to be preferred, at least until another model comes along more adequate to the task.

It should be evident that this volume is not a commentary on Galatians, at least in any ordinary sense. It is designed to explain the forest more than the trees and the trees only insofar as they explicate the forest.[35] It is an endeavor to explain the argument or thought of the letter and is unlike a commentary in this way (though it might be beneficial if such commentaries were occasionally written, and Charles Cousar's is to be commended on this ground). My ongoing decisions regarding which details to include or exclude are consistently guided by this one consideration: That I wish to offer an alternative reading to both the dominant Protestant understanding and the New Perspectives understanding. I therefore include those details that I regard as significant in demonstrating either the inadequacy of the other positions or the comparative

---

34. I remain completely flummoxed, for instance, about the precise identity of the στοιχεῖα in 4:3 or 4:9. (I suspect it is a reference to mothers-in-law, but this is mere speculation.)

35. A responsible commentary expends so much of its space detailing the various arguments in the history of interpretation (including arguments about the more-detailed matters of language and history), that it is often difficult for the commentary to impress its readership with the distinctive approach of its author. As helpful as James D. G. Dunn's commentary on Galatians is, for instance, it is somewhat difficult to benefit from his distinctive perspective on Galatians (and on Paul) from reading the commentary; his case is better made in his other various monographs and articles. My intention here is to avoid, wherever possible, commenting on those aspects of Galatians that are unrelated to my primary thesis: which is to provide an overall approach to Galatians that is an alternative both to the dominant Protestant reading and to the New Perspective on Paul reading. I therefore intend to call attention to those details that highlight the differences in these respective approaches, suggesting that the alternative promoted herein is more satisfactory than these other two alternatives.

adequacy of mine. Some readers will think I have included unnecessary detail; others will judge that I have excluded necessary detail—and I do not flatter myself that I will please all. But I do owe to all a candid discussion of what considerations informed my decisions, even if the judgment I exercise in the process is quite imperfect. Similarly, this volume is not intended as a survey of recent scholarship on the questions of Paul and the law; others have covered this material ably.[36] Rather, I attempt to interact (primarily in the notes) with recent scholarship sufficiently to indicate awareness of the discussion and/or where my perspective differs from other known perspectives. Although I attempt to avoid/evade cluttering the manuscript with such references, again, some will understandably claim that there are too many such references while others will equally understandably claim that there are too few. (I had hoped Goldilocks would edit the manuscript, but she was busy furniture shopping and porridge making.)

After I mention several introductory matters and briefly survey the historical narrative in Galatians 1 and 2, I will present a pericope-by-pericope discussion of the central argument of the letter in Galatians 3 and 4, followed by an abbreviated discussion of chapters 5 and 6.[37] For the student of Galatians, this work needs to be supplemented by the standard commentaries, which continue to appear faster than either my mind or wallet can accommodate them. If this work contributes at all to understanding Galatians, it will not do so because it comments exhaustively on each of the letter's respective details. To the contrary, I deliberately intend to omit mentioning those details (and the arguments about them in the secondary literature), except insofar as they are necessary to establish what I judge to be an overall way of reading Galatians that is more adequate than the known alternatives.

While I will endeavor to state my case positively, offering the reasoning for why I believe this covenant-historical approach illuminates Galatians well, implicit throughout is my dissatisfaction with two other approaches: the dominant Protestant approach prior to E. P. Sanders, and the so-called New Perspective(s) approach. The first always tended to misunderstand Galatians in two ways: First, it tended to read "between the lines," rather than the lines themselves,[38] assuming that Palestinian Judaism taught

---

36. Thomas R. Schreiner, *The Law and Its Fulfillment: A Pauline Theology of Law* (Grand Rapids: Baker, 1993); Stephen Westerholm, *Perspectives Old and New on Paul*; Guy P. Waters, *Justification and the New Perspective on Paul: A Review and Response* (Phillipsburg, NJ: P & R, 2004).

37. The brevity with which I address chapters 5 and 6 is not because I regard them as unrelated paraneses. To the contrary, I have been persuaded for over twenty-five years of the thesis of Frank J. Matera: that these chapters are, in fact, the "culmination" of Paul's argument in Galatians. I treat them more briefly only because they are largely exhortative; they are the imperatival consequences of the rationale articulated in Galatians 3 and 4. They are not less important; they are simply less discursive/argumentative and more imperatival. Far from being unimportant (to my thesis), I judge that they substantiate it. When Paul finally delivers the imperatival consequences of what he has been arguing for in four chapters, those consequences say little about justification (other than at 5:4–5) and everything about freedom from the Sinai covenant and its marking ceremonies, especially circumcision (there are ten references to circumcision or uncircumcision between Gal. 5:2 and 6:15), a matter that Calvin considered "trifling," though it is the very matter whose resolution occupied the entire letter. Cf. Frank J. Matera, "The Culmination of Paul's Argument to the Galatians: Gal 5.1–6.17," *Journal for the Study of the New Testament* 32 (1988): 79–91.

38. Francis Watson refers to what I call "reading between the lines" as "prejudice against historical particularity." He accuses Luther (rightly, in my judgment) of taking Paul's actual

a meritorious theory of justification, and that Paul was correcting such an error at Galatia. Paul's negative comments about ὁ νόμος were assumed to be negative comments about alleged first-century legalism, rather than negative comments about the law itself. While I do not believe the dust has settled yet on the nature of Palestinian Judaism of the first century, Sanders has demonstrated, at a minimum, that this older Protestant view was a caricature. The dominant Protestant approach therefore never appreciated properly how significant the Gentile-excluding nature of Sinai was to the apostle to the Gentiles.[39] F. C. Bauer's criticism of the dominant Protestant perspective on this point was just:

> Thus, not only was he the first to lay down expressly and distinctly the principle of Christian universalism as a thing essentially opposed to Jewish particularism. . . . In his Christian consciousness his own call to the apostolic office and the destination of Christianity to be the general principle of salvation for all people were two facts which were bound up inseparably in each other, and could not be disjoined.[40]

Second, and related, the dominant Protestant approach never really understood Paul's reasoning in Galatians correctly; it viewed the passages regarding justification as though Paul were arguing *for* the doctrine, whereas I read those passages as though Paul is arguing *from* the doctrine. As we will see at the appropriate points, my judgment is that Paul in Galatians does not argue *for* justification as though it were disputed, but *from* justification (as undisputed) in order to argue *for* the full inclusion of the Gentiles in the church, without their observing Mosaic ceremonies (wherein the dispute truly resided). In Galatians, "We who are Jews by nature" are those who know "that a man is not justified by observing the law" (Gal. 2:15–16). Since the Jews know this, Paul reasons, they see no barrier to the justification of the non-law-observing Gentiles. What distinguished the Jews (the law) did not justify anyway, so there is no reason that the Gentiles need to observe a law that never justified the Jews anyway.

Regarding the New Perspectives on Paul, three matters (that appear with differing emphases among different representatives) that characterize that approach strike me as

---

stated objection to circumcision and making a universal truth out of it. Watson takes issue with Luther's saying (regarding circumcision in Gal. 5:1–2), "Paul is not discussing the actual deed in itself, which has nothing wrong in it if there is no trust in it or presumption of righteousness" (from *LW*, 27:10). Watson rightly objects: "Thus, Paul's reference to circumcision is stripped of its particularity. . . . Operating here, it seems, is a prejudice against historical particularity. It is assumed that the historically particular is in itself theologically irrelevant, only becoming theologically relevant insofar as it symbolizes the general and ultimate concern of the conscience here and now." Watson, *Paul, Judaism, and the Gentiles*, 355, 357. Luther, Calvin, and many other representatives of the dominant Protestant approach singularly failed to appreciate how problematic the Israel-segregating, Gentile-excluding Mosaic law was for the apostle to the Gentiles. They therefore had to overlook what Watson called the "historical particularity" and "read between the lines" (as I say) to make Paul criticize what he did not criticize and not criticize what he did criticize.

39. This dominant Protestant approach has been duly corrected on this score by Krister Stendahl and James D. G. Dunn, among others.

40. Allan Menzies, trans. and ed., *The Church History of the First Three Centuries*, vol. 1, 3rd ed. (London: Williams and Norgate, 1878), 47. Francis Watson rightly observes regarding Baur: "Modern interpreters in the Reformation tradition have made little use of Baur's insights in this area, despite his influence in other respects." *Paul, Judaism, and the Gentiles*, 43.

unsatisfactory. First, Professor Dunn's "sociological" discussion of Galatians is largely right and helpful, but this is not the right term and is a tad off in substance. While it is true that Jews and Gentiles were members of different societies, and while it is true that the unity of believing Jews and Gentiles is an important Pauline concern in the letter (indeed, in all of Paul's letters), what separated Jew and Gentile (in Paul's mind) was not their ethnic or cultural differences, but the Sinai covenant itself—a *covenant* God made with the Israelites that deliberately *excluded* the Gentiles, proscribed inter-marriage with them, and even proscribed much of the Gentile diet.[41]

A second feature that often appears in the New Perspectives on Paul is an express or implicit monocovenantalism—a tendency to perceive only one covenant in the Hebrew Bible, or at least to define "covenant" as some single, overarching plan to redeem. Many authors within the New Perspectives approach are aware of the importance of "covenant" in understanding the Scriptures. Regarding Galatians 3, for instance, note how N. T. Wright in one of his earlier writings called attention to this:

> The basic thesis I wish to argue here hinges on Paul's use of the covenantal theme. . . . First, the chapter as a whole should be seen as an extended discussion of Genesis 15. This is one of the great covenantal chapters in the Jewish scriptures. . . . Second, Paul's use of the "curse" terminology here belongs exactly within this overall covenantal exposition, since it comes from one of the other great covenantal sections, Deuteronomy 27–8.[42]

Wright correctly observed the "covenantal" theology of Galatians 3, and he was right to refer to Genesis 15 and Deuteronomy 27–28 as among the "great covenantal chapters" or "great covenantal sections" of the Scriptures. But Wright's overall approach makes it difficult for him to see that these are not only different "sections" or "chapters," but different *covenants* in their own respective rights: one (Genesis 15) made with Abraham and another, of a different kind, later instituted through Moses that segregated Israel from the nations (Deut. 27–28). In his volume on justification, note how Wright defines "covenant":

> Here we have it: *God's single plan, through Abraham and his family, to bless the whole world.* This is what I have meant by the word *covenant* when I have used it as shorthand in writing about Paul. . . . The "covenant," in my shorthand, is not something other than God's determination to deal with evil once and for all and so put the whole creation (and humankind with it) right at last.[43]

Wright understands "covenant" to be God's eternal redemptive plan, a misdefinition not entirely unlike the misdefinition found in the Reformed confessional literature (which,

---

41. I join N. T. Wright in considering Ephesians to be authentically Pauline, and its sentiment on this point, whether the letter is authentically Pauline or not, is a virtual two-verse commentary on Galatians: "But now in Christ Jesus you [Gentiles] who once were far off have been brought near by the blood of Christ. For he himself is our peace, who has made us both [τὰ ἀμφότερα] one and has broken down in his flesh the dividing wall of hostility by abolishing the law of commandments and ordinances, that he might create in himself one new man in place of the two [τοὺς δύο], so making peace, and might reconcile us both [τοὺς ἀμφοτέρους] to God in one body through the cross, thereby killing the hostility" (Eph. 2:13–16).

42. Wright, *Climax of the Covenant*, 140.

43. Wright, *Justification*, 67, 95 (emphases original).

ironically, Wright routinely chastises). Wright's definition of "covenant" is very like the Reformed confessional "covenant of grace"; but both are misleading, because biblically, "covenant" is never some eternal plan but always some ratified-in-space-and-time treaty. Since the nature of Paul's argumentation in Galatians is to compare and contrast the new covenant with the Abrahamic and Sinai covenants, any monocovenantalism, or any tendency to confuse "covenant" with a timeless or eternal plan, is fated beforehand to misunderstand Paul significantly. Note again Wright's comments on Galatians 3:10–14:

> He is expounding covenant theology, from Abraham, through Deuteronomy and Leviticus, through Habakkuk, to Jesus the Messiah. . . . For Paul, then, the covenant is not detached from the realities of space and time, of the this-worldly orientation which was characteristic of Israel's covenant. Rather, the covenant was precisely working its way out through exile and restoration.[44]

Wright refers to several covenants (inaugurated with Abraham, Moses, and Christ) as "the covenant" or "Israel's covenant." But Abraham's covenant (which was also Israel's) threatened no one with exile; the threat of exile was exclusively associated with the Sinai covenant. Wright's view differs from that of interpreters such as Charles Talbert:

> When employed theologically, covenant can describe very different types of relationships. On the one hand, there are covenants in which God binds himself. When talking about such promissory types, covenant and oath are often synonymous (Testament of Moses 1:9; 3:9; 11:17; 12:13), as are covenant and promise (1 Kgs. 8:25). Such covenants are not conditional. On the other hand, there are covenants in which Israel is bound. When talking about such obligatory types, covenant and law are often synonymous. . . . Such covenants are conditional on the people's obedience.[45]

Beginning with E. P. Sanders, the expression "covenantal nomism" has come to be one of the most common errors in contemporary Pauline studies, because the expression ends up homogenizing the several covenants found in the *Tanakh*.[46] The promissory covenant with Abraham, the works-demanding, curse-threatening, Israel-segregating covenant instituted with Moses, the covenant with Phinehas that his descendants would offer sacrifices, and the pledge to David to put a descendant on an everlasting throne, are all tossed into a theological Waring blender, out of which emerges a single slurry that, ironically, bears almost no resemblance to *any* of the particular covenants found in the *Tanakh*. Indeed, from my perspective, much of the discussion of what we call "the Quest for Second Temple Judaism" is crippled by the fact that so many participants in the quest—on either side of the conversation—are monocovenantal. Are there some Second Temple texts that demand rigorous obedience to the laws of Moses? Of course; the covenant instituted via Moses demanded such. Are there some Second Temple texts that regard the pledges Yahweh made to

---

44. Wright, *Climax of the Covenant*, 150.

45. Charles H. Talbert, "Paul on the Covenant," *Review & Expositor* 84, no. 2 (March 1, 1987): 299.

46. For a fuller discussion of why I judge that "covenantal nomism" cannot make sense of the Sinai covenant, cf. my "Getting Out and Staying Out—Israel's Dilemma at Sinai," in the excursus at the end of this book.

Abraham as entirely gracious? Of course; that covenant was a promissory covenant. Are there Second Temple texts that require the strictest observance of the holiness code? Of course; both the Mosaic covenant and the one with Phinehas demanded such. Whatever one calls the monocovenantal slurry that emerges from a blended *Tanakh*—whether it is called "covenantal nomism" by Sanders et al. or "the covenant" by Wright et al.—it will never make adequate sense of Paul's reasoning in Galatians, which was rigorously polycovenantal. Paul perceived more difference between the Abrahamic covenant and the Sinai covenant than, perhaps, Friar Martin Luther did between the Sinai covenant and the new covenant.

A third area in which I find the New Perspectives approach unsatisfactory in Galatians resides in its teaching about justification and the covenant community.[47] Here are two representative samples, from James D. G. Dunn and N. T. Wright, respectively:

> God's justification is rather God's acknowledgement that someone is in the covenant.[48]

> Justification in this setting, then, is not a matter of how someone enters the community of the true people of God, but of how you tell who belongs to that community. . . . Within this context, "justification," as seen in 3:24–26, means that those who believe in Jesus Christ are declared to be members of the true covenant family.[49]

The problem with this view is that throughout most of its history, Israel plainly was in a covenant relationship with Yahweh that condemned it rather than justified it.[50] To be in the Sinai covenant community placed the nation under conditional cursings as well as conditional blessings. So there is not only a lexical problem here (it is not at all clear that the δικ- language means anything about covenanting or covenant communities; we will see that it was and is routinely ethical or forensic language, as I discuss in the lengthiest excursus in this volume), but also a historical problem of great significance: Israel was united covenantally to God by the Sinai covenant, but it was routinely condemned (and almost never justified) by the prophets who were the executors of that covenant. Indeed, both the Hebrew Bible and the New Testament Scriptures record the relationship of the Israelites to their prophets as murderous:

---

47. Of course, I have a number of other occasional differences with the New Perspective on Paul, but these are often less significant to Galatians. N. T. Wright, for example, attempts to find the narrative substructure of Paul's thought in the promises to Abraham. The Abrahamic narrative is indeed a significant part of that narrative substructure; but the Abrahamic narrative is itself grounded in the Adamic narrative, and Wright's tendency is to avoid/evade the importance of that Adamic narrative. "When we ask how it was that Jesus' cruel death was the decisive victory over the powers, sin and death included, Paul at once replies: because it was the fulfilment of God's promise that through Abraham and his seed he would undo the evil in the world." Wright, *What Saint Paul Really Said*, 48. What Wright omits here, in his reference to the seed of Abraham, is the "seed" of the woman mentioned earlier in Genesis 3. Cf. my "Paul on His Own Terms? A Review of N. T. Wright on Justification," *Ordained Servant Online* (May 2010), https://opc.org/os.html?article_id=204&issue_id=55.

48. James D. G. Dunn: "The New Perspective on Paul," *Jesus, Paul and the Law* (Louisville, KY: John Knox, 1990), 190.

49. Wright, *What St. Paul Really Said*, 119, 129.

50. See my excursus later in this volume, "Getting Out and Staying Out: Israel's Dilemma at Sinai."

He said, "I have been very jealous for the LORD, the God of hosts. For the people of Israel have *forsaken your covenant*, thrown down your altars, and *killed your prophets* with the sword, and I, even I only, am left, and they seek my life, to take it away."[51] (1 Kings 19:10)

"Nevertheless, they were disobedient and rebelled against you and cast your law behind their back and *killed your prophets*, who had warned them in order to turn them back to you, and they committed great blasphemies." (Neh. 9:26)

"Thus you witness against yourselves that you are sons of those who *murdered the prophets*." (Matt. 23:31)

"Woe to you! For you build the tombs of *the prophets whom your fathers killed*." (Luke 11:47)

"You stiff-necked people, uncircumcised in heart and ears, you always resist the Holy Spirit. As your fathers did, so do you. *Which of the prophets did not your fathers persecute? And they killed those* who announced beforehand the coming of the Righteous One, whom you have now betrayed and *murdered*, you who received the law as delivered by angels and did not keep it." (Acts 7:51–53)

For you, brothers, became imitators of the churches of God in Christ Jesus that are in Judea. For you suffered the same things from your own countrymen as they did from the Jews, who *killed both the Lord Jesus and the prophets*, and drove us out. (1 Thess. 2:14–15)

Why would the Israelites have murdered the prophets if the prophets exonerated them, acquitted them, or justified them? Would they not rather have welcomed them with open arms? But the pervasive witness of the Hebrew Bible is consistently the same: The Sinai covenant (and its "servants the prophets") ordinarily *condemned* the covenant people; it did not acquit/justify them. By the standards of that covenant itself, the covenant people were judged to be *un*righteous, not righteous, as even a small representation of prophetic testimony against that covenant people (not against the nations) demonstrates:

I know Ephraim, and Israel is not hidden from me; for now, O Ephraim, you have played the whore; Israel is defiled. Their deeds do not permit them to return to their God. For the spirit of whoredom is within them, and they know not the Lord. The pride of Israel testifies to his face; Israel and Ephraim shall stumble in his guilt [ταῖς ἀδικίαις]; Judah also shall stumble with them. (Hos. 5:3–5)

When I would heal Israel, the iniquity [ταῖς ἀδικίαις] of Ephraim is revealed. (Hos. 7:1)

As for my sacrificial offerings, they sacrifice meat and eat it, but the LORD does not accept them. Now he will remember their iniquity [τὰς ἀδικίας] and punish their sins; they shall return to Egypt. For Israel has forgotten his Maker and built palaces, and Judah has multiplied fortified cities; so I will send a fire upon his cities, and it shall devour her strongholds. (Hos. 8:13–14)

Behold, the LORD's hand is not shortened, that it cannot save, or his ear dull, that it cannot hear; but your iniquities have made a separation between you and your God, and your sins have hidden his face from you so that he does not hear. For your hands are defiled

---

51. All emphases added.

with blood and your fingers with iniquity; your lips have spoken lies; your tongue mutters wickedness [ἀδικίαν]. No one enters suit justly [οὐδεὶς λαλεῖ δίκαια]; no one goes to law honestly; they rely on empty pleas, they speak lies, they conceive mischief and give birth to iniquity. (Isa. 59:1–4)

Though you wash yourself with lye and use much soap, the stain of your guilt [ταῖς ἀδικίαις σου] is still before me, declares the LORD God. (Jer. 2:22)

Only acknowledge your guilt [γνῶθι τὴν ἀδικίαν σου], that you rebelled against the LORD your God. (Jer. 3:13)

They have turned back to the iniquities of their forefathers [τὰς ἀδικίας τῶν πατέρων αὐτῶν], who refused to hear my words. (Jer. 11:10)

To be sure, the Sinai covenant also provided the covenant community with a means of atonement. But if such atonement was necessary, then the covenant community otherwise stood condemned as "unrighteous" (ἀδικία). Atonement is not needed for the righteous but for the unrighteous:

And Aaron shall lay both his hands on the head of the live goat, and confess over it all the iniquities [πάσας τὰς ἀνομίας] of the people of Israel, and all their transgressions [πάσας τὰς ἀδικίας], all their sins [πάσας τὰς ἁμαρτίας]. And he shall put them on the head of the goat and send it away into the wilderness by the hand of a man who is in readiness. The goat shall bear all their iniquities [τὰς ἀδικίας] on itself to a remote area, and he shall let the goat go free in the wilderness. (Lev. 16:21–22)

Thus, before offering the required atoning sacrifice, the covenant people were *un*righteous; and after offering such sacrifice, they were (for the moment) acquitted. But both before the atonement/acquittal and after the atonement/acquittal, they were still the covenant people. They were the covenant people before atonement; they were the covenant people after. They were the covenant people when they were declared unrighteous; they were the covenant people when they were declared righteous, both when they were condemned and when they were acquitted. Therefore, any suggestion that there is some lexical or theological relation between justification/δικαιοσύνη and being in a covenant with God has profoundly misunderstood the covenant God made with Israel through Moses and enforced through the prophets.[52] Israel would have avidly welcomed such a new "perspective" in their day; they would have been more than delighted to know that merely by being in the Sinai covenant, they were regarded as righteous or justified. And surely the prophets they murdered would have been much happier to have been able to declare "peace, peace," when there was none (Jer. 6:14; 8:11).

Ironically perhaps, there is a tendency shared by both the dominant Protestant approach and by the New Perspectives in which I believe they are both mistaken. Each, at times, suggests that Palestinian Judaism of the era misunderstood the Mosaic law. One suggests they misunderstood it by attempting to keep its commands (ostensibly in order to be justified), and the other suggests they misunderstood its "badges" as segregating them from the nations. But while I do not deny that Palestinian Judaism

---

52. Again, this is a matter I address in the excursus "Getting Out and Staying Out: Israel's Dilemma at Sinai."

believed both, neither is erroneous. The Mosaic covenant *required* comprehensive obedience: "Cursed is everyone who does not abide by all the things written in the book of the Law, to do them [τοῦ ποιῆσαι αὐτά]" (Deut. 27:26 cited in Gal. 3:10), and "The one who does them [ὁ ποιήσας αὐτὰ] shall live by them" (Lev. 18:5 cited in Gal. 3:12). And the Mosaic covenant *required* Israel to remain separate from the nations:

"When the LORD your God brings you into the land that you are entering to take possession of it. . . . You shall make no covenant with them and show no mercy to them. You shall not intermarry with them, giving your daughters to their sons or taking their daughters for your sons. . . . Then the anger of the LORD would be kindled against you, and he would destroy you quickly. . . . For you are a people holy to the LORD your God. The LORD your God has chosen [προείλατο] you to be a people for his treasured possession, out of all the peoples [παρὰ πάντα τὰ ἔθνη] who are on the face of the earth." (Deut. 7:1–6)

The stipulations of Israel's covenant *required* them to be distinct from the other peoples of the earth: "You shall not eat anything that has died naturally. You may give it to the sojourner [τῷ παροίκῳ] who is within your towns, that he may eat it, or you may sell it to a foreigner [τῷ ἀλλοτρίῳ]. For you are a people holy to the LORD your God" (Deut. 14:21). Regarding the various laws (e.g., diet, Sabbath, circumcision), James D. G. Dunn in his original "New Perspective" address said,

Covenant works had become too closely identified as *Jewish* observances, *covenant* righteousness as *national* righteousness. But to maintain such identifications was to ignore both the way the covenant began and the purpose it had been intended to fulfill in the end.[53]

But the Jews did not "ignore" the teachings of Moses nor how the Sinai covenant began. It began when the Israelites were separate and wandering in an uninhabited region between Egypt and Canaan; and the covenant required the Israelites to *remain* separate from the peoples of the land they would inherit.[54] Dunn's confusion is due to his conflating the Abrahamic covenant *with* the Sinai covenant (the paragraph previous to the quote above referred to the pledge to Abraham to be a blessing to the nations). But the Sinai covenant itself required the Israelites to be separate from the nations about them (for reasons I will discuss later). So, ironically, both approaches believe that Paul needed to correct Jewish misunderstandings of the Sinai covenant; whereas I think the Jews understood that covenant correctly, and it is Paul's *interpreters* who misunderstand it (and therefore him). It *did* require works (it was not "of faith," Gal. 3:12); and it *did* require that the Israelites segregate themselves from the nations around them. Eagerly pursuing the righteousness it demanded and rigorously separating themselves from the *am ha-aretz* were precisely what the Mosaic covenant required; they were not misunderstandings of what it required.

My voice, then, differs both from the dominant Protestant approach to Galatians and from the New Perspectives on Paul approach. I suppose mine could be regarded

---

53. Dunn, "The New Perspective on Paul," 197 (emphases original).
54. Indeed, the covenant required that the inhabitants of the land be "devoted to destruction," a rather permanent form of separation (Num. 21:2; Deut. 2:34; 3:6; 7:2; 20:17; Josh. 2:10; 6:21; 7:12; 8:26; 10:1, 28, 35, 37, 39, 40; 11:20–21; Judg. 1:17; 1 Sam. 15:3, 8, 18; 2 Chron. 32:14; 34:2; Isa. 34:2, 5; Jer. 25:9; 50:21).

as a "third perspective on Paul." I regard each of those approaches as containing many interesting and valuable insights and truths, but I also regard them each as being incapable of making sense of Paul's theological reasoning in Galatians. I offer this alternative reading as merely that: an alternative that I have found satisfactory since I began teaching the Greek text of Galatians in 1984. If others find this approach more satisfactory than other approaches, then I invite them to join me in this way of reading Galatians.

I should make a final introductory comment about my perspective and its relation to the two other prevailing perspectives. My understanding of Galatians antedated most of the New Perspective discussion; it grew out of my sense of the inadequacy of the dominant Protestant approach, but without any reference to the (then-emerging) New Perspective. As time has passed, I have recognized that my view is as far from the one as it is from the other; it is largely independent of the other approaches and was developed largely independently of them. As I look at the matter now, however, I recognize that my viewpoint may have the unintended benefit of bridging the gap that now separates those two points of view, because I think there is something in my perspective that each may find harmonious with its own views.

The New Perspective approach will probably appreciate my understanding of the importance of the Jew-Gentile issues in Paul's writings (and specifically in his negative comments about ὁ νόμος), and will probably appreciate my unwillingness to believe that one must "scold a first-century Jew to be a Christian"; one can embrace the teachings of the new covenant without accusing anyone else of having misunderstood the Sinai covenant. Further, they will probably appreciate the corporate approach I take to a number of interpretive matters; I ordinarily regard ἡμεῖς and ὑμεῖς throughout Galatians 3 and 4 as referring, respectively, to Jews and Gentiles, as they irrefragably do in Ephesians 2.[55]

The dominant Protestant approach may appreciate the fact that I regard Paul's soteriology as being essentially that of the Protestant confessions, and that I regard δικαιοσύνη to denote ethical uprightness (and, by extension, to denote declarative/forensic statements or judgments about such), and not "covenant faithfulness" or "apocalyptic power." If the two find it possible to regard ὁ νόμος as a synecdoche for the Sinai covenant, then all three of us will be able to find a congenial meeting place.

2. On the Greek and English of Galatians

I must explain to the reader three points about this work. First, I routinely refer to the Greek text. Almost always, the English will also appear, at least parenthetically (or vice versa), so even those whose Greek is rusty or nonexistent will ordinarily be able to follow

---

55. I observe an irony here. Due to my understanding of amanuensis as essentially collaborator (not mere stenographer or even mere editor), and due to Paul's insistence on his particular authority (and due to Eusebius's entire silence on the matter), I regard Ephesians as genuinely Pauline. Many/most proponents of the New Perspective do *not* regard Ephesians as genuine, but they *do* embrace its Jew/Gentile focus (and what that means for the genuine letters). Many/most opponents of the New Perspective, on the other hand, *do* regard Ephesians as genuine, but they appear to be largely unfazed by its Jew/Gentile focus.

my reasoning. But I have all but given up on attempting to make sense of Paul (or any other New Testament author) from English translations, for two reasons. Second, their name is legion, for they are many. There are so many different English translations, each with its own respective strengths and weaknesses, that it is no longer realistic to expect that there will be a single, common translation to which all public discourse refers. The Greek text may simply have to serve as the common text for academic discussion of the New Testament. Third, the sheer number of English translations that has appeared since the Second World War is rather significant; and the market niche of each depends, obviously, on its being different from existing translations. Therefore, each newer translation (with some occasional exceptions) has tended to be remarkably adventurous, to justify commercially its raison d'être.

For the sake of illustration, consider several translations of the fairly straightforward comment in Galatians 3:10, Ὅσοι γὰρ ἐξ ἔργων νόμου εἰσίν, ὑπὸ κατάραν εἰσίν. The Authorized/King James Version translated this in a fairly straightforward and literal manner: "For as many as are *of the works of the law* are under the curse." The KJV translators followed the similar substantive use of the preposition ἐκ from the previous verses οἱ ἐκ πίστεως εὐλογοῦνται σὺν τῷ πιστῷ Ἀβραάμ (3:7 and 9), which the KJV similarly translated: "So then they which be *of faith* are blessed with faithful Abraham." But note what other translations have done with this:

> For all who *rely on* works of the law are under a curse. (Revised Standard Version, New Revised Standard Version, English Standard Version; mild variation: "All who *rely on* observing the law are under a curse," New International Version)

> But those who *depend on the law to make them right with God* are under his curse. (New Living Translation)

> Anyone who *tries to please God by* obeying the Law is under a curse. (Contemporary English Version)[56]

> A curse is on all people who are *trying to become good by* obeying the law. (Worldwide English New Testament)[57]

> But those who *depend on following the law to make them right* are under a curse. (New Century Version)

Note that, beginning with the RSV, the simple "ἐκ /of" became "*rely on*," suggesting, I suppose, some inappropriate (legalistic?) self-reliance.[58] But this unsubstantiated and gratuitous mis-translation is mild compared to what followed, when the simple sub-

---

56. One hesitates here to wonder if the translators considered it right to try to please God by *dis*obeying the law, but the simple fact is that the clause ἀρέσκειν θεῷ just isn't in the text.

57. Again, one wonders if we should try to become good by *dis*obeying the law, or if we should try to become *evil* by obeying the law.

58. Had Paul desired to talk about relying on the law, he could have and would have done so; indeed, he said such a thing at Rom. 2:17: "But if you call yourself a Jew and rely on the law [ἐπαναπαύῃ νόμῳ] and boast in God." But he did not say any such thing at Gal. 3:10 by employing the mere preposition ἐκ. Nowhere anywhere else in the New Testament do any of the above translations translate the preposition ἐκ as they do at Gal. 3:10, nor do any of them even translate ἐκ at Gal. 3:7 and 3:9 as they do at Gal. 3:10.

stantive use of the preposition ἐκ became such things as "depend on . . . to make them right," "tries to please God by," "trying to become good by," and "depend on following . . . to make them right." And none of these translations felt any obligation to translate the preposition in the previous verses in a consistent manner; so Paul's parallel, by employing ἐκ characteristically ("of faith" and "of works of the law," or "characterized by faith" and "characterized by works of the law"), is almost entirely camouflaged. I join Alice here when she cried, "Curiouser and curiouser!"

It is often easier, therefore, simply to refer to the original text as our common text, with enough surrounding information (such as a verse reference) so that the reader can check the English if unsure about the Greek. For the sake of consistency, however, some English translation must be selected as the default translation to which I ordinarily refer, unless I indicate otherwise. To serve this purpose, I have selected the English Standard Version. It has its flaws (which I point out whenever pertinent to interpreting Galatians), as do the other English translations; but since its editors claim that it is "literal where possible" (gratuitously, I might add, in light of what they did with Gal. 3:10), it is a tad less adventurous (less "curious") than many other contemporary translations. The New Revised Standard Version is also a fairly restrained translation. Overall, it is probably as good as the ESV and more widely used in academic circles, so I had intended to employ it in this book. Its commitment to gender-inclusive language, however, is a liability in Galatians,[59] where so often Paul refers to Abraham's progeny, yet does so by employing different terms for different purposes. He employs "seed/ offspring" (σπέρμα, 3:16 [thrice], 19, 29), "children" (τέκνα, 4:25, 27, 28, 31), or "sons" (υἱοί, 3:7, 26; 4:6, 7, 22, 30), the latter of which the NRSV cannot employ by its own strictures, even though it is interpretively significant in a letter where inheritance is an important consideration, and the relationship between the κληρονομ- language and the υἱο- language is almost certainly intentional for Paul, yet *verboten* for the NRSV (which translates both υἱοί and τέκνα as "children"). My choice of ESV, therefore, is merely due to my judgment that it obscures Paul's reasoning in Galatians less frequently than do other contemporary English translations, which, admittedly, I am damning with faint praise. On those occasions where I judge it to be necessary, I simply provide my own English translation, and notify the reader of doing so.

Some lament the absence of a common vernacular translation as the basis of public discourse, and I suppose I find the absence somewhat lamentable myself. But there was always some price to be paid for vernacular translations, even when they were fairly restrained;[60] and now they tend to be so imaginative and unrestrained as to be unreliable on their good days and misleading on others. As there may be some advantage in making the original text our common text anyway, I will often do so here.

---

59. It is a liability elsewhere also, of course, though well-intended. Malachi's vision (3:3) of a messianic future included the moral renewal of the priesthood; but he did not envision that Messiah would purify "the descendants of Levi" (NRSV), as though contemplating a general purification of his lineage. Rather, he envisioned a purification of the Levitical priesthood, and "sons of Levi" is the correct rendering of the Hebrew here and an honest testimony to the patriarchal nature of that society, however unenlightened or inegalitarian some may regard it to have been.

60. Cf. Elizabeth L. Eisenstein, *The Printing Revolution in Early Modern Europe*, 2nd ed. (New York: Cambridge University Press, 2005), esp. ch. 6, "Western Christendom Disrupted," 164–208.

CHAPTER 1

Introductory Issues

In the next chapter, we will consider several historical issues that are pertinent to understanding Paul's reasoning in Galatians 3 and 4. Here, however, I wish to introduce three matters that inform my understanding of those chapters. First, I regard ὁ νόμος throughout the Galatian letter to be a synecdoche for the Sinai covenant.[1] Second, I regard Paul's reasoning in Galatians 3 and 4 to be covenant-historical in its nature. Third, I believe Paul argues *from* justification by faith (as a settled doctrine), not *for* justification by faith (as though it were a disputed doctrine). It will help the later discussion to introduce these three briefly here, since they govern my approach throughout.

1.1. ὁ νόμος as Synecdoche for the Sinai Covenant

On several occasions over the past thirty years or so, some hapless individual has felt constrained by the bounds of courtesy to ask me what my dissertation topic was. When I have responded, "Paul's understanding of the law," the eyes glaze over, disclosing only regret for having asked the question. Reading through the glaze and regret, I believe I can surmise what is going through the person's mind: "Oh no, another arcane dissertation on some Pauline minutia. I wish I hadn't asked." Not entirely immune to the demands of courtesy myself, I ordinarily change the topic and enjoy watching that glaze disappear with a satisfaction perhaps matched only by that of Ananias, when he saw the scales disappear from Paul's. At the risk of sounding defensive, however, I would suggest that my topic is not as arcane as most think. If we evaluate the vocabulary of Romans and Galatians and dismiss words that have no particular religious or theological meaning (e.g., prepositions, conjunctions, the verb εἰμί, and so on), we then find that only one term appears with greater frequency than νόμος in Romans, and that is θεός. If we undertake the same search for frequency in Galatians, we find that, again, only one term appears with more frequency than νόμος, though in this case it is Χριστός. Only terms for the Godhead appear with greater frequency in these two letters. Here are the data:

Romans	Galatians
θεός = 153	Χριστός = 38
νόμος = 74	νόμος = 32
Χριστός = 65	θεός = 31
ἁμαρτία = 48	πίστις = 22
κύριος = 43	πνεῦμα = 1

---

1. With few and obvious exceptions, such as τὸν νόμον τοῦ Χριστοῦ at Gal. 6:2 where the genitive deliberately and paradoxically qualifies the previous noun. The others will be addressed as they occur.

In each case, νόμος appears more frequently than some terms for the Godhead itself (more frequently than Χριστός or κύριος in Romans; more frequently than θεός in Galatians). At least in these two letters, then, νόμος is a significant concern for Paul and a significant part of his thought. To grasp his thought, we must understand what he means by νόμος. That is, we study νόμος in Paul not merely because it is a "problem" or conundrum to be solved—Paul says both positive and negative things about it. We study νόμος because it figures so prominently in these two important letters. We might state the matter negatively and say: Insofar as one misunderstands Paul's use of νόμος, one misunderstands Romans and Galatians.[2]

One of the controlling factors in my reading of Galatians is my belief that the prevailing usage of ὁ νόμος throughout the letter is as a synecdoche for the Sinai covenant in its entirety. In this sense, Galatians 3:17 has profound interpretive consequences, because in this verse, ὁ νόμος not only appears to be used as such a synecdoche, but almost no other understanding of the term would make any sense at all. "This is what I mean: the law, which came 430 years afterward, does not annul a covenant previously ratified by God, so as to make the promise void." Suppose the word *law* here were replaced with the word *giraffe*. Then the sentence would read, "This is what I mean: the giraffe, which came 430 years afterward, does not annul a covenant previously ratified by God." But what able-minded person would suppose that the arrival of a giraffe could have the consequence of annulling a covenant? Suppose, then, a less fanciful example of replacing the word *law* with *moral directions*. We then get this: "This is what I mean: moral directions, which came 430 years afterward, do not annul a covenant previously ratified by God." Well, zoologically this is less problematic, but logically it is just as difficult. Who would imagine that the arrival of moral information would annul a previous treaty? What kind of moral information would require one to renege on one's commitments? The only thing that might reasonably be expected to nullify a *previous* treaty is a *new* treaty. For all I know, the Treaty of Westphalia is routinely broken today, as is the Treaty of Versailles. Why? Because the relevant parties entered subsequent treaties by which they related to one another on different terms. So what understanding of *nomos* makes sense of Galatians 3:17? I suggest that it only makes sense to take it as referring to the *covenant* God made with the Israelites at Mount Sinai, a covenant characterized by law-giving and by the threats of severe sanctions upon those who violate those laws/commands.[3]

Paul appears here to be alluding to Exodus 12:40–41, which also enumerates the time between the patriarchal/Abrahamic covenant and the Sinai covenant the same way: "The time that the people of Israel lived in Egypt was 430 years. At the end of 430 years, on that very day, all the hosts of the LORD went out from the land of Egypt."[4]

---

2. Indeed, one could make a case that this term is important to understanding Paul per se. νόμος appears 121 times in his letters, whereas ἀγάπη/ἀγαπάω appear 109 times and δικαιοσύνη/δικαιόω/δίκαιος appear 102 times. As a mere matter of lexical statistics, the term concerns Paul more than love and more than justification.

3. As we shall see when we get to the text, other covenantal language is present also, including the verbs ἀκυρόω and προκυρόω, as well as the obvious διαθήκη.

4. Actually, Moses' record, adequate by the standards of his day, is not quite precise. The Abrahamic covenant was ratified in Abraham's generation, sometime before Joseph (and/or other descendants of Abraham) was enslaved in Egypt. The time of the original covenant with

Further, Paul in this text refers to a "*covenant* previously ratified by God," a matter also implied by the two verbs προκεκυρωμένην and ἀκυροῖ.[5] And Paul characterizes that previously ratified covenant as one of "promise." Implicit in Galatians 3:17 is that ὁ νόμος is itself a covenant, but a different *kind* of covenant than the one characterized by "promise." And, as we all know from Exodus and Deuteronomy, it was not just a single "law" that came 430 years later, or even a *body* of such laws, but a covenant: "The LORD our God made a covenant with us in Horeb (Deut. 5:2; cf. also Deut. 29:1; 1 Kings 8:9; 2 Chron. 5:10). Whatever else was true about this covenant made at Horeb, it did not annul the previous promissory covenant made with the patriarchs.

Note also that in Galatians 3:17, Paul employs the synecdoche "promise" (ἐπαγγελία) for the Abrahamic covenant. He could have spoken otherwise; he could have spoken of "the covenant made with your fathers" (Deut. 4:31; 5:3; 7:12; 8:18, et al.), for instance, but he did not. He called it "the promise." Was only a single promise made to Abraham? No, several promises were made: to make his descendants numerous, to give him a land, and through one of his descendants to bless all the nations of the earth (Gen. 12:1–3, 7; 15:4–7; 17:1–8; 28:14). Nevertheless, promise-giving so characterized the Abrahamic covenant that the word *promise* could justly be employed as a synecdoche for the covenant itself.

By its very nature, synecdoche is a figure of speech employed to designate a reality by a dominant or characteristic feature.[6] Twice in Galatians 3 (verses 23 and 25), Paul refers to the new covenant by the word *faith*, because faith in Christ is such a dominant or an important feature. Luke employs such a synecdoche when he describes the early meetings of the apostolic church: "On the first day of the week, when we were gathered together *to break bread*, Paul talked with them" (Acts 20:7; emphasis mine). We know from other records of the early assemblies of the apostolic church that they were characterized not exclusively by the breaking of bread, but also by apostolic instruction, prayers, and collections (Acts 2:42). But because the Supper was such a dominant, perhaps even climactic, feature of those assemblies, they could be spoken of, by synecdoche, with such an expression as "to break bread."

The Sinai covenant is therefore justly spoken of as ὁ νόμος.[7] The dominant feature of the covenant made at Sinai was law-giving. Of the ten covenantal words Moses

---

Abraham (Gen. 15:18) until the covenant at Sinai was closer to five hundred years. Paul probably cites the "430 years" figure by attraction to Exod. 12:40–41.

5. English has difficulty preserving the Greek wordplay, because our word *annul* differs from our word *ratify*. We could only preserve the Greek by employing a neologism, saying, "The law, that comes 430 years after, cannot de-ratify a covenant previously ratified by God."

6. Actually, synecdoche can be employed also to refer to less-dominant features; but insofar as synecdoche and metonomy differ from each other, it may be that metonomy can employ almost anything associated with a reality for the reality itself, even if that associated thing is not central to the reality; whereas synecdoche tends to refer to an aspect of a reality that is essential to it. Examples of such metonomy might be "the White House" for the executive branch of government, since the branch could exist elsewhere and often does (e.g., in Air Force One). Similarly, the "arm of the law" as a metonomy for the police department has almost nothing to do with arms and everything to do with radar guns, cameras at intersections, and snide state police officers.

7. In saying this, I am not suggesting that there is any difference between the anarthrous νόμος and the articulated one. With most contemporary students of Paul, I believe the presence or absence of the definite article is irrelevant. In Gal. 3:11–12, for instance, the term can be used

brought down from Horeb, nine were commands.[8] And later these nine were expanded into a body of legislation consisting of over 600 commandments. Because a dominant feature of this covenant was law-giving,[9] Paul refers to the covenant itself as ὁ νόμος.

Paul did not invent this covenantal understanding of ὁ νόμος out of whole cloth. Twice in the LXX, διαθήκη is used to translate the Hebrew *torah*:

> As it is written in the Law of Moses [בתורת משה; LXX: ἐν διαθήκῃ Μωσῆ], all this calamity has come upon us; yet we have not entreated the favor of the LORD our God, turning from our iniquities and gaining insight by your truth. (Dan. 9:13)

The Masoretic text plainly says, "in the Torah of Moses," but the LXX translators say, "in the *covenant* of Moses." A similar translation occurs at 2 Chronicles 25:4:

> But he did not put their children to death, according to what is written in the Law, in the Book of Moses [בתורה בספר משה; LXX: κατὰ τὴν διαθήκην τοῦ νόμου κυρίου καθὼς γέγραπται].

Note here that there are two parallel prepositional phrases in the original Hebrew:

"In the Torah" [בתורה]

"In the Book of Moses" [בספר משה]

But the LXX renders the first one: "according to the *covenant* [κατὰ τὴν διαθήκην] of [not "in"] the law of the Lord." It is even possible that the genitive in the expression τὴν διαθήκην τοῦ νόμου κυρίου is appositive, "the covenant that *is* the Law of the Lord." These LXX realities may have influenced Paul, for whom Torah was not merely moral wisdom of a timeless character, but a *covenant* administration that had a good deal of moral wisdom in it. Or perhaps Paul never noticed these two unusual translations of תורה with διαθήκη. But whether he noticed this or not, or whether he was lexically

---

either with or without the definite article, as it can in the LXX. Cf. the discussion by Moo, "'Law,' 'Works of the Law,' and Legalism in Paul," 75–76; and Thomas R. Schreiner, *The Law and Its Fulfillment: A Pauline Theology of Law* (Grand Rapids: Baker, 1993), 33–34. Note also J. Louis Martyn's recognition that only eight of the 32 uses of *nomos* in the letter are articulated, yet "as the contexts show, all are definite references to the Law, except for 3:21a, a condition contrary to fact." *Galatians*, 555n40.

8. It is not necessary to our purposes here for me to indicate why I agree with the Jewish enumeration of the Decalogue, rather than with the three different Christian enumerations. But I do agree that the Jewish enumeration, whereby the first word is the word of preamble and historical prologue ("I am the Lord your God who brought you out of the land of Egypt") is the correct enumeration, and that all three of the Christian enumerations (the Roman Catholic, Lutheran, and Reformed) have serious difficulties. These difficulties are self-inflicted; in the effort to universalize the Decalogue, the various Christian traditions have attempted to find "ten" words that omit the opening words (since these opening words so evidently describe the peculiar relationship between Yahweh and Israel). Once these words are omitted, however, it is difficult to find "ten" words; only nine are left. So the Reformed tradition divides into two different words the prohibiting of having any gods before Yahweh and the making of images, despite the fact that the explanatory clause ("for I the Lord your God am a jealous God") appears to govern the first at least as much as the second. The Roman Catholic and Lutheran enumerations face their own difficulty; each attempts to make two separate words out of the anti-coveting prohibitions.

9. And perhaps because of the highly conditional nature of the Sinai covenant, in which Yahweh pledged either to bless or to curse Israel on the condition of Israel's obedience or disobedience.

influenced or not, he joined the LXX translators in *regarding* Torah covenantally. For both the LXX and for Paul, Torah was not mere wisdom (though it was wise) and Torah was not mere law (though it contained many laws). Torah was a covenant, filled with wise stipulations, made with the Israelites alone at Mount Sinai, segregating them from the Gentiles and threatening them with curses if they disobeyed.

These LXX translations are doubly striking. First, they are remarkable for the fact that they diverge from the literalism so common in the LXX translation.[10] While there is indeed a range of translation within the LXX, its overall tendency is fairly literal, creating a number of somewhat awkward renderings in Greek that have often been called, for lack of a better designation, "Semitisms" or "Hebraisms." To diverge from this pattern is somewhat bold, especially on so well-known and religiously important a term as *torah*. One would have thought that here especially the literal/conservative tendency of the LXX would have been preserved by translating with the ordinary νόμος.[11] Second, they are striking because, in each case, the divergence is identical; תורה is translated by διαθήκη. That is, if each diverged in a different way (e.g., if one had substituted ἡ σοφία, "the book of the wisdom of Moses"), it might merely indicate the kind of idiosyncrasy associated with scribal transmission—too little light, too little sleep, too much wine, and so on. Translating late at night, wearied by the process, perhaps a translator simply got careless and made a mistake, and no one else noticed and corrected the idiosyncrasy. But the divergent, less-literal translations are less literally translated in the identical manner, suggesting that the translators at this point recognized that תורה always had the overtones of the Sinai covenant about it, but that the Greek νόμος did not necessarily have the same lexical overtones. Thus to preserve the covenantal associations with תורה, they felt compelled to substitute διαθήκη for the ordinary (and expected) νόμος.

Consider also the Greek title for the fifth book of Moses: "Deuteronomy." What is contained in that book? Merely a second law? No, the book contains the account of the renewal of the Sinai covenant itself, after the Israelites had broken it. It contains, as it were, a second covenant (and indeed διαθήκη appears therein 28 times, whereas νόμος appears there 24 times), even though the LXX refers to it as τὸ δευτερονόμιον and Odes refers to Deuteronomy 32 as ᾠδὴ Μωυσέως ἐν τῷ Δευτερονομίῳ. As Deuteronomy 29:1 itself says, "These are the words of the covenant [οἱ λόγοι τῆς διαθήκης] that the Lord commanded Moses to make with the people of Israel in the land of Moab, besides the covenant that he had made with them at Horeb [πλὴν τῆς διαθήκης ἧς διέθετο αὐτοῖς ἐν Χωρηβ]." Of course the law was republished therein, but only because the original law covenant had been violated. Therefore, even the nomenclature of τὸ δευτερονόμιον associated a "second law" and a "second covenant."

---

10. I am not suggesting that all portions of the LXX are translated in the same manner, nor equally literally. I merely suggest that, taken as a whole, the LXX is ordinarily fairly literal and in many cases, surprisingly so.

11. An example of this conservative tendency in the LXX resides in the "righteousness" language. According to David Hill, of the 476 uses of the צדק- group in the Hebrew Bible, the LXX employs the δικ- root to translate them 462 (97 percent) times. Cf. Hill, *Greek Words and Hebrew Meanings: Studies in the Semantics of Soteriological Terms*, Society for New Testament Studies Monograph Series 5 (Cambridge: Cambridge University Press, 1967), 104.

Much confusion has occurred in Galatians studies (and Pauline studies more generally) when people assumed that Paul uses ὁ νόμος in many differing ways, even within the same context. While it is possible for this to be done with words, there is a simpler explanation.[12] Ordinarily, Paul uses the term as he does at Galatians 3:17, where it manifestly refers to the covenant made at Sinai. This prevailing usage, however, can also lead to slightly extended uses. An expression such as "the law says" can refer either to the covenant/treaty itself, which requires certain behaviors or rites, or it can refer, by extension, to the treaty *document*, wherein such words can be found. Referring to Clement's use of *diatheke*, for instance, A. H. J. Gunneweg says, "The term means both the covenant, the establishment of divine salvation, and also the *documents* which belong to it and bear witness to it."[13] It would have been unusual (if not impossible) in the ancient Near East to have a treaty without a treaty document, and therefore the one can often be spoken of as the other.[14] Paul followed Moses in associating closely the covenant itself and its written record.

> Then Moses wrote this law [LXX, "Moses wrote this law *in a book*," ἔγραψεν Μωυσῆς τὰ ῥήματα τοῦ νόμου τούτου εἰς βιβλίον] and gave it to the priests, the sons of Levi, who carried the ark of the covenant of the LORD [τοῖς αἴρουσιν τὴν κιβωτὸν τῆς διαθήκης κυρίου], and to all the elders of Israel. . . . Take this Book of the Law [τὸ βιβλίον τοῦ νόμου τούτου] and put it by the side of the ark of the covenant of the LORD your God [τῆς κιβωτοῦ τῆς διαθήκης κυρίου τοῦ θεοῦ ὑμῶν], that it may be there for a witness against you. (Deut. 31:9, 12)

Thus with verbs of communication (speaking, reading, writing), ὁ νόμος can refer either to what the *treaty* "says" or to what the treaty *document* "says," since there is little practical difference.[15] We do a similar thing in English when a banker reminds someone who is late paying the mortgage, "Don't forget; we have a *contract* here." The word *contract* in such a sentence can refer to the business relationship itself or to the written document in which the contract has been formally recorded. While it is true, therefore, in such circumstances, that ὁ νόμος has more than one usage, the latter use is but an extension of the more basic usage. Some would suggest that an expression such as ὁ νόμος λέγει could/should be translated "the Scripture says," and the suggestion is not farfetched. I am suggesting, however, that even in such an expression, it is the covenant document that is being referred to, and it just happens, in this case, that the covenant document is part of the Jewish/Christian Scriptures. To say that

---

12. Whether we join philosophers in approving "Ockham's razor," or join empiricists in treasuring "parsimony," join them we do. If a simpler explanation makes sense of the data, whether philosophically, empirically, or exegetically, then there is no good reason to prefer a more complicated explanation.

13. A. H. J. Gunneweg, *Understanding the Old Testament*, trans. John Bowden (Philadelphia: Westminster, 1978), 36 (emphasis mine).

14. Note how easily Paul can say, "For to this day, when they *read the old covenant* [τῇ ἀναγνώσει τῆς παλαιᾶς διαθήκης], that same veil remains unlifted" (2 Cor. 3:14), because when they read "the old covenant" they are reading what was written on "tablets of stone" (2 Cor. 3:3), "carved in letters on stone" (2 Cor. 3:7). The Sinai covenant itself was so associated with the stone tablets that when one "reads" what is inscribed there, one "reads the old covenant." At least in 2 Cor. 3, what Paul regards as being contained on the "tablets of stone" is "the old *covenant*," not God's moral will and surely not legalism.

15. Cf., e.g., Rom. 3:19; 7:7; 1 Cor. 9:8; 14:21; Gal. 3:10; 4:21.

ὁ νόμος *means* "the Scriptures" in such an expression, while not entirely objectionable, is an extension of an extension ("covenant" extends to "covenant document," which extends to "Scripture") that simply is not necessary and that may obscure the deeply covenantal nature of Paul's thought.[16]

I am especially resistant to the once-common habit of "solving" the problem of Paul and the law by arguing that ὁ νόμος is an arbitrarily polyvalent term in Paul that can have different meanings in different settings. The dominant Protestant approach, for instance, "solved" the tension between Paul's positive and negative statements about the law by defining the term differently: when Paul viewed the law positively, he was referring to the rich moral wisdom found in Torah; whereas when he viewed it negatively, he was referring to a meritorious/legalistic abuse thereof. Douglas J. Moo observed that students of Paul have suggested that Paul uses the term to have as many as seven different meanings.[17] I do not object to polyvalency per se, nor do I insist that Paul employs ὁ νόμος without any variation. However, I am nervous about solving the tension between Paul's negative and positive statements about the law in this manner, and my nervousness is due to three considerations.

First, polyvalent terms are not capriciously so. When a term (or expression) has more than one usage, almost always this is due to its having a different use within different semantic settings (or, as some call them, within different "language games" or semantic fields/domains). As Mark A. Seifrid has observed regarding another lexical stock, "All too frequently, scholars investigating צדק terminology continue to overlook the semantic insight that any proper definition of a word or word group must describe the *contexts* which call forth the various meanings of the terms."[18] That is, one could say that the English word *run* is polyvalent, but this could be misleading. When one is returning an item to a hosiery store, it has only one meaning; when one looks at a baseball scoreboard, it has only one meaning; and when one is discussing a cold-ridden nose, again it has but a single meaning. The word may be employed in many different ways, but it is ordinarily employed only one way in a given semantic setting. So the real question is whether Paul, when in mid-argument about the law somewhere, can simply change his meaning "on the fly," with any hope that his audience could possibly know that he is doing so. In most of Paul's uses of ὁ νόμος, the expression appears several times within a sustained argument, and I regard it as highly unlikely that Paul could continue to discuss the same thing while switching the definition of one of the more important vocabulary terms he employs. This is especially so when one looks at the logical connections in his reasoning: in 3:17, it is evidently the law "that came 430

---

16. Additionally, though somewhat irrelevant to my purposes, to translate ὁ νόμος with "Scripture" might contribute to misunderstanding the public nature of writing in early manuscript cultures. In such cultures, due to the expense of writing material and scribal activity, things that were written were ordinarily matters of significant public importance (such as treaties) or of significant cultural heritage (e.g., *The Iliad*). For this reason, we ought to treat ἡ γραφή with special care and ordinarily translate it as "Scripture" or "what is written," and *not* confuse it with a particular treaty that happens to have a large amount of commanding in it.

17. Moo, "'Law,' 'Works of the Law,' and Legalism in Paul," 73–100.

18. Mark A. Seifrid, "Righteousness Language in the Hebrew Scriptures and Early Judaism," in *Justification and Varied Nomism, Vol. 1: The Complexities of Second Temple Judaism*, ed. D. A. Carson, Peter T. O'Brien, and Mark A. Seifrid (Grand Rapids: Baker, 2001), 422.

years after [the promissory covenant]" that is being referred to, and commentators have routinely conceded that ὁ νόμος is a synecdoche for the Sinai covenant there. But note, rhetorically, that Paul begins with "I give a human example" (3:16) to illustrate what he said before in 3:10-14; so ὁ νόμος almost certainly has the same meaning in each case. And then he raises a rhetorical question in 3:19: Τί οὖν ὁ νόμος; Why raise this question unless to answer a perceived question about what he had already said about ὁ νόμος? And when, in the remainder of the third chapter, he refers to ὁ νόμος six times, it is unlikely that he would change the definition in the answer to his own rhetorical question. In such a tightly reasoned passage, ὁ νόμος most likely has the same meaning every time: the covenant God made with the Israelites alone through Moses at Sinai, a covenant characterized by a large amount of law.

A second consideration grows out of the ordinarily conservative nature of the LXX translators and the particular caution they would have accorded to תורה. By my count, תורה appears 208 times in the Hebrew Bible in the singular. Of those, I could only find 19 that were not translated by ὁ νόμος in the LXX. Three of those, by their own contextual qualifications, are manifestly not "the Law of Moses":

Hear, my son, your father's instruction, and forsake not your mother's *teaching* [תורת אמך, θεσμοὺς μητρός σου]. (Prov. 1:8)

Keep my commandments and live; keep *my teaching* [ותורתי, τοὺς δὲ ἐμοὺς λόγους] as the apple of your eye. (Prov. 7:2)

And the *teaching of kindness* [ותורת חסד, τάξιν] is on her tongue. (Prov. 31:26)

And four others are translated with a derivative of ὁ νόμος:

And when he sits on the throne of his kingdom, he shall write for himself in a book a copy of this law [את משנה התורה הזאת, δευτερονόμιον], approved by the Levitical priests. (Deut. 17:18)

"You shall say to them, 'Thus says the Lord: If you will not listen to me, to walk in my law [בתורתי, ἐν τοῖς νομίμοις μου] that I have set before you.'" (Jer. 26:4)

Were I to write for him my laws [תורתי, νόμιμα] by the ten thousands, they would be regarded as a strange thing. (Hos. 8:12)

My son, do not forget my teaching [תורתי, ἐμῶν νομίμων], but let your heart keep my commandments. (Prov. 3:1)

If we remove these seven, we find only 12 (5.7 percent) that are translated with anything other than ὁ νόμος; the other 94.3 percent are translated with ὁ νόμος. I regard it as unlikely, therefore, that Paul, trained under Gamaliel, would have monkeyed around a good deal with ὁ νόμος. It was, in Paul's circles, simply the Greek equivalent of תורה, and the likelihood of Paul introducing substantively new denotations to such a theologically important term is slender. For Paul, תורה was the distinctive gift delivered by God to the Israelites, the covenant he made with them at Sinai recorded on the "tablets of the covenant" and stored in the "ark of the covenant." Note several texts where תורה is employed by texts that refer to the covenant itself:

And the LORD will single him out from all the tribes of Israel for calamity, in accordance with all the curses of the covenant [τὰς ἀρὰς τῆς διαθήκης] written in this Book of the Law [τῷ βιβλίῳ τοῦ νόμου τούτου]. (Deut. 29:21)

Then Moses wrote this law [τὰ ῥήματα τοῦ νόμου τούτου] and gave it to the priests, the sons of Levi, who carried the ark of the covenant [τὴν κιβωτὸν τῆς διαθήκης] of the LORD, and to all the elders of Israel. (Deut. 31:9)

"Take this Book of the Law [τὸ βιβλίον τοῦ νόμου τούτου] and put it by the side of the ark of the covenant [τῆς κιβωτοῦ τῆς διαθήκης] of the LORD your God, that it may be there for a witness against you." (Deut. 31:26)

Set the trumpet to your lips! One like a vulture is over the house of the LORD, because they have transgressed my covenant [τὴν διαθήκην μου] and rebelled against my law [τοῦ νόμου μου]. (Hos. 8:1)

They did not keep God's covenant [τὴν διαθήκην τοῦ θεοῦ], but refused to walk according to his law [ἐν τῷ νόμῳ αὐτοῦ]. (Ps. 78:10)

A third concern relates to those who have argued that Paul employs ὁ νόμος sometimes to refer to legalism, to a meritorious/legalistic abuse of the law.[19] This I regard as extremely unlikely, bordering on semantically impossible. Why would Paul employ ὁ νόμος to mean both the good law that God gave to the Israelites and to mean an *abuse* of the same good thing? Could ὁ νόμος mean both "God's law, *rightly* understood and used," and "God's law, *wrongly* understood and used"? I doubt any language could do such a thing with a single word. Could the term "antibiotic" refer to that which kills microorganisms and to the microorganisms themselves? Far more likely for a first-century Palestinian Jew such as Paul, ὁ νόμος meant what it did when he defended himself in Jerusalem: "I am a Jew, born in Tarsus in Cilicia, but brought up in this city, educated at the feet of Gamaliel according to the strict manner of the law of our fathers [τοῦ πατρῴου νόμου], being zealous for God as all of you are this day" (Acts 22:3). It would hardly have served Paul's defense to have accused himself here of misunderstanding or misusing the law; to the contrary, his law observance was evidence of his zeal for God. Paul would have employed ὁ νόμος as did the LXX before him, as the Greek term for the Hebrew תורה that God gave the Israelites at Sinai. The only thing I suggest beyond this is that I view ὁ νόμος (in Paul's usage) not primarily as a compendium of moral wisdom, but as a covenant; the "tablets of the covenant" (Deut. 9:9, 11, 15) were placed in the "ark of the covenant," because what was inscribed

---

19. Ernest de Witt Burton, *A Critical and Exegetical Commentary on the Epistle to the Galatians*, ICC (Edinburgh: T & T Clark, 1921), 458; Daniel P. Fuller, *Gospel and Law: Contrast or Continuum?* (Pasadena, CA: Fuller Theological Seminary, 1990), 97–99. Perhaps ironically, James D. G. Dunn does a similar thing regarding "works of the law" when he claims that it can mean, generally, "what the law requires" (355), but also "Israel's misunderstanding of what her covenant law required" (366). Dunn, *The Theology of Paul the Apostle* (Grand Rapids: Eerdmans, 1998). This is R. Barry Matlock's criticism of Dunn: "How exactly can Dunn have 'works of the law' signify *both* 'what(ever) the law requires' *and* a particular perversion of the law, the 'misunderstanding' and its characteristic emphases and effects?" Cf. Matlock, "Sins of the Flesh and Suspicious Minds: Dunn's New Theology of Paul," *Journal for the Study of the New Testament* 72 (1998): 78 (emphasis original).

on those tablets was the covenant God instituted at Sinai. And even here, I argue that this is what it sometimes meant *before* Paul also.

Further, as I will suggest at appropriate places, not only does ὁ νόμος, by synecdoche, suggest "the Sinai covenant," but it also suggests "the Sinai covenant that excludes Gentiles." That is, Paul is deeply aware of the segregationist nature of the Sinai covenant.[20] The previous (Abrahamic) covenant would one day bring blessings to "all the families/nations of the world" (Gen. 12:3; 22:18). But the Sinai covenant segregated the descendants of Abraham from such families and nations. When Paul asks the rhetorical question Τί οὖν ὁ νόμος in Gal. 3:19, he could be paraphrased as asking this, "Why was there an Israel-segregating covenant for so many years, since the earlier covenant comprehended all the nations in its pledged blessings?"[21] His question was not merely, "Why have *another* covenant?" His question was, "Why have a *different* covenant that segregated the descendants of Abraham from the nations? What was the purpose of this segregation? What good could possibly come from such a segregationist covenant, when the earlier covenant had pledged one day to employ the 'seed of Abraham' to bless all of those other nations?"[22]

---

20. This segregationist nature of Sinai is even disclosed in the circumstances under which it was inaugurated. Yahweh did not make covenant with the Israelites while they were slaves to the large civilization of Egypt, nor did he make covenant with them while they were in the well-populated and highly civilized land of Canaan; rather, he made covenant with them in a deserted wilderness. If it had been Yahweh's intention for this covenant to have comprehended other nations, or for its ten words to have been ten timeless words of moral counsel given to the human race per se, then his publicist ought to have been fired. If the Egyptians were to have been benefactors of these ten words, then Yahweh should have given them while the Israelites were still there; and were the Canaanites to have been its benefactors, it should have been delivered after the crossing of the Jordan. But they manifestly were not, because the Sinai covenant was made with God's "chosen people," *with* them alone *when* they were alone.

21. James D. G. Dunn has rightly called attention to this segregating aspect of the Sinai covenant itself: "In sociological terms the Law functioned as an identity marker and boundary, reinforcing Israel's sense of distinctiveness and distinguishing Israel from the surrounding nations." Dunn, "The New Perspective on Paul," in *The Romans Debate*, ed. Karl P. Donfried (Peabody, MA: Hendrickson, 1991), 303. Heikki Räisänen also rightly notices that "in summary, *nomos* in Paul refers to the authoritative tradition of Israel, anchored in the revelation on Sinai, which separates the Jews from the rest of the mankind." Räisänen, *Paul and the Law* (Philadelphia: Fortress, 1983), 16.

22. I have been surprised recently to encounter occasional individuals who deny that the Sinai covenant segregated Israel from the nations. I had anticipated many objections, but not this one. Were the Israelites not prohibited from intermarrying with the people of the land before they entered it (Deut. 7:3ff.)? Was not the entire program of return from exile threatened because they had done this very thing (Ezra 9:14), to the point that the Israelites were required to put away their wives and children? Does not Ephesians 2 regard the law as creating a wall between Israel and the nations, saying that Christ "has broken down in his flesh the dividing wall of hostility [τὸ μεσότοιχον τοῦ φραγμοῦ] by abolishing the law [τὸν νόμον] of commandments and ordinances (2:13–14)? Segregation was so necessary that Yahweh demanded that the *am ha-aretz* be put to death: "But in the cities of these peoples that the LORD your God is giving you for an inheritance, you shall save alive nothing that breathes, but you shall devote them to complete destruction, the Hittites and the Amorites, the Canaanites and the Perizzites, the Hivites and the Jebusites, as the LORD your God has commanded, that they may not teach you to do according to all their abominable practices that they have done for their gods, and so you sin against the LORD your God" (Deut. 20:16–18).

That is, Paul asked precisely the opposite question that Luther and Calvin asked when they formulated three uses of the law. Luther and Calvin effectively asked this question: "What are three good uses of the law that it universally and always has *today*?" But Paul asked just the opposite question, "What was the *temporary* purpose of a covenant that appeared, in some ways, to be a disruption of the Gentile-including covenant that antedated it?" Luther and Calvin asked, "What are the uses of the law that it *still* has?" Paul asked, "What was the purpose of the Sinai covenant that it *no longer* has [οὐκέτι, Gal. 3:25]?" The dominant Protestant approach has not merely misunderstood Paul's answer to this question; it has entirely misunderstood his question and therefore *could* not answer it correctly. Paul was asking what purpose the law had "*until* the coming faith would be revealed" (Gal. 3:23); Luther and Calvin were asking what uses it had *after* the coming faith was revealed. Framing a question rightly does not guarantee a right answer, but framing it wrongly ordinarily does guarantee getting a wrong answer. We cannot frame Paul's question differently than he did and make any sense of his answer.

Few people dispute the presence of synecdoche in the New Testament writings, and people routinely acknowledge that Paul employs "faith" as a synecdoche for the new covenant in Galatians 3:23 and 25 ("before faith came . . . after faith came"). Systematic-theological concerns, however, appear to cause some interpreters to be nervous about Paul characterizing these three covenants as "promise," "law," and "faith," because they fear that doing so will imply too much discontinuity or difference between the various covenants. Were not some imperatives (e.g., circumcision) given to Abraham? And did not Moses encourage the Israelites to believe in Yahweh (e.g., to deliver them from the Egyptians)? Yes and yes; but the way synecdoche works is to describe a reality by a dominant or characteristic feature, without implying that said dominant feature is an exclusive feature. A covenant characterized by law-giving could also encourage faith and could also remind of previous promises. Its dominant feature is not and need not be its exclusive feature. Much of the hesitance, I would argue, to acknowledge Paul's synecdoches in the Galatian letter has been due to this reluctance to suggest that the Sinai covenant is exclusively about law, or that the Abrahamic covenant is exclusively about promise, or that the new covenant is exclusively about faith. But when synecdoche is employed to describe the prevailing or dominant feature of a thing, it does not necessarily exclude other, subsidiary characteristics. When we refer to police officers as "the law," for instance, this is because they do indeed enforce the law; but they also assist us when our automobiles break down by the side of the road, they escort us to the hospital during emergencies, they help us find lost children, and so on (though they do not help with treed cats).

When I attempt to unpack Paul's reasoning in chapters 3 and 4, I suggest that ὁ νόμος is used throughout Galatians as it is in Galatians 3:17, to refer to the (Israel-segregating, Gentile-excluding, obedience-demanding, curse-threatening) covenant God instituted at Sinai with the Israelites.[23] Much later, I will suggest that what is true of Galatians is

---

23. I also suggest later that this is Paul's ordinary use of νόμος in his other letters. Exceptions to this usage can appear (in Galatians and elsewhere), but ordinarily not when νόμος is used absolutely. When νόμος is followed by some qualifying genitive, that qualifying genitive can alter the ordinary referent of νόμος. So, e.g., in Gal. 6:2, τὸν νόμον τοῦ Χριστοῦ does not

largely true of Paul's other letters also. When ὁ νόμος is understood as a synecdoche for the Sinai covenant, much light is spread over Paul's letters and his thought.[24]

1.2. Covenant-Historical Argumentation ("Covenant" or "Covenants")

Throughout my detailed discussion of Galatians 3 and 4, I argue that Paul's reasoning is covenant-historical. That is, he discusses the realities of church life within the new covenant by discussing the realities of the Abrahamic and Sinai covenants, respectively. He argues that the ceremonies of the Sinai covenant were/are temporary, because that covenant itself was temporary. There was a covenant before the Sinai covenant, with important differences. The Abrahamic covenant, while pledging to make Abraham's descendants numerous and give them a land, also pledged to bless all the nations of the world through a single descendant of Abraham (Gal. 3:16). That is, the Abrahamic covenant, unlike the Sinai covenant, comprehended the nations within its pledged blessings. More than four centuries before God made a (segregationist) covenant with a single nation, he had made a covenant that pledged to bless *all* nations. Sinai, rightly understood, was temporary—a temporary covenant with Abraham's descendants that distinguished one nation *from* the other nations for a season of time, until the time would come when one of Abraham's descendants would bless all nations. If the Gentile-excluding Sinai covenant were permanent, it would prevent the fulfilling of what was pledged to Abraham; it was only temporary, *"until* [ἄχρις] the offspring should come to whom the promise had been made" (3:19). The Abrahamic covenant, in this sense, *temporalizes* and thereby *relativizes* the Sinai covenant. The Sinai covenant is secondary to it and is only understood rightly as an instrument by which the earlier covenant reaches its fruition.[25]

---

refer to the covenant made through Moses, because the qualifying genitive alters what the term ordinarily means otherwise. At Rom. 3:27, this is also the case with νόμου πίστεως, and this occurs as well at Rom. 8:2, ὁ γὰρ νόμος τοῦ πνεύματος τῆς ζωῆς ἐν Χριστῷ Ἰησοῦ ἠλευθέρωσέν σε ἀπὸ τοῦ νόμου τῆς ἁμαρτίας καὶ τοῦ θανάτου. But without such qualification, νόμος ordinarily refers to the Sinai covenant in Paul's letters. In a separate work on Romans, I would suggest that, even in chapters 3 and 8, the Pauline association of νόμος and the Sinai covenant does not entirely recede, and the genitives in question probably distinguish the Sinai covenant from the new covenant, which is characterized by such realities as faith, life, and the eschatological Spirit. So while the genitives in such texts change the referent from the Sinai covenant to something else, the "something else" is still a covenant-administration, but a different one.

24. Using some of the simplest features of word processing, I prepare a few handouts for my students to illustrate this. First, I search for all of the 121 Pauline uses of ὁ νόμος. I then print them several times, once in which it is translated "God's moral will," once in which it is translated "legalism," and once in which it is translated "the Sinai covenant." I then ask them to read these over, marking "Y" or "N" or a question mark in the margin beside each, indicating whether the translation does, does not, or might make sense of the text. What they discover is they get far more "Ys" on their handouts for "Sinai covenant" than they do for the other renditions. They realize after this exercise that perhaps this should indeed be the controlling way of understanding the term in Paul's letters.

25. Early covenant theologians recognized this and some, such as Samuel Bolton (1605–54), a commissioner to the Westminster Assembly, therefore referred to the Sinai covenant as a

Paul's language throughout Galatians 3 and 4 was/is remarkably temporal: the Abrahamic covenant preceded the Sinai covenant by 430 years; the Abrahamic covenant was "previously ratified by God." The Sinai covenant, therefore, comes *after* one covenant and *before* another. It (and its Gentile-excluding ceremonies) was in place only "*until* the offspring should come to whom the promise had been made" (3:20), "*until* the coming faith would be revealed" (3:23), and "*until* Christ came" (3:24). But in these passages, Paul also indicated that the new covenant realities are similar in kind to the Abrahamic realities and dissimilar in kind to the Sinai covenant realities. The Abrahamic and new covenants comprehend Gentiles within their blessings; whereas the Sinai covenant is made with a single nation. The Abrahamic and new covenants are promissory, dependent for their fruition only on the faithfulness of the promising God (3:16–17); whereas the Sinai covenant is legal/conditional, dependent for its fruition on the obedience of the Israelites. In this sense, the Sinai covenant "is not of faith" (3:12). The Abrahamic and new covenants pledge to bless (3:6–9); the Sinai covenant threatens to curse (3:10–13). Much of what Paul argues in these chapters is that the Abrahamic covenant was different from, and preferable to, the Sinai covenant in many ways, and it reaches its full expression and blessedness in the new covenant. The differences between the Abrahamic covenant and the Sinai covenant are so stark that Paul anticipated his readers raising the question, "Why then the Law?" (3:19). His answer to this was somewhat complex and somewhat difficult, but effectively he answers that there was a season in the history of redemption during which memory of the promise to Abraham (to bless the nations through one of his descendants) was in jeopardy of being forgotten, during which time the integrity of Abraham's lineage was also threatened (by intermarriage with the *am ha-aretz*). During this season, the Sinai covenant, precisely *by* its prohibitions of such intermarriage (and other ceremonies that distinguished Jew and Gentile) preserved both the basic integrity of Abraham's lineage and the memory of the pledge to bless the nations through that lineage's coming Seed. The law, during this period, was a "guardian" (3:24–25); its Gentile-excluding ceremonies guarded Israel from their own tendency to be like the nations around them and to intermarry with them.[26] The

---

"*Foedus subserviens*," to what they called the covenant of grace. Referring to the Sinai covenant, Bolton said, "It was given by way of subserviency to the Gospel and a fuller revelation of the covenant of grace; it was temporary, and had respect to Canaan and God's blessing there, if and as Israel obeyed. It had no relation to heaven, for that was promised by another covenant which God made before He entered the subservient covenant. This is the opinion which I myself desire modestly to propound, for I have not been convinced that it is injurious to holiness or disagreeable to the mind of God in Scripture." *The True Bounds of Christian Freedom* (repr., Edinburgh: Banner of Truth Trust, 1964), 99.

26. Cf. my "A Note on ΠΑΙΔΑΓΩΓΟΣ in Gal. 3. 24–25," *New Testament Studies* 35, no. 1 (January 1989): 150–54. In this I acknowledged, with many others, that the "child-servant" had different functions in different households. In some, to be sure, the παιδαγωγός was, as Luther thought, disciplinary; and in others, the παιδαγωγός was, as Calvin thought, tutorial/instructive. But in yet others, the παιδαγωγός was manifestly a bodyguard, whose role was to protect or guard. In Galatians, therefore, it is this latter, protecting/guarding role to which Paul refers by the analogy. Sinai's Gentile-excluding regulations protect/preserve both memory of the Abrahamic promise and the basic integrity of his biological lineage from the Israelite tendency to intermarry with the *am ha-aretz*.

Sinai covenant "guarded" Israel against their own prevailing tendency to intermarry with the *am ha-aretz* and follow their deities, forgetting their own covenant marriage to Yahweh. Of course, it guarded them only imperfectly, and some generations less well than others. But at least when the coming Seed of Abraham appeared, Matthew could trace Jesus' lineage back to Abraham. In this sense, the first chapter of Matthew's Gospel, in which Christ's lineage is traced back to Abraham, testifies that the law had fulfilled its "guardian" function adequately.

Precisely here, James D. G. Dunn's various discussions of Paul are tantalizingly close to being exactly right. He rightly focuses on the Gentile-excluding dimensions of Torah as the primary reason for Paul's negative statements about ὁ νόμος. For the dominant Protestant approach, Paul's negative comments about ὁ νόμος were attributed to people's (alleged) attempts to justify themselves by obedience thereto; for Dunn's approach, Paul's negative comments about ὁ νόμος are attributed to how it separates Jew from Gentile. On this point, Dunn's contribution to Pauline scholarship[27] is, in my opinion, both substantial and salutary. But his "sociological" language suggests that the separation of Jew and Gentile was due to ordinary sociological, ethnic, or even xenophobic reasons. Paul's point is that ὁ νόμος *required* this separation, a separation that the Israelites, throughout much of their history, did not desire. Paul's point is that ὁ νόμος not only protected/guarded Israel from the *am ha-aretz*; it also protected Israel from their characteristic desire to intermarry with them.

1.3. Arguing *from* Justification or *for* Justification

Many competent and helpful authors have addressed Galatians in terms of Greco-Roman rhetoric, both generally and specifically. I make no attempt to address any of those here, though the literature is both erudite and fascinating. Rather, I merely wish to introduce one controlling feature of my understanding of the rhetoric of Galatians 3 and 4 in an extremely general and nontechnical way.[28] As far as I can tell after thirty

---

27. With a little assistance from Krister Stendahl's *Paul among Jews and Gentiles* (Philadelphia: Fortress, 1976).

28. By "nontechnical," I mean that I ordinarily make no effort to interact with the secondary literature about Greco-Roman rhetoric and the various technical terms and devices associated with such study, useful as it is. Nor do I distinguish "rhetorical" analysis from "epistolary" analysis. Rather, I use "rhetoric" in its general sense of understanding the logic employed in the letter: What case is Paul making, and how is he making that case? For an introduction to the more technical study of Galatians in light of Greco-Roman rhetoric, cf. Hans Dieter Betz, "The Literary Composition and Function of Paul's Letter to the Galatians," *New Testament Studies* 21:3 (1975): 353–79, and *Galatians: A Commentary on Paul's Letter to the Churches in Galatia*, Hermeneia Series (Philadelphia: Fortress, 1979); George A. Kennedy, *New Testament Interpretation through Rhetorical Criticism* (Chapel Hill: University of North Carolina Press, 1984); David E. Aune, "Review of Galatians: Dialogical Response to Opponents," *Catholic Bible Quarterly* 46 (1984); Wilhelm Wuellner, "Where Is Rhetorical Criticism Taking Us?," *Catholic Bible Quarterly* 49 (1987): 448–63; Burton L. Mack, *Rhetoric and the New Testament* (Minneapolis: Augsburg/Fortress, 1990), 66–73; Walter B. Russell, "Rhetorical Analysis of the Book of Galatians," *Bibliotheca Sacra* 150 (July-September 1993), 341–58; Carl Joachim Classen, *Rhetorical Criticism of the New Testament*, Wissenschaftliche Untersuchungen zum Neuen Testament 128 (Tübingen:

years of reading Galatians, I believe that Paul does not argue *for* the doctrine of justification by faith in the letter; rather, he argues *from* the doctrine of justification by faith. In ordinary rhetoric, whether Greco-Roman or otherwise, people attempt to settle disputed matters by appealing to some commonly shared, nondisputed matters. The nature of such reasoning is to draw out the implications or consequences of the nondisputed matters as a means of settling the disputed matters. Throughout the Galatian letter, I not only find no evidence that the Galatians misunderstood the doctrine of justification by faith in Christ, but the contrary: I find express evidence that Paul refers to it as a settled doctrine, and a settled doctrine that enables him to address what is unsettled—namely, what ceremonies to require of Gentiles.

The issue is not one of refined, technical issues in rhetoric; it is simpler than that. There is a difference between a premise, an argument, and a conclusion. The dominant Protestant approach to interpreting Paul has conceived the doctrine of justification in Galatians as an argument or conclusion; I conceive it as a premise. Paul refers to the doctrine of justification as a settled matter (as a premise) upon which he makes arguments that lead to his conclusion (that the gospel, not just his mission, is νόμος-free) and its practical consequences (that no one—Jew *or* Gentile—needs to observe the law).

Because the doctrine of justification by faith alone was unsettled in Luther's and Calvin's day, much Protestant interpretation of the Galatian letter has (erroneously, in my judgment) assumed that Paul's issue was the same as Luther's and Calvin's. But it was not. Paul's issue was quite different from that of Luther and Calvin. Paul's issue was virtually identical to the issue addressed at the Jerusalem Council: Which, if any, of the ceremonies of the Mosaic law are Gentiles required to observe in the New Testament church? Must they be circumcised? Shall they be required to observe the Jewish calendar or dietary laws? These were the questions the apostles addressed in Acts 15, and they were similar to the questions Paul addressed at Galatia, though Galatians adds the additional consideration of whether even Jews (such as Peter) *may* observe those aspects of the Mosaic law that require separation from table fellowship with Gentiles. As Paul looked for a rhetorical lever in this circumstance, he selected (among others) the doctrine of justification by faith alone. If Abraham was justified by faith (even before he was circumcised; Gen. 15 precedes Gen. 17), then those who have faith are his spiritual progeny (Gal. 3:7, 9), regardless of whether they are circumcised. If Abraham was justified by faith 430 years before the Mosaic law (with its calendar and dietary laws) was given, then people can be justified apart from that calendar and apart from those dietary laws. And if people can be justified apart from such ceremonies, then perhaps it is not necessary to require them at all.

So, while Paul addresses and affirms the doctrine of justification by faith in Galatians, he does not argue *for* it as a doctrine disputed at Galatia. He argues *from* it as a doctrine/premise as old as Abraham, as a doctrine/premise that Abraham—not

---

Mohr Siebeck, 2000), esp. 1–28; Lauri Thurén, *Derhetorizing Paul: A Dynamic Perspective on Pauline Theology and the Law* (Tübingen: Mohr Siebeck, 2000); Ben Witherington III, "The Rhetoric of Galatians," *Grace in Galatia: A Commentary on Paul's Letter to the Galatians* (New York: T & T Clark, 2004), 25–36; D. Francois Tolmie, *Persuading the Galatians: A Text-Centred Rhetorical Analysis of a Pauline Letter*, Wissenschaftliche Untersuchungen zum Neuen Testament 2, Reihe 190 (Tübingen: Mohr Siebeck, 2005); Duane F. Watson, *The Rhetoric of the New Testament: A Bibliographic Survey*, Tools for Biblical Study (Blandford Forum, UK: Deo, 2006).

Paul—originated. Some of the post-Sanders discussion of the nature of first-century Palestinian Judaism is, in this limited and particular sense, irrelevant. Is it possible that some first-century Jews had confused ideas about the relation between the Abrahamic promises and the Mosaic laws? Certainly, but Mr. Gallup was not around to take a poll to determine the matter, and even the relevant literature may only reflect the opinions of those first-century Jews who were familiar with that literature. And, in a prevailingly oral culture in which written material was extremely rare and extremely expensive, we just do not and cannot ever know what Joe Israelite actually believed in the first century, nor do we need to know this. It does not matter to Paul. Paul, rhetorically, refers to the Abrahamic doctrine of justification by faith as a settled matter, without any speculation about whether his entire audience agrees with him or not (or had ever thought about the matter). This is a routine part of human rhetoric, whether ancient or modern. We routinely refer to ideas, attitudes, or values that we judge to be well known and publicly recognized without speculating as to whether 100 percent of our audience actually functions entirely consistently with the same. We say things such as "As we all know, our founding fathers were committed to the idea of freedom of speech," without any consideration at all as to whether our audience may or may not contain a handful of bigots or parochials who actually do *not* believe in freedom of speech.[29]

I am not denying that the post-Sanders discussion of first-century Palestinian Judaism is useful and important in its own right; indeed, it is both useful and important. I am merely denying that such study substantially illuminates the rhetoric of Galatians. That rhetoric can be discovered by the nature of the reasoning itself, with or without reference to our always tentative historical judgments about an ancient culture. Paul reasoned with Peter (and therefore with his audience) by saying, "We who are Jews by birth, and not Gentile sinners, knowing [εἰδότες] that a man is not justified by observing the law" (Gal. 2:15–16; my translation). As with virtually every use of οἶδα or γινώσκω in the first person plural in Paul's letters, the rhetoric here refers to the matter as settled. Whether it was actually settled, intellectually or psychologically, in the minds of every individual in Paul's audience was and is entirely irrelevant (as strange as that seems), because the nature of human rhetoric was and is always this way. No author and no speaker can actually know the contents of the minds of each individual member of the audience; all an author or speaker can know is what is publicly and widely acknowledged within the community that is being addressed. Paul therefore assumed, rhetorically, that his audience was familiar with Father Abraham and with the promises God made freely to him, which Abraham and Sarah received by faith (albeit imperfect faith in what Sarah regarded as risible promises). Paul also assumed, rhetorically, that his audience would not have regarded as a novelty his routine reference to Genesis 15:6, that Abraham "believed God, and it was counted to him as righteousness" (Gal. 3:6).

---

29. According to Mark Bauerlein, "In a 2003 survey on the First Amendment commissioned by the Foundation for Individual Rights in Education, only one in 50 college students named the first right guaranteed in the amendment, and one out of four did not know *any* freedom protected by it." Cf. Mark Bauerlein, *The Dumbest Generation: How the Digital Age Stupefies Young Americans and Jeopardizes our Future (Or, Don't Trust Anyone under Thirty)* (New York: Jeremy P. Tarcher / Penguin, 2008), 10.

This is simply the nature of human rhetoric: we refer to well-known, publicly acknowledged ideas or values to settle unsettled matters. In doing so, we assume nothing about the actual ideas or values of each of the particular members of our particular audience. When we refer to Lincoln's Gettysburg address, or his (more eloquent) Second Inaugural address, we know perfectly well that there may be some Southern sympathizers in our audience, but we don't care (at least not rhetorically). We refer to Lincoln's sentiments as sentiments that are widely known and publicly acknowledged as an important part of our cultural ethos and history, without any concern for the particular opinions of, in this case, the descendants of John Wilkes Booth. Indeed, part of the skillful use of rhetoric is to refer to some matters as settled, even if we know or suspect that there are a few dissenting opinions within our audience. When Christian clergy refer to Holy Scripture in a sermon, for instance, they do not assume that every individual in the audience knows or believes in every sentence in the Scriptures; but the Scriptures, in that context, are regarded as religiously authoritative and can be referred to as such, employing the adjective "holy."

Paul's reasoning with Peter, then, is significant, because Paul articulated as a *settled* matter between them exactly the opposite thing that the dominant Protestant view had long taught. The dominant Protestant understanding had taught that first-century Judaism commonly or routinely taught that people are justified by observing the Mosaic law rather than by faith. But Paul said precisely the opposite of this: "We who are Jews by nature, and not sinners of the Gentiles, knowing that a man is not justified by the works of the law" (Gal. 2:15–16 KJV). Many English translations (e.g., RSV, ESV) obscure this somewhat by translating "*yet* we know," but the original is fairly straightforward: Ἡμεῖς φύσει Ἰουδαῖοι καὶ οὐκ ἐξ ἐθνῶν ἁμαρτωλοί· εἰδότες [δὲ] ὅτι οὐ δικαιοῦται ἄνθρωπος ἐξ ἔργων νόμου. While the "yet" may suggest that Paul's beliefs were contrary to ordinary Jewish belief, the "yet" depends on two very thin lines of evidence. First, it must assume that the [δὲ] following εἰδότες is in fact genuine, despite considerable evidence to the contrary.[30] And second, it must assert an aggressively adversative meaning *to* the disputed δὲ. My search program counts 636 uses of δέ in Paul's letters (if we include the disputed epistles). Yet a translation such as the ESV translates only eight of those 636 as "yet." In only seven other places, out of 636, is the δέ translated with the strongly adversative "yet."[31] Even if we granted the textually suspect δὲ to be original, and even if we approved this extremely rare adversative translation of it, this would still not undo the rhetorical power of the participle itself, εἰδότες. However we attempt to evade/avoid what Paul said, it can-

---

30. I regard the textual evidence as a virtual dead heat here: the δὲ is included by ancient and diverse textual traditions such as ℵ, B, C, D*, F, and some Latin versions, omitted by P46, A, D2 Ψ, the Majority texts, and the Syriac versions.

31. "*Yet* among the mature we do impart wisdom" (1 Cor. 2:6).
    "*Yet* those who marry will have worldly troubles, and I would spare you that" (1 Cor. 7:28).
    "*Yet* in my judgment she is happier if she remains as she is" (1 Cor. 7:40).
    "As it is, there are many parts, *yet* one body" (1 Cor. 12:20).
    "As sorrowful, *yet* always rejoicing" (2 Cor. 6:10).
    "*Yet* because of false brothers secretly brought in" (Gal. 2:4).
    "*Yet* we know that a person is not justified by works of the law" (Gal. 2:16).
    "*Yet* she will be saved through childbearing" (1 Tim. 2:15).

not be disputed that he says at Galatians 2:16 that Jews know/knew that a person was not justified by observing the law.[32] All of the rhetorical power of that clause would be lost if the clause following εἰδότες were debated. Paul asserted in this passage that one thing Jews knew (in contrast to "Gentile sinners") was that an individual was not justified by observing the law.[33]

Some have attempted to deflect this clause by another effort. They have suggested that the "we" who know that a person is not justified by observing the law are Christian believers. While, as a pure conjecture, it might be plausible for a Pauline "we" to refer to believers, this passage does not do so; it refers to those who are Jews and not Gentiles: "We who are Jews by nature/training and not Gentile sinners, having known that a man is not justified by observing the law" (my own free translation of Ἡμεῖς φύσει Ἰουδαῖοι καὶ οὐκ ἐξ ἐθνῶν ἁμαρτωλοί· εἰδότες [δὲ] ὅτι οὐ δικαιοῦται ἄνθρωπος ἐξ ἔργων νόμου). That is, Paul does not say, "We who are by nature Christians," or "We who are by nature believers," but "We who are by nature Jews." Further, his negative clause does not say "and not unbelievers," but "and not Gentile sinners." Nothing, it seems, but our predetermined belief that first-century Judaism was meritorious causes us to misconstrue Paul's reasoning. Paul appears to be observing a commonplace Jewish recognition, which could be paraphrased something like this:

> Peter, you and I who know the Jewish Scriptures—unlike those *meshugina* Gentiles—have read example after example of the prophets bringing judgment on our fathers because of their disobedience to the commandments of the Torah, and we know perfectly well that the Torah, for all its moral wisdom, never produced the moral wisdom it commended, and therefore was an instrument of condemnation, not justification. Now, if it always brought condemnation (rather than justification) upon us to whom it was given, why on earth would we saddle the hapless Gentiles with it? If we ourselves longed for the blessedness that would come one day through Abraham's Seed, and if many Gentiles join us in believing that Jesus of Nazareth was and is that Seed through whom both they and we are blessed, isn't it enough that we are all baptized into his name?

Further, throughout chapter 3 and 4, Paul argues *from* the canonical Old Testament Scriptures—not from sayings from Jesus or other apostolic letters (or even, remarkably, the Jerusalem Council). That is, the nature of his reasoning in chapters 3 and 4 is to demonstrate that the Jewish Scriptures themselves teach justification by faith and not the law and the temporary nature of the law.

---

32. And it is entirely irrelevant to my purposes whether 2:15–18 contains Paul's reasoning with Peter or Paul's reasoning with his fellow Jews at Galatia; either way he asserts that "we . . . Jews" know perfectly well that the law does not justify, as a means to his pre-arguing his point that the non-law-observing Gentiles are not thereby going to be helped any by observing the law.

33. It is even theoretically possible that Paul was mistaken, and that he projected his view onto others whose beliefs differed from his. Even if this were so, it would not alter my thesis. Even if Paul were entirely delusional, to understand the epistle of a delusional individual we must understand rightly what *he* regards as axiomatic, even if no one else regards it as such. In Socrates' apology, for instance, he regarded pantheism as axiomatic, as did his accusers. We might regard both Socrates and Meletus as being mistaken; but to make sense of their respective arguments, we must rightly understand their premises. The correspondence of those premises to *reality* is an entirely different matter than the correspondence of those premises to their *reasoning*.

When we arrive at the exposition of Paul's reasoning in chapters 3 and 4 (and even when we discuss briefly his reasoning in chapters 1 and 2), my exposition will be guided by these three controlling realities: That ὁ νόμος was regularly employed in Galatians as a synecdoche for the Sinai covenant administration in its entirety; that Paul's reasoning was covenant-historical (and therefore polycovenantal rather than monocovenantal); and that he argued not *for* justification by faith but *from* justification by faith. Readers are invited to judge for themselves whether such a reading of Galatians is more adequate than alternative readings.

CHAPTER 2

Historical Questions Pertinent to Galatians

Several historical questions are pertinent to the interpretation of Galatians, and some more than others. It is no purpose of mine in this book to address all of them. I will express virtually no opinion, for instance, about the North Galatia/South Galatia question and will intentionally offer no new arguments or speculations about that matter. For the narrow purposes of this work, which is to assess the nature of Paul's theological reasoning in Galatians 3 and 4, several other historical matters must be briefly addressed, some more general and some more specific. I am basically introducing those matters here as a means of permitting the reader to understand the method to my madness later. Whether my tentative conclusions on these matters contributes to a more successful reading of Galatians will only be determined later, after the pericope-by-pericope survey of Paul's reasoning in those chapters.

2.1. General Observations about Historical Method

Biblical studies might proceed in a more helpful manner if graduate programs required further study of the concept and methodologies of historical research, rather than jumping right in to resolve specific historical questions or challenges. "History" is not merely a subject matter (e.g., the War of 1812); it is a mode of inquiry, a manner of asking questions about how certain dynamics and events influenced or caused others. Its closest analogous discipline is probably archaeology. Both disciplines ordinarily begin with some givens. In the case of archaeology it is, ordinarily, artifacts. Artifacts are discovered at a site and then, based on what we can know about those artifacts, archaeologists attempt to reconstruct the character of the culture. Archaeological knowledge is always tentative or provisional, because its conclusions are limited twice: once by the available artifacts, and again by the conjectures drawn from them.

These available artifacts limit us not merely because we ordinarily wish we had more of them, but because, in many situations, the artifacts discovered may be misrepresentative of their culture. If a given city were razed by marauders, for instance, the marauders would likely have made off with everything valuable, leaving behind only matters of comparatively little value. Archaeologists, discovering this "impoverished" artifactual heritage, do not always know whether the remaining artifacts accurately reflect life in the former community, or whether (because of theft or looting) they misrepresent that life. In addition to this artifactual limitation, archaeologists are limited by their imaginative ability to reconstruct a culture on the basis of the available artifacts. So, archaeology is a fascinating discipline, but also a difficult one, and its "results" are hardly ever final.[1]

---

1. Some disciplines appear very different to outsiders than to insiders. Outsiders to physics and archaeology probably think of both disciplines as factually based. In truth, some of the most flexible, ingenious minds appear in these disciplines, minds that attempt to make comprehensive

History is not substantially different from archaeology. Both disciplines attempt to understand a past moment in light of the existing evidence. Prior to the printing press, however, the documentary evidence for civilizations was much scantier and much less likely to be representative of the culture as a whole. Since the materials on which manuscripts were written were expensive, comparatively few documents exist from such cultures, and we cannot always know how widely known those documents were.[2] The percentage of individuals who actually read or wrote manuscripts was probably smaller than the percentage of those who teach at the college or university level today, and who would suggest that our academic writings are necessarily representative of our culture? So historians function in a similar fashion to archaeologists, doing the best they can to reconstruct a circumstance by evaluating the evidence that exists, and by speculating about how to make sense of it. What we ordinarily call "historical knowledge," therefore, is substantially speculative or theoretical.

As it pertains to biblical studies, the point is this: What we actually have before us is the text (itself sometimes mildly disputed, depending on the manuscript evidence). The text itself has a certain "factness" or "givenness" to it, and I judge that the text, which is not a theoretical construct, should have veto power over all the theoretical constructs surrounding it. If the text that is conflicts with our various speculations about its historical surroundings, then the evidence of the text should be given more weight than speculations about the culture that produced it, at least in the act of interpreting the text. That is, some interpretations are not only more or less plausible in terms of speculations about the historical circumstances; some are more or less plausible in terms of the text itself. I tend to favor, for instance, an interpretation that is more plausible in terms of the text, even if it is less plausible in terms of my reconstruction of the historical situation. If there are several historically plausible ways of reading the text, I prefer the one that conforms to the most plausible reading of the text itself—the reading that accounts best for the data of the text itself, as it were.

To illustrate this, some years ago I argued that the ellipsis in Romans 9:32 was better supplied by adding the copula than by repeating a verb ("pursued") that had appeared earlier in the text.[3] By supplying the ellipsis differently, the interpretation differs in answering Paul's rhetorical question:

> What shall we say, then? That Gentiles who did not pursue righteousness have attained it, that is, a righteousness that is by faith; but that Israel who pursued a law that would lead to righteousness did not succeed in reaching that law. Why?

Paul wonders why Israel did not attain the law, and in his answer, the Greek has an ellipsis: ὅτι οὐκ ἐκ πίστεως ἀλλ᾽ ὡς ἐξ ἔργων ("because not by faith but as by works"). In English, the two possible answers to this "Why?" would be as follows:

---

sense of a fairly limited amount of data. This is a high level of intelligence that integrates both right brains and left brains, both rationality and imagination.

2. There are occasional exceptions to this. If Milman Parry was right, Homeric "literature" first existed orally, and as such may well have been widely known before it was reduced to writing. Cf. Parry, "Studies in the Epic Technique of Oral Verse-Making: II. The Homeric Language as the Language of an Oral Poetry," *Harvard Studies in Classical Philology*, vol. 43 (1932): 1–50.

3. "Why Israel Did Not Obtain Torah-Righteousness: A Translation Note on Romans 9:32," *Westminster Theological Journal* 54 (1992): 163–66.

Option A: "Because (they did not pursue it) by faith, but as (if it were) based on works."

Option B: "Because (the law is) not by faith, but as by works."

In each case, the supplied ellipsis is indicated by parenthesis marks. Now, every translation must supply the ellipsis somehow, and students of Greek know that when a verb is missing, it can be supplied either by the copula or by repeating some other, already mentioned verb. Almost all translations take Option A above, and I was proposing Option B. On two grammatical grounds, this is preferable to me. First, the alternative translation skips over the more proximate verb ("succeed in reaching," ἔφθασεν), reaching back behind it to a less proximate verb ("pursued," διώκων). Second, the comparative particle (ὡς), which normally is merely comparative ("like" or "as" something), would, on the first translation above, need to bear the weight of creating a condition contrary to fact (or "unreal condition"), which ordinarily requires a secondary tense in the protasis, a secondary tense in the apodosis, and ordinarily the particle ἄν in the apodosis, none of which is present. Now, since the verb is missing, one could supply a verb in the secondary tense. Further, since by the Koiné period the particle ἄν is not *always* necessary in conditions contrary to fact, it is possible grammatically to supply the ellipsis as many English translations do, even though it requires a substantial reach to create a condition contrary to fact on as little ground as the comparative particle ὡς.

Contextually, there is also a Pauline ground for my preference, because this is precisely what he says in Galatians 3:12: "for the law is not of/by faith" (ὁ δὲ νόμος οὐκ ἔστιν ἐκ πίστεως). That is, the reading I prefer grammatically also has the virtue of at least being identical to what Paul expressly *says* elsewhere. Since he elsewhere says that the law is "not of faith," it is not at all a *risky* speculation to suggest that this is what he means at Romans 9:32; whereas the alternative translation is risky and does indeed require a speculation that is otherwise unsubstantiated by Paul's other writings. Further, the alternative translation has Paul faulting Israel for pursuing the law "*as if* it were *not* by faith," when in Galatians 3:12 he expressly says that the law is indeed "*not* by faith." Why would Paul fault Israel for pursuing the law "*as if* it were not by faith," when elsewhere he says that the law *is* "not by faith"? Just a few verses later, he says, "For Moses writes about the righteousness that is based on the law, that the person who *does* the commandments shall live by them," and contrasts such righteousness with "righteousness by faith" (Rom. 10:4–5).

So why does almost every translation prefer what I consider to be the weaker translation? Because, prior to E. P. Sanders, the dominant historical reconstruction of first-century Judaism believed there was good historical evidence that some (if not most) Jews pursued religion wrongly, legalistically, "as if it were based on works." So, on the basis of what was mere historical conjecture, an inferior translation (on grammatical and contextual grounds, to my mind) was preferred to a superior translation. The translation and interpretation of the text were "bent," as it were, in the direction of the historical conjecture, rather than the other way around. It remains entirely plausible (and in my opinion much more likely) that Paul's answer to his own rhetorical question in Romans 9 is that Israel did not attain unto the law because the law required works, not faith—works beyond the reach of any group of sinners, Jew or Gentile. This is a point he also made in Romans 2 when he asserted that the law hypothetically justifies only its *doers*, not its hearers (Rom. 2:13), and saying shortly thereafter that no one will be justified by observing the law (ἐξ ἔργων νόμου οὐ δικαιωθήσεται πᾶσα σάρξ, Rom. 3:20).

Thus my own prejudice regarding historical questions pertinent to biblical interpretation is that I am self-consciously somewhat agnostic. I prefer historical doubt to historical confidence, because I am aware of the power of our theoretical reconstructions of history to injure our ability to understand the various texts well. The texts are givens; Galatians 3 and Romans 9 are givens, for instance; and if Romans 9 has an ambiguity in it, that ambiguity can be resolved better by reference to what is less disputable (Galatians 3) than to what is merely suppositional and therefore more disputable. As we shall see below, this means for me that the benefit of E. P. Sanders is not necessarily that his vision/version of first-century Palestinian Judaism is now a fixed construct that guides our interpretive labors, but that his reconstruction is sufficiently persuasive to call into *doubt* our confidence in the previously dominant reconstruction. The effect of that doubt drives interpreters back to the text, which is, in my judgment, the best place for them to be anyway.

Put in a more straightforward manner: I prefer to read the lines rather than read between the lines. If two interpretations of a text are equally plausible, but one requires our reading between the lines some historical thing the lines themselves do not say, I prefer the reading that reads the lines themselves. This preference, in the study of Galatians, is hermeneutically consequential (albeit, of course, possibly erroneous). From Calvin to the present, the assumption of the dominant approach to Galatians has been this: On the surface, Paul appears to be arguing about Jewish ceremonies, but there is a deeper issue beneath the surface that is Paul's (allegedly) real concern. As Calvin put it, "We must remark, however, that he does not confine himself entirely to Ceremonies, but argues generally about Works, otherwise the whole discussion would be trifling."[4] For Calvin, taken at face value, Paul's Galatian concern is "trifling." Therefore, because Calvin believed that such a trifling concern could not occupy Paul, Calvin read between the lines, as it were, and conjectured that Paul was *really* concerned about something else—in this case, justification by works.[5] But, as much recent scholarship has demonstrated, since the ceremonies of the Mosaic law separated Jew and Gentile, to observe those ceremonies that declare Gentiles to be strangers to God's covenanting purposes (Eph. 2:12) was an enormous problem for the apostle to the Gentiles. We, living two millennia after the apostle, may take it for granted that God is now covenanting with Gentiles as well as with Jews; but it was not taken for granted in Paul's generation. Further, as we shall see in some detail later, Paul argued that proclamation to the Gentiles was itself a fulfillment of the third promise God had made to Abraham: to bless all the nations of the world through Abraham's single descendant, whom Paul identifies as Christ (3:16). For Paul, there was noth-

---

4. John Calvin, *Commentaries on the Epistles of Paul to the Galatians and Ephesians* (Grand Rapids: Baker, 1979), 18.

5. Perhaps the most interesting irony about the dominant Protestant approach to Paul is that it has ordinarily been promoted by those (such as Calvin) who also promote a high doctrine of the inspiration of Holy Scripture. But does a high doctrine of Scripture promote our regarding what it actually says as "trifling"? Does a high doctrine of Scripture encourage reading "between the lines" of said Scripture, rather than Scripture itself?

ing "trifling" about God's fulfilling the third pledge he made to Abraham. It was not trifling when God multiplied Abraham's descendants greatly; it was not trifling when (with some assistance by Joshua and the judges) God gave his descendants their own land. Similarly, it was not and is not trifling that God, in Christ and Paul's proclamation about Christ, blessed all the nations of the world through Abraham's descendant.

Calvin, steeped in Renaissance appreciation for history, might have known better. Though for his own generation, disputes about Jewish ceremonies may have appeared merely trifling, there was ample evidence that the matter was not so in Paul's day. Calvin was not unaware of Paul's comments in Romans 3: "Or is God the God of Jews only? Is he not the God of Gentiles also? Yes, of Gentiles also, since God is one" (Rom. 3:29–30). Similarly, Calvin was not unaware of Paul's thoughts in Ephesians 2 (nor did his generation have any qualms about attributing Ephesians to Paul):

> Therefore remember that at one time you Gentiles in the flesh, called "the uncircumcision" by what is called the circumcision, which is made in the flesh by hands—remember that you were at that time separated from Christ, alienated from the commonwealth of Israel and strangers to the covenants of promise, having no hope and without God in the world. But now in Christ Jesus you who once were far off have been brought near by the blood of Christ. For he himself is our peace, who has made us both one [τὰ ἀμφότερα ἓν] and has broken down in his flesh the dividing wall of hostility by abolishing the law of commandments and ordinances [τὸν νόμον τῶν ἐντολῶν ἐν δόγμασιν καταργήσας], that he might create in himself one new man [ἕνα καινὸν ἄνθρωπον] in place of the two, so making peace. (Eph. 2:11–15)

Calvin's training in Renaissance humanism—a humanism that virtually invented the notion of anachronism[6]—should have and could have been more wary about reading his own circumstances back into Paul's.

Ironically, then, Calvin's position actually strengthens mine. He as much as conceded that the lines themselves (unless we read *between* them) taught that the problem at Galatia was requiring Gentiles to observe Jewish ceremonies. It was only Calvin's failure of imagination that required him to read between the lines, as it were, and posit that something *else*, something not said in the lines themselves, *must* have been the problem. I am suggesting a different hermeneutical posture than that of Calvin: a posture that reads the lines themselves whenever doing so provides a plausible explanation of the text. My reading may be right, wrong, or (more likely) partially right; but I will present it below and candidly state here my hermeneutical bias and why I embrace it.[7]

---

6. "Perhaps the most important result of this shift in the scholarly interest and emphasis was the development of a new sense of historical perspective, the birth (or rebirth) of the sense of anachronism. The medieval Scholastics' preoccupation with timeless and abstract truth reflected the underdeveloped historical sense of the Middle Ages." E. Harris Harbison, *The Christian Scholar in the Age of the Reformation* (New York: Charles Scribner's Sons, 1956), 36–37.

7. My brief explanation here is not designed to be convincing. I do not expect many or any of my readers to concur, on the grounds mentioned here, in my preference of the text over speculative historical reconstruction. I merely intend to be candid about my minority view on the matter, and candid about how/why that influences my interpretation of Galatians. At a minimum, another monograph could be devoted to defending/promoting this minority thesis.

2.2. Specific: Paul, the Law, and E. P. Sanders

The "problem" of Paul and the law is the problem of reconciling his positive statements about the law with his negative statements about the law. Paul can as easily say that the law is "holy" or "good" (Rom. 7:12–13) as that the law "brings wrath" (Rom. 4:15), or that "the power of sin is the law" (1 Cor. 15:56). Prior to E. P. Sanders, this conundrum was rather easily solved: Paul's positive statements contain his true thinking about the law *itself*, as delivered at Sinai, and his negative statements about it express his thinking about a later meritorious/legalistic *abuse* of it in the first century. Even before Sanders, this "solution" required a certain willingness to self-deceive; after all, in Galatians 3 (as we shall see), it is the law itself, which "came 430 years after the promise," that Paul contrasts with Abrahamic faith (Gal. 3:17), not some alleged later abuse of the law. And when Paul contrasts the Abrahamic covenant with the Sinai covenant in Galatians 3, he cites texts in the law itself (Deut. 27:26; Lev. 18:5), not Second Temple Jewish texts. Nonetheless, for a human race prone to self-deception, this was not a grave difficulty, and we went merrily along with the self-deception (pausing occasionally to make flattering observations about the emperor's wardrobe), content that this self-deception at least cleaned up the messy problem of Paul and the law. Paul's brain-teasing paradox—"The very commandment that promised life proved to be death" (Rom. 7:10)—was rather breezily dismissed by reference to an alleged meritorious/legalistic abuse of the law.

And then E. P. Sanders appeared, reiterating arguments that had been made before, challenging the consensus that the religion of Second Temple Judaism could be justly accused of meritorious legalism. Many of the substantial arguments had been made before: Jewish scholars had also made the "patterns of religion" argument that Jewish texts had often been wrested from their overall religious context; and scholars such as W. D. Davies had demonstrated that Second Temple Judaism was not at all unaware of a merciful God. But for Sanders, the timing was right. The post-Holocaust interpreters of Paul were finally (though belatedly) wary of appreciating Paul at the expense of Judaism, finally willing (perhaps eager) to read his letters free from assumptions that were unflattering and unfair to Second Temple Judaism. As Peter Stuhlmacher has said regarding the New Perspective: "We must also keep in mind the apparent goal of these authors to make a new beginning in Pauline interpretation, so as to free Jewish-Christian dialogue from improper accusations against the Jewish conversation partners."[8]

In what follows, it will be apparent that I join Sanders in concluding that the dominant Protestant understanding of Second Temple Judaism prior to him was a distorted caricature of what the (reliably dated) literature presents, and that I concur with those interpreters of Paul who, as Stuhlmacher said, desire to free Jewish-Christian dialogue

---

8. Peter Stuhlmacher and Donald A. Hagner, *Revisiting Paul's Doctrine of Justification: A Challenge to the New Perspective: With an Essay by Donald A. Hagner* (Downers Grove, IL: InterVarsity Press, 2001), 34. Stuhlmacher's judgment is surprisingly similar to what George Foot Moore said nearly a century earlier in the opening sentence of an influential article: "Christian interest in Jewish literature has always been apologetic or polemical rather than historical." The same may be the case in the present day, even though the apologetic is an ecumenical apologetic, and the polemic is directed against overt suggestions that Christianity may be superior to some forms of Judaism, at least in some respects. Moore, "Christian Writers on Judaism," *Harvard Theological Review* 14, no. 3 (July 1921): 197–254.

from such improper accusations against Jewish conversation partners. At the same time, it will become apparent that I do this in a different manner from others. Most of the post-Sanders interpreters of Paul, in an appropriate effort to free Palestinian Judaism from charges of meritorious legalism, have had a tendency to conflate several covenant-administrations into a single covenant, and a gracious one at that. But to understand Palestinian Judaism, and to understand the third and fourth chapters of Galatians correctly, one must recognize that both parties were attempting to make sense of a Hebrew Bible that contains a number of covenant-administrations, some more promissory and some more legal. Indeed, I will argue that the Abrahamic covenant is so promissory that Paul ordinarily refers to it by the synecdoche ἡ ἐπαγγελία, and that the Sinai covenant is so legal that Paul ordinarily refers to it by the synecdoche ὁ νόμος. Yahweh simply promised, or pledged, to bless Abraham and his seed, and indeed to bless all the families of the earth through his seed. But through Moses, the same Yahweh said,

> "But if your heart turns away, and you will not hear, but are drawn away to worship other gods and serve them, I declare to you today, that you shall surely *perish*. You shall *not live long* in the land that you are going over the Jordan to enter and possess. I call heaven and earth to witness against you today, that I have set before you life *and* death, blessing *and* curse." (Deut. 30:17–19; emphases added)

Abraham learned of a deity who pledged to *bless* freely, generously, and sovereignly. Moses learned that the same deity could and would also *curse*, under certain circumstances. Moses learned that Yahweh, at least as regarding temporal blessings in the land of Canaan, would condition such blessings upon Israel's obedience. Both Second Temple Judaism, therefore, and Paul had to wrestle with the *multiple* covenants existing side by side in the Hebrew Bible, and both had to wrestle with how, if at all, Jesus of Nazareth figured into expectations arising from that Bible.

E. P. Sanders (and George Foote Moore and W. D. Davies, for that matter) found many pertinent Second Temple texts that reflected belief in a gracious and merciful God. Sanders's critics have found some pertinent texts that appear to condition blessing on Israel's obedience. Neither Sanders nor his major critics, to my knowledge, have adequately accounted for this matter as I will attempt to account for it. I account for this in the way that I judge Paul did: Within the Hebrew Bible there are several covenants (at a minimum, two with Noah, one with Abraham, one with the Israelites through Moses, one with Phinehas, and one with David).[9] What appears to be tension, therefore, between some Second Temple texts and others is likely due to the varying character of the several covenants that informed Second Temple Judaism, and to the responsible efforts of Second Temple Judaism to make sense of those several covenants.

Both the New Perspective on Paul and its critics, however, often make a crucial mistake at this point: at an implicit level, if not explicitly, they regard these various

---

9. I say "at a minimum," because I am myself persuaded that the Adamic material is covenantal also. But this one is so at a more implicit level; and though Paul appears to regard it as covenantal at Rom. 5:12–21, he makes no reference to it in Galatians (nor does he refer to the Noahic covenants, nor to those with Phinehas or David, in Galatians). Cf. Byron Curtis's chapter on Hos. 6:7 in *The Law Is Not of Faith: Essays on Works and Grace in the Mosaic Covenant*, ed. Bryan Estelle, J. V. Fesko, and David VanDrunen (Louisville, KY: P&R, 2009).

covenants in an aggregate manner, as though they are pieces of the puzzle that constitute Second Temple Judaism. And indeed, in some sense, they are such pieces to a historical puzzle. But in another sense, a theological sense, they are not pieces to a common puzzle; each is its own puzzle. Each of these covenants has its own integrity and its own purpose. They cannot and do not meld into one another regarding their parties, their stipulations, or their benefits. Regarding the parties, for instance, only David's lineage could build the house for Yahweh, only the lineage of Phinehas could serve as priests, and only a portion of Abraham's lineage (not Ishmael and not Esau) would be the vehicle by which God would one day bless all the families of the earth. The benefits also differ: Through the covenant with Phinehas, a sacramental priesthood was given to the Israelites to teach them (and the world) the theological concept of atonement (though the blood of the animals sacrificed was not actually efficient to atone for human sin). Through the Davidic covenant, a "permanent" house for Yahweh could be built. Through the Sinai covenant, temporal prosperity could be secured for the Israelites in the land of Canaan. And through the Abrahamic covenant, eschatological blessings would eventually come to all the nations of the earth through his seed.[10]

When either proponents or opponents of the New Perspective on Paul, therefore, describe the realities of Second Temple Judaism in terms of "the covenant" (in the singular), they are prevented from the outset from making sense of a historic religion that was itself shaped and formed by its efforts to relate properly several distinct covenants. And indeed, it is entirely possible that some of the parties to Second Temple Judaism made the same mistake, though I am an agnostic on that point. But Paul's reasoning in Galatians takes another approach. Speaking through both chapters 3 and 4 of the five differences between the Abrahamic and Sinai covenants, he creates a figure of speech in his concluding verses of chapter 4, discussing Hagar and Sarah, and says of the two women, "These are two covenants" (Gal. 4:24). Throughout Galatians, Paul self-consciously refers to the realities of a new covenant in Christ by referring to other covenants that antedated it. Paul does not refer to Israel's heritage in the singular, as "the covenant," but in the plural, as "the covenants" (cf. Rom. 9:4; Eph. 2:12).

My approach then, if it succeeds, accomplishes two things. First, and most importantly, it provides a way of understanding the covenant-historical argumentation of Galatians better than other proposals. But second, in post-Holocaust discussions, it enables us to recognize why both E. P. Sanders and his opponents appear to be able, at times, to muster textual evidence for their point of view. Second Temple Judaism, like Paul, was attempting to make sense of a canon that contained several different covenants, each of which came from the same God while containing distinctive parties, distinctive stipulations, and distinctive benefits. Any responsible wrestling with such a polycovenantal Hebrew Bible will reflect the same tensions and distinctives that appear in those several covenants themselves.

---

10. It may not be self-evident that the pledges to Abraham are ultimately eschatological, but there are clues that this will be the case, such as the references to his seed being as numerous as the sands of the sea (hinting at cosmological renewal) or as numerous as the stars of heaven, a more overt eschatological hint. In Rom. 4, Paul likened the provision of a child to (old) Abraham and (barren) Sarah to giving "life from the dead" (4:17), and noting that Abraham's body was at that point "as good as dead" (4:19); so Paul at least appears to have regarded the pledges to Abraham as reversing the mortality curse of Gen. 3, which makes them eschatological in character.

2.3. Specific: Jewish Problems/Christian Problems

One semi-hidden assumption that has influenced Pauline studies significantly is the assumption that if there is a problem in the Christian churches, it must reflect an antecedent problem in Jewish synagogues: If there were Judaizers of some sort at Galatia, there must have been similar Judaizers in the Jewish synagogues who were the source of the problem. Prima facie, this is a rather curious line of reasoning. After all, Paul writes to the "*churches* of Galatia [ταῖς ἐκκλησίαις τῆς Γαλατίας]," not to "the *synagogues* of Galatia." Is it not at least possible that the early Christian assemblies generated their own errors, whether behavioral or doctrinal? Does not Paul routinely address other errors in his letters that no one would dream of attributing to Jewish influence? Does anyone blame the synagogues, for instance, for the man who had sexual relations with his stepmother (see 1 Cor. 5)? To raise the question is to answer it.

What makes this assumption more plausible (though still, in my judgment, unwarranted) is that Paul discusses in Galatians so many realities associated with God's covenanting with the Israelites: circumcision, the dietary laws, the Mosaic law itself, and so on. Indeed, Paul uses the language of "Judaizing" at 2:14. It is therefore understandable that interpreters of Galatians would inquire as to whether there might have been an antecedent problem within Second Temple Judaism that was analogous to the problem Paul encountered at Galatia. It is *understandable* that interpreters might look for this, but it would also be understandable for them to have not done so and to have intentionally considered an alternative: that the problem at Galatia was sui generis, just as the immoral Corinthian was, to our knowledge, sui generis and not attributable to some antecedent error in Second Temple Judaism.

I propose an alternative: Rather than base our interpretation of Galatians on the constantly shifting reconstructions of the nature of first-century Palestinian Judaism, we might at least *consider* the possibility that the problem at Galatia was a Christian error in its origins with no corresponding error in Palestinian Judaism.[11] Is it not possible to reconstruct the problem at Galatia from the evidence of the text itself? Is it not possible that the text itself describes what the problem is, regardless of whether the problem existed elsewhere in Jewish or early Christian circles? Is it not at least theoretically possible that the erroneous belief or practice at Galatia was generated by *Christian* misunderstandings of the Mosaic law and not by alleged *Jewish* misunderstandings thereof? When the question is stated so acutely, it is difficult to regard it as anything but rhetorical. But the question is not unimportant. If, as Peter Stuhlmacher observed, many of us are attempting to understand Paul without misconstruing Palestinian Judaism, we could theoretically accomplish this in either of two ways. First, as Sanders and many others have done, we could pore over the reliably dated texts from

---

11. I am not unaware that the term "Judaize" appears outside of Galatians. Some might be inclined to believe that this demonstrates that there was a fairly well-established Jewish error known as "Judaizing." But the verb only appears once in the LXX (Esther 8:17), once in the intertestamental writings (Theodotus 4:1), once in Paul (Gal. 2:14), and once, later, in the apostolic fathers (Ignatius to the Magnesians 10:7–8), which is hardly enough evidence to suggest a common or well-known problem. Further, in some of those other texts, it denotes a virtue, not a vice. Cf. below my discussion of the lexical issues surrounding this uncommon verb.

the era and conclude that those texts do not warrant a legalistic/meritorious under-standing of Second Temple Judaism. Or second, as I propose, we could also discuss Paul's problem at Galatia without the assumption that it must have been spawned by Second Temple Judaism at all: the early Christian churches may have had their own creative genius for inventing behavioral or doctrinal errors without any assistance from the Jewish synagogues. I propose that, barring any evidence that Paul attributes the Galatian error to a common Second Temple synagogue error, there is no need for us to speculate about the matter at all.[12]

One fairly common objection to the reassessment of Palestinian Judaism provoked by E. P. Sanders is that it is novel. The objection is put like this: If Judaism of the first century was not, in fact, meritorious, why did almost everyone from Luther and Calvin until E. P. Sanders believe that it *was* meritorious? Such a question places the burden of proof on Sanders (et al.) to account for why the novel view should be embraced over an older view. To such a question, I propose several answers. First, in point of fact, Sand-ers's view is not novel; many Jewish scholars suggested similar things for many years, and even some notable Christian scholars of the preceding generation (George Foot Moore, David Daube, and W. D. Davies) said similar things. Second, the "dominant" Protestant understanding from Luther until Sanders was largely based on the assump-tion that the Talmudic literature accurately reflected the Palestinian Judaism of Paul's day, an assumption few would concede today. The writing of the *Tannaim* came well over a century after the destruction of the temple, and their writings are not necessarily an accurate reflection of the Temple Judaism that antedated them. And some of the intertestamental literature available to us now (certainly, e.g., the Dead Sea Scrolls) was not known to Luther. That is, Sanders did not merely read the same literature *differently* than Luther and Calvin; he read *different* literature altogether. The view of Luther and Calvin was based upon their reading of literature (the Babylonian Talmud) that they judged to be an accurate reflection of first-century Palestinian Judaism—a view we simply do not share today. Third, while it is not inappropriate to refer to the pre-Sanders approach as the "dominant" Protestant approach, we can only call it "dominant"; we cannot call it "confessional," because, in point of fact, the Protestant confessions make no comment at all about the character of Palestinian Judaism. That is, there is nothing at stake in terms of Protestant confessional orthodoxy in this conversation. No Protestant body was ever so confidant of its speculative reconstruction of Palestinian Judaism as to record a word about the matter in any of its confessional or catechetical literature.

2.4. Specific: "Judaize"

Those who troubled the Galatians have often been called "Judaizers." To the unwary, this expression may suggest a standing, well-known idea or practice associated with a particular, well-known movement, such as Pharisaism, Sadduceeism, or Essenism. As we shall see, such a suggestion would be wrong; the term is remarkably rare in the

---

12. Had this proposal been embraced forty years ago, thousands of pages of such specula-tion might never have been written, which surely would have been a welcome boon to many graduate students.

extant literature, and it is only employed by Pauline scholars because Paul uses the expression in his conversation with Peter: "If you, though a Jew, live like a Gentile and not like a Jew, how can you force the Gentiles to *live like Jews* [εἰ σὺ Ἰουδαῖος ὑπάρχων ἐθνικῶς καὶ οὐχὶ Ἰουδαϊκῶς ζῇς, πῶς τὰ ἔθνη ἀναγκάζεις ἰουδαΐζειν]?" This requirement that Gentiles ἰουδαΐζειν, then, is the source of our term "Judaize." But what constitutes "Judaizing"?

Specifically, we raise this question: Is the problem at Galatia behavioral or doctrinal? The assumption, by so many Pauline interpreters, is that the problem is doctrinal; the "errorists" at Galatia have frequently been referred to as those who "taught x." But such a determination cannot be made as a mere assumption; it must be the result of some evidence or reasoning, because Paul in his letters corrected both doctrinal problems and behavioral problems. Among the things Paul corrected at Corinth, for instance, were incest (1 Cor. 5:1–13), vexatious lawsuits (6:1–11), immorality (6:12–20), celibacy versus marriage (7:1–24), eating food that had been sacrificed to idols (8:1–11:1), headcoverings (11:2–16), mispractice of the Lord's Supper (11:17–34), misuse of spiritual gifts (12:1–14:40), collections for the relief of the saints (16:1–11), and the doctrine of the resurrection (15)—only the last of which was a doctrinal error. The majority of the letter addressed behavioral issues, and only one (important) chapter addressed a doctrine.

It is perfectly fair, and perfectly in accord with the evidence from other Pauline epistles, to inquire as to whether the problem at Galatia is doctrinal or behavioral. In doing so, I do not intend to exclude the middle or to frame the question erroneously. It is entirely possible, prima facie, that the problem will disclose itself to be both doctrinal and practical; and if the evidence for that third, mediating position is substantial, then that mediating position should be embraced. What we cannot do, however, is assume before investigation that the problem is doctrinal in part or whole. The error could be entirely behavioral or partly behavioral, and we must raise the question openly and fairly.

I recognize that it is entirely possible that any behavioral error *implies* a doctrinal one. Any erroneous behavior, that is, implies at least the *idea* that the behavior is acceptable. The behavior of the man at Corinth who had relations with his stepmother, for instance, had implications for the doctrine of marriage, the doctrine of human sexuality, and so on. However, Paul said nothing about these doctrines in his refutation, nor did he object to the behavior *because* of its potential doctrinal implications. The behavior itself was wrong—so shamefully wrong, Paul said, that it even would have embarrassed the pagans. Paul expressed no concern that this behavior would lead to doctrinal error; to the contrary, he feared that tolerating it might cause similar *behavioral* error to spread (1 Cor. 5:6).

So what does the term "Judaize" mean? Well, we note from the language of Gal. 2:14 that the expression is parallel to the expression "live like/as a Jew," and indeed most English translations translate ἰουδαΐζειν just as they translate the parallel expression Ἰουδαϊκῶς ζῇς (from which, as a simple matter of word formation, it appears to be derived). The English translations assume that the two expressions mean essentially the same thing, since the word formation of the verb ἰουδαΐζειν consists of the two separate words of the expression Ἰουδαϊκῶς ζῇς. We note then, prima facie, that Paul does not say anything here about "*believing* like a Jew" but about "*living* like a Jew." And indeed, Paul had indicated what constitutes "living like a Jew" two verses earlier:

"For before certain men came from James, he was eating with the Gentiles; but when they came he drew back and separated himself, fearing the circumcision party." Peter had relaxed the requirement of Kashrut and eaten with Gentiles; in doing so, he had "lived as a Gentile, and not as a Jew." When representatives from Jerusalem came down, out of fear of their reaction, Peter separated himself from the Gentiles in conformity with the dietary laws. If we knew nothing else from Galatians but this contextual information, we would determine that "to live as a Jew" meant to observe the dietary laws of Moses, which was/is a behavioral error. That is, the prima facie contextual evidence, unless the usage of the term in the extant literature of Paul's day is otherwise or technical, suggests that the term designates a practice, not a doctrine. To that extant literature, we now turn.

The first thing one notices in researching ἰουδαΐζειν is how rare the term is. It is a New Testament *hapax*, occurring only in Galatians 2:14. This itself is significant. If the term designated some well-known existing party or viewpoint within Judaism, one might expect that party to appear more frequently in the New Testament. By comparison, "Pharisee" occurs 98 times in the New Testament and "Sadducee" appears fourteen times. The term is even rarer in the LXX, since it appears there, in vaster literature, only once, in the book of Esther:

> Then Mordecai went out from the presence of the king in royal robes of blue and white, with a great golden crown and a robe of fine linen and purple, and the city of Susa shouted and rejoiced. The Jews had light and gladness and joy and honor. And in every province and in every city, wherever the king's command and his edict reached, there was gladness and joy among the Jews, a feast and a holiday. And many from the peoples of the country declared themselves Jews, for fear of the Jews had fallen on them [καὶ πολλοὶ τῶν ἐθνῶν περιετέμοντο καὶ ἰουδάιζον διὰ τὸν φόβον τῶν Ἰουδαίων]. (Esther 8:15–17)

We initially note that many English translations have one verb ("declared themselves Jews," RSV and ESV; "became Jews," KJV), though the LXX has two: περιετέμοντο καὶ ἰουδάιζον. The English translations follow the Hebrew, which has a single verb (מתיהדים, itself a *hapax* in the Hebrew Bible). The LXX translators chose to translate the single Hebrew verb with two Greek verbs, electing to employ hendiadys to represent the meaning of the original. It is not without significance, especially for Galatians, that a literal translation of the LXX rendering would be "*were circumcized* and lived as Jews." That is, if the hendiadys is accurate, the later English translations such as RSV and ESV are preferable to the KJV. Where the King James translated "*became* Jews," the RSV and ESV translated "*declared* themselves Jews," indicating that the behavior referred to being *marked* by circumcision as a Jew and not a Gentile.

We also note another matter significant to interpreters of Galatians. Why did these people of the land mark themselves as Jews by the rite of circumcision? Because "*fear* of the Jews had fallen upon them [διὰ τὸν φόβον τῶν Ἰουδαίων]." Similarly, when Paul objected to Peter's behavior of withdrawing from Gentile table fellowship, Paul accused him of the identical motivation: "For before certain men came from James, he was eating with the Gentiles; but when they came he drew back and separated himself, *fearing* the circumcision party [φοβούμενος τοὺς ἐκ περιτομῆς]." Note especially that these people of the land were not attempting to be justified before God nor was their spiritual condition at stake in any way. They did not "fear" God's judgment;

they "feared" the Jews the way Peter feared the circumcision party. In each case, the error was behavioral; in each case, it consisted of observing those Mosaic laws that distinguished Jew from Gentile; and in each case, it was motivated by concern about status before other (Jewish) human beings, not status before God.

Not surprisingly, this term that is a *hapax* both in the NT and in the LXX is also rare in the intertestamental literature, and I find it only in Theodotus.[13]

> He says that Jacob came from the Euphrates to Hamor in Shechem, and that he welcomed him and gave some of the region to him. He apportioned the land to Jacob, and Jacob's sons—there were eleven of them—tended sheep, while his daughter, Dinah, and his wives worked with the wool. Dinah, still a virgin, wanting to see the city, went to Shechem during a festival. When Shechem, the son of Hamor, saw her, he fell in love with her: taking her as though she was his own, he carried her off and defiled her. But the next day, he came with his father to Jacob and asked to be joined to her in marriage. [Jacob] said he would not give [his consent], until all the inhabitants of Shechem *became like the Jews, by being circumcised* [πρὶν ἂν ἢ πάντας τοὺς οἰκοῦντας τὰ Σίκιμα περιτεμνομένους Ἰουδαῖσαι], and Hamor said that he would persuade them [to do so]. And, concerning the necessity of them being circumcised, Jacob said, "For it is certainly not lawful for Hebrews to bring sons-in-law or daughters-in-law in from elsewhere, to lead them into the house; rather, [they are allowed to bring only] someone who boasts of being from the same race." (Theodotus 4:3; emphases added)

Here ἰουδαΐζειν is translated "became like the Jews," as the KJV translated Esther 8:17. And note here that, as in Galatians and in the LXX, the verb appears with circumcision, possibly as hendiadys. The residents of Shechem "became like the Jews *by being circumcised*." Note also that the behavior was undertaken not out of regard to God, but out of regard for Jews (in this case, Jacob). The term is unusually rare, appearing only once in the LXX, once in the intertestamental literature, and once in the NT.[14] In none of the examples is anything explicitly said about salvation, justification, or any other doctrinal matter at all. It appears to mean something like this: "Identify oneself as a Jew by performing the requisite marking ceremonies, to appease those Jews who would be scandalized otherwise."[15]

Negative evidence may also be significant here. In all of Galatians, of the ordinary four Greek words for "teaching" (διδάσκαλος, διδάσκω, διδαχή, διδασκαλία), only one appears, and only one time when Paul refers to his own Damascus instruction at 1:12: "For I did not receive it from any man, nor was I taught it [οὔτε ἐδιδάχθην], but I received it through a revelation of Jesus Christ." Think of how often the language of "false *teachers* at Galatia" or "false/erroneous *teaching* at Galatia" appears in New Testament

---

13. The root (יהד) from the Hebrew of Esther 8:17 does not appear in Qumran. Qumran does not appear to use the expression.

14. Similarly, in the early church fathers it appears only in Ignatius to the Magnesians 10:3: "It is monstrous to talk of Jesus Christ and to practise Judaism. For Christianity did not believe in Judaism, but Judaism in Christianity, wherein {every tongue} believed and {was gathered together} unto God" [ἄτοπόν ἐστιν Ἰησοῦν Χριστὸν λαλεῖν καὶ ἰουδαΐζειν. ὁ γὰρ χριστιανισμὸς οὐκ εἰς ἰουδαϊσμὸν ἐπίστευσεν, ἀλλ' ἰουδαϊσμὸς εἰς χριστιανισμόν, ᾧ πᾶσα γλῶσσα πιστεύσασα εἰς Θεὸν συνήχθη].

15. Curiously enough, it means largely what James D. G. Dunn thinks "works of the law" means.

studies, and yet Paul never says any such thing in the letter—not even once. He never employs any of the ordinary Greek doctrinal vocabulary to describe the problem at Galatia. To the contrary, he uses almost everything *but* such language:

> But there are some who trouble you [ταράσσοντες ὑμᾶς]. (Gal. 1:7)

> Yet because of *false brothers* secretly brought in—who slipped in *to spy out our freedom* that we have in Christ Jesus. (Gal. 2:4)

> And the rest of the Jews *acted hypocritically* along with him, so that even Barnabas was led astray by their hypocrisy. (Gal. 2:13)

> You *observe* [παρατηρεῖσθε] *days and months and seasons and years*! I am afraid I may have labored over you in vain. (Gal. 4:10–11)

> This *persuasion* [ἡ πεισμονὴ] is not from him who calls you. A little *leaven* leavens the whole lump. (Gal. 5:8–9)

> I wish those who *unsettle* you [οἱ ἀναστατοῦντες] would emasculate themselves! (Gal. 5:12)

> But if you *bite and devour* one another, watch out that you are not consumed by one another. (Gal. 5:15)

> It is those who want to *make a good showing in the flesh* who would force you to be circumcised, and only in order that they may not be persecuted for the cross of Christ. (Gal. 6:12)

> From now on let no one cause me *trouble* [κόπους], for I bear on my body the marks of Jesus. (Gal. 6:17)

Paul referred to the Galatian Judaizers by almost every expression shy of Jude's "waterless clouds" (Jude 12). Couldn't Paul have just said "teach," "doctrine," or "teacher" one time? Instead he uses language such as "unsettle," "bite and devour," "make a good showing in the flesh," and so on, as though he were bending over backward to avoid/evade any appearance that the problem at Galatia was doctrinal. It is, I concede, entirely possible that any behavioral error has doctrinal implications. Early in the first chapter, Paul said: "I am astonished that you are so quickly deserting him who called you in the grace of Christ and are turning to a different gospel—not that there is another one, but there are some who trouble you and want to distort [μεταστρέψαι] the gospel of Christ" (Gal. 1:6–7). So, the purity of the gospel is indeed at stake at Galatia, but is this "distortion" the result of erroneous teaching or the result of erroneous behavioral requirements?

Paul employed no doctrinal language to describe the error at Galatia; but he did employ behavioral language to describe it, referring to circumcision, observing the Jewish calendar, and withdrawing from Gentile table fellowship. If we "read the lines" of Galatians itself rather than read between them, we find that the error of "Judaizing" was a behavioral error—an error that consisted of the specific behavior of continuing to observe the various Mosaic ceremonies that separated Jews from Gentiles. Further, if we read Galatians itself, and the fairly minuscule lexical evidence elsewhere, we note that the Judaizing behavior was motivated by a desire to win *Jewish* approval, not *divine* approval. If you wish to marry Jacob's daughter, you must be circumcised; if the *am ha-aretz* wish to join in Jewish celebrations, they must be circumcised; if Peter desires the approval of the Jerusalem apostles, he must avoid table fellowship with the uncircumcised Gentiles.

A final observation about "Judaize" should be made here. It is entirely possible that ἰουδαΐζειν refers not to Jewish behavior but to Gentile behavior. As counterintuitive as that may seem, the lexical evidence is compelling. At Galatians 2:14, it is unmistakable: "How can you force *the Gentiles* to live like Jews?" Similarly, in both Esther and Theodotus, as we observed earlier, it was Gentiles who performed the action denoted by this verb. With entire justification, therefore, Stephen G. Wilson wrote, "L. Gaston more sensibly argues that we should use the term 'judaizer' only in its ancient and technical sense, i.e., of non-Jews who chose to live like Jews. A judaizer was by definition a Gentile and it is Christian Gentiles of this sort on whom we shall focus."[16] Similarly, James D. G. Dunn has said, "'To judaize' was a quite familiar expression, meaning 'to adopt a (characteristically) Jewish way of life'. The fact that many *Gentiles* in the ancient world 'judaized', that is adopted Jewish customs, attended Jewish synagogues, identified themselves in some measure with Jews, is well attested."[17] While a "Judaizing" Gentile's behavior had reference to winning the *approval* of law-abiding Jews, the behavior itself was a Gentile behavior, and it is even possible that the troublers at Galatia themselves were Gentiles who had already "Judaized" and were now urging their fellow Gentiles to do the same. My interpretation of Galatians does not depend upon this possibility in any substantive manner, but it also does not preclude the possibility.

My reading of Galatians, therefore, is self-consciously suspicious of much of the "reading between the lines" interpretation that has gone before. My interpretation, while largely agnostic on most of the historical issues, is perfectly compatible with a reconstruction that says the problem at Galatia had no antecedents outside of the churches. To the contrary, it could quite possibly be a Christian error alone, not a Jewish one. Those Jews who chose not to follow Christ would necessarily remain disciples of Moses and would enjoin obedience to his commandments. Only Christian churches would be capable of the error of requiring unnecessary rites of their members. The error may have been entirely self-generated by the early churches, and it may have been entirely committed by Gentiles. It is, of course, also possible that Jewish Christians were "troublers," but my reading of Galatians requires no resolution to this issue.

---

16. Stephen G. Wilson, "Gentile Judaizers," *New Testament Studies* 38, no. 4 (1992): 605.

17. James D. G. Dunn, *The Epistle to the Galatians*, Black's New Testament Commentary (Peabody, MA: Hendrickson, 1993), 129. I do not concur with Dunn's reference to the verb as "quite familiar" or even "well attested," since the term is so rare. But he is certainly correct in observing that many Gentiles "Judaized," despite his earlier comment: "That the 'troublemakers' or 'agitators' were Jews is also fairly obvious. It is implicit in the very fact that circumcision was their primary demand" (9). I still think it is possible that even the "troublers" themselves were Gentiles, though indeed every act of "Judaizing" has reference to Jewish approval, as Dunn rightly notes: "In short, though there were clear boundary lines between Jew and Gentile, marked out, not least, by the food laws and the complex of traditional attitudes and practices gathered round them, there were many Gentiles who were eager to cross these boundaries, to at least some extent, and who were welcomed by Jews when they did so" (120).

CHAPTER 3

The Autobiographical/Historical Introduction: Galatians 1–2

While students of Paul have rightly recognized that the theological argumentation in Galatians properly and technically begins in Galatians 3, the first two chapters are closely associated with those later chapters; indeed, one could argue that Paul prepares to argue that case in Galatians 1 and 2. In these introductory chapters, Paul makes important points about the gospel itself and important points about himself (and why the Galatians should listen to him). He makes two essential points about the gospel in this historical narrative: That it was once a commonly agreed upon gospel and that it is a gospel for the Gentiles/Greeks/uncircumcised. Similarly, he makes two important points about himself as one to whom the Galatians should listen: First, he was no less called by Christ than the other apostles; and second, Paul has held steadfastly to this gospel while others (e.g., the Galatians and Peter) have not.

3.1. Salutation and Present Circumstance (Gal. 1:1–12)

3.1.1. The Introduction/Salutation (Gal. 1:1–5)

> Paul, an apostle—not from men nor through man, but through Jesus Christ and God the Father, who raised him from the dead—and all the brothers who are with me, To the churches of Galatia: Grace to you and peace from God our Father and the Lord Jesus Christ, who gave himself for our sins[1] to deliver us from the present evil age, according to the will of our God and Father, to whom be the glory forever and ever. Amen.

Following his ordinary custom, Paul referred to himself as an apostle.[2] What is profoundly distinctive to Galatians, however, is that the third word of the letter is οὐκ: "Paul, an apostle—*not* from men nor through man, but through Jesus Christ and God the Father." Methinks the apostle doth protest too much—but his protest is, in fact, necessary. If his detractors could either deny outright his apostolic authority or suggest that he was a "sub-apostle" of some sort (that is, subordinate in authority to those who were instructed

---

1. Paul's reference to Christ as having given himself "for our sins" (ὑπὲρ τῶν ἁμαρτιῶν ἡμῶν) may be formulaic; the same expression appears in 1 Cor. 15:3 where Paul recites that what he had himself received he handed on to the Corinthians, that Χριστὸς ἀπέθανεν ὑπὲρ τῶν ἁμαρτιῶν ἡμῶν. It may even be that ὑπὲρ ἡμῶν in several Pauline texts is an abbreviated form of ὑπὲρ τῶν ἁμαρτιῶν ἡμῶν. It is plausibly so at Rom. 5:8; 8:32; 2 Cor. 5:21; Eph. 5:2; 1 Thess. 5:10; and Titus 2:14. That the death of Christ was an act of giving is affirmed not only here in Galatians but also at 2:20, where Paul refers to Christ as the one who "loved me and gave himself for me."
2. This designation as an apostle does not appear in Philippians, Philemon, or 2 Thessalonians; and it does not appear in the salutation of 1 Thessalonians (though it does appear there at 1 Thess. 2:7).

by Jesus in his earthly ministry), then they could effectively dismiss his attempt to correct them. Whether such detractors had already made such claims—or whether Paul merely anticipated, rhetorically, the possibility of their doing so—is not critical to my understanding of the letter.[3] It is critical, however, that Paul asserted his authority here as being equal to that of the other apostles (notably to that of the cowardly and vacillating Peter); he is commissioned by Christ no less than they.[4] Just as importantly, he denied that he was commissioned by any merely human authority: Παῦλος ἀπόστολος οὐκ ἀπ᾽ ἀνθρώπων οὐδὲ δι᾽ ἀνθρώπου. This is the only Pauline salutation where this denial is registered; not even the Corinthians provoked such a statement from him.

This denial of a human origin of Paul's apostleship anticipated his similar denial that his gospel was of human origin in verses 11 and 12:

> For I would have you know, brothers, that the gospel that was preached by me is not man's gospel [οὐκ ἔστιν κατὰ ἄνθρωπον]. For I did not receive it from any man [παρὰ ἀνθρώπου], nor was I taught it, but I received it through a revelation of Jesus Christ.[5]

Both the Pauline gospel and his apostolic authority to proclaim it came from Christ himself and not from any mere human agent or agents, and this is why both his general ministry and his specific ministry to the Galatians in this letter were unconcerned with pleasing such humans:

> For am I now seeking the approval of man [ἀνθρώπους πείθω], or of God? Or am I trying to please man [ζητῶ ἀνθρώποις ἀρέσκειν]? If I were still trying to please man [ἀνθρώποις], I would not be a servant of Christ. (1:10)

ESV's "man" here is curious, since the noun is manifestly plural.[6] While there may be all sorts of reasons that might justify such a collective use of "man," I fear that this translation may obscure that to which this entire historical/autobiographical section is tending: the riveting confrontation of Paul and Peter in chapter 2, where Paul says regarding Peter: "For before certain men came from James, he was eating with the

---

3. Johan S. Vos argues that there is no reason to regard these statements as "defensive," in response to an allegation about Paul such as happened in the Corinthian correspondence; but that they can be understood as "offensive" language equally well. See his "Paul's Argumentation in Galatians 1–2," *Harvard Theological Review* 87, no. 1 (January 1, 1994): 1–16, esp. 13: "In contrast to the letters to the Corinthians, for example, nowhere in the letter to the Galatians did Paul explicitly present the legitimacy of his apostolate as the controversial point. . . . [T]he supporting statements about his ethos as an apostle and the heavenly origin of his apostolate have more an offensive than a defensive function."

4. Later, in verses 15–17, Paul goes beyond this and suggests that his authority is perhaps greater than that of the other apostles, by likening his call to that of OT prophets such as Jeremiah and Isaiah (see below). Here, however, he is content merely to assert that he received his commission from Christ himself and not from any human agent.

5. While the strategic and rhetorical significance of this claim has been observed by many, its paradigmatic significance for Paul's overall theology awaited Seyoon Kim's *The Origin of Paul's Gospel, Wissenschaftliche Untersuchungen zum Neuen Testament* 2, Reihe 4 (Tübingen: J. C. B. Mohr, 1984).

6. KJV and RSV have "men," which satisfies the plural but dissatisfies the demand for so-called inclusive language. NRSV satisfies that concern but employs "human" three times and "people" twice in this text, which probably obscures that the same Greek word is beneath all five.

Gentiles; but when they came he drew back and separated himself, fearing the circumcision party." That is, unlike Paul, Peter was entirely too concerned to please and
be approved by other *people*—specifically, the Jerusalem apostles, the circumcision
party associated with James. Just as Paul's "if *we*" (ἐὰν ἡμεῖς) of 1:8 anticipated his later
statement to Peter, "*we* ourselves are Jews by birth" (ἡμεῖς φύσει Ἰουδαῖοι), so also his
denial that he pleased or sought the approval of "men" here in chapter 1 anticipated
his condemnation of Peter for doing precisely that in chapter 2. The mere statistical
fact that Paul employs ἄνθρωπος five times in verses 10–12 is significant. The implicit
alternative, at least rhetorically, is humans or God. Is Paul an apostle from humans
or from God? Is Paul seeking the approval of humans or of God? Is Paul seeking to
please humans or to please God? Did Paul receive his gospel from humans or from
God? Once this alternative of humans-or-God is established, it becomes a criterion
by which Peter's vacillating behavior can be condemned.

Paul here, as elsewhere, cleverly turned his detractors' accusations into his defense.
His detractors were displeased with Paul, Peter was none too happy with him, and the
Galatians probably regarded him as a "troubler." But Paul wasn't interested in pleasing
humans—whether his Galatian detractors or Peter. He was interested in pleasing God.
And he turned the tables on those detractors and suggested that, in the truest sense,
they were the "troublers" (1:7; 5:10). When the Corinthians accused Paul of being less
powerful than their wonder-working hyper-apostles, Paul responded by "boasting" in
his comparative weakness (2 Cor. 11:30; 12:5, 9), turning the tables on his accusers.
Similarly, when many Galatians regarded him as troublesome and uncooperative, he
turned these tables also, suggesting that the *really* troublesome people were Galatian
(and Petrine) human pleasers.

3.1.2. The Present Galatian Circumstance (Gal. 1:6–12)

Just after the salutation, Paul announced without further ado[7] what occasioned his
sending of the letter: the Galatians had effectively and practically abandoned the gospel. In these seven verses, εὐαγγ- language appears seven times, so nothing less than
the gospel itself is at stake. And we note that it is "*the* gospel," not "*a* gospel," that is at
stake. The Galatians are "turning to a different gospel—not that there is another one"
(1:6–7).[8] Much of the remainder of the historical narrative proper will substantiate
this claim that there was/is a single Christian gospel, one that was once unanimously
agreed upon by all the apostles (and by the Galatians).

Further, as though the situation were not already profoundly consequential, Paul's
initial accusation of the Galatians declares that they have not merely abandoned the
gospel but God himself: "I am astonished[9] that you are so quickly deserting him who

---

7. As many commentators have noted, there is no thanksgiving section in the Galatian letter.

8. Commentators are right to notice the deliberate Pauline play on the subtle, but important,
lexical difference between ἕτερον and ἄλλο here. The so-called gospel to which the Galatians
have turned is not merely an acceptable variety (ἄλλο) of the gospel; it is fundamentally different
in kind (ἕτερον) from the true, apostolic gospel.

9. Johan S. Vos's comment is apt: "θαυμάζω is here—as often in Greek letters—less an expression of real astonishment than of irritation and rebuke; the word is equivalent to μέμφομαι."
Cf. his "Paul's Argumentation in Galatians 1–2," 4.

called you in the grace of Christ" (1:6). For Paul, the gospel is *God's* gospel; not merely a message *about* God, but a message *from* God (1:11–12).[10] Therefore, one cannot abandon this gospel without abandoning God himself, from whom it comes. This is what accounts for the rather extreme language in these verses, especially the repeated ἀνάθεμα ἔστω in verses 8 and 9. Indeed, in the only other place where Paul employs this expression, the circumstance also involves a rejection of God himself—not merely some fine point of theology. "If anyone has no love for the Lord, let him be accursed" (εἴ τις οὐ φιλεῖ τὸν κύριον, ἤτω ἀνάθεμα; 1 Cor. 16:22).

Cleverly embedded in this curse is a pre-argument of Paul's confrontation with Peter:

> But even if we [ἡμεῖς] or an angel from heaven [ἄγγελος ἐξ οὐρανοῦ] should preach to you a gospel contrary to the one we preached to you, let him be accursed. As we have said before, so now I say again: If anyone [τις] is preaching to you a gospel contrary to the one you received, let him be accursed. (1:8–9)

The τις alone would and should be sufficient; the indefinite pronoun universalizes the category. But Paul goes further: if even a *heavenly* emissary of some sort were to preach contrary to what Paul had preached, such an emissary would also receive Paul's ἀνάθεμα. But the "we" (ἡμεῖς) is rhetorically brilliant. First, Paul is willing to place a conditional curse upon himself, were he to preach a contradictory gospel. But in extending the hypothetical ἀνάθεμα to himself and *other apostolic ministers*, Paul anticipates the conflict with Peter that will be narrated in the latter half of chapter 2. Effectively, he asserts here that the gospel trumps ecclesiastical office. *Any* messenger— heavenly or earthly, apostolic or otherwise—who proclaims a contradictory message to that proclaimed by Paul is worthy of malediction.

3.2. The Historical Narrative Proper: Paul's Life in Judaism to the Present (Gal. 1:13–2:21)

The structure of the historical narrative in Galatians is fairly straightforward, and the presence of temporal adverbs delineates each subsection from the others.[11] The only significant question of the structure of this portion of the narrative appears at Galatians 2:15, which some take as part of the confrontation with Peter in 2:11–14, and others take as a separate pericope.[12] In these six (or seven) subsections, Paul's narrative substantiates two things about the gospel (that it was once commonly agreed upon, and that it was a gospel for the Gentiles) and two things about Paul (that Christ called

---

10. For this reason, it may not be possible to resolve with any final confidence the proper understanding of the expression τὸ εὐαγγέλιον τοῦ Χριστοῦ at the end of verse 7. It is equally plausible, in this context, to regard τοῦ Χριστοῦ as either an objective genitive or as a *genitivus auctoris*. The gospel is both *about* Christ and *from* Christ, as we have already observed.

11. Ὅτε, 1:15; Ἔπειτα, 1:18, 21; 2:1; Ὅτε, 2:11.

12. Most who take 2:15–21 as a separate pericope recognize, however, that it contains the rationale or explanation for Paul's confronting Peter. The only question is whether that rationale was actually stated to Peter, as part of the Antioch event, or whether it was unstated to Peter, yet put into the Galatian letter to explain why the confrontation took place. Either way, 2:15ff. is closely related to 2:11–14.

him no less than the other apostles, and that he never vacillated in his gospel proclamation). The historical narrative, therefore, pre-argues the case of Galatians 3 and
4 by establishing Paul's credentials to address the Galatian error, and by establishing
the gospel reality that so distinguishes the Abrahamic covenant (which promised to
bless all the nations/Gentiles through Abraham's descendant) from the Sinai covenant
(which was not only made with a single nation, but whose laws excluded intermarriage
and table-fellowship with the Gentiles).

This autobiographical narrative of Galatians falls into the following divisions:

- Paul's life in Judaism (1:13–14)
- Paul's apostolic call (1:15–17)
- Paul's first Jerusalem visit (1:18–20)
- Paul's visit to Syria and Cilicia (1:21–24)
- Paul's second Jerusalem visit, with Barnabas (2:1–10)
- Paul's encounter with Peter at Antioch: Part 1 (2:11–14)
- Paul's encounter with Peter at Antioch: Part 2 (2:15–21)

3.2.1. Paul's Life in Judaism (Gal. 1:13–14)

For you have heard of my former life in Judaism, how I persecuted the church of God
violently and tried to destroy it. And I was advancing in Judaism beyond many of my own
age among my people, so extremely zealous was I for the traditions of my fathers.

Paul was entirely candid about his activity prior to his Damascus calling. Both here and
at 1:21–23, Paul reminded his audience that what he had been doing had been publicly
reported (Ἠκούσατε, v. 13; ἀκούοντες, v. 23) in many regions north of Jerusalem:
He had persecuted the churches (ἐδίωκον τὴν ἐκκλησίαν τοῦ θεοῦ, v. 13; ὁ διώκων
ἡμᾶς ποτε, v. 23). Indeed, the verb διώκω in Paul's case almost achieves the status of a
technical term, because of its repeated use in both Luke's narratives and in Paul's own:

And falling to the ground he heard a voice saying to him, "Saul, Saul, why are you persecuting me? [τί με διώκεις;]" And he said, "Who are you, Lord?" And he said, "I am Jesus,
whom you are persecuting [ὃν σὺ διώκεις·]." (Acts 9:4–5)

"I am a Jew, born in Tarsus in Cilicia, but brought up in this city, educated at the feet of
Gamaliel according to the strict manner of the law of our fathers, being zealous for God as
all of you are this day. I persecuted this Way to the death [τὴν ὁδὸν ἐδίωξα ἄχρι θανάτου],
binding and delivering to prison both men and women, as the high priest and the whole
council of elders can bear me witness. . . . As I was on my way and drew near to Damascus,
about noon a great light from heaven suddenly shone around me. And I fell to the ground
and heard a voice saying to me, 'Saul, Saul, why are you persecuting me? [τί με διώκεις;]'
And I answered, 'Who are you, Lord?' And he said to me, 'I am Jesus of Nazareth, whom
you are persecuting [ὃν σὺ διώκεις].'" (Acts 22:3–4, 6–8)

"And I punished them often in all the synagogues and tried to make them blaspheme, and
in raging fury against them I persecuted them [αὐτοῖς ἐδίωκον] even to foreign cities. . . .
And when we had all fallen to the ground, I heard a voice saying to me in the Hebrew

language, 'Saul, Saul, why are you persecuting me? [τί με διώκεις] It is hard for you to kick against the goads.' And I said, 'Who are you, Lord?' And the Lord said, 'I am Jesus whom you are persecuting [ὃν σὺ διώκεις].'" (Acts 26:11, 14–15)

For I am the least of the apostles, unworthy to be called an apostle, because I persecuted the church of God [ἐδίωξα τὴν ἐκκλησίαν τοῦ θεοῦ]. (1 Cor. 15:9)

As to zeal, a persecutor of the church [διώκων τὴν ἐκκλησίαν]; as to righteousness, under the law blameless. (Phil. 3:6)

Both Luke and Paul regarded the charge of Paul's persecuting (διώκω) the church as a dominical saying, and each candidly reported it as such.

One might regard Paul's candid statement about his prior reputation as being injurious, rhetorically, to his purposes in Galatians. How could Paul's reputation as a persecutor of the churches possibly make the Galatians listen to him? Does this not, and should it not, diminish his stature? Here again, Paul turns accusation to defense and recrimination to validation. Unlike others (Peter and the Galatians),[13] Paul's once zealous persecution of those who did not observe the Mosaic law *ceased* once he embraced the gospel. When he encountered the resurrected Christ, he recognized that the one whom the Mosaic law judged to be accursed (Gal. 3:13) had in fact been vindicated by resurrection from the dead and that, therefore, the entire Mosaic era of tutelage was over—with the logical correlate that those Gentiles judged outsiders by such a law were no longer so. Paul never persecuted the church for any reason other than devotion to the Mosaic law, zeal for "the traditions of the fathers" (Gal. 1:14).

Paul's double reference to his former life "in Judaism" (ἐν τῷ Ἰουδαϊσμῷ), while not seemingly unusual to our ears, may have been so to his generation and may well have communicated a different thing than it does to us. To us, "Judaism" is a world religion that appeared in the first century of the Common Era, just as "Christianity" is a world religion that appeared in the same century. The term, however, had not yet attained that meaning in Paul's generation. The expression itself, Ἰουδαϊσμός, appears only here in the New Testament; Paul's usage in this instance is the first known Christian use of it. In the LXX and intertestamental Jewish literature, it appears only in Maccabean literature: three times in 2 Maccabees and once in 4 Maccabees.[14] Two of these are interesting to students of Galatians. Second Maccabees 14:37–38 says:

A certain Razis, one of the elders of Jerusalem, was denounced to Nicanor as a man who loved his fellow citizens and was very well thought of and for his good will was called father of the Jews. For in former times, *when there was no mingling with the Gentiles* [lit., "in the times of separation," χρόνοις τῆς ἀμειξίας, cf. 4 Macc. 14:3] he had been accused of Judaism [Ἰουδαϊσμοῦ], and for Judaism [Ἰουδαϊσμοῦ] he had with all zeal risked body and life.

---

13. Not only was there a virtual identity between the Galatian behavior and Peter's, but Peter's vacillating behavior probably encouraged the Galatian behavior. As Betz says, "In other words, Cephas shifted his position, and this must have become one of the preconditions for the Galatians' own plans to shift." Betz, *Galatians*, 107.

14. Second Macc. 2:21; 8:1; 14:38; 4 Macc. 4:26. It is also rare in the early fathers, appearing only three times: twice in Ignatius to the Magnesians (8:1; 10:3), and once in Ignatius to the Philadelphians (6:1).

Note here that those who did not mingle with the Gentiles were "accused of Judaism," as though "Judaism" was not a general reference to Mosaic religion per se but to those aspects of the Mosaic faith and life that required separation from Gentiles. Four Maccabees 4:22b–26 is similar:

> He [Antiochus Epiphanes] speedily marched against them, and after he had plundered them he issued a decree that if any of them should be found observing the ancestral law [τῷ πατρίῳ πολιτευόμενοι νόμῳ] they should die. When, by means of his decrees, he had not been able in any way to put an end to the people's observance of the law, but saw that all his threats and punishments were being disregarded, even to the point that women, *because they had circumcised their sons*, were thrown headlong from heights along with their infants, though they had known beforehand that they would suffer this—when, then, his decrees were despised by the people, he himself, through torture, tried to compel everyone in the nation to eat defiling foods and to renounce Judaism [μιαρῶν ἀπογευομένους τροφῶν ἐξόμνυσθαι τὸν Ἰουδαϊσμόν; lit., "*by* eating defiling foods to renounce Judaism"].

While Antiochus's decree ostensibly prohibited all following of "the ancestral law," students of Galatians cannot help but notice that fidelity to circumcision and the dietary laws of Moses are what specifically constituted Ἰουδαϊσμός in this passage. If one eats defiling foods, then one renounces Judaism; by contrast, if one refuses to do so, and if one circumcises one's sons, then one practices Judaism.[15]

The early Christians considered themselves to be followers of the God of Abraham and Moses. Prior to the synagogue ban of the late 80s or early 90s of the first century, Christianity and Judaism had not yet entirely or clearly diverged as separate "religions," in the contemporary sense of the term. Paul consistently claimed Abraham as the father of believing Christians and called such believers Abraham's sons (Gal. 3:7). Thus when he spoke of his behavior "in Judaism," he probably did not intend to suggest that "Judaism" and "Christianity" were, in his mind, two distinct religions. Rather, for Paul, "Judaism" was a term he employed to describe not general faith in the God of Abraham and Moses, but zealous insistence on the Gentile-excluding dimensions of the Mosaic law, a zeal that had characterized the Maccabees before:

> The story of Judas Maccabeus and his brothers, and the purification of the great temple, and the dedication of the altar, and further the wars against Antiochus Epiphanes and his son Eupator, and the appearances which came from heaven to those *who strove zealously on behalf of Judaism* [ὑπὲρ τοῦ Ἰουδαϊσμοῦ], so that though few in number they seized the whole land and pursued [διώκειν] the barbarian hordes. (2 Macc. 2:19–21)

The Maccabean zeal required separation of Jew and Gentile, so the Maccabees "pursued [διώκειν] the barbarian hordes." Similarly, when Paul was ἐν τῷ Ἰουδαϊσμῷ he pursued (ἐδίωκον, 1:13; ὁ διώκων, 1:23) those who abrogated the Mosaic distinctions between Jew and Gentile. So Paul was no stranger of such Maccabean zeal for the Gentile-excluding aspects of the Mosaic law; he had himself been an exemplary (notorious?) practioner

---

15. That is, according to these admittedly few examples, it appears that Ἰουδαϊσμός means what James D. G. Dunn believes "works of the law" means. In Maccabean literature and in the only usage in the New Testament, Ἰουδαϊσμός appears to be fidelity to those aspects of the Mosaic law that distinguished Jew and Gentile. I will argue later, however, that τὰ ἔργα τοῦ νόμου is not so restricted; that it refers to *all* of the works required by Torah.

thereof: "I persecuted the church of God violently and tried to destroy it. And I was advancing in Judaism beyond many of my own age among my people, so extremely zealous was I for the traditions of my fathers." But something, or someone, changed this.

3.2.2. Paul's Apostolic Call (Gal. 1:15–17)

But when he who had set me apart before I was born, and who called me by his grace, was pleased to reveal his Son to me,[16] in order that I might preach him among the Gentiles, I did not immediately consult with anyone; nor did I go up to Jerusalem to those who were apostles before me, but I went away into Arabia, and returned again to Damascus.

Several aspects of this abbreviated account of Paul's call are significant for the book of Galatians: its location (outside of Jerusalem), its agent (God himself), its nature (prophetic), and its intended benefactors (the Gentiles).

The location of Paul's call was almost certainly already known to the Galatians. Indeed, this is implied in verse 17 when he says that he "returned again [πάλιν] to Damascus," even though he had not mentioned Damascus earlier. Apparently, his readers would already have known that the call was extended to him there. Yet it is nearly as important where the call was *not* extended: "nor did I go up[17] to Jerusalem." This is already the third pairing of οὐ with οὐδὲ in Galatians 1:

Paul, an apostle—not from men nor through man [οὐκ ἀπ' ἀνθρώπων οὐδὲ δι' ἀνθρώπου].

The gospel that was preached by me is not man's gospel. For I did not receive it from any man [οὐκ ἔστιν κατὰ ἄνθρωπον· οὐδὲ γὰρ ἐγὼ παρὰ ἀνθρώπου παρέλαβον].

I did not immediately consult with anyone; nor did I go up to Jerusalem [οὐ προσανεθέμην σαρκὶ καὶ αἵματι οὐδὲ ἀνῆλθον εἰς Ἱεροσόλυμα].

This may appear to be a lot of negativity (not only to have three denials in the first seventeen verses but also to double each one), yet the negatives are purposeful. Paul here establishes his independence of the Jerusalem apostles on the perfectly cogent ground that his call *originated* elsewhere. Generally, he consulted with no one, and specifically, he did not go up to Jerusalem. Not only was he not in Jerusalem when he initially received his call, but he visited elsewhere (Arabia) and returned to Damascus, bypassing Jerusalem altogether. "Arabia" can refer to the entire region south and east

---

16. ESV "to me" is a plausible interpretation, but it is equally plausible, and I judge more likely, that it is instrumental: "through me" or "by me." The KJV "in me" may retain in English the ambiguity of the Greek.

17. From Damascus, Paul would have actually traveled south to get to Jerusalem, and the expected verb would have been κατῆλθον, not ἀνῆλθον ("went up"). Whether ἀνῆλθον is a recognition of Jerusalem's elevation or is a convention denoting deference is not essential to my thesis. But the New Testament rather consistently observes the convention that "go up" and "go down" ordinarily mean "go north" and "go south," unless Jerusalem is involved. One "goes up" to Jerusalem and "goes down" from Jerusalem, regardless of cartographic designations, such as "north" and "south." Philip, for instance, "went down" from Jerusalem to Samaria, even though Samaria was north of Jerusalem (Acts 8:5). Similarly, prophets "went down" from Jerusalem to Antioch (Acts 11:27).

of Palestine and west of the Mesopotamian region, which was a fairly deserted, nonarable region. It can also refer to the smaller area of that region immediately south and east of Damascus. Either way, there would be no particularly good reason to travel there at all (though some commentators have suggested that he went here to clear his head, to make sense of the Damascus revelation, and so on, as a kind of retreat); and there were no apostles or established churches there when Paul was called. To travel there, instead of traveling to Jerusalem, was an action that communicated an entire independence of the Jerusalem apostolate.[18] Paul did not need to go up to Jerusalem to confirm his call or to make sense of it.

The agency of Paul's call is equally important. Since the other apostles were called by Jesus himself (Matt. 10:1–4; Mark 3:13–19; Luke 6:12–16),[19] Paul's detractors might conveniently have asserted or implied that he was a "secondary" apostle, a helper or an assistant called by the Jerusalem apostles to assist in the worldwide spread of Christianity. To such an expressed or implied accusation, Paul asserts that he was no less called by God than were the other apostles. He was not and is not sent by humans; he was and is sent by God.

This calling by "God" ("he who . . . was pleased to reveal his Son to me") may first appear somewhat odd, since, as we saw above, the Damascus revelation was clearly a revelation of the ascended Christ ("I am Jesus"; Acts 9:5; 22:8; 26:15). Just as Jesus of Nazareth selected and commissioned the Twelve, so also he selected and commissioned Paul. Here in Galatians 1 Paul refers to the ascended Christ in the third person, which may appear either curious or contradictory to his and Luke's testimony elsewhere. Yet this choice of designation is deliberate, because it permits Paul to liken the *nature* of his call to that of the calling of the significant OT prophets.

Despite the notable efforts of Krister Stendahl,[20] there remains a persisting tendency to describe the narrative of Paul's *call* as a narrative of his *conversion*.[21] Perhaps Stendahl's timing was just bad, or perhaps there were other reasons, but students of Paul are missing something terribly important about Damascus if they do not perceive the intentional efforts by Paul to liken his call to that of the significant Old Testament prophets.

Students of the Old Testament prophetic call narrative have observed that it is a special form/*Gattung* employed to set a prophet apart from other prophets as having a distinctive mediatorial or governmental task. Consider Norm Habel's important observation:

---

18. It is even possible that this would have been construed by some as a willful, or even disrespectful, evasion of Jerusalem.

19. Excepting Matthias (Acts 1:21–26).

20. Esp. "Call Rather than Conversion," *Paul among Jews and Gentiles* (Philadelphia: Fortress, 1976), 7–23; also "The Apostle Paul and the Introspective Conscience of the West," 78–96.

21. Happily, the situation is not entirely bleak. Seyoon Kim, in *The Origin of Paul's Gospel* (Tübingen: J. C. B. Mohr, 1981), provoked a number of serious studies of the Damascus event and its role in shaping Paul's thought. Cf. the collection of eleven essays in Richard C. Longenecker, ed., *The Road from Damascus: The Impact of Paul's Conversion on His Life, Thought, and Ministry* (Grand Rapids: Eerdmans, 1997). So also, Scott J. Hafemann can rightly refer to "the consensus of scholars that the *purpose* of the prophetic call in its canonical form is not primarily autobiographical, but apologetic." Hafemann, *Paul, Moses, and the History of Israel: The Letter/Spirit Contrast and the Argument from Scripture in 2 Corinthians 3* (Peabody, MA: Hendrickson, 1995), 60 (emphasis original).

There can be little doubt that the classical prophets Isaiah, Jeremiah, Ezekiel and II Isaiah appropriate and develop the call traditions reflected in the structure of the calls of Moses and Gideon. By using the same call *Gattung* the prophets in question establish a specific link with the past history of Israel. Their own calls, it would seem, are viewed from the historical perspective of the commission of the ancient mediators of Israel. This proposition agrees with an assertion noted in the call narratives themselves, that the prophets are both messengers and "more than messengers", *both spokesmen and mediators* of Yahweh's historical involvement. In this sense the prophets are successors to the saviors of old. Thus, for Jeremiah it was not only a question of claiming to be a *prophet* like Moses, but also of extending the historical line of continuity from the ancient *mediators* via the divine commission and its form.

In the light of the previous discussion, the prophetic call accounts also seem to be the product of later reflection as the prophets concerned announce their credentials to Israel at large, either orally or in writing, in accordance with the tradition of their predecessors. By employing this form the prophets publicly identify themselves as *God's ambassadors*. The call narratives, therefore, are not primarily pieces of autobiographical information but *open proclamations of the prophet's claim to be Yahweh's agent at work in Israel.*[22]

If Habel's observation is correct, then the purpose of employing this particular form/ *Gattung* is to mark a prophet not merely as a prophet but as a special *kind* of prophet, a prophet who had a special mediatorial or ambassadorial role in the history of redemption. Luke plainly appears to have understood Paul to have been called in such a manner and to such a role, because even the structure of the Acts of the Apostles, no less than its content, is so "weighted" as to give Paul prominence in the work of discipling the nations. Paul, in my judgment, concurred with Luke, and regarded himself in such a manner. His own personal sense of contrition for his previous prosecution, coupled with his savvy recognition of the strategic value of self-deprecation, caused him, overtly, to use other language for himself: "For I am the *least* of the apostles, unworthy to be *called* an apostle, because I persecuted the church of God" (1 Cor. 15:9).

Yet in a less overt way, having made public statements of his unworthiness to the office, Paul recognized (with Moses, the meekest of all men) that his was a distinctively important voice and that he held a distinctly important office. As modestly and indirectly as was possible, Paul compared his call to that of the major Old Testament prophets:

"Before I formed you in the womb [ἐν κοιλίᾳ] I knew you, and before you were born [ἐκ μήτρας] I consecrated you; I appointed you a prophet to the *nations* [εἰς ἔθνη]. (Jer. 1:5)

"Listen to me, O coastlands, and give attention, you peoples from afar. The LORD called me from the womb [ἐκ κοιλίας μητρός μου ἐκάλεσεν], from the body of my mother [ἐκ κοιλίας] he named my name. . . . And now the LORD says, he who formed me from the womb [ἐκ κοιλίας] to be his servant, . . . I will make you as a light for the nations [εἰς φῶς ἐθνῶν], that my salvation may reach to the end of the earth." (Isa. 49:1, 5–6)

---

22. Norm Habel, "The Form and Significance of the Call Narratives," *Zeitschrift für die alttestamentliche Wissenschaft* 77, no. 1 (January 1965): 297–323 (all emphases mine). Cf. also Gerhard von Rad, *Old Testament Theology*, vol. 2, 54ff.; Walther Zimmerli, *Ezekiel 1: A Commentary on the Book of the Prophet Ezekiel, Chapters 1—24*, trans. Roland E. Clements (Philadelphia: Fortress, 1979), 100; and William Baird, "Visions, Revelation, and Ministry: Reflections on 2 Cor. 12:1–5 and Gal. 1:11–17," *Journal of Biblical Literature* 104, no. 4 (December 1985): 651–62.

But when he who had set me apart before I was born [lit., "from my mother's womb"], and who called me by his grace [v. 16], was pleased to reveal his Son to me, in order that I might preach him among the Gentiles. (Gal. 1:15–16)

Ὅτε δὲ εὐδόκησεν[23] [ὁ θεὸς] ὁ ἀφορίσας με ἐκ κοιλίας μητρός μου καὶ καλέσας διὰ τῆς χάριτος αὐτοῦ ἀποκαλύψαι τὸν υἱὸν αὐτοῦ ἐν ἐμοί, ἵνα εὐαγγελίζωμαι αὐτὸν ἐν τοῖς ἔθνεσιν

Modesty may very well have prevented Paul from making the claim more overtly. Or perhaps contrition over his former persecution of the church may have caused the reticence. But the literary parallels between his call and those of Isaiah and Jeremiah are unmistakable. Note especially the striking similarity between Paul's ἐκ κοιλίας μητρός μου καὶ καλέσας and Isaiah's ἐκ κοιλίας μητρός μου ἐκάλεσεν, an almost perfect verbal correspondence. There can be little doubt that Paul's call is analogous to that of Isaiah and Jeremiah—just as their calls were analogous to those of Moses (Exod. 3:1–6), Gideon (Judg. 6:11–18), and Samuel (1 Sam. 3:1–14).[24]

What Paul achieved by this narrative, at a minimum, was the legitimacy of his apostolic call; his voice was equal to that of the Jerusalem apostles. But, to his readers who might have understood the significance of his references to the calls of Jeremiah and Isaiah (and Moses, Samuel, and Gideon), Paul would have achieved more. He would have been claiming a *distinctive* ambassadorial role to the Gentiles, one that not merely equaled but surpassed that of the other apostles. By framing the narrative in this way, he claimed a *special* authority to settle matters related to the Gentile mission—not merely a seat at the table or a voice in the conversation.

This leads to a brief consideration of the fourth aspect of the Damascus narrative in Galatians: its intended beneficiaries. The purpose clause in this abbreviated narrative is "in order that I might preach him among the Gentiles" (1:16).[25] The previous

---

23. As Seyoon Kim points out, εὐδόκησεν here seems to come from Isa. 42:1, because in portions of the textual tradition, προσεδέξατο is replaced with εὐδόκησεν. Kim, *Paul and the New Perspective: Second Thoughts on the Origin of Paul's Gospel* (Grand Rapids: Eerdmans, 2002), 102.

24. So Karl Olav Sandnes, *Paul: One of the Prophets? WUNT* 2, no. 43 (Tübingen: Mohr-Siebeck, 1998): "Paul presents his commission in a manner reminiscent of the literary form that is used in the OT to depict the call of the prophets. . . . Paul here actually describes his Christophany in the form of a prophetic call. Attention has to be paid to this form critical observation, for it defines the framework for the interpretation of the overloaded subordinate clause" (58–59). So also Seyoon Kim: "Since Gal 1:24 seems to allude to Isa 49:3 and Gal 2:2 to Isa 49:4, the call of the Ebed of Isa 49 appears to be in the forefront of Paul's mind while he recalls his own call to apostleship on the road to Damascus." *Paul and the New Perspective*, 101.

25. Paul's claim in 1:16 need not necessarily be taken as reflecting Paul's understanding at the time of the Damascus epiphany. That is, he does not explicitly affirm that he understood at the time of the epiphany that he would play a critical role in the Gentile mission. I leave open the possibility that Francis Watson et al. are correct in suggesting that Paul's role in the Gentile mission may have become clearer to him at a later date. But for his purposes here in Galatians, he asserts that God called Paul to "preach him among the Gentiles." Cf. Watson, *Paul, Judaism and the Gentiles beyond the New Perspective*. On the other hand, the similarity of the language to that of the call of Isaiah in Isa. 49 and Isa. 42, where the servant would be "a light to the nations" (εἰς φῶς ἐθνῶν, v. 6), suggests that Paul's recognition of a distinctive call to the Gentiles was early, as argued by Seyoon Kim in *Paul and the New Perspective* esp. 103–4, where Kim argues that when Paul went away "immediately to Arabia," this means that "his interpretation of his call in the light of Isa 42 must have been equally immediate!"

consideration (the likeness of Paul's distinctively ambassadorial call to that of the calls of Jeremiah and Isaiah) should have been sufficient to establish Paul's distinctive qualification to address the Gentile mission; this consideration goes even further. As Paul later indicated, Peter was authorized to evangelize the circumcised, but Paul to evangelize the uncircumcised (Gal. 2:7). Here he reminds his readers that the entire purpose of his Damascus encounter was "that I might preach him among the Gentiles." This claim anticipates the incident with Peter at Antioch (closely analogous to the Galatian situation itself) and establishes beforehand Paul's jurisdiction over this matter.

From our point of view, it is easy to miss the importance of the Damascus narrative in Galatians entirely, because Paul's claims here are far more implicit than explicit. He did not explicitly claim that he had *more* authority than that of other apostles to address the matter at hand; he did not explicitly say that the Jerusalem apostles had nothing to do with his call (though he came close); he did not explicitly claim the kind of epochal ambassadorial role as that of Isaiah or Jeremiah, who envisioned the end of rebellious Israel as the exclusive "people of God" and the inclusion of Gentiles therein; and he did not explicitly claim distinctive authority or exclusive jurisdiction over the Gentile question. But he came precariously close, and only a kind of tone-deafness to inference and implication would cause his hearers (then or now) to miss his point: that the Damascus revelation granted him not only divine *authority* to promote the Gentile mission, but it also placed him under divine *obligation* to do so, in the face of any opposition, from within or without the church. Whether modesty, contrition, deference, or a desire for church unity motivated him to address the matter implicitly rather than explicitly, we may never know. But the gentle, understated, and abbreviated manner of the narrative nevertheless positions Paul early in the letter as the rightful person to correct this problem, and positions his opponents as opponents of the God who disclosed himself to Paul (as God had earlier disclosed himself to several OT prophets) at Damascus.

Equally important to the Damascus revelation was that it established Paul's *gospel*, not just his mission. He did not merely receive a commission at Damascus; he also claimed to have received there his gospel message:

> I would have you know, brothers, that the gospel that was preached by me [τὸ εὐαγγέλιον τὸ εὐαγγελισθὲν ὑπ' ἐμοῦ] is not man's gospel. For I did not receive it from any man, nor was I taught it, but I received it through a revelation of Jesus Christ. (1:11–12)

Paul does not provide a summary here of what this gospel was that he began proclaiming shortly after Damascus, but he does provide some hints. In 1:23, for instance, he mentions that the Judean churches heard that the one who once persecuted them was "now preaching the faith he once tried to destroy [νῦν εὐαγγελίζεται τὴν πίστιν ἥν ποτε ἐπόρθει]." Note that while the verb is not expressly defined (any more than the noun in 1:11), it suggests that its fundamental content was that which the other apostles had preached before him, that which he had formerly attempted to destroy. Similarly, verse 16 provides some clues, because Paul there claimed that God "was pleased to reveal his Son to me, that I might preach him [ἵνα εὐαγγελίζωμαι αὐτὸν] among the Gentiles." The verb is probably deliberate throughout this passage; he did not employ κηρύσσω until 2:2, where it is qualified by τὸ εὐαγγέλιον: "the gospel that I proclaim [τὸ εὐαγγέλιον ὃ κηρύσσω] among the Gentiles." What Paul proclaimed, then, was "the gospel" and "him." By employing εὐαγγελίζω six times from 1:8 to 1:23, and εὐαγγέλιον seven times between 1:7 and 2:14, Paul identifies his own proclamation substantially with that of those who preceded him (though he denies being *taught* it by them). Indeed, in 2:7, he suggests that he and Peter preached the same gospel, albeit to different audiences: "They saw that I had been entrusted with the gospel to the uncircumcised, just as Peter had been entrusted with the gospel to the circumcised." This should temper somewhat the claims of those (e.g., James D. G. Dunn, T. L. Donaldson, and Francis Watson) who suggest that much or most of Paul's soteriology—particularly, his doctrine of justification—was a late development, or an expedient necessitated by or derived from the Gentile mission.[26] Paul claims that, from the beginning, his "gospel" was essentially the same as that of the other apostles. Though he did not say particularly what he proclaimed about "him" (Christ) in this passage, it could not have been substantially different from what was proclaimed by the other apostles, and it was probably something similar to the summary about Christ's death and resurrection found in 1 Corinthians 15:3–5.

3.2.3. Paul's First Jerusalem Visit (Gal. 1:18–20)

> Then after three years I went up to Jerusalem to visit[27] Cephas and remained with him fifteen days. But I saw none of the other apostles except James the Lord's brother. (In what I am writing to you, before God, I do not lie!)

By this point, readers of Galatians are learning to take careful notice of Paul's denials; his ἕτερον . . . οὐκ εἶδον here is undoubtedly significant (as is the οὐ ψεύδομαι). On his first visit to Jerusalem, Paul made it clear that he was not commissioned by the Jerusalem apostles, because he saw only Cephas (and James, the Lord's brother, who was not technically an apostle, but who was an important leader of the Jerusalem church). He expressly denied seeing any other of the apostles: ἕτερον δὲ τῶν ἀποστόλων οὐκ εἶδον, a curious enough thing to say. Name-droppers, for instance, routinely mention as many perceived-to-be-significant acquaintances that they have. One might think that Paul would *strengthen* his authority to settle the Galatian matter if he could prove he was commissioned by the Jerusalem apostles and was bringing their authoritative message. Paul thought otherwise, however, and believed that it was precisely his independent calling that granted him all the authorization he needed.

This independent calling may account for Paul's adding to the narrative two temporal qualifiers that are pertinent. First, he specified that three entire years passed between the Damascus revelation and his first visit to Jerusalem. If Jerusalem concurrence were

---

26. James D. G. Dunn. "'A Light to the Gentiles,' or 'The End of the Law'? The Significance of the Damascus Road Christophany for Paul," *Jesus, Paul, and the Law: Studies in Mark and Galatians* (Louisville, KY: Westminster / John Knox, 1990), 89–107; T. L. Donaldson, *Paul and the Gentiles: Remapping the Apostle's Convictional World* (Minneapolis: Fortress, 1997); Watson, *Paul, Judaism and the Gentiles beyond the New Perspective*. For a detailed critique, cf. Seyoon Kim, *Paul and the New Perspective*, 1–57.

27. ἱστορῆσαι is a NT hapax, and in the LXX is found only in the first chapter of 1 Esdras, where it is translated "reported" or "recorded."

necessary to Paul's commission, he certainly dawdled for quite a while before soliciting such concurrence. The passage of three years certainly indicated that he was in no hurry to solicit Jerusalem approval, which he regarded as entirely unnecessary. Second, he was only in Jerusalem for fifteen days. The inclusion of this detail may be entirely incidental, or its inclusion may be a subtle way of suggesting that Paul was not there long enough for the meeting to have been significant in forming his understanding of his mission or the gospel itself. Little catechesis or correction could have been done in just over two weeks.

Considering how brief (and apparently insignificant) this sub-narrative is, the most remarkable part is the oath, "In what I am writing to you, before God (ἐνώπιον τοῦ θεοῦ),[28] I do not lie!" One might ordinarily employ οὐ ψεύδομαι only in circumstances where what one says is highly improbable ("No lie, I had three birdies on the back nine!") or likely to be disputed. Paul says this in only three other places. At the beginning of the section of Romans 9–11, Paul articulates that according to God's own purposes, many Gentiles have been grafted onto God's tree, though some Jews have been pruned from it. He begins that entire remarkable discussion this way:

> I am speaking the truth in Christ—I am not lying [οὐ ψεύδομαι]; my conscience bears me witness in the Holy Spirit—that I have great sorrow and unceasing anguish in my heart. For I could wish that I myself were accursed and cut off from Christ for the sake of my brothers, my kinsmen according to the flesh.

The matter of Gentile inclusion and Jewish exclusion is so mysterious, and so likely to offend the sensibilities of portions of Paul's audience, that he prefaces the entire discussion with this solemn statement. Similarly, he employs the expression toward the end of 2 Corinthians, in this case to testify that his ironic "boasting" attests to his apostolic credentials:

> If I must boast, I will boast of the things that show my weakness. The God and Father of the Lord Jesus, he who is blessed forever, knows that I am not lying [οὐ ψεύδομαι].

He appends a similar statement to 1 Timothy 2:7:

> For this I was appointed a preacher and an apostle (I am telling the truth, I am not lying [οὐ ψεύδομαι]), a teacher of the Gentiles in faith and truth.

To the Corinthians and to Timothy, the statement is employed to verify his apostolic authority. In Galatians, however, to say this after such an apparently inconsequential observation that Paul saw only Peter and James seems misplaced. But it isn't. Paul declared that his initial visit to Jerusalem was emphatically *not* for the purpose of attaining or confirming any commission from the Jerusalem apostles. As if to buttress his earlier positive statement that he received his commission from God himself, Paul anticipated that someone may recall his visit to Jerusalem as counterevidence; however, he solemnly refuted any such counterevidence.

---

28. ESV omits ἰδοὺ before ἐνώπιον τοῦ θεοῦ; the omission is not entirely consequential, but the expression is more striking if included: "Behold, before God, I do not lie." Perhaps ESV attempts to include this via the exclamation mark.

3.2.4. Paul's Visit to Syria and Cilicia (Gal. 1:21–24)

> Then I went into the regions of Syria and Cilicia. And I was still unknown in person to the churches of Judea that are in Christ. They only were hearing it said, "He who used to persecute us is now preaching the faith he once tried to destroy." And they glorified God because of me.

After this initial visit to Jerusalem, Paul traveled north once more, probably following well-traveled trade routes to the northeast corner of the Mediterranean before heading east into Cilicia. Since those churches were at such a distance from Jerusalem, Paul could rightly say that he was "still unknown in person"[29] to them. Since they did not know him personally, they knew him only by reputation: "They only were hearing it said."[30]

What these portions of the church knew about Paul's reputation could be succinctly stated, "He who used to persecute [ὁ διώκων] us is now preaching the faith he once tried to destroy [ἐπόρθει]." This reputation initially found its way further north and east to Galatia, so the Galatians would have been familiar with what was reported/ reputed in Syria and Cilicia. Recall 1:13: "For you have heard of my former life in Judaism, how I persecuted [ἐδίωκον] the church of God violently and tried to destroy it [ἐπόρθουν]." There is nothing new in this point of the narrative; the same reputation Paul had among the Galatians at one time was the reputation he had in Syria and Cilicia: he was a persecutor/destroyer (ἐδίωκον/ἐπόρθουν) of the church and its faith.

But Paul added one small strategic addition to this brief narrative: "And they glorified God because of me." This addition performs two functions: First, it plainly suggests that it accrues to God's glory when Saul, a then-persecutor, becomes Paul, a now-propagator. But second, it reminds the Galatians of their own experience—that they, no less than those in Syria and Cilicia, also once recognized the legitimacy of Paul's ministry: "Though my condition was a trial to you, you did not scorn or despise me, but received me as an angel of God, as Christ Jesus" (4:14).

3.2.5. Paul's Second Jerusalem Visit, with Barnabas (Gal. 2:1–10)

As Paul's autobiographical narrative moves into chapter 2, the plot thickens. The pericopes of chapter 2 are longer, more detailed, and therefore more significant to the subsequent arguments made in Galatians 3 and 4. The first of these is the sub-narrative of Paul's second Jerusalem visit, which is a narrative that falls into four parts:

1. Paul set the gospel "to the Gentiles" before the Jerusalem "seemers." (vv. 1–2)
2. The Greek Titus was not compelled to be circumcised. (vv. 3–5)
3. The three added *nothing* to Paul's gospel but rather extended to Paul the right hand of fellowship. (vv. 6–9)

---

29. Literally, "by face" or "by appearance" (τῷ προσώπῳ); RSV, NRSV "by sight."

30. The ESV in "they were hearing" attempts to retain the force of the periphrastic: ἀκούοντες ἦσαν, which itself is parallel to the periphrasis in the previous sentence: ἤμην δὲ ἀγνοούμενος. Most ETs are content with "they heard." Whether the periphrasis is mere "corruption" or an intentional way of suggesting that this reputation was commonly repeated or well-known would be difficult to determine; though the latter would certainly make good rhetorical sense.

4. The only "addition" was a reminder of Paul's ordinary practice regarding the poor. (v. 10)

> Then after fourteen years I went up again to Jerusalem with Barnabas, taking Titus along with me. I went up because of a revelation and set before them (though privately before those who seemed influential) the gospel that I proclaim among the Gentiles, in order to make sure I was not running or had not run in vain.[31] (Gal. 2:1–2)

Verse 1 begins with a temporal adverb and temporal prepositional phrase ("then after fourteen years") that functions similarly with the similar expression in 1:18 ("then after three years"). Together, these expressions reiterate the claim made in 1:16b, "I did not immediately [εὐθέως] consult with anyone." There is even a verbal parallel between "did not consult" (προσανεθέμην) in 1:16 and "set before them" (ἀνεθέμην) in 2:2.[32] Three years passed before Paul visited Jerusalem at all, and another fourteen years passed before his second visit. The citation of the amount of time in each case is not a mere fine point of timekeeping; it is rhetorically significant as a means of establishing that Paul's call was independent from Jerusalem. In his first visit, as he had made clear, he didn't even see any apostles other than Peter and the Lord's brother James; and he might not have even made a second visit had it not been for a divine revelation.

The purpose of the second Jerusalem visit was not to receive any authorization or approval, but to inform them of Paul's Gentile mission: "I . . . set before them . . . the gospel that I proclaim among the Gentiles."[33] Paul's qualification of "the gospel" is significant here. The gospel that he set before the Jerusalem leaders was not "the gospel of justification," or "the gospel of justification by faith," or "the gospel of free grace," but "the gospel that I proclaim *among the Gentiles*." The dominant Protestant approach to Galatians from Luther onward tended to overlook the importance of this qualification, as though it were little more than a matter of a division of labor: Peter, you go here; Paul, you go there. But the Gentile mission, from Paul's point of view, was part of the gospel *itself*. The gospel, as Paul understood it, constituted the fulfillment of the third part of God's promise to Abraham: to bless all the nations through one of his descendants. Later, in 3:16, Paul would say, "Now the promises were made to Abraham and to his offspring. It does not say, 'And to offsprings,' referring to many, but referring to one, 'And to your offspring,' who is Christ." This is a reference to Genesis 28:13–14:

---

31. For convenience, I separate verses 1 and 2 from 3–5. But I have sympathies with including all five verses together, and with the argument of William O. Walker that δὲ κατὰ ἀποκάλυψιν in verse 2 and διὰ δὲ τοὺς παρεισάκτους ψευδαδέλφους of verse 4 are syntactically parallel, each linked to the main verb, ἀνέβην. If Walker is correct, Paul then provides two reasons for the first visit to Jerusalem. Cf. William O. Walker, "Why Paul Went to Jerusalem: The Interpretation of Galatians 2:1–5," *Catholic Biblical Quarterly* 54, no. 3 (July 1, 1992): 503–10. My interpretation does not rest on any particular resolution of this matter.

32. Paul employs ἀνατίθημι here only; and he employs προσανατίθημι here only and at 2:6, where the Jerusalem "seemers" are the subject: "those, I say, who seemed influential added [προσανέθεντο] nothing to me."

33. The English translations face a bit of a challenge here. RSV, NRSV, and ESV place the qualifying phrase ("privately before those who seemed influential") between the verb and its object; whereas the original adds the qualifying phrase as an afterthought. The difference is small, but in the original the emphasis is on the verb and its object: "placed before them the gospel which I preach among the Gentiles—privately, to those who seemed to be something."

And behold, the L ORD stood above it and said, "I am the L ORD, the God of Abraham your father and the God of Isaac. The land on which you lie I will give to you and to your offspring. Your offspring shall be like the dust of the earth, and you shall spread abroad to the west and to the east and to the north and to the south, and *in you and your offspring shall all the families of the earth be blessed.*

Plainly enough, Abraham's descendants became numerous ("like the dust of the earth") in their four hundred years in Egypt. Equally plainly, his descendants inherited the land during the time of Joshua. But the families/nations of the earth were not blessed until the appearance of the single "seed" of Abraham, whom Paul identified as Christ (more on this later). One-third of the tripartite pledge to Abraham was fulfilled in Egypt when his descendants became numerous; another third was fulfilled hundreds of years later during the period of the conquest of the land. But the final third awaited the arrival of Christ and Paul's preaching him to the Gentiles. From Paul's point of view, the very purpose of the dying and rising of Christ was "that in Christ Jesus the blessing of Abraham might come to the *Gentiles*" (Gal. 3:14). In a very real sense, though Paul is too modest/contrite to say it, Paul's mission to the Gentiles *constituted* the fulfillment of God's pledge to Abraham. Paul's Gentile mission, that is, was the inaugural fulfillment of the third aspect of the Abrahamic promise. The gospel itself, which Paul placed before the Jerusalem leaders, was a gospel τοῖς ἔθνεσιν, just as the purpose of the Damascus revelation was that Paul would preach to the Gentiles, as he had said earlier at 1:16, that God "was pleased to reveal his Son to me, in order that I might preach him among the Gentiles."

If Paul showed appropriate deference to the Jerusalem leaders by informing them of his Gentile mission, then he also showed his independence by refusing to accord them any special status, which he did with the clever use of the verb δοκέω here. Four times (once in 2:2, twice in 2:6, and once again in 2:9) in this passage, Paul referred to the Jerusalem "seemers." In his initial use of this expression here in verse 2, he doesn't even specify what they "seemed" to be. Later, he concedes that they "seemed" to be "something" (τι), and even later he suggests that they "seemed" to some to be "pillars." But Paul asserted that this was *mere* appearance; they might have "seemed" to be something, but "what they *were* makes no difference to me" (2:6).[34]

Paul skirted the edge of a dangerous precipice here. On the one hand, he knew that the Jerusalem leaders were highly regarded by some both in Jerusalem and in Galatia. On the other hand, he was persuaded that he himself had equal or superior authority regarding the Gentile mission by virtue of the Damascus call. Paul conceded that *some* regarded the Jerusalem leaders as something special, without conceding that *he* regarded them as special. For him, they were fellow laborers in the gospel; nothing more nor less. Paul cleverly shrouded them in double anonymity;[35] he qualified the

---

34. While not critical to my thesis, I regard as more probable the view of Betz (*Galatians*, 87), Longenecker (*Galatians*, 48), et al., that the use of δοκέω here is, as Longenecker says, "ironic." It is a way of acknowledging that they enjoyed a special status without necessarily concurring that one agrees with the special status accorded. This is preferable, in my judgment, to the view of Lightfoot (*Galatians*, 103), Burton (*Galatians*, 71), Bruce (*Galatians*, 109), et al., that the use of δοκέω here is neutral.

35. As he did with the Galatian troublers: "there are some [τινές] who trouble you (1:7)," and "the one who is troubling you will bear the penalty, *whoever he is*" (5:10). The first of these

"seemed" with the ambiguous "to be something," and he did not even name them until verse 9, where the narrative says nothing about Paul's regard for them (they merely "seemed" to be "pillars" or "something"), but everything about *their* regard for Paul: "When James and Cephas and John . . . perceived the grace that was given to me, they gave the right hand of fellowship to Barnabas and me."

> But even Titus, who was with me, was not forced to be circumcised, though he was a Greek. Yet because of false brothers[36] secretly brought in—who slipped in to spy out our freedom[37] that we have in Christ Jesus, so that they might bring us into slavery—to them we did not yield in submission even for a moment,[38] so that the truth of the gospel might be preserved for you. (Gal. 2:3–5)

This is the first of thirteen references to circumcision in Galatians.[39] Apart from the circumstances, verse 3 appears not only unusual but perhaps inappropriate; Titus might have even regarded the matter as a tad personal. This section also contains the first of eleven references to the ἐλευθ- language in the letter.[40] Here, then, his autobiographical narrative anticipates the substance of the argumentation proper, and he introduces matters that dominate the discussion in the theological reasoning in Galatians 3 and 4. Paul places before the Galatians an indisputable part of the historical record: That when Paul took along Barnabas and Titus with him to Jerusalem, the Greek Titus was not required to be circumcised. Some anonymous "false brothers," some anonymous enemies of Christian liberty, may have *wished* that he had been circumcised, but Paul and his co-laborers did not yield to such "even for a moment."

And why did they not yield even for a moment? To preserve Titus's comfort? To protect his pride in his own ethnic heritage? To get on with more important matters? No, the purpose clause is very telling: They did not yield to any expressed or implied

---

employs the indefinite pronoun—τινές—and the same ambiguity appears at 2:6: Ἀπὸ δὲ τῶν δοκούντων εἶναί τι, literally, "from those who appear to be something [τι]." The second reference is even more uncertain: "whoever he is," as though Paul will not dignify the troubler with a proper noun. H. D. Betz thinks the same intentional ambiguity toward Paul's opponents is communicated with the "certain men [τινας] from James" in 2:12. Betz, *Galatians*, 107.

36. NRSV's "false believers" is misleading here apart from the explanatory note in some printings that rightly represents the Greek as saying "false brothers." The πίστ- group in Galatians is too important to confuse with ἀδελφοί- language.

37. We will encounter the ἐλευθ-language again in Galatians; this is the first of eleven uses thereof (Gal. 2:4; 3:28; 4:22, 23, 26, 30, 31; 5:1 twice; 5:13 twice). While we might justly think of "freedom" or "liberty" in a positive sense, it is also the case that the language always implies freedom *from* something: from Egyptians, from oppression, or from some other bondage. Paul, in his first usage of the term in Galatians, determined to define the matter only implicitly, rather than explicitly. Implicitly, the opponents of Christian freedom might have insisted on Titus's obedience to the Mosaic law, but Paul does not here expressly describe the freedom as ἀπὸ τοῦ νόμου, though perhaps he does at Rom. 8:2.

38. Many contemporary ETs (RSV, NRSV, ESV) translate πρὸς ὥρα as "for a moment," which grasps the sense of the original better than the more-literal KJV, "for an hour." Before the advent of watches and clocks, minutes and seconds could not be measured; the hour was the smallest measure of time. But had a smaller unit of measure been available to Paul, he almost certainly would have employed it, so "for a moment" is a justifiable paraphrase.

39. Cf. also Gal. 2:7–9, 12; 5:2, 3, 6, 11; 6:12–13, 15.

40. Also Gal. 3:28; 4:22–23, 26, 30–31; 5:1, 13.

requirement that Titus be circumcised "so that [ἵνα] the truth of the gospel [ἡ ἀλήθεια
τοῦ εὐαγγελίου] might be preserved for you." How or why could the truth of the gospel be at stake here, unless the gospel *itself* had something to do with the nations, the
uncircumcised Gentiles, and the families of the earth being blessed through Abraham's
descendant? Paul's reasoning here is identical to his reasoning in Ephesians 3:4 and
6, where he also affirmed that the gospel itself, in its very nature, blesses the various
nations of the earth:

> When you read this, you can perceive my insight into the *mystery of Christ*. . . . This *mystery*
> is that the Gentiles are fellow heirs, members of the same body, and partakers of the *promise*
> in Christ Jesus through the *gospel*.[41]

Paul's logic is that the truth of the gospel is entirely at stake: If Gentiles are not blessed
by Abraham's (singular) descendant, then the promise to Abraham remains unfulfilled.
For Paul, the purpose of the election of Abraham and his descendants was not that
they would monopolize God's blessings, but that they would one day be the vehicle of
bringing those blessings to all the nations/families of the earth.[42]

This narrative regarding Titus is critical precedent. If the Jerusalem leaders had
regarded circumcision as necessary, this was their opportunity to have said something;
but they didn't. Their not requiring anything of Titus was tacit agreement with Paul's
νόμος-free understanding of the Gentile mission. If Titus could be a co-laborer with
Paul (2 Cor. 8:23) without observing the Mosaic law, then surely other Gentiles were
also free from its requirements.

> And from those who seemed to be influential (what they were makes no difference
> [οὐδέν] to me; God shows no [οὐ] partiality)[43]—those, I say, who seemed influential
> added nothing [οὐδέν] to me. On the contrary, when they saw that I had been entrusted
> with the gospel to the uncircumcised, just as Peter had been entrusted with the gospel

---

41. It is not essential or critical to my thesis that Paul authored Ephesians; the point is the same
if a Pauline disciple, influenced by Paul's understanding of the gospel mystery, wrote Ephesians.
But Pauline scholarship, for more than a century now, has overestimated the stylistic grounds
for denying Pauline authorship of Ephesians, and it has underestimated the role of amanuensis
in chirographic cultures. Paul referred to adding a greeting in his "own hand" three times in
his letters (1 Cor. 16:21; Col. 4:8; and 2 Thess. 3:17), and indicated that this was his practice "in
every letter of mine." Paul as much as indicated thereby that an amanuensis wrote the rest of
such letters; and if he employed different amanuenses at different times, then this would easily
account for lexical and syntactical differences.

42. We will pursue this in greater detail when we discuss Galatians 3. I merely mention the
matter now to demonstrate how the autobiographical narrative in chapters 1 and 2 anticipates
some of the reasoning in chapters 3 and 4, preparing the Galatians to understand that reasoning
in its best light. Paul did not merely perceive the Gentile mission to be part of the church's *mission*; he perceived the Gentile mission to be part of the church's *gospel*, part of its *message*. Her
gospel itself declared that God had now fulfilled the third pledge made to Abraham: through
his descendant to bless all the nations of the earth. If God, in Christ, merely blesses Israel (and
non-Israelites who enter its Gentile-excluding covenant), then Abraham's descendant has not
blessed the nations, the pledge to Abraham remains only two-thirds fulfilled, and therefore there
is no (Abrahamic) news, good or otherwise.

43. Paul here employs a verbal expression: πρόσωπον . . . λαμβάνει, employing two
words. Elsewhere, he communicates the same by forming the two words into a single word,
προσωπολημψία (Rom. 2:11; Eph. 6:9; Col. 3:25).

to the circumcised (for he who worked through Peter for his apostolic ministry to the circumcised worked also through me for mine to the Gentiles), and when James and Cephas and John, who seemed to be pillars, perceived the grace that was given to me, they gave the right hand of fellowship to Barnabas and me, that we should go to the Gentiles and they to the circumcised. Only, they asked us to remember the poor, the very thing I was eager to do. (Gal. 2:6–10)

The polemical nature of the letter is disclosed here by two things: the three negatives (no difference, no partiality, and no addition) and the caveat in verse 10. Paul was aware that the autobiographical portion of his letter was crucial to settling the issue at Galatia itself. Therefore, he was at pains to ensure that no portion of it would suffer rebuttal. So, when he recorded that the highly regarded members of the Jerusalem churches "added nothing to me," he anticipated an objection. Apparently, at some point in this meeting, the Jerusalem leaders reminded Paul (ἵνα μνημονεύωμεν) about the poor;[44] and Paul was concerned that, if he did not make express acknowledgment of this, his detractors might have grounds to refute his saying that they "added nothing." He therefore dutifully acknowledged their reminder in his narrative, while also indicating that it was not truly an "addition," since he had always eagerly labored to this end (ὃ καὶ ἐσπούδασα αὐτὸ τοῦτο ποιῆσαι) anyway.[45]

While the primary event recorded in this sub-narrative is negative—"added nothing"—the overwhelming positive point made is the agreement between Paul and the Jerusalem leaders that the Christian gospel embraces Jew and Gentile equally. Six times in this brief narrative, Paul employed the language that ordinarily distinguished Jew and Gentile.[46]

Having denied that the Jerusalem leaders added anything to him, Paul asserted just the opposite. "On the contrary," he said, indicating that what followed would communicate just the opposite of any suggestion that there was some correction or addendum to him and his Gentile mission.[47] To the contrary of any suggestion that the Jerusalem leaders were obliged to add anything to Paul's Gentile-embracing gospel, the apostles did just the opposite. Omitting the parenthetical expressions, Paul said this:

---

44. Perhaps especially the poor *in* Jerusalem, who suffered severely from the famine of 46–48. And perhaps the "reminder" had a dual message: "Remember that if, according to your preaching, Jews and Greeks are alike members of the body of Christ—marked by baptism into him rather than by observance of Mosaic ceremonies—then Gentiles must regard the Jewish believers as brothers, and prove this regard by their monetary collections." Dunn rightly says here that "the principle of covenant obligation on those claiming membership of the assembly of God's people should be safeguarded and affirmed." *Galatians*, 113.

45. Here and elsewhere, there is not an especially facile English rendering for σπουδάζω. Most ETs translate "be eager," which suggests an attitude, but σπουδάζω is a verb and a verb that communicates diligent, perhaps even arduous, labor. ESV sometimes translates "endeavor" or "strive" (1 Thess. 2:17; Heb. 4:11), "be diligent" (2 Pet. 1:10; 3:14), or "do one's best" (2 Tim. 2:15; 4:9, 21; Titus 3:12), which are better.

46. περιτομή appears three times, τὰ ἔθνη twice, and ἀκροβυστία once.

47. By itself, ἀλλά might not warrant the strong adversative translation of RSV, NRSV, ESV, "on the contrary," but the combination, ἀλλὰ τοὐναντίον, does warrant the strong adversative, since either by itself suggests fairly strong disjunction. τοὐναντίον is rare in the NT; cf. 2 Cor. 2:7; 1 Pet. 3:9.

When they saw [ἰδόντες] that I had been entrusted with the gospel to the uncircumcised,
. . . and when James and Cephas and John . . . perceived [γνόντες] the grace that was given
to me, they gave the right hand [δεξιὰς ἔδωκαν] of fellowship to Barnabas and me,[48] that
we should go to the Gentiles and they to the circumcised.

Paul indicated a double ground for the extension of the right hand of fellowship to
him,[49] using two almost synonymous terms (ἰδόντες, γνόντες) to describe what they
saw/perceived in him. They recognized that he had been entrusted with the "gospel
to the circumcised," and they recognized the ministerial grace that had been given to
him.[50] Paul would have had no psychic access to the inner workings of their minds, so
these verbs of perception suggest that the Jerusalem leaders *acknowledged* that Paul
had been entrusted with the gospel and that ministerial grace had been given to him.

Critical to the situation at Galatia and to the reasoning in the letter is the special
qualification added here. What the Jerusalem leaders acknowledged was not merely
that Paul was entrusted with the gospel, but with the gospel "to the uncircumcised"
(τὸ εὐαγγέλιον τῆς ἀκροβυστίας), and that this ministry of declaring the gospel to the
uncircumcised was recognized as equivalent to the work of Peter: "I had been entrusted
with the gospel to the uncircumcised just as [καθὼς] Peter had been entrusted with the
gospel to the circumcised." This claim was repeated in the parenthetical sentence: "For
he who worked through Peter for his apostolic ministry to the circumcised worked also
through me for mine to the Gentiles." Paul thereby established that, at this moment in
the church's history, the Jerusalem leaders recognized and overtly acknowledged Paul's
mission to the uncircumcised Gentiles no less than Peter's mission to the circumcised
Jews. Implicit in this recognition (though later to be explicated in the incident at
Antioch and in Gal. 3) was that the reign of ὁ νόμος was over; the law's requirement
of circumcision was over; the law's distinction between "Jew and Greek" had ended
(anticipating Gal. 3:28).

One small rhetorical flourish should be noted. When Paul recorded that the ones
who "seemed" gave the right hand of fellowship to him, he changed his tune a little.
Having merely described them before as those who "seemed/appeared" to be something
(τοῖς δοκοῦσιν, 2:2), and having said earlier, "What they were makes no difference to
me" (2:6), he now acknowledged that they "seemed to be pillars" (οἱ δοκοῦντες στῦλοι

---

48. NRSV and ESV follow the English convention that in compound subjects or objects,
one deferentially puts self in the second position: "gave the right hand of fellowship to Barnabas
and me." KJV and RSV preserve the original better: "gave . . . to me and Barnabas," because what
is critical in this narrative is the relation between Paul and the Jerusalem leaders; Barnabas is
a kind of afterthought.

49. The expression "right hand of fellowship" may be somewhat commonly used in ecclesiastical circles in the present day, but this is the only use of the expression in the New Testament.

50. "Grace," surely, is sometimes soteric in Paul's letters, as at Rom. 3:24, where Paul says
we "are justified by his grace as a gift, through the redemption that is in Christ Jesus." But
"grace" is also sometimes ministerial—the special grace that is associated with varying forms of
ministerial service, as at Rom. 12:6, "Having gifts that differ according to the grace given to us,"
or 1 Cor. 3:10, "According to the grace of God given to me, like a skilled master builder I laid
a foundation," or esp. Eph. 3:7–8, "Of this gospel I was made a minister according to the gift
of God's grace, which was given me by the working of his power. To me, though I am the very
least of all the saints, this grace was given, to preach to the Gentiles the unsearchable riches of
Christ" (also Rom. 12:3; 15:15; Gal. 1:15; Eph. 3:1–3).

εἶναι) as though, in their act of recognizing the equal legitimacy of the Gentile mission, they had truly come to be pillars in the house of God.

3.2.6. Paul's Encounter with Peter at Antioch: Part 1 (Gal. 2:11–14)

> But when Cephas came to Antioch, I opposed him to his face, because he stood condemned. For before certain men came from James, he was eating with the Gentiles; but when they came he drew back and separated himself, fearing the circumcision party.[51] And the rest of the Jews acted hypocritically along with him, so that even Barnabas was led astray by their hypocrisy. But when I saw that their conduct was not in step with the truth of the gospel, I said to Cephas before them all, "If you, though a Jew, live like a Gentile and not like a Jew, how can you force the Gentiles to live like Jews?"

For sheer drama, this brief narrative is probably as arresting as any post-ascension narrative in the New Testament. While there were matters to be settled in the New Testament church (Jerusalem Council, Acts 15:1–29), and while there were occasional disruptions in ministerial labor (Paul and Silas separating from Barnabas and John Mark, Acts 15:36–40), there was nothing to compare with a narrative like this, where one apostle publicly and unequivocally condemned the behavior of another, and even commented on the faulty motivation behind the behavior (φοβούμενος τοὺς ἐκ περιτομῆς). In an already abbreviated historical/autobiographical narrative, in which Paul used only thirty-eight verses to narrate events covering well over seventeen years, Paul employed only four verses[52] to describe one of the most profound encounters

---

51. ESV translates τοὺς ἐκ περιτομῆς as "the circumcision party," suggesting that it was a (recognized or well-established?) subgroup within the church. While it is not critical to my thesis in any way, I am inclined to think that the expression is essentially identical to ἡ περιτομή in verses 7, 8, and 9, where it refers simply to Jews. That is, the contrast between ἡ περιτομή and ἡ ἀκροβυστία is not between two parts of the Christian church; the terms designate Jews and Gentiles. So Watson, *Paul, Judaism, and the Gentiles*, 106–7; and Bruce, *Galatians*, 106.

52. It is plausible that the narrative includes verses 15–21; indeed, I have considerable sympathies with such a position, as do those who regard the section as formally addressed to Peter, although intended, materially, to be directed toward the Galatians (Burton: "Having in mind the Antioch situation and mentally addressing Peter, if not quoting from what he said to him," *Galatians*, 116). Since uncial Greek manuscripts made no effort to indicate the beginnings and endings of direct discourse, the original manuscripts do not indicate whether verses 15–21 are a record of what Paul said to Peter, or whether they are Paul's commentary on the rationale that led him to confront Peter, or, as George Kennedy thinks, they are Paul's commentary on the entire autobiographical narrative that began at 1:13. H. D. Betz, persuaded that Paul is following the typical form of an apologetic letter, believes the *narratio* section ends at 2:14 and that 2:15–21 consists of the *propositio*, a position with which Longenecker appears to concur (Longenecker, *Galatians*, 82). Undoubtedly, the language shifts between 2:14 and 2:15 from the second-person singular (σύ) to the first-person plural (ἡμεῖς). This need not indicate that the pericope ends at 2:14, however, for several reasons. First, Paul ordinarily addresses his Galatian recipients in the second-person plural, not the first-person plural, especially in the following verses, 3:1–5, where he does so consistently. So, who are the "we" of 2:15ff., if not Paul and Peter? Second, shifts of person need not be indicative of shifts from direct to indirect discourse; since, within 2:15–21, there is also a shift from first plural in verses 15–17 to first singular in verses 18–21. Third, there are two word chains that connect verses 14 and 15, since each verse includes both the ιουδα- stock and the ἐθν- stock. Therefore, I find it impossible to determine with any

in apostolic Christianity. Its very brevity contributes to its laconic force: "But when Cephas came to Antioch, I opposed him to his face, because he stood condemned."[53]

Many historical questions surround the sub-narrative of Galatians 2:11–21; fortunately, the resolution of most of them is inconsequential to my thesis. Many students of Galatians have wrestled with the question of what, if any, relation exists between the event narrated here and the Jerusalem Council narrated in Acts 15. It appears to me that the majority report distinguishes the two as separate events, for the following reasons:

- A public meeting (Acts 15) versus a private meeting (Gal. 2).
- Correcting doctrine ("were teaching the brethren," Acts 15:1) versus correcting behavior (Gal. 2).
- Peter, the champion of the narrative (Acts 15:9–10), versus Peter, the "goat" of the narrative (Gal. 2).
- Peter, one of the resolvers of the problem (Acts 15:7–11), versus Peter, the source of the problem (Gal. 2).
- The issue settled by the assembled church (Acts 15) versus the issue settled by an individual, Paul (Gal. 2).
- The issue settled by official decree versus the issue settled by an informal rebuke.

I concur with the majority that it is unlikely that the two narratives record the same event. To the contrary, with H. D. Betz et al.,[54] I regard it as likely that the Jerusalem Council antedated the Antioch incident, which accounts for two things in the narrative of Galatians 2. First, if the Jerusalem Council antedated the incident at Antioch, it helps account for Peter's custom of eating with the Gentiles, as recorded in Galatians 2. Since the Jerusalem Council had freed the Gentiles from the obligation of circumcision, they were no longer to be regarded as ceremonially unclean and were, therefore, appropriate company for table fellowship. Second, if the Jerusalem Council antedated the incident at Antioch, this may also account for Paul's apparently severe language in Galatians 2, wherein he bluntly accused Peter of being condemned[55] and charged him with cowardice and hypocrisy. Such acute language is more appropriate if it occurs after the Jerusalem Council, especially if Peter was one of the resolvers of the issue there. That is, if Peter were present at the Jerusalem Council and one of the central figures in the resolution regarding the Gentiles, then his withdrawal from

---

degree of confidence whether we should regard the direct discourse with Peter as ending at 14 or continuing through 21; I actually lean toward the latter. All commentators recognize a close connection between 2:15–21 and what precedes, since the reasoning of 2:15–21 explains, theologically, the narrative since 1:13 and especially the narrative of 2:11–14 (while also anticipating the arguments in chapters 3 and 4). Perhaps all agree with F. F. Bruce's understated comment: "It is difficult to decide," (*Galatians*, 136). I will therefore treat them separately, simply for the sake of convenience, since 2:15–21, by itself, contains so many challenging matters.

53. Though, as Betz suggests (*Galatians*, 105), the incident was likely widely known, and perhaps this is why it could be referred to so briefly, as a mere reminder of a well-known incident.

54. Betz, *Galatians*, 105n436.

55. Which Longenecker (*Galatians*, 72), following Ulrich Wilckens (*Theological Dictionary of the New Testament* 8:568n1), takes as being "severe" language and meaning "condemned before God," not merely "be blamed," "in the wrong," or "self-condemned by the inconsistency of his own actions."

Gentile fellowship is not a mere social faux pas, nor a mere personal inconsistency, but a vacillation regarding an important public issue in the life of the nascent church with which Peter was well acquainted.

The narrative is interestingly constructed by a form of bracketing. Verses 11 and 14 record Paul's act of opposing Peter at Antioch itself, whereas verses 12 and 13 record the rationale for his doing so: that the behavior was hypocritical/inconsistent in itself, that it was contrary to the truth of the gospel, that it was ill-motivated, and that it had ill consequences.

The initial record of the encounter, as suggested above, is remarkably laconic: "But when Cephas came to Antioch, I opposed him to his face, because he stood condemned." Presumably, the incident was publicly known (v. 14 reminds the reader: "I said to Cephas before them all"), sufficiently so that Paul's record could be so brief. The verbal summary of the encounter (v. 14) is also brief, almost enigmatic: "If you, though a Jew, live like a Gentile and not like a Jew, how can you force the Gentiles to live like Jews?" The rationale, to which we will turn our attention shortly, makes clear what Paul meant by the expression "live like a Gentile." At some point (whether after Peter's visions and before the Jerusalem Council, or after both), Peter developed the custom[56] of eating with Gentiles, a matter forbidden by the Mosaic law. Thus Peter had abandoned the Kashrut laws that had proscribed table fellowship with Gentiles; he had, in short, "lived like a Gentile" without regard for the Mosaic prescriptions and proscriptions regarding such matters. Paul's reasoning, indisputable in its abbreviated form, is straightforward: "If even you, a Jew, do not observe the Mosaic ceremonies, how can you require the hapless Gentiles to do so? You surely do not expect Gentiles to be more circumspect in observing the laws of Moses than Jews, do you?"

It has been common among Pauline interpreters to refer to the errorists at Galatia as "Judaizers," or "the Judaizing party," and those who make such reference suggest that the problem at Galatia was analogous to the problem Paul encountered at Antioch with Peter. I largely concur (or at least I can see no good reason not to concur). Unfortunately, those who recognize the analogy between Peter and the Galatian "Judaizers" sometimes make a number of other assumptions that the text does not warrant: that "Judaizers" were a well-known Jewish phenomenon or party; that "Judaizers" taught some sort of false doctrine; and/or that "Judaizers" specifically taught an erroneous view of the doctrine of justification. It is not to my purposes to give an exhaustive list of the participants in this tendency. I would like to take the opportunity of commenting on the term's only appearance in Galatia (or in the New Testament, for that matter) to raise questions about each of these assumptions.

First, there is no historical evidence that "the Judaizers" were a well-known phenomenon or party within Palestinian Judaism, though ironically, there is evidence that they existed among first-century *Christian* congregations (at Galatia and possibly also at Philippi).[57] As we noted earlier, the term is a *hapax legomenon* in the New Testament (appearing only here), a *hapax* in the LXX (appearing only at Esther 8:17), and a *hapax* in

---

56. Many commentators rightly recognize that the imperfect tense of συνήσθιεν is almost surely intended to indicate that the behavior was ongoing and common.

57. Phil. 3:2–3 "Look out for the dogs, look out for the evildoers, look out for those who mutilate the flesh [τὴν κατατομήν]. For we are the real circumcision."

the intertestamental Jewish Greek literature (occurring only at Theodotus 4:0). If, in the combination of these rather substantial bodies of literature, the term appears only thrice, it was either a rare phenomenon or an extremely well-concealed one.[58] It is even entirely possible that Paul thought he was coining a term, since it is possible that he either had not encountered or had not remembered its other two known occurrences before him.

Second, contrary to so many assertions, it is not at all clear that Paul employs the term ἰουδαΐζειν to describe a *doctrine*, at least in any ordinary sense. He cites a change in Peter's *behavior*—he once ate with Gentiles, then later withdrew, and separated himself from them. Both in terms of word formation and the parallel clause in the sentence, the verb ἰουδαΐζειν appears to be nothing more than a combination of Ἰουδαϊκῶς and ζάω. If Paul were aware of other uses of the term, he would have known that it described a behavior, not a doctrine. Note again the usage in Esther 8:17:

> Then Mordecai went out from the presence of the king in royal robes of blue and white, with a great golden crown and a robe of fine linen and purple, and the city of Susa shouted and rejoiced. The Jews had light and gladness and joy and honor. And in every province and in every city, wherever the king's command and his edict reached, there was gladness and joy among the Jews, a feast and a holiday. And many from the peoples of the country declared themselves Jews, for fear of the Jews had fallen on them [καὶ πολλοὶ τῶν ἐθνῶν περιετέμοντο καὶ ἰουδάιζον διὰ τὸν φόβον τῶν Ἰουδαίων]. (Esther 8:15–17)

While ESV translates "*declared* themselves Jews," suggesting some sort of verbal activity, if the two verbs are hendiadys, then something like "were circumcised and lived in other ways as Jews" would be a perfectly acceptable translation. The only specific thing we know about these Gentiles was that they were circumcised. Similarly, in Theodotus 4, when Shechem wished to marry Jacob's daughter Dinah, Jacob "said he would not give [his consent], until all the inhabitants of Shechem *became like the Jews, by being circumcised* [πρὶν ἂν ἢ πάντας τοὺς οἰκοῦντας τὰ Σίκιμα περιτεμνομένους Ἰουδαῖσαι], and Hamor said that he would persuade them [to do so]." In each case, the issue was behavioral and the term ἰουδαΐζειν referred to performing those specific behaviors that distinguished Jews from Gentiles, setting the Jews apart as a "holy" people. Further, as we noted above, this Gentile behavior of being circumcised and living as Jews was motivated out of a concern to please Jews. In the one case, it was expressly because of "fear of the Jews" (διὰ τὸν φόβον τῶν Ἰουδαίων), an expression that is remarkable for its similarity to Paul's description of Peter's motivation, "fearing the circumcision party" (φοβούμενος τοὺς ἐκ περιτομῆς). In the other, it was in order to overcome Jewish resistance to intermarriage with the unclean nations. But in neither of the two situations before Antioch did the term refer to a doctrine per se, nor did Paul say anything about what Peter said or taught in any way. To be sure, Paul said that Peter's behavior was incompatible with the "truth of the gospel" (Gal. 2:14), but what he actually objected to was Peter's behavior and its motivation. And, of course, if the matter complained of was behavioral (rather than doctrinal), then there is no warrant for the common assertion that the Judaizers taught an erroneous view of justification.[59]

---

58. Φαρισαῖος, by contrast, appears ninety-eight times in the New Testament.

59. If Peter's behavior was inconsistent with "the truth of the gospel," then such behavior left unchallenged was an implicit challenge to the truth; so I do not deny that Peter's behavior,

Here we often encounter what I have described as a tendency to "read between the lines" of Galatians, rather than to read the lines themselves. In the texts antecedent to Paul where this rare term appeared, nothing at all suggests that the behavior in question had anything to do with justification; to the contrary, the behavior was motivated by a concern to please the Jews (and their Gentile-excluding ceremonies), not to please God. The behavior, in other words, was not motivated by a concern to pass the bar of God's judgment; it was motivated by a concern to pass the bar of Jewish judgment. And it appears that the behavior was the same here: Peter was "fearing the circumcision party," not "fearing God."

In verses 12–13, Paul indicated why he had confronted Peter and why he regarded Peter's behavior as being "condemned." First, he noted the inconsistency of Peter's behavior. One who had apparently eaten with Gentiles for some time (consistently with the events of Acts 10–11 and Acts 15) later withdrew and separated himself from them. When Peter ate with the Gentiles, his behavior suggested that the Mosaic proscriptions regarding eating were passé and that table fellowship between Jews and Gentiles was therefore now permissible. But when he withdrew from them, his behavior did an about-face, with just the opposite implications. Not surprisingly, then, Paul twice referred to the behavior as "hypocrisy."

In the second place, Paul indicated that Peter's behavior was incompatible with the truth of the gospel: "But when I saw that their conduct was not in step with [οὐκ ὀρθοποδοῦσιν] the truth of the gospel, I said to Cephas . . ." As I have indicated earlier (and will argue again in the pertinent passages in Galatians 3), for Paul, the Gentile mission was not merely an aspect of the church's *mission*; it was an aspect of its *message*.[60] Its message itself included the fulfillment of the third pledge made to Abraham:

---

if unchallenged, would ultimately have consequences for Christian doctrine. But is it necessary, historically or logically, to assume that the particular consequences are necessarily for the doctrine of justification, rather than for other doctrines? To provide a contemporary analogy, some Protestant communions (e.g., Presbyterians and Anglicans) baptize infants, whereas others (the various Baptistic communions) do not. But neither party, on either side of that issue, suggests that the baptism of infants has any consequences for their justification (I deliberately omit the Lutheran position for the sake of the illustration, since, for at least some Lutherans, there is an important relation between infant baptism and justification). It is merely a debate about whom the church should mark by which ordinance. I've never encountered either party to this particular debate raising the question of justification or accusing the other party of having a faulty view thereof. So, as regards marking ordinances (circumcision or baptism), one can hold to a view perceived to be erroneous without that error necessarily having anything to do with justification. For Paul, it was wrong per se to reestablish those Sinai ceremonies that distinguished Jew and Gentile; but it was entirely possible (in light of his reasoning in Galatians 3) that the more essential problem was that such activity would suggest that the seed of Abraham had not yet brought blessings to the Gentiles.

60. We could also say that the Gentile mission was not merely or primarily a *strategic* concern; it was a *biblical-theological* concern. If God is not blessing the Gentiles through the single "seed of Abraham" (3:16), then the pledge to do so has not yet been fulfilled. So for Paul, the Gentile mission proves that God has indeed fulfilled the third of the three pledges to Abraham. One might even say that the Gentile mission is therefore essential also to the mission to the Jews; it is simply part of what Paul understands the person and work of Christ to have accomplished. If God has not fulfilled this third part of the pledge to Father Abraham, then both Jews and Gentiles must await his doing so.

that one day, through Abraham's (single) "seed," God would bless all the nations. Note what he would later say at Galatians 3:8, "And the Scripture, foreseeing that God would justify the Gentiles by faith, *preached the gospel* beforehand [προευηγγελίσατο] to Abraham, saying, 'In you shall all the nations be blessed [ἐνευλογηθήσονται ἐν σοὶ πάντα τὰ ἔθνη].'" For Paul, the gospel *itself* was defined, in part, by the blessing of the nations by Abraham's seed. Any behavior suggesting that the Gentiles remain *outside* the arena of God's blessing denies the gospel itself, as it was earlier preached/pledged to Father Abraham. Peter's behavior of withdrawing from them—as though they were still unclean and/or "strangers to the covenants of promise" (Eph. 2:12)—denied that Christ, Abraham's single "seed" (Gal. 3:16), had brought them blessedness.

In the third place, Paul reasoned that Peter was worthy of open condemnation because his behavior was ill-motivated. By describing his behavior as cowardly (φοβούμενος τοὺς ἐκ περιτομῆς) and hypocritical (καὶ συνυπεκρίθησαν), Paul removed the behavior from the arena of acceptable Christian liberty or honest difference of opinion and placed it in the arena of shame.[61] On a matter so central to the "truth of the gospel," Peter should not have been concerned to please men and avoid/evade their disapproval; with Paul, he should have been willing to take his lumps, as it were.

The fourth reason Paul supplied for his opposing Peter publicly was that the behavior had dire consequences. Others were emboldened by Peter's cowardice; they, too, yielded to those confused members of the circumcision party who had not yet understood the gospel correctly: "And *the rest of the Jews* acted hypocritically along with him." This is a rather sweeping accusation and could either refer to other Jews who may have traveled with Peter or to those who had been present at Antioch earlier. Probably, Paul did not intend to employ οἱ λοιποὶ Ἰουδαῖοι absolutely as though it comprehended every single Jewish Christian at Antioch. Rhetorically, however, it does suggest that large numbers of the Jewish Christians joined Peter's confused and cowardly behavior. The extent of this widespread effect was so great that even Barnabas was caught up in the hypocrisy—the very Barnabas who had been with Paul and Titus for the second visit to Jerusalem (Gal. 2:1–3) and who should therefore have known (as Peter should have) that the Greek Titus was not required to be circumcised then.

If there were merely some individual xenophobic or parochial Jewish Christian somewhere reticent to have a ham sandwich with a Gentile, Paul would not have included this narrative in this autobiographical section. But his comments on Peter's motivation (φοβούμενος τοὺς ἐκ περιτομῆς) suggest that it was not xenophobia that was being corrected, but a misunderstanding of whether Sinai's distinction between Jew and Gentile was still pertinent to the definition of the new covenant community. Further, because Peter was a significant leader in the early church, his behavior also emboldened

---

61. One of the helpful insights in Francis Watson's interpretation of Paul is his awareness of the sociological dimensions. If, as he suggests, the early Christian church requires "an ideology legitimating its state of separation" (from the synagogue), then any such ideology delegitimates, by necessary inference, Peter's insistence on *not* separating from Judaism. Additionally, however, sociologists recognize that all cultures and subcultures perpetuate standards of shame and honor. The language Paul employs here is not merely the rational/academic language of "truth" or "error," but the sociological conveying of what is honorable or shameful; and he plainly employs language suggestive that Peter's behavior is shameful and dishonorable. Cf. Watson, *Paul, Judaism, and the Gentiles*, 52.

others to separate from the Gentiles. Paul apparently believed that the churches may have been nearing a tipping point, where so many Jewish believers would separate from Gentile believers that it would appear that nothing new had happened; that the centuries-old distinction between Jew and Gentile had not been eradicated, and that the Gentiles were still strangers to the promissory covenants. If so, then nothing less than the "truth of the gospel" was at stake. And, as the earlier parts of the narrative made clear, it was not merely the Pauline gospel that was at stake, but the Jerusalem gospel also (Gal. 2:1–10)—the gospel communicated to Paul by divine revelation (Gal. 1:16).

The dominant Protestant approach to Galatians has manifested a certain failure of imagination here. It has so identified "the gospel" with the doctrine of justification by faith that it has had difficulty imagining that "the truth of the gospel" could be at stake *unless* the doctrine of justification by faith were at stake.[62] Anticipating Paul's own later reasoning in Galatians, however, we note two things that will be argued at greater length then: First, the doctrine of justification by faith was not "new" for Paul. It may have been "good," but it was not "good *news*," since nearly every time he discussed the matter he referred to Abraham.[63] The first time Paul referred to Abraham in Galatians he said, "Abraham 'believed God, and it was counted to him as righteousness [Ἀβραὰμ ἐπίστευσεν τῷ θεῷ, καὶ ἐλογίσθη αὐτῷ εἰς δικαιοσύνην]'" (Gal. 3:6, citing Gen. 15:6). Second, the Abrahamic reality that *was* new for Paul was the fulfillment of God's pledge to bless the nations through his seed: "So that in Christ Jesus the blessing of Abraham might come to the Gentiles" (Gal. 3:14). The truth, therefore, of *this* good news that God was/is now blessing the nations through Abraham's single seed (whom Paul identified as Christ, Gal. 3:16) was certainly jeopardized by any behavior that suggested that the Sinai-erected barrier between Jew and Gentile still stood.

Rhetorically and strategically, Paul committed an enormous blunder in recalling the incident with Peter at Antioch in Galatians 2:11–14, *unless* his description of it was

---

62. For Paul, however, τὸ εὐαγγέλιον is so rich that there could be many threats to it, from a variety of directions. To the Corinthians, for example, he said, "Now I would remind you, brothers, of the *gospel* I preached to you [τὸ εὐαγγέλιον ὃ εὐηγγελισάμην ὑμῖν], which you received, in which you stand" (1 Cor. 15:1); he followed this with a traditional formula about the death and resurrection of Christ that said nothing expressly about justification by faith, *sola* or otherwise.

63. So Richard B. Hays: "Paul did not invent the doctrine of justification by faith. He could assume it as the common conviction of Jewish Christianity, as Gal. 2:15–16 unmistakably shows." Cf. "'Have We Found Abraham to Be Our Forefather According to the Flesh?' A Reconsideration of Rom. 4:1," *Novum Testamentum*, vol. 27 (January 1985), 85. Also, and rightly, James D. G. Dunn: "Justification by faith, it would appear, is not a distinctively Christian teaching. Paul's appeal here [Gal. 2:16] is not to Christians who happen also to be Jews, but to Jews whose Christian faith is but an extension of their Jewish faith." Cf. "The New Perspective on Paul," in *Jesus, Paul, and the Law: Studies in Mark and Galatians* (Louisville, KY: John Knox Press, 1990), 191. Some of Dunn's critics suggest that he overstresses the continuity between Judaism and Christianity on this point. So, e.g., Heikki Räisänen, objecting to Dunn's "The New Perspective" essay, said: "πίστις does not denote just any 'trust' in Gal. 2.16. It is faith in *Jesus Christ*, and *this* is something *novel* in Judaism." Cf. "Galatians 2.16 and Paul's Break with Judaism," *New Testament Studies* 31, vol. 4 (1985): 546 (emphasis original). Räisänen is correct. As we will see below in chapter 3, while Jewish faith, informed by the Jewish Scriptures, would rightly have believed that we are justified by faith and that all the nations would one day be blessed by Abraham's single "seed," they would *not* have known beforehand that this "seed" would incarnate as Jesus of Nazareth, the child of Mary.

widely known and believed in. To bring up the confrontation with Peter at Antioch—if Peter did not acknowledge the rebuke, and if Peter remained a recalcitrant member of an ongoing apostolic division on the matter—would have been disastrous to Paul's purposes. The Galatian troublers could simply reply by saying, "Okay, Paul, you go your way, and we'll go Peter's way. You eat with the Gentiles whenever you wish—we'll turn a blind eye to it—but we, along with Peter, Barnabas, and the rest (οἱ λοιποὶ Ἰουδαῖοι) will continue to observe the Mosaic distinctions between Jews and Gentiles." That is, in order for this pericope to have had its intended effect, Paul must have known that Peter was widely acknowledged to have been in the wrong (and almost certainly acknowledged it himself). If there were any substantial party that was consciously refuting Paul's initial statement that Peter stood condemned (ὅτι κατεγνωσμένος ἦν, Gal. 2:11), then Paul's rhetoric was extremely clumsy. If, on the other hand, Peter accepted the Pauline rebuke and admitted his error to those who publicly witnessed the confrontation, then Paul's rhetoric was well advised if not brilliant. It set the stage for the remainder of his reasoning with the Galatians this way (permit a paraphrase):

> If, as we all know, even Peter was not beyond rebuke and correction when he separated from Gentiles; if, as we all know, even Peter acknowledged his behavior to be erroneous and contrary to the truth of the gospel, do you Galatians think it improper or inappropriate if I correct you? If I will oppose and correct anyone—even a fellow apostle—who denies the blessedness that Abraham's seed has brought to the Gentiles, do you think for a minute that I will not oppose and correct you?

3.2.7. Paul's Encounter with Peter at Antioch: Part 2 (Gal. 2:15–21)

> We ourselves are Jews by birth and not Gentile sinners; yet we know that a person is not justified by works of the law but through faith in Jesus Christ, so we also have believed in Christ Jesus, in order to be justified by faith in Christ and not by works of the law, because by works of the law no one will be justified. But if, in our endeavor to be justified in Christ, we too were found to be sinners, is Christ then a servant of sin? Certainly not![64]

> For if I rebuild what I tore down, I prove myself to be a transgressor. For through the law I died to the law, so that I might live to God. I have been crucified with Christ. It is no longer I who live, but Christ who lives in me. And the life I now live in the flesh I live by faith in the Son of God, who loved me and gave himself for me. I do not nullify the grace of God, for if justification were through the law, then Christ died for no purpose.

3.2.8. The Relation of Galatians 2:11–14 to 2:15–21

As we observed earlier, it is entirely possible that verses 15–21 continue Paul's discourse with Peter in verse 14.[65] The early uncial manuscripts included no quotation marks or paragraph marks, and therefore gave no certain clues for where direct discourse ended. Those who believe that the direct discourse with Peter ended at verse 14 call attention

---

64. I begin a new paragraph before verse 18, because at this point the first-person plural becomes a first-person singular. While the pericope remains a unified pericope, it does divide itself into these two portions rhetorically.

65. So Dunn: "Paul is probably at this point still recalling (if not actually repeating) what it was he said to Peter at Antioch." Cf. "The New Perspective on Paul," 189.

to the shift in person—from second-person singular to first-person plural—as the primary reason for believing that Paul began a new section at verse 15. But Paul ordinarily addressed the Galatians in the second-person plural, so who constitutes the "we" of verses 15–17?[66] If Paul was continuing to address Peter, then the first-person plural would be a reference to the Jewish Christians, as it is elsewhere in the letter. Further, verses 18–21 shift person again; this time to the first-person singular, yet without this necessitating a new pericope. Fortunately, virtually all commentators have noticed a close relation between the reasoning of verses 15–21 and the reasoning that anticipated it (whether proximately, in 2:11–14, or more distantly, comprehending matters since 1:13). A. Andrew Das summarizes the matter well:

> Paul is certainly retelling the events at Jerusalem (2:1–10) and Antioch (2:11–14) with an eye toward the Galatian opponents. Verse 15's "we Jews by birth" harks back and includes the various "Jews" identified in 2:1–14—Peter, Barnabas, "the circumcision faction"/"men from James," Paul—as well as the Jewish Christian teachers in Galatia.[67]

For the sake of convenience, I treat it separately here, even though I regard its logical relation to the preceding verses as being very close.

3.2.9. Galatians 2:15–16—Who Are the "We"?

The opening words of this section identify the "we," at least rhetorically: "We who are Jews by birth [φύσει Ἰουδαῖοι] and not Gentile sinners." After the nature/nurture discussions of the twentieth century, φύσις has become awkward to translate.[68] Almost certainly, Paul did not mean that there was something in Jewish genes that would cause them, at birth, to know the things he mentioned following the participle εἰδότες in verse 16. Rather, he probably meant what was "natural" to a particular upbringing within a given cultural context, which D. J. Verseput aptly translates as "by heritage."[69] Paul was distinguishing what was commonly known by Jews in his day,[70] though Gentiles, bereft

---

66. Don Garlington rightly refers to it as "the emphatic ἡμεῖς at the beginning of 2:13. This is the first of several instances in which the first person plural is used to denote Jewish Christians of the Pauline sort, who had been nurtured in Judaism and taught the Torah. The impact of ἡμεῖς is thus: even we know that justification is not ἐξ ἔργων νόμου, but rather ἐκ (sic) πίστεως Ἰησοῦ Χριστοῦ." Cf. Garlington, "Role Reversal and Paul's Use of Scripture in Galatians 3.10–13," Journal for the Study of the New Testament, no. 65 (March 1, 1997): 88.

67. "Another Look at ἐὰν μὴ in Galatians 2:16," Journal of Biblical Literature 119, no. 3 (Autumn 2000): 536.

68. KJV "by nature"; RSV/ESV/NRSV "by birth."

69. D. J. Verseput, "Paul's Gentile Mission and the Jewish Christian Community: A Study of the Narrative in Galatians 1 and 2," New Testament Studies 39, no. 1 (January 1993): 53.

70. Martinus C. de Boer makes an intriguing suggestion that what follows the ὅτι clause in 2:16 is a pre-Pauline justification tradition that Paul cites. De Boer's five arguments for this are not entirely compelling. While, of course, what follows εἰδότες "may be a quotation," surely de Boer is not suggesting that every Pauline use of οἶδα introduces a quote. A better case could be made for γινώσκω introducing a quote, because it shares its root with ἀναγινώσκω. Similarly, while it is true that Paul "does not pause to explain or to define the meaning of the verb δικαιοῦσθαι," this may be due to the fact that when *Paul* preached there earlier *he* had explained justification, and this would also account for why it appeared here "without introduction or

of training in the Scriptures, would not ordinarily know the same things. We note also that it was Jews, in their distinction from Gentiles, with whom Paul identified in the first-person plural.[71] There is no reason to assume that the "we" meant Jewish Christians, though they may well have been. Paul's point is that they were Jews-not-Gentiles; he said nothing about whether they were Jewish/Christian-not-Gentile/Christian, and his use of the modifier φύσει suggests that he intended to assert that it was the Jewish heritage that shaped "our" beliefs.

What this heritage knew, according to Paul, was this: "that a person is not justified by works of the law."[72] Now, this clause in verse 16 is so contrary to what the dominant Protestant approach to Paul had always taught that the translations themselves have worked ingeniously to avoid/evade the matter. ESV/NRSV says "yet we know" as though it were surprising that someone who was φύσει Ἰουδαῖοι would believe such a thing. RSV says "yet who know," and New Jerusalem Bible managed to be both creative and archaic: "have nevertheless learnt." The Authorized Version, informed only by the majority text, managed to stay above the fray with a fairly literal translation: "Knowing that a man is not justified by the works of the law." And the New International Version, ordinarily prone to paraphrase, was quite restrained here: "We who are Jews by birth and not 'Gentile sinners' know that a man is not justified by observing the law."

Most of the resistance to a straightforward translation of the perfect participle rests upon the overburdened shoulders of the textually uncertain δὲ following the participle.[73] The translations that add "yet" or its equivalent, do so entirely on the ground of this textually debatable δὲ.[74] Even if the δὲ were original, however, it would

---

elaboration." Cf. Martinus C. de Boer, "Paul's use and interpretation of a justification tradition in Galatians 2.15–21," *Journal for the Study of the New Testament* 28, no. 2 (December 1, 2005): 189–216, esp. 195.

71. There is no dispute that in Ephesians 2:1–5 ὑμεῖς refers to Gentiles and ἡμεῖς refers to Jews; the parallel between ὑμᾶς ὄντας νεκροὺς τοῖς παραπτώμασιν in verse 1 and ὄντας ἡμᾶς νεκροὺς τοῖς παραπτώμασιν in verse 5 is unmistakable. I regard Paul as doing the same thing here in Galatians 2, and also throughout most of chapters 3 and 4, following T. L. Donaldson, Michael Bachmanm, et al. Cf. Donaldson, "The 'Curse of the Law' and the Inclusion of the Gentiles: Galatians 3:13–14," *New Testament Studies* 32 (1986): 95–99; and Bachmann, *Anti-Judaism in Galatians? Exegetical Studies on a Polemical Letter and on Paul's Theology*, trans. Robert L. Brawley (Grand Rapids: Eerdmans, 2008), 78–80.

72. For a discussion of ἔργα νόμου, see "Excursus 1: ἔργα νόμου" at the end of this chapter, where I give grounds for why the expression should be understood comprehensively, for whatever works the law required, rather than in the narrower sense that Dunn has often suggested, as referring exclusively (or even primarily) to the "marking" ordinances.

73. The textual evidence is split: the δὲ is included by ancient and diverse textual traditions such as ℵ, B, C, D*, F, and some Latin versions; yet it is omitted by P46, A, D2, Ψ, the Majority texts, and the Syriac versions.

74. The translations may also be motivated by the qualifying phrase "but through faith in Jesus Christ," since manifestly not every first-century Jew would have affirmed this. But there are two adequate explanations for this objection that do not require a translation that is so paraphrastic. First, it is entirely possible that the participle (εἰδότες) governs the initial clause itself (οὐ δικαιοῦται ἄνθρωπος ἐξ ἔργων νόμου) and not necessarily its qualifying phrase. Second, it is also possible that the first-person plural means "Jewish Christians" in this sense: "We (Christians) who are Jews by heritage know." The point would still be that φύσει Ἰουδαῖοι governs the participle, and it is their Jewishness that accounts for what they know. This is especially likely since verse 17 appears to cite Psalm 143:2.

not necessarily be adversative. Outside of our passage, there are seven places where Paul uses a post-positive δὲ following οἶδα:

οἴδαμεν δὲ ὅτι τὸ κρίμα τοῦ θεοῦ ἐστιν κατὰ ἀλήθειαν ἐπὶ τοὺς τὰ τοιαῦτα πράσσοντας. [We know that the judgment of God rightly falls on those who do such things.] (Rom. 2:2)

οἴδαμεν δὲ ὅτι ὅσα ὁ νόμος λέγει τοῖς ἐν τῷ νόμῳ λαλεῖ [Now we know that whatever the law says it speaks to those who are under the law], ἵνα πᾶν στόμα φραγῇ καὶ ὑπόδικος γένηται πᾶς ὁ κόσμος τῷ θεῷ. (Rom. 3:19)

οἴδαμεν δὲ ὅτι τοῖς ἀγαπῶσιν τὸν θεὸν πάντα συνεργεῖ εἰς ἀγαθόν [And we know that for those who love God all things work together for good], τοῖς κατὰ πρόθεσιν κλητοῖς οὖσιν. (Rom. 8:28)

οἶδα δὲ ὅτι ἐρχόμενος πρὸς ὑμᾶς ἐν πληρώματι εὐλογίας Χριστοῦ ἐλεύσομαι. [I know that when I come to you I will come in the fullness of the blessing of Christ.] (Rom. 15:29)

οἴδατε δὲ ὅτι δι᾽ ἀσθένειαν τῆς σαρκὸς εὐηγγελισάμην ὑμῖν τὸ πρότερον. [You know it was because of a bodily ailment that I preached the gospel to you at first.] (Gal. 4:13)

οἴδατε δὲ καὶ ὑμεῖς, Φιλιππήσιοι, ὅτι ἐν ἀρχῇ τοῦ εὐαγγελίου, ὅτε ἐξῆλθον ἀπὸ Μακεδονίας, οὐδεμία μοι ἐκκλησία ἐκοινώνησεν εἰς λόγον δόσεως καὶ λήμψεως εἰ μὴ ὑμεῖς μόνοι. [And you Philippians yourselves know that in the beginning of the gospel, when I left Macedonia, no church entered into partnership with me in giving and receiving, except you only.] (Phil. 4:15)

οἴδαμεν δὲ ὅτι καλὸς ὁ νόμος, ἐάν τις αὐτῷ νομίμως χρῆται [Now we know that the law is good, if one uses it lawfully], εἰδὼς τοῦτο, ὅτι δικαίῳ νόμος οὐ κεῖται, ἀνόμοις δὲ καὶ ἀνυποτάκτοις, ἀσεβέσι καὶ ἁμαρτωλοῖς, ἀνοσίοις καὶ βεβήλοις, πατρολῴαις καὶ μητρολῴαις, ἀνδροφόνοις. (1 Tim. 1:8)

In none of these is there the slightest suggestion of an adversative use of the δὲ. To the contrary, the verb in each case appears to be employed to describe something commonly known—shared knowledge between Paul and his audience.[75] Indeed, those

---

75. And so Longenecker believes it should be understood here at 2:16: "It is best translated as a coordinate verb with καὶ ('and we know'). Its use here suggests that what follows is commonly held knowledge. In fact, the appearance of ὅτι, which is probably a ὅτι-*recitativum*, signals that what follows could even be set in quotes as something widely affirmed." *Galatians*, 83 (parentheses original). So also Richard B. Hays: "Paul did not invent the doctrine of justification by faith. He could assume it as the common conviction of Jewish Christianity, as Gal. 2:15–16 unmistakably shows." Hays, " 'Have We Found Abraham to Be Our Forefather According to the Flesh?' A Reconsideration of Rom. 4:1," *Novum Testamentum*, vol. 27 (January 1985), 85. Frank J. Matera understands the rhetorical importance of the statement: "Paul begins by establishing common ground between himself and other Jewish Christians; even they acknowledge that a person is justified by God on the basis of faith in Christ rather than by the works of the law." Cf. Matera, "Galatians and the Development of Paul's Teaching on Justification," *Word & World* 20, no. 3 (June 1, 2000): 242. H. D. Betz refers to 2:15–16 as "the points of presumed agreement," in *Galatians*, 114. Ian W. Scott disagrees. Referring to the similarity between 5:4–5 and 2:15–16, Scott says, "We find the position of 2:16 being treated once again as a disputed point in need of defense . . . the idea of justification apart from νόμος was controversial in Galatia. . . . There is no indication that the Apostle intended the verse to express convictions he held in common

English translations that insist on adding "yet" (or its equivalent) at Galatians 2:16 do not translate *any* of the other seven passages with such an adversative. To the contrary, we find in ESV such translations as "*Now* we know . . ." (Rom. 3:19, RSV also; 1 Tim. 1:8), "*And* we know . . ." (Rom. 8:28), "*And* you Philippians yourselves know" (Phil. 4:15, RSV also), if they translate the δὲ at all. The RSV is similar: "*and* I know . . ." (Rom. 15:29). The only time in the Pauline letters these translations assert a "yet" (or its equivalent) as a translation for the post-positive δὲ following some form of οἶδα is here at Galatians 2:16 (where the δὲ is textually disputed). Elsewhere it has either a purely conjunctive force or no force at all, in compliance with its ordinary usage.[76]

Though the δὲ could introduce an adversative clause, this would be contrary to the ordinary use of οἶδα and contrary to the final clause of verse 16, which appears to quote Psalm 143:2 (LXX 142:2). Paul said, "By works of the law no one will be justified" (οὐ δικαιωθήσεται πᾶσα σάρξ); whereas the psalm said, "for no one living is righteous before you" (οὐ δικαιωθήσεται ἐνώπιόν σου πᾶς ζῶν). Whether Paul intended an allusion, a partial quotation, or was merely influenced by the teaching of the psalm, the point is the same: Anyone familiar with the heritage of the Scriptures knows that the Israelites fell under God's judgment again and again. Though Torah was given to Israel, they were not obedient to it, and their lot was consistently one of cursing, rather than blessing.[77]

More damaging than the textually questionable (and even then, not necessarily adversative) δὲ is the verb εἰδότες itself. The entire rhetorical weight of either οἶδα or γινώσκω in the first-person plural (and often in the second-person plural) is to assert a matter as beyond dispute. In the other twenty-two cases where Paul employs the perfect participle of οἶδα, it is correctly translated by the same translators as "knowing," referring to an agreed upon matter that Paul can mention as a means of advancing some other argument.[78] Thus if Paul were to assert as a commonplace (among those who were Jews by heritage) a belief that in fact was commonly disputed, his argument would lose all its force. It would be equivalent to saying today, "Now, as we all know, the earth is flat," which would lose its rhetorical force. Such rhetorical language, however, serves a useful purpose. One asserts a matter as commonly known on the assumption that even if there may be those who do not yet know it, they would not dispute it, at least not publicly. Thus we are led to conclude that Paul's initial affirmation here is simply incompatible with the dominant Protestant approach, which for many generations claimed that first-century Palestinian Judaism (Ἡμεῖς φύσει Ἰουδαῖοι) commonly

---

with his Galatian audience and their new teachers." Cf. Ian W. Scott, "Common Ground? The Role of Galatians 2.16 in Paul's Argument," *New Testament Studies* 53, no. 3 (2007): 431–33. Scott's reasoning does not take into account the differences in the pronouns in the two passages and what this implies for Paul's reasoning. Paul was addressing Peter in 2:16 yet addressing the Galatians in 5:4–5. The largely Gentile Galatians may *not* have known what Peter and Paul, as φύσει Ἰουδαῖοι, knew.

76. So Bauer, Arndt, Gingrich, *A Greek-English Lexicon of the New Testament and Other Early Christian Literature*, 2nd ed. (1979) : "Very freq. as a transitional particle pure and simple, without any contrast intended"; also "freq. it cannot be translated at all" (1974), p. 170, col. 2.

77. A point Paul developed more fully in Gal. 3:10–13, with its fivefold reference to cursing and reference to the curse sanctions of Deut. 21 and 27.

78. Rom. 5:3; 6:9; 13:11; 1 Cor. 15:58; 2 Cor. 1:7; 4:14; 5:6, 11; Gal. 4:8; Eph. 6:8–9; Phil. 1:16; Col. 3:24; 4:1; 1 Thess. 1:4; 4:5; 2 Thess. 1:8; 1 Tim. 1:9; 2 Tim. 2:23; 3:14; Titus; 3:11; Philem. 21.

taught that people were justified by observing the Mosaic law. Not only does such a view read "between the lines" of Galatians (presuming that some other problem, not expressed by Paul, was his "real" concern); it reads *against* the lines of Galatians, where Paul asserted the opposite—that those who were Jewish by heritage knew that a person was not justified by observing the works of the Mosaic law.

3.2.10. Galatians 2:15–17—Not Justified by Works of the Law

> We ourselves are Jews by birth and not Gentile sinners; yet we know that a person is not justified by works of the law but through faith in Jesus Christ, so we also have believed in Christ Jesus, in order to be justified by faith in Christ and not by works of the law, because by works of the law no one will be justified. But if, in our endeavor to be justified in Christ, we too were found to be sinners, is Christ then a servant of sin? Certainly not!

The δικ- language appears for the first time in Galatians at 2:16. Further, five of the thirteen Galatian[79] uses of this vocabulary appear in 2:15–21, and four of those within 16 and 17. This pericope therefore contains both the *initial* use of this important theological vocabulary and a fairly *concentrated* use (in Galatians, only comparable to 3:6–11).[80] Further, this pericope is instructive because the verb (δικαιόω) is employed four times and the noun (δικαιοσύνη) once, and the terms appear to be interchangeable in their basic lexical meaning. Three times here, Paul employed the *verb* to deny that we are justified by works of the law (οὐ δικαιοῦται ἄνθρωπος ἐξ ἔργων νόμου . . . ἵνα δικαιωθῶμεν ἐκ πίστεως Χριστοῦ καὶ οὐκ ἐξ ἔργων νόμου . . . ἐξ ἔργων νόμου οὐ δικαιωθήσεται πᾶσα σάρξ), and then he summarized the passage by framing a contrary-to-fact condition using the *noun* to deny the same thing (εἰ γὰρ διὰ νόμου δικαιοσύνη). At least in this passage, the verb and noun that formed from a common root appear to have substantially the same meaning.[81]

---

79. Also Gal. 3:6, 8, 11 (twice), 21, 24; 5:4–5 (twice).

80. A concentration, I might add, that diminishes some of the force of the argument that πίστεως Ἰησοῦ Χριστοῦ likely means something different from εἰς Χριστὸν Ἰησοῦν ἐπιστεύσαμεν, on the ostensible ground that otherwise the passage would be redundant. Redundancy for emphasis is a common part of both human language per se and of the apostle Paul in particular; e.g., "For I am not ashamed of the gospel, for it is the power of God for salvation to everyone who believes [παντὶ τῷ πιστεύοντι], to the Jew first and also to the Greek. For in it the righteousness of God is revealed from faith [ἐκ πίστεως] for faith [εἰς πίστιν], as it is written, 'The righteous shall live by faith [ἐκ πίστεως]'" (Rom. 1:16–17). In Gal. 2:17 alone, for instance, ἐξ ἔργων νόμου appears three times. Must this prepositional phrase mean a different thing each time, or is redundancy for emphasis simply a common linguistic reality?

81. This is a matter that is often confounded in English. As J. Louis Martyn justly complains, "Whereas in Greek the verb *dikaioo* and the noun *dikaiosyne* are linguistically cognate, most of the verbs and nouns by which these terms have been translated are not. To render the verb with the English expression 'to justify' while translating the noun as 'righteousness'—the most common way of proceeding—is to lose the linguistic connection that was both obvious and important to Paul." *Galatians* (New York: Doubleday, 1997), 249. I am not suggesting, as a general principle, that the verb and noun must *always* have the same meaning. Sam K. Williams argues that we must "maintain a careful distinction among *dikaioun, dikaiosyné,* and *dikaiosyné theou.*" Williams, "The 'Righteousness of God' in Romans," *Journal of Biblical Literature* 99, no. 2 (1980), 260. Perhaps in Romans that is the case; but in our particular passage, Paul denies that

Interestingly, then, and in entire accord with the polemical nature of the letter, the first time Paul addressed justification in the letter was by denial more than affirmation: οὐ δικαιοῦται ἄνθρωπος ἐξ ἔργων νόμου . . . ἵνα δικαιωθῶμεν ἐκ πίστεως Χριστοῦ καὶ οὐκ ἐξ ἔργων νόμου . . . ἐξ ἔργων νόμου οὐ δικαιωθήσεται πᾶσα σάρξ . . . εἰ γὰρ διὰ νόμου δικαιοσύνη. Paul appears to assume, rhetorically, that his audience understood the concept of justification as he did (Ἡμεῖς φύσει Ἰουδαῖοι . . . εἰδότες), so that his comments were largely reminders of what was already known. The Galatians would not have disputed Paul's fourfold denial that justification came through observing the law. What we observe here in chapter 2 is what we will observe again in chapter 3: That the doctrine of justification was not disputed at Galatia. To the contrary, this undisputed doctrine was employed by Paul to resolve what remained disputed: Whether the law's practices that distinguished Jews from Gentiles should still be observed.

We will have more occasion to discuss justification later, but this first appearance of the topic is significant in two ways. First, by employing εἰδότες, Paul referred to a common understanding with his fellow Jews at Galatia (and Antioch) that no one is justified by observing the law.[82] Second, in his first discussion of justification, he used the expression manifestly in a juridical manner.[83] Most commentators rightly recognize

---

neither "being justified" (δικαιωθῆναι) nor "righteousness" (δικαιοσύνη) comes from νόμου. In our passage, then, it is not necessary to maintain such a distinction.

82. Though, of course, this is not universally recognized. Ian W. Scott says, "The idea that justification cannot come ἐξ ἔργων νόμου is treated as highly controversial in the Galatian conflict" (431). Cf. his reasoning in Scott, "Common Ground? The Role of Galatians 2.16 in Paul's Argument," *New Testament Studies* 53, no. 3 (2007): 425–35. Similarly, Thomas R. Schreiner believes that Paul's negative statement implies that some *did* believe the negated statement: "When Paul writes that no one can be righteous by works of law, these words are presumably directed against some people who thought they could be righteous by doing what the law commanded." Schreiner, *The Law and Its Fulfillment: A Pauline Theology of Law* (Grand Rapids: Baker, 1993), 94. Schreiner's reasoning is plausible, but not (for me) compelling. A person can employ a negated statement for logical and rhetorical purposes, not merely to refute an actually existing error. Consider an analogous example from Rom. 2:28: "For no one is a Jew who is merely one outwardly, nor is circumcision outward and physical." Must we assume here that Paul was refuting a common teaching that being a Jew was merely an outward thing? Is it not just as likely that Paul knew that it was a well-established and noncontroverted OT teaching that anyone familiar with Deut. 10:16, 30:6, or Jer. 4:4 would have affirmed?

83. See "Excursus 2: δικαιοσύνη et cetera in Galatians" for a fuller discussion of the language that informed Paul's conception. I argue there that δικαιοσύνη is ordinarily an ethical term; that its antonyms and synonyms in all five pertinent bodies of literature (Hebrew OT, LXX, Pseudepigrapha, Apocrypha, and Qumran) are common ethical terms. I also argue there that, by extension, the terms and concept are often juridical, since the purpose of systems of justice is to promote orderly societies by condemning the wicked and exonerating the innocent. In the antecedent literature, I find no evidence of a so-called relational meaning of the δικ- vocabulary, and only rare occasions where it might reasonably construed as "saving power" (I found seventeen plausible such out of 1,829 uses, and an ethical or forensic construal is also plausible in those seventeen). Here I merely observe that in its first usage in Galatians, it is manifestly forensic, as Paul's citation of Ps. 143:2 (LXX 142) makes clear: "Enter not into judgment [εἰς κρίσιν] with your servant, for no one living is righteous before you." After examining these nearly two thousand passages, I became increasingly confident of the essentially ethical meaning of the δικ- vocabulary (extended to a forensic meaning in some contexts). Because justice systems in various cultures are to condemn the wicked and exonerate the righteous, the language is frequently juridical, but even such usages are small extensions from its ordinary

that the final clause of Galatians 2:16 (ἐξ ἔργων νόμου οὐ δικαιωθήσεται πᾶσα σάρξ) is an allusion to or quotation of the second clause of Psalm 143:2 (LXX 142:2): "Enter not into judgment with your servant, for no one living is righteous before you" (καὶ μὴ εἰσέλθῃς εἰς κρίσιν μετὰ τοῦ δούλου σου ὅτι οὐ δικαιωθήσεται ἐνώπιόν σου πᾶς ζῶν).[84] While Paul quotes only the second clause, that clause is causally connected (ὅτι, following the כִּי-clause in Hebrew) in the LXX to the previous: "Enter not into judgment [εἰς κρίσιν] with your servant." Why does the psalmist appeal to Yahweh not to enter into such judgment? "Because [ὅτι] no one living is righteous before you [οὐ δικαιωθήσεται ἐνώπιόν σου πᾶς ζῶν]." If Yahweh were to enter into judgment with the servant, or with any other living being, the servant would not be acquitted/justified.

In its original context, the speaker is likely a Hebrew monarch, and indeed, the psalm is identified as ψαλμὸς τῷ Δαυιδ ὅτε αὐτὸν ὁ υἱὸς καταδιώκει. Thus the language is not the language of some despairing, God-forsaken pagan or Gentile; it is the language of a monarch of the covenant people. Yet even he pleads with Yahweh not to enter into judgment with the royal servant, because "no one living is righteous before you." This is why Paul felt free to add the prepositional phrase ἐξ ἔργων νόμου to the citation. If even David feared Yahweh's entering into judgment because no one would be justified before him, surely observing the law was no means of avoiding/evading God's condemnation. οὐ . . . πᾶς ζῶν is comprehensive and includes both (law-observant) Jews and (law-ignorant) Gentiles. Neither those who had Torah nor those who did not have Torah could survive if God entered into judgment with them; and Paul asserted that those who were φύσει Ἰουδαῖοι knew this. As the letter progressed, Paul would say more about the implications of this doctrine that no one was justified by works of the law; but what he would later say built upon what he said in 2:16: That it was a nondisputed matter among Jews that no one was justified by observing the law.[85]

---

ethical usage. When Jesus told a parable about an "unjust judge" (ὁ κριτὴς τῆς ἀδικίας, Luke 18:6), the parable was striking precisely because a judge ought to have promoted righteousness and did not. My view is nearly opposite that of J. Louis Martyn, for instance, who said, "All of the translation options listed above have one weighty liability: they are at home either in the language of the law—where 'to justify' implies the existence of a definable legal norm—or in the language of religion and morality—where 'righteousness' implies a definable religious or moral norm. As we will see, Paul intends his term to be taken into neither of these linguistic realms." Martyn, *Galatians*, 250.

84. The translation "is righteous" (RSV, NRSV, ESV) is a little peculiar, since both the Hebrew and the LXX have the verb "is justified." KJV somewhat more accurately translates it as "in thy sight shall no living man be justified."

85. The alternative to law observance is believing in Christ. Even those, such as Richard B. Hays, who argue that πίστεως Ἰησοῦ Χριστοῦ here means "faithfulness of Jesus Christ," recognize that the verbal expression is also present, and that Paul here affirms "so we also have believed in Christ Jesus." The only issue at stake in the precise question of the nominal expression is whether that expression affirms that Christ was faithful. Indeed, part of the argument of Hays et al. is that the nominal expression probably does (or must) mean something different from the verbal expression or it would be redundant. Space does not permit a full engagement of the question here, but several brief comments are in order. First, redundancy is a perfectly ordinary part of language generally and also of Paul's language, as I indicated earlier in reference to Rom. 1:16: "For I am not ashamed of the gospel, for it is the power of God for salvation to everyone who believes [παντὶ τῷ πιστεύοντι], to the Jew first and also to the Greek. For in it the righteousness of God is revealed from faith [ἐκ πίστεως] for faith [εἰς πίστιν], as it is written, 'The righteous

Galatians 2:16 is not merely the first place where the δικ- vocabulary appears in
Galatians; it is also the first place where ὁ νόμος appears. It appears three times, all
negated: "*not* justified by works of the *law* . . . in order to be justified by faith in Christ
and *not* by works of the *law*, because by works of the *law no one* will be justified." As
Paul assumes that his readers understand what he means by ὁ νόμος, he does not supply a definition. Later, in 3:17, it is fairly clear that the term is used (by synecdoche)
to mean the Sinai covenant in its entirety: "The law, which came 430 years afterward,
does not annul a *covenant* previously ratified by God."[86] What happened, historically,
430 years after the Abrahamic covenant was the inauguration/institution of the Sinai
covenant. Also here at Galatians 2:16, that understanding, at a minimum, makes good
sense of the text. While Paul distinguishes "Jews" from "Gentiles" in verse 15, it is clear
that the distinction is not a moral distinction, because he designates both groups as
ἁμαρτωλοί—calling the Gentiles ἁμαρτωλοί in verse 15 and the Jews ἁμαρτωλοί in
verse 17. So what is it that distinguishes Jews and Gentiles? God made a covenant with
the one group at Sinai and expressly excluded the other group from that covenant.
But the various practices and stipulations ("works") required by that covenant did
not justify the Jewish people with whom the covenant was made. And, Paul says here,
Jews such as himself and Peter knew that this was the case, because Psalm 143:2 and

---

shall live by faith [ἐκ πίστεως].' " Second, Paul frequently employs the verb πιστεύω with Christ
as the object and ourselves as the subject thereof; and he also sometimes employs the noun
πίστις with prepositions that indicate that faith is "in" or "toward" Christ. Lexically, then, there
are no unambiguous examples of Paul using the πίστ-vocabulary in such a manner that Christ
is its subject; yet there are numerous unambiguous examples of his using the stock in a manner
that Christ or God is its object. Third, one could agree with Hays's notion of Christ as narrative
hero without concluding that Christ is presented as such in order that we would *emulate* him. He
could equally be plausibly presented as such in order that we would *believe* in him. I would think
that God, for instance, is the narrative hero of the Genesis creation account; but I also think that
Moses narrates this in order that we would *believe* in a divine creator, not to *be* one or emulate one.
Cf. Richard B. Hays, *The Faith of Jesus Christ: The Narrative Substructure of Galatians 3:1–4:11*
(Grand Rapids: Eerdmans, 2002). This matter will remain discussed for some time, but I have
not found any compelling reason to take the expression differently than did the ancient church
fathers (whose language was that of Paul's), none of whom took it or similar expressions to mean
anything other than human faith in Christ. Cf. Roy A. Harrisville III, "*Pistis Christou*: Witness
of the Fathers," *Novum Testamentum* 36, no. 3 (July 1, 1994): 233–41. Harrisville's reasoning is
quite compelling. How could it be that all of the apostolic fathers misunderstood Paul's Greek
(which was their own)? And how could it be that we, removed by two millennia and speaking
other languages natively, now understand correctly what none of them understood correctly?
Was Paul simply so linguistically incompetent that he miscommunicated his thought for two
millennia? Theologically, of course, there is nothing objectionable about the idea of Christ being
faithful, as long as we specify that to which he was faithful (his people, his redemptive mission,
or his father's commissioning?). I tend to agree with Stephen Westerholm here: "I have no
objection whatever to the πίστις Χριστοῦ formula other than that it is wrong." *Perspectives Old
and New on Paul: The "Lutheran" Paul and His Critics* (Grand Rapids: Eerdmans, 2004), 305n18.

86. So Douglas J. Moo: "Paul sometimes (perhaps often) . . . uses *nomos* with reference
to the Mosaic dispensation or covenant. . . . It is surprising that Paul only once (2 Cor. 3:14)
clearly uses *diatheke* of the Mosaic economy; *nomos*, it seems, is preferred instead. This implies
that it would not be falling into the error of J. Barr's 'illegitimate totality transfer' to suggest that
Paul uses *nomos* of the Mosaic economy precisely because he views the commanding aspect of
it as so prominent." " 'Law,' 'Works of the Law,' and Legalism in Paul," *Westminster Theological
Journal* 45 (1983): 82.

the entire history of the Jewish people (routinely condemned by the prophets) taught them that this was the case.

The pre-Sanders dominant Protestant approach to Paul and to Galatians denied what Paul affirmed in Galatians 2:16—that those who were φύσει Ἰουδαῖοι *knew* that a person was not justified by works of the law. Galatians 2:16 was grounded in Psalm 143:2, and that psalm was grounded in two large realities that accounted for it. First, Israel's atonement system would have been entirely unnecessary if justification before God could have been secured by observing the law. Built into the law itself was a recognition that it would likely be broken, and therefore provision was made for atonement when such breaches occurred. One-twelfth of the Israelites literally had a full-time job offering atonement for the sins of their own plus those of the other eleven tribes. For those whose religious life was centered on the tabernacle and (later) the temple, atonement was central to their religious consciousness, and atonement was needed only when the divine will had been broken.

A second reason those who in Paul's day were φύσει Ἰουδαῖοι would not have been surprised by his citation of Psalm 143 is this: They would have known their history. Oh, they may not have known its fine points, but they could not have forgotten that one nation had been divided into two, and they surely could not have forgotten the Babylonian exile. That is, theirs was a memory of Israelite-disobedience-and-divine-chastisement. The hapless prophets, whose duty was to present the divine lawsuit against the Israelites, often found themselves victims of impenitent Israel, as their Scriptures recorded:

> He said, "I have been very jealous for the LORD, the God of hosts. For the people of Israel have *forsaken your covenant*, thrown down your altars, and *killed your prophets* with the sword, and I, even I only, am left, and they seek my life, to take it away." (1 Kings 19:10)

> "Nevertheless, they were disobedient and rebelled against you and cast your law behind their back and *killed your prophets*, who had warned them in order to turn them back to you, and they committed great blasphemies." (Neh. 9:26)

Western Christians (and perhaps some Western Jews) may romanticize Israel's history now, because we are so conveniently far from it. But those closer to that history were well aware that the "land flowing with milk and honey" often flowed with the blood of the prophets. They were therefore well aware, with both the psalmist and with Paul, that Torah had not protected Israel from divine judgment; nor had it protected the hapless prophets who declared that divine judgment—no one was justified before God by observing the Torah.

The first-person plural continues in verse 17: "But if, in our endeavor to be justified in Christ, we too were found to be sinners [εὑρέθημεν καὶ αὐτοὶ ἁμαρτωλοί], is Christ then a servant of sin? Certainly not!" Note that ἁμαρτωλοί functions as an *inclusio* that relates 15 and 17. In verse 15, Paul had declared that "we Jews" (Ἡμεῖς φύσει Ἰουδαῖοι) were *not* "Gentile sinners" (οὐκ ἐξ ἐθνῶν ἁμαρτωλοί). In verse 17, he concedes that their pursuit of justification in Christ proves that such justification is needed and must be found outside of the self; that "we Jews" are *also* ἁμαρτωλοί—Gentiles no, sinners yes. Having just denied that "we" are "Gentile sinners," it may appear rhetorically odd to state that "we" are "sinners." But it is not odd at all in this letter. The same Paul who *distances* himself throughout from law-observing Jews *identifies* himself throughout with (non-law-observing) Gentile sinners who are blessed and justified in Christ. The law regards Jew and Gentile differently; sin, faith, and justification in Christ regard them as the same. The law distinguished Jew and Gentile ceremonially but justified neither (2:16); faith in Christ does not distinguish Jew and Gentile ceremonially but justifies both (2:17).

If Jews like Paul pursue justification by faith in Christ, they discover that they are not so different from the "Gentile sinners" after all. Believing in Christ for justification does not distinguish the good from the bad, the righteous from the sinners; it "discovers" (in the archaic sense of "discloses") all to be ἁμαρτωλοί in themselves. This recognition of universal human sin does not mean that Christ approves of sin or that he is its minister (διάκονος).

3.2.11 Galatians 2:18–21—Dead to the (Nonjustifying) Law/Alive to God

> For if I rebuild what I tore down, I prove myself to be a transgressor. For through the law I died to the law, so that I might live to God. I have been crucified with Christ. It is no longer I who live, but Christ who lives in me. And the life I now live in the flesh I live by faith in the Son of God, who loved me and gave himself for me. I do not nullify the grace of God, for if justification were through the law, then Christ died for no purpose.

There is a mild rhetorical shift at verse 18 because the language shifts from the first-person plural to the first-person singular. There are ten first-person singular verbs and six first-person pronouns. Despite this rhetorical shift, the reasoning is the same: the law does not justify. ὁ νόμος appears thrice and righteousness (δικαιοσύνη) once. I regard the shift as rhetorical rather than autobiographical.[87] Paul here works through the *logic* of Christian faith and its relation to the Mosaic law, not his own *experience* thereof. Paul has not, himself, "rebuilt" what he tore down; Peter has.[88] The point of the first-person singular rhetorically is that the same logic by which Peter is condemned would condemn Paul also (and any other Jewish Christian who had table fellowship with Gentiles) if Paul did what Peter had done. So, even though the language is first-person singular, it is rhetorical and probably corporate—analogous to that of the first-person singular in Romans 7, where "I" is Israel before, under, and after the law/Sinai covenant.

One of the more surprising, if not puzzling, aspects of this passage is Paul's statement that he died *to* the law *through* the law (ἐγὼ γὰρ διὰ νόμου νόμῳ ἀπέθανον, 2:19),

---

87. So Bruce, 142. Though Debbie Hunn argues plausibly for the alternative: that it is Paul himself. Cf. Debbie Hunn, "Christ versus the Law: Issues in Galatians 2:17–18," *Catholic Biblical Quarterly* 72, no. 3 (July 1, 2010): 537–55.

88. Many commentators have rightly recognized that ἃ κατέλυσα here refers to the demands of the Torah. Cf. D. Lührmann, *Der Brief an die Galater* (Zürich: Theologischer Verlag, 1978), 45; A. Oepke, *Der Brief des Paulus an die Galater* (Leipzig: Deichert, 1937), 61; H. Schlier, *Der Brief an die Galater* (Gottingen: Vandenhoeck & Ruprecht, 1962), 60; F. Mußner, *Der Galaterbrief* (Freiburg: Herder, 1974), 178; Dunn, *Galatians*, 142; Longenecker, *Galatians*, 90; Martyn: "That the edifice is the Law, seen as the wall that separates Jews from Gentiles," in *Galatians*, 256.

an expression that has cultivated a number of ingenious explanations.[89] While there is plausibility to a number of these, I suggest it is merely Paul's introduction of what is about to follow: Paul's doctrine that the law is a *temporary* covenant; a covenant to which the people of God would one day "die" is a doctrine he derives from his reading of the OT law itself. That is, within the Torah, within the five books of Moses, within the book of the covenant, we learn that the Mosaic covenant has covenantal anteced- ent and successor.[90] Through the five books of Moses themselves, we learn that the tutelage of Moses is temporary, even parenthetical. Especially from those five books, we learn that the antecedent Abrahamic covenant was characterized by a divine pledge to bless *all* the nations/Gentiles one day through a descendant of Abraham—a reality that could never take place as long as a Gentile-excluding covenant was in force. Paul did not die to the law because a better covenant or better master came along (though both are true), nor was his death to the law any more painful or unnatural than one's death to a marriage covenant after one's spouse has died (Rom. 7:1–4); he died to the law because the law taught him to do so. Just as we burn the mortgage note when we send the last payment after twenty or thirty years without violating that mortgage covenant in any way, so also Paul understood from the Torah itself that any Gentile- excluding covenant *had* to be temporary. In the remainder of chapter 3, with its seven OT citations (all but one from the Pentateuch), Paul substantiated this claim.

Paul's dying to the law is also rhetorical here: the "I" is not merely Paul; it is also Peter and all other Jewish Christians. His language in Romans 7, while not necessarily determinative, is surely *instructive*:

> Or do you not know, brothers—for I am speaking to those who know the law—that the law is binding on a person only as long as he lives? Thus a married woman is bound by law to her husband while he lives, but if her husband dies she is released from the law [κατήργηται ἀπὸ τοῦ νόμου] of marriage. Accordingly, she will be called an adulteress if she lives with another man while her husband is alive. But if her husband dies, she is free from that law [ἐλευθέρα ἐστὶν ἀπὸ τοῦ νόμου], and if she marries another man she is not an adulteress. Likewise, my brothers, you also have died to the law [ἐθανατώθητε τῷ νόμῳ] through the body of Christ, so that you may belong to another, to him who has been raised from the dead, in order that we may bear fruit for God.

---

89. I use "ingenious" advisedly here, because some of these explanations require a certain creative genius, some creativity in inventing something that simply is not said in the text. Some, but not all, of the dominant Protestant interpretations have done substantial "reading between the lines" (e.g., Burton), saying that Paul refers here to the law as "divine law as a legalistic system, a body of statutes legalistically interpreted." *Galatians* (London: T&T Clark, 2001), 132. F. F. Bruce: "It was Paul's zeal for the law that made him so ardent a persecutor of the church. . . . After his conversion, his persecuting activity was seen by him to have been unspeakably sinful. . . . In the revelation of Jesus Christ on the Damascus road the moral bankruptcy of the law was disclosed." *Galatians*, 143. As we will see, especially in 3:10–25, it is not any perversion/abuse/misunder- standing of the law that concerned Paul, but the law itself as a Gentile-excluding covenant. He cited no first-century rabbis in the chapter but rather cited the OT seven times. It was the law itself, as encountered in the OT writings—and no alleged abuse thereof—to which Paul died.

90. So Longenecker: "Paul simply says that it was the intention of the Mosaic law (διὰ νόμου) to bring us to a place of being no longer dependent on its jurisdiction." *Galatians*, 92. Even Lightfoot recognized the plausibility of this view—"The law bore on its face the marks of its transitory character" (*Galatians*, 118)—though he did not embrace it.

Note that there is nothing anguished in this statement, nor anything personal or individual; to the contrary, he says, "Likewise, my brothers, you also have died to the law." Paul views marriage (and its covenant) as an institution ordained by God, and he does not regard it as painful, anguished, frustrating, or something from which one seeks deliverance. He does regard the marriage covenant as obliging the parties only until the death of one or the other; after that, it is naturally discarded.

The reasoning here, in other words, is not substantially different from what we will see in 3:19ff. Paul's reasoning is *covenant*-historical, not *personal*-historical. It was not Paul's anguish over having persecuted the church out of zeal for the law that caused him to die to the law; it was not Paul's frustrated efforts at self-justification (Luther?) that caused him to die to the law. It was not even the fact that the law cursed Christ (3:13) that caused him to die to the law (though this explanation is closer). It was the law's own teaching about its temporary character that caused him to expect a day to arrive when its tutelage would end. If Torah teaches that God pledged to Abraham to bless all the nations/Gentiles through one of his descendants, then a later covenant (430 years later) that excludes Gentiles *must* be temporary.

Similarly, in this context, the first-person singular language regarding life in Christ is also rhetorical[91] and not autobiographical. The "I" throughout verses 18–21 is the "I" who might have rebuilt what he had torn down (the law), and therefore could only be a rhetorical/gnomic reflection about what is true for all who once lived to God under the tutelage of the Sinai covenant and who now live to God under the governance of the new covenant. Christ's crucifixion and death became their crucifixion and death; his dying to the law became their dying to the law; and his resurrection to new life with God became their resurrection to new life with God in Christ.

In English, Galatians 2:20 may suggest a similar reality to Galatians 1:4, where Paul referred to Christ as the one "who gave himself for our sins," and in 2:20, he refers to him as the one "who loved me and gave himself for me." But the verb here is noticeably different from the τοῦ δόντος ἑαυτὸν in 1:4; here it is παραδόντος ἑαυτὸν, employing the same verb ordinarily employed in the NT to refer to Judas, who was known as ὁ καὶ παραδοὺς αὐτόν (Matt. 10:4; 26:25; John 12:4; 18:2). Paul's use here may be influenced by an early tradition[92] represented at Romans 4:25—"who was delivered up for our trespasses [ὃς παρεδόθη διὰ τὰ παραπτώματα ἡμῶν] and raised for our justification" (cf. Rom. 8:32, where it is the not-sparing Father who "handed

---

91. Longenecker says, "Gnomic . . . referring to all who by an act of personal commitment have based their hopes on Christ" (*Galatians*, 91), and perhaps "gnomic" is better than "rhetorical." My only quibble with Longenecker is that his "referring to all" must be constrained to mean "all Jewish Christians," since Gentiles never *were* under the law and therefore never did die to it. But I concur heartily with Longenecker that Paul is not describing his own individual experience, agonized or otherwise, here. Had he intended/desired to do so, it would have appeared at Gal. 1:11–17, where he provided a brief narrative of his own individual life before Damascus.

92. Peter Stuhlmacher refers to Rom. 4:25 as "an old christological formula built on the basis of the Hebrew text of Is. 53.11," *Paul's Letter to the Romans*, trans. Scott J. Hafemann (Louisville, KY: John Knox/Westminster, 1994), 71. We would not wish to overlook the influence of the LXX in the formula, especially the repeated παρεδόθη in Isa. 53:12, which is identical to its form in Rom. 4:25; in Isa. 53:6, the form is παρέδωκεν. I concur with James D. G. Dunn that "the influence of Isa 53 LXX is hard to dispute." Dunn, *Romans 1–8*, vol. 38a, Word Biblical Commentary (Dallas: Word, 1988), 224.

over" Christ to his death). At a minimum, Galatians 2:19–20 affirms that somehow Christ's death became Paul's (and other believers') death to the law: "For through the law I died *to the law* [νόμῳ ἀπέθανον], so that I might live to God. I have been crucified with Christ [Χριστῷ συνεσταύρωμα]. . . . I live by faith in the Son of God, who loved me and gave himself for me [παραδόντος ἑαυτὸν]." In the reasoning of Galatians 2 (like the reasoning in Rom. 7:1–7), Paul asserts *more* than the union of believers with Christ's death and resurrection; in each case, the death is death *to the law* (Gal. 2:19, νόμῳ ἀπέθανον; Rom. 7:4, ὑμεῖς ἐθανατώθητε τῷ νόμῳ διὰ τοῦ σώματος τοῦ Χριστοῦ).

3.2.12. *Galatians 2:21—The Law Could Not Justify*

The condition contrary to fact in 2:21 is just that: a condition contrary to fact. "If justification were through the law [εἰ γὰρ διὰ νόμου δικαιοσύνη], then Christ died for no purpose [δωρεὰν ἀπέθανεν]." This expression is not as cryptic as it may appear. Paul has already asserted, as an uncontested matter that "we" know that no one is justified by observing the law (2:16). He has, therefore, already said that the law *did* not justify (as OT history made plain). Here he merely implies another degree of the same reality: that the law *could* not justify. There is a kind of *a fortiori* reasoning here: If there were some *less* costly manner of God providing justification other than the death of his Son, then surely such a less costly provision would have been made. If the Sinai covenant, which required only the death of bulls and goats, could possibly have justified us, Paul reasons, then a covenant that required the death of God's own Son would surely have been not needed. Such a costly provision implies that other provisions were insufficient. Later, he will say that if the law had the power to give life, then it would have had the power also to justify (εἰ γὰρ ἐδόθη νόμος ὁ δυνάμενος ζωοποιῆσαι, 3:21); but in that context, he denies that the law could make alive or justify. In his early efforts to persuade the Galatians to relinquish the law, he testifies not only to common knowledge of what it *did* not do (εἰδότες ὅτι οὐ δικαιοῦται ἄνθρωπος ἐξ ἔργων νόμου), but he testifies also to what it *could* not do (εἰ γὰρ διὰ νόμου δικαιοσύνη).

Paul's reasoning here (as elsewhere in Galatians) is all or nothing: Either we observe ὁ νόμος in its entirety or not at all. We either live to Torah in its entirety or we die to Torah in its entirety. If Paul (or Peter or anyone else) reestablishes those stipulations of the Sinai covenant, such as the prohibitions against table fellowship with Gentiles, they constitute themselves transgressors thereof. If Peter now regards the Kashrut laws as obligatory, then all of his previous violations of those laws count as transgressions.[93]

This all-or-nothing evaluation of ὁ νόμος is reflected in the stark, death-or-life language Paul employs in verses 19–21: ἀπέθανον . . . ζήσω . . . συνεσταύρωμαι . . . ζῶ . . . ζῇ . . . ζῶ . . . ζῶ . . . παραδόντος . . . Χριστὸς . . . ἀπέθανεν. For Paul, we either now live to/in Christ or to/in Torah—"I died to the law, so that I might live to God." The purpose clause (νόμῳ ἀπέθανον, ἵνα θεῷ ζήσω) implies that the law was a barrier to

---

93. And while Peter's eating with the Gentiles in 2:12 was possibly/probably regular meals and not the Lord's Supper, the celebration of the Supper would cause a problem with Kashrut any time that Gentile believers were present.

life with God.[94] This death to the law can be spoken of as union with the crucifixion of Christ: "I have been crucified with Christ." Paul is dead *to* Torah (νόμῳ ἀπέθανον), crucified *with* Christ (Χριστῷ συνεσταύρωμαι), and alive *to* God (θεῷ ζήσω). This is a profound claim, and one that he does not explicate entirely until later in the letter.

3.2.13. Galatians 2:15–21 as **Propositio?**

The technical question of whether these verses form a kind of *propositio* that introduces the remainder of the letter,[95] while fascinating, is inconsequential to my thesis. Surely, the passage reflects on the incident with Peter at Antioch, explaining why Paul's rebuke was so severe; and equally surely, the introduction of justification and observing the law here anticipate the arguments in chapters 3 and 4. In manuscript cultures, where one did not mark paragraphs with indentation or chapters by titles, any portion of a written document can, in theory, either conclude a previous section, introduce the next, or both. For my purposes, I am content to read these verses as both concluding the historical narrative that constitutes chapters 1 and 2 and as an introduction to the theological reasoning that constitutes chapters 3 and 4.

In their entirety, the historical narratives in chapters 1 and 2 establish two things about Paul and two things about the gospel he proclaimed: That Paul was commissioned no less (and in some senses more) than the other apostles and never vacillated in the clarity with which he proclaimed the gospel; and that this gospel itself was once commonly agreed upon by Paul and the other apostles and that it included the Gentiles, something the law did not and could not do.

---

94. A similar reality is indicated using the rhetorical first person in Rom. 7:9: "I once was alive apart from the law, but when the commandment came, sin came alive and I died."
95. The thesis argued by H. D. Betz, *Galatians*, 113–14.

CHAPTER 4

Promise, Law, Faith: Galatians 3

4.1. Galatians 3:1–5

O foolish Galatians! Who has bewitched you?[1] It was before your eyes that Jesus Christ was publicly portrayed as crucified. Let me ask you only this: Did you receive the Spirit by works of the law or by hearing with faith?[2] Are you so foolish? Having begun by the Spirit, are you now being perfected by the flesh?[3] Did you suffer so many things in vain[4]—if indeed it was in vain? Does he who supplies the Spirit to you and works miracles among you do so by works of the law, or by hearing with faith?

Paul shifts personal pronouns here at the beginning of Galatians 3. In the previous verses, he employed the first-person plural (2:15–17) and the first-person singular (2:18–21), but now he shifts to the second-person plural, distinguishing himself from

---

1. The use of ὑμᾶς here suggests a deliberate move from the first-person plural and first-person singular of the previous chapter. Many commentators rightly conclude that the first plural in Gal. 3 ordinarily means the same as it did in 2:15—Ἡμεῖς φύσει Ἰουδαῖοι—and that the second plural refers to the (predominantly Gentile) Galatian church. For bibliography, cf. T. L. Donaldson, "The 'Curse of the Law' and the Inclusion of the Gentiles: Galatians 3.13–14," *New Testament Studies* 32, no. 1 (January 1986): 94–112, and esp. 107n2–3. My interpretation throughout is that, absent contextual reason to do otherwise, the first plural refers to Jewish Christians and the second plural to Gentile Christians.

2. The expression (vv. 2, 5), ἐξ ἀκοῆς πίστεως contrasted with ἐξ ἔργων νόμου is very difficult. Translating in any sensible fashion to preserve the parallel seems near to impossible. Also, ἀκοή can mean "report," "message," and "obedience" in and of itself. There is help by the parallel in 2:16ff, where the ἐξ ἔργων νόμου is contrasted with διὰ πίστεως Ἰησοῦ Χριστοῦ. It is certainly the case throughout that the Torah and its requirements are contrasted with faith in Christ. *BAG* suggest translating, "as the result of preaching which demanded faith" (30).

3. ἐναρξάμενοι . . . ἐπιτελεῖσθε should not be understood in terms of the *ordo salutis*, as a reference to justification and sanctification. Paul expresses no such concern in the letter, but rather concern for their overall congregational experience: where they "began" with a clear understanding of the Gentile-embracing gospel and then later "continued" in a different direction. Garlington writes: "'Flesh', in this place, by way of contrast with 'Spirit', is not 'the sinful nature' or 'human effort' (as per NIV); it is, rather, the era of the flesh, that is, the old covenant/old creation." Don Garlington, "Role Reversal and Paul's Use of Scripture in Galatians 3.10–13," *Journal for the Study of the New Testament*, no. 65 (March 1, 1997): 93.

4. ἐπάθετε is preferably translated "experienced," not "suffered," as KJV and here ESV. Better is RSV, NRSV: "Did you experience" so much for nothing? There is no indication that the Galatians had suffered anything, and, more importantly, it appears to be a reference to the experience of the Spirit and miracles. In favor of the KJV/ESV, however, is that every other of the forty-one occurrences in the NT suggests "suffer." All thirty appearances in the Pseudepigrapha appear to mean "suffer." Similarly, the LXX uses appear always to mean "suffer," except at the apocryphal Baruch 6:34, "Whether one does evil to them or good [lit., "whether they suffer evil or good," οὔτε ἐὰν κακὸν πάθωσιν ὑπό τινος οὔτε ἐὰν ἀγαθόν], they will not be able to repay it." In earlier Greek, the term was apparently more neutral, as Liddell-Scott say, "to suffer or be affected by anything whether good or bad, opp. to acting of oneself." *Liddell and Scott's Greek-English Lexicon*, abridged (Oxford: Clarendon Press, 1974), 536.

the (predominately Gentile) Galatians and their behavior.[5] The "you/we" throughout Galatians 3 continues to distinguish the predominately Gentile Galatians from Jewish Christians, as at Ephesians 2.

Paul raises only one rhetorical concern (τοῦτο μόνον) with the Galatians, although he expresses this one reality in the form of several specific questions. The fact that the contrast of ἐξ ἀκοῆς πίστεως and ἐξ ἔργων νόμου[6] appears in verse 2 and again in 5 suggests that the other questions are variations of this basic one: If your initial embracing of the message of the crucified Christ was attended by the eschatological gift of the outpoured Spirit, and if this happened merely by your hearing with faith the apostolic report of the Crucified One and his resurrection—and not by your observing the law—then why would you *now* observe the law, which (covenant) governed pre-eschatological life?

We note the eschatological language here, though it is somewhat implicit. First, there are three references to the Galatian experience of the Holy Spirit: τὸ πνεῦμα ἐλάβετε . . . ἐναρξάμενοι πνεύματι . . . ὁ οὖν ἐπιχορηγῶν ὑμῖν τὸ πνεῦμα. Consistent with OT expectations, the apostles believed that the eschaton was a great re-creative work of God's Spirit (as Peter's Pentecost sermon surely affirmed), poured out by the agency of God's exalted Christ. In the contrast between the fallen condition and the eschatological condition in 1 Corinthians 15, the two Adams stand, representatively, for others, and Paul says: "Thus it is written, 'The first man Adam became a living being [ψυχὴν ζῶσαν]'; the last Adam became a life-giving spirit [πνεῦμα ζῳοποιοῦν]." As Herman Ridderbos says,

> There (in the OT) the Spirit appears repeatedly in the closest relationship with the acting of God in history. The Spirit represents the creating and re-creating power of God that governs the world and history and conducts them to their final goal. He is the Creator and Precursor of the great future, he equips the coming Messiah-Savior for his task, and he will pour out his gifts without measure on the eschatological people of God.[7]

---

5. My reasoning throughout is that, unless contextual considerations dictate otherwise, the first-person plural after 2:16 refers to Jewish Christians and the second-plural refers to Gentile Christians, for the reasons stated by T. L. Donaldson, in "'The 'Curse of the Law' and the Inclusion of the Gentiles," 94–112. For Paul, when he discusses the distinctive privileges of the Jews, he mentions "the giving of the law" (ἡ νομοθεσία, Rom. 9:4), among other things. He also distinguishes Jews and Gentiles in this manner, even while describing their common circumstance beneath God's judgment: "For God shows no partiality. For all who have sinned without the law [ἀνόμως] will also perish without the law [ἀνόμως], and all who have sinned under the law [ἐν νόμῳ] will be judged by the law" (διὰ νόμου, Rom. 2:11–12).

6. I discuss the proposals for understanding ἔργα νόμου in the brief excursus on that matter at the end of this chapter. There, I attempt to demonstrate that ἔργα νόμου refers neither to legalistic works nor merely to the identifying/marking works, but simply to whatever the Law requires to be done.

7. Herman Ridderbos, *Paul: An Outline of His Theology*, trans. J. R. DeWitt (Grand Rapids: Eerdmans, 1975), 67. Cf. also Geerhardus Vos, who proposed to investigate "to what extent Paul's doctrine of the Holy Spirit shows interdependence with his eschatology" (94), surveyed four specific ways in which this was the case, and concluded, "In the combination of these two ideas, that the Spirit belongs to the μέλλων αἰών, and that He determines the present life, we have the most impressive witness for the thoroughgoing supernaturalness of Paul's interpretation of Christianity" (125). "The Eschatological Aspect of the Pauline Conception of the Spirit," in *Redemptive History and Biblical Interpretation: The Shorter Writings of Geerhardus Vos*, ed. Richard B. Gaffin, Jr. (Phillipsburg, NJ: Presbyterian and Reformed, 1980), 94, 125.

The mention of miracles (ἐνεργῶν δυνάμεις ἐν ὑμῖν) is also eschatological. From the time of the prophets, miracles came to be—not only as an attestation to an individual's prophetic authority but also as an irruption of the heavenly into the earthly, of the eschatological into the present. When John the Baptist questioned from prison whether Jesus really was the eschatological "one to come," Jesus sent John's disciples back, telling them to report in Isaiah's language what they saw: "Go and tell John what you hear and see: the blind receive their sight and the lame walk, lepers are cleansed and the deaf hear, and the dead are raised up, and the poor have good news preached to them" (Matt. 11:4–5, citing Isa. 26:19; 29:18; 35:5–7; 42:18; 61:1).

Thus both by the threefold reference to the experience of the heavenly, eschatological Spirit and by the reference to those miracles associated with the Messianic era, Paul effectively reminded the Galatians that they had already experienced the realities of the age to come. Why would they now live as though that moment had not dawned? If they experienced the realities of the Messianic age without observing the law, what could they possibly gain by observing the law now? What becomes more explicit later in Galatians 3 is hinted at here: The Sinai covenant (ὁ νόμος) governed God's visible people on earth *before* the eschatological age. It was associated, temporally, with sin and the flesh, with the pre-eschatological order: "In the same way we also, when we were children, were enslaved to the elementary principles of the world. But when the fullness of time had come, God sent forth his Son, born of woman, born under the law, to redeem those who were under the law, so that we might receive adoption as sons" (Gal. 4:3–5).

Paul also hinted here at another difference, which he would make more explicit later (esp. at 3:12), that the Sinai covenant is characterized by law-giving and the *works* it requires, and that the new covenant is characterized by the dying-and-rising Christ and *faith* in him. Twice in this passage, a contrast is made between ἐξ ἀκοῆς πίστεως and ἐξ ἔργων νόμου, because Paul will later state more explicitly, "But the law is *not* of faith, rather 'The one who does them [ὁ ποιήσας αὐτὰ] shall live by them'" (3:12).

More will be said about ἔργα νόμου in the first excursus at the end of this book. But here we observe that the two references to ἔργα νόμου introduce much of the remainder of Paul's reasoning. I suggest that even here, ὁ νόμος refers to the Sinai covenant in its entirety. In Galatians 3:17, by referring to ὁ νόμος as that which came 430 years after the promise, it appears evident that he refers there to the inauguration of that covenant in its entirety. I suggest that it is helpful to understand such a usage of ὁ νόμος not only in 3:17 but throughout Galatians. For much of Israel's history, one could argue that tabernacle/temple was the center of their religious life; and indeed, scholars conventionally refer to "Pre-Temple Judaism," "First Temple Judaism," "Second Temple Judaism," and "Post-Temple Judaism" to communicate this. But after the Babylonian captivity, for a variety of reasons, the temple came to recede in comparative importance and Torah to grow in comparative importance. James A. Sanders rightly said that "Paul could use *nomos* to mean the Jewish religion."[8] In fact, Torah had become so central to Judaism during this period that Sanders could properly say that Torah is Judaism and Judaism Torah *sensu lato*.[9] It is the

---

8. James A. Sanders, "Torah and Paul," in *God's Christ and His People*, ed. Jacob Meeks and Wayne A. Jervell (Oslo: Universitetsforlaget, 1977), 137.

9. Ibid., 137. As Jacob Neusner says, "To be a Jew may similarly be reduced to a single, pervasive symbol of Judaism: Torah. To be a Jew meant to live the life of Torah, in one of the

recognition of the centrality of Torah for the Judaism of the New Testament period that provides a means of understanding Paul's comments accurately.

Here in Galatians 1–5, Paul effectively asks the predominately Gentile congregation at Galatia if they were Torah-observers when the blessings of the eschaton came upon them. Were they Jews? Were they participants in the covenant God made with the Jews at Sinai, a covenant that excluded Gentiles? Paul's reasoning (here and throughout Galatians) is this: Was the Sinai covenant and observance thereof (ἔργα νόμου) the means by which either Jews or Gentiles emerged from the pre-eschatological into the eschatological age? Was the Sinai covenant and observance thereof the means by which the blessings of the nations pledged to Abraham actually came to those nations/Gentiles? Did the Sinai covenant ever have any power to make alive (ὁ δυνάμενος ζῳοποιῆσαι, 3:21) in the eschatological sense? Did that Sinai covenant ever do anything other than govern the people of God in that pre-eschatological moment when Jew and Gentile had not yet become one? Was it ever intended to be anything other than a temporary measure?

Paul raises these questions, because he is confident there is only one answer to them. Surely, the many Gentiles at Galatia were not followers of Moses when Paul and others first preached about Christ to them. Surely, many were uncircumcised Gentiles at the time; they were not Torah-observant. Yet the blessings of the age to come came upon them just the same; the blessings of Abraham came upon them, despite the fact that they were not parties to the Sinai covenant.

4.2. Galatians 3:6–9

Just as[10] Abraham "believed God, and it was counted to him as righteousness"? Know then[11] that it is those of faith[12] who are the sons of Abraham. And the Scripture, foreseeing that God would justify the Gentiles by faith, preached the gospel beforehand to Abraham,

---

many ways in which the masters of Torah taught." *Judaism in the Beginnings of Christianity* (Philadelphia: Fortress, 1984), 13.

10. ESV takes καθώς here as comparative, relating the sentence back to the previous verse. UBS4 also takes verse 6 as belonging to the previous pericope, whereas NA27 takes verse 6 with what follows. KJV permits the beginning of a new sentence, while still retaining a comparative aspect: "Even as Abraham . . ." RSV/NRSV also begin a new sentence, but one that could either be comparative or an introduction to the Scripture quote: "Just as Abraham. . ." Each is entirely possible grammatically, but the καθώς could be employed as an introductory formula to the scriptural citation. Eighteen times, Paul introduces an OT citation with the formula καθὼς γέγραπται (Rom. 1:17; 2:24; 3:4, 10; 4:17; 8:36; 9:13, 33; 10:15; 11:8, 26; 15:3, 9, 21; 1 Cor. 1:31; 2:9; 2 Cor. 8:15; 9:9); καθὼς can also be employed with some form of λέγω to the same effect (1 Cor. 14:34; 2 Cor. 6:16; 9:3; Eph. 4:17). It is entirely possible, then, that καθὼς can be employed as a shorthand way of saying καθὼς γέγραπται. Nothing crucial to my thesis hinges on the resolution of this, but I think the logic of 9–6 is so thoroughly Abrahamic that it makes better sense to retain 6 with 9–7.

11. ESV takes γινώσκετε as an imperative ("Know then that . . . ," so KJV); RSV/NRSV take it almost as resultative, "so you see." I think the verb may be taken as an indicative and therefore rhetorical; Paul asserts that the Galatians *know* (or ought to know) that those who have faith are Abraham's descendants.

12. This is one of many "characteristic" uses of ἐκ in Galatians; οἱ ἐκ πίστεως means "those characterized by faith." *BAG* prefers to regard it as a matter of membership: "In these cases the idea of belonging often completely overshadows that of origin" (234). This is plausible, esp. when

saying, "In you shall all the nations be blessed." So then, those who are of faith are blessed along with Abraham, the man of faith.[13]

Abraham appears for the first time in Galatians here; and here also Paul begins his temporalizing/relativizing argument regarding the Sinai covenant, by establishing some of the realities of the covenant that antedated it. The structure of this pericope is in five parts: an A-B-B-A followed by a conclusive (ὥστε) clause. Each A-clause is a Scripture quote, and each B-clause is an interpretation thereof:

A[1]   Abraham "believed God, and it was counted to him as righteousness" (Gen. 15:6)

B[1]   Know then that it is those of faith who are sons of Abraham

B[2]   And the Scripture, foreseeing that God would justify the Gentiles by faith, preached the gospel beforehand to Abraham, saying

A[2]   "In you shall all the nations be blessed." (Gen. 12:3)

CONCLUSION: So then, those who are of faith are blessed along with Abraham, the man of faith.

Two extremely well-known Abrahamic texts bracket the ABBA section: Genesis 15:6 and Genesis 12:3. These texts, taken by themselves, appear to do different things. One indicates that justification by faith is an old Abrahamic doctrine (a point Paul makes also in Rom. 4); whereas the other expressly refers to the third (prior to Paul, unfulfilled) aspect of the tripartite pledge God made to Abraham, to bless the nations/Gentiles[14] through him. The other two parts, becoming numerous and inheriting the land, had been fulfilled many years before.

ἐκ is used with well-known groups or parties, as at 2:12, e.g.: φοβούμενος τοὺς ἐκ περιτομῆς, "fearing those of the circumcision party." The matter is discussed further in the text itself.

13. ESV is not alone in the compulsion to make a simple adjective do extra duty. The phrase σὺν τῷ πιστῷ Ἀβραάμ could/should simply be translated "with faithful Abraham" (KJV). But ESV says, "Abraham, the man of faith," which is similar to RSV saying "Abraham who had faith" and NRSV "Abraham who believed." Each of these rather expansive treatments of a simple adjective makes the text a tad more hagiographic than Paul intended. Paul's faith/works contrast in Gal. 3:6–14 is a covenantal contrast, not a personal contrast. Paul did not argue that Abraham, as an individual, had faith; whereas Moses, as an individual, did works. He referred to each as the one by whom God inaugurated two respective covenants. And the one *covenant* (not merely the individual with whom it was made) was characterized by faith; whereas the other *covenant* was characterized by the works it commanded. Abraham's faith was not necessarily exemplary; he was not a "man of faith," if we mean by that a man whose faith was especially unusual or exemplary. After all, had he believed God would keep his promise to him and Sarah, he would not have attempted to fulfill the promise by having relations with Hagar (Gen. 16:4), nor laughed out loud when God pledged to give him descendants (Gen. 17:17). And had he believed God would preserve him, Sarah, and their seed, he would not have twice prevaricated about it (Gen. 12; 20). Paul's point was that the covenant God made with Abraham did not depend in any substantive way on Abraham (or the chuckling Sarah, Gen. 18:20). It depended, for its fruition, merely upon the fidelity of Yahweh to fulfill his pledges. The covenant made at Sinai, as we see below, depended for its fruition, upon the obedience of the Israelites.

14. Paul employs τὰ ἔθνη to translate the LXX's αἱ φυλαὶ τῆς γῆς, perhaps conflating Gen. 12:3 with Gen. 17:4 ("You shall be father of a multitude of *nations*, πλήθους ἐθνῶν) or Gen. 26:4

But the two B parts of this passage unite the two, because Paul's comments on the two texts make both texts pertinent to the Gentiles who believe in Christ, and both texts are pertinent to the doctrine of justification.[15] Those who have faith (whether Jew or Gentile) are Abraham's children, the nations God pledged to bless through Abraham. Further, as B² makes clear, the *particular* "blessing" pledged to the nations through Abraham was the justification that would come through the Christian "gospel."

Whether the γινώσκετε is indicative mood and rhetorical or not, the citations of the two Genesis passages clearly *are* rhetorical. Paul effectively says that his gospel-including proclamation was not only a matter commonly agreed upon by other apostles (chapters 1 and 2), but that it was/is the fulfillment of what was pledged to Abraham. In chapter 1, Paul had effectively implied that his call was *different* from that of the other apostles, different in a way that made him analogous to those prophetic mediators who received similar calls: Moses, Samuel, Jeremiah, and Isaiah. Because of his unique vocation, he would have been authorized to introduce new revelation or instruction to the Christian assemblies. Nonetheless, he not only did not go beyond the earlier apostolic proclamation (rather, he received the right hand from the other apostles regarding his Gentile mission), but he professes here not to be going even beyond what was pledged to Abraham: the twin doctrines of Gentile inclusion and justification by faith are Abrahamic doctrines. Paul is no innovator. To be sure, Abraham did not specify beforehand *which* of his numerous descendants would be the one[16] by whom blessings would come to τὰ ἔθνη (just as the Dalai Lama does not tell us now who his successor will be). But from Abraham, we did learn that some seed of Abraham would one day bless the nations/Gentiles, and that they, like Father Abraham, would enjoy the specific blessing of being justified by faith.

There are implicit truths affirmed here in 3:6–9 that are not explicated until 3:10–14, especially the five contrasts between the Abrahamic covenant and the Sinai covenant. Paul, however, prepares for those contrasts by making statements that anyone familiar with the Genesis narrative ought to have known:

- Those who have faith are the sons of faithful Abraham;
- Those who have faith are justified as was Abraham;
- The pledges to Abraham comprehended the nations/Gentiles; and
- Abraham's covenant was replete with blessings and pledges of blessings.

One small linguistic matter Paul employs here deserves special notice, because of how it is employed later (and so badly mistranslated by so many translations). In verses 7 and 9, Paul employs the expression οἱ ἐκ πίστεως. He creates a substantive, using the definite article with the preposition ἐκ. Earlier, he had employed such a construction at

---

("And in your offspring all the *nations* of the earth shall be blessed," ἐνευλογηθήσονται ἐν τῷ σπέρματί σου πάντα τὰ ἔθνη τῆς γῆς).

15. And we note here, as we did in 2:15–21, that either the noun (δικαιοσύνην, v. 6) or the verb (δικαιοῖ, v. 8) can be employed to mean the same thing. At least here, the verb does not mean something substantially different from the noun formed from the same root.

16. In 3:16, Paul makes it quite clear that it is through a *single* descendant that such blessing would come.

2:12, when he described Peter's vacillating behavior as being attributable to his "fear-ing the circumcision party" (φοβούμενος τοὺς ἐκ περιτομῆς). Literally, the text says, "fearing those of circumcision," and it could be translated "those who are circumcised" or "those who are characterized by circumcision." Most prefer to retain some sense of the idea of origin in ἐκ and to translate it as "belonging to," or some similar expression, which is entirely plausible in cases such as these:

> Tebtunis Papyri, vol. 1.40 (BCE 117): αὐτὸς προθυμούμενος εἶναι ἐκ τῆς οἰκίας ["being myself eager to be a *member* of your house"].

> Paris Papyri, vol. 26.32 (BCE 163–162): ἄλλοι τῶν ἐκ Σαραπειου καὶ ἕτεροι τῶν ἐκ Ασκληπιειου ["others *belonging to* the Sarapeum and Asclepium"].

If so, an expression such as οἱ ἐκ νόμου (or, as Paul actually puts it in 3:10, Ὅσοι γὰρ ἐξ ἔργων νόμου εἰσίν) might mean something like "belonging to the works of the law." But I think its use in these substantive occurrences makes more sense if we understand ἐκ as merely "characterized by" or "identified by." Here are examples that I think make slightly better sense that way:

> τοὺς ἐκ περιτομῆς, "those characterized by circumcision." (Gal. 2:12)

> ἐξ ἐθνῶν ἁμαρτωλοί, "those characterized as Gentile sinners." (Gal. 2:15)

> οἱ ἐκ πίστεως, "those who are characterized by faith." (Gal. 3:7, 9)

> οὐ γὰρ πάντες οἱ ἐξ Ἰσραὴλ οὗτοι Ἰσραήλ, "for not all who are identified as Israel are in fact Israel." (Rom. 9:6)

> διεκρίνοντο πρὸς αὐτὸν οἱ ἐκ περιτομῆς, "those who were identified by circumcision criticized him." (Acts 11:2)

In our two places, then, οἱ ἐκ πίστεως could be translated "those who have faith" or "those who are characterized by faith," rather than "those who belong to faith," which makes less sense.[17] The reason this matter becomes important will appear at 3:10—Ὅσοι γὰρ ἐξ ἔργων νόμου εἰσίν. Many English translations translate the substantive use of ἐκ in verse 10 profoundly differently than they do in verses 7 and 9, suggesting that it is a false *reliance* upon observing the law or other abuse of the law that is intended. This is not only unwarranted (as we shall see), but profoundly misleading, because Paul intends to contrast the two covenant administrations *themselves*, not any alleged abuse thereof.

Further, whatever merit the "faith of Christ" view[18] has elsewhere (and I think it has none), it cannot work here where it is parallel to the Ὅσοι γὰρ ἐξ ἔργων νόμου in

---

17. Don Garlington uses the language of "belonging to," but I believe in substance he means what I mean: "Once more, in keeping with the way Paul tends to use ἐκ in Galatians, οἱ ἐκ πίστεως are the people who belong to the new community of faith identified with Jesus the crucified Messiah." Garlington, "Paul's 'Partisan ἐκ' and the Question of Justification in Galatians," *Journal of Biblical Literature* 127, no. 3 (September 1, 2008): 580.

18. E.g., G. Howard, *Paul: Crisis in Galatia: A Study in Early Christian Theology* (Cambridge: Cambridge University Press, 1979), 57; and Richard B. Hays, *The Faith of Jesus Christ: An Investiga-tion of the Narrative Substructure of Galatians 3:1–4:11* (Grand Rapids: Eerdmans, 2002), 296–97.

the next verse. The two substantive expressions employing ἐκ describe the members of two different covenant administrations and what is notable about them and their respective covenants. The οἱ ἐκ πίστεως denotes the same people in verse 7 and in verse 9, and verse 6 made it clear that it meant those who had faith as Abraham did: "Abraham 'believed God [Ἀβραὰμ ἐπίστευσεν τῷ θεῷ], and it was counted to him as righteousness.' Know then that it is those of faith [οἱ ἐκ πίστεως] who are the sons of Abraham."

4.3. Galatians 3:10–14

For all who rely on[19] works of the law are under a curse; for it is written, "Cursed be everyone who does not abide by all things written in the Book of the Law, and do them." Now it is evident that no one is justified before God by the law, for "The righteous shall live by faith." But the law is not of faith, rather "The one who does them shall live by them." Christ redeemed us from the curse of the law by becoming a curse for us—for it is written, "Cursed is everyone who is hanged on a tree"—so that in Christ Jesus the blessing of Abraham might come to the Gentiles, so that we might receive the promised Spirit through faith.[20]

4.3.1. Structure of the Passage

The passage appears to be structured by groupings of comments and Scripture citations, followed by a final comment. If so, the structure is this:

---

19. There is no justification for the addition of the English "rely on" here in the ESV (or RSV/NRSV). ESV professes to be "literal where possible," but the Authorized Version had little trouble translating the verse both literally and correctly: "For as many as are *of* the works of the law are under the curse." Moisés Silva's suggestion is similar and more elegant: "as many as are characterized by works of law." Cf. Silva, "Abraham, Faith, and Works: Paul's Use of Scripture in Galatians 3:6–14," *Westminster Theological Journal* 63, no. 2 (September 1, 2001): 259. Cf. also Joseph P. Braswell, "For as many as are characterized by Torah-works" (73), "'The Blessing of Abraham' Versus 'the Curse of the Law': Another Look at Gal 3:10–13," *Westminster Theological Journal* 53, no. 1 (March 1, 1991): 73–91.

20. ESV takes τὴν ἐπαγγελίαν τοῦ πνεύματος epexegetically ("the promised Spirit"), as argued by Meyer, Betz, Burton, et al., and by Sam K. Williams, "Promise in Galatians: A Reading of Paul's Reading of Scripture," *Journal of Biblical Literature* 107, no. 4 (December 1, 1988): 709–20. Williams not only takes the genitive τοῦ πνεύματος epexegetically, he argues that throughout Gal. 3, ἐπαγγελία refers to the Spirit. This appears to be an unnecessary reduction of the promise to Abraham, until Williams argues that what was essentially (and initially, in Gen. 15:5–6) pledged was that Abraham would have innumerable descendants: "The promise of numerous descendants is, for Paul, the promise of the Spirit. . . . On the one hand, it refers to the divine pledge to Abraham that he would have innumerable descendants. But since God keeps his word, fulfills his pledge, through the operation of the Spirit, the promise of many descendants is, at the same time, the promise of the Spirit." Williams, "Promise in Galatians," 714, 716. On this reading, Williams's understanding is much more plausible and consistent with Paul's concerns in Galatians. The Judaizing reduction of God's people to the circumcised necessarily limits the number of Abraham's children, reducing them to the mere number of the faithful within a single nation.

COMMENT A   Ὅσοι γὰρ ἐξ ἔργων νόμου εἰσίν, ὑπὸ κατάραν εἰσίν.
SCRIPTURE A   ἐπικατάρατος πᾶς ὃς οὐκ ἐμμένει πᾶσιν τοῖς γεγραμμένοις ἐν
              τῷ βιβλίῳ τοῦ νόμου τοῦ ποιῆσαι αὐτά. (Deut. 27:26)

COMMENT B   ἐν νόμῳ οὐδεὶς δικαιοῦται παρὰ τῷ θεῷ δῆλον.
SCRIPTURE B   ὁ δίκαιος ἐκ πίστεως ζήσεται. (Hab. 2:4)

COMMENT C   ὁ δὲ νόμος οὐκ ἔστιν ἐκ πίστεως.
SCRIPTURE C   ὁ ποιήσας αὐτὰ ζήσεται ἐν αὐτοῖς. (Lev. 18:5)

COMMENT D   Χριστὸς ἡμᾶς ἐξηγόρασεν ἐκ τῆς κατάρας τοῦ νόμου
              γενόμενος ὑπὲρ ἡμῶν κατάρα.
SCRIPTURE D   ἐπικατάρατος πᾶς ὁ κρεμάμενος ἐπὶ ξύλου. (Deut. 21:23)

CONCLUSION   ἵνα εἰς τὰ ἔθνη ἡ εὐλογία τοῦ Ἀβραὰμ γένηται ἐν Χριστῷ Ἰησοῦ,
              ἵνα τὴν ἐπαγγελίαν τοῦ πνεύματος λάβωμεν διὰ τῆς πίστεως.

Rhetorically, the point of these scriptural comments is to buttress what Paul had earlier claimed: that he died to the law *through* the law (2:19). But the point of that statement and these combined statements is *to bring the law onto Paul's side* in the debate, a matter he expresses somewhat tartly in 4:21: "Tell me, you who desire to be under the law, do you not listen to the law?" Throughout the remainder of Galatians 3, Paul *relativizes* the law by *temporalizing* it. He positions it, historically, squarely between the Abrahamic covenant and the new covenant; between its antecedent and its successor. Unlike Marcion, however, Paul accomplishes this relativizing of the law precisely by appealing *to* the Pentateuch, *to* the books of Moses. It is the law itself (understood as Paul understands it) that teaches its own transitory/temporary jurisdiction over God's visible people; and to this law Paul turns in Galatians 3:10–14 by appealing to Deuteronomy 27:26, Habakkuk 2:4, Leviticus 18:5, and Deuteronomy 21:23. As he pries each clutching Galatian finger from the Mosaic law, he employs a Mosaic lever to do so.

In the process of doing this, Paul also temporalizes the Sinai covenant by contrasting it, in five specific ways, from the Abrahamic covenant that antedated it.[21] If we compare Galatians 3:6–9 to Galatians 3:10–14, we note these five differences between the covenant administrations, differences disclosed in the law itself, as the citations from the Old Testament Scriptures attest.

Abrahamic Covenant	**Sinai Covenant**
"those who are characterized by faith"	"those who are characterized by works of the law"
includes the nations	excludes the nations
blesses	curses
justifies	justifies no one
promise	law

---

21. Cf. also my "Abraham and Sinai Contrasted in Galatians 3:6–14," in *The Law Is Not of Faith: Essays on Works and Grace in the Mosaic Covenant*, ed. Bryan D. Estelle, J. V. Fesko, and David VanDrunen (Phillipsburg, NJ: P&R, 2009), 240–58.

We will examine each of these in turn as we look at each of the subsections in the order that Paul presents them. For now, it is enough to observe that, in Paul's reasoning, the law/Sinai covenant was so different from the Abrahamic covenant that its very existence temporarily disrupted the pledges of the Abrahamic covenant. The Sinai covenant, for Paul, either *permanently* ended the Abrahamic covenant or *temporarily* delayed its fulfillment; but it was not and could not be compatible with it.

4.3.1.1. First Comment/Scripture

> For as many as are of the works of the law are under the curse: for it is written, "Cursed is every one that continueth not in all things which are written in the book of the law to do them." (KJV)[22]

Twice in the previous pericope, Paul had spoken of the *blessing* to the nations that was pledged to Abraham and enjoyed by those who shared his faith. In this passage, the first thing Paul says about those who observe the Sinai covenant is that they are under a *curse*.[23] And, almost as though Paul anticipated the later dominant Protestant (mis) interpretations of his letters, he did his level best to say that he was not talking about any curse generated by his own generation (i.e., alleged meritorious/legalistic abuse of the law), nor was he talking about any teaching or teachers in his own generation.[24] The curse referred to by Paul is the curse sanction of the Sinai covenant itself, as the citation of Deuteronomy 27:26 demonstrates.[25] Paul did not make statements such as this:

---

22. I employ the KJV to evade/avoid the ESV. There is no justification for the addition of the English "rely on" here in the ESV (or RSV/NRSV). Each of the translations that gratuitously adds "rely on" here does not translate the parallel in the previous verses (οἱ ἐκ πίστεως in 7 and 9), "those who *rely on* faith." The translation "*rely on* works of the law" is therefore both gratuitous and inconsistent. If ἐκ needed "rely on" to make a sensible translation, then it would have needed it in both substantives, in both verse 9 and verse 10. Further, if Paul had wanted to say something like "rely on," he would have used the language he chose to use in Rom. 2:17, where he *does* say "rely/rest on the law" by saying ἐπαναπαύῃ νόμῳ. We rarely find such breathtaking theological prejudices in the translations, so I suppose we should savor this one here. "Rely on" does not come from Paul or from his Greek; it is simply an intrusion of the pre-Sanders prejudice into the translations. And here, especially, it disrupts the parallel expression οἱ ἐκ πίστεως in verses 7 and 9. Much better is Garlington's insistence: "What is glaringly obvious is that Paul will not let go of ἐκ as he continues to contrast οἱ ἐκ πίστεως with Ὅσοι γὰρ ἐξ ἔργων νόμου." Garlington, "Paul's 'Partisan ἐκ' and the Question of Justification in Galatians," 382.

23. Indeed, "curse" language appears five times in this pericope.

24. Contra, e.g., Timothy G. Gombis, who says, "The group designated by ὅσοι γὰρ ἐξ ἔργων νόμου εἰσίν is those who hold to the doctrine of the Judaizers—the teaching that one must believe in Christ Jesus for salvation *and* submit to the Mosaic Law." Gombis, "The 'Transgressor' and the 'Curse of the Law': The Logic of Paul's Argument in Galatians 2–3," *New Testament Studies* 53, no. 1 (2007): 90.

25. Martin Noth, "For All Who Rely on Works of the Law Are under a Curse," *The Laws in the Pentateuch and Other Studies* (Edinburgh: Oliver & Boyd, 1966), 118–31. Noth raised the question of whether Paul "has not wrongly appealed to the passages he quotes from Deuteronomy in support of his judgment on the law in general" and suggested that Paul "has broadly generalized what was a statement of specific, limited, application" (119). Noth also expressed concern that Paul referred only to the curse, when Deuteronomy held forth blessing also. Noth's concerns, and those of others like him, are due to his assuming that Paul is speaking compre-

As many as misinterpret the law individually versus corporately or meritoriously versus graciously are under a curse.

As many as (individually or corporately) attempt to keep the law and fail to do so are under a curse.

Rather, he said, "As many as are of the works of the law are under a curse," because his point was to contrast the Abrahamic/promissory covenant with the Sinai/conditional covenant. This is why the contrast is not perfect. He did not contrast the "shall be blessed" (ἐνευλογηθήσονται, 3:8) and "are blessed" (εὐλογοῦνται, 3:9) of the Abrahamic covenant with "are cursed" with the Sinai covenant;[26] rather, he said that those who are of the law "are *under* a curse" (ὑπὸ κατάραν, 3:10), because the point is not that the Sinai covenant curses per se. Rather, the Sinai covenant places its recipients[27] under a *conditional* curse, a *threatened* curse.[28] Abraham's covenant threatened with no curses

---

hensively here of the Sinai covenant. I assume otherwise: that Paul is here speaking of what was *distinctive* to the Sinai covenant *in comparison to* the Abrahamic. That it shared "blessings" with the Abrahamic covenant is not as important, for Paul's purpose, as it also, distinctively from the Abrahamic, introduced cursing.

26. What Moisés Silva calls "the very paradox that troubles scholars in this verse (those who do the works of the law are cursed because Deuteronomy says that those who do not do the works of the law are cursed!)" is self-created by those who do not distinguish "are cursed" from "are *under* a curse." To be sure, being "under a curse" is no bargain (just ask Damocles about Dionysius's sword); but to be cursed is still conceptually a different thing than to be *under* a curse. Cf. Silva, "Abraham, Faith, and Works," 263. Joseph P. Bradwell rightly argues that " 'under a curse' is parallel to the later expressions 'under law' and 'under tutors and governors.' . . . All of these expressions describe spheres . . . to which people therein enclosed are made subject and under whose sway, reign, and jurisdiction they live. The ἔργα νόμου are not said to be *accursed*; they are merely under a curse (threat) as those living within the sphere in which the curse principle is operative." Bradwell, " 'The Blessing of Abraham' Versus 'the Curse of the Law': Another Look at Gal 3:10–13," *Westminster Theological Journal* 53, no. 1 (March 1, 1991): 76. The early Protestant confessional literature therefore rightly employed the term "threatenings" to indicate that the curse sanction threatened only if the Israelites disobeyed; they were not "cursed" by being part of that covenant, but they were "threatened" by a curse: "Although true believers be not under the law, as a covenant of works, to be thereby justified, or condemned; yet is it of great use to them . . . and the *threatenings* of it serve to show what even their sins deserve" (WCF 19:6, cf. also 14:2; emphases mine).

27. Readers will now rightly expect me to argue that the Sinai covenant placed under a threatened curse only those who were its recipients. The hapless Gentiles were "strangers" to the covenants and therefore "strangers" to its threatened curse sanctions. I concur entirely with Joseph P. Bradwell, who comments about this verse: "The sphere of the law's dominion and authority therefore extends only to the Jews and it is only those who are under the law who could be under a curse pronounced by that law. . . . The reference is not to legalists, Judaizers, or all of unredeemed humankind, but to Jews in their special identity and distinctiveness provided by a *torah* lifestyle" (75, 77). Bradwell, " 'The Blessing of Abraham' Versus 'the Curse of the Law,' " 73–91.

28. So Normand Bonneau: "Paul does not say that those of works of the law are cursed, but that they are under a curse. Only the failure to observe the law will incur the curse, not the fact of being ἐξ ἔργων νόμου." Bonneau, "The Logic of Paul's Argument on the Curse of the Law in Galatians 3:10–14," *Novum Testamentum* 39, no. 1 (January 1, 1997): 73. This probably accounts for the Ὅσοι γὰρ ἐξ ἔργων νόμου, rather than the simpler form of the substantive in the previous verse, οἱ ἐκ πίστεως. The Ὅσοι extends the threat of Sinai's curse sanction indefinitely, even to

at all; Moses' threatened with many; in the "dodecalogue," there are twelve curse sanc-tions the Israelites said "Amen" to in Deuteronomy 27; the final one is what Paul cited here.[29] Israel may have had a "decalogue" with ten covenantal words, but they also had a "dodecalogue" with twelve covenantal curses. Most contemporary English transla-tions obscure the parallel with the previous verse. The KJV was closer to preserving the parallel: "They which be *of faith* [οἱ ἐκ πίστεως] are *blessed* with faithful Abraham. For as many as are *of the works of the law* [Ὅσοι γὰρ ἐξ ἔργων νόμου] are *under the curse.*" Those who are "of faith" are blessed with faithful Abraham; those who are "of the works of the law" live under threats of curse.

In Deuteronomy 27, Moses prepared the Israelites for the next phase of their post-wandering history, when they would cross the Jordan into the land promised to their fathers. In preparation for this, a solemn ceremony occurred in which the Levitical priests were divided into two sections of six each, to warn the Israelites that either blessing or cursing awaited them across the Jordan:

> That day Moses charged the people, saying, "When you have crossed over the Jordan, these shall stand on Mount Gerizim to bless the people: Simeon, Levi, Judah, Issachar, Joseph, and Benjamin. And these shall stand on Mount Ebal for the curse: Reuben, Gad, Asher, Zebulun, Dan, and Naphtali." (Deut. 27:11–13)

We note the perfect parity: two mounts with six tribes of Israelites on each. What fol-lows is equally solemn: twelve specific warnings regarding twelve specific behaviors are made by the twelve branches of Israelites, and in each case the twelve tribes of Israel must acknowledge their willingness to submit to this conditional curse. In each of the twelve, the pattern is identical to the first:

> "Cursed be the man who makes a carved or cast metal image, an abomination to the LORD, a thing made by the hands of a craftsman, and sets it up in secret." And all the people shall answer and say, "Amen." (Deut. 27:15)

The next chapter of Deuteronomy continues this solemn warning, and again the Levitical priests hold out to the Israelites the stipulations of the covenant, pledging blessings to their obedience and cursings to their disobedience, again in almost perfect parity.

Gentiles who might be unwary enough to submit themselves to it. As Norman H. Young has said, "Paul's use of Ὅσοι in Galatians and elsewhere would indicate that Paul is not restricting those ἐξ ἔργων νόμου to the Jews." Young, "Who's Cursed—and Why? (Galatians 3:10–14)," *Journal of Biblical Literature* 117, no. 1 (March 1, 1998): 81.

29. The solemn "And all the people shall say 'Amen,'" repeated twelve times in the dodeca-logue of Deuteronomy 27, is foreboding enough in its own right, especially as we look back on the history of what happened afterward. The liturgical practice of repeating these words now in Christian worship—worship in which the Deuteronomic curse has been borne by Christ—especially at such trivial liturgical places as after so-called special musicstrikes me as being as ill-considered a liturgical practice as could possibly be. Even Israel probably wished within a week that they could renege on this solemn oath of self-malediction; and one might think that no other people would ever desire to take the same upon themselves or to trivialize its solemnity by making it the liturgical equivalent of applause.

And if you faithfully obey the voice of the LORD your God, being careful to do all his commandments that I command you today, . . . all these blessings shall come upon you and overtake you, if you obey the voice of the LORD your God.

But if you will not obey the voice of the LORD your God or be careful to do all his commandments and his statutes that I command you today, then all these curses shall come upon you and overtake you.

Blessed shall you be in the city, and blessed shall you be in the field. Blessed shall be the fruit of your womb and the fruit of your ground and the fruit of your cattle, the increase of your herds and the young of your flock. Blessed shall be your basket and your kneading bowl. Blessed shall you be when you come in, and blessed shall you be when you go out. (Deut. 28:1–5)

Cursed shall you be in the city, and cursed shall you be in the field. Cursed shall be your basket and your kneading bowl. Cursed shall be the fruit of your womb and the fruit of your ground, the increase of your herds and the young of your flock. Cursed shall you be when you come in, and cursed shall you be when you go out. (Deut. 28:15–19)

In each of these cases, the matter continues, listing numerous plagues and disasters, and especially the description of Israel's relation to the other nations *from* whom God will deliver them if they obey and *by* whom God will curse them if they disobey. This is an enormous contrast to the Abrahamic covenant, wherein the only time the language of cursing appears it is not a threat to Abraham at all but a pledge: "I will bless those who bless you, and him who dishonors you I will curse, and in you all the families of the earth shall be blessed" (Gen. 12:3).

We observe, then, that in Deuteronomy itself—not in some later generation—a significant aspect of the Sinai covenant is the threatened curse sanctions. Indeed, if we think of Deuteronomy 5 as containing "ten commandments,"[30] then we observe that Deuteronomy 27 has twelve curses. Even a Greek professor (not noted for arithmetical abilities) can tell in Deuteronomy's solemn assemblies that there are more *curses* than *commandments*. The later Western tradition may have isolated the covenant stipulations from their covenantal context (and from the covenant sanctions); but Paul's generation does not appear to have done so yet, and surely Moses' generation did not do so.[31]

This is why the various English translations are so profoundly misleading when they translate the first clause of 3:10 as "those who rely on works of the law are under a curse." The problem is not merely that it is a pure conjecture invented out of whole

---

30. Though it is not pertinent to my thesis, I am entirely at odds with referring to the "ten words" at Sinai as "ten commandments." In addition to being an erroneous translation of דברים that confuses it with מצות, denoting the ten words as "ten commandments" has the effect of overlooking the importance of the covenant preamble and prologue (the first word) and the occasional curse sanctions embedded therein ("visiting the iniquity of the fathers on the children to the third and fourth generation . . . for the LORD will not hold him guiltless who takes his name in vain").

31. Martin Noth suggested that the origin for this significant cursing section in ANE treaties was Hammurabi's Code, saying, "That a law should end with blessing and curse had its pattern in the Code of Hammurabi." Cf. Noth, "For All Who Rely on Works of the Law Are under a Curse," 122.

cloth (where else among the other 913 uses in the NT does ἐκ mean "rely on"?), nor is the problem merely that it obscures the parallel between the two ἐκ clauses (οἱ ἐκ πίστεως of verses 7 and 9 and Ὅσοι γὰρ ἐξ ἔργων νόμου of verse 10). The problem is graver: The translation suggests that some attitude or idea about the works of the law brings a curse, when Paul's point is that the covenant administration in Deuteronomy 27 itself threatens twelve curses in its very inception—long before anyone can, does, or did frame any attitude or idea about it at all. It is not one's posture, attitude, or idea about the law that places anyone "under a curse": it is the Sinai covenant administration itself, as mediated to the Israelites through the hand of Moses and the Levites, that places Israel under a threat of curse. The *dodekas* of Deuteronomy 27 deserve far more attention than they have ordinarily been given (and are two in number more than the "ten words" that have received so much attention): Twelve tribes, twelve sets of Levites, twelve threatened curses, and twelve solemn maledictory oaths. Deuteronomy has only ten so-called (and mistranslated) commandments, but it has twelve solemn curses. For Moses (and Paul), the "curses" are literally more numerous than the "words" and equally important for assessing the covenant rightly. Nor did the next generation forget the significance of the curse sanction to the covenant itself. Joshua reminded the Israelites of this significance: "And afterward he read all the words of the law, the blessing and the curse [הברכה והקללה] according to all that is written in the Book of the Law" (Josh. 8:34). There is no "and" between "the words of the law" and "the blessing and the curse." Since all of the Mosaic law was attended by threatened curse sanctions, Joshua can speak summarily of "all the words of the law," by apposition, as virtually consisting of "the blessing and the curse."

Both the LXX and Paul translate *ad sensum* when they add πᾶσιν to Deuteronomy 27:26. The Hebrew text does not say "all" here, but it does commonly, as in the following examples, where the Hebrew has כל in each case:

"And you shall observe all my statutes and all my rules [πάντα τὸν νόμον μου καὶ πάντα τὰ προστάγματά μου], and do them: I am the LORD." (Lev. 19:37)

"The whole commandment [πάσας τὰς ἐντολάς] that I command you today you shall be careful to do, that you may live and multiply, and go in and possess the land that the LORD swore to give to your fathers." (Deut. 8:1)

"Take care, in a case of leprous disease, to be very careful to do according to all that the Levitical priests shall direct you [κατὰ πάντα τὸν νόμον ὃν ἐὰν ἀναγγείλωσιν ὑμῖν οἱ ἱερεῖς οἱ Λευῖται]. As I commanded them, so you shall be careful to do." (Deut. 24:8)

"'Cursed be anyone who does not confirm the words of this law [πᾶσιν τοῖς λόγοις τοῦ νόμου τούτου] by doing them.' And all the people shall say, 'Amen.'" (Deut. 27:26)

"If you are not careful to do all the words of this law [πάντα τὰ ῥήματα τοῦ νόμου τούτου] that are written in this book, that you may fear this glorious and awesome name, the LORD your God." (Deut. 28:58)

"The secret things belong to the LORD our God, but the things that are revealed belong to us and to our children forever, that we may do all the words of this law [πάντα τὰ ῥήματα τοῦ νόμου τούτου]." (Deut. 29:29)

"When you obey the voice of the LORD your God, to keep his commandments [πάσας τὰς ἐντολὰς αὐτοῦ] and his statutes that are written in this Book of the Law, when you turn to the LORD your God with all your heart and with all your soul." (Deut. 30:10)

"Assemble the people, men, women, and little ones, and the sojourner within your towns, that they may hear and learn to fear the LORD your God, and be careful to do all the words of this law [πάντας τοὺς λόγους τοῦ νόμου τούτου]." (Deut. 31: 12)

When Moses had finished writing the words of this law [πάντας τοὺς λόγους τοῦ νόμου τούτου] in a book to the very end . . . (Deut. 31:24)

He said to them, "Take to heart all the words by which I am warning you today, that you may command them to your children, that they may be careful to do all the words of this law [πάντας τοὺς λόγους τοῦ νόμου τούτου]." (Deut. 32:46)

"This Book of the Law shall not depart from your mouth, but you shall meditate on it day and night, so that you may be careful to do according to all that is written [πάντα τὰ γεγραμμένα] in it." (Josh. 1:8)

"Therefore, be very strong to keep and to do all that is written in the Book of the Law of Moses [πάντα τὰ γεγραμμένα ἐν τῷ βιβλίῳ τοῦ νόμου Μωυσῆ], turning aside from it neither to the right hand nor to the left." (Josh. 23:6)

"To offer burnt offerings to the LORD on the altar of burnt offering regularly morning and evening, to do all that is written in the Law of the LORD [πάντα τὰ γεγραμμένα ἐν νόμῳ κυρίου] that he commanded Israel." (1 Chron. 16:40)

"And I will no more remove the foot of Israel from the land that I appointed for your fathers, if only they will be careful to do all that I have commanded them [πάντα ἃ ἐνετειλάμην αὐτοῖς], all the law [πάντα τὸν νόμον], the statutes, and the rules given through Moses." (2 Chron. 33:8)

"The rest of the people . . . join with their brothers, their nobles, and enter into a curse and an oath to walk in God's Law that was given by Moses the servant of God, and to observe and do all the commandments of the LORD [πάσας τὰς ἐντολὰς κυρίου] our LORD and his rules and his statutes" [Hebrew does not qualify the commandments with כל]. (Neh. 10:28–29)

The point of adding "all" is to refer to the comprehensiveness of the demand for obedience that characterized the covenant relationship at Sinai.[32] It is not merely coincidental

---

32. Comprehensiveness is not the same as perfection. Whether, and to what degree, others had the same understanding of moral perfection disclosed by Jesus in the Sermon on the Mount (where even motivations and thoughts come under moral inspection) is a fair matter for discussion. My point, however, is that the "all" statements are probably comprehensive. Those who covenant with Yahweh at Sinai are required to do *whatever* the law says; they are not permitted, as Don Garlington put it, "to pick and choose from the variety of the commandments." In the rhetoric of Galatians, such comprehensive statements (as at 5:3 also) are designed to remind that if one observes part of the law (circumcision), on the ostensible assumption that the law remains authoritative, then one is then obliged to observe all of it and to reside under its threatened curse sanctions for noncompliance. Garlington, "Role Reversal and Paul's Use of Scripture in Galatians 3.10–13," 97. For the alternative view, that "all" denotes the demand for

that the same language appears in the *Shema*: "Hear, O Israel: The LORD our God, the LORD is one. You shall love the LORD your God with *all* your heart and with *all* your soul and with *all* your might" (Deut. 6:4–5). The curse sanctions of the Sinai administration hovered over *every* commandment and, therefore, over the entirety of Israel's history after that covenant was inaugurated; whereas to Abraham, God promised, "In you shall all the nations be *blessed*."

This curse sanction, then, was a significant feature of the Sinai administration, as both Moses and Paul understood it.[33] The two major interpretations of Paul (the dominant Protestant view and many New Perspective on Paul views) have both had difficulty with it, for different reasons. The dominant Protestant view has ordinarily attempted to suggest that the curse comes from misunderstanding the law, from an inappropriate/legalistic pursuit thereof. But Paul does not cite any mispursuit of the law when he cites Deuteronomy 27. The law itself, as a covenant, brings threatened curse sanctions with it. As Richard Longenecker says,

> Israel had willingly placed herself under the stipulations of the covenant, and in so doing had accepted the threat of being cursed for nonfulfillment. Coming under a curse was therefore inextricably bound up with receiving the law, and Paul seeks to make that point explicit in his treatment of Deut 27:26.[34]

All those (Ὅσοι γὰρ ἐξ ἔργων νόμου εἰσίν) who are "under the law," as a covenant administration, live under its threatened sanctions, not just those who pursue it wrongly or legalistically.[35] We see here again how important it is to interpreters of Galatians to consider that ὁ νόμος throughout Galatians (not just at 3:17) is a synecdoche referring to the covenant made at Sinai itself.

Similarly, some of the particular New Perspectives on Paul have difficulty with what Paul says about the curse sanctions, but for differing reasons than the dominant Protestant interpretation. First, some representatives of the New Perspectives on Paul blend the various OT covenants together and routinely speak of "being in the covenant" or "the covenant people," without specifying *which* specific OT covenant they are speaking about. In his volume on justification, for instance, N. T. Wright says:

> Here we have it: *God's single plan, through Abraham and his family, to bless the whole world.* This is what I have meant by the word *covenant* when I have used it as shorthand in writing about Paul. . . . The "covenant," in my shorthand, is not something other than

---

perfect obedience, cf. Thomas R. Schreiner, "Why the Works of the Law Cannot Save," *The Law and Its Fulfillment: A Pauline Theology of Law* (Grand Rapids: Baker, 1993), 41–72.

33. George E. Mendenhall said this about the blessing/cursing formula: "In some ways this is the most interesting feature of the covenant." Mendenhall, "Covenant Forms in Israelite Tradition," *The Biblical Archaeologist* 17, no. 3 (September 1954): 59.

34. Longenecker, *Galatians*, 117.

35. This may account for the imperfect nature of the parallel ἐκ clauses in verses 9 and 10. The first is a mere substantive use of the prepositional phrase (οἱ ἐκ πίστεως); the second employs a pronoun that calls attention to comparative quantity (Ὅσοι γὰρ ἐξ ἔργων νόμου). Cf. Louw-Nida: "pertaining to a comparison of a quantity," 59.19. It is also possible that the correlative pronoun makes the matter slightly less definite, extending it (in this case) to "whoever" is characterized by observing the law—including Gentile converts to Judaism.

God's determination to deal with evil once and for all and so put the whole creation (and humankind with it) right at last.[36]

Biblically, covenants are not extrahistorical "plans." They are inaugurated-in-space-and-time *treaties* between particular parties. And they have particular benefits that differ from each other, particular parties that often differ from each other, particular sanctions (or not) that differ from each other, and so on.

It is now somewhat common to observe that the two major (known) forms of treaty from the ancient Near East were the suzerainty treaty and the land-grant treaty (Mendenhall's original article referred to "parity treaty" as the second type). It is also common to observe that some OT covenants demonstrate profound structural similarities to one or the other of these and also to observe that, while the formal structure of ANE treaties may account for the formal structures of some OT treaties, this does not and need not mean that the substance of any particular OT treaty must be identical to any known type of ANE treaty, or even that classification of those treaties is always easy. Indeed, Mendenhall himself said, "It is important to observe that the Hittite treaties cannot be classified on the basis of terminology alone. It is only by examination of the *text* of the covenant that a classification can be carried out."[37] I am content with this caveat in every way. I do not insist that each biblical covenant be identical, in substance, to any particular ANE treaty. But each ANE treaty and each OT treaty was a true, ratified-in-space-and-time treaty, not some ahistorical decree or eternal plan. Further, the Sinai covenant, as Mendenhall et al. have noted, has profound similarities to the ANE suzerainty treaty. As John Bright put it, "Parallels with the covenant form as we know it from the Bible leap to the eye; we cannot discuss them all here."[38]

The Sinai covenant, for instance, envisions only one people in one land, not Wright's "whole creation (and humankind with it)." And the repeated sanctions for Israelite disobedience through many generations "dealt with" evil, but not "once for all;" it was plainly a *sub*-eschatological covenant, and Paul routinely refers to it as the covenant that governed the people of God before the eschaton, "until faith came" (Gal. 4:4). In a passage such as we have before us in which Paul contrasts the Abrahamic covenant with the Sinai covenant in five ways, any "monocovenantal" viewpoint (common among NPP interpreters) that does not distinguish between the various OT covenants is disastrous. *Some* of the biblical covenants do *some* of the things Wright spoke about; but some did not, and they did not all do the *same* things. Those who are parties to the covenant with Abraham, for instance, are most definitely *not* under the curse sanctions of the (later) Sinai covenant; to the contrary, they are "*blessed* with faithful Abraham."

Second, some New Perspective authors discuss membership in the covenant as though it constituted justification. James D. G. Dunn has said,

> Paul therefore prefaces his first mention of "being justified" with a deliberate appeal to the standard Jewish belief, shared also by his fellow Jewish Christians, that the Jews as a race

---

36. N. T. Wright, *Justification: God's Plan & Paul's Vision* (Downers Grove, IL: IVP, 2009), 67, 95 (emphases original).

37. Mendenhall, "Covenant Forms in Israelite Tradition," 56 (emphasis original).

38. John Bright, *A History of Israel*, 2nd ed. (Philadelphia: Westminster), 147.

are God's covenant people. . . . God's justification is rather God's acknowledgement that someone is in the covenant.[39]

But the Israelites, those who said "Amen" to the threatened sanctions of the covenant, were inescapably members of that Sinai covenant, and yet were rarely (if ever) justified thereby. They experienced the curse sanctions throughout their history, as the prophets routinely adjudged that they were *un*righteous. It was about the covenant people that Hosea returned this repeated verdict:

> When I would heal Israel, the iniquity of Ephraim [ἡ ἀδικία Εφραιμ] is revealed, and the evil deeds of Samaria; for they deal falsely; the thief breaks in, and the bandits raid outside. (Hos. 7:1)

> As for my sacrificial offerings, they sacrifice meat and eat it, but the LORD does not accept them. Now he will remember their iniquity [τὰς ἀδικίας αὐτῶν] and punish their sins; they shall return to Egypt. (Hos. 8:13)

> The days of punishment have come; the days of recompense have come; Israel shall know it. The prophet is a fool; the man of the spirit is mad, because of your great iniquity [ὑπὸ τοῦ πλήθους τῶν ἀδικιῶν σου] and great hatred. (Hos. 9:7)

> They have deeply corrupted themselves as in the days of Gibeah: he will remember their iniquity [ἀδικίας αὐτοῦ]; he will punish their sins. (Hos. 9:9)

So they *were* members of the Sinai covenant, but they were *not* justified. Insofar as some individual members of the Sinai covenant *were* justified before God, they were justified by the terms of the *Abrahamic* covenant: faith in God.

In the first paired comment/Scripture in this passage, Paul has introduced one of five contrasts between the Abrahamic covenant and the Sinai covenant: the one pledged blessings (for both Abraham's descendants and all the families of the earth), and the other threatened with curses. Although Martin Noth's objection to Paul's comments here are understandable, they are not correct:

> It is moreover noteworthy that the Old Testament itself does not appear to share Paul's judgment upon the law, for from the law it apparently opens out the perspectives, "blessing *and* curse", i.e. *either* blessing *or* curse, according as the individual or the group fulfils or does not fulfil the requirements of the law.[40]

But Paul's point in Galatians is not to describe the law comprehensively. He says little to nothing about its atonement system or Levitical priests in this letter, for instance. Paul's point is to compare the Abrahamic covenant to the Sinai covenant historically and to observe that, while *blessings* are pledged to Abraham (with no threatened curses), the Sinai administration *adds* the additional reality of threatened *curse* sanction.

---

39. Dunn, "The New Perspective on Paul," 190.
40. Noth, "For All Who Rely on Works of the Law Are under a Curse," 119.

4.3.1.2. Second Comment/Scripture

> Now[41] it is evident[42] that no one is justified before God by the law, for[43] "The righteous shall live by faith."[44]

Paul earlier (2:16) cited Psalm 143:2 as ground for his observation that no one is justified by observing the law. There, the rationale was that *no* flesh (Torah-observant or otherwise) was righteous before God. Here, the rationale is somewhat different: Paul's citation of Habakkuk 2:4 suggests that the Old Testament taught not merely that righteousness (negatively) is not by the law, but that the righteous one (positively) is so by *faith*, which is a matter also taught in Genesis 15:6 and just cited in Galatians 3:6.

It would probably not have been "evident" to everyone in Paul's generation that his was the only plausible construal of Habakkuk 2:4. However, the use of δῆλον does suggest that Paul would be surprised if anyone disputed his basic assertion that no one is justified before God by the law. And, since Genesis 15:6 had already been cited by Paul as teaching that Abraham was justified by his faith in God's promise, Paul probably assumed that such teaching was generally well known and that Habakkuk 2:4 was just another example of the kind of OT teaching about the limits of the law. He had earlier said (by contradiction, contrary to fact in 2:19) that righteousness is not by the law; that it is by faith. Here, he provides a reminder that the Sinai covenant did not justify.

4.3.1.3. Third Comment/Scripture

> But the law is not of faith, rather "The one who does them shall live by them."

Earlier (3:7, 9) Paul twice referred to those who were characterized by faith (οἱ ἐκ πίστεως), and here he expresssly asserts that the law is *not* so characterized: ὁ δὲ νόμος οὐκ ἔστιν ἐκ πίστεως. The law is characterized, not by faith, but by the *works* that it demands to be *done*, as Leviticus 18:5 says: ὁ ποιήσας αὐτὰ ζήσεται ἐν αὐτοῖς. Contextually, Yahweh addressed Moses, instructing him to tell the Israelites to be separate in all of their behavior from either the Egyptians, from whom they were recently delivered, or from the Canaanites, among whom they were about to dwell. They were not to *do* as the Egyptians and Canaanites did; they were to *do* what God commanded:

---

41. ὅτι δὲ is a *peculiar* introduction, even awkward; but I do not judge that it its peculiarity especially favors one interpretation of the passage or another.

42. δῆλον is at the end of the clause, though RSV/NRSV/ESV place it at the beginning.

43. Perhaps the causal force of ὅτι is stronger than "for" suggests. Perhaps "because" would introduce the Habakkuk citation more accurately.

44. The textual tradition for Hab. 2:4 is difficult. The Masoretic text appears to have a third singular suffix: "the righteous shall live by *his* faith." The LXX tradition has two readings, each of which reads a shorter, first-person suffix "my" (μου). In one, pronoun modifies πίστεώς "by *my* faith." In the other, the pronoun modifies δίκαιος, "my righteous one will live by faith." Paul omits the pronoun altogether, which can either mean he agrees with the third singular but leaves it unexpressed, or that he works from a defective textual tradition. Curiously enough, he also omits the pronoun when he cites Hab. 2:4 at Rom. 1:17.

"You shall not do [οὐ ποιήσετε] as they do in the land of Egypt, where you lived, and you shall not do [οὐ ποιήσετε] as they do in the land of Canaan, to which I am bringing you. You shall not walk [οὐ πορεύσεσθε] in their statutes. You shall follow [ποιήσετε] my rules and keep [φυλάξεσθε] my statutes and walk [πορεύεσθαι] in them. I am the LORD your God. You shall therefore keep [φυλάξεσθε] my statutes and [do] my rules [καὶ πάντα τὰ κρίματά μου καὶ ποιήσετε]; if a person does [αὐτά ἃ ποιήσας ἄνθρωπος] them, he shall live by them: I am the LORD." (Lev. 18:3–5)

We observe that ποιέω is employed not only in verse 5 but also four other times in this passage, where it is interchangeable with synonyms such as φυλάσσω or πορεύομαι. In these few lines of text, verbs of "doing" appear nine times, so Paul's summary of it by verse 5 is entirely apt. Notably missing from this grand occasion where Israel is about to enter the promised land is the verb πιστεύω.

This is not to say that none of the Israelites believed in Yahweh; *some*one had provided manna, quail, and water from a rock, and *some*one had drowned the Egyptian army (and, for that matter, sent the occasional fiery serpent among the Israelites themselves), and presumably the Israelites knew *who* that someone was. This is also not to say that the Sinai covenant, or any of its officers or servants, *discouraged* faith in God. To the contrary, they appear to have encouraged it heartily. But Paul is not assessing these covenant administrations in their respective entireties; he assesses them in their distinctives. What is *distinctive* to each? What *characterizes* each (the Abrahamic and now the Sinaitic) that distinguishes it from the other? Later, Paul will wonder aloud why one covenant would be "added" to another already-existing covenant (3:19), unless it did/does something distinctive that the other did not do.

Since faith in God, and the promises God made to Abraham, had already been well revealed in the Abrahamic administration, the Sinai covenant would do something else. It would hold before the twelve tribes of Abraham's descendants a conditional matter: If they would obey (i.e., *do* what he commanded), then God would bless them in the land of Canaan; and if they would not obey (*do* contrary to what he commanded), then God would curse them there.

This demand for obedience (with its attendant threatened curse sanctions) is different from Abraham who, with Sarah, was told to *believe* that God would keep his promises, remarkable though they were. Abraham and Sarah actually believed fairly badly. They cooked up a (nonmonogamous) scheme with Hagar to provide Abraham with a child, disbelieving that Sarah could conceive. Sarah laughed at God when he pledged that within a year she would be pregnant and then prevaricated also about her laughter. Abraham twice endangered the pledged seed by prevaricating about whether Sarah was his wife and thereby endangering the one who would eventually give birth to Isaac (Gen. 12:20). All told, then, Abraham and Sarah were fairly indifferent believers; I would give them a "gentleman's C" for their faith. But since their covenant was not about performance, nor conditioned on anyone's performance, their faith was good enough. By contrast, the post-Sinai history of the Israelites was a history of disobedience and subsequent cursing, because the Sinai covenant was conditioned on their *performance*. As *believers*, those subsequent Israelites did about as well as Sarah and Abraham and deserve another "gentleman's C" for their faith. But their covenant was *not* characterized by faith—good, bad, or indifferent. It was characterized by (and conditioned on) *doing* what was commanded.

Paul may or may not have had an opinion on whether the Mosaic law *could* be kept. Perhaps it was enough for him that Israel's history plainly indicated that it ordinarily *was* not kept. But in this particular place, he simply wished to contrast the works-character of the Sinai administration with the faith-character of the Abrahamic. It is not essential to his argument or reasoning to specify *whether* the law could have been kept.[45]

4.3.1.4. Fourth Comment/Scripture

> Christ redeemed us from the curse of the law by becoming a curse for us—for it is written, "Cursed is everyone who is hanged on a tree."

Paul continues to distinguish Jewish Christians from Gentile Christians through the use of the first-person plural and the second-person plural.[46] Note that the "curse" referred to here is the curse previously spoken of: the threatened curse sanction of the Sinai covenant, to which the twelve tribes of Israelites attached their ceremonial "Amen," and to which *no* Gentiles attached theirs. Speaking as a Jewish Christian, then, Paul can say that Christ redeemed "us" (ἡμᾶς) from the curse of the law, because "we Jews" were *parties* to the Sinai covenant, and therefore "we" (and "we alone") were subject to its threatened curse sanction.

Paul's actual theological reasoning here is so brief as to be almost nonexistent. The "comment" has two clauses, and it appears that the second clause especially ("by becoming a curse for us") is substantiated by the citation of Deuteronomy 21:23. The point of Deuteronomy 21:22–23 is to preserve the holiness of the land by the proper disposal of certain recipients of capital punishment:

> And if a man has committed a crime punishable by death and he is put to death, and you hang him on a tree, his body shall not remain all night on the tree, but you shall bury him the same day, for a hanged man is cursed by God [κεκατηραμένος ὑπὸ θεοῦ πᾶς κρεμάμενος ἐπὶ ξύλου]. You shall not defile your land that the LORD your God is giving you for an inheritance.

In the Deuteronomy text, the emphasis is on the preservation of the land's holiness by removing from it what is defiled—in this case an individual who has been hanged on a tree. But the reason that the hanged individual would defile the land is because the hanged man is "cursed by God."[47]

---

45. Among those who believe that Paul had a "rigorist" view of the law such that it could not be kept are Burton, Schoeps, Hübner, Räisänen, and Noth, "For All Who Rely on Works of the Law Are under a Curse." Many argue, especially on the basis of Phil. 3, that Paul thought the law could be kept: Stendahl, "Paul and the Introspective Conscience of the West," in *Paul, the Law, and the Jewish People*, 23–24, ed. E. P. Sanders. A mediating view can be found in Christopher D. Stanley, "'Under a Curse': A Fresh Reading of Galatians 3.10–14," *New Testament Studies* 36, no. 4 (October 1990): 481–511.

46. In-Gyu So Hong, "Does Paul Misrepresent the Jewish Law? Law and Covenant in Gal 3:1–14," *Novum Testamentum* 36, no. 2 (April 1, 1994): 178.

47. A rather significant body of interpreters believes that Christians were persecuted in the first century because their proclamation of a crucified messiah conflicted with Deut. 21:23. Resolving that issue is beside my thesis here. For a thorough survey (and cogent critique) of the matter, cf. Kelli S. O'Brien, "The Curse of the Law (Galatians 3.13): Crucifixion, Persecution,

Paul reasons, therefore, that if one who is hanged on a wooden tree is cursed, then when Christ was crucified on a wooden cross, he was cursed. Paul does not explain or develop the implicit idea of substitution here, how Christ's becoming a curse was "for us" (ὑπὲρ ἡμῶν). Elsewhere, this particular prepositional phrase is comparatively infrequent (only twelve other places in the Pauline letters). But where it occurs, it is often associated with substitutionary atonement, explicitly or implicitly:

> While we were still sinners, Christ died for us [ὑπὲρ ἡμῶν ἀπέθανεν]. (Rom. 5:8)

> He who did not spare his own Son but gave him up for us all [ὑπὲρ ἡμῶν πάντων παρέδωκεν αὐτόν], how will he not also with him graciously give us all things? (Rom. 8:32)

> For our sake he made him to be sin [ὑπὲρ ἡμῶν ἁμαρτίαν ἐποίησεν] who knew no sin, so that in him we might become the righteousness of God. (2 Cor. 5:21)

> And walk in love, as Christ loved us and gave himself up for us [παρέδωκεν ἑαυτὸν ὑπὲρ ἡμῶν], a fragrant offering and sacrifice to God. (Eph. 5:2)

> Who died for us [τοῦ ἀποθανόντος ὑπὲρ ἡμῶν] so that whether we are awake or asleep we might live with him. (1 Thess. 5:10)

> Who gave himself for us [ὃς ἔδωκεν ἑαυτὸν ὑπὲρ ἡμῶν] to redeem us from all lawlessness and to purify for himself a people for his own possession who are zealous for good works. (Titus 2:14; nonsubstitutionary uses are found at Rom. 8:31, 34; 2 Cor. 1:11; 5:12; 7:12)

If Peter Stuhlmacher is correct in his reading both of Paul and of the Christian community that antedated Paul, the idea of substitutionary atonement was common:

> Even before the call of Paul to be an apostle, the members of the early church made these Jesus sayings (Mk. 10:45, Mt. 20:28, Mk. 14:22, 24) their own and interpreted his death on the cross in terms of atonement theology. This is shown not only by the Last Supper tradition but also by the early christological formulas that Paul cites in 1 Corinthians 15:3–5, 2 Corinthians 5:21, Romans 3:25–26 and Romans 4:25. . . . Jesus' vicarious death is interpreted in them not only from the Suffering Servant tradition of Isaiah 53:10–12, but also from the ransom or exchange tradition in Isaiah 43:3–4 and the sin offering tradition in Leviticus 4, 16. God demonstrates his own saving righteousness by delivering his Christ to death on Golgotha "for the many," by making atonement for their sins.[48]

Stuhlmacher is probably correct. Paul's citation of traditions that antedated him suggests that the idea of substitutionary atonement was well known. Perhaps it was so well known that Paul could make the kind of assertion he makes here ("becoming a

---

and Deuteronomy 21.22–23," *Journal for the Study of the New Testament* 29, no. 1 (September 1, 2006): 55–76, esp. 58n11.

48. Stuhlmacher, "The Process of Justification," *Revisiting Paul's Doctrine of Justification: A Challenge to the New Perspective* (Downers Grove, IL: IVP Academic, 2001), 58 (parenthesis mine, to refer to the texts just cited by Stuhlmacher). For a refutation of this notion of atonement in Paul's thought, cf., e.g., Bradley H. McLean, "The Absence of an Atoning Sacrifice in Paul's Soteriology," *New Testament Studies* 38, no. 4 (October 1992): 531–53. For a survey of some of the intertestamental literature, cf. Sydney H. T. Page, "The Suffering Servant between the Testaments," *New Testament Studies* 31, no. 4 (October 1985): 481–97.

curse for us") in passing, without any perceived need to argue, develop, or substantiate the assertion. Stuhlmacher's view is more satisfying than that of David Brondos, who denies that "notions such as substitution, representation and participation played an important role in ancient Jewish thought concerning redemption or in the primitive Jesus-tradition Paul received."[49] Brondos's view appears to overlook Passover and the entirety of the Levitical sacrificial system, and/or to suggest that these were not well known in Second Temple Judaism. But surely the author of the Fourth Gospel did not regard it that way, when he records John the Baptist's initial greeting of Jesus: ἴδε ὁ ἀμνὸς τοῦ θεοῦ ὁ αἴρων τὴν ἁμαρτίαν τοῦ κόσμου (John 1:29). If such a comment did not allude to the hundred-plus LXX uses of ἀμνός, it would have been as meaningless as had the Baptist said, "Look, the giraffe of God."

What is even less likely is Wright's suggestion that the passage refers to how Jesus' death led to covenant renewal for Israel:

> In the cross of Jesus, the Messiah, the curse of exile itself reached its height, and was dealt with once and for all, so that the blessing of covenant renewal might flow out the other side, as God always intended.[50]

Far from Christ's death *renewing* the Sinai covenant, Paul will argue comprehensively in what follows that Christ's death *terminated* the Sinai covenant. It did away with the temporary (and Gentile-excluding) covenant by bringing into existence what had been promised to Abraham—namely, blessings to *all* the nations/families of the earth. Note how Paul put it in 13b and 14: " 'Cursed is everyone who is hanged on a tree'—so that in Christ Jesus the blessing of Abraham might come to the Gentiles, so that we might receive the promised Spirit through faith." The purpose of the cross, far from *renewing* the Israel-segregating/Gentile-excluding Sinai covenant, was to *terminate* its temporary governance over Abraham's descendants by blessing all the nations of the earth through his single "seed." As I will argue below, there was a season in redemptive history when it was necessary to preserve both the integrity of Abraham's lineage and the memory of the promise made to him to bless all nations through his single seed one day. To this end, God instituted the Israel-segregating/Gentile-excluding Sinai covenant, to prevent intermarriage with the "people of the land," which would have destroyed Abraham's lineage and probably destroyed memory of what was promised to him. Once it had protected Abraham's "seed" and promise, once the "seed" brought about the promise, then this temporary, Israel-segregating, Gentile-excluding covenant would be terminated, not renewed.

The only way to be redeemed from the curse of the law is for that covenant to be terminated. By the reasoning of Galatians 3:10–14, whoever is part of that covenant administration is "under a curse." Christ's death—in the reasoning here, at Romans 7:1–7, and at Galatians 2:19–20—terminates the Sinai covenant. Those who are united to Christ died to the law when Christ died: "For through the law I died *to the law* [νόμῳ ἀπέθανον]. . . . I have been crucified with Christ [Χριστῷ συνεσταύρωμαι]" (Gal. 2:19–20). Here, the language of death is only implicitly present, because Christ in some

---

49. David A. Brondos, "The cross and the curse: Galatians 3.13 and Paul's doctrine of redemption," *Journal for the Study of the New Testament*, no. 81 (March 1, 2001): 10.

50. N. T. Wright, *Climax of the Covenant* (Philadelphia: Fortress, 1992), 141.

sense became a curse "for us," and this is related to the language of cursing associated with Deuteronomy 21:22–23. But the Deuteronomy text clearly refers to execution:

> And if a man has committed a crime *punishable by death* and he is *put to death*, and you *hang* him on a tree, his body shall not remain all night on the tree, but you *shall bury him the same day*, for a hanged man is cursed by God. You shall not defile your land that the LORD your God is giving you for an inheritance.

Christ's death terminated the Sinai covenant's reign over God's people and simultaneously inaugurated a new covenant, and this accounts for the covenantal language in the institution of the Lord's Supper, where Jesus referred to τὸ αἷμά μου τῆς διαθήκης (see Matthew and Mark), and where he said τοῦτο τὸ ποτήριον ἡ καινὴ διαθήκη ἐν τῷ αἵματί μου (see Luke and 1 Cor. 11). We need not explore the entire historical/theological background to the role of death in covenant inaugurations, but some explanation will help. The language employed in the institution of the Lord's Supper almost certainly is a deliberate allusion to Exodus 24, where the covenant-ratification ceremony required bloody death:

> Moses came and told the people all the words of the LORD and all the rules. And all the people answered with one voice and said, "All the words that the LORD has spoken we will do." And Moses wrote down all the words of the LORD. He rose early in the morning and *built an altar* at the foot of the mountain, and twelve pillars, according to the twelve tribes of Israel. And he sent young men of the people of Israel, who offered burnt offerings and sacrificed peace offerings of oxen to the LORD. And Moses took half of the *blood* and put it in basins, and half of the *blood* he threw against the altar. Then he took the *Book of the Covenant* [τὸ βιβλίον τῆς διαθήκης] and read it in the hearing of the people. And they said, "All that the LORD has spoken we will do, and we will be obedient." And Moses took the blood [τὸ αἷμα] and threw it on the people and said, "Behold the blood of the covenant [τὸ αἷμα τῆς διαθήκης] that the LORD has made with you in accordance with all these words." (Exod. 24:3–8)

The author of Hebrews understood this close relation between covenant inauguration and the sacrificial blood and made these comments about Christ by reference to the realities recorded in Exodus 24:

> Therefore he is the mediator of a new covenant [διαθήκης καινῆς μεσίτης], so that those who are called may receive the promised eternal inheritance, since a death has occurred [ὅπως θανάτου γενομένου] that redeems them from the transgressions committed under the first covenant [τῇ πρώτῃ διαθήκῃ]. . . . Therefore not even the first covenant was inaugurated without blood [χωρὶς αἵματος]. For when every commandment of the law had been declared by Moses to all the people, he took the blood of calves and goats, with water and scarlet wool and hyssop, and sprinkled both the book itself and all the people, saying, "This is the blood of the covenant [τὸ αἷμα τῆς διαθήκης] that God commanded for you." And in the same way he sprinkled with the blood both the tent and all the vessels used in worship. Indeed, under the law almost everything is purified with blood, and without the shedding of blood there is no forgiveness of sins. (Heb. 9:15, 18–22)

Hebrews evidently understands covenant inaugurations to require this blood shedding, and appears to recognize that it is a "death" that enabled Christ to be "the mediator of a new covenant." Paul appears familiar with the reasoning of Exodus 24, the allusions to it in the words of the Lord's Supper, and the kind of reasoning evident in the Epistle to the Hebrews. David Brondos is almost surely mistaken, therefore, when he comments about Galatians 3:13,

> Yet the purpose for which God's Son had been sent was not that he might *die*, but that he might *redeem* God's people from the law's curse. . . . Thus, for Paul, it is not *Jesus' death* that brings about deliverance from the law's curse.[51]

What Brondos overlooks is death/blood-as-covenant-inauguration; he does not perceive what is implicit in Paul: that one covenant is terminated when another is inaugurated, and in each case there is a bloody death essential to the covenant inauguration itself.

While Paul's explicit language is cryptically brief ("Christ redeemed us from the curse of the law by becoming a curse for us"), the brevity may be due to the fact that he regarded the role of bloody death in covenant inaugurations as well known. Those of us who live after the printing press may be prone to exaggerated estimates of the typical first-century Christian's knowledge of Holy Scripture, but we may fairly assume that the prominence of the Lord's Supper liturgically was such that people would have been familiar with the language of its institution. Many students of the New Testament and early Christianity believe the Supper was celebrated weekly in the early church, as Luke appears to suggest: "On the first day of the week, when we were gathered together to break bread [κλάσαι ἄρτον], Paul talked with them" (Acts 20:7). And while the Corinthians managed to make a botch of the matter, there is little doubt that their gatherings included this important rite:

> When you come together, it is not the Lord's supper that you eat. For in eating, each one goes ahead with his own meal. One goes hungry, another gets drunk. What! Do you not have houses to eat and drink in? Or do you despise the church of God and humiliate those who have nothing? (1 Cor. 11:20–22)

If the Galatians were familiar with the Lord's Supper, then it is not a stretch to assume they would have understood the relation between bloody death and covenant inauguration. Ironically, then, when Christ suffered the particular curse sanction of the Sinai covenant that pertained to execution, he inaugurated a new covenant at the same time and by the same act; and in so doing, he terminated the previous covenant with its threatened curse sanctions. There was no provision in the Sinai administration for a representative human substitute to shed blood for others, but there was provision in the Sinai administration for the shedding of blood to inaugurate a covenant. While I affirm the theological truth of penal substitution, I do not believe Paul appeals to it here. I believe he appeals to the role of death in covenant inauguration, reasoning that when Christ "became a curse" by being executed in a particularly shameful and accursed way, he did so "for us" (that is, the Jews who lived under Sinai's threatened curses), in order that he might inaugurate another, nonthreatening covenant and free "us" (Jews) from one that threatened with curses.

If this suggestion for reading Galatians 3:13 is correct, then it demonstrates again how important covenantal reasoning is throughout the letter and how difficult it is to unpack Paul's letter apart from such reasoning.

---

51. Brondos, "The Cross and the Curse," 29.

4.3.1.5. Fifth Comment/Scripture

> So that in Christ Jesus the blessing of Abraham might come to the Gentiles, so that we
> might receive the promised Spirit through faith.

Previously in this passage, the "we" was Jewish Christians and the "you" was Gentile Christians, and I have done little more than refer to T. L. Donaldson's reasoning
to make the case. I am not sure it is critical to anything in my thesis, so I leave it to
others to make the case. But I do observe here that Paul appears in this comment to
create two purpose clauses (ἵνα is repeated), with different benefactors to each: *to the
Gentiles* the blessing of Abraham might come, and "*we* might receive the promised
Spirit through faith." The twin purpose clauses and their twin benefactors, however,
are not soterically distinguished. The eschatological ("promised") Spirit will not come
upon the Jews until that day when the eschatological blessings come to the Gentiles.
For Paul the eschaton, like love, is a many-splendored thing. When the eschaton arrives, many realities will attend it. In this particular place, Paul mentions two things
that will attend the eschaton: Gentiles will receive the blessings pledged to Abraham,
and the Jews will receive the promised Spirit.

It is interesting that Paul refers here to the single "blessing of Abraham" (ἡ εὐλογία
τοῦ Ἀβραάμ). In point of fact, the language of blessing and blessedness is fairly common in the Genesis account of Abraham (12:2–3; 14:19–20; 17:16, 20; 18:18; 22:17–19;
24:1). Further, the entire Abraham narrative is bracketed with such language, from
Genesis 12 to Genesis 24:

> "And I will make of you a great nation, and I will *bless* you and make your name great, so
> that you will be a *blessing*. I will *bless* those who *bless* you, and him who dishonors you I
> will curse, and in you all the families of the earth shall be *blessed*." (Gen. 12:2–3)

> Now Abraham was old, well advanced in years. And the LORD had *blessed* Abraham *in all
> things*. (Gen. 24:1)

Indeed, even beginning students of the Abraham narrative associate Abraham with three
promises (to become numerous, to inherit a land, and to bring blessings to all nations/
families of the earth), so why does Paul mention a single "blessing"? Because Paul is
referring here and throughout Galatians to the third pledge God made to Abraham:
that through Abraham's seed, all nations/families of the earth would be "blessed." In a
special sense, then, this third pledge to Abraham comprehended Gentiles (εἰς τὰ ἔθνη),
not Jews. Thus, in keeping with Paul's distinguishing of "we" and "you" since 2:16, "we"
Jews have indeed received the Holy Spirit as many of the prophets had predicted, but
"you" Gentiles have received the third promise to Abraham: that the nations/families
of the earth would be blessed in him.

If the Spirit is the active agent who produces faith in Jew and Gentile alike, then
the argument of Sam K. Williams is pertinent here. Williams not only takes the genitive
τοῦ πνεύματος epexegetically, he argues that throughout Galatians 3 ἐπαγγελία refers
to the Spirit. This appears to be an unnecessary reduction of the promise to Abraham,
until Williams argues that what was essentially (and initially, in Gen. 15:5–6) pledged
to Abraham were innumerable descendants:

> The promise of numerous descendants is, for Paul, the promise of the Spirit. . . . On the one hand, it refers to the divine pledge to Abraham that he would have innumerable descendants. But since God keeps his word, fulfills his pledge, through the operation of the Spirit, the promise of many descendants is, at the same time, the promise of the Spirit.[52]

On this reading, Williams's understanding is much more plausible and consistent with Paul's concerns in Galatians. The Judaizing reduction of God's people to the circumcised necessarily limits the number of Abraham's children, reducing them to the mere number of the faithful within a single nation.

For Paul, then, the eschaton brings some realities that Gentiles and Jews experience the same way (e.g., forgiveness of sins and the breaking down of the wall of hostility that separated them). But it also brings some distinctive realities to each: Jews are redeemed from the "curse of the law," a curse that never threatened the Gentiles. And Gentiles receive the third reality pledged to Abraham, becoming his sons in a distinctive, nonethnic manner. Each participates in such eschatological realities "by faith." Gentiles who have faith are Abraham's children (3:7), and "we" Jews receive the promised Spirit διὰ τῆς πίστεως (3:14).

This is all well and good, but by contrasting the Abrahamic covenant to the Sinai covenant here in Galatians 3:10–14, Paul has some explaining to do. Perhaps many in his day would not have thought in such stark terms about these two covenant administrations (as many in our day do not), even though his thorough citation of the OT texts themselves seems to be somewhat irrefragable. Is not each of these covenants sovereignly instituted by Yahweh? Is not each made either with Abraham or with his descendants? Have we not heard of each in tabernacle, temple, and synagogue? To answer these and other questions, Paul reasons covenantally in 3:15–18.

4.4. Galatians 3:15–18

> To give a human example, brothers: even with a man-made covenant, no one annuls it or adds to it once it has been ratified. Now the promises were made to Abraham and to his offspring. It does not say, "And to offsprings," referring to many, but referring to one, "And to your offspring," who is Christ. This is what I mean: the law, which came 430 years afterward, does not annul a covenant previously ratified by God, so as to make the promise void. For if the inheritance comes by the law, it no longer comes by promise; but God gave it to Abraham by a promise.

4.4.1. Structure

The passage begins with a nominative employed as vocative, and the noun of address begins the new section. The next section (beginning at 3:19) begins with a rhetorical question, so the limits of the passage are fairly evident. The reasoning in this passage is also fairly straightforward. Paul advances a human analogy to what he has been saying and will continue to say: Covenants/treaties cannot be altered

---

52. Sam K. Williams, "Promise in Galatians: A Reading of Paul's Reading of Scripture," *Journal of Biblical Literature* 107, no. 4 (December 1, 1988): 714, 716.

once they have been ratified. He then draws two pertinent conclusions from this general principle, applied to the two earlier-mentioned covenants made with Abraham and with Moses.

4.4.2. The Human Analogy (Gal. 3:15): No One Alters a Covenant after It Is Ratified

Paul establishes a human analogy (κατὰ ἄνθρωπον λέγω): Even with human[53] covenants/treaties, changes cannot be made once the covenant is formally ratified. The purpose of the *human* analogy is not merely to make an otherwise-difficult matter clear, since there is nothing especially mysterious about covenant ratification. The purpose is rhetorical to establish a kind of *a fortiori* reasoning: If even human covenants[54] cannot be changed after ratification, surely divine covenants cannot be.

Paul continues the "negativity" that has particularly distinguished this letter, whose third word in the original is οὐκ. Here also οὐδείς figures prominently: κεκυρωμένην διαθήκην οὐδεὶς ἀθετεῖ ἢ ἐπιδιατάσσεται ("No one, without exception, changes a covenant once it is ratified"). The language of ratification is important to this passage. Each of the three verbs is comparatively rare in the NT literature; between them, κυρόω,

---

53. NRSV is peculiar here: "an example from *daily* life." This is not only untrue (none of us enters contracts on a "daily" basis, and some humans in Paul's culture would *never* have entered one, much less have done so "daily"), it also misses Paul's implied contrast between human (κατὰ ἄνθρωπον) and divine covenants. Paul expressly said that no one alters a "man's covenant" (RSV) or a "man-made covenant" (ESV, Greek ἀνθρώπου . . . διαθήκην; I would prefer "human covenant"), in order to develop an *a fortiori* argument regarding the *divinely* made Abrahamic covenant. Paul will say in verse 17 that the Abrahamic covenant was ratified "by God" (προκεκυρωμένην ὑπὸ τοῦ θεοῦ); and in verse 20, he will distinguish the Abrahamic and Sinai covenants on precisely this ground that the former is unmediated and directly from God, whereas the latter is indeed mediated through a human mediator (ὁ δὲ μεσίτης ἑνὸς οὐκ ἔστιν, ὁ δὲ θεὸς εἷς ἐστιν). So the distinction between divine and human covenanting is important to Paul's reasoning here, and NRSV needlessly obscures the matter by translating κατὰ ἄνθρωπον as "daily." "Daily" forms a nice antonym to "rarely," or even, perhaps, "occasionally." But it is not the antonym to "divine" that Paul intends here. NRSV follows Betz (et al.), who approves of Burton's "I draw an illustration from common human practice." Betz, *Galatians*, 154. Among those who concur with my construction are Charles Cosgrove, "Arguing Like a Mere Human Being Galatians 3.15–18 in Rhetorical Perspective," *New Testament Studies*, 34 (1988): 542ff.; and Scott Hahn, "Covenant, Oath, and the *Aqedah: diathēkē* in Galatians 3:15–18," *Catholic Biblical Quarterly* 67, no. 1 (January 1, 2005): 87–88. Hahn also argues convincingly that διαθήκη here does not mean "testament" but covenant, as it does throughout the LXX and NT (with the "one possible exception" of Heb. 9:16–17), 80–88.

54. While we mentioned two well-established types of covenant in the ANE above, the land-grant covenant and the suzerainty covenant, here Paul's particular reasoning appears to be governed substantially by the Greco-Roman provenance of διαθήκη as "last will and testament." That is, he is establishing an *a fortiori* argument from human covenants to divine covenants, and the particular human covenants he envisions here are neither of the two types of ANE covenants but the Greco-Roman *testamentum*, by which provision is made for one's estate—a matter also implicit in his subsequent use of the κληρονομ- language of 3:18, 29; 4:1, 7, 30. See the discussion in S. M. Baugh, "Galatians 3:20 and the Covenant of Redemption," *Westminster Theological Journal* 66, no. 1 (March 1, 2004): 49–70; section III, "The Testamentary Analogy: Galatians 3:15," 54–58.

προκυρόω, and ἀκυρόω appear only six times in the NT, half of them here.[55] But they are critical to the reasoning in this critical passage, because Paul will argue throughout that a later (Sinai) covenant cannot annul or alter another (Abrahamic) covenant after the first one has been ratified.

Rhetoric, both ancient and contemporary, can be used nobly or ignobly, by which I do not mean merely that it can be put either to noble or ignoble *purposes*. I mean that it can be used to obfuscate, deceive, or manipulate, on the one hand; or to make clear, on the other hand. Paul, in my judgment, does the latter. What could be a clearer principle of treaty making than this? That once a covenant is formally ratified, it cannot be altered or amended. The process that leads to treaty ratification may be complex, even (at times) tedious. But however convoluted the process, once the treaty is in place, it is solemnly ratified, often with deities called as witnesses and/or solemn ceremonies of self-malediction[56] by the parties involved. However the particularities of the solemnification process may differ from circumstance to circumstance, once the treaty is ratified, it is inalterable: *Nobody* modifies it then.

The purpose for Paul making this fairly obvious point is this: The remainder of his covenant-historical reasoning depends on this principle being clearly established. Paul's evaluation of the Sinai covenant is covenant-historical: whatever the Sinai covenant does, it cannot (indeed it *may* not) in any manner annul or alter the Abrahamic covenant that antedated it by 430 years.[57] Paul's reasoning is partly negative: Whatever else we think about the Sinai covenant, we cannot construe it in such a manner that it violates or alters the integrity of an antecedent covenant.

---

55. The others are Matt. 15:6 and Mark 7:13 (both ἀκυρόω), and 2 Cor. 2:8 (κυρόω).

56. According to Adolph Berger, in Roman law this was called the *Exsecratio*. Cf. *Encyclopedic Dictionary of Roman Law*, Transactions of the American Philosophical Society, vol. 43 (repr., Philadelphia: American Philosophical Society, 1953), pt. 2, 465. For ANE backgrounds to self-malediction in OT covenants, cf. Dennis J. McCarthy, *Treaty and Covenant: A Study in Form in the Ancient Oriental Documents and in the Old Testament*, Analecta Biblica 21A (Rome: Biblical Institute Press, 1963); Meredith G. Kline, *Treaty of the Great King: the Covenant Structure of Deuteronomy* (Grand Rapids: Eerdmans, 1963); Meredith G. Kline, *By Oath Consigned: A Reinterpretation of the Covenant Signs of Circumcision and Baptism* (Grand Rapids: Eerdmans, 1968); Noel Weeks, *Admonition and Curse: The Ancient Near Eastern Treaty/Covenant Form as a Problem in Inter-Cultural Relationships* (London: T & T Clark, 2004), esp. 143–50.

57. Paul denies those Second Temple sources that suggest that the law was eternal, predating Abraham, and that Abraham obeyed it perfectly. Jubilees 16:10, 21 states that Abraham even observed the Feast of Tabernacles: "After these things, departing from the oak of Mambre, Abraham was dwelling at the Well of the Oath. For himself and for his house servants, by relation, having put up tents, then first Abraham celebrated the feast of tabernacles for seven days [τότε πρῶτον Ἀβραὰμ τῆς σκηνοπηγίας ἐπὶ ἑπτὰ ἡμέρας ἐπιτελεῖ τὴν ἑορτήν]." Similarly, Sirach 44:19–20 affirms that the law antedated Abraham, who obeyed it: "Abraham was the great father of a multitude of nations, and no one has been found like him in glory; he kept the law of the Most High [ὃς συνετήρησεν νόμον ὑψίστου], and was taken into covenant with him." Paul disputes such claims here and reiterates the language from the narrative of Exod. 12:40–41: "The time that the people of Israel lived in Egypt was 430 years. At the end of 430 years, on that very day, all the hosts of the LORD went out from the land of Egypt." Cf. the discussion of this important matter in Hong, "Does Paul Misrepresent the Jewish Law?," 164–82.

4.4.3. Two Pertinent Conclusions (Gal. 3:16–18)

4.4.3.1. CONCLUSION ONE: THE (THIRD ASPECT OF THE) PROMISE TO ABRAHAM WILL BE FULFILLED BY ONE INDIVIDUAL DESCENDANT OF ABRAHAM (GAL. 3:16).

> Now the promises were made to Abraham and to his offspring [τῷ σπέρματι]. It does not say, "And to offsprings [τοῖς σπέρμασιν]," referring to many [ὡς ἐπὶ πολλῶν], but referring to one [ὡς ἐφ᾽ ἑνός], "And to your offspring [τῷ σπέρματι]," who is Christ [ὅς ἐστιν Χριστός].

From the time God first made pledges to Abraham until the translation of the LXX (and perhaps afterward), there was some ambiguity in the pledge to bless all the families/nations of the earth through Abraham's "seed." In the Hebrew of Genesis 13:15; 17:8; 22:18; and 24:7, the divine pledge is expressed as being "to you" and "to your seed" (לזרעך). Since the Hebrew noun זרע is a collective noun, one cannot be sure whether the original suggests "to your descendants" or "to your descendant," which is not an insignificant matter at all for OT theology. If God pledged to Abraham that one day he would bless all the nations/families of the earth through Abraham's "seed," was this "seed" to be understood individually or collectively? If collectively, then the pledge might be understood something like this (I paraphrase freely):

> "One day, Abraham, your descendants will be a numerous people in a fine, arable land. Between now and then—yet unknown to you—I will deliver Torah to them, divine wisdom full of justice. If they multiply greatly in this bountiful land, and if they pursue the wisdom I will give them in Torah, their culture will be a haven for strangers, orphans, and widows; their courts will establish justice; the bountiful land in good seasons will sustain them in difficult times; and they will live in Shalom. Other nations will see their culture, with its justice, prosperity, compassion and wisdom, and will emulate them; and thus, your descendants will be exemplary to the whole world, ultimately refining the entire earth and filling it with *Shalom*."

Undoubtedly, many people from Abraham's day until ours understood the third part of the Abrahamic pledge in precisely this manner. Abraham's "seed" is the collective group of his numerous, Torah-observing descendants whose well-ordered society will be a "light to the nations."

Another reading of "seed" is also possible, though much less likely, prima facie. It is possible that through a single, unusual descendant of Abraham, God would bring blessings to all the nations/families of the earth. When the decision was made to translate the LXX in the third century BCE, the translators faced an interesting choice. The Greek σπέρμα can be used collectively, but since σπέρμα so easily admits of a plural, would it be wiser to translate it with a plural or a singular form? The plural probably catches the sense that many would naturally derive from the Hebrew collective, but the singular would permit the LXX translators to retain their ordinarily conservative/literalist tendency, while still permitting a collective understanding of the Greek noun. Undoubtedly, there would have been some discussion of the matter, before they decided to translate the word precisely as Paul cites it. The decision to translate with the Greek singular does not exclude a corporate understanding of "seed." To the contrary, in chapters 13 and 15 of Genesis, σπέρμα is manifestly corporate, even though the singular form is employed:

"I will make your offspring as the dust of the earth, so that if one can count the dust of the earth, your offspring [τὸ σπέρμα σου] also can be counted." (Gen. 13:16)

And he brought him outside and said, "Look toward heaven, and number the stars, if you are able to number them." Then he said to him, "So shall your offspring be [οὕτως ἔσται τὸ σπέρμα σου]." (Gen. 15:5)

The use of the Greek singular, then, permits either a singular or corporate reading of the Abrahamic promises regarding Abraham's "seed," but a plural translation would not have the same flexibility; it would permit only a corporate understanding.

Paul surely understood that the first pledge to Abraham's "seed" was manifestly corporate and numerous; Yahweh would make his "seed" as numerous as the sands of the sea or the stars of the sky. Paul probably understood the second pledge to be corporate and numerous also: that to this large group of descendants a great, arable land would be given (after all, a single descendant could hardly inhabit/cultivate or militarily defend such a large piece of real estate). But he understood the third pledge singularly, as finding its focus in one particular descendant of Abraham. We might be inclined to regard this as arbitrary, especially if we failed to distinguish definition from referent. Surely, we might say, Paul cannot define τὸ σπέρμα willy-nilly, as Abraham's numerous progeny in one place and as a single descendant in another. But referent is a different reality than definition. When a term has a particular referent in mind, the identity of the referent necessarily trumps ordinary definition. In the 1982 film *The Year of Living Dangerously*, for instance, Linda Hunt played the role of Billy (quite convincingly). Discussing the role, one might say, "The man is a woman." Definitionally, it would make little sense to define "man" as "woman." Referentially, however, it would make perfect sense in that context, because the "man," Billy, was played by a woman actor.

Paul legitimately understood the third Abrahamic pledge by reading the LXX in a straightforward manner, without any collective overtones. He not only reminded (twice) that the pertinent LXX texts have the dative singular (τῷ σπέρματι); he also expressly denied (οὐ λέγει) that the pertinent texts have the plural (τοῖς σπέρμασιν). He went even further to indicate what significance he derived from what is not there and what is there, saying that the pledge is not to offsprings, referring to many (ὡς ἐπὶ πολλῶν), but rather, "referring to one [ὡς ἐφ᾽ ἑνός], 'And to your offspring [τῷ σπέρματι].'"[58] Paul, of course, said nothing here about whether the LXX translators thought through the matter and actually shared Paul's belief. Perhaps he merely thought that the LXX was just a fairly literal translation, and so they literally (and consistently) translated the collective Hebrew noun with a singular Greek noun, leaving *open* the interpretive question of what to do with it. Nevertheless, Paul does an enormous amount with it, and he expressly affirms that the singular "seed" of Abraham by whom the nations will be blessed "is Christ" (ὅς ἐστιν Χριστός).

It is entirely possible that this is interpretation after the fact; Paul recognized, obviously, that the Gentile Galatians had received the blessings of the eschaton, and that this had happened because of the apostolic proclamation about Christ. Paul was perhaps as surprised as anyone that God had brought blessings to the world through

---

58. Note also the chiastic structure of "not seeds [σπέρμασιν]" referring to many but referring to one τῷ σπέρματι.

a *single* descendant of Abraham; but, surprised or not, he affirms that this did indeed happen, and so he identifies the Abrahamic "seed who will bless the nations" with Christ. It is also possible that it is *not* interpretation after the fact; that Paul understood the Abraham material in Genesis in terms suggested by the earlier chapters. In the curse sanction of Genesis 3, for instance, God pledged to destroy one day the unholy alliance between the woman and the serpent that had provoked the curse: "I will put enmity between you and the woman, and between your offspring [τοῦ σπέρματός σου] and her offspring [τοῦ σπέρματος αὐτῆς]; he [αὐτός] shall bruise your head, and you [σὺ] shall bruise his [αὐτοῦ] heel." The "seed" here is singular, and the remainder of the Genesis narrative will concern itself, in part, with how this might come to pass. It surely will not come to pass through Abel, who is slain by Cain, and it surely will not come to pass through the murderous Cain, as Genesis 4:25 says: "And Adam knew his wife again, and she bore a son and called his name Seth, for she said, 'God has appointed for me another offspring [σπέρμα ἕτερον] instead of Abel, for Cain killed him.'" In Genesis 3 and 4, therefore, "seed" had a more singular understanding than a collective understanding; so the remainder of Genesis, even when narrating the numerous progeny of Abraham, may have also left open the expectation of a single "seed" of the woman who would one day reverse the curse. Paul surely took it this way.

Paul was not entirely alone in this belief. Matthew's Gospel also traces the genealogy of Jesus back to Abraham. For Matthew, it was important enough in the first verse to declare that Jesus was "the son of David, the son of Abraham," and then to proceed in the very next verse to say, "Abraham was the father of Isaac" and to trace the matter all the way to "Jacob the father of Joseph the husband of Mary, of whom Jesus was born, who is called Christ" (Matt. 1:16). It was important, in other words, to some in the apostolic generation that Jesus was "a" descendant of Abraham; but Paul's Gentile mission caused him to see the matter as more significant than that. In a very real sense, Jesus is "the" descendant of Abraham, the particular descendant in whom all the blessings pledged to fall upon the nations/Gentiles would actually arrive. He suggested, then, not so much a "singular" reading of τῷ σπέρματι, but a focal reading, a concentrated reading, something like this: Of all the descendants of Abraham by which history crept closer and closer to its fructive, eschatological moment, the great breakthrough "descendant" was not David, Solomon, Hezekiah, Ezra, the Maccabees, or the Baptist; the great, single "descendant" of Abraham by which the Gentiles finally and fully received adoption as children of God was Jesus the Christ. He was and is, in fact, the seed in whom the richest eschatological blessings pledged to Abraham have come to earth, in whom the curses of Genesis 3 are reversed.

The roots of such a reading reside implicitly in the Genesis narrative itself. One of the curious paradoxes of the patriarchal narrative in Genesis is that the pledges are routinely made to Abraham "and your seed," yet in the earliest generations "seed" is narrowed from meaning "all of your descendants" to, effectively, "*some* of your descendants." Abraham's firstborn son is Ishmael (a point Paul develops later in Galatians), yet Ishmael is plainly excluded from the line of promise. In the next generation, Abraham's first grandson is Esau, who is also excluded from the line of pledge/promise in favor of Jacob. So, not only is the law of primogeniture violated, as it were, in the first two generations, but also a division within Abraham's "seed" takes place in those two generations, indicating already that Abraham's "seed" does *not* mean the collective of *all* of his descendants, but some subgroup within that. Paul, of course, narrows that subgroup much further in this text, narrowing it to a single seed. The process of narrowing the meaning of Abraham's "seed," however, goes back to Abraham's generation itself, which is a point Paul similarly made in Romans 9:6–8.

The Abrahamic narrative also introduces the element of surprise or counter-expectation to the narrative about the "seed." Considering the widespread adoption of the principle of primogeniture, it is actually surprising that neither Ishmael nor Esau is the "seed" by which the pledged/promised blessing is passed along to subsequent generations. Indeed, the narrative of Jacob and Esau is replete with surprise twists, from the unusual circumstances of their birth, to the difference between Rebekah and Isaac about which son each loved, to the implausible bartering away of the birthright for a bowl of soup,[59] to Isaac's inability to recognize his own ("beloved") son. If the narrative were not bound in leather, it would be curious enough to expect to find it in *The Canterbury Tales*. So, though unstated, perhaps Paul knew not only that Abraham's "seed" was not the collective entirety of his descendants, but he also knew that Abraham's "seed" was and always would be a surprising entity, an unexpected entity. If so, then Paul's reasoning rests on a good deal more than the LXX's translation of the Hebrew collective noun זרע with the Greek τῷ σπέρματι. It rests on interpretive trajectories resident in the original Abrahamic narrative, though it surely develops those trajectories further.

4.4.3.2. CONCLUSION TWO: THE LAW IS NOT (AND CANNOT BE) AN ALTERNATIVE WAY OF INHERITING THE ABRAHAMIC PROMISE (GAL. 3:17–18)

> This is what I mean: the law, which came 430 years afterward, does not annul[60] a covenant [διαθήκην] previously ratified by God, so as to make the promise void. For if the inheritance comes by the law, it no longer comes by promise; but God gave it to Abraham by a promise.

If Romans 1:16–17 contains in a nutshell the entirety of the book of Romans, then Galatians 3:17–18 does the same thing for the entirety of the book of Galatians. Both lexically and rhetorically, my reading of Galatians is profoundly influenced by this portion thereof. Lexically, it is difficult to construe ὁ νόμος here as anything but the Sinai *covenant* itself, a covenant that was made at least 430 years after the previous covenant made with Abraham. My interpretation of the letter, then, suggests that this definition is the controlling definition elsewhere in the letter, unless some contextual consideration suggests otherwise. That is, the natural ease with which Paul uses ὁ νόμος as a synecdoche for the Sinai covenant here suggests that this is how Paul uses the term elsewhere in Galatians.[61] There is no evidence that he is now discussing something

---

59. Were it an exceptional lobster bisque, the choice may have been understandable, if not excusable.

60. English translators have difficulty construing this sentence in a manner that demonstrates Paul's juxtaposition of ἀκυροῖ and προκεκυρωμένην. I suppose they could coin a new word and translate it as "the law . . . does not de-ratify a previously ratified covenant," but this would perhaps raise eyebrows.

61. Except, of course, where he intentionally adds a qualifying genitive to do something different with νόμος, as he does at 6:2 when he speaks of τὸν νόμον τοῦ Χριστοῦ.

different from what he has been discussing since he first introduced the expression in 2:16, and here it is manifestly the "covenant" made over four hundred years after the one made with Abraham. Further, the introductory τοῦτο δὲ λέγω demands that we take what Paul says here as explaining what he has said earlier, which could hardly happen if he were to change his definition of νόμος here. The τοῦτο δὲ λέγω could almost be paraphrased, "This is what I am saying about the law." Here in 3:17, Paul roots ὁ νόμος historically; the figure/synecdoche is not *merely* a figure of speech, or a parable of some sort. The figure/synecdoche is figurative *language* for a *historical* reality.

Paul roots ὁ νόμος here not only in *history* ("430 years afterward"), but in *covenant* history: "the law, which came 430 years afterward, does not annul a *covenant* [διαθήκην] previously ratified [προκεκυρωμένην] by God." What came 430 years after the Abrahamic covenant was not (as the dominant Protestant approach has often suggested) legalism; nor was what came 430 years afterward God's moral will (as so many Protestant confessions have suggested in places; e.g., Westminster Confession of Faith 19:1–2); nor was what came 430 years afterward "identity markers" that distinguished Jew and Gentile (though this is closer). What came 430 years after a "previously ratified *covenant*" was another *covenant.* "Ratify" (κυρόω), "previously ratify" (προκυρόω), and "de-ratify/annul" (ἀκυρόω), as well as διαθήκη itself, are all covenant terms, and for Paul, ὁ νόμος is that covenant reality that appeared 430 years after the ratification of the Abrahamic covenant.

We note that Paul has no interest in computing the actual time that elapsed from the covenant with Abraham to the covenant with Moses. From Exodus 12, he knows that the Israelites were in Egypt for 430 years: "The time that the people of Israel lived in Egypt was 430 years. At the end of 430 years, on that very day, all the hosts of the LORD went out from the land of Egypt" (Exod. 12:40–41). But of course, Abraham's covenant was made some time *before* his descendants were enslaved in Egypt, and the covenant made at Horeb took place some time *after* the Exodus, so the actual figure would likely be much closer to five hundred years, or roughly half a millennium. But whether one employs Stephen's round figure of four hundred years (Acts 7:6), the "at least 430" figure from Exodus 12, or half a millennium, the rhetorical point is the same. No Sinai-come-lately has any business altering a covenant that had been in effect for half a millennium before it.

Paul's Greek communicates this wonderfully, but our English has some difficulty putting the matter quite as he did. Paul separates the definite article from its noun by a good distance, adding important modifiers in between the article and its noun (à la 1 Peter, where the construction is as frequent as it is eloquent). He defines the law this way here: ὁ μετὰ τετρακόσια καὶ τριάκοντα ἔτη γεγονὼς νόμος: "the-after-four-hun-dred-and-thirty-years-having-come-law." We just cannot do this in English, but it's fun to try, and the effort (albeit clumsy) discloses Paul's mind wonderfully. It isn't merely that "the law" does not annul a previously ratified covenant; it is that the law *that comes 430 years later* does not (and surely cannot) annul a previously ratified covenant. If, in terms of Paul's human analogy of 3:15, *no one* (οὐδείς) alters or adds to even a *human* covenant after it is ratified, then surely no one is going to alter a *divine* covenant half a millennium later. This is an *a fortiori* argument on steroids.

Before he goes any further, then, Paul accomplishes a substantial rhetorical feat. Even before he discusses what the purpose of ὁ νόμος is (3:19ff.), he declares here what its purpose is *not* (οὐκ). Its purpose is not to alter, modify, or annul the Abrahamic covenant in any manner whatsoever. Whatever else Moses' covenant is and does, it may not lay a finger on the Abrahamic covenant. Abraham's covenant is promissory; Abraham's covenant embraces all the families of the earth; Abraham's covenant is characterized by faith; and Abraham's covenant justifies by faith. Whatever the Sinai covenant *will* do, what it will *not* do is violate any of the realities of the Abrahamic covenant.

It is not essential to my discussion to determine which aspect of the Abrahamic covenant Paul focuses on, nor to address whether there were several covenants with Abraham. Surely, the pledges to Abraham were threefold: numerous descendants, land inheritance, and the blessing of all the families/nations of the earth through Abraham's seed. Ordinarily, God's three-part pledge to Abraham is referred to as "the Abrahamic covenant," and I do so here. But the matter could be refined more acutely. There are two events in the life of Abraham that are referred to with the designation διαθήκη:

> On that day the Lord made a covenant [διαθήκην] with Abram, saying, "To your offspring I give this land, from the river of Egypt to the great river, the river Euphrates." (Gen. 15:18)

> When Abram was ninety-nine years old the Lord appeared to Abram and said to him, "I am God Almighty; walk before me, and be blameless, that I may make my covenant [τὴν διαθήκην μου] between me and you, and may multiply you greatly." Then Abram fell on his face. And God said to him, "Behold, my covenant [ἡ διαθήκη μου] is with you, and you shall be the father of a multitude of nations. . . . I will make you exceedingly fruitful, and I will make you into nations, and kings shall come from you. And I will establish my covenant [τὴν διαθήκην μου] between me and you and your offspring after you throughout their generations for an everlasting covenant, to be God to you and to your offspring after you. And I will give to you and to your offspring after you the land of your sojournings, all the land of Canaan, for an everlasting possession, and I will be their God. . . . This is my covenant [αὕτη ἡ διαθήκη], which you shall keep, between me and you and your offspring after you: Every male among you shall be circumcised." (Gen. 17:1–10)

Each of these events is explicitly referred to as a "covenant," and each expressly refers to Abraham's descendants and their inheritance of the land. The third aspect of the pledge-making to Abraham, that God would bless all the families/nations of the earth, appears elsewhere:

> "By myself I have sworn [κατ᾽ ἐμαυτοῦ ὤμοσα]," declares the Lord, "because you have done this and have not withheld your son, your only son, I will surely bless you, and I will surely multiply your offspring as the stars of heaven and as the sand that is on the seashore. And your offspring shall possess the gate of his enemies, and in your offspring [ἐν τῷ σπέρματί σου] shall all the nations of the earth be blessed, because you have obeyed my voice." (Gen. 22:16–18)

Should this also be referred to as part of the covenant made with Abraham? The answer is yes, on three grounds. First, it is a sheer gracious pledge, analogous to the pledges of numerous descendants and the land. Second, though Galatians 3:15–18 deals with the relation of the Abrahamic and Sinai covenants, and though Paul in 3:16 refers to "the promises" (αἱ ἐπαγγελίαι), the only specific reference Paul makes to Genesis here is to the pledge to bless the nations through the seed of Abraham in Genesis 22:18. And third, as Scott Hahn has argued, "oath" and "covenant" are closely related, and Genesis 22 is expressly referred to as an "oath" by Zechariah in Luke 1:72–73:

"That we should be saved from our enemies and from the hand of all who hate us; to show the mercy promised to our fathers and to remember his holy covenant [μνησθῆναι διαθήκης ἁγίας αὐτοῦ], the oath that he swore [ὅρκον ὃν ὤμοσεν] to our father Abraham."[62]

I believe Hahn makes a compelling case that, at a minimum, the pledge to bless the nations through a single seed of Abraham is an aspect of what Paul regards as "the covenant with Abraham"; at a maximum, it is the focal part, because it is the part so crucial to the argument of Galatians that the Abrahamic covenant remains partly unfulfilled until the seed of Abraham blesses the nations of the world.

What Paul affirms emphatically in 3:17 is this: ὁ νόμος is not and cannot be an alternative way of arriving at the blessings associated with the Abrahamic covenant: "the law, which came 430 years afterward, does not annul a covenant previously ratified by God, so as to make the promise void. For if the inheritance comes by the law, it no longer comes by promise; but God gave it to Abraham by a promise." The specific reason the law does not annul/de-ratify the Abrahamic promise is that if it were an alternative means of arriving at that promise it would "make the promise void. For if the inheritance comes by the law, it no longer comes by promise; but God gave it to Abraham by a promise." The law, with over six hundred commands, cannot become the means to attaining that which was promised to Abraham without voiding its promissory nature altogether. The law, whose recipients live under the threatened *curse* sanction, cannot be the means of inheriting the *blessings* that were promised to Abraham without corrupting entirely what "promise" means. The law, which separates Jews from Gentiles, cannot possibly be the means by which Abraham's seed brings the promised blessings *to* the nations. Four times in three verses (3:16–18), Paul employs the language of "promise," because the Abrahamic covenant (which came 430 years earlier than the Sinai covenant) was and is essentially promissory. And for Paul, "promise" and "law" are as different as a "free woman" is from a "slave woman" (4:22ff.).

4.5. Galatians 3:19–22

Why[63] then the law? It was added because of transgressions, until[64] the offspring should come to whom the promise had been made, and it was put in place through angels by an

---

62. Hahn mentions other examples of the NT and Second Temple sources that refer to Gen. 22 as "oath" and/or "covenant." Cf. his extended argument in "Covenant, Oath, and the *Aqedah*," 79–100.

63. "*What* is the law?" is also, of course, a possible construal of the Greek. But the answer Paul gives sounds like the answer to a "why" question rather than to a "what" question. And, of course, this adverbial use of τί is common enough, as in "Why do you worry? [τί μεριμνᾶτε]" at Matt. 6:28; "Why do you see the speck? [τί δὲ βλέπεις τὸ κάρφος]" at Matt. 7:3; "Why are you afraid? [τί δειλοί ἐστε]" at Matt. 8:26; "Why do you stand looking? [τί ἐστήκατε (ἐμ) βλέποντε]" at Acts 1:11; or Paul's "Why do you boast? [τί καυχᾶσαι]" at 1 Cor. 4:7, or "Why are people baptized? [τί καὶ βαπτίζονται]" at 1 Cor. 15:29.

64. This is the right translation of ἄχρις οὗ here. While ἄχρις can sometimes be used to describe extent, it also has plainly temporal uses ("until") at places such as Matt. 24:38; Luke 1:20; 4:13; 17:27; Acts 1:2; 3:21; 7:18; 20:11; 23:1; 26:22; Rom. 5:13; 8:22; 1 Cor. 4:11; 11:26; 15:25;

intermediary. Now an intermediary implies more than one, but God is one. Is the law then contrary to the promises of God? Certainly not! For if a law had been given that could give life, then righteousness would indeed be by the law. But the Scripture imprisoned everything under sin, so that the promise by faith in Jesus Christ might be given to those who believe.

4.5.1. Structure of the Passage

The structure of these verses seems to consist of two portions of three parts each. There is a question/answer/further elaboration followed by another question/answer/ further elaboration:

Question 1: Why then the law?
>   *Answer 1*: It was added because of transgressions, until the offspring should come to whom the promise had been made.
>   *Further Elaboration 1*: and it was put in place through angels by an intermediary. Now an intermediary implies more than one, but God is one.

Question 2: Is the law then contrary to the promises of God?
>   *Answer 2*: Certainly not! For if a law had been given that could give life, then righteousness would indeed be by the law.
>   *Further Elaboration 2*: But the Scripture imprisoned everything under sin, so that the promise by faith in Jesus Christ might be given to those who believe.

These few verses contain not a little ambiguity. The reasoning here is extremely terse and not always self-evident. Some (but not all) of this ambiguity can be relieved by framing the initial rhetorical question correctly. Indeed, many of the misunderstandings of the passage come from framing the question wrongly. Τί οὖν ὁ νόμος; is, admittedly, somewhat unclear. Paul could be asking a total or a comprehensive question: "What is the *entire* purpose of the law in God's saving purposes?" If he is perceived as asking such a question, then his answer will be not only disappointing and possibly confusing, but also potentially in conflict with what he says in related texts elsewhere. Yet suppose he is framing a narrower question. Suppose ὁ νόμος means the same thing it has meant since 2:16, to wit: "A Gentile-excluding, works-based and curse-threatening covenant that came 430 years after the Abrahamic covenant"? Suppose, that is, Paul is saying something like this: Well, if God pledged blessings to Abraham, and through his single descendant to all the nations, and all by faith; and if 430 years later the same God instituted a covenant that segregated Israel from the Gentiles entirely and threatened even the included Israelites with curses unless they obeyed comprehensively, why would God do such a thing? What would be the point of inaugurating such a covenant at that moment? What good could such a covenant accomplish? Why not go straight

---

2 Cor. 3:14; Gal. 4:2; Phil. 1:5–6; Heb. 6:11; Rev. 2:25–26; 17:17; 20:3, 5. In our context, where the preceding verses specified the 430 years between the Abrahamic and Sinai covenants, we are on safe ground to assume that the reasoning is still historical and temporal here.

from the promissory covenant with Abraham to its fulfillment, without this curious thing in between? This, in my opinion, is what Paul means by Τί οὖν ὁ νόμος here. He is not asking (as we so often do) the general *theological* question of what all the law accomplishes; he is asking a question following the previous passage, a question that flows out of the reasoning of the previous passages, which candidly narrates the differences between the Abrahamic covenant and the Sinai covenant—differences so great that, as Paul says, it is unthinkable that the Sinai covenant could become the means by which the blessings pledged to Abraham come. The natural question that occurs after such reasoning is this: Well, then why have the Sinai covenant at all? What is the point, in covenant history, of having a covenant between the promissory covenant and a "new" covenant that consists of its fruition? Why have anything in between, especially an anything that is so different in *kind* from the other two?

Note also that Paul is not redefining ὁ νόμος here to mean something different than it did at 3:17, where it manifestly referred to the covenant inaugurated more than 430 years after the Abrahamic covenant. The question that begins this pericope at 3:19 flows out of what was said earlier, so ὁ νόμος here means what it did before; it is still a synecdoche for the covenant made with the Israelites at Sinai. That is, if we wanted to expand Τί οὖν ὁ νόμος by paraphrase, we would say this: "Why then have this particular curse-threatening-and-Israel-segregating-and-law-characterized covenant 430 years after the promissory Abrahamic covenant, if it does not and cannot have the effect of nullifying or amending the previous covenant? What is its purpose, then?" Indeed, we should assume that ὁ νόμος continues to mean this throughout the reasoning of the remainder of the letter unless some contextual consideration demands otherwise.

If Paul is asking a covenant-historical question here, and yet we think he is asking a general theological question, then we will tend to misunderstand him, especially in a passage that is fairly cryptic on its own merits. One could make a plausible case (from, e.g., Rom. 7) that the law has the effect of *revealing* sin to be sin; or, less likely but still plausibly, one could argue that the law *restrains* sin by defining and promoting virtue. For such perspectives, Paul's τῶν παραβάσεων χάριν προσετέθη means, "It was added to *disclose/suppress* transgressions." Still others have suggested, with entirely cogent theological reasoning, that the works-character of the Sinai covenant is a reminder of the obedience required of the first Adam and of the curse that followed his transgression. I suggest, however, that Paul is reasoning otherwise here.[65] His rhetorical question is the question he assumes will be on the mind of every intelligent auditor or reader of his letter: If Paul is right that the Abrahamic covenant and Sinai covenant are different in kind in five ways, and if he is right that the second covenant cannot be an alternative method—therefore, of attaining what was pledged in the first—then why have that second covenant at all? This, I suggest, is what Τί οὖν ὁ νόμος means here.

---

65. I actually think there is an element of theological truth in all three of the above answers, and an element of theological truth, disclosed in Hebrews, that the law also teaches about substitutionary atonement through its various "types." So I am not foreclosing here on the ongoing legitimate systematic-theological question about what functions the law has. I am merely saying that Paul is not addressing that comprehensive, systematic-theological question here. He is merely answering a covenant-historical question that arises from his own covenant-historical statements in the preceding verses.

So what is the answer to the question? If God had pledged to bless *all* the nations through a seed of Abraham one day merely by *faith*, then why would the same God have later instituted a covenant with a *single* nation—a covenant that prohibited ordinary dietary and marital relations with other nations—and why would such a covenant threaten *curses* upon the one nation with which it was made? Answer: Because it is also entirely possible that the law is added to *insulate* the covenant people from those *particular* transgressions that would destroy memory of the Abrahamic covenant and that would destroy the integrity of Abraham's "seed." Since the Israelites exhibited a recurring tendency to intermarry with the *am ha-aretz*,[66] there was the real possibility that, apart from some covenant threatening such activity with severe sanctions, the entire Abrahamic promise and Abrahamic seed might be lost to history. So, if this reading is correct, the Gentile-excluding Sinai covenant is instituted (in part) to preserve Israel from this tendency (albeit imperfectly), by including many marking regulations that restrict relations with the Gentiles. If this view is correct, then it anticipates the "guardian" language of the paidagogue later in the chapter.

Contemporary readers of the Bible are a little embarrassed about what they regard as the xenophobia of the Old Testament. In our pluralistic moment, we regard ethnocentrism (and even perhaps nationalism?) with disdain, and we find the divine demand for Israel's segregation somewhat off-putting. But this isolating of Abraham's seed, so that when blessings would one day come to all the nations of the earth they would do so through a descendant of his, was crucial to God's program. Paul was not the first to notice how important Israel's segregation was. Note how Ezra recalls Deuteronomy 7:

> And now, O our God, what shall we say after this? *For we have forsaken your commandments*, which you commanded by your servants the prophets, saying, "The land that you are entering, to take possession of it, is a land impure with the impurity of the peoples of the lands, with their abominations that have filled it from end to end with their uncleanness. Therefore *do not give your daughters to their sons, neither take their daughters for your sons*, and never seek their peace or prosperity, that you may be strong and eat the good of the land and leave it for an inheritance to your children forever." And after all that has come upon us for our evil deeds and for our great guilt, seeing that you, our God, have punished us less than our iniquities deserved and have given us such a remnant as this, *shall we break your commandments again and intermarry with the peoples* who practice these abominations? Would you not be angry with us until you consumed us, so that there should be no remnant, nor any to escape? O Lord the God of Israel, you are just, for we are left a remnant that has escaped, as it is today. Behold, we are before you in our guilt, for none can stand before you because of this. (Ezra 9:10–15)

For Ezra, what comprehensively constituted "forsaking" or "breaking" God's commandments was intermarriage with the nations. Of all the commands that he could have selected from Deuteronomy, he selected chapter 7's prohibition of intermarrying with the *am ha-aretz*. And indeed the entire program of return to the land was jeopardized by such intermarriage:

---

66. A tendency by which Israel was less tempted when in its servile role with the Egyptians, who would not likely have wished to intermarry with them.

> While Ezra prayed and made confession, weeping and casting himself down before the house of God, a very great assembly of men, women, and children, gathered to him out of Israel, for the people wept bitterly. And Shecaniah the son of Jehiel, of the sons of Elam, addressed Ezra: "We have broken faith with our God and have married foreign women from the peoples of the land, but even now there is hope for Israel in spite of this. Therefore let us make a covenant with our God to put away all these wives and their children, according to the counsel of my LORD and of those who tremble at the commandment of our God, and let it be done according to the Law. Arise, for it is your task, and we are with you; be strong and do it." Then Ezra arose and made the leading priests and Levites and all Israel take oath that they would do as had been said. So they took the oath. (Ezra 10:1–5)

I doubt the wives and children who were put away were very impressed with the Sinai covenant, a covenant that effectively made widows and orphans of them. But Israel's segregation from the nations preserved Abraham's lineage, and it was therefore necessary. An Israel-segregating covenant was needed to preserve the integrity of Abraham's lineage and memory of the pledge to bless the nations of the world thereby.

Recall how inadequate the Abrahamic covenant was to accomplish this purpose of protecting/preserving Abraham's lineage. Abraham himself twice (Gen. 12; 20) prevaricated about Sarah being his (half) sister rather than his wife, and in each case, the prevarication could have had the result of Sarah becoming part of an Egyptian harem, and therefore either producing children that were not Abraham's children, or children whose lineage could not have been traced to Abraham. Similarly, Sarah and Abraham concocted a plan to employ the slave Hagar as the means to provide a "seed" for Abraham (Gen. 16), but this would not have been the seed of Abraham and Sarah, and it also would have prevented the fulfillment of God's purposes for them. So we note that—apart from the Israel-segregating laws of the (later) Mosaic administration, and the severe threatenings of cursing for noncompliance—the entire program to bless all the families of the earth through a single seed of Abraham (so important to Paul, albeit perhaps curious to us, 3:16) might easily have been frustrated. Only God's divine intervention rescued the seed pledge *to* Abraham and Sarah *from* Abraham and Sarah themselves! Slavery to the Egyptians for over four centuries also helped, because it would have been unlikely, by the conventions of the second millennium, for the Egyptians to have intermarried with their slaves. But the covenant made at Sinai, with its Israel-segregating laws and severe curse sanctions, would and could be an excellent means of preserving the integrity of Abraham's biological lineage and of preserving the memory of the pledge made thereto. Why then the law covenant? To preserve the integrity of Abraham's seed from the tendency of transgressors like Sarah, Abraham, and Hagar to forget and jeopardize God's pledges regarding Abraham's seed. "It was added because of transgressions."

I am not suggesting here that the term παράβασις is technical, a virtual synonym of what James D. G. Dunn believes ἔργα νόμου means. To the contrary, παράβασις is a fairly general term, and if there is any lexical tendency, it leans toward the pre-Sinai Adamic situation. It only appears three times in the LXX (2 Macc. 15:10; Ps. 101:3; Wis. 14:31), each fairly general. In the twelve instances in the Pseudepigrapha, eight appear to be Adamic:

> And slavery was not given to a woman, but because of the works of her hand; for it was not ordained that a slave should be a slave. It was not given from above, but came about through

oppression. Likewise neither was iniquity given from above, but it came from transgression [ἐκ παραβάσεως]. Likewise a woman was not created barren, but because of her wrong-doings she was punished with childlessness; [and] childless she will die. (1 Enoch 98:5)

And the prophet said: "Who made Adam the first-formed?" And God said: "My undefiled hands. And I put him in paradise to guard the food of the tree of life; and thereafter he became disobedient and did this in transgression [ἐν παραβάσει]." (Esdras 2:10–12)

Know therefore, O Baruch, that as Adam through this very tree obtained condemnation, and was divested of the glory of God, so also the people who now drink insatiably the wine that is begotten of it, transgress worse than Adam [χεῖρον τοῦ Ἀδὰμ τὴν παράβασιν ἀπεργάζονται], and are far from the glory of God, and are surrendering themselves to the eternal fire. (3 Baruch 4:16)

And at the transgression of the first Adam [ἐν τῇ παραβάσει τοῦ πρώτου Ἀδάμ], it was near to Sammael when he took the serpent as a garment. And it did not hide itself but increased, and God was angry with it, and afflicted it, and shortened its days. (3 Baruch 9:7)

The wild animals and the four-footed animals and the reptiles . . . spoke the same language before the transgression of the first-formed people [πρὸ τῆς παραβάσεως τοῖς πρωτοπλάστοις]. Therefore . . . the snake spoke in a human voice to Eve. . . . In the seventh year he transgressed and in the eighth they had cast (them) from Paradise . . . after forty-five days since the transgression [τῆς παραβάσεως], in the rising of Pleiades. Adam made in Paradise a calendar (consisting of) three hundred sixty five days. And he was cast out with the woman Eve, on account of the transgression [διὰ τὴν παράβασιν] on the tenth (day) of the month of May. (Jubilees 3:28, 32)

And he says to her: "Call all our children and our children's children and tell them the manner of our transgression [τὸν τρόπον τῆς παραβάσεως ἡμῶν]." (Life of Adam and Eve 14:3)

"And after the transgression inseparable [μετὰ τὴν παράβασιν ἀχώριστος], thus also should no one separate us." (Life of Adam and Eve 42:7)

Further, in the other four uses by Paul, two of those appear to be Adamic:

Yet death reigned from Adam to Moses, even over those whose sinning was not like the transgression of Adam [ἐπὶ τῷ ὁμοιώματι τῆς παραβάσεως Ἀδάμ], who was a type of the one who was to come. (Rom. 5:14)

And Adam was not deceived, but the woman was deceived and became a transgressor [ἐν παραβάσει γέγονεν]. (1 Tim. 2:14)

Thus the term παράβασις itself is probably the most general term possible for the kind of rebellion against God's purpose and will that began with Adam. But if humans have this tendency to revolt against the divine purpose, then what will Abraham's descendants likely do if they are delivered from bondage to the Egyptians and enter the land of Canaan? Will they remember the promises made to Father Abraham and pass them along from generation to generation? Will they retain their genetic/ethnic purity by preserving the integrity of that "seed" who will one day bless the nations? Or, by contrast, will they likely (as other humans) rebel against God's purposes, decide to get along by going along, intermarry with the Gentiles, forget their distinctive past and compromise (thereby) their distinctive future? To raise the question is to answer it. Apart from the Sinai covenant's stringent Gentile-excluding regulations, and apart from the severity of the curse sanctions that enforced them, the Israelites might have disappeared as a distinctive people within the first century or two in Canaan. Matthew would never have been able to write his first chapter as he did: "The book of the genealogy [Βίβλος γενέσεως] of Jesus Christ, the son of David, the son of Abraham [υἱοῦ Ἀβραάμ]." Abraham and Sarah would have long ago been forgotten as the Israelites intermarried with the Canaanites and served their gods, forgetting Yahweh and the pledges he made to the world through Abraham and his seed to come. Indeed, this pattern or tendency disclosed itself even before the Sinai covenant, within the Abrahamic narrative itself. Twice Abraham endangered his own lineage by prevaricating about whether Sarah was his wife or sister—a prevarication that could have had the effect of her serving as a concubine, and disrupting any possibility that the pledge to bless the world through their "seed" would ever be fulfilled (Gen. 12; 20). Only divine intervention rescued Abraham's "seed" from Abraham himself, and only the curse-threatening, Israel-segregating Sinai covenant continued to preserve that seed later.

Paul's answer to his own rhetorical question ("Why then the law?") is this: "It was added temporarily, because of the human tendency to rebel against God's purposes, *until* the Seed should come to whom the promise had been made." Once the seed would arrive, the Gentile-excluding Sinai covenant would no longer be necessary, because Abraham's lineage would by then have *been* preserved, and a people who remembered the pledges made to him would have been preserved. Matthew could write his first chapter; Paul could write Romans 4 and Galatians 3; and then the apostolic church would have the duty for the remainder of human history to tell the world about how Abraham's seed has brought blessings to all. This, I submit, is how the question and answer of this passage should be understood; not as a general, systematic-theological answer to "why then the law?"—because such an answer would require a discussion of tabernacle/temple, Levitical sacrifices, and many other things. Rather, here Paul is merely answering the specific question that would have been raised by anyone intelligently following his covenant-historical reasoning since 3:6. So, with that introduction, we now turn briefly to each of the two clusters of question/answer/further elaboration.

4.5.2. First Cluster

> Why then the law? It was added because of transgressions, until the offspring should come to whom the promise had been made, and it was put in place through angels by an intermediary.[67] Now an intermediary implies more than one, but God is one.

---

67. ESV follows RSV by translating ἐν χειρὶ μεσίτου as "by/through an intermediary." So also NRSV translates "by a mediator." Wiser (if not always cooler) heads prevailed in the seventeenth century, and the KJV rightly preserved the original: "in the *hand* of a mediator." While that exact expression does not appear in this form in the LXX, ἐν χειρὶ Μωυσῆ appears 18 times (Lev. 26:46; Num. 4:37, 42, 45; 9:23; 10:13; 15:23; 33:1; 36:13; Josh. 21:2; 22:9; Judges 3:4; 1 Kings 8:56; 1 Chron. 16:40; 2 Chron. 33:8; Neh. 9:14; 10:29; Ps. 77:20), and a similar expression, διὰ χειρὸς Μωυσῆ, appears twice (Lev. 10:11; 2 Chron. 34:14). Paul's expression is likely informed by this, and the more literal translation is preferable, because the Sinai narrative expressly in-

Paul had earlier argued that the "offspring" (σπέρμα) was singular (3:16), and he refers here to the singular "offspring" (τὸ σπέρμα) also. But the ἄχρις οὗ ἔλθη is not merely temporal; it is not mere accident or coincidence that the law is added, as a covenant administration, until the seed would come. Rather, this is woven into covenantal *purposes*: The law would manage and preserve the covenant people until the seed would come "to whom the promise had been made." That is, the law, though different in kind from the promissory covenant, served the purposes of that covenant. By preserving the integrity of Abraham's lineage through its Gentile-excluding regulations (enforced by the threatened curses), Sinai's job was to preserve such integrity until it was no longer needed. Sinai's role was to prevent the Israelites from hopelessly and irretrievably intermarrying and committing idolatry with the *am ha-aretz*; once it had preserved the integrity of Abraham's lineage until the seed came, it would no longer be needed; its purpose would have been fulfilled. From its outset, Paul argues, the law was ἄχρις οὗ ἔλθη τὸ σπέρμα ᾧ ἐπήγγελται. Since its goal/τέλος was to preserve the lineage of Abraham and the memory of pledges made to the world through that lineage, it would necessarily remain in place until the seed arrived, and not a moment longer. That is, the *terminus*/τέλος of the Sinai covenant coincided with the most important covenantal *purpose*/τέλος of the same covenant. Its covenantal purpose was to preserve the integrity of Abraham's seed and the memory of the pledges made thereto; and therefore when the pledged seed arrived, Sinai could (like an old general) retire honorably, move to Florida, and sip daiquiris for the remainder of his days.

Dominant Protestant interpretations of Galatians have misunderstood Paul's reasoning by underappreciating the "seed" theology of Paul and the biblical narrative that informed him. For Calvin to have dismissed the discussion of "ceremonies" in Galatians as "trifling,"[68] he must not have had categories at hand by which their true importance could have been properly weighed. Calvin (and those who embraced his misinterpretation of Galatians) failed to appreciate how important "offspring/seed" was to biblical theology. Note the repetition of such "offspring" language in the promises of the Abrahamic covenant. Seventeen times in Genesis, such seed language occurs in texts that convey the reality of God's promissory covenant with Abraham:

> Then the LORD appeared to Abram and said, "To your offspring [לְזַרְעֲךָ] I will give this land." So he built there an altar to the LORD, who had appeared to him. (Gen. 12:7)

---

dicated that Moses had the tablets of the covenant in his *hand*: "Moses turned and went down from the mountain with the two tablets of the testimony in his hands [ἐν ταῖς χερσὶν αὐτοῦ]" (Exod. 32:15; cf. also Exod. 32:19; 34:29; Deut. 9:15, 17; 10:3). Since the narrative records that the tablets of the covenant were carried by Moses in his hands, the expression "in the *hand* of" a mediator is a much more apt expression for the realities of the Sinai covenant than "by" or "through" a mediator/intermediary.

68. Calvin says, "We must remark, however, that he does not confine himself entirely to Ceremonies, but argues generally about Works, otherwise the whole discussion would be trifling." In John Calvin, *Commentaries on the Epistles of Paul to the Galatians and Ephesians* (Grand Rapids: Baker, 1979), 18. This statement by Calvin is doubly surprising; because even if he did not understand how or why the discussion of ceremonies was important, he surely knew that they had all been instituted by God for *some* purpose (however inscrutable the purpose may have been), so one would expect Calvin not to refer to divine institutions as "trifling."

"For all the land that you see I will give to you and to your offspring [ולזרעך] forever."
(Gen. 13:15)

On that day the LORD made a covenant with Abram, saying, "To your offspring [לזרעך] I
give this land, from the river of Egypt to the great river, the river Euphrates." (Gen. 15:18)

"And I will establish my covenant between me and you and your offspring [זרעך] after you
throughout their generations for an everlasting covenant, to be God to you and to your
offspring [ולזרעך] after you. And I will give to you and to your offspring [ולזרעך] after you
the land of your sojournings, all the land of Canaan, for an everlasting possession, and I
will be their God." (Gen. 17:7–8)

God said, "No, but Sarah your wife shall bear you a son, and you shall call his name Isaac.
I will establish my covenant [בריתי] with him as an everlasting covenant for his offspring
[לזרעו] after him." (Gen. 17:19)

"The LORD, the God of heaven, who took me from my father's house and from the land
of my kindred, and who spoke to me and swore to me, 'To your offspring [לזרעך] I will
give this land,' he will send his angel before you, and you shall take a wife for my son from
there." (Gen. 24:7)

"Sojourn in this land, and I will be with you and will bless you, for to you and to your
offspring [ולזרעך] I will give all these lands, and I will establish the oath that I swore to
Abraham your father. I will multiply your offspring [זרעך] as the stars of heaven and will
give to your offspring [לזרעך] all these lands. And in your offspring [בזרעך] all the nations
of the earth shall be blessed." (Gen. 26:3–4)

"May he give the blessing of Abraham to you and to your offspring [ולזרעך] with you, that you
may take possession of the land of your sojournings that God gave to Abraham!" (Gen. 28:4)

And behold, the LORD stood above it and said, "I am the LORD, the God of Abraham your
father and the God of Isaac. The land on which you lie I will give to you and to your offspring [ולזרעך]." (Gen. 28:13)

"The land that I gave to Abraham and Isaac I will give to you, and I will give the land to
your offspring [ולזרעך] after you." (Gen. 35:12)

"And [he] said to me, 'Behold, I will make you fruitful and multiply you, and I will make
of you a company of peoples and will give this land to your offspring [לזרעך] after you for
an everlasting possession.'" (Gen. 48:4)

We observe also how often in Genesis the narrative tension centers on the question
of the continuation of Abraham's seed. Abraham laughed in disbelief about the promise
that he would have offspring (Gen. 17:17). Sarah also disbelievingly laughed about the
pledge of offspring and then prevaricated about her laughter and was corrected by God
(Gen. 18:10–15). Sarah conspired with Hagar to provide an offspring for Abraham (Gen.
16; 21). Abraham prevaricated about Sarah being his sister (Gen. 12; 20), thus endangering her and the offspring she would bear (and God delivered her). Judah failed in his
Levirate duty toward providing a descendant for Er through Tamar; he would have had
Tamar put to death unjustly, yet eventually recognized that she had rightly taken action
to preserve the lineage, and so he confessed, "She is more righteous than I" (Gen. 38).

And, of course, the literary and redemptive-historical backdrop to all this discussion of Abraham's offspring is the Adamic narrative, and especially the curse-and-pledge-of-redemption of Genesis 3:15: "I will put enmity between you and the woman, and between your *offspring* [זרעך] and her *offspring* [זרעה]; he shall bruise your head, and you shall bruise his heel." And while the collective noun for "offspring" may be indeterminate in Genesis 3:15, leaving open the possibility that it is Adam's or Eve's offspring collectively or individually understood, it is less ambiguous in its next occurrence at 4:25, where Eve said, "God has appointed for me another offspring [זרע] instead of Abel, for Cain killed him." Thus the Pauline understanding of "offspring" as singular was a possibility not only before Paul but also before any pledges were made to Abraham and to *his* "offspring."

All of this discussion of offspring may strike our ears as peculiar, and we may dismiss it or overlook it at our pleasure. But it is undoubtedly a significant part of the theology of Genesis and therefore of the entire theology of the Hebrew Bible informed by it. It is equally significant to the theology of Matthew, who titled his Gospel, "The book of the *genealogy* [Βίβλος γενέσεως] of Jesus Christ, the son of David, the son of Abraham [υἱοῦ Ἀβραάμ]." And what is the initial clause of a Gospel so titled? "Abraham was the father of Isaac." When Matthew concluded this section, and before he began the narrative of Jesus's earthly life, he wrote, "So all the generations from Abraham to David were fourteen generations, and from David to the deportation to Babylon fourteen generations and from the deportation to Babylon to the Christ fourteen generations" (1:17).

In Paul's theology also, the preservation of Abraham's lineage is crucial. The narrative that leads ultimately to the blessing of "all the nations of the earth" (Gen. 26:4) is a narrative that consistently runs *through* Abraham's offspring *to* those nations. As the nations/Gentiles/benefactors of the Abrahamic pledge, we may merely be concerned *that* we ourselves are blessed; Moses, Matthew, and Paul were also concerned that such blessing would come through Abraham's offspring. The Sinai covenant, by segregating Abraham's descendants from the *am ha-aretz*, therefore served a crucial role in the history of redemption. Had Abraham's descendants intermarried willy-nilly with the people of the land, the Abrahamic pledge—in its particular form—could never have been fulfilled. By this reasoning, the Sinai covenant was *both* necessary (to preserve the Abrahamic lineage) *and* temporary (because the ultimate goal was to bless all nations, not just one). It was therefore "added . . . until the offspring [τὸ σπέρμα] should come to whom the promise had been made." The Sinai ceremonies that Calvin regarded as "trifling" were not that at all; they were *essential* to protecting and preserving the lineage of Abraham from their rebellious tendency to intermarry with the people of the land.[69]

The "further elaboration" part of this cluster of three parts is even more cryptic, but I think not inscrutably so: "And it was put in place through angels by an intermediary.[70]

---

69. Even Calvin's language reveals his tone deafness about this point. He referred to "ceremonies," rather than to "Israel-segregating ceremonies" or "Gentile-excluding ceremonies." He perceived these as mere ceremonies and therefore regarded the issue of ceremonies as "trifling." But had he perceived the ceremonies of circumcision, diet, and calendar as Paul did—as ceremonies that distinguished Israel from the nations—he might have regarded them by some term other than "trifling."

70. ESV translates μεσίτης as "intermediary," as does RSV, though the KJV/NRSV have "mediator." I am not sure much is gained or lost with either, but I suspect "mediator" is a slightly

Now an intermediary implies more than one,[71] but God is one." Recall that just a few verses earlier in 3:15, Paul began to distinguish human covenants (ἀνθρώπου κεκυρωμένην διαθήκην) from divine covenants (διαθήκην προκεκυρωμένην ὑπὸ τοῦ θεοῦ), so he has already begun distinguishing the superiority of divine covenants over human ones. Since the mediator/μεσίτης by whom the Sinai covenant was made was/is the well-known Moses, we know here who the mediator was.[72] We are unsure who the angels are; we are sure who Moses was, but then the curious tautology is articulated: "Now an intermediary implies more than one, but God is one." Well, of course, an intermediary implies more than one; so the tautology appears to be an unnecessary one, until the next clause appears: "but God is one"—a reference to the *Shema* that, at first glance, seems peculiar or gratuitous. But if Paul is answering his own question, a question that arises from his covenant-historical reasoning in the earlier verses, then the matter is not so difficult. The Sinai covenant has two parties, Yahweh and Israel, and it depends on both for whatever fruition it will achieve. Yahweh will either bless or curse, dependent upon Israel's obedience or disobedience; and Moses stands as mediator between these two parties. When Israel obeys, Moses cries out to Yahweh as mediator on their behalf; when they disobey, he explains to them why (e.g.) fiery serpents come upon them. But the Abrahamic covenant has no such provision. Yahweh appears to Abraham and simply pledges, univocally, to bless him, his descendants, and the world through them. Period. No threats about what Yahweh will do if Sarah laughs at the promises (and then prevaricates about having laughed at them). No threats about what Yahweh will do if Sarah and Abraham drag Hagar in as an alternate means of getting what they don't believe Yahweh can provide. No threats are made if Abraham prevaricates about whether Sarah is his wife or sister. No, nothing is contingent on

---

more technical term suggestive of a legal matter; if so, it is to be preferred here, since the passage deals throughout with the solemnizing of a treaty. In a passage that employs the language of "ratify," "ratify before," and "de-ratify," it may be better to say "mediator."

71. ESV is mildly paraphrastic here, adding "*implies* more than one," as does RSV. NRSV is a shade more paraphrastic: "Now a mediator involves more than one party." The Greek says, "a mediator is not of one" (ὁ δὲ μεσίτης ἑνὸς οὐκ ἔστιν), as does the KJV, which never shied away from fairly straightforward literalism. The reasoning in each case is clear: A mediator is needed only between two parties; a single party would not need mediation.

72. Though more sleuthing will need to be done to answer satisfactorily who the angelic beings at Sinai actually were or where the tradition suggesting such originated. The solution is not critical for my purposes, however, since angelic beings are also not deities. Moses' covenant arrives mediated by two created parties: angels and Moses; Abraham's covenant has no such intermediaries at all. It could be a reference to Deut. 33:2: "The LORD came from Sinai, and dawned from Seir upon us; he shone forth from Mount Paran, he came from the ten thousands of holy ones [ἄγγελοι], with flaming fire at his right hand." There are references to Moses and angels on the mount in the Testament of Moses 6 and 9, but these appear to refer to the end of Moses' life, not to the covenanting at Sinai. Similarly, Jubilees 2:10 refers to God addressing Moses through an angel, and the content of that is the Sabbath command. Cf. the thorough survey of Second Temple material in Hindy Nahman, "Angels at Sinai: Exegesis, Theology and Interpretive Authority," *Dead Sea Discoveries* 7, no. 3 (January 1, 2000): 313–33. Hans Hübner's suggestion that the angels are, effectively, demons is intriguing but not compelling (though a version of the theory is proposed also by J. Louis Martyn, *Galatians*). It is just as possible that Paul views the angels as reminding of the *heavenly* origin, not a demonic origin, of the Sinai covenant. Cf. Hübner, *Law in Paul's Thought*, trans. James C. G. Greig (Edinburgh: T & T Clark, 1984), 26–27.

Abraham and Sarah, and no mediator is needed between Yahweh and them. This one is "all on Yahweh," as it were; he either keeps his pledges or he doesn't, but Abraham and Sarah *do* not have and do not *need* to have a mediator. All they have, and all they need to have, is the one true and living God whom Israel confesses in the *Shema*. This appears to be how Lightfoot understood the matter:

> The very idea of mediation supposes two persons at least, between whom the mediation is carried on. The law then is of the nature of a contract between two parties, God on the one hand, and the Jewish people on the other. It is only valid so long as both parties fulfil the terms of the contract. It is therefore contingent and not absolute. . . . ὁ δὲ θεὸς εἷς ἐστιν *"but God (the giver of the promise) is one."* Unlike the law, the promise is absolute and unconditional. It depends on the sole decree of God. There are not two contracting parties. There is nothing in the nature of a stipulation. The giver is everything, the recipient nothing.[73]

4.5.3. Second Cluster

> Is the law then contrary to the promises of God? Certainly not! For if a law[74] had been given that could give life,[75] then righteousness would indeed be by the law. But the Scripture imprisoned[76] everything under sin, so that the promise by faith in Jesus Christ might be given to those who believe.

Though the law covenant is different in five ways from the promise covenant, Paul argues that it is not contrary to it, because it is not a different means of attaining the same thing. Note also that two realities of the eschaton are associated here: making alive and acquittal/righteousness. Any instrument that could inaugurate one aspect of the eschaton could inaugurate the other aspects, but the law is not able (δυνάμενος) to do so. Paul's reasoning here, perhaps as cryptic as in the first cluster of question/ answer/further elaboration, is clear enough on at least one point: the Sinai covenant

---

73. Lightfoot, *Commentary*. Parentheses and italics are his, so note that the parenthetical comment discloses Lightfoot's opinion that what was unstated was that God was "the giver of the promise." Since the Abrahamic covenant is promissory, it does not depend on Abraham's or Sarah's obedience to any stipulations; it depends for its fruition only on the fidelity of the promising God. My interpretation focuses, then, on the contrast between the mediated-because-conditional Mosaic covenant and the unmediated-because-unconditionally-pledged Abrahamic covenant. This interpretation does not exclude the possibility of S. M. Baugh's inter-Trinitarian interpretation (a pledge between the Father and the Son): "No one can mediate between these two parties to the covenantal agreement, for they are both members of the one, triune God. They are not, in fact, two separate parties, but represent the one God originating and effecting our redemption." Cf. Baugh, "Galatians 3:20 and the Covenant of Redemption," 66.

74. KJV, RSV, NRSV, and ESV all translate the first νόμος here as "a law" yet translate the second (νόμου) as "the law," though both are anarthrous. Paul is not speaking hypothetically about some other law in the first clause; he is still continuing the reasoning he began earlier, contrasting the Sinai covenant to the Abrahamic covenant. It would be just as well to render it in such a manner that this is clear, such as: "If the law that was given was able to make alive, then righteousness would be by the law." This contrary-to-fact condition is defective only by not including the particle ἄν, but this "defect" is common in the NT.

75. ESV (similarly KJV) renders ζῳοποιῆσαι as "give life" that, while not objectionable per se, unnecessarily evades/avoids a more straightforward rendering, "make alive" (so RSV, NRSV).

76. Since the verb συγκλείω appears again in the next verse, I reserve discussion about its meaning to that point.

was sub-eschatological. The "life" available by that administration was only temporal life in the land of Canaan; it was not Edenic life, free of sin and mortality: "Justice, and only justice, you shall follow, that you may live and inherit the land that the LORD your God is giving you" (Deut. 16:20). The pair of "life and death" that Yahweh set before Israel (Deut. 30:19) was not eschatological life or death but earthly well-being in the temporal land of Canaan:

> If you obey the commandments of the LORD your God that I command you today, by loving the LORD your God, by walking in his ways, and by keeping his commandments and his statutes and his rules, then you shall live and multiply [ζήσεσθε καὶ πολλοὶ ἔσεσθε], and the LORD your God will bless you in the land that you are entering to take possession of it. But if your heart turns away, and you will not hear, but are drawn away to worship other gods and serve them, I declare to you today, that you shall surely perish. You shall not live long [οὐ μὴ πολυήμεροι γένησθε] in the land that you are going over the Jordan to enter and possess. (Deut. 30:16–18)

Obedience to Sinai's statutes would give the Israelites a legitimate covenantal claim to a long tenure in the land; disobedience would lead (and did lead) to exile.[77] But original Edenic life, forfeited by Adam, could not be restored by the terms of the Sinai administration; Sinai could not "make alive" those who had become mortal through Adam's transgression.

The life pledged in the Abrahamic administration, however, was real eschatological life (though Paul only implies such here; he does not elucidate).[78] For Abraham and Sarah to have natural children at their advanced point in life was virtually miraculous, a point Paul made elsewhere at Romans 4:17: "'I have made you the father of many nations'—in the presence of the God in whom he believed, who gives life to the dead [θεοῦ τοῦ ζωοποιοῦντος τοὺς νεκρούς] and calls into existence the things that do not exist." In this text, Paul associated Abraham and Sarah's descendants with the affirmation

---

77. One frequently encounters the assumption that whenever Paul speaks of curses or blessings he means eschatological ones, but this need not be so; the curses/blessings at Mount Ebal and Mount Gerizim were temporal and earthly, not eternal or heavenly. In unpacking Paul's reasoning at Gal. 3:10, for example, Thomas R. Schreiner even adds the assumption to his translation: "Therefore, those who rely on the works of the law *for salvation* are cursed" (emphasis mine). Neither "rely on" nor "for salvation" are in the original text, and the assumption that they are leads to misunderstanding many of Paul's statements about the Sinai covenant. Cf. Schreiner, *The Law and Its Fulfillment*, 44.

78. Some of the evidence of this eschatological character may be found in the pledge that Abraham's descendants would be as numerous as "the stars of heaven" (Gen. 15:5; 22:17; 26:4), which appears to be glossed eschatologically by the author of Hebrews, who said of Abraham: "Therefore from one man, *and him as good as dead*, were born descendants as many as the stars of heaven" (Heb. 11:12), a passage that surely suggests resurrection life as does Rom. 4:17. Similarly, the eschatological nature is disclosed in the reversal of the Adamic curse of Gen. 3:14–18. In the narrative of Genesis, the looming question is: What or who can deliver mortal humanity from the curses of Genesis 3? The answer begins to appear in Abraham's first encounter with God, who pledges to him: "I will make of you a great nation, and I will bless you and make your name great, so that you will be a blessing. I will bless those who bless you, and him who dishonors you I will curse, and in you all the families of the earth shall be blessed" (Gen. 12:2–3). Contextually, this is not merely earthly blessing in the land of Canaan; it is a global reversal of the Adamic curse itself.

that God makes alive those who are dead. What is cryptic about our Galatians passage is that Paul does not expressly say here what he did in Romans 4: that God makes alive the dead, and that this is a reality pledged in the Abrahamic promise. Rather, in our text, Paul denies that the Sinai covenant can make alive and hopes/assumes that, in a context where he has already contrasted the two administrations, his audience will understand his implications (a pious wish that has not proven entirely true in the history of interpretation).

Underneath this reasoning is the deeply Adamic structure of Paul's thinking disclosed in texts such as Romans 5:12–21, in which there is a relationship between sin/trespass/disobedience-condemnation-death in Adam, and righteousness/obedience-acquittal-life in Christ:

> If, because of one man's trespass, death reigned [ὁ θάνατος ἐβασίλευσεν] through that one man, much more will those who receive the abundance of grace and the free gift of righteousness reign in life [ἐν ζωῇ βασιλεύσουσιν] through the one man Jesus Christ. Therefore, as one trespass led to condemnation [κατάκριμα] for all men, so one act of righteousness leads to justification and life [εἰς δικαίωσιν ζωῆς] for all men. (Rom. 5:17–18)

Those familiar with this underlying structure therefore understand why Paul states that if the law could *make alive*, then it could also provide *righteousness*; but it can, in fact, do neither. What is pledged to Abraham, however, is nothing less than the reversal of the Adamic curse by Abraham's seed.[79] In our context, Paul says that the law is not "contrary to" the promise, because it is not a would-be alternative means of providing what only the fruition of the Abrahamic pledge could provide.

The further elaboration of Paul's statement in verse 22 continues to be cryptic: "But the Scripture imprisoned everything under sin, so that the promise by faith in Jesus Christ might be given to those who believe." Paul's personification of Scripture here is both unusual and unspecified. *Which* Scripture "imprisoned everything [τὰ πάντα] under sin"? "Scripture" here is singular (ἡ γραφὴ) not plural (αἱ γραφαὶ), though the singular could be a reference to Scripture as a totality. Since the "everything" (NRSV "all things") here is neuter plural, it is probably more than merely humans, and it probably suggests the curse of Genesis 3 that brought curses on the natural creation in addition to the humans. Paul does not seem as concerned to identify which Scripture consigns the created order "under sin" as he is to indicate that the ultimate purpose of this consignment was/is that the Abrahamic promise might be given by faith in Jesus Christ to those who believe, continuing his contrast between the faith characteristic of the Abrahamic administration (which needs no mediator, since it depends upon God only) and the works characteristic of the Sinai administration (which needs a mediator, since it depends upon Israelite obedience), a contrast that has been reiterated unabated since Galatians 3:6.

---

79. Moses provided some background to understanding "seed" correctly in the Abrahamic narrative. Before recording God's pledges to Abraham in Gen. 12:7—"To your offspring [לזרעך] I will give this land"—Moses had already introduced the idea of "seed" initially in Gen. 3:15, where plainly it refers to a reversal of the Adamic curse: "I will put enmity between you and the woman, and between your offspring and her offspring; he shall bruise your head, and you shall bruise his heel."

New Perspective authors have rightly reminded us that the faith/works antithesis in Paul's thought is not, ordinarily, a mere or bare contrast between faith in the abstract and works in the abstract; rather, it is a contrast between faith in *Christ* (or of Christ) and works of the *law*, a point I made in a 1987 essay on the problem at Galatia.[80] What some New Perspective authors overlook, however, is that this contrast itself reflects a divine/human antithesis beneath it. The contrast is faith in what the unique God-man has done to reverse the Adamic curse versus works required by the Mosaic covenant of mere mortal (and sinful) humans. So, while on the exegetical level in its strictest sense, I heartily concur that it is not just *any* faith that Paul contrasts with *any* works; on a theological level, there is a real antithesis between what God can alone do in rescuing his creation and what mortal, sinful humans can do to extend their tenure in the land of Canaan. The Sinai covenant was never intended to reverse Adamic mortality; it could not make alive. But what God pledged to do for and through Abraham was indeed to make alive; first, through an old barren couple having numerous descendants, and later, through resurrecting their (singular) seed and all who are united to him.

4.6. Galatians 3:23–25

> Now before faith came, we were held captive under the law, imprisoned until the coming faith would be revealed. So then, the law was our guardian until Christ came, in order that we might be justified by faith. But now that faith has come, we are no longer under a guardian.

These three verses could easily be understood as part of a pericope that continues through verse 29, since at 4:1 the Λέγω δέ appears to begin a distinct unit. On the other hand, verse 26 does appear to begin a slight shift, since the first-person plural of 23–25 shifts there to seven instances of the second-person plural (five verbs, two personal pronouns). Further, the logic of this brief pericope is contained in the two temporal clauses that have the same noun, ἡ πίστις. The pericope is bracketed by "before faith came" (Πρὸ τοῦ δὲ ἐλθεῖν τὴν πίστιν) and "now that faith has come" (ἐλθούσης δὲ τῆς πίστεως). Somewhat oddly, ESV, RSV, NRSV, and Nestle-Aland all take verse 26 as part of 23ff. and begin a new subunit at 27. The resolution of the matter is not critical, since either way the concluding verses of chapter 3 are all conclusions that genuinely derive from what is said earlier in the chapter. Since I regard the shifts from first to second person to be fairly intentional in Galatians, and since I regard the two temporal clauses employing ἡ πίστις as intentionally bracketing the subsection, I will follow KJV in beginning the next section at verse 26 rather than verse 27.

Here, in these brief several lines, we perceive the value of reading the Pauline synecdoches correctly. Here, for Paul, ἡ πίστις is not some existential human capacity; in this passage, as many commentators have rightly observed, it is a synecdoche for the new covenant, a covenant that is characterized by faith in the dying and rising Christ. Four times Paul uses the noun in this brief passage, and four times he refers to the law either by ὁ νόμος itself or by the figure he employs for it, παιδαγωγός. Note also that Paul employs five temporal modifiers in this brief section: "*before* faith came

---

80. "The Problem at Galatia," *Interpretation* 41 (January 1987): 32–43.

. . . imprisoned *until* the coming faith . . . *until* Christ came . . . *now* that faith has come
. . . *no longer* under a guardian," even though the fourth of these is merely implicit in
the genitive absolute construction ἐλθούσης δὲ τῆς πίστεως. Since Paul indicated
earlier that Abraham had faith and that all who had faith are his children, plainly Paul
knew that "faith" in the human existential sense was here long before the law; "faith"
as synecdoche for the new covenant came later. But the "faith" he refers to here is a
historical reality: "until the coming faith would be revealed" (εἰς τὴν μέλλουσαν πίστιν
ἀποκαλυφθῆναι). Both μέλλουσαν and ἀποκαλυφθῆναι are often profoundly historical
terms for Paul, and they surely are here, with the five temporal qualifiers. Note several
other uses of these terms to describe historical, even epochal, matters:

> Yet death reigned from Adam to Moses, even over those whose sins were not like the
> transgression of Adam, who was a type of the one who was to come [τύπος τοῦ μέλλοντος].
> (Rom. 5:14)

> For I consider that the sufferings of this present time are not worth comparing with the
> glory that is to be revealed [τὴν μέλλουσαν δόξαν ἀποκαλυφθῆναι] to us. (Rom. 8:18)

> For I am sure that neither death nor life, nor angels nor rulers, nor things present nor things
> to come [μέλλοντα],[81] nor powers . . . (Rom. 8:38)

> Each one's work will become manifest, for the Day will disclose it, because it will be re-
> vealed by fire [ἐν πυρὶ ἀποκαλύπτεται], and the fire will test what sort of work each one
> has done. (1 Cor. 3:13)

> Whether Paul or Apollos or Cephas or the world or life or death or the present or the future
> [εἴτε ἐνεστῶτα εἴτε μέλλοντα]—all are yours. (1 Cor. 3:22)

> Let no one deceive you in any way. For that day will not come, unless the rebellion comes
> first, and the man of lawlessness is revealed [καὶ ἀποκαλυφθῇ ὁ ἄνθρωπος τῆς ἀνομίας],
> the son of destruction. (2 Thess. 2:3; also 2:6, 8)

The underlying covenant-historical structure to Paul's reasoning is, I suggest, promise-
law-faith. Three covenants appear at different moments in history, all tending toward
the same ultimate goal of reversing the Adamic curse but each having distinctive proximate purposes. The three synecdoches describe their distinctive roles and distinctive
natures, even though they ultimately serve a common end. In our particular pericope,
he moves from discussing the relation between the Abrahamic and the Sinai covenants
to discussing the relation of the Sinai covenant to the new covenant. That is, he earlier
placed Sinai as "430 years after the promise"; here he places it "before" and "until" faith.
    Verse 23 continues matters raised in the previous pericope, as is evident from the
repetition of the verb συνέκλεισεν . . . συγκλειόμενοι. Translators of the verb in either
verse 22 or verse 23 face the challenge of whether to render the verb connotatively

---

81. The participle μέλλοντα is somewhat surprisingly anarthrous: οὔτε θάνατος οὔτε ζωὴ
οὔτε ἄγγελοι οὔτε ἀρχαὶ οὔτε ἐνεστῶτα οὔτε μέλλοντα οὔτε δυνάμεις. Perhaps μέλλοντα as a
reference to the future had become sufficiently technical in Paul's day that it, like ἐνεστῶτα, did
not need the definite article either to make it substantive or to make it technical. Note that the
other nouns here (e.g., θάνατος and ζωὴ) are also anarthrous.

positive ("guarded/preserved"), connotatively negative ("locked up"), or connotatively neutral ("under lock and key"). It is not an easy matter for the translators, since the verb appears only here in the NT and in two other places, Luke 5:6 and Romans 11:32. In the latter of which the context indeed suggests a negative connotation: "For God has consigned [συνέκλεισεν] all men to disobedience, that he may have mercy upon all." The former is slightly less negative, and merely refers to the fishing nets encircling the catch of fish: "And when they had done this, they enclosed a great shoal of fish [συνέκλεισαν πλῆθος ἰχθύων]." Now, from the fish's point of view, this was surely imprisonment; but the verb itself refers to the way the nets encircle them and is fairly neutral. The verb is a compound of σύν and κλείω, and the question for translators is whether this "locking" is to be regarded as a positive, negative, or neutral thing; a matter that appears again in a moment with the main verb φρουρέω. I suggest that the main verb should have some control over the dependent verb, so let us consider φρουρέω first.

Three times φρουρέω appears elsewhere in the NT, twice in Paul. In 2 Corinthians 11:32, Paul mentions that the governor of Damascus had the city guarded (ἐφρούρει τὴν πόλιν) in order that he might arrest Paul. In this context, it appears not so much that the city was locked up/imprisoned, but that guards were posted to be on lookout for Paul. In Philippians 4:7, Paul says that God's peace, which surpasses understanding, will "keep," or "preserve," or "protect" the hearts and minds of the Philippians (φρουρήσει τὰς καρδίας ὑμῶν καὶ τὰ νοήματα ὑμῶν). Here also, the idea of preserving or protecting is more prominent than that of "locking up," "confining," or "restricting." In 1 Peter 1:5, Peter speaks of the saints as those who are, by the power of God, "kept," "preserved," or "protected" through the agency of faith in Christ for a salvation that is prepared to appear in the last season (τοὺς ἐν δυνάμει θεοῦ φρουρουμένους διὰ πίστεως εἰς σωτηρίαν ἑτοίμην ἀποκαλυφθῆναι ἐν καιρῷ ἐσχάτῳ). Like the other NT uses, this one has to do with protection or preservation, but not with imprisonment. In each of these cases, the force of the term has to do with guarding or protecting; it does not have the negative connotation of confinement or restriction.

For this reason, I believe that συνέκλεισεν . . . συγκλειόμενοι should also be translated in either a connotatively neutral or positive manner.[82] When we lock our homes, we do so not to imprison ourselves but to preserve/protect ourselves from harm. And while the prefix can make the verb mean a different thing, its usage in the LXX can be neutral or positive. Sometimes, it is merely a reference to a thing being "shut" or "closed," such as a womb (Gen. 16:2; 20:18; 1 Sam. 1:6). Sometimes it refers to the "overlay" of gold on the sanctuary or altar (1 Kings 6:20; 7:49). But it also used to mean the locking up of a city as a defensive/protective measure when under military siege:

> Now Jericho was shut up inside [συγκεκλεισμένη] and outside because of the people of Israel. None went out, and none came in [οὐθεὶς ἐξεπορεύετο ἐξ αὐτῆς οὐδὲ εἰσεπορεύετο]. (Josh. 6:1)

> When Holofernes, the general of the Assyrian army, heard that the people of Israel had prepared for war and had closed [συνέκλεισαν] the passes in the hills and fortified all the high hilltops and set up barricades in the plains . . . (Jdt. 5:1)

---

82. So Dunn, "This role attributed to the law is essentially positive. . . . So what Paul had in mind was almost certainly a *protective* custody." *Galatians*, 197 (emphasis his).

He [Judas] set fire to the harbor by night, and burned the boats, and massacred those who had taken refuge there. Then, because the city's gates were closed [συγκλεισθέντος], he withdrew, intending to come again and root out the whole community of Joppa. (2 Macc. 12:6–7)

Consider also these uses of the related noun, συγκλεισμός.

Foreigners lost heart and came trembling out of their fortresses [ἐκ τῶν συγκλεισμῶν αὐτῶν]. (2 Sam. 22:46)

They shall lick the dust like a serpent, like the crawling things of the earth; they shall come trembling out of their strongholds [ἐν συγκλεισμῷ αὐτῶν]. (Mic. 7:17)

And you, take an iron griddle, and place it as an iron wall between you and the city; and set your face toward it, and let it be in a state of siege [ἐν συγκλεισμῷ], and press the siege against it [συγκλείσεις]. (Ezek. 4:3)

A third part you shall burn in the fire in the midst of the city, when the days of the siege [τῶν ἡμερῶν τοῦ συγκλεισμοῦ] are completed. (Ezek. 5:2)

In each of these texts, the protective/guardian nature of the word is emphasized, more than the restrictive/punitive use (though the word can also be used for those who lay siege to a city). Note, in the case of military siege, that the same act of locking one party *in* is an act that locks another party *out*. But neither party, to use our contemporary language, is being locked *up*. My concern regarding "imprison" or "constrain" language is that I believe it suggests to our contemporary ears the notion of locking *up*. If the usage of the vocabulary to refer to military sieges informs Paul's usage, then the import is on locking someone (Jews?) in and someone (Gentiles?) out. In light of everything else said in this letter about the law, and in light of Paul's specific references to the "marking" dimensions of the law, I suggest this is the best way to understand the matter here. The Israel-segregating Sinai covenant (ὁ νόμος) was like the gates of Jericho: "Now Jericho was shut up [συγκεκλεισμένη] inside and outside because of the people of Israel. None went out [ἐξεπορεύετο], and none came in [εἰσεπορεύετο]" (Josh. 6:1). The Sinai covenant, like a reversal of Jericho's gates, would not allow the Jews outside (to intermarry with the Gentiles) nor the Gentiles inside (to intermarry with the Jews).

In light of the fact that the main verb φρουρέω appears to have a positive (protective/ guardian) sense elsewhere in the NT, and in light of the occasional usage of συγκλείω or συγκλεισμός in the LXX to refer to a protective/preservative/guardian lock, I propose that we read the language that way here in Galatians. We considered earlier in the previous pericope that when the law was added "*because* of transgressions," this need not be understood as "*punishment for* transgressions" or even "*revealer* of transgressions," but more "*protection* from transgression," especially the particular transgression of intermarrying with the Gentiles and thereby destroying both the genealogical integrity of Abraham's seed and the memory of the promises made thereto. That is, the Sinai covenant, as a Gentile-excluding covenant, had a purpose for excluding Gentiles; and that purpose was to protect/preserve/promote the integrity of Abraham's seed and the memory of the pledges made thereto, "until the seed would come."

So, when Paul speaks here of the temporary nature of the Sinai covenant, he also speaks of the good and important role this temporary covenant played in preserving the integrity of Abraham's lineage and memory of the pledge to bless the world one day through a single member of that lineage. Had Israel not locked their doors to the Gentiles, as it were, they would have intermarried, destroyed or diluted Abraham's line of descent, and probably forgotten any specific pledges made to those descendants. Therefore, just as φρουρέω ordinarily has a positive, protective denotation in the other NT texts, and just as συγκλείω (and its related noun) can be used in the same protective senses, I believe it is better to understand Paul as simultaneously speaking of both a temporary and yet positive role of the Sinai administration. In other words, Sinai was not temporary because it failed (though perhaps the Israelites were exiled under its conditional curse sanction), nor was it merely temporary because its punitive/chastening purposes had now ended; it was temporary because its *preservative* function had now ended. Abraham's seed was born, lived, died, and was raised, and blessings are now proclaimed in his name to all nations. In this sense, the Sinai administration succeeded in its purpose; it did indeed preserve/ protect the lineage of Abraham sufficiently that Jesus of Nazareth could be identified as the Abrahamic seed to whom the pledge to bless the nations came.

To put this differently, the interpretive issues in this pericope are similar to those in the previous one. When Paul asked "Why then the law?" (3:19), he was not asking a general question of systematic theology. He was asking a covenant-historical question in light of the five contrasts he had earlier made between the Abrahamic and Sinai covenants. If these covenants differ in five important ways, then why have the second one at all? What could possibly have been the purpose of a works-based, curse-threatening, Gentile-excluding covenant if God had pledged to bless all the nations/Gentiles by faith one day? Paul began answering that specific question in 3:19–22, and he continued to answer it again here by calling attention to the important protective/guarding role that this Gentile-excluding covenant played. Oddly enough, excluding the Gentiles for a *season* was beneficial and necessary in order to bless the Gentiles (and Jews) *later*.

This understanding is not substantially different from that expressed in the Letter of Aristeas (137–139):

> The makers and authors of these myths think that they are the wisest of the Greeks. Why need we speak of other infatuated people, Egyptians and the like? . . . Now our Lawgiver [ὁ νομοθέτης], being a wise man and specially endowed by God to understand all things, took a comprehensive view of each particular detail, and fenced us round [περιέφραξεν] with impregnable ramparts and walls of iron [ἀδιακόποις χάραξι καὶ σιδηροῖς τείχεσιν], that we might not mingle at all [ἐπιμισγώμεθα κατὰ μηδέν] with any of the other nations [τῶν ἄλλων ἐθνῶν], but remain pure in body and soul, free from all vain imaginations, worshiping the one Almighty God above the whole creation.

The Letter of Aristeas associates Moses "the lawgiver" with making fences and ramparts to prevent the Jews from mingling with the other nations. Aristeas goes on to argue that this law was to protect them from the idolatry so associated with the other peoples; whereas for Paul, the law preserves the integrity of the "seed" of Abraham. But in each case, separation from the nations around them was both necessary and a servant to a high and positive end.

This understanding also helps us in identifying the twice-mentioned παιδαγωγός of verses 23 and 24, a matter I have addressed in greater detail elsewhere.[83] It is well

---

83. "A Note on ΠΑΙΔΑΓΩΓΟΣ in Gal. 3. 24–25," *New Testament Studies* 35, no. 1 (January 1989): 150–54. Cf. also, Linda L. Belleville, "'Under Law': Structural Analysis and the Pauline

established in the primary literature that παιδαγωγός was a general term for any in-dividual (ordinarily a slave) who had responsibilities for the care of children in some way; and it is reasonably well agreed upon that the term itself, therefore, can be used to designate a variety of different roles that such slaves played in the Greco-Roman world. Among common roles that the παιδαγωγός might play were an instructional role, a disciplinary role, and a bodyguard role. On two grounds, I suggest that the last understanding is preferable here, even though the other two would make theological sense in other theological contexts. First, I believe the temporal language here ("before," "until," "no longer") suggests that Paul is referring not to some eternal reality about the law, but a temporary reality. Second, as we observed above, Paul's teaching about the law here is designed to explain why it was necessary for the law to exclude ("lock out") Gentiles for a season of history.

Luther is well known for understanding the law as a harsh, disciplinary "taskmaster" that drives us to find relief in grace. To be sure, the Mosaic law could indeed and did indeed function in such a manner, and perhaps does so today. Calvin was about as well known for talking about the law's third use to teach us how to live. I have no dogmatic-historical interest, however, in settling or perfecting that discussion here; my point is to argue that Paul did not address any such question or questions here, which I do by reminding of the temporal language he uses. Whatever the law-as-pedagogue did, it did it only "before" (Πρὸ) or "until" (εἰς, three times) Christ, and does so "no longer" (οὐκέτι). That is, whatever we would conclude about Luther's or Calvin's theology, or that of their respective confessional traditions, both Luther and Calvin would insist that the law *still has* a disciplinary and/or didactic use, however much they may have differed in emphasis. That is, while Luther and Calvin were discussing what three uses the law *still* has in our Christian churches or lands, Paul was discussing what use the law "no longer" has, what it did "before," and what it did "until Christ" (εἰς Χριστόν).

So what did the law do "before" and "until" Christ that it does "no longer" after Christ? It no longer distinguishes Jew and Gentile, or at least we no longer observe its requirements that do so. It no longer "locks in" the Jews and "locks out" the Gentiles. It no longer preserves/protects the lineage of Abraham, because the seed to whom the Abrahamic pledges were made has now come; Sinai's preservative/protective role was temporary, until the seed to whom the pledges were made would come (ἄχρις οὗ ἔλθη τὸ σπέρμα ᾧ ἐπήγγελται, 3:19). Thus that child slave who functioned as a bodyguard—protecting his charges from corruption, molestation, or theft—was the kind of παιδαγωγός Paul was speaking of here: an individual placed in protective charge of a child until the child reached maturity, anticipating what he will say in the initial verses of chapter 4 also about the various custodians who care for individuals in the state of minority.[84]

Concept of Law in Galatians 3:21–4:11," *Journal for the Study of the New Testament*, no. 26 (February 1, 1986): 53–78.

84. My view is similar to that expressed by David J. Lull, who correctly recognizes that Paul regarded the law as temporary. Lull, however, still views even that temporary pedagogy as being primarily moral: "As a 'pedagogue,' the Law was limited to the task of curbing 'the desires of the flesh' of those who were kept in its custody" (497). While I do not deny that the Sinai covenant may have had such an effect, I believe the "pedagogue," as Paul perceived it, was the entire Gentile-excluding covenant. As with Aristeas, Paul throughout Galatians wrestles with

To understand the reasoning of Galatians, we need to imagine a "fourth use of the law," a temporary use, put in place 430 years after the Abrahamic promise, "before" faith came, and "until Christ." This fourth use is the guardian/protecting/preserving-from-intermarrying-with-the-Gentiles use. This preservative use, to guard and protect Abraham's lineage and the pledges made thereto, is what Paul discusses in Galatians. This explains therefore why he can speak of it favorably and unfavorably; it was wise and necessary to preserve the Abrahamic seed and promise by having a Gentile-excluding covenant. But it is unwise to continue such a covenant once its purpose is fulfilled. It was not the law per se that troubled the apostle to the Gentiles; it was the law that excluded the Gentiles that troubled him. So, throughout Galatians, he reasoned that this Gentile-excluding role must end in order for Abrahamic blessings to come to them; but he argued here that the Gentiles *did* need to be excluded for a season of redemptive history. Paul affirms this "fourth use of the law" as utterly necessary to achieve the purposes earlier expressed to Abraham; but, at the same time, he affirms that this utterly necessary purpose was temporary. Like a good παιδαγωγός, it guarded/protected Abraham's lineage until that protection was "no longer" (οὐκέτι) needed, and then it retired.

Since the terms of the Sinai covenant were entire obedience, that covenant would have excluded the Gentiles and judged the Israelites if it had remained standing; exile would have followed exile. It guarded the Jews from the Gentiles while they needed to be so guarded, and it threatened them with curse sanctions while doing so. This is why Paul said that the "law was our guardian until Christ came, in order that we [Jews] might be justified by faith." If the law were still our guardian against the Gentiles, then not only would Abraham's pledges to bless them not be here, but "we Jews" would still be under a curse-threatening covenant administration. The termination of the Sinai covenant unlocks the doors of God's house to the Gentiles, while simultaneously ending the threatened curse sanction upon Israel.

4.7. Galatians 3:26–29

For in Christ Jesus you are all sons of God, through faith. For as many of you as were baptized into Christ have put on Christ. There is neither Jew nor Greek, there is neither slave nor free, there is neither male nor female,[85] for you are all one in Christ Jesus. And if you are Christ's, then you are Abraham's offspring, heirs according to promise.

---

the Abrahamic pledge to bless "all the nations," juxtaposed to a later covenant that segregates Abraham's descendants *from* those nations. So I regard the focus of the analogy to be similar to how Aristeas understood the matter. The law separated the Jews from the people of the land, protecting them from their tendency both to intermarry with them and commit idolatry with them, and it thereby preserved the integrity of Abraham's genealogy and the memory of the pledges made to him. Cf. Lull, "'The Law Was Our Pedagogue': A Study in Galatians 3:19–25," *Journal of Biblical Literature* 105, no. 3 (September 1, 1986): 481–98.

85. The first two "either/or" categories are distinguished as οὐκ . . . οὐδὲ, but the third (male or female) is rendered οὐκ . . . ἄρσεν καὶ θῆλυ. Some have suggested that this is influenced by the LXX of Gen. 1:27: "In the image of God he made them, male *and* female he made them" (κατ᾽ εἰκόνα θεοῦ ἐποίησεν αὐτόν ἄρσεν καὶ θῆλυ ἐποίησεν αὐτούς).

My hapless students recall that for twenty-five years I have suggested that this text hasn't seen its context since it left the hand of Paul's amanuensis.[86] I exaggerate. But it has *rarely* seen its context in a populist American culture. Our American ears cannot help but hear some egalitarian mandate here, even though Paul never thought about such a concept, as intellectual history well proves.[87] The "Abraham" of this pericope is the "Abraham" of Galatians 3:6–9, 14, 16, and 18. The "promise" is the "promise" of Galatians 3:14, 16–18, and 21–22. The "Greek" here is the "Greek" of Galatians 2:3 and the "Gentile" of Galatians 1:16; 2:2, 8–9, 12, 14–15; 3:8 and 14. And the "Jew" here is the "Jew" of Galatians 2:13–15. That is, to put it mildly, Paul is not interrupting his thought at this critical juncture to provide social commentary on the Greco-Roman world and its public policies. To the contrary, he is drawing into conclusive summary the reasoning throughout chapter 3, returning to his earlier claim in 3:7 that "those who have faith, these are Abraham's sons." He does so not merely by repetition but by now making a distinctly Christian affirmation: It is those who are baptized into Christ who have put on Christ; and, implicitly therefore, it is *not* those who are circumcised who have put on Christ. Messiah is the benefactor of the baptized, regardless of whether the baptized are circumcised or not. The text naturally breaks itself into two smaller parts. The first (3:26–28) affirms the union of all who are Christ's through faith and baptism; the second (3:29) extrapolates from this that those who are Christ's are therefore Abraham's offspring and therefore heirs/inheritors of the things promised to him.

The first section itself has two parts. In the first of these, Paul makes a statement that echoes 3:7: "For in Christ Jesus you are all *sons* of God, through *faith* (3:26)." This echoes 3:7: "It is those of *faith* who are the *sons* of Abraham." To be sure, the "sons" of

---

86. The γὰρ in Πάντες γὰρ υἱοὶ θεοῦ ἐστε cannot simply be discarded. Paul is *concluding* the argument about the relation of Jews and Gentiles under three covenant administrations that has occupied the entire chapter; he is not beginning a new interest (civic lessons, social policy in the Roman Empire, or general political theory). He is concluding his thoughts about how the Mosaic law distinguished Jew and Gentile, temporarily, in service to the earlier pledged promise to bless all nations one day through Abraham's descendant.

87. Our egalitarian zeitgeist reveals itself by the frequency with which one hears "equality" spoken of with regard to Gal. 3:28. So Ben Witherington, "Rite and Rights for Women—Galatians 3.28," *New Testament Studies* 27 (1981): 600: "An affirmation of the ontological *equality* of these pairs"; J. Keir Howard, "Neither Male nor Female: An Examination of the Status of Women in the New Testament," *Evangelical Quarterly* 55, no. 1 (1983): 31: "*equality* of status is given to all"; Paul K. Jewett, *Man as Male and Female* (Grand Rapids: Eerdmans, 1975), 112: "He thought of the woman as *equal* to the man in all things," and 142: "in Galatians 3:28, when speaking of her *equality* with the man"; Aída Besançon Spencer, *Beyond the Curse: Women Called to Ministry* (Grand Rapids: Baker Academic, 1989), 67: "Justification by faith creates an *equality* between Jew and Gentile, slave and free, male and female." Paul's point here is *unity*, not equality. You are "one" in Jesus Christ. In both Greek and English, there is a distinction (both lexicographic and semantic) between "unity" and "equality." On other occasions, Paul employs the terms ἴσος and ἰσότης, when he wishes to speak of equality. This demonstrates his awareness of the terms, lexically (Phil. 2:6; 2 Cor. 8:13–14; Col. 4:1). Thus Paul knew how to use the ordinary Greek words for "equal" and "equality," and he did indeed use them when he wished to speak about such matters. By contrast, Paul employs the term "one" to indicate unity, as in Eph. 2:14–16, where he affirms that God has made "one new human" out of the formerly divided and separated Jew and Gentile. Whether redemption establishes equality of function is a separate question, which is simply not addressed by the employment of the term "one." The problem with the law for Paul was not that Jew and Gentile were unequal but that the Gentiles were excluded *entirely*.

Galatians 3:7 were υἱοὶ Ἀβραάμ; whereas in Galatians 3:26, they are υἱοὶ θεοῦ. Also, the "sons" of Galatians 3:7 were spoken of in the third person; in 3:26, they are spoken to in the second-person plural: "*you* are all sons of God" (υἱοὶ θεοῦ ἐστε). If the "you" here is the same "you" that was distinct from "*we* who are Jews by birth" earlier (2:15), it is the predominately Gentile Galatians that Paul now addresses as God's sons.

In the second part of this first section, Paul contrasts the new covenant ceremony with the Sinai covenant ceremonies. The new covenant rite of baptism unites all in a common reality; whereas the Sinai covenant ceremonially distinguished Jew from Greek, male from female, and slave from free. Surely, the Sinai law and ceremonies regarded the Jew as clean and the Gentile as ceremonially unclean. Similarly, the law of Moses made ceremonial distinctions between males and females:

> "Speak to the people of Israel, saying, 'If a woman conceives and bears a male child, then she shall be unclean seven days. As at the time of her menstruation, she shall be unclean. Then she shall continue for thirty-three days in the blood of her purifying. She shall not touch anything holy, nor come into the sanctuary, until the days of her purifying are completed. And if she cannot afford a lamb, then she shall take two turtledoves or two pigeons, one for a burnt offering and the other for a sin offering. And the priest shall make atonement for her, and she shall be clean.'" (Lev. 12:2, 4, 8)

> When a woman has a discharge, and the discharge in her body is blood, she shall be in her menstrual impurity for seven days, and whoever touches her shall be unclean until the evening. (Lev. 15:19)

Similarly, the law distinguished between being a slave and being free:

> If a man lies sexually with a woman who is a slave, assigned to another man and not yet ransomed or given her freedom, a distinction shall be made. They shall not be put to death, because she was not free. (Lev. 19:20)

> If your brother becomes poor beside you and sells himself to you, you shall not make him serve as a slave. (Lev. 25:39)

> When you buy a Hebrew slave, he shall serve six years, and in the seventh he shall go out free, for nothing. (Exod. 21:2)

> When a man strikes his slave, male or female, with a rod and the slave dies under his hand, he shall be avenged. But if the slave survives a day or two, he is not to be avenged, for the slave is his money. (Exod. 21:20–21)

Thus the three pairs of Jew/Greek, slave/free, and male/female are not universal categories, nor are they categories distinguished by Greco-Roman law; they are categories distinguished by the Mosaic law. Christian baptism, Paul says, makes no such distinctions between these pairs; all belong to Christ by faith and are baptized into his church. They have all "put on" Christ.

Not only does the Mosaic law distinguish these three pairs, Troy W. Martin has made a compelling argument that the Mosaic law distinguishes these three pairs regarding circumcision itself. Unlike some other cultures, Israel never practiced female circumcision, and only the slaves owned by Hebrews were required to be circumcised

(Gen. 17:12–13), whereas free men living in the Jewish community were regarded as sojourners or resident aliens and were not required to be circumcised. As Martin put it:

> The covenant of circumcision distinguishes between Jew and Greek, slave and free, male and female. In these antithetical pairs, those described by the first member of the pair have an obligation to be circumcised in a Jewish community while those described by the second member do not. . . . Christian baptism recognizes neither Jew nor Greek, slave nor free, and it does not distinguish between male and female.[88]

This is contrary to three other interpretations of this passage: that the three pairs are derived from Paul's society,[89] that the pairs are derived from a misunderstanding of the Torah,[90] and that the final of the three pairs is a reference to the creation distinctions of Genesis 1:27.[91] The first of these errs not because it misrepresents Paul's society,[92] but because it misrepresents the connection between 3:28 and the preceding argument. Paul's preceding argument, as we demonstrated above, asserts that what the Torah (not the society) required is no longer required. It is the claims of *Torah* that concern Paul, not the claims of his *society*. The second of these options is far better, because it brings Torah into the picture. Regrettably, it also misunderstands the nature of Paul's previous argument, which is not that Torah has been *misunderstood*, but that Torah *properly understood* excludes the Gentiles.[93] The third, while cogently accounting for the language of the third pair, fails to appreciate the preceding argument, which is not addressed toward any problem or limitation in the *created* order, but to a problem or limitation in the specific provisions of the *Sinai* order.[94]

The second part of this pericope draws a conclusion from this. If the distinctions made by the Mosaic law/covenant are not made in the new covenant, which regards all of these former categorical distinctions as passé, and if they have put on Christ,

---

88. Troy W. Martin, "Whose Flesh? What Temptation? (Galatians 4.13–14)," *Journal for the Study of the New Testament*, no. 74 (June 1, 1999): 121.

89. So, e.g., Spencer, *Beyond the Curse*, 66–67; Howard, "Neither Male nor Female," 31; Daniel P. Fuller, "Paul and Galatians 3:28," *TSFB* 9, no. 2 (1985): 9; Paul K. Jewett, *Man as Male and Female* (Grand Rapids: Eerdmans, 1975), 143.

90. Ben Witherington, "Paul is arguing against the religious abuse, not the use, of these distinctions," in "Rite and Rights for Women—Galatians 3.28," *New Testament Studies* 27 (1981): 600.

91. So Witherington, "Rite and Rights for Women," 597–98; and Krister Stendahl, *The Bible and the Role of Women* (Philadelphia: Fortress, 1966), 32. Stendahl and Witherington are probably correct in arguing that the *language* of the LXX of Gen. 1:27 accounts for the presence of the καὶ between the third pair, as opposed to the οὐδὲ; between the other two pairs.

92. In fact, for our limited purpose here, historical reconstruction of the practices of first-century Greco-Roman or Jewish culture is unnecessary, since Paul is not addressing the practice of the *culture* but the specific practice of requiring Torah observance in the church.

93. Here the bias of generations of Protestant interpretation probably accounts for this interpretation. Assuming that the Jews legalistically misinterpreted their Torah, interpreters conclude that they misunderstood it here. The problem (in addition to the assumption itself) is that any fair interpretation of the Sinai covenant must concede that it excludes Gentiles and marks Israel off as a distinct nation and people. Thus it is no misinterpretation of the Torah that leads to excluding Gentiles; rather, it is precisely fidelity to the Torah that requires their exclusion.

94. I am not sure that any of these other three interpretations is fatal, or even harmful, to my thesis; but I think that my approach makes better contextual sense of the passage than do these alternatives.

who was earlier designated as Abraham's "seed," then all baptized Christians are Abraham's offspring and heirs of the eschatological blessings pledged to him: "And if you are Christ's, then you are Abraham's offspring, heirs according to promise." This relies on the reasoning made earlier in chapter 3, but especially at 3:7 and 3:16—the former identifying as Abraham's sons those who have faith, and the latter identifying Christ as the single "Seed" through whom blessings would come to all the nations without distinction.

One of the interesting things about this brief pericope is the interchangeable nature of υἱοὶ θεοῦ and τοῦ Ἀβραὰμ σπέρμα. Of course, Abraham's children are God's, but the interesting thing here—in a text that plainly denies the Sinai distinguishing of "male and female"—is that the females who are baptized into Christ are regarded as God's "sons." One might have expected simply a double use of σπέρμα here, but since the law of primogeniture designated the eldest male son as the heir/inheritor, Paul says regarding both sexes, "You are Abraham's offspring, heirs according to the promise" (τοῦ Ἀβραὰμ σπέρμα ἐστέ, κατ᾽ ἐπαγγελίαν κληρονόμοι).

The primary point of this concluding pericope in chapter 3 is to state unequivocally the consequence of what the rest of the chapter says about the temporary nature of the Sinai covenant: There is neither Jew nor Greek. By extension, other ceremonial distinctions of the Sinai covenant (male/female, slave/free) disappear also, along with others that Paul does not even mention here (e.g., Levitical/non-Levitical). As the apostle to the Gentiles, Paul's primary concern throughout the letter is to assure and remind that, if Gentiles are still "strangers to the covenants of promise," as it were (Eph. 2:12), then there is no good news for anyone, whether Jew or Greek. Paul's thinking is deeply Abrahamic, and Paul continually recalls the pledge to Abraham that the ultimate purpose of the lineage of Abraham is that, one day through one of his descendants, God would bless all the nations of the earth. For Paul, the death and resurrection of Christ now erased the centuries-old distinction between Jew and Gentile, between Israel and the nations, and between "my people" and the *am ha-aretz*.

CHAPTER 5

Promise, Law, Faith: Galatians 4:1–5:1

Chapter 4 of Galatians could as easily be read as the remainder of chapter 3; and there was little reason, other than convenience, to divide the book where it is now divided. The first seven verses of chapter 4 are closely related to the last verse of chapter 3, where the last words described the Galatians as "heirs according to the promise" (κατ᾽ ἐπαγγελίαν κληρονόμοι). Indeed, verses 1 and 7 of chapter 4 bracket the subunit by the discussion of the relation between κληρονόμος and δοῦλος in each verse. Throughout Galatians, Paul undertakes the delicate job of arguing, from the OT Scriptures themselves, that it is not the observers of the Sinai covenant who are Abraham's "children," "descendants," "heirs," or "sons" (τέκνα, σπέρμα, κληρονόμοι, υἱοί). His thesis throughout the section is what he affirms in the first pericope where Abraham is mentioned (3:6–9), in which 3:7 states one of the recurring theses of Galatians 3 and 4: οἱ ἐκ πίστεως, οὗτοι υἱοί εἰσιν Ἀβραάμ. Indeed, the concluding ten verses of chapters 3 and 4 contain the illustration of Sarah and Hagar, in which Paul introduces that section with the reminder: "Abraham had two sons, one by a slave woman and one by a free woman" (Ἀβραὰμ δύο υἱοὺς ἔσχεν, ἕνα ἐκ τῆς παιδίσκης καὶ ἕνα ἐκ τῆς ἐλευθέρας).

Throughout Galatians 3 and 4, that is, Paul makes both a negative and a positive observation. Negatively, he argues that those who observe the Sinai covenant are not necessarily Abraham's heirs (any more than Ishmael and Esau were heirs); positively, he argues that those who have faith are in fact his sons and therefore heirs, even if not his genetic descendants. Most of Galatians 3 carries the negative argument, as Paul consistently argues there that the Sinai covenant was only temporary, its curses were only temporary, and its separation of Jew and Gentile was only temporary. But before that covenant administration was instituted (indeed, nearly a half millennium before), God had disclosed purposes for Abraham and his seed that would both precede and follow the temporary Sinai administration. We might say that Paul puts Sinai "in its place," covenant-historically, by reminding that Abraham and his seed had a history for nearly five hundred years *before* Sinai, and that he and his true seed would (therefore) also have a history *after* Sinai.

Paul poses this question throughout Galatians 3 and 4: Who will inherit the third reality pledged to Abraham and Sarah? We know that they, their children, and their grandchildren began the process of becoming numerous; we also know that after four centuries in bondage to Egypt, this vast group inherited the great arable land promised to Abraham and Sarah. But was not something else pledged?

> "And I will make of you a great nation, and I will bless you and make your name great, so that you will be a blessing. I will bless those who bless you, and him who dishonors you I will curse, and in you all the families of the earth shall be blessed." (Gen. 12:2–3; cf. also Gen. 18:18; 22:18; 26:4; 28:14).

The language employed is sometimes "all the *families* of the earth" (πᾶσαι αἱ φυλαὶ τῆς γῆς, Gen. 12:2–3, 28:14) and sometimes "all the *nations* of the earth" (πάντα τὰ ἔθνη τῆς γῆς, Gen. 18:18; 22:18; 26:4). The substance, however, is the same: that from one elderly and barren couple, God will one day bless a great host from all the nations/ tribes of the earth.

In the course of history, God later made a covenant at Sinai with the descendants of Abraham, in pursuit of which covenant the Israelites separated from the *am ha-aretz* and kept alive the memory of the patriarchs and the pledges made to them. Later, threatened by the globalization and pluralization of the Greco-Roman era and empire, it was especially necessary for the followers of (Abraham and) Moses to resist absorption into the greater Greco-Roman empire. All of this Paul understands. But after Damascus, Paul perceived with a clarity rare in his generation that through apostolic proclamation of the death and resurrection of Christ, the pledge to bless the nations/families of the earth through Abraham's Seed had arrived, so he was eager to remind his auditors of the history that antedated the Sinai covenant so that they could understand the history that postdates it.

5.1. Galatians 4:1–7

I mean[1] that the heir [ὁ κληρονόμος], as long as he is a child [νήπιός], is no different from a slave [δούλου], though he is the owner of everything [κύριος πάντων], but he is under guardians[2] and managers until the date set by his father.[3] In the same way we also, when we were children [νήπιοι], were enslaved to the elementary principles of the world. But when the fullness of time had come, God sent forth his Son [τὸν υἱὸν αὐτοῦ], born of woman, born under the law, to redeem those who were under the law, so that we might receive adoption as sons [τὴν υἱοθεσίαν]. And because you are sons [υἱοί], God has sent the Spirit of his Son [τὸ πνεῦμα τοῦ υἱοῦ αὐτοῦ] into our hearts, crying, "Abba! Father!" So you are no longer a slave [δοῦλος], but a son [υἱός], and if a son [υἱός], then an heir [κληρονόμος] through God.

---

1. "I mean" (ESV/RSV) is a curious translation of Λέγω, as is "my point is this" (NRSV) since "I say" (KJV) is not difficult in English.

2. "Guardians" (ESV) is a perfectly acceptable translation of ἐπιτρόπους, but it should be observed that this is the same English word that ESV employs to translate παιδαγωγός in 3:24. Insofar as Paul employed the different terms to denote slightly different ideas, it might be preferable to find English terms that are also distinct. NRSV uses distinct terms (disciplinarian/ guardian), and while I do not care for "disciplinarian" as a translation for παιδαγωγός, at least NRSV preserves a difference. KJV preserved a difference by employing schoolmaster/tutor, though those two are fairly close, semantically.

3. I do not regard as either persuasive or important to Paul's argument James A. Scott's thesis that Paul refers here to Israel's enslavement in Egypt, or to the variations on that thesis, such as Hafemann's, that it refers to the exile. The "we" of the passage are the Jews under the administration of the Sinai covenant, as it has been throughout, and cannot therefore refer to their period in Egypt before that covenant, nor is it restricted to their experience in exile later. Cf. James M. Scott, *Adoption as Sons of God: An Exegetical Investigation into the Background of ΥΙΟΘΕΣΙΑ in the Pauline Corpus*, Wissenschaftliche Untersuchungen zum Neuen Testament 2, no. 48 (Tübingen: J. C. B. Mohr, 1992); Scott J. Hafemann, "Paul and the Exile of Israel in Galatians 3–4," in *Exile: Old Testament, Jewish, and Christian Conceptions*, ed. James M. Scott (Leiden: E. J. Brill, 1997), 329–71.

Verses 1 and 7 bracket this pericope by the repeated mention of heirs and sons in each, recalling that in 3:26–29 the Galatians had also been designated as υἱοὶ, Ἀβραὰμ σπέρμα, and κατ᾽ ἐπαγγελίαν κληρονόμοι. Having just said that in Christ there is neither "male nor female," the use of υἱοὶ here may appear curious; but it is merely a reflection of the law of primogeniture, by attraction to κληρονόμοι. Equally interesting, but not especially germane to my thesis, is the use of υἱός to designate either the Galatians or Jesus of Nazareth; to keep the matter clear, the special relation of Christ to God the Father is indicated by the qualification "his" (αὐτοῦ) in each case.

Paul continues an argument similar to the one made in Galatians 3:22–25: that being under the Sinai covenant was like being under special and temporary care,[4] the kind of care that is extended to children before and until they reach maturity. There, the figurative language was ὑπὸ παιδαγωγόν; here, it is ὑπὸ ἐπιτρόπους ἐστὶν καὶ οἰκονόμους. The comparative point, however, in each case was largely the same: being ὑπὸ νόμον was like a child being under special care and guardianship, which is necessary to the child's minority circumstance but not necessary upon the age of majority (which, in the second comparison, is expressly said to be a time "set by his father"). Here, however, Paul employs paradox: that a child designated not only κληρονόμος but κύριος πάντων is no different than a servant (οὐδὲν διαφέρει δούλου). The analogy is not entire; of course, the designated heir does not assume the same household responsibilities as a servant/slave. But as regards the point of the analogy—that is, inheritance—the heir receives no more of the inheritance than a slave would, until the proper time. Paul thereby describes Israel's tutelage under the Mosaic covenant as a kind of servitude or slavery, a time of comparative poverty and yet-unrealized privilege: "In the same way we also, when we were children [νήπιοι], were enslaved [ἤμεθα δεδουλωμένοι] to the elementary principles of the world." The first-person plural cannot be universalized here; the "we" are still those who were "under the law," a condition that was never true for the Gentiles. Paul does not specify what kind of servitude/enslavement is implied here; possibly, it is a reference to the curse sanctions he mentioned earlier in 3:10–13; but contextually, it is possible that it is neither more nor less than unfulfilled aspiration—the longing for the shalom pledged to Abraham, while suffering national disunity, military defeat, and exile.

The reasoning turns eschatological in verses 4 and following:

> But when the fullness of time had come [ὅτε δὲ ἦλθεν τὸ πλήρωμα τοῦ χρόνου], God sent forth his Son, born of woman, born under the law, to redeem those who were under the law, so that we might receive adoption as sons.

Though he does so almost in passing, Paul's thought is similar to that of the apostle John, who constantly perceived the mission of Christ in terms of commissioning by his Father, forty-four times recording that Jesus was "sent" by the Father: "God sent forth [ἐξαπέστειλεν] his Son."[5] The Jews awaited deliverance from their slavery/servitude under the law, and the work of Christ manumitted them (ἵνα τοὺς ὑπὸ νόμον ἐξαγοράσῃ)

---

4. The temporal language here is frequent and reminiscent of Gal. 3: ἐφ᾽ ὅσον χρόνον (v. 1), ἄχρι (v. 2), ὅτε, (vv. 3–4), τὸ πλήρωμα τοῦ χρόνου (v. 4), and οὐκέτι (v. 7).

5. I would prefer the more literal "sent out" here to emphasize that the commissioning was heavenly, but "sent forth" works sufficiently.

therefrom. Only then, manumitted from the covenant that separated Jew from Gentile, could they receive their full inheritance/adoption as mature sons. As long as the Gentiles were outsiders, even Abraham's descendants had not yet witnessed what was pledged to him and Sarah; Gentile exclusion entailed Israelite servitude and minority.

The eschatological language is indeed striking. In the fullness of time (τὸ πλήρωμα τοῦ χρόνου), the heavenly Father "sent out" (ἐξαπέστειλεν) his Son from heaven to earth; who manumitted (ἐξαγοράσῃ) those previously enslaved and granted to them the long-awaited privileges of inheritance (υἱοθεσίαν), including the heaven-sent Spirit (also ἐξαπέστειλεν ὁ θεὸς τὸ πνεῦμα τοῦ υἱοῦ αὐτοῦ). Two heavenly gifts (Son and Spirit) are sent in quick succession, resulting in the transition of the Jews from (Mosaic) slave to (Abrahamic) son, and full son at that, with all the rights of υἱοθεσίαν and κληρονόμος.

5.2. Galatians 4:8–11

> Formerly, when you did not know God, you were enslaved to those that by nature are not gods. But now that you have come to know God, or rather to be known by God, how can you turn back again to the weak and worthless elementary principles of the world, whose slaves you want to be once more? You observe days and months and seasons and years! I am afraid I may have labored over you in vain.

In two particular ways, this pericope reminds us of the first in Galatians 3. First, in each, Paul addresses the Galatians in the second-person plural (maintaining the tendency to use "us" for Jewish Christians and "you" for the predominately Gentile Galatians that began at 2:15); and, in each, he fears that his labors or that the Galatians' faith may have been "in vain" (εἰκῇ, 3:4; 4:11). The references to the Sinai covenant are only implicit here, and apart from context we might not notice them at all. However, there are three lines of evidence that he is referring to it here. First, he employs the language of slavery/ servitude (ἐδουλεύσατε, v. 8; δουλεύειν, v. 9), which he has just employed three times in the previous pericope in such a manner (4:1, 3, 7) and will do so unmistakably in the figure of 4:21–31, where he contrasts Abraham's "free" son from his "slave" son and later refers to their mothers, saying, "These women are two covenants. One is from Mount Sinai, bearing children for slavery" (μία μὲν ἀπὸ ὄρους Σινᾶ εἰς δουλείαν γεννῶσα, 4:24). Second, however we understand the "elementary principles of the world" (πτωχὰ στοιχεῖα, 4:9), it appears to be a reference back to 4:3 (τὰ στοιχεῖα τοῦ κόσμου ἤμεθα δεδουλωμένοι), where it referred to either the same *reality* or the same redemptive-historical *moment* as the season in which Israel was ὑπὸ νόμον. Third, the reference to "days and months and seasons and years" is almost certainly a reference to the Jewish calendar, which had annual celebrations, seasonal observances, monthly observances, and special days as well. Along with the food laws and circumcision, the calendar was one of the Sinai realities that marked Israel as a distinct nation.[6] Additionally, though

---

6. In fact, most sociological groups—whether nations or subgroups within them—have calendars that mark them as distinct from other groups. Americans, for example, observe the Fourth of July differently than do Britons (and perhaps more enthusiastically). Israel's only difference is that hers was substantially characterized by celebrations/observances that Yahweh instituted, such as Passover and Tabernacles.

also implicitly, it would be quite surprising if Paul turned here to a new consideration altogether, despite the linguistic ties to 4:1–7 and to 3:1–5.

That Paul addresses the predominately Gentile Galatians is probably disclosed in his saying, "Formerly, when you did not know God, you were enslaved to those that by nature are not gods." The Gentiles, before the death and resurrection of Christ, were "strangers to the covenants of promise" (Eph. 2:12) and pantheistic idolaters, yet their pantheon contained no true divinities; they were merely τοῖς φύσει μὴ οὖσιν θεοῖς. Now that they have come to know God (and/or be known by God), why would they observe the very covenant that had *excluded* them for centuries?[7]

5.3. Galatians 4:12–20—The "Pathetic Appeal"

Brothers, I entreat you, become as I am, for I also have become as you are. You did me no wrong. You know it was because of a bodily ailment that I preached the gospel to you at first, and though my condition was a trial to you, you did not scorn or despise me, but received me as an angel of God, as Christ Jesus. What then has become of the blessing you felt? For I testify to you that, if possible, you would have gouged out your eyes and given them to me. Have I then become your enemy by telling you the truth?

They make much of you, but for no good purpose. They want to shut you out, that you may make much of them. It is always good to be made much of for a good purpose, and not only when I am present with you, my little children, for whom I am again in the anguish of childbirth until Christ is formed in you! I wish I could be present with you now and change my tone, for I am perplexed about you.

Many have rightly observed that this pericope contains a "pathetic" appeal—a perfectly ordinary aspect of Greco-Roman rhetoric; along with *ethos* and *logos* went *pathos*. Large portions of Galatians 1 and 2 might be categorized as *ethos*, and most of 2:15–4:11 would be regarded as *logos*; this pericope is primarily *pathos*. The three parts are not unrelated, especially in this letter. Not only does Paul regard the Christian gospel to be at stake; his authority to address/settle the matter is *also* at stake (which is why so much time is expended on the *ethos* matter in Gal. 1–2). Here in the *pathos* section, Paul steps back from his reasoning about the gospel (and its relation to two antecedent covenants) to discuss his former relationship with the Galatians, in hopes that this may jar them into recognizing that a change has happened. Verses 12–16 address Paul's relation to the Galatians, and then 17–20 contrast this with the "troublers'" relation to the Galatians.

Paul begins with an appeal (δέομαι) for the Galatians to regard him with the affectionate concern he has for them: "Become as I am, for I also have become as you are."[8] This is followed by a litotes ("You did me no wrong") and an elaboration on the

---

7. Before the cooler head of his amanuensis prevailed, one can easily imagine the apostle having said, "This is no time for you *meshugginah* Gentiles to be donning yarmulkes!," though there is no evidence for this in the textual tradition.

8. It is also likely that Paul, the Jew, by rejecting the Kashrut and enjoying table fellowship with the predominately Gentile Galatians had "become as you [Gentiles] are," and is here calling the Gentiles to be just as "law-free" as he is. If so, he is employing similar language to what he employed in the familiar 1 Cor. 9:22: "To the weak I *became* weak [ἐγενόμην τοῖς ἀσθενέσιν ἀσθενής], that

litotes. Far from having wronged Paul, the Galatians went out of their way to care for him in a season of significant physical illness:

> You know it was because of a bodily ailment that I preached the gospel to you at first, and though my condition was a trial to you, you did not scorn or despise me, but received me as an angel of God, as Christ Jesus. . . . For I testify to you that, if possible, you would have gouged out your eyes and given them to me.

Many have speculated whether this refers to a problem with Paul's eyesight; I judge it more likely that it is mere hyperbole, analogous to our saying, "He would give you the shirt off his back." Eyesight is perhaps universally regarded as the most important of the five senses, and to be willing to surrender this important sense for another would be a matter of extraordinary sacrifice.[9]

Paul's point is that, whatever his medical ailment was, it caused considerable hardship (πειρασμὸν) for the Galatians, who might have rejected him but did not (οὐκ ἐξουθενήσατε οὐδὲ ἐξεπτύσατε);[10] they did not shrink from the responsibility of caring for him. To the contrary, he reminds them, they received him as they would have received "an angel of God, as Jesus Christ" (ὡς ἄγγελον θεοῦ ἐδέξασθέ με, ὡς Χριστὸν Ἰησοῦν). There may be mild hyperbole here, as an expression of Paul's gratitude; but the hyperbole, if present, could not be great or the rhetorical point would be lost. Unless the Galatians concurred largely with Paul's narration, the narration would lose its rhetorical force. As it is, he hopes the Galatians, upon reading this, will respond in this way: "You know, Paul's right. When he first came here, he was extremely ill; some of us were even concerned whether he would make it. But we arranged to care for him in shifts and gave him our best effort, and eventually he recovered. Remember how relieved we all were when he began to recuperate?" If Paul can strike this sort of responsive "pathetic" appeal, then he hopes thereby to gain attention to the actual argumentation he has employed to this point. But here, he is appealing for a *hearing*; he is asking the Galatians to *receive* him now as they first received him.

This is what makes the almost universal mistranslation of the first part of verse 15 not only inexplicable but almost risible. This is not difficult Greek,[11] and there is no

---

I might win the weak. I have *become* all things to all people [τοῖς πᾶσιν γέγονα πάντα], that by all means I might save some." Paul effectively became a Gentile, a non-Torah observer; so he calls on the Torah-observing Gentiles to become as non-Torah observing as he has become: "I (the Jew) became as you (nonobservant Gentiles), so you (observant Gentiles) should become as I am."

9. I do not deny the possibility that Paul also may have had a problem with his eyesight. I merely observe that biblical interpreters are sometimes a little tone-deaf to figurative language, and perhaps assume without contextual warrant that language is literal when it may be figurative. I also observe that Goddard and Cummins make a plausible argument that the reference to a "weakness of the flesh" here was the physical trauma Paul had incurred as a result of persecution. A. J. Goddard and Stephen Anthony Cummins, "Ill or Ill-Treated? Conflict and Persecution as the Context of Paul's Original Ministry in Galatia (Galatians 4.12–20)," *Journal for the Study of the New Testament*, 52 (1993): 93–126.

10. Does Paul use this language of scorn and "spitting out" (the literal rendering of ἐκπτύω) to suggest that the Galatians *are* treating him in such a manner now?

11. I've taught the Greek text of Galatians almost every year since 1984, and my third-semester Greek students have translated it correctly almost every time; they (and their instructor) are puzzled at the inability of the translators to get such simple Greek right.

reason to render ποῦ οὖν ὁ μακαρισμὸς ὑμῶν; as anything other than: "Where then is your (former) approval?" Many translations effectively regard 4:15 as appearing straight out of the magician's hat with no contextual connections. Here are several that miss Paul's point almost entirely:

> "What has happened to all your joy?" (NIV)

> "What has become of the satisfaction you felt?" (RSV)

> "You were so happy! What has happened?" (TEV)

> "What then has become of the blessing you felt?" (ESV)

> "Have you forgotten how happy you thought yourselves in having me with you?" (NEB, better)

Only NRSV gets the basic sense, though even it is too subjective: "What has become of the goodwill you felt?" There is simply no valid reason to translate μακαρισμὸς as though it were a description of the Galatian emotional state (nor any reason to think anyone in Paul's pre-Freudian generation *thought* in such terms), though NRSV's use of "goodwill" is close. The following sentence (v. 15b: "For I testify to you that, if possible, you would have gouged out your eyes and given them to me"), causally (or possibly explicatively) connected to verse 15a by the γὰρ, *also* indicates that Paul's concern in this immediate context is for how the Galatian congregation formerly *treated/regarded* Paul. In this sentence, Paul argues that had it been possible, the Galatians would have plucked out their own eyes and given them to Paul. What possible sense does it make, in such a context, to interject a sentence inquiring about the sense of joy or happiness the Galatians experienced? Paul is not here inquiring about how much happier they were when they were orthodox; he is inquiring about the how they once regarded *him* as a messenger.

The term μακαρισμός (and its cognates) is routinely used as an expression of approval or commendation. Outside of the New Testament, the term can have reference to "the admiring praises with which the people exalt honoured men."[12] In Psalm 72:17, speaking of the king, the people say, "May his name endure forever, his fame continue as long as the sun! May people be blessed in him, all nations call him blessed! [πάντα τὰ ἔθνη μακαριοῦσιν αὐτόν]." In Song of Solomon 6:9, the synonymous parallelism renders it as the virtual equivalent of "praise": "The maidens saw her and called her blessed [καὶ μακαριοῦσιν αὐτήν]; the queens and concubines also, and they praised her [καὶ αἰνέσουσιν αὐτήν]."

The Apocryphal writings have many examples of this use of the lexical stock:

> On this anniversary it is fitting for me to praise [ἐπαινεῖν] for their virtues those who, with their mother, died for the sake of nobility and goodness, but I would also call them blessed [μακαρίσαιμι] for the honor in which they are held. (4 Macc. 1:10).

> O man of blessed [μακαρίου] age and of venerable [σεμνῆς] gray hair and of law-abiding life, whom the faithful seal of death has perfected! (4 Macc. 7:15)

---

12. *Theological Dictionary of the New Testament*, vol. 4, ed. Gerhard Kittel and Gerhard Friedrich, trans. Geoffrey W. Bromily (Grand Rapids: Eerdmans, 1964–1976), 363.

What person who lives as a philosopher by the whole rule of philosophy, and trusts in God, and knows that it is blessed [μακάριόν ἐστιν] to endure any suffering for the sake of virtue, would not be able to overcome the emotions through godliness? (4 Macc. 7:21–22)

No, by the blessed death of my brothers [τὸν μακάριον τῶν ἀδελφῶν μου θάνατον], by the eternal destruction of the tyrant, and by the everlasting life of the pious, I will not renounce our noble brotherhood. (4 Macc. 10:15)

In texts like these, it is almost impossible to make sense of them as a reference to a happy, subjective state. Can "blessed death" mean "death that feels joyous"? And how can it be "happy" or "joyous" "to endure any suffering"?

Similarly, in Romans 14:22, Paul addresses the necessity of the Christian's conscience being right before God. The believer is not to do anything the believer thinks is wrong. Paul says, μακάριος ὁ μὴ κρίνων ἑαυτὸν ἐν ᾧ δοκιμάζει. Perhaps this is best translated, "*Blessed* is the one whose behavior is not condemned by his or her stated principles." The point here as well is not so much that such an individual is subjectively happy as that such a one is *approved* by God or evidences that such a one is blessed by God. In 1 Corinthians 7:40, Paul says it is "more blessed" for the unmarried individual to remain that way (μακαριωτέρα δέ ἐστιν ἐὰν οὕτως μείνῃ); again, he is almost certainly not arguing that the individual will be happier but, contextually, more useful (and therefore approved) as a Christian under the present circumstances. When Paul uses this term to designate God, he almost certainly means that God is praiseworthy, not that God is happy, as in 1 Timothy 1:11, "According to the glorious gospel of the blessed God" (κατὰ τὸ εὐαγγέλιον τῆς δόξης τοῦ μακαρίου θεοῦ, cf. 1 Tim. 6:15; and, similarly, Titus 1:13). Paul's entire rhetorical point in this section is this: "Where is your former reception and *approval* of me and my ministry?"[13]

Each of these mistranslations betrays a rather ham-fisted handling of the pathetic appeal, an almost entire misunderstanding of what is happening rhetorically, as Paul challenges the Galatians to recognize that they once "received" him ministerially as they would have received angels, or Christ himself. Now, however, they consider him to be a troublemaker and a nuisance (ἐχθρὸς); and Paul, far from concealing or overlooking this changed estimation of him, calls *attention* to it in hopes that it will awaken in the Galatians a reassessment of him *and* his message: "Have I then become your enemy by telling you the truth?" The Galatians may not like what Paul says in this letter (and they almost surely felt uncomfortable with its tone at times), but Paul has already made it clear (Gal. 1–2) that he has not changed his message at all. Therefore, if the Galatians are now at odds with him (i.e., they regard him as an "enemy"/ἐχθρὸς), then it is *they* who have changed, not Paul.

Paul's employment of the *pathos* argument here is therefore unusually skillful. It is not merely that he checks off the list of rhetorical requirements and discovers

---

13. This follows the common usage outside of the NT where the term has to do with congratulation or approval. "Parents are congratulated on their children, the well-to-do on their wealth, the wise on their knowledge, the pious on their inward well-being, initiates on their experience of God and the dead on their escape from the vanity of things." *New International Dictionary of New Testament Theology*, vol. 1, A-F, ed. Colin Brown (Grand Rapids: Zondervan, 1975–1978), 215.

that he has covered *ethos* and *logos* but not *pathos*. To the contrary, he realizes that a skillful use of *pathos* here, calling attention to the change in the Galatian estimate of him, may rouse them out of their sense of complacency and force them to recognize that their changed estimation of Paul is due to their changed estimation of the gospel Paul proclaimed.[14]

5.4. Galatians 4:21–31—A Concluding Illustration

Tell me, you who desire to be under the law, do you not listen to the law? For it is written that Abraham had two sons, one by a slave woman and one by a free woman. But the son of the slave was born according to the flesh, while the son of the free woman was born through promise. Now this may be interpreted allegorically: these women are two covenants. One is from Mount Sinai, bearing children for slavery; she is Hagar. Now Hagar is Mount Sinai in Arabia; she corresponds to the present Jerusalem, for she is in slavery with her children. But the Jerusalem above is free, and she is our mother. For it is written, "Rejoice, O barren one who does not bear; break forth and cry aloud, you who are not in labor! For the children of the desolate one will be more than those of the one who has a husband." Now you, brothers, like Isaac, are children of promise. But just as at that time he who was born according to the flesh persecuted him who was born according to the Spirit, so also it is now. But what does the Scripture say? "Cast out the slave woman and her son, for the son of the slave woman shall not inherit with the son of the free woman." So, brothers, we are not children of the slave but of the free woman.

This figure of speech does not conclude the letter as a whole, but it does conclude the argumentative section thereof.[15] Figurative language can be employed for a number of purposes; in the case of parables, the language is deliberatively enigmatic and ambiguous, as an expression of judgment; it quite often appears in such contexts with no discursive context to make its meaning clear. In other places, such as the analogy of the cave in Book VII of Plato's *Republic*, it is employed more illustratively, and in such contexts it tends to conclude a substantial discursive context; I take it that way

---

14. This is something Socrates could not do at his trial before the Athenians, because the majority of the Athenians present at his trial never *did* like him. Some regarded him as a charlatan, others as a gadfly, and still others with envy (because of his popularity); but most of those present disliked him and always *had* disliked him. The Galatians, however, unlike the Athenians, *had* once liked Paul a good deal and were extremely attentive to both his message and his physical/medical needs. Paul therefore, unlike hapless Socrates, could appeal to the *changed* estimation and ask why the change had occurred.

15. I recognize that the determination of where the paraenesis begins is not an easy matter. Otto Merk noted that cogent arguments had been made for six different locations of the beginning of the paraenesis: 4:12, 4:21, 5:1, 5:2, 5:7, and 5:13. For those such as myself who are persuaded by Frank Matera's thesis that Galatians 5 and 6 are the "culmination" of the arguments in 3 and 4, the determination is not as critical. But I take the illustration/analogy here as a concluding analogy and so treat the argumentative portion of the letter as ending here, while acknowledging that there are plausible reasons for each of the other five suggested beginnings. See Otto Merk, "Der Beginn der Paränese im Galaterbrief," *Zeitschrift für die neutestamentliche Wissenschaft und die Kunde der älteren Kirche* 60 (1969): 83–104; and Frank J. Matera, "The Culmination of Paul's Argument to the Galatians: Gal 5:1–6:17," *Journal for the Study of the New Testament*, no. 32 (February 1, 1988): 79–91.

here. Paul introduces nothing new to his reasoning that began in 3:6, where he began discussing the differences between the Abrahamic covenant and the Sinai covenant; rather, he illustrates the reasoning with a fairly pointed use of a well-known event in the life of Abraham.

The structure of the passage appears to be as follows: in verse 21, Paul introduces a rhetorical question, and in verses 22–23, he alludes to the Genesis narrative, reminding that there were two sons to Abraham (not one)—one born of a free woman and one of a slave woman; one who is merely related to Abraham by the flesh and another who is additionally related as the heir of the promise. In verses 24–27, Paul applies this OT allusion to the present situation, arguing that these two sons correspond to two covenants, only one of which he then discusses at any length—namely, the Sinai covenant, which begets children for slavery and which corresponds to the current Jerusalem. There is an "above Jerusalem," *our* mother, who is free. In verses 28–31, Paul applies this analogy of Abraham's sons and the two covenants to the believers at Galatia, whom Paul affirms to be Isaac's children, according to the promise. As then, and also now, the merely fleshly descendant pursued the descendant who would inherit the promise. As then, and also now, the merely fleshly descendant who does not accept the promissory descendant excludes himself from blessing.

The rhetorical question is well framed: "Tell me, you who desire to be under the law, do you not listen to the law? For it is written . . ." Here, Paul extends his ordinary use of ὁ νόμος; the second use referring not to the covenant per se but to the covenant document, something that could be read audibly (οὐκ ἀκούετε),[16] something that is "written."[17] This introduction reiterates the Pauline position throughout Galatians 3 and 4: If one understands rightly the relationship between the Abrahamic and Sinai covenants—a relationship articulated in the books of Moses themselves—then one will candidly recognize both the limits of the Sinai administration and its temporary character. So Paul introduces a well-known narrative and does something with it that few would necessarily have understood to be an ordinary interpretation. Paul, in other words, could probably not have *proved* his argument from this narrative; he can, however, *illustrate* that argument in a convincing fashion, because a correct understanding of the Abrahamic administration recognized that it ultimately anticipated blessings on all people (not just Abraham's biological descendants), and that such blessings would be purely promissory, requiring no obedience to Mosaic commandments.[18]

Paul abbreviates the narrative of Hagar and Sarah, recording only what he regards as especially pertinent: "Abraham had two sons, one by a slave woman and one by a free woman. But the son of the slave was born according to the flesh, while the son of the

---

16. We note here that in a manuscript culture, most people would not have had access to manuscripts, or even the ability to read them; they would have encountered them through public *reading*, so Paul says οὐκ ἀκούετε, not οὐκ ἀναγινώσκετε.

17. Here also, note that the expression "it is written" in a manuscript culture is more than a mere "introductory formula" (though it may be that). Prior to inexpensive paper and movable type, the inscribing of anything on papyrus or animal skins was both laborious and expensive. Anything that was "written," therefore, was a matter of significant public consequence.

18. Contra Jubilees 16:21, which both erroneously and gratuitously affirmed that Abraham observed the Feast of Tabernacles.

free woman was born through promise." He makes no mention of the fact that Hagar was an Egyptian (Gen. 16:1, 3), nor does he mention that Sarah blamed Yahweh for her barrenness ("The LORD has prevented me from bearing children," Gen. 16:2). No mention was made of Hagar's "contempt" (ἠτιμάσθη) for Sarah, or of Sarah's wishing that her own "wrong" would come upon Abraham (who, after all, had not originated the plan; Sarah had). Paul cuts through these otherwise-interesting narrative details to call attention to only two things: the distinction between slave and free, and the distinction of flesh and promise. He has argued throughout Galatians that life under the Sinai administration was/is a kind of bondage; and he has argued throughout that the fruition of the Abrahamic covenant depended only on God's pledge/promise, whereas any fruition of the Sinai covenant depended upon Israelite works: "But the law is not of faith, rather 'The one who does them shall live by them'" (Gal. 3:12).

We observe also that the language suggests that Paul intends to illustrate what he has been saying about the difference between the Abrahamic covenant and the Sinai covenant; not the difference between the Sinai covenant and the new covenant. He indeed addresses all three covenants in the letter; but, just as the early parts of chapter 3 (vv. 6–14) contrast the Abrahamic and Sinai covenants, so also his conclusion of this part of the letter addresses the same two. "Abraham had two sons" is far more likely to be a reference to two covenant administrations made with his lineage than it is a reference to one covenant (Sinai) made with his lineage and another (the new) that is plainly not made with his lineage. So, while the implications of Paul's elucidation of these two covenants have profound consequences for his understanding of the new covenant, in this particular passage it is the two covenants (δύο διαθῆκαι, 4:24) made with Abraham's "sons" that are the point of this figure of speech.

Paul then suggests that there is something figurative[19] to be found in the story:

> Now this may be interpreted allegorically: these women are two covenants. One is from Mount Sinai, bearing children for slavery; she is Hagar. Now Hagar is Mount Sinai in Arabia; she corresponds to the present Jerusalem, for she is in slavery with her children. But the Jerusalem above is free, and she is our mother. For it is written, "Rejoice, O barren one who does not bear; break forth and cry aloud, you who are not in labor! For the children of the desolate one will be more than those of the one who has a husband."[20]

Paul's initial statement about this figure is covenant-historical: "These women are two covenants. One is from Mount Sinai, bearing children for slavery [εἰς δουλείαν]." The two references to "Mount Sinai" in the narrative make it unmistakable that what Paul

---

19. There is no reason to believe that Paul intends by ἀλληγορούμενα what we communicate by our term "allegory." The expression does not yet appear technical in Paul's day. It does not appear in the LXX, and in the Pseudepigrapha its one appearance need not be understood as technical: "The high priest explained to the Greeks who came to him these things concerning the allegorical method in the holy Law [τῆς ἀλληγορουμένης ἐν τοῖς ἱεροῖς νόμοις], even though they would encounter traditional interpretations of the writings. And Aristobulus was also acquainted with Aristotelian philosophy, in addition to [that of his] ancestors" (Aristobulus 2:1).

20. The "slavery" language in Gal. 4:21–31 is especially interesting, because it does not appear in the Hagar narrative in Gen. 16 and 21, where Hagar is referred to as a "servant" (παιδίσκη, 16:1–3, 5–6, 8; 21: 10, 12–13) or an "Egyptian" (Αἰγυπτία, 16:1, 3; 21:9), but not as a "slave" (δούλη).

is discussing is the Sinai covenant itself, as delivered by the hand of Moses on Mount Sinai—not some later perversion thereof, which is a point the dominant Protestant approach has characteristically misunderstood. It is not two interpretations of that covenant he discusses, but "two covenants"—one of which is specified to be the covenant made on Mount Sinai. The dominant Protestant approach has had enormous difficulty allowing Paul to speak for himself in Galatians. But we note that by two devices (one temporal, one geographic) he locates the "covenant" that he critiques as being geographically inaugurated on Mount Sinai and temporally inaugurated 430 years after the Abrahamic promise (διαθήκην προκεκυρωμένην ὑπὸ τοῦ θεοῦ ὁ μετὰ τετρακόσια καὶ τριάκοντα ἔτη γεγονὼς νόμος οὐκ ἀκυροῖ, 3:17). The "slavery" that concerned Paul in Galatians was the slavery he associated with the covenant administration inaugurated at Sinai over 430 years after the promissory Abrahamic covenant; it was not some alleged "slavery" associated with some rabbi, zealot, or cultist in Paul's own generation. The dominant Protestant approach to Paul therefore not only reads, as I say, "*between* the lines" (assuming the existence of a phenomenon for which little or no historical evidence exists), it reads "*against* the lines" by suggesting that Paul is discussing a first-century Palestinian CE reality rather than a second-millennium BCE reality on the Sinai Peninsula.

While I concur therefore with Sanders (et al.) that the dominant Protestant approach made an historical error, misconstructing first-century Palestinian Judaism on the basis (largely) of reading later texts, I go further than Sanders and argue that the dominant Protestant approach also made/makes an enormous exegetical error. The Letter to the Galatians is not silent about what Paul means by νόμος; it is a reality that came about 430 years after Abraham's descendants were enslaved (Gal. 3:17) and that took place at Sinai (4:24–25). It is a "covenant" (Gal. 3:17; 4:24), not a perversion or misunderstanding of one. The dominant Protestant approach has not merely misread the (constantly shifting) historical data pertinent to the period; it has misread what Paul's (never-shifting) letter expressly says, which I regard as an even greater liability for Pauline scholarship.

Most of the "slavery" language in Galatians is clustered here in chapter 4. Outside of Galatians 1:1 and 5:13, the other nine references are either in chapter 4 or nearly contiguous to it (the penultimate verse of Gal. 3 and the first verse of Gal. 5). Paul's understanding of the language is clear: "Now this may be interpreted allegorically: these women are two covenants. One is from Mount Sinai, bearing children for slavery; she is Hagar." There was and is only one "covenant . . . from Mount Sinai," and Paul affirms that said covenant bears children "for slavery." As I indicated earlier, it is less clear whether the precise definition of the "slavery" is Sinaitic separation from Gentiles, Sinai's curse sanctions, or merely the frustrated aspirations regarding the third pledge to Abraham that each of these entailed (or all three).[21] Since all three are part of Paul's reasoning in the letter, it may not be necessary to decide. What is unmistakable here in chapter 4, however, is that Paul regards being "under the law" (ὑπὸ νόμον, 4:21) as being enslaved:

---

21. However, since Paul's initial negative comparison between the Abrahamic and Sinai covenants distinguishes them, because one blesses and the other curses, I "lean" in the direction of judging that Paul's reference to enslavement is primarily because of the threatened curse sanctions at Sinai.

Now this may be interpreted allegorically: these women are two covenants. One is from Mount Sinai, bearing children for *slavery*; she is Hagar. Now Hagar is Mount Sinai in Arabia; she corresponds to the present Jerusalem, for she is in *slavery* with her children. But the Jerusalem above is *free*, and she is our mother. . . . But what does the Scripture say? "Cast out the *slave* woman and her son, for the son of the *slave* woman shall not inherit with the son of the *free* woman." So, brothers, we are not children of the *slave* but of the *free* woman. For *freedom* Christ has set us free; stand firm therefore, and do not submit again to a yoke of *slavery*. (Gal. 4:24–5:1)

Note that Sinai's "children" (unlike Abraham's) are of one kind; Mount Sinai bears children "for slavery" (εἰς δουλείαν γεννῶσα). Paul does not say that Mount Sinai "has two children," one who observes the covenant rightly and one who observes it wrongly; or one who understands it rightly and another who misunderstands it legalistically. It is Abraham (not Sinai) who has "two" sons—one unbounded by the enslaving realities of the Sinai administration, and the other bounded by those same realities. But Sinai has only one category of children: those who are εἰς δουλείαν γεννῶσα.[22] Note, then, that this is the near opposite of the dominant Protestant approach, which rests persistently on the notion that there is a right way and a wrong way to observe the Sinai covenant, and a right way and a wrong way to understand it; and that Paul in Galatians corrects those in his own generation, miles away from Sinai, who understand/observe it the wrong way. Yet in the heart of his most vigorous reasoning, the νόμος to which he objects is located squarely on the Mount Sinai 430 years after the Abrahamic promise; and he states that while Abraham had two sons (one slave/one free), Sinai's children, comprehensively considered as a unit, are born for slavery.

The dominant Protestant approach has routinely suggested that the reason the Sinai covenant produced children for bondage is because, as sinners, the Israelites either approached/understood the covenant the wrong way or failed to keep it because they were sinful. What the dominant Protestant approach has not explained is how/why/whether the same people did not also misunderstand the Abrahamic covenant. If the "bondage" associated with the Sinai covenant is due to human sinfulness or

---

22. Even defenders of the so-called Lutheran Paul are too generous to Sinai for my taste. Stephen Westerholm tends to join E. P. Sanders and the New Perspective in saying what I would contest. Referring to the law of Moses, Westerholm says, "It is a divine gift to Israel, a signal token of God's favor to his people." In *Perspectives Old and New*, 411. Similarly, James D. G. Dunn asks, "After all, had not the law been given to Israel as Israel's special prerogative, given to the chosen people as a mark of God's favour and thus to distinguish them from the other nations?" In "Works of the Law and the Curse of the Law," *Jesus, Paul, and the Law: Studies in Mark and Galatians* (Louisville, KY: Westminster/John Knox, 1990), 218. I believe sovereignty and grace/favor are being confused here (by many Pauline interpreters of every stripe). Yes, Yahweh sovereignly elected Israel to covenant with him. But I would not refer to a curse-threatening covenant as a "gift" or as any indication of God's "favor," especially if one reads the actual history of Israel, which was routinely a history that witnessed judgment after judgment, curse after curse. Surely the Israelites did not regard it as a "gift" when they expressed their considered preference to return to Egyptian bondage (e.g., Num. 11:18–20). Equally surely, they did not regard this curse-threatening covenant as an expression of Yahweh's "favor," as Moses reminded them: "And you murmured in your tents and said, 'Because the LORD hated us he has brought us out of the land of Egypt, to give us into the hand of the Amorites, to destroy us'" (Deut. 1:27). Cf. also my excursus, "Getting Out and Staying Out: Israel's Dilemma at Sinai," which appeared in *Pittsburgh Theological Review* 3 (2011–12): 3–37, and which is the final excursus in this book.

misunderstanding on the part of the Israelites, then why did not the same (alleged) sinfulness or misunderstanding produce bondage with the Abrahamic covenant? He refers to "*two* covenants" (αὗται γάρ εἰσιν δύο διαθῆκαι), only *one* (μία) of which produces bondage. From what we know from the Genesis passage, Abraham, Sarah, and Hagar were just as sinful as their later descendants would be. Abraham and Sarah doubted (and/or laughed at) God's promise; the three connived to produce a seed for Abraham that bypassed Sarah (and the ordinary conventions of sexual fidelity); and Abraham prevaricated twice about Sarah being his "sister" rather than his "wife." So why didn't the Abrahamic covenant produce children for bondage? Because it was a promissory covenant, dependent for its fruition only on the promise-keeping God's fidelity to his pledge.

What is somewhat less clear in this passage to some is whether the second "covenant" is the Abrahamic covenant or the new covenant; commentators have made cogent cases for each. One would think, for my covenant-historical approach to Galatians, that it would be critical to resolve this question, but it is not entirely so. It is evident throughout the reasoning of chapters 3 and 4 that the Abrahamic covenant and the new covenant have profound similarities: each embraces/includes all the nations/Gentiles of the earth; each is characterized by faith in the God who keeps his pledges; each is free of any threatened curse sanctions; and finally, the new covenant is regarded as the fulfillment/historical arrival of the reality pledged in the Abrahamic covenant. If we ask, then, whether the "our mother" of 4:26 is the figurative mother of members of the Abrahamic or the new covenant, the answer is probably "both." After all, Paul began this reasoning with this statement in 3:6–7: "Abraham 'believed God, and it was counted to him as righteousness.' Know then that it is those of faith who are the sons of Abraham" (Gal. 3:6–7). Paul has already indicated that those in Abraham's generation and those in Paul's generation who have faith in Abraham's God are his progeny.

Therefore, it is not necessary here to determine whether the allegory/figure intends to designate the second "son" as a member of the Abrahamic or the new covenant; rather, what is necessary for Paul is to designate the slave son as a child of Sinai. Paul's primary argumentative purpose in Galatians 3 and 4 is negative, not positive: to temporize and relativize the Sinai covenant, in order to put an end to the practice of requiring Gentile obedience to its ceremonies. Thus in this concluding illustration, it is far more important for Paul to identify which covenant is the "slave" than which is the free. Having said this, however, there is some good reason to think that the first-person plural here ("*our* mother") refers to those who are members of the new covenant. And, as we indicated above, "Abraham had two sons" is far more likely to introduce an illustration about the two covenants made with his sons/descendants than it is to introduce a discussion of the international and multiethnic new covenant.

Whereas the "our mother" in verse 26 is somewhat ambiguous (does it include Paul and other Jewish Christians, or all believers?), the second-person plural in verse 28 is unambiguous: "Now *you*, brothers, like Isaac, are children of promise." The predominately Gentile Galatians are described in three ways in this brief sentence—the first two being the ordinary term of address for Christian believers (ἀδελφοί, again in verse 31) who are "like Isaac" and who are "children of promise." Plainly, the third of these cannot be construed to mean "the children such as Isaac to whom the promises were originally given." Rather, it means the later descendants who ultimately receive the *substance* of what was earlier promised. And, of course, if it is the largely Gentile Galatians who are "like Isaac," then these new covenant believers are likened to the free son in the illustration. It is also possible that the "then/now" comparison of verse 29 also suggests that the "free son" is intended to be the new covenant believers in Paul's day. And the concluding statement in verse 31 surely suggests that it is new covenant believers who are represented by the free woman and the free child of the analogy: "So, brothers, we are not children of the slave but of the free woman." Even if the "we" here is the Jewish Christian "we" of earlier in chapters 2 and 3 (which I question, because the noun of address, ἀδελφοί, includes the Galatians), the "are" (ἐσμέν) surely indicates a present reality, the realities of the apostolic era.

Much of the rhetorical weight of the illustration falls toward the end of the comparison, where Paul extends the as-then/as-now comparison in two ways: Just as the child of the flesh pursued/persecuted (ἐδίωκεν) the child of the Spirit in that generation, "so also now . . ." (οὕτως καὶ νῦν)—a tantalizingly unfinished comparison. Paul does not expressly say, "So also now, the troublers at Galatia are persecuting you (and me)." Here, the power of suggestion is more useful than an express comment, but every hearer of the letter would have understood his meaning. He then extends the comparison in a second way: "But what does the Scripture say? 'Cast out the slave woman and her son, for the son of the slave woman shall not inherit with the son of the free woman.'" Whether Paul suggests here a formal ecclesiastical act (such as that in 1 Cor. 5), or merely a figurative act of ridding the Galatian churches of the error, he concludes the discussion of the comparison by insisting that the two parties must be separated, since the one party is intent on injuring the other.

5.5. Galatians 5:1—End of 4 or Beginning of 5?

> For freedom Christ has set us free; stand firm therefore, and do not submit again to a yoke of slavery.

Translators, commentators, and interpreters of Galatians are unsure whether to regard Galatians 5:1 as the conclusion of chapter 4 or the beginning of chapter 5.[23] The problem is partly due to the practices of early manuscript culture, which provide neither punctuation nor indentations at the beginnings of paragraphs. Because of this convention, whenever thought flows coherently from what we would call pericope to pericope, there is always the possibility that a given sentence could both end one section and begin another, analogous to enjambment in poetry. The conventions of manuscript culture simply did not force one to regard sentences as belonging to one paragraph or another, and the matter may be unsolvable.

Certainly, Galatians 5:2 appears to begin another section of some sort: "Look: I, Paul, say to you" (Ἴδε ἐγὼ Παῦλος λέγω ὑμῖν). The Ἴδε, combined with two subjects

---

23. Indeed, at least six different suggestions have been made for where the paranetical section of the epistle begins: 4:12; 4:21; 5:1; 5:2; 5:7; 5:13. See Merk, "Der Beginn der Paränese im Galaterbrief," 83–104; and the discussion of these options in Matera, "The Culmination of Paul's Argument to the Galatians," 79–91.

being supplied to a verb that already contains one in its ending, indicate a shift from what has preceded. Therefore, 5:1 could plausibly be construed as conclusive of the previous, rather than as a part of what continues through 5:2 and following. Surely, the language of slavery and freedom in 5:1 is closely related to the discussion of Hagar and Sarah in the previous section, and "yoke" is fairly likely a reference to the yoke of the Sinai covenant or the yoke of the Torah.[24] This appears to be how it was used in Acts 15, where it was reported that Gentiles were being circumcised "according to the custom of Moses," and Peter's reasoning about the matter was this: "Now, therefore, why are you putting God to the test by placing a yoke (ζυγὸν) on the neck of the disciples that neither our fathers nor we have been able to bear?" (Acts 15:10). Contextually there, the unbearable yoke appears to have been the covenant administration of Moses and its threatening curse sanctions.

While in itself "yoke" is a fairly neutral term to refer to an apparatus that permits two animals to work in tandem, it also developed some uses that were connotatively negative. It is sometimes used in the LXX to refer to oppressive political leadership; Egyptian bondage was spoken of this way in Leviticus 26:13, as was Babylonian bondage in Jeremiah 27:8, 11; 28:2, 4, 11, 14. Rehoboam even boasted of his oppressive rule by employing such language,

> "Your father made our yoke [τὸν ζυγὸν ἡμῶν] heavy. Now therefore lighten the hard service of your father and his heavy yoke [τοῦ ζυγοῦ αὐτοῦ] on us, and we will serve you." . . . "My father made your yoke [τὸν ζυγὸν ὑμῶν] heavy, but I will add to it. My father disciplined you with whips, but I will discipline you with scorpions." (2 Chron. 10:4, 14)

Not surprisingly, then, Maccabean literature refers to Hellenistic dominion this way: "In the one hundred and seventieth year the yoke of the Gentiles [ὁ ζυγὸς τῶν ἐθνῶν] was removed from Israel" (1 Macc. 13:41). In addition to a figure for political bondage, "yoke" is also occasionally employed to refer to the Sinai covenant between Yahweh and Israel: "For long ago I broke your yoke [τὸν ζυγόν σου] and burst your bonds; but you said, 'I will not serve.' Yes, on every high hill and under every green tree you bowed down like a whore" (Jer. 2:20; cf. 5:5).

It is entirely likely, therefore, that Paul intended what we know as 5:1 to be the exhortative summary of what he had argued in Galatians 3 and 4: The Sinai covenant, a burdensome yoke to those who lived under it, has disappeared with the appearance of the new covenant, and Paul commanded the Galatians to submit to it no more.

If Frank Matera is right,[25] the paraenetic material in Galatians 5 and 6 is the "culmination" of the argument made in the earlier parts of Galatians; it is not "bare" paraenesis with no relation to the previous material. I regard his reasoning as compelling, and because of this I do not believe it is critical to determine where the "arguments" of Galatians 3 and 4 end and the paraenesis of 5 and 6 begin. The difference is merely the rhetorical move from rationale to imperative. In chapters 5 and 6, Paul's

---

24. While the dating of Aboth 3:5 is a matter of some uncertainty, the sentiment expressed is likely old: "He who takes the yoke of Torah on himself shall have lifted from him the yoke of kingdom and the yoke of the world's way. But he who takes the yoke of Torah off himself shall find laid on himself the yoke of kingship and the yoke of the world's way."

25. Matera, "The Culmination of Paul's Argument to the Galatians," 79–91.

imperatives are more frequent; he regards his reasoning prior to this to be sufficient to permit him now to articulate the behavioral consequences of the earlier reasoning. Of the twenty-one imperatives in Galatians, there is one in chapter 1, zero in chapter 2, and one in chapter 3. Six appear in chapter 4 (but only three of those are Paul's; the other three are from his citation of the OT). Five imperatives appear in chapter 5 and seven in chapter 6. Only three imperatives appear before 4:12; the other eighteen after. Understood this way, 5:1 functions both as the summary of the reasoning in chapters 3 and 4 and the introduction to the remainder of the exhortations in chapters 5 and 6, which, as Matera has demonstrated, focus so much on circumcision, the "badge" that distinguished Jew from Gentile (5:2, 3, 6, 11; 6:12, 13, 15). To conclude what he has said to this point and to introduce the remainder, Paul says: "For freedom Christ has set us free; stand firm therefore, and do not submit again to a yoke of slavery."

Paul might have said the same thing to Peter at Antioch, and Galatians 5:1 could have concluded his reasoning with Peter in chapter 2. He also might just as aptly have placed it after Galatians 3:10–14, where he had said that those who were under the law were "under a curse," that no one was justified by the law, and that the law was not of faith. At each such point, he might have said, "For freedom Christ has set us free; stand firm therefore, and do not submit again to a yoke of slavery." He might have said it justly after 3:23, "Now before faith came, we were held captive under the law, imprisoned until the coming faith would be revealed." But now we are free from that law, imprisoned under it no more. In these and in other places, we can easily perceive that the sentiment contained in 5:1 is where Paul has been aiming throughout the previous reasoning. The practical result of arguing that the Sinai covenant was a temporary, curse-threatening, nonjustifying, Gentile-excluding, and fulfillment-of-Abraham's-third-promise-delaying covenant is that we should get out from under it as soon as possible and that we should refuse to be placed back under it again—which I judge to be what Paul says in Galatians 5:1.

CHAPTER 6

The Exhortations: Galatians 5–6

The exhortations of the fifth and sixth chapters of Galatians are neither random nor general. They grow out of the contest in which Paul has been engaged since the first chapter, and are what Frank J. Matera has rightly called the "culmination" of the argument of Galatians:

> Thus, although these chapters contain a great deal of moral exhortation, they should not be viewed exclusively as paraenesis. They are the climax of Paul's deliberative argument aimed at persuading the Galatians not to be circumcised. If this thesis is correct, Paul employs the paraenesis of these chapters to support his argument and bring it to its culmination.[1]

Therefore, when these exhortations are read correctly, they confirm one's reading of the rest of the book. My comments on this part of Galatians are briefer than on the other chapters, because these exhortations "culminate" the previous argument but do not make that argument, at least not in the same manner or detail. And it has been my purpose to explain the nature of Paul's theological reasoning, especially in chapters 3 and 4. As we observed earlier, only three of the twenty-one imperatives in Galatians appear before 4:12; the other eighteen appear from there onward.

It may be useful, however, albeit briefly, to observe how the exhortations in these chapters culminate the reasoning in the others. In the remainder of this chapter, I will attempt to demonstrate that the concerns of the rest of the book appear here also—but in the form of exhortations, more than in covenant-historical reasoning. Even a superficial glance at some of the lexical matters discloses this: Of the sixteen appearances of the language of circumcision and uncircumcision, six appear in chapter 2 and ten appear from 5:2 to 6:15 (as well as the delightfully sarcastic pun ἀποκόψονται in 5:13). Similarly, Paul speaks of those who "spy out our freedom . . . so that they might bring us into slavery [καταδουλώσουσιν]" in 2:4; and in 5:1 he exhorts the Galatians, "For freedom Christ has set us free; stand firm therefore, and do not submit again to a yoke of slavery [ζυγῷ δουλείας]." Similarly, the νόμος that has appeared twenty-five times in the reasoning of the first four chapters makes seven more appearances in the exhortations of chapters 5 and 6. The following observations from these chapters are not intended to be comprehensive; they are merely designed to demonstrate the culminating relationship between the exhortations of these chapters and the reasoning that preceded them.

6.1. Galatians 5:2–6

> Look: I, Paul, say to you that if you accept circumcision, Christ will be of no advantage to you. I testify again to every man who accepts circumcision that he is obligated to keep the

---

1. Matera, "The Culmination of Paul's Argument to the Galatians: Gal 5.1–6.17," *Journal for the Study of the New Testament* 32 (January, 1988), 80.

whole law. You are severed from Christ, you who would be justified by the law; you have fallen away from grace. For through the Spirit, by faith, we ourselves eagerly wait for the hope of righteousness. For in Christ Jesus neither circumcision nor uncircumcision[2] counts for anything, but only faith working through love.[3]

The three references to circumcision here (and the one to uncircumcision) disclose plainly that Paul's exhortation has the same concern as his six comments about the matter in chapter 2. This "badge" of Israelite belonging, this ceremony that distinguished Jew and Greek, no longer "counts for anything"; and for those who submit to the rite, "Christ will be of no advantage to you."

Paul even uses "again" (πάλιν) here, either to call attention to the general culminating nature of this exhortation or to refer back specifically to his citation earlier of Deuteronomy 27:26 in Galatians 3:10. Note the similarity between 3:10 and 5:3:

ἐπικατάρατος πᾶς ὃς οὐκ ἐμμένει πᾶσιν τοῖς γεγραμμένοις ἐν τῷ βιβλίῳ τοῦ νόμου τοῦ ποιῆσαι αὐτά. (Gal. 3:10)

μαρτύρομαι δὲ πάλιν παντὶ ἀνθρώπῳ περιτεμνομένῳ ὅτι ὀφειλέτης ἐστὶν ὅλον τὸν νόμον ποιῆσαι. (Gal. 5:3)

In addition to the reference to circumcision in each passage is the relationship between circumcision and "doing" the *entirety* of the Mosaic law, πᾶσιν . . . τοῦ νόμου τοῦ ποιῆσαι

---

2. The term ἀκροβυστία is peculiar. One would have expected a privative alpha in front of περιτομή, something like ἀπεριτομή, literally "un-circumcision." But the word, in fact, is formed from ἄκρος (topmost, highest, or outermost) and ποσθία or πόσθη (the male organ), cf. B-A-G, p. 33. The term is not only peculiar; it is comparatively rare, appearing sixteen times in the LXX, not at all in the Pseudepigrapha, and twenty times in the NT. Its two appearances in the Fathers (Barn. 9:4 and 13:7) both appear to be OT citations.

3. Hung-Sik Choi argues that ἐνεργέω in Gal. 5:6 is a reference to divine love, in part because "the verb ἐνεργέω itself usually has a supernatural connotation. . . . The fact that the verb is employed in Paul's letters to refer to effective divine and supernatural action points to πίστις in 5:6 as a divine power working for justification." In "*Pistis* in Galatians 5:5–6: neglected evidence for the faithfulness of Christ," *Journal of Biblical Literature* 124, no. 3 (September 1, 2005): 483. The verb does commonly enough have God as its subject (1 Cor. 12:6, 11; Gal. 2:8; 3:5; Eph. 1:11, 20; 3:20; Phil. 2:13; Col. 1:29; possibly 1 Thess. 2:13). But Paul also employs the verb with something other than God as its subject, including these examples (subject italicized):
"For while we were living in the flesh, *our sinful passions*, aroused by the law, were at work in our members [ἐνηργεῖτο ἐν τοῖς μέλεσιν ἡμῶν] to bear fruit for death." (Rom. 7:5)
"If we are afflicted, it is for your comfort and salvation; and if we are comforted, it is for your *comfort*, which you experience [τῆς ὑμῶν παρακλήσεως τῆς ἐνεργουμένης] when you patiently endure the same sufferings that we suffer." (2 Cor. 1:6)
"So *death* is at work in us, but *life* in you [ὥστε ὁ θάνατος ἐν ἡμῖν ἐνεργεῖται, ἡ δὲ ζωὴ ἐν ὑμῖν]." (2 Cor. 4:12)
"In which you once walked, following the course of this world, following the prince of the power of the air, the *spirit* that is now at work [τοῦ πνεύματος τοῦ νῦν ἐνεργοῦντος] in the sons of disobedience." (Eph. 2:2)
"For *the mystery of lawlessness* is already at work [ἤδη ἐνεργεῖται]. Only he who now restrains it will do so until he is out of the way." (2 Thess. 2:7)
These strike me as sufficiently clear and numerous that the verb itself does not settle the matter; and since the alternative (circumcision or uncircumcision) is a human behavioral matter, I am content that "faith working through love" here is human faith expressing itself in charity.

and ὅλον τὸν νόμον ποιῆσαι. As I argued earlier at 3:10, I take the πᾶσιν there and the ὅλον here as demanding *comprehensive* obedience, not necessarily *perfect* obedience. In covenantal terms, all of the stipulations are stipulations, and the covenant Suzerain may require obedience to the entirety of the body of stipulations. I have no objection to the idea that the law required perfect obedience; I just do not believe that Paul is arguing for such here.[4] What he is arguing is that the law (as a covenant administration) requires obedience to *all* that it requires and does not permit picking and choosing. That is, one cannot elect to observe circumcision without electing to observe other regulations, including those that segregate Israel from the Gentiles more generally.

Three times here, Paul affirms the mutual exclusivity of the law and circumcision on the one hand and Christ on the other: "If you accept circumcision, Christ will be of no advantage to you. . . . You are severed from Christ, you who would be justified by the law. . . . For in Christ Jesus neither circumcision nor uncircumcision counts for anything." The second of these poses a bit of a challenge for the translators, many of whom add "would be" before "justified by the law."[5] The translators who make this addition apparently do so because Paul has elsewhere in the letter denied that one can be justified by the law before God (2:16, 21; 3:11, 21). This translation is reasonable, but it is also possible that Paul is content to let the language stand as it is (lit., "you who are justified by the law") either as a sarcasm (in light of the prophetic judgments on Israel in almost every generation) or as a reference to the law's own pledge to justify its doers (which amounts to a kind of sarcasm, or taunt, also). It is also possible that Paul believed in a kind of "sub-eschatological" justification, which he appears to have affirmed at Philippians 3:6: "as to righteousness under the law, blameless" (κατὰ δικαιοσύνην τὴν ἐν νόμῳ γενόμενος ἄμεμπτος).

Therefore, I prefer the Authorized (King James) Version's translation, "whosoever of you who are justified by the law," because it challenges the audience to wrestle with whether they are justified, and/or in what degree, and/or by what instrument. That is, in theory, the Sinai covenant could and would justify/bless had the Israelites obeyed its commands; its curses fell only on disobedience, but blessings were pledged to obedience. So rather than fault them for a pretense ("who *would be* justified by the law"), or even an *improper* effort (as the dominant Protestant approach might), Paul simply reminds of the *terms* of that covenant—that it requires obedience to ὅλον τὸν νόμον ποιῆσαι. He says, effectively,

> All who wish to obey the law yourselves, and reap whatever temporal reward you may achieve thereby in the land of Canaan, go right ahead. But Christ has nothing to do with any of that—nothing to do with temporal prosperity for one nation in Canaan, and nothing to do with the obedience by which some degree thereof might be attained.

---

4. I actually believe that the most fundamental ethical duty is imbedded in creation. The human as *imago Dei* has the lifelong privilege/duty of *imitatio Dei*; and any of the various ethical commands in the Scriptures are merely specific, concrete instances of what constitutes such imitation. God didn't create fish to swim on occasion, or birds to fly on occasion, nor did he create humans to imitate him on occasion. Every justifiable human act (including thoughts and speech) imitates divine acts, and of course God requires entire/perfect compliance with our (original) created nature and purpose. But Paul is not talking about such creational realities in Galatians; he is talking about the stipulations of the Sinai covenant.

5. RSV, NRSV, ESV all take δικαιοῦσθε as a conative present, "would be" or "want to be."

Note that he employs ποιέω here, as he did elsewhere in Galatians (3:10 and 3:12, citing Lev. 18:5) and elsewhere generally (Rom. 2:14; 7:16, 21; 10:5, citing Lev. 18:5), because Paul understood the Sinai covenant's proffered blessings as being dependent upon obedience/works/doing, not upon faith.

The rationale for Paul's threefold distinction between Christ and the law/circumcision here is the principle of substitution: the blessings/cursings of the Sinai covenant are conditioned upon the obedience of the people themselves; if they obey they will be blessed in Canaan, and if they disobey they will be cursed there. But Paul has argued that, in Christ, the principle of substitution enters: "Christ redeemed us from the curse of the law by becoming a curse for us—for it is written, 'Cursed is everyone who is hanged on a tree'" (Gal. 3:13).[6] So Paul forces an either/or reasoning in order that we might paraphrase this way: "Evade (if you can) the curse sanctions of Sinai by your own behavior, or evade the same through the substitutionary work of Christ. But you cannot do both; you must choose."

By contrast to Sinai's temporal cursing/blessing based on obedience to the entirety of the law, Paul posits the Christian alternative: "For through the Spirit, by faith, we ourselves eagerly wait for the hope of righteousness" (5:5). The expression is highly eschatological: we *wait* for (ἀπεκδεχόμεθα) the *hope* of righteousness (ἐλπίδα δικαιοσύνης). This does not mean that Paul elsewhere cannot or does not refer to righteousness/acquittal/justification as something that is already ours by union with Christ (Rom. 3:24; 4:2; 5:1, 9 [δικαιωθέντες νῦν]; 6:7; 1 Cor. 6:11). Rather, the statement implies two things, in no particular order: that justification itself is an eschatological doctrine, and that Israel's covenant was merely temporal.[7]

First, justification is itself essentially an eschatological doctrine.[8] To be acquitted/justified in the ultimate sense is to survive God's final act of judgment that inaugurates the eschaton. Since the last Adam's resurrection and ascension both participate in that eschatological reality and guarantee it to others by union with Christ, texts such as the ones mentioned above refer to justification as a past and a present reality also.

Second, Israel did not wait for the hope of acquittal; if they were obedient, then they prospered temporally in the land of Canaan right then and right there. The curse they wished to evade/avoid similarly was not some far-off threat; it was immediate. "We," by contrast, *wait* for a righteousness (and its concomitant blessings) that remains future to us.

In 5:6, Paul says a similar thing to what he later says in 6:15, "For in Christ Jesus neither circumcision nor uncircumcision counts for anything [τι ἰσχύει], but only faith working through love [πίστις δι' ἀγάπης ἐνεργουμένη]." Note that early in the exhortations, and also right at the end of them (6:15), Paul asserts that the distinction between

---

6. Paul does not expressly, in Galatians, affirm that Christ's obedience/righteousness is also substitutionary, though he does so in Rom. 5:12–21, where the obedience is not Sinaitic but Adamic.

7. This is not to say that individual members of that covenant would not, did not, or will not participate in eschatological blessings; it is merely to say that if they do so, they will do so by the terms of the Abrahamic covenant (as fulfilled in Christ) rather than by the terms of the Sinai covenant.

8. Cf. Heinz-Dietrich Wendland, *Die Mitte der paulinischen Botschaft* (Göttingen: Vandenhoek & Ruprecht, 1935); "Der eschatologische Charakter der Rechtfertigung," 25–30, and "The Eschatological Character of Justification" (Section 27) in Herman Ridderbos, *Paul: An Outline of His Theology*, trans. J. R. De Witt (Grand Rapids: Eerdmans, 1975), 161–66.

circumcision and uncircumcision means nothing. As Frank Matera has argued, such exhortations are not mere appendages or general counsel; they are the "culmination" of Paul's argument in Galatians.[9] Here, as elsewhere in Galatians, it is Abrahamic faith that characterizes God's true people—those who have faith are the sons of Abraham (3:7). But here, in the exhortations section, Paul adds the qualifier "working through love." Throughout the exhortation portion of the letter, Paul is eager to indicate that "νόμος-free" does not mean "ethics free" or "licentious." While free from the obligation to observe the entirety of the Mosaic law (ὅλον τὸν νόμον), believers are not free from the fundamental ethical duty of love.[10]

6.2. Galatians 5:7–12

You were running well. Who hindered you from obeying the truth?[11] This persuasion is not from him who calls you.[12] A little leaven leavens the whole lump. I have confidence in the Lord that you will take no other view than mine, and the one who is troubling you[13] will bear the penalty, whoever he is. But if I, brothers, still preach circumcision,[14] why am I still being persecuted? In that case the offense of the cross has been removed. I wish those who unsettle you would emasculate themselves!

Circumcision, mentioned four times between Galatians 2:7 and 2:12, appears here again. Throughout the letter, Paul has demonstrated a concern to remove from the churches the ceremonial distinction between Jew and Gentile. Here, Paul observes that his law-free proclamation has exposed him to persecution from those who are unwilling to make a clear choice between the new covenant and its baptismal rite and the Sinai covenant with its circumcision. Paul does not specify the persecution here, but we know from Luke's account that Paul's detractors had accused him of lawbreaking. Both in Achaia[15] and in Jerusalem[16] his detractors had accused him of violating the law.

---

9. Matera "The Culmination of Paul's Argument to the Galatians," 79–91.

10. Many aspects of the Mosaic law reflect/demand the duty of love, as Rom. 13:8–10 and Gal. 5:14 demonstrate. While the distinction between positive law and moral law may have been unknown to Paul, and a later development in Western philosophy, Paul evidently believed that while the Sinai legislation in its entirety disappeared with the covenant itself, some of its particular commands reflected the fundamental creational imperative to imitate (the loving) God by loving others.

11. ἀλήθεια has not appeared in the letter since it twice appeared, qualified as τοῦ εὐαγγελίου, in 2:5 and 14. Note, then, how these exhortations "culminate," as Matera has observed, the concerns of the remainder of the epistle.

12. The participle τοῦ καλοῦντος ὑμᾶς recalls the similar τοῦ καλέσαντος ὑμᾶς in 1:6.

13. ὁ δὲ ταράσσων ὑμᾶς, cf. 1:7, οἱ ταράσσοντες ὑμᾶς.

14. The adverb ἔτι modifying κηρύσσω is, as Douglas A. Campbell has pointed out, problematic and has occupied the attention of interpreters for some time. Note the lengthy bibliographic footnote 32 on p. 335 in Campbell's "Galatians 5.11: Evidence of an Early Law-observant Mission by Paul?," *New Testament Studies* 57, no. 3 (July 2011): 325–47. The adverb implies that, at some point, Paul *did* proclaim circumcision, unless it is an unreal (contrary to fact) supposition, for rhetorical purposes (option #4 in Campbell's taxonomy, and the one I favor).

15. "This man is persuading people to worship God contrary to the law" (Acts 18:13).

16. "Men of Israel, help! This is the man who is teaching everyone everywhere against the people and the law and this place. Moreover, he even brought Greeks into the temple and has defiled this holy place" (Acts 21:28).

Circumcision was the rite that especially segregated the Jews from the Gentiles, and Paul's opinion about the matter is exactly what one would expect at this point in the letter: "For in Christ Jesus neither circumcision nor uncircumcision counts for anything [τι ἰσχύει], but only faith working through love [ἀλλὰ πίστις δι᾽ ἀγάπης ἐνεργουμένη]." Toward the end of the letter (6:15), Paul will say something similar, "For neither circumcision counts for anything [τί ἐστιν], nor uncircumcision, but a new creation [ἀλλὰ καινὴ κτίσις]." The pithy statement appears also in a slightly different manner in 1 Corinthians 7:19: "For neither circumcision counts for anything [οὐδέν ἐστιν] nor uncircumcision, but keeping the commandments of God [ἀλλὰ τήρησις ἐντολῶν θεοῦ]."

Calvin may have regarded Paul's discussion of circumcision as "trifling," but it was far from a trifling matter in Paul's day. The Israelites, for much of their history, did not want to be the "separate" people God had called them to be. They did not wish to commit *cherem* warfare when they originally dispossessed the *am ha-aretz*; they were frequently tempted to intermarriage and idolatry by them, and the entire program of return from exile was jeopardized by intermarriage with them. Therefore, whenever the Israelites *were* faithful to the separating ordinances (circumcision or diet), this was regarded as especially virtuous, as 4 Maccabees makes clear in describing the reaction of the faithful to Antiochus IV:

> And when he [Antiochus] could by no means destroy [καταλῦσαι] by his decrees the obedience to the law of the nation, but saw all his threats and punishments without effect, for even women, because they continued to circumcise their children [περιέτεμον τὰ παιδία], were flung down a precipice along with them, knowing beforehand of the punishment. When, therefore, his decrees were disregarded by the people, he himself compelled by means of tortures every one of this race, by tasting forbidden meats [ἀπογευομένους τροφῶν], to abjure the Jewish religion. (4 Macc. 4:24–26)

For Paul to say in his context that the rite for which faithful Israelite women gave their lives was "nothing" would have been anything but trifling; it might have been understood as disrespect, not only for the law but for the law's martyrs. Yet Paul persists in the point he has made throughout: Sinai's tutelage over God's visible people on earth was temporary; it only segregated Abraham's descendants from the nations until his nation-blessing "Seed" arrived, after which it was necessarily passé because it had completed its temporary task.

While Paul has no particularly new arguments to make here, his rhetoric is still significant; in two ways, he expresses contempt for those at Galatia who insist on circumcision. First, as was true in the beginning of the letter, he does not dignify his opponent(s) with a name; to the contrary, he says, "The one who is troubling you will bear the penalty, *whoever he is*" (ὅστις ἐὰν ᾖ, 5:10). And second, in a deliciously satirical insult, he says, "I wish those who unsettle you would emasculate themselves" (ἀποκόψονται, v. 12). The root of the verb is κόπτω, which appeared earlier in the pericope at verse 7: "Who hindered [ἐνέκοψεν, "cut you off"] you from obeying the truth?" While the more extended translations here are fine, the root often means simply "to cut":

> That place was called the Valley of Eshcol, because of the cluster that the people of Israel cut down [ὃν ἔκοψαν ἐκεῖθεν] from there. (Num. 13:24)

As when someone goes into the forest with his neighbor to cut wood [κόπτοντος τὸ ξύλον], and his hand swings the axe to cut down a tree, and the head slips from the handle and strikes his neighbor so that he dies—he may flee to one of these cities and live. (Deut. 19:5)

How he attacked you on the way when you were faint and weary, and cut off your tail [ἔκοψέν σου τὴν οὐραγίαν], those who were lagging behind you, and he did not fear God. (Deut. 25:18)

Then the men of the town said to Joash, "Bring out your son, that he may die, for he has broken down the altar of Baal and cut down the Asherah [ἔκοψεν τὸ ἄλσος] beside it." (Judges 6:30)

Most of the crowd spread their cloaks on the road, and others cut branches [ἄλλοι δὲ ἔκοπτον κλάδους] from the trees and spread them on the road. (Matt. 21:8)

The bracketing of the pericope with two different verbs from the same root is both artful and meaningful: the foreskin-cutting troublers at Galatia have "cut off" the Galatians from the full blessedness of the truth of the gospel; and in a moment of ironic and sarcastic judgment, Paul wishes that those who promote cutting off the foreskin would cut off the entire male sexual organ. The English translations have difficulty retaining the play on "cut," and perhaps ESV (and others) is a tad too Victorian in translating "emasculate themselves." Paul's point is more ribald, clever, and insightful; it could be rendered vernacularly: "As for those who trouble you by insisting that the foreskin of the male organ be cut off, I hope they cut the whole organ off!" Such a way of understanding the figure accomplishes two things: It understands that Paul's language here is intentionally contemptuous; and that Paul's language communicates disdain not only by being ribald but also by suggesting that, if they dismember themselves, the troublers will not be able to reproduce their kind in another generation. So the reference to the organ of reproduction is doubly significant.[17] Different cultures employ different euphemisms for referring to human sexuality, as when David told Uriah to "go down to your house and *wash your feet*," and Uriah understood him to be suggesting that he "go to my house, to eat and to drink and *to lie with my wife*" (2 Sam. 11:8, 11). Such differing cultures also have differing standards of how to refer to human sexuality in public or formal settings. It is understandable, therefore, that the English translations have attempted to avoid/evade violating public expectations; but it is also unfortunate that, in the process, they present a translation that is less pointed and less sarcastic/contemptuous than what Paul probably intended.

6.3. Galatians 5:13–15

Only do not use your freedom as an opportunity for the flesh, but through love serve one another. For the whole law [ὁ γὰρ πᾶς νόμος] is fulfilled in one word: "You shall love your neighbor as yourself." But if you bite and devour one another, watch out that you are not consumed by one another.

---

17. It may even be trebly significant. If it is an allusion to the same verb in Deut. 23:1, it effectively is a kind of anathema: "No one whose testicles are crushed or whose male organ is cut off [ἀποκεκομμένος] shall enter the assembly of the LORD."

The "freedom" Paul refers to here is the "freedom" from the Sinai covenant that has been his concern in his use of the ἐλεύθ- group seven times (of the nine in Galatians) from 4:22 until here. He has anticipated, as at Romans 6:1, that his declaration of freedom from the tutelage of the Mosaic law may lead some to believe he is a proponent of licentiousness, so he is quick to refute such a belief here. Paul anticipates what he will say next by his passing reference to the "flesh" here. The last thing one would do in this redemptive-historical moment, in which the temporary tutelage of Sinai yields to the inbreaking of the eschaton, is return to behavior characteristic of the old order.[18]

Neither Paul nor Jesus was the first to consider Leviticus 19:18 as a possible summary[19] of the entire ethical obligation of the Mosaic law. Other Second Temple sources did a similar thing:

> Therefore, guard the law of God [Φυλάξατε οὖν νόμον θεοῦ], my children, and acquire generosity, and walk in innocence; do not meddle in the commandments of the Lord and the business of your neighbor; but love the Lord and your neighbor [ἀγαπᾶτε κύριον καὶ τὸν πλησίον]; show mercy to the poor and weak. (Testament of Issachar 5:1–2)

Issachar here almost surely alludes to Leviticus 19:18 (ἀγαπήσεις τὸν πλησίον σου) and the *Shema* of Deuteronomy 6 (καὶ ἀγαπήσεις κύριον)—the same two commands Jesus referred to when replying to the question of which of the commandments in the law was the greatest (Matt. 22:36–40). Also note Sibylline 8:48: "And your neighbor love [ἀγαπᾶν τὸν πλησίον] wholly, even as yourself," which is a similar allusion to Leviticus 19:18, as is the double allusion in Testament of Benjamin 3:3–4:

> Fear the Lord and love your neighbor [φοβεῖσθε κύριον καὶ ἀγαπᾶτε τὸν πλησίον]. If the spirits of Beliar seek to oppress you with wicked tribulation, they will not overcome you,

---

18. Walt Russel, "The Apostle Paul's Redemptive-Historical Argumentation in Galatians 5:13–26," *Westminster Theological Journal* 57 (1995): 333–57. Russel takes the σάρξ/πνεῦμα contrast in Paul, not as his equivalent of the rabbinic *yetzer ha-ra* and *yetzer ha-tov*, but as a redemptive-historical contrast between the two ages, à la Herman Ridderbos, *Paul: An Outline of His Theology*, trans. J. R. De Witt (Grand Rapids: Eerdmans, 1975), 64–68.

19. I take πληρόω here as "summary" rather than as "prophetic fulfillment," even though I recognize that in Paul's overall theology he probably did believe that new covenant obedience fulfilled prophetically Jeremiah's longed-for new covenant in which the law of God would be written on the heart. However, in light of the statements in the intertestamental literature, and in light of Jesus' use of the verb κρέμαται ("hangs"), I think he is referring to a "summary" of the ethical demands of the Sinai covenant rather than to a prophetic fulfillment of them in this text. In Rom. 13:8–9 Paul can employ either πληρόω or ἀνακεφαλαιόω largely interchangeably: "The one who loves another has fulfilled [πεπλήρωκεν] the law. The commandments, 'You shall not commit adultery, You shall not murder, You shall not steal, You shall not covet,' and any other commandment, are summed up [ἀνακεφαλαιοῦται] in this word: 'You shall love your neighbor as yourself.'" Westerholm observes that while Paul routinely says that those under the law are required "to do" (ποιέω) it; when he refers to Christians and the law he routinely says (descriptively, not prescriptively) that they "fulfill" (πληρόω) it and observes that "such a consistent distinction in usage is striking indeed." Westerholm concludes his discussion by saying, "Thus statements of the law's 'fulfillment' should not be thought to compromise Paul's claim that the law does not bind believers. . . . The righteousness that divine commands could not elicit from a rebellious humanity becomes a possibility first for those transformed through the drama of divine redemption and the gift of the divine Spirit." In Westerholm, *Perspectives Old and New on Paul*, 436–37.

any more than Joseph my brother. Many people wished to kill him, but God watched over him. For the person who fears God and loves his neighbor [ὁ γὰρ φοβούμενος τὸν θεὸν καὶ ἀγαπῶν τὸν πλησίον αὐτοῦ] has on him the fear of God.

Paul, therefore, was not going out very far on a limb in asserting that the one who loves his neighbor fulfills the entirety of the law. Such an individual, more than one who is circumcised but does not love his neighbor, comes closer to fulfilling the demand of ὅλον τὸν νόμον ποιῆσαι of Galatians 5:3.[20]

It is not necessary to my purposes to express an opinion on whether Paul reasserts here the enduring obligation to (the moral portions of) the Mosaic law. He may very well be arguing that, even within the ethical commands of the Mosaic law (now defunct as a whole, as are the other aspects of that covenant), loving one's neighbor was considered to be a summary of other duties. If this is the case, his reasoning is something like this: "If you are unwilling to let go of Sinai and its laws, don't forget that it is love—not circumcision—that is regarded as the summary of what Torah requires."[21] Citing a well-known source of cultural ethical wisdom does not necessarily mean that one regards the source as morally authoritative. Rather, if one assumes that certain human behaviors have been widely (if not universally) approved, then one can simply appeal to a source that one's *audience* regards as authoritative or informative to substantiate one's exhortations. As Debbie Hunn put it, "Paul may appeal to Greek poets, gentile morality, or a desire for happiness to bolster an argument without establishing them as general standards for doctrine or praxis."[22]

---

20. So Matera: "Clearly, Paul is developing the argument against circumcision mounted in 5.1–12. There he said that the circumcised Galatians will be responsible to *do* all the prescriptions of the Law (ὅλον τὸν νόμον). Here he says that uncircumcised Galatians, living by the Spirit, *fulfill* the Law in its totality (ὁ πᾶς νόμος) through the love commandment (5.14), what Paul calls in 5.6, 'faith working through love.'" Matera, "Culmination," 85–86.

21. It would require a separate monograph to engage the question of whether Paul cites some portions of the Decalogue (e.g. at Rom. 13:8–10 or Eph. 6:2) as obligatory per se, or as obligatory because they reflect the creational duty of *imitatio Dei*. Both positions have been evident in dogmatic history; and in Reformed theological history, they have ordinarily been known respectively as the "law in the hand of Moses" view and the "law in the hand of Christ" view. I embrace the latter view; technically considered, the ten words oblige only the covenant people to whom they were given. Their obligation extends to others insofar (but only insofar) as they reflect the original creational mandate to imitate (the loving) God. John Gill represented this tradition when he said, "Christ is king and lawgiver in his house and kingdom, the church and besides some positive commands which he has delivered out, there is a repetition of the law in the New Testament; a new edition of it, published under the authority and sanction of Christ; so that we are now under the law to him (1 Cor. 9:21) and under new obligations to obey it, as held forth by him. . . . Upon the whole, let it be an instruction and direction to you to look to the law only as in Christ; viewed otherwise it is a terrible law, a fiery one, working wrath and threatening with it; throwing out its menaces, curses, damnation and death; but view it in Christ, and there it is fulfilled, its curse is removed, its demands answered, and that itself magnified and made honourable: and appears lovely and amiable, to be delighted in and served with pleasure." John Gill, "The Law in the Hand of Christ: A Sermon Preached May 24, 1761, at Broad-Mead, in Bristol."

22. Debbie Hunn, "Christ versus the Law: Issues in Galatians 2:17–18," *Catholic Biblical Quarterly* 72, no. 3 (July 1, 2010): 553. While it is not essential or especially pertinent to my reading of Galatians, it is consistent with my reading to recognize that a covenant-historical reading tends to recognize that covenants are wholes. The conditions of a covenant, the parties

I suspect that Paul intended an irony in the closing warning of this section: "But if you bite and devour one another, watch out that you are not consumed by one another." Effectively he says something ironic like this: "You will bite, devour, and consume one another, but will not take table fellowship *with* one another."

6.4. Galatians 5:16–24

But I say, walk by the Spirit, and you will not gratify the desires of the flesh. For the desires of the flesh are against the Spirit,[23] and the desires of the Spirit are against the flesh, for these are opposed to each other, to keep you from doing the things you want to do. But if you are led[24] by the Spirit, you are not under the law. Now the works of the flesh[25] are evident: sexual immorality, impurity, sensuality, idolatry, sorcery, enmity, strife, jealousy, fits of anger, rivalries, dissensions, divisions, envy, drunkenness, orgies, and things like these. I warn you, as I warned you before, that those who do such things will not inherit the kingdom of God. But the fruit of the Spirit[26] is love, joy, peace, patience, kindness, goodness, faithfulness, gentleness, self-control; against such things there is no law. And those who belong to Christ Jesus have crucified the flesh with its passions and desires.

---

of a covenant, the stipulations of a covenant, the ceremonies of a covenant, etc., are all integrated parts of the covenant itself; and when a covenant disappears, it disappears in its entirety. This perspective, while perhaps not common, is not new. In the nineteenth century, it was articulated by Stuart Robinson, who said regarding the Decalogue: "This is a covenant transaction, and this law, so called, constitutes simply the stipulations of that covenant. So it is expressly declared of it, 'The Lord our God made a covenant with us at Horeb.' It was ratified formally, as a covenant, when first received, the people being called upon solemnly to swear it, after it had been written down in a book." Stuart Robinson, *Discourses of Redemption* (Richmond: Committee on Education, 1866), 124. By analogy, my mortgage contract obliges no one but me; when it is paid off in full, it will no longer oblige even me. So also covenant stipulations per se oblige no one but the parties to the covenant. Insofar as those stipulations reflect or reiterate "natural law," they are obligatory—but for that reason and not because they appeared as stipulations of a given covenant.

23. ESV (also RSV, NRSV) elects to make a nominal expression here ("are against"), rather than a true verbal one: "For the flesh desires against [ἐπιθυμεῖ κατὰ] the Spirit." The KJV reliably (and quaintly) translates the verb as a verb: "For the flesh lusteth against the Spirit." Paul twice elsewhere (Rom. 7:7; 13:9) employs ἐπιθυμέω to translate the final command of the Decalogue, following the LXX.

24. The construction of the conditional clause is significant. Paul employs εἰ with an indicative mood, present-tense verb: εἰ δὲ πνεύματι ἄγεσθε. Such a condition is a condition of fact and could be translated, "Since you are led by the Spirit, you are not under the law." It is similar to Rom. 8:11 or 25: "If [εἰ] the Spirit of him who raised Jesus from the dead dwells [οἰκεῖ] in you, he who raised Christ Jesus from the dead will also give life to your mortal bodies through his Spirit who dwells in you. . . . But if we hope [εἰ . . . ἐλπίζομε] for what we do not see, we wait for it with patience." Each could be translated "Since the Spirit . . . dwells" or "Since we hope."

25. τὰ ἔργα τῆς σαρκός. This is probably a play on the ἔργων νόμου that appear at 2:16 (three times) and 3:2, 5, and 10. Other than here and at 6:4, ἔργα in Galatians are always "works" of the law because the law requires *doing*; recall 3:12: "But the law is not of faith, rather 'The one who *does* them shall live by them' [ὁ δὲ νόμος οὐκ ἔστιν ἐκ πίστεως, ἀλλ' ὁ ποιήσας αὐτὰ ζήσεται ἐν αὐτοῖς]." The realm of both law and flesh is the realm of human work; the realm of faith and Spirit is the realm of God's work in Christ.

26. Similarly, Paul refers to the "fruit" (καρπὸς) of the Spirit, because he understands the Spirit to be the enlivening agent of the new eschatological era; the behaviors/virtues that appear in believers are the fruit of the Spirit's activity, not their own "work."

The passage begins and ends with a discussion of that "fleshly" behavior (or slavery) from which believers have been delivered. The two interior sections disclose what characterizes fleshly behavior and the behavior of the Spirit. The opposition of Spirit and flesh is not in the first place anthropological: σάρξ and πνεῦμα are not anthropological terms for Paul, and they are not the equivalent of the rabbinic *yetzer ha-ra* and *yetzer ha-tov*; they do not refer to different parts or aspects of every human. Rather, here as elsewhere, σάρξ refers to the entirety of fallen human existence and experience; it designates the entirety of the era under the curse sanctions of Genesis 3. By contrast, πνεῦμα is language of the new age, the "age to come" (ὁ μέλλων αἰών), an age revivified by the same Spirit that hovered over the face of the deep in the original, pre-fallen created order. The enmity spoken of between flesh and Spirit (ἀλλήλοις ἀντίκειται) is, in my judgment, redemptive. I take the purpose clause, as does the ESV: "to keep you from doing the things you want to do." Apart from the re-creating Spirit, humans are under bondage to sin and mortality, and this bondage is ordinarily spoken of by the convenient Pauline shorthand, "flesh." In the flesh, humans do whatever they wish (ἃ ἐὰν θέλητε), often with disastrous consequences. When the risen Christ sends the Spirit to the church, there is now resistance to this fleshly impulse—a resistance that is redemptive, albeit imperfectly so in this life. Consistently with his reasoning in chapter 3, he places νόμος in the pre-eschatological era and πνεῦμα in the eschatological era: "If (since) you are led by the Spirit, you are not under the law."

6.4.1. The Works of the Flesh

Verses 19–21 contain what some scholars call a "vice list."[27] Others appear at Romans 13:13, 1 Corinthians 6:9–10, Ephesians 5:5, Colossians 3:5, 1 Peter 4:3, and Revelation 21:8 and 22:15 (and in the early fathers, *Didache* 2:1–7 and 3:1–6). Typically, such Christian lists (also common in the Greco-Roman world) include idolatry (εἰδωλολατρία) and sexual impurity (πορνεία, ἀκαθαρσία, ἀσέλγεια). Paul includes fifteen items on his list (his longest), seven of which (the three just mentioned, plus φαρμακεία, μέθη, and κῶμος, sorcery, drunkenness, and carousing) are fairly common on other lists in other places. Eight of the terms on this list, however, are uncommon: ἔχθραι, ἔρις, ζῆλος, θυμοί, ἐριθεῖαι, διχοστασίαι, αἱρέσεις, φθόνοι (enmity, strife, jealousy, fits of anger, rivalries, dissensions, divisions, and envy). These distinctive terms describe fleshly behavior, especially insofar as it becomes divisive or partisan, which is precisely the issue between the circumcised and uncircumcised at Galatia.

---

27. B. S. Easton, "New Testament Ethical Lists," *Journal of Biblical Literature* 51 (1932): 1–12; J. T. Fitzgerald, "Virtue/Vice Lists," in *Anchor Bible Dictionary*, ed. David Noel Freeman, vol. 6 (New York: Doubleday, 1992): 857–59; C. G. Kruse, "Virtues and Vices," *Dictionary of the New Testament* 1:962–63; N. J. McEleney, "The Vice Lists of the Pastoral Epistles," *Catholic Biblical Quarterly* 36 (1974): 203–19; G. Mussies, *Catalogues of Sins and Virtues Personified*, Nag Hammadi Codices 2.5 (Leiden: E. J. Brill, 1981); D. Schroeder, "Lists, Ethical," *The Interpreter's Dictionary of the Bible Supplement*, ed. George A. Buttrick (New York: Abingdon, 1962), 546–47; J. D. Charles, "Vice and Virtue Lists," in *Dictionary of New Testament Background: A Compendium of Contemporary Biblical Scholarship*, ed. Stanley E. Porter and Craig A. Evans, electronic ed. (Downers Grove, IL: InterVarsity Press, 2000).

6.4.2. The Fruit of the Spirit

In contrast to such works of the flesh, Paul mentions the fruit characterized by the Spirit: love, joy, peace, patience, kindness, goodness, faithfulness, gentleness, and self-control. While some of these are general virtues, they are virtues of an especially irenic kind; these are the traits that would prevent the Galatians from biting and devouring one another.

6.5. Galatians 5:25–26

If we live[28] by the Spirit, let us also walk by the Spirit. Let us not become conceited, provoking one another, envying one another.

Paul returns to where he began earlier in 5:16 where he urged, "Walk by the Spirit [πνεύματι περιπατεῖτε], and you will not gratify the desires of the flesh." Here also, "Since we live by the Spirit, let us also walk by the Spirit [πνεύματι καὶ στοιχῶμεν]."

Since "empty" (κενὸς) can mean "vain" or "pointless," by extension it could mean "conceited," as ESV and NRSV take it here. But "empty" or "pointless" is still a substantial part of the root, and I suspect this is what Paul means here. He often uses it to refer to his fear that own ministerial work will come to no good end:

But by the grace of God I am what I am, and his grace toward me was not in vain [οὐ κενὴ]. (1 Cor. 15:10)

And if Christ has not been raised, then our preaching is in vain [κενὸν] and your faith is in vain [κενὴ]. (1 Cor. 15:14)

Therefore, my beloved brothers, be steadfast, immovable, always abounding in the work of the Lord, knowing that in the Lord your labor is not in vain [οὐκ ἔστιν κενὸς]. (1 Cor. 15:58)

Working together with him, then, we appeal to you not to receive the grace of God in vain [μὴ εἰς κενὸν]. (2 Cor. 6:1)

I went up because of a revelation and set before them (though privately before those who seemed influential) the gospel that I proclaim among the Gentiles, in order to make sure I was not running or had not run in vain [μή πως εἰς κενὸν]. (Gal. 2:2)

Holding fast to the word of life, so that in the day of Christ I may be proud that I did not run in vain or labor in vain [οὐκ εἰς κενὸν]. (Phil. 2:16)

For you yourselves know, brothers, that our coming to you was not in vain [οὐ κενὴ]. (1 Thess. 2:1)

For this reason, when I could bear it no longer, I sent to learn about your faith, for fear that somehow the tempter had tempted you and our labor would be in vain [εἰς κενὸν]. (1 Thess. 3:5)

---

28. The same condition of fact is established here as at 5:18 by the use of εἰ with the indicative: "Since we live by the Spirit."

I judge that what he means here is something similar: "Do not reason and think so unproductively, in your divisive provoking and envying; I wonder if I've done any good among you at all." Each of the participles (προκαλούμενοι and φθονοῦντες) is a *hapax*, but the nominal form of the second just appeared in 5:21, φθόνοι—"envy." Contextually, it is probably the envying of the circumcised and the uncircumcised at Galatia; perhaps the circumcised envy those who "got off easy" without the Mosaic ceremonies; and perhaps the uncircumcised envy those who are Abraham's physical descendants. But for Paul, for whom neither circumcision nor uncircumcision is anything, this is an entirely empty and futile (κενός/κενόδοξος) exercise. Now that the Spirit—the eschatological gift—is here, the Mosaic covenant is over, its marking ceremonies are over, and this is simply no time for Jews and Gentiles to envy one another; the very distinction is now moot.

6.6. Galatians 6:1–5

Brothers, if anyone is caught in any transgression, you who are spiritual[29] should restore him[30] in a spirit of gentleness. Keep watch on yourself, lest you too be tempted. Bear one another's burdens, and so fulfill the law of Christ.[31] For if anyone thinks he is something, when he is nothing, he deceives himself. But let each one test his own work, and then his reason to boast will be in himself alone and not in his neighbor. For each will have to bear his own load.

There is some difficulty in discerning what unites this passage (if anything). It would be easiest to separate the first two verses from the latter three; this would have the first two verses dealing with the general matter of congregational burden-bearing, especially bearing the burden of restoring someone caught in a trespass, and thus fulfilling the law of Christ; and the last three verses dealing with ministerial labor. But the γάρ in verse 3 suggests that the matters there are germane to the two earlier verses and the use of βαστάζετε in verse 2 and βαστάσει in verse 5 suggests a single pericope also.

The "if anyone" at the beginning suggests that the text addresses an issue that may be germane to any member of the Galatian congregations; but some of the later

---

29. "You who are spiritual" is probably the best way to render the English, rather than something like "the spiritual among you," since Paul regards the NT community as the community of the Spirit. That is, ὑμεῖς οἱ πνευματικοὶ designates the Galatian congregation(s), not some smaller subset of unusually spiritual ones within. The CEV translates it correctly: "My friends, you are spiritual. So if someone is trapped in sin, you should gently lead that person back to the right path."

30. RSV/ESV rightly translates τὸν τοιοῦτον as "him" (NIV "restore that person"), since Paul does not mean merely "someone like this" but "this one and others like him." KJV translates "restore such an one," and NRSV translates "restore such a one."

31. This unusual expression appears twice in the Apostolic Fathers. Ignatius, *To the Magnesians*, refers to "my fellow-servant the deacon Sotio, whose friendship may I ever enjoy, inasmuch as he is subject to the bishop as to the grace of God, and to the presbytery as to the law of Jesus Christ" (νόμῳ Ἰησοῦ Χριστοῦ). Barnabas also said, "These things therefore he annulled, in order that the new law of our Lord Jesus Christ [ὁ καινὸς νόμος τοῦ Κυρίου ἡμῶν Ἰησοῦ Χριστοῦ], being without the yoke of necessity [ἄνευ ζυγοῦ ἀνάγκης ὤν], might not have its offering by human hands" (2:6).

language "test his own work," "reason to boast," may suggest ministerial activity. The only other place, for instance, where ἔργον and δοκιμάζω appear together in Paul's writings is at 1 Corinthians 3:13, "The fire will test what sort of work each one has done" (τὸ ἔργον ὁποῖόν ἐστιν τὸ πῦρ δοκιμάσει), where the context plainly discusses ministerial ἔργον. Similarly, the καυχ- vocabulary in Paul ordinarily refers to "boasting" in ministerial labor. Of the fifty-five uses of this vocabulary, at least thirty-three refer to ministerial labor.[32] So it is possible that the particular "transgression" here is the transgression of the Galatian error itself, a reference to the "troubler" (or one troubled) who needs to be corrected and restored. This would, however, be a somewhat unusual understanding of παράπτωμα.[33]

If verse 1 is separated out by itself, then some (but by no means all) of the difficulty is relieved. Verse 1 could stand on its own as a general, aphoristic exhortation: "Brothers, if anyone is caught in any transgression, you who are spiritual should restore him in a spirit of gentleness. Keep watch on yourself, lest you too be tempted." If so, then a new pericope begins with verse 2: "Bear one another's burdens [Ἀλλήλων τὰ βάρη βαστάζετε], and so fulfill the law of Christ."[34] This would make the matter somewhat easier, because the "burdens" borne at Galatia might very well be caused by the "troublers" and their divisiveness.

Part of the difficulty of relating the two uses of βαστάζω in verses 2 and 5 is due to the translation of φορτίον in verse 5, a NT *hapax*. Why is this the direct object of the second verb, while τὰ βάρη is the object of the first use of the verb? Are these synonyms, or does this suggest that Paul is saying something different in verse 5 than in 2? Paul's usage of βάρος twice elsewhere (2 Cor. 4:17; 1 Thess. 2:7) is hardly sufficient to establish the range of meaning, but its usage at the Jerusalem Council may be pertinent: "For it has seemed good to the Holy Spirit and to us to lay on you no greater burden [μηδὲν πλέον . . . βάρος πλὴν τούτων] than these requirements" (Acts 15:28). For Paul (and the Jerusalem Council), the Christian moment is a moment of burden-bearing and burden-relieving, not a moment of burden-increasing. The Sinai covenant, with its Israel-segregating and curse-threatening nature, is now gone.

The expression τὸν νόμον τοῦ Χριστοῦ has intrigued commentators for some time and will probably continue to do so. What I regard as least likely, among proposed interpretations, is any interpretation suggesting that Paul refers here to the Mosaic law. While I have argued throughout this monograph that ὁ νόμος ordinarily refers to the Mosaic covenant, the usage here is distinct from the other uses. Of the thirty-two uses of νόμος in Galatians, this is the only one that is qualified by an adjective or qualifying genitive. Paul goes out of his way to employ ὁ νόμος paradoxically here to mean something *other* than what it means in its unqualified sense. It is also entirely possible that the presence of the reciprocal pronoun (Ἀλλήλων τὰ βάρη βαστάζετε) is intended to allude to the "new commandment" of Jesus in John 13:34: "A new commandment

---

32. Rom. 15:16–17; 1 Cor. 3:21; 9:15–16; 15:31; 2 Cor. 1:12, 14; 5:12; 7:4, 14; 8:24; 9:2–3; 10:8, 13, 15–16; 11:10, 12, 16–18, 30; 12:1, 5–6; Phil. 2:16.

33. It is not impossible that ἔν τινι παραπτώματι here refers to those "works of the flesh" earlier mentioned, many of which denoted behavior or attitudes that were of a divisive or partisan nature. If so, Paul is urging the Galatians to reject Judaizing while restoring Judaizers.

34. NA 27 and UBS 4 take this approach, capitalizing Ἀλλήλων at the beginning of verse 2. Few English translations follow this lead, however.

I give to you, that you love one another [ἀλλήλους]: just as I have loved you, you also
are to love one another [ἀλλήλους]."

Certainly, the referent of τὸν νόμον τοῦ Χριστοῦ cannot be the same referent as
the unqualified use of ὁ νόμος throughout the letter. The unqualified "law" throughout the reasoning of Galatians was the one that came 430 years after the promise (Gal.
3:17). So those interpreters who wish to retain some sense of the Mosaic law here
can only plausibly do so by suggesting that the expression means something like "the
Mosaic law as understood and/or interpreted by Christ and his apostles." There is
nothing objectionable per se to such a suggestion, since both Christ and his apostles
did reiterate some of the commandments of Moses (e.g., Rom. 13:8–10). It strikes me
as much more likely, in the Galatian context where Paul has expressly stated that the
Galatians are not ὑπὸ νόμον (3:23; 4:21; 5:18), that his language is deliberately both
neologistic and somewhat ironic.

Although it would take a separate monograph to demonstrate the matter, Paul's
ethical teaching is surprisingly independent of the Mosaic traditions when one
considers how well trained Paul was therein. While he indeed makes reference to
several of the Mosaic commands in Romans 13:8–10, and while he reiterates the
duty of Leviticus 19:18 there and also here in Galatians 5:14, much of Paul's most
substantive ethical teaching makes no reference to the Mosaic law at all, perhaps
most notably Philippians 2 and 1 Corinthians 13. Insofar as we discover Paul's ethical
teaching, it will never be merely that of another rabbi, expounding the Mosaic law
from a (to him) contemporary perspective. Paul can "do ethics," as it were, entirely
without the Mosaic law; and, in my judgment, when he does refer to it, it is for the
strategic reason of indicating that the stipulations of the Christian covenant are, in
some particulars, not different from the stipulations of the Mosaic covenant. But he
can also exert his apostolic authority as a minister of the new covenant in places such
as 1 Corinthians 13 without any reference to the Mosaic law at all. I therefore regard
it as extremely unlikely that τὸν νόμον τοῦ Χριστοῦ means anything like "the Mosaic
law as interpreted by Christ." The statement is far more polemical and ironic, and it
means something like this: "The important thing now is to live as followers of Christ,
following the stipulations of his covenant; if we need a νόμον now, it is Christ's law."

6.7. Galatians 6:6–10

One who is taught the word must share all good things [ἐν πᾶσιν ἀγαθοῖς] with the one
who teaches. Do not be deceived: God is not mocked, for whatever one sows [σπείρῃ], that
will he also reap [θερίσει]. For the one who sows [ὁ σπείρων] to his own flesh will from
the flesh reap [θερίσει] corruption, but the one who sows [ὁ δὲ σπείρων] to the Spirit will
from the Spirit reap [θερίσει] eternal life. And let us not grow weary of doing good [τὸ δὲ
καλὸν ποιοῦντες], for in due season we will reap [θερίσομεν], if we do not give up. So then,
as we have opportunity, let us do good [τὸ ἀγαθὸν] to everyone, and especially[35] to those
who are of the household of faith.

---

35. It is not at all pertinent or germane to my overall thesis how to take the μάλιστα in verse
10. I do observe, however, that the translation "especially" is not the only way to take the term.
Elsewhere in Paul, the term could better be translated as "namely" or "specifically." T. C. Skeat

The unity in this pericope is indicated both by the *inclusio* language of "doing good" in verses 6, 9, and 10 and by the word-chains of "sowing" and "reaping" in the interior lines. Further, Paul inserts a conclusion in his own hand (apart from his amanuensis) in verse 11 that separates that verse from these. For three reasons, I regard this pericope as teaching the duty of supporting the Christian ministry financially: the mention of κατηχούμενος τὸν λόγον in the first line; Paul's financial usage of the κοινωνέω vocabulary; and Paul's financial usage of the vocabulary of doing good.

We observe that the introduction of the pericope evidently exhorts to a financial compensation for Christian ministry: "One who is taught the word must share all good things with the one who teaches." The meaning of the verse here suggests an appropriate care for Christian instructors, and the interpretive question is then whether Paul changes direction to discuss more general Christian duties in the following verses, or whether he continues to discuss this particular duty in those verses.

If the ἀγαθοῖς here denotes the same thing as the τὸ ἀγαθὸν in verse 10 (and, probably, the synonym τὸ δὲ καλὸν in verse 9), then the particular well-doing is the financial/material care for the well-being of Christian instructors. Elsewhere, the expression "to do good" in the NT sometimes has the notion of such material benevolence. Contextually, there is little doubt that this is the meaning at 2 Corinthians 9:8: "And God is able to make all grace abound to you, so that having all sufficiency in all things at all times, you may abound in every good work [πᾶν ἔργον ἀγαθόν]." Throughout that chapter, Paul has urged the Corinthians to participate in material relief for those other saints who are suffering, and his point is summarized in verse 7: "Each one must *give* as he has made up his mind, not reluctantly or under compulsion, for God loves a cheerful *giver*." The particular "good work" he invokes is the good work of ministering to the material needs of other saints, which he also describes using the sowing/reaping language employed in our pericope: "The point is this: whoever sows sparingly will also reap sparingly [ὁ σπείρων φειδομένως φειδομένως καὶ θερίσει], and whoever sows bountifully will also reap bountifully" (ὁ σπείρων ἐπ᾽ εὐλογίαις ἐπ᾽ εὐλογίαις καὶ θερίσει, 2 Cor. 9:6). This appears to be the meaning of doing good also at 2 Thessalonians 3:11–13: "For we hear that some among you walk in idleness, not busy at work, but busybodies. Now such persons we command and encourage in the Lord Jesus Christ to do their work quietly and to earn their own living. As for you, brothers, do not grow weary in doing good" (καλοποιοῦντες). The opposite of not being busy at work is those who "work quietly" and "earn their own living," which permits such brothers to do "good" in the almsgiving sense of the word.

The "sharing" language (Κοινωνείτω) of verse 6 is also employed elsewhere to denote material sharing:

---

has argued, correctly I think, that in 2 Tim. 4:13, the term means "namely." "Bring the books, that is to say more specifically, the parchments." Skeat understands the term to be employed this way also in Titus 1:10–11, "In other words, the Jewish converts." He adduces a third NT example from 1 Tim. 4:10, "We have set our hope upon the living God, who is the saviour of all people, namely of those who believe" (especially apt, because there also μάλιστα qualifies πᾶς). Skeats offers other examples from the papyri. Cf. " 'Especially the Parchments': A Note on 2 Timothy IV.13," *Journal of Theological Studies* 30, no. 1 (1979): 173–77. I prefer understanding Paul to say that we ought to provide material support ("to do good") for all categories (Jews and Gentiles?)—namely, within the household of the faith.

Contribute to the needs of the saints [ταῖς χρείαις τῶν ἁγίων κοινωνοῦντες] and seek to show hospitality. (Rom. 12:13)

For Macedonia and Achaia have been pleased to make some contribution for the poor [κοινωνίαν τινὰ ποιήσασθαι εἰς τοὺς πτωχοὺς] among the saints at Jerusalem. They were pleased to do it, and indeed they owe it to them. For if the Gentiles have come to share [ἐκοινώνησαν] in their spiritual blessings, they ought also to be of service to them in material blessings. (Rom. 15:26–27)

Begging us earnestly for the favor of taking part in the relief of the saints [τὴν κοινωνίαν τῆς διακονίας τῆς εἰς τοὺς ἁγίους]. (2 Cor. 8:4)

By their approval of this service, they will glorify God because of your submission flowing from your confession of the gospel of Christ, and the generosity of your contribution [ἁπλότητι τῆς κοινωνίας] for them and for all others. (2 Cor. 9:13)

And you Philippians yourselves know that in the beginning of the gospel, when I left Macedonia, no church entered into partnership [ἐκοινώνησεν] with me in giving and receiving, except you only. [And probably 1:5, "Because of your partnership in the gospel (τῇ κοινωνίᾳ ὑμῶν εἰς τὸ εὐαγγέλιον) from the first day until now."] (Phil. 4:15)

I thank my God always when I remember you in my prayers, because I hear of your love and of the faith that you have toward the Lord Jesus and all the saints, and I pray that the sharing of your faith [ἡ κοινωνία τῆς πίστεώς] may become effective for the full knowledge of every good thing that is in us for the sake of Christ. [N.B. that the "love . . . for all the saints" precedes "sharing your faith."] (Philem. 4–6)

Such language is employed also by Paul's travel partner, Luke:

And they devoted themselves to the apostles' teaching and fellowship [τῇ κοινωνίᾳ],[36] to the breaking of bread and the prayers. . . . And all who believed were together and had all things in common [κοινὰ]. (Acts 2:42, 44)

The particular "sharing" envisioned in this passage is almost certainly the sharing in the ministerial work of the gospel, which sharing is a kind of "sowing" to the Spirit, an investment in the Spirit's work of giving life through Christian instruction.

Now, of course, the language of "doing good" does not always denote material giving, and the language of "sharing" does not always denote material sharing, and the language of sowing to/reaping from the Spirit does not always denote such material sharing. The combination of them all here, combined with Paul's expressed concern for those who are instructors in the word (τῷ κατηχοῦντι) in verse 6, suggests that this is what Paul is saying in this pericope.

We may also see in this pericope another example of what Frank J. Matera has called the "culmination" of the argument at Galatians. Earlier, in the autobiographical section, Paul indicated that the Jerusalem apostles added nothing to his gospel;

---

36. Calvin understood κοινωνίᾳ here to refer not exclusively to material giving, but to all those duties of fellowship that included almsgiving: "I do rather refer it [κοινωνίᾳ] unto mutual society and fellowship, unto alms, and unto other duties of brotherly fellowship." Calvin, *Commentary on Galatians* (repr., Grand Rapids: Baker, 1979), 126.

they only reminded him to care for the poor (2:10). In these verses, Paul effectively reminds his readers (and the Jerusalem apostles, if they are overhearing this) that it is also important to provide fiscal support for the Christian ministry.

6.8. Galatians 6:11–16

See with what large letters I am writing to you with my own hand.

It is those who want to make a good showing in the flesh who would force you to be circumcised, and only in order that they may not be persecuted for the cross of Christ. For even those who are circumcised do not themselves keep the law, but they desire to have you circumcised that they may boast in your flesh. But far be it from me to boast except in the cross of our Lord Jesus Christ, by which the world has been crucified to me, and I to the world. For neither circumcision counts for anything, nor uncircumcision, but a new creation. And as for all who walk by this rule, peace and mercy be upon them, and upon the Israel of God.

From now on let no one cause me trouble, for I bear on my body the marks of Jesus.

The grace of our Lord Jesus Christ be with your spirit, brothers. Amen.

This text can be divided into four parts. The bulk appears in verses 12–16, which are preceded by a Pauline authentication and followed by a final warning and benediction. The initial clause has been variously interpreted, but the most natural interpretation is simply to recognize the common practice of amanuensis in the ancient world.[37] Paul was not trained to etch letters skillfully onto papyrus or animal skins, and so he undoubtedly employed an amanuensis to craft his letters with/for him. On several other occasions, he mentioned his appending a greeting/authentication in his own hand (1 Cor. 16:21; Col. 4:18; 2 Thess. 3:17; Philem. 19). Further, his amanuensis appears to identify himself at the end of the Letter to the Romans: "I Tertius, who wrote this letter [ὁ γράψας τὴν ἐπιστολὴν], greet you in the Lord" (Rom. 16:22). The "large letters" need not be a reference to failing eyesight or even emphasis; Paul simply was not trained in the fine art of crafting neat letters, so his greeting was noticeably less artful than that of the rest of the manuscript.

---

37. For a brief introduction to the practice, cf. the following: Gordon J. Bahr, "Paul and Letter Writing in the First Century," *Catholic Biblical Quarterly* 28 (1966): 465–77; Richard Bauckham, "Pseudo-Apostolic Letters," *Journal of Biblical Literature* 107, no. 3 (1988): 469–94; William G. Doty, *Letters in Primitive Christianity*, Guides to Biblical Scholarship: New Testament, ed. Dan O. Via, Jr. (Philadelphia: Fortress, 1988); Harry Y. Gamble, "Amanuensis," *Anchor Bible Dictionary*, vol. 1., ed. David Noel Freedman (New York: Doubleday, 1992); Richard N. Longenecker, "Ancient Amanuenses and the Pauline Epistles," *New Dimensions in New Testament Study*, ed. Richard N. Longenecker and Merrill C. Tenny (Grand Rapids: Zondervan, 1974), 281–97; E. Randolph. Richards, *The Secretary in the Letters of Paul* (Tübingen: Mohr Siebeck, 1991); E. Iliff Robson, "Composition and Dictation in New Testament Books," *Journal of Theological Studies* 18 (1917): 288–301; Stanley K. Stowers, *Letter Writing in Greco-Roman Antiquity*, Library of Early Christianity, vol. 8, ed. Wayne A. Meeks (Philadelphia: Westminster, 1989); Robert W. Wall, "Introduction to Epistolary Literature," *New Interpreter's Bible*, vol. 10., ed. Leander E. Keck (Nashville: Abingdon, 2002), 369–91.

It is not at all surprising that the concluding pericope would "culminate" so much of the rest of the letter. Several of the recurring matters in the letter appear here also. The references to circumcision and uncircumcision in 12, 13, and 15 surely reflect the concern with the matter elsewhere in the book:

ἀλλ᾽ οὐδὲ Τίτος ὁ σὺν ἐμοί, Ἕλλην ὤν, ἠναγκάσθη περιτμηθῆναι· (Gal. 2:3)

ἀλλὰ τοὐναντίον ἰδόντες ὅτι πεπίστευμαι τὸ εὐαγγέλιον τῆς ἀκροβυστίας καθὼς Πέτρος τῆς περιτομῆς, ὁ γὰρ ἐνεργήσας Πέτρῳ εἰς ἀποστολὴν τῆς περιτομῆς ἐνήργησεν καὶ ἐμοὶ εἰς τὰ ἔθνη, καὶ γνόντες τὴν χάριν τὴν δοθεῖσάν μοι, Ἰάκωβος καὶ Κηφᾶς καὶ Ἰωάννης, οἱ δοκοῦντες στῦλοι εἶναι, δεξιὰς ἔδωκαν ἐμοὶ καὶ Βαρναβᾷ κοινωνίας, ἵνα ἡμεῖς εἰς τὰ ἔθνη, αὐτοὶ δὲ εἰς τὴν περιτομήν· (Gal. 2:7-9)

πρὸ τοῦ γὰρ ἐλθεῖν τινας ἀπὸ Ἰακώβου μετὰ τῶν ἐθνῶν συνήσθιεν· ὅτε δὲ ἦλθον, ὑπέστελλεν καὶ ἀφώριζεν ἑαυτόν φοβούμενος τοὺς ἐκ περιτομῆς. (Gal. 2:12)

Ἴδε ἐγὼ Παῦλος λέγω ὑμῖν ὅτι ἐὰν περιτέμνησθε, Χριστὸς ὑμᾶς οὐδὲν ὠφελήσει. μαρτύρομαι δὲ πάλιν παντὶ ἀνθρώπῳ περιτεμνομένῳ ὅτι ὀφειλέτης ἐστὶν ὅλον τὸν νόμον ποιῆσαι. (Gal. 5:2-3)

ἐν γὰρ Χριστῷ Ἰησοῦ οὔτε περιτομή τι ἰσχύει οὔτε ἀκροβυστία ἀλλὰ πίστις δι᾽ ἀγάπης ἐνεργουμένη. (Gal. 5:6)

Ἐγὼ δέ, ἀδελφοί, εἰ περιτομὴν ἔτι κηρύσσω, τί ἔτι διώκομαι; ἄρα κατήργηται τὸ σκάνδαλον τοῦ σταυροῦ. (Gal. 5:11)

The reference to "(not) keep the law" in verse 12 reminds of the thirty-two uses of νόμος in the letter, and the pregnant little formula in verse 15—οὔτε γὰρ περιτομή τί ἐστιν οὔτε ἀκροβυστία ἀλλὰ καινὴ κτίσις—is nearly identical to its earlier appearance at 5:6—ἐν γὰρ Χριστῷ Ἰησοῦ οὔτε περιτομή τι ἰσχύει οὔτε ἀκροβυστία ἀλλὰ πίστις δι᾽ ἀγάπης ἐνεργουμένη.

Similarly, the book continues with the interesting question of who is persecuting whom for what. Earlier, Paul had candidly referred to himself as a former persecutor:

Ἠκούσατε γὰρ τὴν ἐμὴν ἀναστροφήν ποτε ἐν τῷ Ἰουδαϊσμῷ, ὅτι καθ᾽ ὑπερβολὴν ἐδίωκον τὴν ἐκκλησίαν τοῦ θεοῦ καὶ ἐπόρθουν αὐτήν. (Gal. 1:13)

μόνον δὲ ἀκούοντες ἦσαν ὅτι ὁ διώκων ἡμᾶς ποτε νῦν εὐαγγελίζεται τὴν πίστιν ἥν ποτε ἐπόρθει. (Gal. 1:23)

In his discussion of the Hagar/Sarah narrative in chapter 4, he also referred to the persecution of the one brother by the other: ἀλλ᾽ ὥσπερ τότε ὁ κατὰ σάρκα γεννηθεὶς ἐδίωκεν τὸν κατὰ πνεῦμα, οὕτως καὶ νῦν (Gal. 4:29). In 5:11, he raised the matter of his own persecution to prove that he remained faithful to his apostolic call: Ἐγὼ δέ, ἀδελφοί, εἰ περιτομὴν ἔτι κηρύσσω, τί ἔτι διώκομαι; ἄρα κατήργηται τὸ σκάνδαλον τοῦ σταυροῦ. Here he raises the question of persecution again; only now it is his opponents whom he accuses for an unwillingness to experience the kind of persecution he once did and now suffers from: οὗτοι ἀναγκάζουσιν ὑμᾶς περιτέμνεσθαι, μόνον ἵνα τῷ σταυρῷ τοῦ Χριστοῦ μὴ διώκωνται.

These culminating comments demonstrate how far off the dominant Protestant approach to the letter really was. Calvin's reference to ceremonies as a "trifling" concern in itself failed to estimate how important the realizing of the Abrahamic pledge to bless all the nations by his seed really was for Paul. Not merely the rite of circumcision, but even the distinction of "circumcised" and "uncircumcised" is refuted in this concluding part of the letter: οὔτε γὰρ περιτομή τί ἐστιν οὔτε ἀκροβυστία. Paul once persecuted those who did not distinguish Jew and Gentile; now he is persecuted because he refuses to acknowledge the distinction. There is nothing "trifling" about whether one is a persecutor or persecutee, and nothing trifling about whether God has kept his pledge to bless *all* the nations of the world through Abraham's single seed.

The culminating comments also revive part of the earlier polemic, because Paul again questions the motives behind Judaizing. Earlier, he had accused Peter and others of cowardice (φοβούμενος τοὺς ἐκ περιτομῆς, 2:12) and hypocrisy (συνυπεκρίθησαν αὐτῷ . . . καὶ Βαρναβᾶς συναπήχθη αὐτῶν τῇ ὑποκρίσει, 2:13); here he says his opponents only wish "to make a good showing in the flesh" (6:12) or to "boast in your flesh" (6:13).

Before his concluding warning and blessing (oddly juxtaposed in verses 17 and 18, and exclusively here in the Pauline corpus), Paul presents a penultimate (and somewhat puzzling) blessing: καὶ ὅσοι καὶ ὅσοι τῷ κανόνι τούτῳ στοιχήσουσιν, εἰρήνη ἐπ᾽ αὐτοὺς καὶ ἔλεος καὶ ἐπὶ τὸν Ἰσραὴλ τοῦ θεοῦ. Peace and mercy are expressed to those who walk by "this rule/canon" (τῷ κανόνι τούτῳ): to wit, that there is no distinction between circumcision and uncircumcision. Then Paul adds the much disputed καὶ ἐπὶ τὸν Ἰσραὴλ τοῦ θεοῦ. The expression Ἰσραὴλ τοῦ θεοῦ does not appear elsewhere in the NT or in the LXX or the Pseudepigrapha. Thus what is true of τὸν νόμον τοῦ Χριστοῦ in Galatians 6:2 is also true here: the qualifying genitive is both deliberate and surprising, thereby intentionally altering the ordinary understanding of the word's referent without the genitive qualifier. The unqualified term Ἰσραήλ ordinarily refers to the genetic descendants of Abraham, in Paul's usage or elsewhere.[38] But Paul was the first to qualify the term with the genitive—τοῦ θεοῦ—and this qualification of a term that was so common in its unqualified form was almost certainly disjunctive in some way. This is especially so since the two terms are frequently paired with one another in reverse order.

The expression "God of Israel" (אלהי ישראל) appears 198 times in the Hebrew Bible. "God of Israel" appears 103 times in the LXX, and once in the Pseudepigrapha. That is, the two terms appearing in construct relation are quite common in the Hebrew Bible, and therefore also in the LXX, where Ισραηλ, though uninflected, is in the construct state/genitive case. Thirty-three of the LXX uses are fairly general, as when the Levites are distinguished from the other tribes: "The God of Israel [ὁ θεὸς Ισραηλ] has separated you from the congregation of Israel" (Num. 16:9), or "The Lord God of Israel [κύριος ὁ θεὸς Ισραηλ] fought for Israel" (Josh. 10:42), or "The Lord, the God of Israel, has given rest [κατέπαυσεν κύριος ὁ θεὸς Ισραηλ] to his people" (1 Chron. 23:25).[39]

---

38. Though at the perplexing Rom. 9:7, Paul also indicates that Ἰσραὴλ may not be a reference to Abraham's natural descendants, οὐ γὰρ πάντες οἱ ἐξ Ἰσραὴλ οὗτοι Ἰσραήλ. Here, at least, not all who are ἐξ Ἰσραὴλ are, in fact, Ἰσραήλ. So the Galatian enigma may have a friend or cousin in Romans.

39. The general uses can be found at: Exod. 34:23; Num. 16:9; Josh. 10:40, 42; 22:16; 24:25; Judg. 4:6; 11:21, 23; 1 Sam. 1:17; 5:7, 8, 10–11; 1 Chron. 5:26; 15:12; 23:25; 24:19; 28:4; 2 Chron.

But the paired words also appear in more formal ways: three times in oaths (1 Sam. 20:12; 25:34; 1 Kings 17:1), ten times in formal blessings expressed to God, such as when David said to Abigail, "Blessed be the Lord, the God of Israel [εὐλογητὸς κύριος ὁ θεὸς Ισραηλ], who sent you this day to meet me!" (1 Sam. 25:32; also 1 Kings 1:48; 8:15; 1 Chron. 16:36; 29:10; 2 Chron. 2:12; 6:4; Ps. 41:13; 72:18; 106:48); and eighteen times in formal address being made to God, such as when the Israelites inquired, "O Lord, the God of Israel [κύριε ὁ θεὸς Ισραηλ], why has this happened in Israel, that today there should be one tribe lacking in Israel?" (Judg. 21:3; cf. also 1 Sam. 14:41; 23:60; 1 Kings 8:23, 25–26, 28; 18:36; 2 Kings 19:15; 2 Chron. 6:4, 16–17; Ezra 9:15; Jdt. 13:7; Isa. 37:16; Bar. 2:11; 3:1, 4). And thirty times the expression "God of Israel" appears in the formulaic, "Thus says the Lord, the God of Israel." (Ordinarily τάδε λέγει κύριος ὁ θεὸς Ισραηλ, but there are variants, such as τάδε εἶπεν κύριος ὁ θεὸς Ισραηλ or even οὕτως εἶπεν κύριος ὁ θεὸς Ισραηλ. Cf. Exod. 5:1; 32:27; Josh. 7:13; 24:2; Judg. 6:8; 1 Sam. 2:30; 10:18; 2 Sam. 12:7; 23:3; 1 Kings 11:31; 20:28; 2 Kings 9:6; 19:20; 21:12; 22:15, 18.) So the pairing of these two terms is entirely commonplace in the Old Testament, where the expression "God of Israel" appears over a hundred times.

But the converse never happens; for words that appear over a hundred times in construct relation with one another, the construct noun is always Ισραηλ and never θεοῦ. Paul's juxtaposition of the two terms, however, reverses this consistent trend in the Hebrew Bible and in the LXX. "God" is no longer qualified by "Israel," but "Israel" is qualified by "God." This can hardly be an oversight or undeliberate. To qualify "Israel" with "God" (rather than the other way around) must have been intentional, and an effort to refer not to what the unqualified "Israel" ordinarily means (to wit, the ethnic descendants of Abraham), but to "Israel" as the true inheritors of the promises made to Abraham (3:29; 4:28; and to the nations through his single descendant, 3:14, 16), to "Israel" as the true people of God, and to "Israel" as those who have the faith of Abraham (Gal. 3:7). In Romans 9:6–7 (NRSV), Paul indicated that "Israel" can mean something other than the genetic descendants of Abraham, when he said, "It is not as though the word of God had failed. For not all Israelites truly belong to Israel [οὐ γὰρ πάντες οἱ ἐξ Ἰσραὴλ οὗτοι Ἰσραήλ], and not all of Abraham's children are his true descendants."

What was true at Galatians 6:2 (τὸν νόμον τοῦ Χριστοῦ) is also true at Galatians 6:16. Here, a term that has significant theological consequences is used with remarkable regularity and consistency in its unqualified form; but the same term, when qualified, can have a different referent altogether. In English, "Mother" probably refers to one's biological female parent over 99 percent of the time; but in Roman Catholic thought and liturgy, "Mother of God" refers to someone else altogether. When I am preparing a meal in the kitchen and say, "Mother, could you put the salad bowls on the table?," I am not soliciting any aid from the Virgin Mary. "Law" routinely and regularly refers to the Mosaic covenant, and "Israel" in Paul's letters regularly refers to the genetic descendants of Abraham. But each term (τὸν νόμον and Ἰσραὴλ, respectively), when qualified by a genitive noun that is also theologically significant (τοῦ Χριστοῦ and τοῦ θεοῦ, respectively), can and does thereby refer to another thing altogether. "Law of Christ" does not refer to the Mosaic covenant; and "Israel of God" does not refer

---

13:5; 36:13; 1 Esdr. 5:48; 8:3; Ezra 6:22; 7:6; Ps. 59:5; 68:8, 35; Sir. 47:18; Zeph. 2:9; Isa. 24:15; 41:17; 52:12.

to the genetic descendants of Abraham. In each case, the addition of the qualifying genitive creates a kind of intentional neologism—a deliberate way of saying a new thing with old language; a purposeful "play" not merely *on* words but *with* words. In this case, then, τὸν Ἰσραὴλ τοῦ θεοῦ is a play that is also paradoxical: Contrary to all expectations, the true "Israel of God" is actually constituted of those who recognize the rule that οὔτε γὰρ περιτομή τί ἐστιν οὔτε ἀκροβυστία.

Paul concludes the letter as he does in no other, combining a warning with a blessing: "From now on[40] let no one cause me trouble,[41] for I bear on my body the marks of Jesus. The grace of our Lord Jesus Christ be with your spirit, brothers. Amen." The irony in the warning could hardly be more apt: "You who wish to mark bodies with the rites of Abraham and Moses should not forget that my body is marked with the result of my being persecuted for my consistent testimony about the Gentile-including new covenant." Paul challenges his troublers mark for mark, as it were. His blessing is common; most of his letters (as with Galatians) begin and end with a similar greeting that refers to "the grace of the Lord" or "the grace of the Lord Jesus Christ," or sometimes χάρις ὑμῖν καὶ εἰρήνη ("grace to you and peace"), combining both. Paul still regards the Galatian congregations as being true Christian congregations, despite the presence of the troublers in their midst. Throughout the letter, he writes as though the troublers are a minority faction, which may be merely rhetorical or may be his true estimate. Either way, he does not afflict the congregation with his repeated ἀνάθεμα ἔστω of chapter 1; he reserves that for the troublers themselves, still wishing the grace of Christ on the remainder of the assembly.

---

40. ESV's translation (also NRSV, RSV "henceforth," perhaps out of deference to KJV "from henceforth") of Τοῦ λοιποῦ as "from now on" strikes me as somewhat tone-deaf to the rhetoric of the letter. "Finally," or more literally, "my remaining comment" suggests that this is right at the end of what one has to say. At Eph. 6:10, ESV translates the identical expression "Finally," as it does the almost-identical Λοιπόν at 2 Cor. 13:11 and Phil. 3:1 and 8. While the consequence is not grave, it is significant. Is the point that Paul is telling his troublers not to do so any more, or is the point that the last thing he's going to *say* is that he is not putting up with their burdens?

41. The combination of παρέχω and κόπος is without precedent in Paul and appears in the NT only on four other occasions. Both Matthew and Mark employ the combination when the woman anoints Jesus' feet and the disciples object, to which Jesus says, "Why do you trouble her?" (τί αὐτῇ κόπους παρέχετε; Matt. 26:10; Mark 14:6). In the parable of the visitor at night and of the importunate woman (Luke 11:7; 18:5), the expression also appears, referring to the bothersome or inconvenient behavior.

CHAPTER 7

Quo Vadis: Where Do We Go from Here?

Some of the exegetical matters I have discussed in Galatians might be smaller points of exegetical observation with little significance beyond their own role in construing the letter. But some of the observations—and my overall approach to the letter—may have broader implications, implications that others may elect to pursue elsewhere. For the sake of candor, if nothing else, here are what I regard to be some of the implications of this approach in several other areas.

7.1. For Pauline Studies

7.1.1. νόμος as Synecdoche for the Sinai Covenant

While my primary interest has been to understand the nature of Paul's reasoning in Galatians—and while his reasoning there is not necessarily his reasoning elsewhere, nor his vocabulary necessarily his vocabulary elsewhere—I have taught and studied the book of Romans for over twenty-five years and have found that, with few exceptions, the prevailing use of νόμος in Paul's other letters, including Romans, is the same as for Galatians. I even regard it as the "default use" for Paul. To be sure, "Torah" is part of "Tanakh," so there are passages where "the law" is a reference to the covenant *document* itself, the written Torah. But even here, the use is one of extension, because even the "Torah" that is part of "*Tanakh*" is the written record of the covenant itself. In the following texts, for instance, νόμος may well designate that written record:

> Now we know that whatever the law says it speaks to those who are under the law, so that every mouth may be stopped, and the whole world may be held accountable to God. (Rom. 3:19)

> What then shall we say? That the law is sin? By no means! Yet if it had not been for the law, I would not have known sin. I would not have known what it is to covet if the law had not said, "You shall not covet." (Rom. 7:7)

> For Moses writes about the righteousness that is based on the law, that the person who does the commandments shall live by them. (Rom. 10:5)

> Do I say these things on human authority? Does not the law say the same? For it is written in the Law of Moses, "You shall not muzzle an ox when it treads out the grain." Is it for oxen that God is concerned? (1 Cor. 9:8–9)

> In the law it is written, "By people of strange tongues and by the lips of foreigners will I speak to this people, and even then they will not listen to me, says the Lord." (1 Cor. 14:21)

> The women should keep silent in the churches. For they are not permitted to speak, but should be in submission, as the law also says. (1 Cor. 14:34)

> Tell me, you who desire to be under the law, do you not listen to the law? (Gal. 4:21)

But I suggest that even in texts such as these, "law" does not become some general moral will or ethical truth; even in these texts, the "law" is the written record of the stipulations of the *covenant* Yahweh made with the Israelites, and so the covenantal overtones of νόμος remain in these texts. This understanding might prove especially helpful in instances where the expression ὑπὸ νόμον appears. In such passages, it may also prove helpful to paraphrase "under (the) law" as "under the Sinai covenant administration."

I might even recommend to students of Paul that they spend an afternoon doing the assignment I have done with my students, an assignment easily aided by computers. First, find the 121 uses of νόμος in Paul's letters and then copy them (in English) into a word processor. Then run a search/replace to replace "law" with "God's moral will" and repeat this procedure for two other documents, replacing "law" with "legalism" in one and "Sinai covenant" in the other. Then go through each of the documents, writing "Y," "N," or "?" in the margin of each usage, asking if the text would make plausible sense construed this way. What one inevitably finds is that the fewest "Ns" go to "Sinai covenant." Many Pauline texts make no sense at all translated by the other words; but nearly all will make sense translated as the "Sinai covenant" (especially when it is extended to mean the document in which that covenant was recorded).

Now, of course, it is entirely possible that for Paul, νόμος has a range of meanings; polyvalency is a well-established lexical reality. But it is less likely that Paul would change his use of such a theologically significant term without some contextual clue, and it is entirely unlikely that he would do so within a brief context in which the term is employed several times. Where, for instance, within Galatians 3 does he change his definition from "Sinai covenant" (which it evidently means at 3:17) to something else? Those many Pauline students, who for years have suggested that νόμος has a wide range of usage in Paul, did so largely because none of the other proposed definitions could make even plausible sense of many of its uses. They were forced, in other words, to find multiple definitions, because no single definition could make much sense of the majority of his texts. But this is because they did not consider "Sinai covenant" as one of the uses. When one does, one finds that it accounts for a substantial majority of his texts.[1]

Such an understanding of νόμος evades/avoids a common criticism that νόμος does not translate Torah adequately, because Torah is (ostensibly) more comprehensively "instruction" and includes priestly ceremonies, commandments, and many other things.[2] Well, "instruction" has its own problems as well, because Torah was

---

1. I do not think my definition works particularly well at Rom. 3:27—διὰ ποίου νόμου; τῶν ἔργων; οὐχί, ἀλλὰ διὰ νόμου πίστεως. Similarly, I do not believe it makes especially good sense of Rom. 8:2—ὁ γὰρ νόμος τοῦ πνεύματος τῆς ζωῆς ἐν Χριστῷ Ἰησοῦ ἠλευθέρωσέν σε ἀπὸ τοῦ νόμου τῆς ἁμαρτίας καὶ τοῦ θανάτου. On the other hand, these two texts are difficult for almost *any* definition of νόμος. A plausible construal is possible on my terms, however, so this is not enough for me to abandon my thesis that Paul's ordinary or controlling use of νόμος is as a synecdoche for the covenant made at Sinai. Further, in such cases, the word is defined by a qualifying genitive noun, as though Paul were deliberately employing it other than he ordinarily did.

2. So Pinchas Lapide and Peter Stuhlmacher: "To debase divine *instruction* (a concept which linguistically, as well as regarding content, corresponds to Torah) by equating it with the narrow-minded word *nomos* (the law)—all of this is an absurd caricature which finds its source in Paul. . . . Torah is the instruction or teaching of God," *Paul: Rabbi and Apostle*, trans. W. Denef (Minneapolis: Augsburg, 1984), 39 (parenthesis and emphases original). Since the LXX almost always translates *Torah* with *nomos*, I don't understand why Lapide and Stuhlmacher suggest

not universal wisdom or instruction; it was divinely instituted instruction *to* the Is-raelites via the *covenant* Yahweh made *with* the Israelites. As we saw much earlier in Daniel 9:13 and in 2 Chronicles 25:4, νόμος was not used in those two passages (as ordinarily) to translate תורה. Rather, in those texts, διαθήκη was employed. We note, then, not only that νόμος was not used but διδασκαλία was not employed either; in fact, διδασκαλία was/is *never* employed to translate Torah in the LXX.[3] But at least twice, the ordinarily conservative LXX translators elected not to employ the expected νόμος, instead employing διαθήκη. They did this, I suggest throughout this work, because a covenant was made at Horeb: "The Lord our God made a covenant with us in Horeb" (Deut. 5:2; cf. also Deut. 29:1; 1 Kings 8:9; 2 Chron. 5:10). I have suggested throughout that no aspect of that covenant was more prominent or characteristic than lawgiving. Ask any hundred people what God gave the Israelites at Sinai and at least ninety-five will say "the law," "the commandments," or "the Decalogue." Because this trait was so prominent, Paul could employ the word νόμος as a synecdoche for it; but in his actual reasoning, he refers not merely to lawgiving but to the covenant in its entirety, including (especially in Galatians) its Israel-segregating dimension and its cursing dimension. When interpreters consider the possibility that νόμος refers to the entirety of that covenant made with the Israelites 430 years after the Abrahamic covenant, many difficult Pauline texts become less so.

This is especially pertinent because of the frequency with which νόμος appears in some of Paul's other letters. This word appears 74 times in Romans. Only the following words appear more frequently in Romans: καί (279), ἐν (173), αὐτός (158), θεός (153), δέ (148), γάρ (144), οὐ (122), εἰς (119), εἰμί (113), ἐγώ (92), διά (91), ὅς (90), ὑμεῖς (83), and μή (80). Of these, only one (θεός) is theological. Apart from "God," no other theological term appears as frequently in Romans. Indeed, πίστις (40), δικαιοσύνη (34), πνεῦμα (34), ἔθνος (29), and χάρις (24) all appear substantially less frequently, half or less than νόμος. If my judgment is right (that, ordinarily, νόμος is a synecdoche that refers to the Sinai covenant in its entirety), then Romans also needs to be reinterpreted. I doubt I will have occasion to do so, with the kind of technical reasoning I have em-ployed here; but perhaps I will write a nontechnical "romp" through Romans, just to demonstrate how the letter would make sense if its second most frequent theological term was understood as a synecdoche for the Sinai covenant.

7.1.2. Covenant-Historical Reasoning

The lexical reality that νόμος ordinarily means "Sinai covenant" also reveals an im-portant truth about Paul's theology: that his theology itself is deeply covenantal. If

---

that this "finds its source in Paul." It found its source in the translators of the Septuagint, and Paul merely followed that well-established convention.

3. It does, occasionally, translate the various forms of the root למד, as at Isa. 29:13. "Talmud," I might suggest, always implies instruction; but "Torah" could denote the covenant itself, includ-ing any substantial parts thereof, including the conditional blessings and cursings, as at Josh. 8:34: "And afterward he read all the words of the law, the blessing and the curse, according to all that is written in the Book of the Law." Here, what constitutes the "words of the law" written in the "Book of the Law" is the blessings and cursings.

one searched a concordance for the term διαθήκη in Paul's letters, one would find only nine occurrences. One might conclude from this that Paul's thinking is rarely covenantal, but one would be mistaken. If even half of the 121 occurrences of νόμος refer to the Sinai covenant (and I believe the matter is 75 percent or higher), then things appear differently. If even half of the twenty-six occurrences of ἐπαγγελία are synecdoches for the Abrahamic covenant, then the reality of covenant thinking in Paul is disclosed again.

That is, while Paul's purposes do not always require that he speak as explicitly in covenantal language as he does (e.g., in Gal. 3:10–17), his understanding of the covenants that antedate the new covenant is always present in his thinking, even where less explicitly stated. Note the appearance of covenantal language in several remarkably comprehensive Pauline statements.

> They are Israelites, and to them belong the adoption, the glory, the covenants, the giving of the law, the worship, and the promises. (Rom. 9:4)

> Remember that you were at that time separated from Christ, alienated from the commonwealth of Israel and strangers to the covenants of promise, having no hope and without God in the world. (Eph. 2:12)

Jews and Gentiles are distinguished precisely by this issue of those to whom the covenants are given and those who were, on the other hand, "strangers" to such covenants.

> Such is the confidence that we have through Christ toward God. Not that we are sufficient in ourselves to claim anything as coming from us, but our sufficiency is from God, who has made us competent to be ministers of a new covenant, not of the letter but of the Spirit. (2 Cor. 3:4–6)

Here in a comprehensive statement about the apostolic ministry, it is as easy for Paul to refer to "ministers of a new covenant" as to say something like "ministers of the gospel" or "ministers of Christ."

> But their minds were hardened. For to this day, when they read the old covenant, that same veil remains unlifted, because only through Christ is it taken away. (2 Cor. 3:14)

We might have expected Paul to have said here, "For to this day, when they read the Scriptures," but he did not say that; he said "when they read the old covenant," as though this comprehensively describes the situation of those who lived between Sinai and the resurrection of Christ. We would never say this, and I don't believe I have personally *ever* heard anyone say this, unless they were reading this passage. I've heard "read the Bible," "read the Scriptures," "read *Tanakh*," "read the Torah," and "read the law," but I've never heard anyone say "read the old covenant." Paul's thinking is simply more richly covenantal than ours is, and so an expression that we students of Paul do not use fell from his lips as easily as saying, "Mother."

This may seem counterintuitive or wrong: that if Paul uses διαθήκη only nine times, then surely his thinking cannot be so richly covenantal. But James Barr was right that words and concepts are not the same things; and often in human undertakings, the most significant determinants of one's thoughts are so commonplace that they remain unexpressed. Unless writing about the history of science, for instance, most biologists never utter the word *Darwin* in their day-to-day activity; yet the *concept* of natural selection influences nearly everything they do, from how they frame their questions to how they conceive their experiments, to how they conduct them. After the first week of a semester, I probably never use the word *college* in one of my lectures, and rarely do so in anything I write. Does this suggest that I do not teach at a college, or does it merely reflect that the academic context is so obvious and pervasive that it does not ordinarily need to be expressed?[4]

Closely related to this, and a point I have attempted to make throughout this volume, is that Paul's thinking is not merely covenantal but polycovenantal. As we saw above in Romans 9 and Ephesians 2, Paul employs αἱ διαθῆκαι in the *plural*, even when referring to the pre-Christ, pre-new-covenant era. One of the unfortunate circumstances in contemporary Pauline studies is that many of those who do acknowledge the covenantal nature of Paul's thinking construe his thinking monocovenantally, repeatedly referring to the pre-Christ era as "the covenant," rather than (as Paul did) "the covenants."

The five differences Paul articulates between the Abrahamic and Sinai covenants in Galatians 3 indicate that Paul's thinking is not merely numerically polycovenantal, but also qualitatively polycovenantal. It is not at all surprising, then, that many proponents of the New Perspectives on Paul speak so disapprovingly of Luther; their monocovenantalism cannot accommodate a law/gospel paradigm such as that proposed by Luther; and if they cannot easily distinguish the Sinai covenant from the new covenant (as Paul did in 2 Cor. 3), then they surely will not find it easy to distinguish the Abrahamic covenant from the Sinai covenant. And because they do not distinguish the gracious, promise-giving Abrahamic covenant from the legal, curse-threatening Sinai covenant, they end up with a blending of faith-and-works in both their understanding of first-century Palestinian Judaism and in their understanding of apostolic Christianity—and they are in error both times. The great promise that the New Perspective on Paul held forth thirty years ago has shipwrecked itself on the monocovenantalism that pervades so much New Perspective thinking. They do not misunderstand Paul in the same *manner* that the dominant Protestant approach did; but, in my judgment, they misunderstand Paul in a similar, if not greater, *degree*. Exegesis is an imperfect endeavor, and all interpretations—including my own—are merely provisional. However, we may say with entire confidence that "these are two covenants" (Gal. 4:24) can never be responsibly construed as "these are one covenant." The word δύο can never mean εἷς.

---

4. A monograph could be written on terms that exist in a given language that are rarely used and how this reflects common matters in the culture—matters so common that they are unstated. We rarely use the term "banal" in the United States, perhaps because most of our popular culture is so pervasively banal. I rarely hear the expression "paedocentric" in our culture, but who would deny that it has become so in the last half century? I coined the term "contemporaneity" in a book I recently wrote, because it appears so evident to me that ours is a culture without regard for the past or future. Sometimes what is not said reflects what is pervasive; Paul was trained by and rooted in a culture that was pervasively covenantal, even though διαθήκη is comparatively rare in the New Testament, appearing only thirty-three times.

7.1.3. "Law-Free Gospel" Is Not an Obedience-Free Gospel or a Command-Free Gospel

For centuries, the doctrine of justification *sola fide* has raised fear of antinomianism (as it did for Paul in Rom. 6:1: "What shall we say then? Are we to continue in sin that grace may abound?"). But Paul's "νόμος-free" gospel is a gospel that ends the Sinai covenant administration and, therefore, it is a gospel of a covenant that includes Gentiles in the Messiah's blessings. To be "law-free" in this covenantal sense says nothing, in and of itself, about the role of obedience in the new covenant administration. A "Sinai-free" gospel says nothing, in and of itself, about new life, new obedience, or even "a new commandment I give to you, that you love one another: just as I have loved you, you also are to love one another" (John 13:34). If, for Paul, νόμος is a synecdoche for the Sinai covenant, "νόμος-free" does not and need not mean imperative-free or duty-free.

The Galatian letter contains many imperatives (21), as do the remainder of Paul's letters (422 total). Paul even reiterated many of the imperatives from the Old Testament Scriptures, so he regarded many of them as containing abiding moral wisdom and authority. He never, however, enumerated those commands as "ten," nor did the Hebrew or Greek Bibles before him. The Sinai revelation was referred to three times as "ten words,"[5] but never as "ten commandments" in either the Hebrew Bible or the LXX. None of the biblical witnesses perceived the Sinai revelation as so much of the Western tradition has: as timeless moral counsel. They perceived the words as covenantal words, as "words of the covenant" (Exod. 34:28; Deut. 28:69; 2 Chron. 34:31), inscribed on the "tablets of the covenant" (Deut. 9:9, 11, 15), which were placed in the "ark of the covenant." For them, the Decalogue was the center of the *covenant* God made with the Jews at Sinai; it was not the center of timeless moral instruction (though a substantial amount of moral instruction is contained therein). It would require another monograph to explain the nature of Paul's understanding of ethics and what, if any, role the Decalogue plays in that understanding. My point here is that νόμος-free means "Sinai-covenant-free," not "ethics-free" or "command-free."

7.1.4. The Problem of the Law Is Intrinsic, Not Extrinsic

In Galatians (and I believe elsewhere), the problem of the law resides not in its misperception nor in its mispractice, however possible it may be that some in Paul's generation (or earlier generations) did either or both. The problem inheres in the covenant itself and in its five traits that distinguish it from the Abrahamic covenant. If the "problem of the law" in academic or theological circles has always been the issue of relating Paul's positive and negative statements about the law, then the Galatian solution is straightforward: As a covenant administration with the characteristics distinctive[6] to it (most

---

5. In Exod. 34:28 and Deut. 10:4, the LXX has τοὺς δέκα λόγους, and at Deut. 4:13, τὰ δέκα ῥήματα, following the Hebrew עשרת הדברים.

6. And when I say "distinctive," I mean "distinctive" as Paul viewed the matter. That is, the Epistle to the Hebrews develops the typology of that covenant in substantial detail, discussing priests, sacrifices, tents, and so on. But Paul gave less attention to this in his extant writings. For the apostle to the Gentiles, the Israel-segregating dimension was more frequently discussed.

notably, its segregating of Israel from the nations and its threatened curse sanctions), it could never be anything but a temporary juncture in redemptive history until God *blessed all nations* by Abraham's seed. Whether every Israelite from Moses to Paul misunderstood or mispracticed the law, or whether not a single Israelite from Moses to Paul misunderstood or mispracticed the law, the law would still be problematic. Consider this inherent dilemma, for instance: If the right practice of Torah segregates Israel from the nations, then how can the seed of Abraham be a vehicle for blessing the nations? Conversely, if the Sinai community does not segregate from the nations (e.g., as when they refused to execute *cherem* warfare on the peoples of the land or intermarried with them when they returned from exile), then they will themselves be cursed for disobedience to the segregating requirements. There is simply no way, within the confines of that covenant administration, for the blessings pledged to Abraham to ever fall upon both Jews and Gentiles.

Nearly all of the dominant Protestant approaches to Paul through the centuries have failed on this score. However the dust finally settles on the nature of Second Temple Judaism—whether Sanders's or a more modified view prevails—is irrelevant to the criticism of the law as we find it in Galatians. Paul does not fault the Judaizers for *mis*-following Torah, but for following it; not for *mis*understanding it (and its Gentile-excluding rites), but for understanding it. Throughout Galatians, the νόμος Paul concerns himself with is the one that came "430 years after" the covenant that was previously ratified by God (Gal. 3:17). It is not some later covenant, nor even some later misunderstanding of that covenant, but it is the covenant itself—the one that came half a millennium after the covenant with Abraham—that is the focus of Paul's critique.

Similarly, nearly all of the New Perspective approaches fail in the same direction; because the "covenantal nomism" they promote is inherently monocovenantal, they end up with a Paul who is only a little different from Second Temple Judaism and little different from any Judaism that appeared earlier. Paul wanted nothing to do with any nomism of any sort, covenantal or otherwise. The only νόμος he knew excluded Gentiles and cursed Jews, and he wanted no part of any νόμος that did such a thing. For Paul in Galatians, the only stated good that came out of the Sinai covenant was that, for a necessary season of time, it preserved the integrity of Abraham's line of descendants (and, probably, memory of the pledges made to Abraham) "until the Seed would come to whom the promise had been made" (3:19). The very rites that excluded Gentiles, and the stern threatenings of curses if these rites were not observed, served an important-but-temporary (παιδαγωγός) purpose in God's designs. But Paul knew of no way to remove the Gentile-excluding rites or the threats from the law. He could not, like a fisherman, scale them away; they were inherent to it. The whole fish of nomism, "covenantal" or otherwise, had to be returned to the sea.

If the New Perspective authors rightly condemn dominant Protestant approaches for their tendency to abstract "works" from their historical setting, then I would gently condemn some new perspectivalists for their own tendency to abstract "nomism" from the Sinai covenant with its Gentile-excluding, Jew-threatening realities. If Bultmann (et al.) abstracted "works" to mean human efforts to achieve God's approval, then the New Perspective often abstracts "nomism" from the Mosaic law. But the "works of the law" to which Paul objected were not abstract in either of those two ways; the "works of the law" were those *particular* works required by that *particular* (Gentile-excluding and Israel-threatening) covenant. Ironically, then, each of the major approaches to Paul not only fails to understand Galatians but fails to do so in a similar way by avoiding/ evading the stark particularity of his problem with one particular covenant.[7] Paul, as a matter of pure intellectual history, did not consider for one moment "covenantal no-mism" or a "pattern of religion"; he inherited two things that placed him at the crucible of religious history. On the one hand, he was reared from childhood in a covenant administration that required his separation from Gentiles and threatened him (and its other adherents) with curses if they did not do so. On the other hand, the Damascus theophany (and Paul's later reflection on the meaning of it) persuaded him that the risen Jesus of Nazareth was the "Seed of Abraham" by whom God's pledge to bless *all* the nations of the world had come, and by whom God had therefore inaugurated a "new covenant." Paul's concern was to understand those two mutually exclusive covenants from the perspective of the earlier covenant made with Abraham. The very last thing that would have occurred to him was the possibility of mixing these three together in a Waring blender to create some homogenized "covenantal nomism" that miraculously permitted Jews to remain segregated from Gentiles while still blessing the same Gentiles, that neither cursed some Jews if they did not segregate from Gentiles (Paul?) nor cursed others (Peter?) if they did segregate from them. Paul knew nothing of such a benevolent (non-curse-threatening) νόμος.[8]

Precisely because the only νόμος Paul knew was inseparable from the covenant of which it was a part, Paul himself (but not the New Perspective) was genuinely cov-enantally nomistic. That is, his "nomism" was not some abstraction or a mere "pattern of religion." His νόμος was the νόμος that first appeared to the human race in the hand of a mediator, who descended from a thunder-and-smoke-enshrouded mountain with "tablets of the covenant" in his hand. And as this mediator's ministry continued with those to whom this covenant was made, the "ten words" inscribed on those tablets would be complemented by "twelve words" of threatened cursing (Deut. 27), to each of which the twelve tribes solemnly ascribed their "Amen." That is, one can describe Paul as "covenantally nomistic" only if one is particular about it; Paul knew of a νόμος that was part and parcel of a particular covenant made with one people alone, which threatened them with severe curse sanctions. He knew nothing of "covenantal" as a vague theological term, nor were "works of the law" vague. His covenantalism was particular; as apostle to the Gentiles, he liked some covenants and some more than others, comparing one to Sarah but another to Hagar, calling the children of one "free" and the children of the other "in bondage." He knew of no sleight of hand that could blend free and enslaved children into a single pattern of a half-free/half-enslaved religion.

In differing ways, then, each of the major attempts to understand Galatians has failed by abstracting a letter that was and is very concrete and instead attempting to

---

7. I have substantial sympathies therefore with Francis Watson's suggestion that we must move "beyond the new perspective" on the ground that it *and* its predecessors have avoided/ evaded historical particularity. Watson's concern was primarily related to the proper interpreta-tion of Romans; mine is related to the nature of Paul's reasoning in Galatians; but his and my concerns are easily harmonized and not very different on this score. Francis Watson, *Paul, Judaism, and the Gentiles: Beyond the New Perspective*, rev. ed. (Grand Rapids: Eerdmans, 2007), 354–57.

8. For fuller development, cf. my "Getting Out and Staying Out: Israel's Dilemma at Sinai," in the excursus at the end of this book.

generalize what was originally quite particular. Luther and Calvin effectively overlooked the Gentile-excluding ceremonies and assumed that there must have been something else (some meritorious, self-justifying activity?) that provoked Paul's critique of the law. And the New Perspective has tended to overlook Paul's profound contrasts between the Abrahamic and Sinai covenants throughout the letter, effectively blending the unblendable into a single, generalized pattern of religion called "covenantal nomism" that could somehow integrate the Abrahamic covenant, the Sinai covenant, and the new covenant. Paul's (and Moses') statement of "Cast out the slave woman and her son, for the son of the slave woman shall not inherit with the son of the free woman" (Gal. 4:30) has become, for them, "Isn't this great? The son of the slave woman and the son of the free woman—and anybody else who may come along at some later date—can all inherit together." Paul's statement of "So, brothers, we are not children of the slave but of the free woman" (Gal. 4:31) has become "So, brothers, we are indeed children of both the slave and the free woman."

Until and unless we think covenant-historically, we cannot think Paul's thoughts after him. His reasoning will remain enigmatic to us, unless we take into consideration the frequent temporal language in his discussion of covenants: His "whens" (4:3, 3, 8), "befores" (3:23), "afters/nows" (3:17, 25; 4:9), and "untils" (3:19) must become ours. He did not speak in Galatians of eternal, timeless, general realities, true and binding for all time; he spoke there of realities that had beginnings or ends or both. He did not speak of a "pattern of religion" or of a "covenant of grace," nor of what was common to Judaism and Christianity or to many biblical covenants. He spoke of three distinct covenant administrations; two of which reside in *Tanakh*, and a third of which resides in apostolic proclamation (though it fulfilled one and terminated the other).

Closely related to this, then, is my suggestion that one purpose of the curse-threatening, Israel-segregating Sinai covenant was to preserve the lineage of Abraham.[9] By separating the descendants of Abraham from the *am ha-aretz*, and by threatening them with severe temporal consequences if they did not remain separate, the Sinai covenant preserved the integrity of Abraham's lineage "until the Seed would come, to whom the promise had been made" (3:19). Without this covenant, Israel's twin tendencies toward intermarrying with the people of the land and committing idolatry with their deities would almost surely have removed from the earth a lineage to Abraham or memory of anything pledged to him. The lineage of Abraham might have disappeared in the first millennium before the Common Era. But the Sinai covenant, the faithful paidagogue, guarded Abraham's lineage against such. That covenant so utterly necessary to preserving Abraham's lineage needed to disappear once Abraham's Seed—the one who would bring blessings to all the nations—had come. And once the Seed had come, then the covenant—including its segregating ordinances, its curse sanctions, and everything else about it—disappeared in its entirety: "I died to the law in order that I might live to God" (Gal. 2:19; cf. Rom. 7:1–4). Paul and other Christians died to the Israel-segregating Sinai covenant in order to live to the God who is One, who is not the God of the Jews only (Gal. 3:20; Rom. 3:9).

---

9. I say "one purpose" because I believe other purposes were achieved by the Sinai administration. But the one that has Paul's attention is the Gentile-excluding/Israel-segregating dimension. I can think quickly of at least three other achievements by the Sinai administration in the history of redemption, but they were not Paul's concern in this letter.

7.1.5. N. T. Wright's Single Plan through Israel to Bless the World

While there is little need to elaborate on the point here, this is certainly the place to express appreciation for one of the consistent features of N. T. Wright's thought, which is to read the Hebrew Bible as a lengthy, complex (at times), and perplexing (many times) development of a single theme: God's single plan through Israel to bless the world. God's plan for Abraham's descendants included blessing them (with progeny and land) but did not end there; his ultimate goal was to bless all the nations of the world through Abraham's seed. This welcome aspect of Wright's thinking is not only amenable to my reading of Galatians, but it also echoes it on many points (though I surely do not fault him for any of the other idiosyncracies present here). The Abrahamic covenant came a half millennium before the (Israel-segregating/Gentile-excluding) Sinai covenant, and its pledge to bless all the nations through Abraham's seed would not be and could not be defeated by the (later) Sinai covenant. Indeed, Sinai's preserving/guardian role actually served the purposes of preserving Abraham's seed and of preserving the memory of the pledges made to them, and to the world through them.

7.2. For the Ecumenical Dialogue[10]

Much of the New Perspective on Paul consists of an attempt to carry on the conversation between Judaism and Christianity in a manner that is fair to the Jewish conversation partner.[11] In and of itself, this is a perfectly laudable goal, as is the goal to be candid about the manner in which the Hebrew Bible informs both conversation partners. And indeed, there are many formal similarities between Judaism and Christianity. Especially, as E. P. Sanders had indicated, there is little or no reason to believe that Palestinian Judaism was any more "legalistic" than Christianity. Paul's Letter to the Galatians was written to a Christian assembly, after all, not to a Jewish synagogue. So we know there were "Judaizers" in the Christian congregations in at least one region, yet few of us believe it would be fair to characterize Christianity as "legalistic." Each religion taught the importance of faith in God and in God's promises. Each religion taught that God's commands were to be obeyed.

Beyond such formal similarities, however, there is the question of Jesus of Nazareth. Paul claimed that Jesus—the Christ, the crucified and resurrected one—was the single seed promised to Abraham and his descendants, by whom God would bless all the nations of the world. Most Jews reject this claim, as to embrace it would make them Christian. Further, while both Jews and Christians recognize the formative importance of both the Abrahamic and Sinai covenants, only Christians observe a "new covenant" ratified by the death of Jesus of Nazareth. Historical fairness demands

---

10. Throughout, I have employed "ecumenical" synonymously with "interfaith." While technically, one could argue that "ecumenical" ought to be employed narrowly to refer to discussions within the Christian church, I employ the term more broadly to include both those discussions and the discussions between Christians and Jews.

11. So Watson, *Paul, Judaism, and the Gentiles*, 1–2; Peter Stuhlmacher, *Revisiting Paul's Doctrine of Justification: A Challenge to the New Perspective: With an Essay by Donald A. Hagner* (Downers Grove, IL: IVP Academic, 2001), 34.

that we be equally candid about both the differences and the similarities.[12] Especially needful, if my reading of Galatians is correct, is to recognize that the Sinai covenant itself requires such division of Jew and Gentile. It is no first-century "misreading" of the antecedent Scriptures to recognize that the Israelites were the exclusive nation with whom God covenanted at Sinai. Any respect for that covenant's integrity requires that we are faced with an either-or: either that covenant administration is passé, in which case Jews and Gentiles are *all* "law-free"; or that covenant administration *is* still in effect, and therefore requires Jews to do the very thing that Paul insisted Peter not do.

The post-Holocaust ecumenical situation has caused Christian scholars to be careful not to suggest that the Israelite religion was defective or primitive, compared to the Christian religion, and they have also been careful not to suggest that the Jews of the first century characteristically misunderstood (legalistically) their own religion. I am in entire agreement with both of these concerns. This ecumenical situation, however, has had the unfortunate effect of causing the same Christian scholars to be hesitant to affirm, with Paul, that the Sinai covenant is entirely passé in light of the Christ event, out of fear that this will sound disparaging of the Jewish religion. In Galatians, Paul candidly states that the Sinai covenant had its drawbacks: notably, its exclusion of the nations and its covenant curse sanctions. However, the same Paul equally candidly states that this covenant, with these two characteristics, served an important role in the history of redemption—a role that ultimately had the effect of bringing blessings to both Jew and Greek. His argument throughout is that there was a season in redemptive history in which the preservation of the integrity of Abraham's "seed"/lineage was utterly necessary, and perhaps nothing short of severe threats of temporal sanctions would have achieved this purpose. His figurative images for the Sinai covenant—παιδαγωγός, ἐπίτροπος, οἰκονόμος—are fairly benevolent in themselves, even though the *effect* of that guardianship on a sinful people was often curse/exile and servitude. But had Israel more frequently obeyed the covenant, it would still have fulfilled its benevolent (though Gentile-excluding) role as παιδαγωγός/ἐπίτροπος/οἰκονόμος, yet without exile and without slavery. Paul never hints, even for a moment, that the history would have been different with any other people. To the contrary, he said that the Scripture "consigned *all* things to sin" (Gal. 3:22), so that the negative effects of this covenant administration would have been the same had the covenant been made with any *other* clan on earth, whether Abraham's or Gordon's. So, while I appreciate the reticence of Christian scholars to speak as candidly as Paul did about the temporary nature of the Sinai administration, and/or about the curse and servitude/slavery that were its consequences for Israel, I believe we can affirm these as candidly as Paul without fear of saying anything that could fairly be construed as anti-Semitic. As long as we view Israel

---

12. There would have been no synagogue ban of CE 93–94 had not the synagogues by this point determined that the two groups were dissimilar, and most scholars believe that from the Bar Kochba revolt on, reunion was practically impossible. It would be better to recognize—warts and all—that Paul was one of the first to perceive the necessity of this, as Francis Watson has observed: "As we shall see, *the social reality underlying Paul's discussions of Judaism and the law is his creation of Gentile Christian communities in sharp distinction from the Jewish community. His theological reflection legitimates the separation of church from synagogue.*" Cf. Watson, *Paul, Judaism, and the Gentiles,* 51 (emphases original).

as a microcosm of the sinful human race per se, recognizing that the Sinai covenant would have excluded all but the chosen people (whoever that people would have been) and would have ended up exiling *any* sinful people to whom it was given, there is no reason to fear that our comments will be construed as anti-Semitic.

One individual who has been candid about both the similarities and dissimilarities between Christianity and Judaism has been Rabbi Jacob Neusner, and I remain convinced that his approach to the Jewish-Christian dialogue is probably still the best solution to the situation.[13] Over twenty-five years ago, he proposed a way of understanding the matter that still strikes me as elegant. Neusner suggested several matters that would promote fair-minded Jewish-Christian dialogue, yet without the liabilities of the E. P. Sanders tendency to confuse the two religions.

First, Neusner rightly reminded that two (not one) new world religions appeared in the first century of the Common Era:

> Let me at the outset explain why formative Christianity demands to be studied in the context of formative Judaism, and formative Judaism in the context of formative Christianity. . . . [W]hile most people are familiar with the story of the development of Christianity, few are fully aware that Judaism constitutes a separate and distinctive religious tradition.[14]

Neusner was surely right that Post-Temple Judaism is a new thing in its own right. Neither Christianity nor Judaism of the Common Era resorted to the Jerusalem Temple nor to the sacrifices there made, and to recognize this is to understand how genuinely new or "formative" each religion was. Students of the Bible commonly refer to "Pre-Temple," "Temple," and "Second Temple" Judaism, because the temple was so central to the religion. Whatever we call these two things that emerge in the first century of the Common Era, *neither* one is Temple Judaism; each is a new religion in its "formative" stage, a religion that can function without the Jerusalem Temple.

Second, Neusner rightly observed that the Hebrew Bible was regarded as Scripture by both of these formative religions, yet each tradition read this Scripture through the interpretive grid of another, growing literature: the Babylonian Talmud on the one hand and the apostolic writings on the other.

> Both Judaism and Christianity claim to be the heirs and products of the Hebrew Scriptures. . . . Yet both great religious traditions derive not solely or directly from the authority and teachings of those Scriptures, but rather from the ways in which that authority has been mediated, and those teachings interpreted, through other holy books. The New Testament is the prism through which the light of the Old comes to Christianity. The canon of rabbinical writings is the star that guides Jews to the revelation of Sinai, the Torah. . . . The claim of these two great Western traditions, in all their rich variety, is for the veracity not merely of the Scriptures, but also of Scriptures as interpreted by the New Testament or the Babylonian Talmud.[15]

Third, because the Hebrew Bible was read through the interpretive matrix of these other two religious texts, the Hebrew Bible was read differently by each tradition.

---

13. Jacob Neusner, *Judaism in the Beginning of Christianity* (Philadelphia: Fortress, 1984).
14. Ibid., 10–11.
15. Ibid., 11.

Both the apostles and the rabbis thus reshaped the antecedent religion of Israel, and both claimed to be Israel. That pre-Christian, prerabbinic religion of Israel, for all its variety, exhibited common traits: belief in one God, reverence for and obedience to the revelation contained in the Hebrew Scriptures, veneration of the Temple in Jerusalem (while it stood), and expectation of the coming of a Messiah to restore all the Jews to Palestine and bring to a close the anguish of history. The Christian Jews concentrated on the last point, proclaiming that the Messiah had come in Jesus; the rabbinic Jews focused on the second, teaching that only through the full realization of the imperatives of the Hebrew Scriptures, Torah, as interpreted and applied by the rabbis, would the people merit the coming Messiah.[16]

Two new, formative religions thus emerged, based on a common history and common Scripture, yet they each read that common Scripture with a different focus:

> For the Christian, therefore, the issue of Messiah predominated; for the rabbinic Jew, the issue of Torah; and for both, the question of salvation was crucial.[17]

Rabbi Neusner's proposal strikes me as being entirely and equally fair to each tradition. For twenty-five years now, I have proposed his manner of assessing the matter to my (predominately Christian) students, asking them if they found anything objectionable in Rabbi Neusner's proposal. To date, not one of my students has found his proposal objectionable. It is candid about the similarities and candid about the dissimilarities.[18] For our purposes, note that each of these traditions taught "belief in one God," an idea as old as Abraham; and each taught "obedience to the revelation contained in the Hebrew Scriptures," a matter at least as old as Moses, who brought the first written revelation to his people.[19] Note then that these two realities of "belief" and "obedience" resided in the Hebrew Bible itself, and therefore they appeared again in the two new religions in their "formative" stage. The New Perspective, however, tends to blend the two covenants with Abraham and Moses in such a manner that is indistinguishable from legalism, and in a manner far more meritorious than anything taught by medieval Catholicism. This is because it tends to confuse or mix the two covenants together and to describe the mixture as "the covenant," when there were in fact two of them as different in what they birthed as the children of Hagar and Sarah (Gal. 4:21–31). The alternative I have proposed throughout is to distinguish the Abrahamic covenant (promise) from the Sinai covenant (law), and to recognize with Rabbi Neusner that each formative religion in the first century of the Common Era was informed by both covenants.

While I have addressed the matter only briefly, I also suggest that the Jewish-Christian dialogue has been injured when Paul's interpreters assume without argumentation that errors in Christian churches reflect antecedent errors in Jewish synagogues. In

---

16. Ibid., 12.

17. Ibid., 13.

18. Those interested in a fuller discussion of Neusner's understanding of the differences may consult his *A Rabbi Talks with Jesus* (Montreal: McGill-Queens University Press, 2000).

19. Indeed, most Christian confessional literature contains an exposition of the Decalogue. Luther's Small Catechism begins with such an exposition in Section 1; the *Catechism of the Catholic Church* contains such an exposition in Part Three, Section Two; and it appears in various other Protestant confessions, such as the Westminster Larger Catechism and the Heidelberg Catechism.

my discussion titled "Judaize" in chapter 2, I observed two realities that should correct this. First, the term itself was extremely rare in Paul's day; he may even have believed he was coining a new term.[20] If the term was rare, then it cannot properly be taken to be a common designation for a common problem in the synagogues. Second, in the rare texts that employed the term before Paul, it always described Gentile (not Jewish) behavior, and it appears to have referred to compliance with Jewish ceremonies in order to get along with *Jews* who were required to keep them; the other texts suggest nothing about any notion that in doing so one would please *God*.

The ecumenical conversation has another front, of course, in the discussion between Catholicism and Protestantism; and this second front energizes the New Perspective on Paul as much as the first (perhaps none more so than Bishop Wright, whose Church of England has witnessed the occasional [!] friction between Catholicism and Protestantism). If there is any doctrinal distinctive (as opposed to the historical question of the nature of first-century Palestinian Judaism) that characterizes the New Perspective, it is its entire redefining of the Pauline doctrine of justification.[21] It is not merely that the NPP tends to blur/blend faith and works, but the very question of what *constitutes* justification is changed entirely—from a *judicial* question of how the created order (in part or whole) will survive the Creator's judgment thereof at the close of history, to an *ecclesiastical* question of who/what constitutes the visible covenant people on earth before that judgment. The motivation that prompts such redefinition is perhaps admirable, but the attempt is simultaneously ambitious and naive.

I regard it as ambitious in the extreme to suggest that we can resolve the debate between Rome and Protestantism by suggesting that there is hardly a shred of truth in the way in which *either* tradition has articulated the matter before. The difference was always extremely refined:

1. Each tradition affirms that God was/is/will be the judge of all that he has made;
2. Each affirms that humans since Adam have sinned and (therefore) merit God's judgment;
3. Each affirms that if any sinner or sinners survive that judgment, it will be entirely due to God's grace alone, since those who merit his judgment could not, by definition, merit his favor; and
4. Each affirms that such justifying grace comes by the instrument of faith.

The only difference (albeit a significant one) is that Catholicism teaches that God's grace comes via the instruments of faith *and* obedience, whereas Protestantism teaches that God's grace comes via the instrument of faith *alone* (*sola fide*). The gospel obedience (for Protestantism) that surely, always, and necessarily *attends* saving faith is nonetheless no part of the instrument by which justification is received; whereas for Catholicism, such gospel obedience is part of the instrument by which justification is received.

---

20. It appeared only once in the LXX (Esth. 8:17), once in the intertestamental writings (Theodotus, *On the Jews* 4:1), once in Paul (Gal. 2:14), and once, later, in the Apostolic Fathers (Ignatius, *To the Magnesians* 10:7–8).

21. And, curiously within the literature, there is far more objection to a "Lutheran" reading of Paul than of a "Reformed" or "Calvinist" reading, even though the Lutheran and Reformed confessions are identical on this doctrine.

The New Perspective does not take one side or the other on this one disputed point; rather, it denies all four of the points that the previous Catholic and Protestant doctrine affirmed. Note, then, in effect, what the New Perspective offers: If both parties will recognize that everything either party has ever affirmed about justification is entirely wrong (the four agreed-upon theses and the one disagreed-upon thesis), then perhaps the barrier to their ecclesiastical union can be overcome. All they have to do (I speak ironically here) is both admit that they divided the entire tradition of the Western church for over half a millennium over a matter that both parties misunderstood entirely. Everything they *both* said for this half-millennium—four things in unison, one not—was entirely mistaken. This is an ambitious undertaking indeed to suggest that everything ever taught about justification in the Western church—including its divergence in the fifteenth century over whether faith alone is the instrument of justification—was and is entirely wrong. I doubt whether such an ambitious undertaking will prove successful, but it is so audaciously ambitious that one cannot but sympathize with it in some measure.

Curiously, this approach to Catholic-Protestant ecumenism is not only ambitious; it is naive, because the doctrine of justification is not the only matter that separates Rome from Protestantism. Every pious Catholic acknowledges the mediation of Mary (in theory and practice); no pious Protestant does. Catholics affirm seven sacraments; Protestants but two. Catholicism promotes the religious use of images; Protestantism denies the same. Catholicism acknowledges the pope as the head of the visible church on earth; Protestantism (with Eastern Orthodoxy) does not.[22] Catholicism regards the Mass as a kind of sacrifice; Protestants deny this. Catholicism affirms transubstantiation; Protestants deny it.[23] Catholicism requires clerical celibacy; Protestantism denies the same. Catholicism affirms ecclesiastical infallibility;[24] Protestantism denies this. In these (and several other, perhaps smaller) matters, Catholics and Protestants remain, tragically and unhappily, divided.[25] Even if the issue of justification by faith (alone or

---

22. Indeed, the common Protestant label for Roman Catholics until the twentieth century was "papists." It even appears in some Protestant confessional literature, such as the Westminster Confession of Faith, chapter 24 (on marriage), section 3: "It is lawful for all sorts of people to marry, who are able with judgment to give their consent. Yet it is the duty of Christians to marry only in the Lord. And therefore such as profess the true reformed religion should not marry with infidels, papists, or other idolaters."

23. Though some forms of Protestantism embrace views that are closer to transubstantiation than others. Lutheran consubstantiation also affirms that Christ is present in the actual elements of bread and wine; whereas other Protestants (Reformed) deny that Christ is present in the elements (though present in the event), and some (Zwinglian) deny his presence in the meal altogether.

24. In qualified ways, to be sure. Not all ecclesiastical statements are regarded by Rome as infallible; and at least since John Henry Cardinal Newman (esp. *Essay on the Development of Christian Doctrine*, 1845), there have been various ways of "historicizing" infallibility in such a manner that a deliverance that might have been infallibly right for its moment may not necessarily be binding in the same manner for subsequent generations.

25. The original division was due to Luther's objection to Tetzel's sale of indulgences. In practice, I believe this wound has been healed, but Luther has not been de-excommunicated. To the best of my knowledge, Rome has ceased from selling indulgences but has not recanted (and cannot recant) its previous practice, since doing so would impinge upon ecclesiastical infallibility. So we now find ourselves in the happy/unhappy predicament that the original cause of

otherwise) were resolved, the two branches of Western Christianity would still not be reunited as many other, equally significant and less nuanced, barriers remain.

Five hundred years of division will not be easily (if ever) overcome; though I surely wish well to all who attempt it. Some of us (both Catholic and Protestant) promote what we call ecumenism with a small "e," because we believe ecumenical progress with a large "E" may be beyond our conceivable grasp. But such ecumenism with a small "e" is not an entire waste of time; making every effort to cooperate in every manner and on every occasion that we possibly can is still right and is still an acknowledgment of the church catholic, in both theory and practice. But some human failure (and its consequences) is grave and, on some occasions, irremediable (a murderer may express sorrow for his deed afterward, but he cannot restore the life that was taken). The fifteenth-century division of the Western church represented a significant failure. Perhaps the vested interests in the (powerful) medieval church were too resistant to appropriate reform; perhaps the Reformers were too zealous in their efforts at reformation. For whatever reasons—and however history eventually assigns respective blame—the present situation is tragic, because the *number* of issues that divide the Western church is large. The difference between the two traditions on the doctrine of justification (a difference so refined that few priests, ministers, or laypersons can even articulate wherein the agreements and disagreements reside) is hardly the only or even most significant difference.

In one area, I hope that my understanding of Galatians will improve Protestant-Catholic dialogues about justification, though without suggesting that both traditions have entirely miscomprehended the matter for half a millennium. If (as I suggested here) the problem at Galatia may have been behavioral (and not doctrinal), and if (as I suggested here) Paul regarded justification as a settled doctrine in his day, *from* which (not *for* which) he resolved other matters, then the common Protestant assertion that the position of medieval Rome was the virtual equivalent of the problem Paul addressed at Galatia is false. If my reading is correct, then there was no specific doctrinal error at Galatia regarding justification, and therefore, whatever medieval Catholicism taught about the matter has little or nothing to do with the error at Galatia. This does not mean differences do not remain between Catholicism and Protestantism regarding the doctrine; but it does mean that we Protestants must come down a little from our rhetorical high horse and stop saying that Rome merely repeated the error at Galatia. It did not. Real differences exist in the confessional literature of both traditions, and real development and refinement took place from Paul's day until the fifteenth century, as seen below in the contrast between the Canons and Decrees from the Council of Trent and the Westminster Confession of Faith.

Catholicism (Trent, Sixth Session)

CANON IX. If any one saith, that by faith alone the impious is justified; in such wise as to mean, that nothing else is required to co-operate in order to the obtaining the grace of Justification . . . let him be anathema.

---

the "Disruption" of the church (as Lord Acton and Bishop Creighton referred to it) has ceased, but those who objected to what caused the Disruption have neither been pardoned for their objections nor invited to return.

CANON XI. If any one saith, that men are justified, either by the sole imputation of the justice of Christ, or by the sole remission of sins, to the exclusion of the grace and the charity which is poured forth in their hearts by the Holy Ghost, and is inherent in them; or even that the grace, whereby we are justified, is only the favour of God; let him be anathema.

CANON XXIV. If any one saith, that the justice received is not preserved and also increased before God through good works; but that the said works are merely the fruits and signs of Justification obtained, but not a cause of the increase thereof; let him be anathema.

Protestantism (Westminster Confession)

WCF 11:2. Faith, thus receiving and resting on Christ and his righteousness, is the alone instrument of justification: yet is it not alone in the person justified, but is ever accompanied with all other saving graces, and is no dead faith, but worketh by love.

WCF 11:3. Christ, by his obedience and death, did fully discharge the debt of all those that are thus justified, and did make a proper, real, and full satisfaction to his Father's justice in their behalf. Yet, inasmuch as he was given by the Father for them; and his obedience and satisfaction accepted in their stead; and both, freely, not for anything in them; their justification is only of free grace; that both the exact justice and rich grace of God might be glorified in the justification of sinners.

The two traditions do differ but in a nuanced and refined way[26]—in a manner that may not even have been expressly addressed (or considered) in Paul's day, or the way the precise questions about the nature of Christ addressed at Nicea may not have been considered in the apostolic generation.

7.3. For First-Century Palestinian Judaism

It is possible that the post-Sanders discussion of "variegated nomism" is explicable by my covenant-historical approach. If Paul's paradigm, as discussed here, distinguishes

---

26. Indeed, the difference is even more refined in the current *Catechism of the Catholic Church* (2nd ed.), where the pertinent language is more subtly different from confessional Protestantism: "Justification has been *merited for us by the Passion of Christ* who offered himself on the cross as a living victim, holy and pleasing to God, and whose blood has become the instrument of atonement for the sins of all men. Justification is conferred in Baptism, the sacrament of faith. It conforms us to the righteousness of God, who makes us inwardly just by the power of his mercy. Its purpose is the glory of God and of Christ, and the gift of eternal life" (section 1992; emphases added). Justification still has a synergistic quality to it in confessional Catholicism: "Justification establishes *cooperation between God's grace and man's freedom.* On man's part it is expressed by the assent of faith to the Word of God, which invites him to conversion, and in the cooperation of charity with the prompting of the Holy Spirit who precedes and preserves his assent" (section 1993; emphases added).

the Abrahamic and Sinai covenants as different in kind—one distinguished by promise, the other by law—then this may account for why pertinent Jewish literature affirms both the unconditioned, gracious promise on the one hand and conditional blessedness on the other, since these two covenants teach such realities. Rather than try to sort through the various documents to determine whether there was a "gracious" party and/or a "legalistic" party, it is entirely likely that all Jews of the period, when reflecting on the Abrahamic narrative, observed the entirely gracious character of the pledges made to the patriarchs; while the same Jews of the same period, when reflecting on the Sinai covenant, rightly called attention to its conditional character and/or its threatened cursings for disobedience.

The question is not whether there are more "legal" texts than "gracious" texts, or vice versa; the question is whether the "legal" texts are commentary on the realities of the Sinai covenant, whereas the "gracious" texts are commentary on the realities of the Abrahamic covenant. If the Mosaic texts themselves said, "Do this and you will live" (Lev. 18:5), should it be surprising that some Palestinian Jews considered how best to fulfill such responsibility? In some circles, there has been a tendency to conflate the various covenants recorded in the *Tanakh* as though there were only one; that is, to speak of "Judaism" as a singular reality, rather than a multifaceted (polycovenantal) one. The children of Abraham were parties to at least two distinct covenants with Yahweh:[27] one that pledged divine blessing entirely by the grace of God, a blessing that would one day comprehend all the nations of the earth; and another covenant that conditioned Israel's tenure in the land on their obedience.

This multicovenantal understanding of the Hebrew Bible has never (or rarely) been overtly denied, to my knowledge; but its consequences for understanding either the Scriptures (Hebrew or Greek) or Palestinian Judaism appear to have been underestimated and underutilized. If I had a nickel for every time I have seen or heard the unqualified expression "the covenant" in scholarly and theological literature without any contextual indication of *which* biblical covenant was being referred to, I could probably have retired some years ago. Sometimes even when there is some qualification, the qualification is inadequate. For instance, I have occasionally encountered an expression such as "God's covenant with the Jews." But God made at least two covenants with the Jews (the covenants with Phinehas and David could be construed either as made with the Jews or with these smaller subparties among them—a matter unnecessary for me to pursue here): one with Abraham, and another through Moses more than 430 years later.

Perhaps this is what confuses so many people. Perhaps it is difficult to imagine God making two different covenants with the same people. If this seems difficult, then perhaps a contemporary analogy will clarify. At one point, I was under two contracts with the same banker. Jim's bank carried the mortgage loan on our house and an automobile loan on a vehicle. The parties, in each case, were the same: Jim's bank and

---

27. I say "at least" two, because it might be more difficult to determine whether the covenant with Phinehas was made with "Abraham's descendants," or merely with one tribe thereof. Similarly, the covenant with David to put a descendant on his throne forever could be regarded as a covenant with Abraham's descendants, or merely a covenant with a representative of the tribe of Benjamin.

yours truly. But the amount borrowed, the interest rate, and the terms (twenty years versus three years) were all different, and what was attained by each was different (a dwelling or an automobile). If I had walked into the bank one day and said, "Jim, I'd like to talk about my loan," Jim would have said, "Sure, Dave. *Which* loan?," because at the time we had two. So also, Yahweh had two covenantal relationships with the Israelites: one inaugurated roughly half a millennium after the other. In the one, Yahweh unconditionally pledged[28] to give innumerable descendants to an elderly couple, to give a great arable land to their descendants, and one day to bless all the families of the earth through their "seed." In the other, Yahweh pledged either to bless or to curse Israel in a temporal manner in the land of Canaan, conditioned on their obedience: blessing or cursing, *shalomic* tenure or exile.

Because of the tenacity with which the Judaizers clung to the Mosaic law, Paul explicated (and some think he even exaggerated) the differences between these two covenants in the Galatian letter. But it would be well to read all of his letters with an awareness of the covenant-historical reasoning that Paul expresses in Galatians. And if we are to understand other Palestinian Jews contemporaneous with Paul, then we should consider that some/many of them may have shared his understanding and may, therefore, have written sometimes about the realities of the one covenant and on other occasions about the realities of the other. When writing about the one, they would undoubtedly acknowledge the utterly gracious pledges made to an old barren couple many years earlier; when writing about the other, they would pursue with all seriousness how best to obey those Mosaic commands, by which obedience alone they could enjoy shalom in the land of Canaan.

7.4. For the New Perspective on Paul

The New Perspective on Paul, like love, is a many-splendored thing. One of its greatest insights—that there is little historical basis for the dominant Protestant caricature of first-century Judaism—is still, in my judgment, a corrective that will continue to bear fruit in Pauline studies. Freed from the assumption that Paul was constantly fighting an invisible Jewish legalism that he never actually said he was fighting, Paul's interpreters have a genuinely new perspective from which to evaluate Paul's negative statements about the law. Even if the dust will never entirely settle on the question of the precise nature of first-century Palestinian Judaism, the mere fact that Paul's interpreters now feel an obligation to justify allegations of legalism (rather than merely *assume* them) has genuinely and fruitfully altered the landscape of Pauline studies.

Two other tendencies within the New Perspective on Paul, however, are neither as overt nor as helpful. In his original essay that coined the term, James D. G. Dunn mentioned Ernst Käsemann only twice, unfavorably, for promoting a "Lutheran" understanding of Paul. I attempt to demonstrate in an excursus in this work that Käsemann

---

28. In the most technical sense, Yahweh did later require circumcision (Gen. 17); but this is not a true condition, for two reasons: first, the pledges made in Gen. 12 and 15 attached no such conditions; and second, had Yahweh not given Isaac to Abraham and Sarah, there would have been no son to circumcise.

was far more influential than Dunn's essay suggested; albeit, perhaps like radon, the influence was largely undetected. Käsemann's reevaluation of God's righteousness, and the consequences of this for understanding justification in Paul's thinking, is as widespread in New Perspective thinking as is E. P. Sanders's reevaluation of Palestinian Judaism. But Käsemann, on this particular point, was almost entirely mistaken. Not only was it gratuitous to assume that Paul had any familiarity with anything happening or written at Qumran, Käsemann misunderstood 1QS 11:12 almost entirely. "Righteousness of God" here was not at all a "ready-made formulation"; as I demonstrate in my excursus, the *zedek*-stock is used eight times in the passage, with profound variety. Further, in that passage, "righteousness of God" was used virtually interchangeably with other expressions, such as "his righteousness," "his lovingkindness," and "his righteous truth." He also stated that "righteousness of God" was used in a "peculiar" manner here when, in fact, it was used there just as it was used throughout the remainder of the Qumran literature, the Old Testament, and the Apocrypha and Pseudepigrapha. Worst of all, Käsemann (and his school of thinking on the matter) confused association with definition; to be sure, within both the canonical and post-canonical literature, God's "righteousness" was associated with the Sinai covenant/relationship by which Yahweh bound himself to Israel and Israel to him. This, however, does not and did not mean that "righteousness" *means* or *meant* "God's faithfulness to a relationship," as a thorough analysis of both the canonical and post-canonical literature demonstrates. As its synonyms and antonyms in all the pertinent literature demonstrate, "righteousness" is an ethical term that designates upright/praiseworthy behavior, including, of course, upright behavior in relationships. From this, by extension, it also can be used forensically, for a court's *judgment* that a behavior is approved or not. And indeed, on rare occasion, particular authors do appear to extend the matter into the eschaton, where God proves himself upright by his final judgment of the wicked and final acquittal of the righteous. But again, that God will powerfully judge the world in righteousness one day does not mean that the term "righteousness" *means* "power" (saving, condemning, or otherwise); the two are merely associated in the eschaton.

On this point, the New Perspective on Paul is strikingly like the nineteenth-century Protestant liberal perspective on Paul, and therefore not especially "new" at all. Neither the New Perspective nor the Protestant liberal interpreters of Paul[29] have understood the theology of justification correctly, because neither has been able to understand the relationship of justification to the related doctrines of creation and judgment. On this point, the inability is surprising, because the biblical teaching is almost common sense and therefore obvious: every intelligent creator, virtually by definition, exercises discriminating judgment in the very *process* of creating. Every stroke of the painter's brush either does or does not achieve what the painter intends it to achieve; and with each stroke, the painter therefore *judges* whether it has or has not succeeded in fulfilling the creative purpose. That is, creators do not merely evaluate their creations *after* they finish creating them (though they do this also); they constantly evaluate their creations in the *process* of crafting them, and necessarily so, because the only alternative is some sort of random, aleatoric "creating." The book

---

29. Käsemann derived his view from that of Cremer, who was an outspoken proponent of the old nineteenth-century Protestant liberalism.

of Genesis presents a narrative of artistic intelligence, as God the Creator evaluates at each creative moment, observing ("and God *saw* . . .") what he had made thus far and rendering a judgment ("and God saw that it was *good*"). When one aspect of that creation rebels against its created purpose, the Creator renders an unfavorable judgment, and all of the remainder of the scriptural record essentially answers (or joins Malachi in asking), "But who can endure the day of his coming, and who can stand when he appears?" (Mal. 3:2). What we ordinarily call the doctrine of justification is merely the answer to Malachi's question, as an answer unfolds and we discover that, contrary to Malachi's and our expectation, something has been done that will permit us to be acquitted in that day, and that something, according to the apostolic testimony, is the dying and rising of Christ. But then if his dying is an enduring of God's righteous judgment and if his resurrection is the vindication for his obedience by the same righteous God, then our justification can only be a gracious gift to those of us who are united to Christ, one with his death-to-sin and one with his resurrection-to-life. God's "righteousness" in such a scheme is that perfect moral righteousness by which he will by no means clear the guilty; a righteousness that therefore demands that death be paid for sin and rebellion, death in our own persons, or death in the person of a substitute (and what did Temple Judaism teach if not substitutionary death? Did goats sin? Did lambs sin?). It is only in exacting this death of the substitute that God can therefore, for Paul, be both "just and the justifier [δίκαιον καὶ δικαιοῦντα] of the one who has faith in Christ Jesus" (Rom. 3:26).

But Protestant liberal interpreters of Paul more than a century ago were just not happy with the idea of judicial wrath and were therefore not happy with substitutionary atonement.[30] They desired a God who was somehow "just" and "upright," but one who did not *care* about *in*justice or doing *wrong*. They wanted a deity who approved and promoted "righteousness," but not a deity who would *judge* his creation *in* righteousness (Ps. 9:4, 8; 35:4; 96:13; 98:9). But could the true and living God possibly care less about his creation than Rembrandt cared about his? Could he possibly be less interested in what he created than Brahms was in what he created? And if Brahms wrote a page of music that was unmusical, would he not judge that it was so and throw the score in the fireplace? Theologically, one cannot discard the doctrine of justification without discarding the doctrine of judgment (upon which it rests), and one cannot discard the doctrine of judgment without discarding the doctrine of creation (upon which it rests). We moderns (and postmoderns) may not like any notion of creation, but many premoderns liked the notion a good deal (sagely judging that chaos was worse); and Paul was a premodern. Paul not only affirmed the idea of intelligent creation; he even employed re-creation language to describe redemption. But neither the psalmist nor Paul, nor any premodern, could or would or did celebrate aleatoric "creation." They celebrated intelligent, purposeful creation and for this reason celebrated discriminating/

---

30. Peter Stuhlmacher has rightly complained that substitutionary atonement is absent in most New Perspective thinking. Cf. Stuhlmacher, *Revisiting Paul's Doctrine of Justification*. H. Richard Niebuhr famously demurred from such Protestant liberalism by characterizing it this way: "A God without wrath brought men without sin into a Kingdom without judgment through the ministrations of a Christ without a cross." *Kingdom of God in America* (New York: Harper & Row, 1937), 193.

judging creativity, expecting God, no less than human artists, to judge what he made.[31] Intellectually, this is easy enough that young children can understand it, so the New Perspective's inability to handle the Pauline understanding of justification must be due to something else. Perhaps it simply shares Protestant liberalism's aversion to the idea of God caring enough about his creation to render judgment, in which case it is not a very new perspective at all; it's just the same old nineteenth-century perspective using slightly modified language.

A second unhappy tendency within the New Perspective that I have mentioned frequently is its monocovenantalism. If Peter Stuhlmacher is right—and I believe he is—then the New Perspective must be understood within our post-Holocaust ecumenical setting. One way of reducing the differences between Judaism and Christianity is to suggest that they really are, after all, basically the same; religions that describe getting in and staying in "*the* covenant" in a similar manner. But in Paul's thinking, the new covenant and the Sinai covenant are not the same covenant; they are not, mingled together, "the covenant." One kills and the other gives life (2 Cor. 3:6). Indeed, in Paul's thinking, the Abrahamic covenant and the Sinai covenant are not the same covenant or "the covenant." One liberates and the other "is in slavery with her children" (Gal. 4:25). Paul's polycovenantal thinking is a round peg that will never fit into the New Perspective's monocovenantal square hole.

To realize its full potential to untie the knot of two strands in Paul's thinking (both positive and negative statements about the law), the New Perspective on Paul will continue in its admirable rejection of the easy way out of the dominant Protestant approach, continuing to be wary of assuming that his negative statements about the law were due to a common legalistic abuse thereof. But to understand the same Paul, the New Perspective will need to become more sensitive to the polycovenantal nature of Paul's thinking; it will need to recognize that justification/acquittal for Paul is a forensic activity, by which some court or judge approves a behavior as being upright. God the Creator expects fish to swim, birds to fly, and humans to imitate him on a creaturely scale; when any fails to fulfill what it was created to do, it comes under his intelligent judgment. "Justification" then for Paul is not about God expressing his faithfulness or his power, nor is it about who is in "the covenant" (whichever unnamed covenant is being referred to at the time). It is a declaration that the Maker and therefore Judge of all things has, through the work of an obedient Substitute, acquitted all who are united to him. The dominant Protestant approach may well have misunderstood almost entirely the historical *context* in which this doctrine was articulated, but it articulated the doctrine *itself* essentially correctly. The New Perspective understands the historical context better but misunderstands the doctrine almost entirely.[32]

---

31. A matter reflected in Bishop Wright's Anglican Book of Common Prayer, whose Prayer of General Confession addresses God as "*Maker* of *all* things, *Judge* of *all* men."

32. The New Perspective has created a virtual cottage industry of authors eager to correct its misapprehensions of justification, including: D. A. Carson, ed., *Right with God: Justification in the Bible and the World* (Grand Rapids: Baker, 1992); Mark A. Seifrid, *Christ Our Righteousness* (Downers Grove, IL: InterVarsity, 2000); Stuhlmacher, *Revisiting Paul's Doctrine of Justification*; Stephen Westerholm, *Perspectives Old and New on Paul: The Lutheran Paul and His Critics* (Grand Rapids: Eerdmans, 2004); Guy P. Waters, *Justification and the New Perspectives on Paul: A Review and Response* (Phillipsburg, NJ: P&R, 2004); *Justification and Variegated Nomism: The*

7.5. For the Dominant Protestant Approach

Lest the previous paragraph suggest an alliance with the dominant Protestant approach to Paul, permit me to reiterate several points that I have made before. The dominant Protestant approach erred, characteristically, in at least three ways: It misconstrued the historical circumstances by reading later, Tannaitic (post-Temple) sources as though they accurately represented late-Temple Judaism; it then assumed that Paul's negative statements about the law were directed at some later, distorted *view* of the law rather than the law itself as instituted at Sinai; and it therefore read "between the lines" of Galatians rather than the book of Galatians itself, which led it to confuse what Paul argued *for* with what Paul argued *from*.

If Neusner was/is right, then in later Tannaitic Judaism the central focus was indeed Torah, not Temple. But this later, "formative" Judaism had not yet emerged (or not emerged entirely) in Paul's day, while the temple still stood. And, if I understand the tip of Neusner's iceberg of writings correctly, it was a persistent thesis of his that the destruction of the temple in CE 70 was, to put it mildly, a significant event in Jewish history—significant enough that it is not only a chronological error but a theological error to assume that post-Temple sources accurately represent Temple Judaism without further argumentation.

The dominant Protestant approach, misarmed by this misdiagnosis of the historical circumstances, read Paul's negative statements about νόμος as negative statements about the mispractice, mispursuit, or misunderstanding of the same νόμος in his day. As I attempted to demonstrate in this work, Paul objected not to the law as it was construed or misconstrued in his generation (or, actually, several generations later in the Tannaitic writings); he objected to that law that came "430 years after" the Abrahamic administration. Throughout the central argument of Galatians 3, Paul persistently quoted Old Testament Scriptures, not contemporary writings, whether of sectarians or rabbis. The "curse" from which Paul desired relief was the curse that came through the hand and mouth of Moses himself in Deuteronomy 27:26—the legal, works-contingent nature of νόμος that he derived from Leviticus 18:5. His beef was neither with Hillel nor Gamaliel nor the Teacher of Righteousness; it was with Moses and Aaron. The dominant Protestant approach to Galatians mislocated the νόμος Paul criticized by a millennium and a half; Paul's negative comments about the law were directed to a reality that came on the scene in the middle of the second millennium BCE—not a reality that later emerged in the third century of the Common Era.

The dominant Protestant approach, therefore, read "between the lines" of Galatians rather than Galatians itself and never fully felt the weight, for the apostle to the Gentiles, of that Gentile-excluding character of the Sinai covenant itself to which Stendahl and Dunn (et al.) have so rightly called attention. It always tended to dismiss the discussion of "ceremonies" as though this were merely the tip of a much larger iceberg that was Paul's "real" concern; and, based on such a misreading, it attempted to read Galatians as though Paul argued there *for* the doctrine of justification (as the alleged problem at

---

Complexities of Second Temple Judaism, vol. 1, ed. D. A. Carson, Peter T. O'Brien, and Mark A. Seifrid (Grand Rapids: Baker, 2001); and *Justification and Variegated Nomism: The Paradoxes of Paul*, vol. 2, ed. D. A. Carson, Peter T. O'Brien, and Mark A. Seifrid (Grand Rapids: Baker, 2004).

Galatia itself) rather than *from* it (as a means to settle what *was* the problem: ceremonially marking as unclean Gentiles whom the new covenant did not regard as unclean).

7.6. For the Practical Application of the Letter

Many students and friends have listened patiently to me for the past thirty years as I have attempted to distinguish my view from both the dominant Protestant view of Galatians and from the New Perspectives on Paul. A gratifying number have found my reasoning to be, at least provisionally, persuasive. A sticking point arises, however, when they inquire about what *practical* difference it makes. At least the dominant Protestant approach was easy to apply: Don't do anything to attempt to justify yourself, don't even obey God's commands in the law in an effort to do so. No muss, no fuss. My understanding of both the problem and the solution at Galatia provides less clear guidelines. This does not distress me as much as it does my auditors, because I assume from the outset that some of the problems encountered in the initial generations of the church may have no contemporary equivalent. For instance, how many people in our churches today are discussing whether to eat food offered to idols (Rom. 14:1–4; 1 Cor. 8:4–13)? The problem at Galatia is nearly identical to the problem at Acts 15, and its applicatory problems are therefore neither greater nor lesser than those encountered there. So let me indicate a few thoughts regarding how Galatians might inform us today.

7.6.1. Paul Affirmed the Doctrine of Justification by Faith

First, I have no objection to allowing Paul's subarguments or premises to have their full weight. Although in my judgment he argues *from* the doctrine of justification rather than *for* the doctrine, he does believe and affirm the doctrine, and he regards it as true from Abraham's day until Christ returns (and after). He does not regard it as a new truth, but as an old truth that originated in Genesis 15:6; but he still regards it as a truth, and there is no reason to think that we cannot join him in affirming its truth, even if there is no evidence to me that anyone at Galatia denied it. In fact, the food offered to idols in 1 Corinthians 8 is instructive here; though we today are not likely to encounter the precise problem Paul encountered there, the theological rationale regarding Christian conscience and Christian charity by which he addressed the matter is still an important rationale.

7.6.2. The Decalogue Is Not Eternal in Se

The prevailing tendency of Christian confessional literature (Catholic or Protestant) has been to eternalize the ten words in two ways. First, they tend to mistranslate "ten words" as "ten commandments," in some/most of the translations, construing *debarim* as though it were *mitzvot*. There are only three places in the Hebrew Bible where the revelation at Sinai is enumerated as "ten"—Exodus 34:28, Deuteronomy 4:13, and Deuteronomy 10:4—and in each case the Hebrew (and the LXX) says "ten words" not "ten commandments." Second, in order to render this construal of *debarim* plausible, the Christian confessions all removed the first word ("I am the LORD your God, who brought you out of the land of Egypt, out of the house of slavery") from the other nine. Whether deliberate or unconscious, the effect of this was/is to eternalize and universalize the ten words by removing them from their covenantal context of Yahweh's dealings with the Israelites. Look again at the grammar: "And God spoke all [כל] these words [הדברים], saying, 'I am the LORD your God, who brought you out of the land of Egypt, out of the house of slavery. You shall have no other Gods before me. You shall not make . . . you shall not bow down . . . for I the LORD your God am a jealous God," and so on. And immediately after the prohibition of covetousness, Deuteronomy 5:22 recorded Moses as saying, "These words [הדברים] the LORD spoke to all your assembly at the mountain out of the midst of the fire, the cloud, and the thick darkness, with a loud voice; and he added no more." For Moses, the narrative (whether in Exod. 20 or Deut. 5) had unbroken divine discourse, beginning with "I am the LORD" and ending with the prohibition of covetousness—all of which constitutes "these words." The preliminary language of covenant preamble and prologue is one of the covenant "words" itself, and this word addresses those who had assembled at Sinai. In and of themselves, the commands no more oblige other nations or peoples than does the historical prologue: "brought you out of the land of Egypt, out of the house of bondage."

The Jewish enumeration of the Decalogue, from as early as *Mekhilta* (the Halakhic Midrash on Exodus), includes the historical preamble and prologue as one of the ten "words." The Jewish enumeration of the "ten words" includes the covenantal context and properly regards the other nine as covenant stipulations that oblige the benefactors of the deliverance spoken of in the historical prologue. The Christian enumerations[33] all remove the first word, leaving the impression that Moses brought ten universal, timeless words of moral counsel to the human race generally considered. This reflects an almost entire disregard for the original historical context, which was so distinctively covenantal and specific:

> And Moses summoned *all Israel* and said to *them*, "Hear, O Israel, the statutes and the rules that I speak in your hearing today, and you shall learn them and be careful to do them. The LORD our God *made a covenant with us* in Horeb. Not with our fathers did the LORD make *this covenant*, but with us, who are all of us here alive today. The LORD spoke with *you* face to face at the mountain, out of the midst of the fire. . . . He said: 'I am the LORD *your* God, who brought *you* out of the land of Egypt, out of the house of slavery.'" (Deut. 5:1–5)

And we note also the distinctly covenantal language Moses employs to refer back to this event:

> And he was there with the LORD forty days and forty nights; he neither ate bread nor drank water. And he wrote upon the tables the words of the covenant [דברי הברית], the ten commandments [*sic*] [עשרת הדברים]. (Exod. 34:28)

---

33. The Roman Catholic numbering (apparently first proposed by Augustine, *Quæstiones in Exodum*, Bk. II, q. 71, but also evident in Codex Alexandrinus) is found in the Baltimore Catechism question/answer no. 1130. The Lutheran numbering (apparently first proposed by Origen) can be found at the beginning (Section One) of either the Small or Large Catechism of Martin Luther. The Reformed enumeration is found, e.g., in the Westminster Shorter Catechism, Q/A 41ff., or Larger Catechism Q/A 98ff.

And he declared to you his *covenant*, which he commanded *you* to perform, that is, the ten commandments [*sic*] [עשרת הדברים]; and he wrote them upon two tables of stone. (Deut. 4:13)

And, of course, the tables or tablets were referred to as "the tablets of the *covenant*" (Deut. 9:9, 11, 15), and they were stored in the "ark of the *covenant*" (appears 43 times).

I mention this misenumeration of the Decalogue by the Christian traditions, not because of its consequences in its own right, but as an illustration of the tendency to disregard the covenantal contexts of biblical material. A tradition that can so blithely overlook that the ten words are "words of the covenant" inscribed on the "tablets of the covenant" and placed in the "ark of the covenant" is a tradition that is somewhat tone-deaf to biblical covenants and therefore incapable of unpacking the densely covenantal reasoning in Galatians. The interminable (and occasionally heated) conversations in the various Christian traditions regarding the Sabbath command, for instance, are partly due to the tension created by attempting to universalize God's covenant stipulations with the Israelites. On the one hand (excepting the Seventh-day Adventists), the Christian traditions all recognize that the apostolic gatherings occurred on the first day of the week; yet on the other, they wish to construe the Decalogue as timeless/universal moral counsel.[34] So they end up with statements such as that found in the Westminster Confession of Faith, 21:7: "He hath particularly appointed one day in seven, for a sabbath, to be kept holy unto him: which, from the beginning of the world to the resurrection of Christ, was the last day of the week; and, from the resurrection of Christ, was *changed* into the first day of the week." But if the "moral" law is "summarily comprehended" in the Ten Commandments, and if the definition of "moral" law is that it is unchanging (as opposed to positive law), then how can a moral law be "changed," whether in part or whole? And, if the specific holy day can be "changed" from one day to another, then why cannot some of the practices required on that holy day also be "changed"? The problem is self-created; treat the stipulations of any particular covenant made with a particular people as though they were universal, and you will end up with difficulty.[35] Whether, or in what degree, any biblical text contains universal moral wisdom is a mini-enterprise in itself. And while we might wish we had a single, convenient summary of God's moral purpose for us somewhere, it may simply be that such a thing does not exist biblically, because the biblical documents are written in order to direct covenant communities, not to provide counsel to those who are "strangers to the covenants."[36]

---

34. E.g., Westminster Larger Catechism, Q/A 98: "The moral law is summarily comprehended in the ten commandments."

35. I do not regard it as misguided for either the Jewish or Christian tradition to seek moral wisdom wherever it may be found in Holy Scripture; and I agree with both traditions that the Decalogue contains a profound concentration of such moral wisdom. But this profound concentration is not entire; some of the stipulations found there can be "changed." Further, it is not the only such concentration found in Holy Scripture. I regard 1 Cor. 13 and Phil. 2 as being similarly rich in moral wisdom.

36. Space surely does not permit a treatise on Christian ethics here in this brief chapter. I am working on such a treatise, in popular language and reasoning, and in that treatise I will suggest that the curse banishment from the garden consists, in part, to being handed over to moral blindness, which I take to be the import of Paul's thrice-repeated παρέδωκεν ("he handed

7.6.3. Christianity Should Be Disassociated from Nationalist Concerns

If Paul desired to disassociate the Christian gospel from geopolitical Israel (believing that the consequences of the new covenant were for all people in all nations), then he would surely wish to disassociate the gospel from nations that *never* enjoyed a special covenantal relationship with God at all. The new covenant is not made with any particular nation, and to suggest that any nation enjoys favored status within that covenant administration would encounter Paul's resistance. As James Davison Hunter has recently argued,[37] we should be intentional about distinguishing Christianity from the United States (and/or other nations). As Peter Berger earlier suggested,[38] we should be equally intentional about distinguishing Christianity from a particular (middle) class *within* such a national experiment. One should not need to embrace, encourage, or defend the geopolitical interests or practices of the United States (or any other nation) in order to be part of the professing Christian church. At a minimum, this might mean things like the following:

- We should remove national flags from churches (Berger: "Making the American flag into a quasi-sacramental object is offensive").

- When we pray regarding wars, we should pray for the protection and preservation of innocents, regardless of whether they are militarily friend or foe.

- We should reconsider whether it is the church's business to address national political issues. Why should we not pray for wisdom and justice in all cultures rather than merely our own, and why should we assume that Christians, *qua* Christians, care more about one nation than another, and therefore about the specifics of public policy issues in a given nation?

- We should not observe national holidays in the churches. Visitors/citizens of other nations share heavenly citizenship (Phil. 3:20) with us and should not be distinguished from us in any ecclesiastical setting.

7.6.4. We Might Want to Rethink Zionism

The Jews were God's chosen people for a particular purpose in a particular time. The apostles did not regard them as continuing to have any such distinctive or particular purpose; God's purpose is now global, and Jesus was regarded by Paul as the "second" and "last" Adam (not the second or last Abraham or Moses). While I understand that there will always be exegetical discussion about what the expression Ἰσραὴλ τοῦ θεοῦ

---

them over . . .") in Rom. 1:24, 26, 28, the last of which says that God handed them over "to a debased mind [ἀδόκιμον νοῦν] to do what ought not to be done." Had the human race in its original state cherished living in the presence of God, in whose image it was made, God's own moral qualities would have been sufficient to have provided all the direction that was needed. Banished from such presence, we grope about in relative moral blindness, into which moral blindness Scripture provides some, but not all, the light we might desire.

37. In the ironically titled *To Change the World: The Irony, Tragedy, and Possibility of Christianity in the Late Modern World* (New York: Oxford University Press, 2010).

38. Peter Berger, "Reflections of an Ecclesiastical Expatriate," *The Christian Century* (October 24, 1990), 964–69.

means in Galatians 6:16, I will happily and peacefully go to my grave suspicious that Paul reversed his opinion in the entire letter in its antepenultimate verse.

There are perfectly good nontheological reasons to be pro-Jewish and/or pro-Israel (and I do not take the two to be the same). Whether compassion for their unmerited persecution for so many centuries—or admiration for their remarkable achievements in industry, commerce, philanthropy, science, or the various arts—there are numerous reasons to look at this heritage and say, "Wow." If one examines the profound disproportion between their numbers and their awards/achievements, even in our own culture, then one cannot but wonder how such an overachieving culture became such. ("Bartender, I'll have whatever they're drinking.") My own opinion on the matter, as a student of the apostolic writings and of history, is this: The Jews not only do not *enjoy* any special favor from God, but I'm not even sure they *need* it. That they have achieved what they have in spite of many centuries of persecution is all the more remarkable.

7.7. Conclusion

I have proposed a *tertium quid*—a third way or third perspective of reading Galatians that avoids/evades what I regard as significant liabilities to the two major alternative readings. If this proposed reading proves to be satisfactory to others, then its ramifications will be such as I have described here.

ἔργα νόμου in Galatians

While it is somewhat less critical to my primary thesis (that Paul discusses the realities of the new covenant by means of his understanding the differences between the Abrahamic and Sinai covenants), James D. G. Dunn's various writings have provoked a substantial discussion of ἔργα νόμου in Galatians. As briefly as possible, I wish to provide an overview of what I regard to be the three major opinions on the matter, and my rationale for preferring one solution to the other two. There has been a "legalistic" approach to the matter among many within the dominant Protestant camp, which has regarded "works of the law" to be "works done in a legalistic manner." There has been Dunn's thesis that "works of the law" is a technical and restricted expression that refers to those particular prescriptions of Torah that distinguish the Jews from the Gentiles. And there has been a fairly unrestricted and commonsense view that the expression means nothing more or less than those works required by the Mosaic law.

1.1. The "Legalistic" View of ἔργα νόμου

Ernest De Witt Burton's commentary on Galatians is a prime example of what E. P. Sanders has called the dominant Protestant approach to Paul.[1] Both the interpretation of the letter as a whole and the particular resolution of ἔργα νόμου reflect the dominant approach. Burton assumed that there was a widespread legalistic element in first-century Judaism, that such an element had insinuated itself at Galatia, and that Paul referred to the requirements of such a party by using the expression ἔργα νόμου:

> By ἔργα νόμου here Paul means deeds of obedience to formal statutes done in the legalistic spirit, with the expectation of thereby meriting and securing divine approval and award, such obedience, in other words, as the legalists rendered to the law of the O.T. as expanded and interpreted by them. Though νόμος in this sense had no existence as representing the basis of justification in the divine government, yet ἔργα νόμου had a very real existence in the thought and practice of men who conceived of the divine law after this fashion.[2]

---

1. Ernest De Witt Burton, *A Critical and Exegetical Commentary on the Epistle to the Galatians*, The International Critical Commentary (Edinburgh: T & T Clark, 1920). More recently, the position is articulated by Richard N. Longenecker, who says that Paul "uses ἔργων νόμου not just to refer to 'the badges of Jewish covenantal nomism,' though that may have been how other Jewish believers thought of them, but as a catch phrase to signal the whole legalistic complex of ideas having to do with winning God's favor by a merit-amassing observance of Torah." Longenecker, *Galatians*, 86. Longenecker also employs the expression "merit-amassing observance of Torah" (102).

2. Burton, *Galatians*, 120. To be fair, Burton qualified the thesis somewhat: "It must, of course, be recognized that different views prevailed among Jewish, and even among Pharisaic thinkers, as is illustrated, e.g., in the more strenuous legalism of the book of Jubilees, and the more liberal views of the almost precisely contemporary Testament of the Twelve Patriarchs.

This dominant view depended also, in part, on assuming that ἔργα νόμου referred not to νόμος in a neutral manner, but in a manner that focused on performing the deeds therein required and achieving some merit before God. Indeed, this also required that the dominant viewpoint skewed the use of νόμος itself, and sometimes regarded even νόμος itself as referring to legalism, as C. E. B. Cranfield said:

> The Greek language of Paul's day possessed no word-group corresponding to our "legalism", "legalist" and "legalistic". This means that he lacked a convenient terminology for express- ing a vital distinction, and so was surely seriously hampered in the work of clarifying the Christian position with regard to the law. In view of this, we should always, we think, be ready to reckon with the possibility that Pauline statements, which at first sight seem to disparage the law, were really directed not against the law itself but against that misunder- standing and misuse of it for which we now have a convenient terminology.[3]

If scholars such as Cranfield were willing to read "legalism" where Paul employed νόμος, it would be an even easier step to read "legalism" where Paul employed ἔργα νόμου, since this expression at least expressly employed "works."

I'm not at all sure we need to make the concession that Cranfield suggests: to wit, that "the Greek language of Paul's day possessed no word-group corresponding to our "'legalism', 'legalist' and 'legalistic.'" It appears to me that the New Testament provides at least some evidence that such a phenomenon could have been described in the existing language of the first century. Here are two examples, one from the Gospels and one from Paul himself.

1. He also told this parable to some who trusted in themselves that they were righteous [τοὺς πεποιθότας ἐφ᾽ ἑαυτοῖς ὅτι εἰσὶν δίκαιοι], and treated others with contempt. (Luke 18:9)
2. But if you call yourself a Jew and rely on the law [ἐπαναπαύῃ νόμῳ] and boast in God . . . (Rom. 2:17)

So it seems to me that, if a widespread legalistic phenomenon existed in the first century, then the Greek of the New Testament could have articulated it.

But let us, for the sake of argument, concede Cranfield's point that, at least, no "convenient" terminology existed at the time. Since languages are fairly flexible, and since loanwords from some languages make their way into common usage in others, when they are deemed useful, we might turn Cranfield's point back upon him and ask this: If legalism, as understood in the late medieval period, was so widespread an issue in Paul's day, then why *didn't* Paul (or someone else) coin a convenient term for it? I am confident, for instance, that there are probably cultures today that have no convenient term for our word *unicorn*. The reason this defect occurs perhaps is

---

. . . Besides that extreme type of legalism which Paul opposed, other views were held then and later, some of them closely approximating certain aspects of Paul's own thought. But the evi- dence seems to indicate that the view against which Paul contended was very influential in his day, and it is in any case that with which in our effort to understand N.T. usage we are chiefly concerned." Ibid., 447–48.

3. C. E. B. Cranfield, *A Critical and Exegetical Commentary on the Epistle to the Romans*, vol. 2 (Edinburgh: T & T Clark, 1979), 853. Cf. also Stephen Westerholm's critique of the Cranfield "legalism" definition of ὁ νόμος in *Perspectives Old and New on Paul: The "Lutheran" Paul and His Critics* (Grand Rapids: Eerdmans, 2004), 330–35.

because that culture has no *need* for a term that describes a nonexistent reality. That is, the dominant Protestant approach encountered some counterevidence to its thesis; no convenient term for legalism even existed. This could have indicated that Greek had no more use for a word like *legalism* than it did for a word like *unicorn*, because neither existed. But rather than modify the thesis to the lexical evidence, they modified the lexical evidence to the thesis and forced the perfectly neutral expression ἔργα νόμου to mean a legalistic perversion of the law.[4]

1.2. ἔργα νόμου as the "Identity Markers" within the Law

James D. G. Dunn has argued that ἔργα νόμου is technical, and that the expression refers to those particular commands within the Mosaic law that served to mark the Israelites as distinct from the nations around them—the kinds of laws that feature so prominently in the Galatian letter: circumcision, the dietary laws, and the Jewish calendar.

> We may justifiably deduce, therefore, that by "works of law" Paul intended his readers to think of *particular observances of the law like circumcision and the food laws*. His Galatian readership might well think also of the one other area of law observance to which Paul refers disapprovingly later in the same letter—their observance of special days and feasts. . . . The phrase "works of the law" in Galatians 2.16 is, in fact, a fairly restricted one: it refers precisely to these same identity markers described above, *covenant* works—those regulations prescribed by the law which any good Jew would simply take for granted to describe what a good Jew did. To be a Jew was to be a member of the covenant, was to observe circumcision, food laws, and sabbath.[5]

Dunn is surely right that the Mosaic covenant *en toto* was made with the Israelites and required their separation and holiness from the nations around them. He is also right in observing that this separation of Jew and Gentile is at the heart of the "problem" of the law for Paul (a point the dominant Protestant approach almost always underestimated). Indeed, this is where his overall approach is so much more satisfactory than the dominant approach that preceded it; Dunn's approach takes exegetical note of which laws specifically trouble Paul (the Gentile-excluding ones) in Galatia, without speculating that some other, unspecified problem is the "real" problem. And Dunn is additionally right in observing that, under the precarious circumstances that followed the exile, for many Israelites the separation laws became a virtual test of their commitment to God per se. Consider Tobit's self-testimony:

> Now when I was carried away captive to Nineveh, all my brethren and my relatives ate the food of the Gentiles [ἤσθιον ἐκ τῶν ἄρτων τῶν ἐθνῶν]; but I kept myself from eating it, because I remembered God with all my heart. (Tob. 1:10–12)

---

4. It does not appear to have occurred to the dominant Protestant approach to answer this question: If ἔργα νόμου meant "legalistic perversion of the law," then how *could* anyone in Paul's day have referred neutrally to the works demanded by Torah? If someone (e.g., a Gentile "God-fearer") had wished to ask what deeds the law required, would it not have been necessary to preface the answer something like this?: "Well, the ἔργα νόμου are these . . ."

5. Dunn, "The New Perspective on Paul," 191, 194.

Or consider the narrative of martyrdom in the beginning of 1 Maccabees:

> According to the decree, they put to death the women who had their children circumcised, and their families and those who circumcised them; and they hung the infants from their mothers' necks. But many in Israel stood firm and were resolved in their hearts not to eat unclean food. They chose to die rather than to be defiled by food or to profane the holy covenant; and they did die. (1 Macc. 1:60–63)

While Dunn's general approach to Galatians is an extremely helpful corrective to the dominant Protestant (mis)understanding, that approach does not require one to believe that ἔργα νόμου refers to the separating/marking/identifying laws. And there are good reasons not to do so. First, the ordinary usage of the ἔργ- language is merely general, not restrictive or particular. Paul, for instance, can say, "Love does no wrong to a neighbor [κακὸν οὐκ ἐργάζεται]; therefore love is the fulfilling of the law [πλήρωμα οὖν νόμου ἡ ἀγάπη]." Further, elsewhere in Galatians, Paul uses ἐργ- language as the virtual synonym of ποιέω/ποίημα- language or ἐμμένω. Note especially Galatians 3:10–12:

> Ὅσοι γὰρ ἐξ ἔργων νόμου εἰσίν, ὑπὸ κατάραν εἰσίν· γέγραπται γὰρ ὅτι ἐπικατάρατος πᾶς ὃς οὐκ ἐμμένει πᾶσιν τοῖς γεγραμμένοις ἐν τῷ βιβλίῳ τοῦ νόμου τοῦ ποιῆσαι αὐτά. ὅτι δὲ ἐν νόμῳ οὐδεὶς δικαιοῦται παρὰ τῷ θεῷ δῆλον, ὅτι ὁ δίκαιος ἐκ πίστεως ζήσεται· ὁ δὲ νόμος οὐκ ἔστιν ἐκ πίστεως, ἀλλ᾽ ὁ ποιήσας αὐτὰ ζήσεται ἐν αὐτοῖς.

In this passage, Paul explains why those who are characterized by ἔργων νόμου are under a curse, by referring to Deuteronomy 27:26 and its threatened curse sanction. But note that the curse comes upon the one who does not "abide by" (ἐμμένει) the things written in the book of the law "to do" (τοῦ ποιῆσαι) them. In verse 12 also, distinguishing this "working" character of the Sinai covenant from the faith associated with the Abrahamic covenant, he summarizes the Sinai covenant by referring to Leviticus 18:5: ὁ ποιήσας αὐτὰ ζήσεται ἐν αὐτοῖς.

We note two things about Paul's language here. First, "works" (ἔργων) of the law appear to be synonymous with "remaining" (ἐμμένει) in the law or "doing" (ποιῆσαι, ποιήσας) the things required in the law. Second, we note that in the OT texts cited, plainly the original reference was to the *entirety* of the Mosaic law, not merely the marking requirements. Note the preface to Leviticus 18:5, for instance:

> And the LORD spoke to Moses, saying, "Speak to the people of Israel and say to them, I am the LORD your God. You shall not do [οὐ ποιήσετε] as they do in the land of Egypt, where you lived, and you shall not do [οὐ ποιήσετε] as they do in the land of Canaan, to which I am bringing you. You shall not walk [οὐ πορεύσεσθε] in their statutes. You shall follow my rules [τὰ κρίματά μου ποιήσετε] and keep my statutes [καὶ τὰ προστάγματά μου φυλάξεσθε] and walk in them [πορεύεσθαι ἐν αὐτοῖς]. I am the LORD your God. You shall therefore keep [φυλάξεσθε] my statutes and my rules; if a person does them, he shall live by them: I am the LORD. (Lev. 18:1–4)

Note how comprehensively Moses contrasted the behavior of the Egyptians in Israel's past with the Canaanites in their near future. Israel was to separate themselves in *all* their behavior from *all* of the behavior of the nations around them by their *entire* obedience to the Mosaic law. What follows Leviticus 18:5 are examples of what Moses intended:

> None of you shall approach any one of his close relatives to uncover nakedness. . . . You shall not give any of your children to offer them to Molech, and so profane the name of your God. . . . You shall not lie with a male as with a woman. . . . And you shall not lie with any animal and so make yourself unclean with it. . . . Do not make yourselves unclean by any of these things. . . . Every one of you shall revere his mother and his father, and you shall keep my Sabbaths. . . . Do not turn to idols or make for yourselves any gods of cast metal. . . . When you reap the harvest of your land, you shall not reap your field right up to its edge, neither shall you gather the gleanings after your harvest. And you shall not strip your vineyard bare, neither shall you gather the fallen grapes of your vineyard. You shall leave them for the poor and for the sojourner. . . . You shall not steal; you shall not deal falsely; you shall not lie to one another. You shall not swear by my name falsely, and so profane the name of your God: I am the LORD. . . . You shall not oppress your neighbor or rob him. . . . You shall not curse the deaf or put a stumbling block before the blind. . . . You shall do no injustice in court. . . . You shall not hate your brother in your heart. . . . You shall not take vengeance or bear a grudge against the sons of your own people, but you shall love your neighbor as yourself.

Some of these behaviors, one might argue, are "marking" laws by which the Israelites would distinguish themselves from the Canaanites (Molech, idolatry, "uncleanness," Sabbath-keeping). But most of them reflect the Mosaic legislation comprehensively and have to do with agriculture, jurisprudence, truth-telling, sexual purity, concern for the poor or dispossessed, and so, concluding with the comprehensive "You shall love your neighbor as yourself."

Both Leviticus 18:5ff. and Deuteronomy 27:26 were comprehensive in their original contexts, as Paul noted by citing this comprehensiveness. Though the word order is somewhat different, the comprehensiveness is affirmed.

> Cursed be anyone who does not confirm the words of this law [ὃς οὐκ ἐμμενεῖ ἐν πᾶσιν τοῖς λόγοις τοῦ νόμου τούτου, KJV "*all* the words of this law"] by doing them. (LXX)

> Cursed be everyone who does not abide by *all* things written in the Book of the Law [οὐκ ἐμμένει πᾶσιν τοῖς γεγραμμένοις ἐν τῷ βιβλίῳ τοῦ νόμου], and do them. (Gal. 3:10)

The Hebrew text of Deuteronomy does not say "all," but both the LXX and Paul add πᾶσιν to make it clear, contextually, that avoidance of the curse sanction requires obedience to the *entirety* of the Mosaic code. "Works of the law" are those works required *by* the law; they include "*all* things written in the Book of the Law," not merely the marking or separating behaviors.

Dunn has felt the weight of the criticism of his construal on this point, and he has conceded that perhaps ἔργα νόμου could be construed more comprehensively:

> "Works of the law" denote *all that the law requires* of the devout Jew, but precisely because it is the law as identity and boundary marker which is in view, the law as Israel's law focuses on these rites which express Jewish distinctiveness most clearly. The conclusion of the previous section is thus confirmed: "works of the law" refer *not exclusively but particularly* to those requirements which bring to sharp focus the distinctiveness of Israel's identity.[6]

---

6. James D. G. Dunn, "Works of the Law and the Curse of the Law (Galatians 3.10–14)," *New Testament Studies* 31, no. 4 (October 1985): 531 (emphases added).

While I might quibble with the "particularly" above, nonetheless I applaud the concession Dunn made by using such comprehensive language as "all that the law requires,"
and "not exclusively" to the identity markers, which concession brings him so much
closer to what I regard as perhaps the majority opinion: that ἔργα νόμου is not technical but comprehensive.

1.3. The Comprehensive View of ἔργα νόμου

In addition to the ordinary lexical considerations and some of the texts mentioned
above, there are other examples of the ἔργα stock being employed comprehensively
of all that the Mosaic law required. Moses himself anticipated his coming death and
expressed his fear that the Israelites would violate the covenant once he was gone:

> For I know that after my death you will surely act corruptly [ἀνομίᾳ ἀνομήσετε] and turn
> aside from the way that I have commanded you [ἧς ἐνετειλάμην ὑμῖν]. And in the days to
> come evil will befall you, because you will do what is evil in the sight of the Lord [ποιήσετε
> τὸ πονηρὸν ἐναντίον κυρίου], provoking him to anger through the work of your hands [ἐν
> τοῖς ἔργοις τῶν χειρῶν ὑμῶν]. (Deut. 31:29)

Several comprehensive expressions occur here, summarized at the end as "the work"
of your hands, work that was contrary to what Moses (comprehensively) commanded,
work that was evil in the Lord's sight, work that was lawless (ἀνομίᾳ ἀνομήσετε, though
obscured by many English translations).

In Jewish literature closer to Paul's time, the ἔργ- stock also reflects this
comprehensiveness:

> And the things which you have heard from your father, share them also with your children,
> so that the savior of the nations may receive you; for he is true and patient, meek and
> humble, and teaches *by his works* the law of God [ἐκδιδάσκων διὰ τῶν ἔργων νόμον θεοῦ].
> (Testament of Dan 6:9; emphasis added)

> And the Lord has kept the calamities ready, and the Lord has brought them upon us, for the
> Lord is righteous in *all his works which he has commanded* us to do [ὅτι δίκαιος ὁ κύριος
> ἐπὶ πάντα τὰ ἔργα αὐτοῦ ἃ ἐνετείλατο ἡμῖν, emphasis mine]. Yet we have not obeyed his
> voice, to walk in the statutes of the Lord which he set before us. (Bar. 2:9–10)

In texts such as these, we observe comprehensive statements referring to "the statutes
of the Lord" or "the law of God," and the "works" that are required thereby. It is not at
all surprising, therefore, that students of Paul and Galatians such as Douglas J. Moo
have understood ἔργα νόμου comprehensively, as a straightforward way of indicating
the behaviors required by the Mosaic law, and as "actions performed in obedience to
the law, works which are commanded by the law."[7] Even though the specific expression
does not appear in the literature, enough parallel passages exist for us to arrive at this
comprehensive understanding of what the expression means, as does J. Louis Martyn:

---

7. Moo, " 'Law,' 'Works of the Law,' and Legalism in Paul," 92.

Although the precise expression *erga nomou* has not been found in any Greek literature prior to Galatians, Jewish Christians of Paul's time . . . would have had little difficulty grasping its meaning. It refers simply to observance of God's Law. There are numerous parallels in the Septuagint, in Jewish traditions, and in traditions we can trace to Jewish Christians . . . [referring to its use in 1QS 5:21]. For the expression simply summarizes the grand and complex activity of the Jew, who faithfully walks with God along the path God has opened up for him in the Law.[8]

As I have attempted to demonstrate, Paul's problem at Galatia was not with particular works of the law per se, but with observing the law *itself* as a still-obligatory covenant. It is true that his primary objection to that covenant was that it was made with only a single nation (temporarily disrupting the Abrahamic pledge to bless all nations); and therefore it is also true that those particular works that separated Jew from Gentile animated his polemical comments in the letter. But, as we shall see, Paul did not believe that any or all of the commands given at Sinai could be extracted from the covenant of which they were a part. All of the laws, from the first to the last, were covenant stipulations, and any member of that covenant was obliged to observe all of them: "I testify again to every man who accepts circumcision that he is obligated to keep the whole law" (ὅλον τὸν νόμον ποιῆσαι, Gal. 5:3). For Paul, if a few Gentile-excluding *commandments* were bad (Dunn's "identity markers"), then a Gentile-excluding *covenant* was even worse. Such a covenant could have only a temporary role in the plans of a God who had pledged to Father Abraham to bless through Abraham's single descendant all the nations of the earth.

---

8. Martyn, *Galatians*, 261. Cf. also Peter Stuhlmacher, "God's Righteousness and God's Kingdom," *Revisiting Paul's Doctrine of Justification: A Challenge to the New Perspective* (Downers Grove, IL: IVP Academic, 2001), 43–44.

δικαιοσύνη et cetera in Galatians

2.1. Introduction

Words and concepts, as James Barr rightly reminded us, are not the same things.[1] At the same time, neither concepts nor any other intellectual realities can be easily communicated apart from words, and therefore any wrestling with justification in Paul requires some attempt to understand his usage of the δικ- group: δικαιόω, δίκαιος, and δικαιοσύνη, even if the result of our study were to disclose that there is little relation between the Greek δικαιοσύνη and the English "justification," between the Greek δικαιόω and the English "justify," or between the Greek δίκαιος and the English "righteous."

From the outset, we observe a Scylla and Charybdis challenge. On the one hand, we join Rudolf Bultmann and many others who rightly warn that the verb, noun, and adjective need not have an identical semantic range, and that each of the three itself need not have a fixed range[2]—while, on the other hand, wishing to understand what holds the root together. That is, on the one hand, we do not wish to restrict our understanding of the usage, forcing Paul into an artificial consistency in which his usage of the noun, adjective, and verb must correspond entirely (or each of the three necessarily be employed to communicate always the identical matter); but on the other hand, we do not wish to dismiss their common lexical root as a mere coincidence. We wish to avoid/evade assuming a "foolish inconsistency" if such is contrary to Paul's actual usage, while also avoiding/evading the suggestion that Paul's employment of a common root for the three terms was a matter of sheer caprice.

We also cannot but notice that in the past century, there has been a shift in the understanding of δικαιοσύνη and its cognates, so that the former majority opinion (which was, in fact, a virtually unanimous opinion) has become secondary; and a formerly

---

1. James Barr, *The Semantics of Biblical Language* (Oxford: Oxford University Press, 1962), esp. ch. 8, "Some Principles of Kittel's Theological Dictionary," 206–62. So, e.g., "The work of the dictionary is to be in the realm of 'concept history'; but the dictionary itself is a dictionary of Greek *words*. The construction of the work thus brings right to the fore the difficult problem of the relation of word and concept." Ibid., 207 (emphasis his).

2. Objecting to Ernst Käsemann's "Gottesgerechtigkeit bei Paulus," in *Zeitschrift für Theologie und Kirche* 58 (1961), 367–78, Bultmann said, "Dass Paulus in verschiedenem Sinn von der Gottesgerechtigkeit redet, ist ohne weiteres daraus verständlich, dass ihm der alttestamentliche Sprachgebrauch vertraut ist. Auch im AT wird der Begriff der Gerechtigkeit Gottes in verschiedenem Sinn gebraucht." Rudolf Bultmann, "*Dikaiosune Theou*," *Journal of Biblical Literature* 83 (1964): 12–13. Far from disagreeing with Bultmann's claim, Käsemann merely objected that he himself had not denied a diverse usage: "Similarly, I do *not* maintain that the concept 'must have the same meaning throughout the Pauline corpus.'" Ernst Käsemann, "'The Righteousness of God' in Paul," *New Testament Questions of Today* (Philadelphia: Fortress, 1969), 169n (emphasis original).

nonexistent opinion has become the dominant scholarly opinion, which accounts for my brief historical statement below. Very little of this change is due to new evidence, though some of it has been due to the increased access to late Jewish sources. Most of the change is due to a different way of construing the sources themselves.[3]

Complicating the matter significantly is that the only way to determine whether the previous dominant view or the current dominant view is correct is to study the primary literature itself, which is not especially easy. By my current count, there are 329 occurrences of the various forms of the root צדק in the Hebrew Bible[4] and 471 in the Qumran literature; as for the relevant δικ- vocabulary (I omit some of the less-pertinent forms, such as δικαίωμα), I find 564 uses in the LXX, 343 in the Jewish Pseudepigrapha, and 122 in the Jewish Apocrypha, bringing the total number of pertinent Jewish texts to 1,829. While some of these are quite straightforward, especially many of the uses in narrative or wisdom literature, others (especially Qumran, because the manuscripts are so fragmented) appear in virtually obscure contexts, and still others appear in contexts that are debatable as to their meaning.[5]

My unappetizing recommendation is that serious students read these texts; only then, I believe, will the student get beyond the various plausible construals to the material itself. Indeed, my own confidence in the previously dominant view is due to the fact that nearly all, if not all, of the original texts use the language in its ethical (and, by extension, forensic) sense, and very few of them can even plausibly be construed otherwise.[6] This does not mean that Paul could not coin a new usage, were he so inclined; indeed, much of the vocabulary of the Hebrew Bible takes on new meaning in the apostolic generation; e.g., the Baptist's calling Jesus the "Lamb of God, who takes

---

3. As we shall see below, though in its contemporary form Käsemann and Stuhlmacher made reference to later Jewish sources (especially Qumran), the real shift in viewpoint was originally generated by Hermann Cremer in 1899, roughly a half century before the Qumran scrolls were discovered, much less made available to scholarly investigation. Further, as I hope to demonstrate, the late Jewish sources are not significantly different from the Hebrew Bible or the LXX. In the Hebrew Bible, the LXX, and the late Jewish sources, we still find unquestioned ethical usages and forensic usages (and that these usages are overwhelmingly dominant), and we also find some texts that could be plausibly capable of a relational/soteric construal (though the number of such texts is comparatively small).

4. Unless necessary to the argument in specific places, my citation of the Hebrew will be unpointed, for several reasons. First, insofar as the Hebrew Bible influenced Paul, it was an unpointed Hebrew Bible; he was unacquainted with the pointed texts of the Masoretes a millennium later. Second, our concern here is lexicographic; we are primarily concerned with the lexical stock that influenced Paul, rather than with finer points of exegesis in those texts.

5. Of those 1,829 texts, I find 205 that are indeterminate. Not surprisingly, of those 205, 122 are in the Qumran literature, some of which are so fragmentary that making a reliable determination in some cases is not possible. In the other four bodies of literature, the texts are rarely fragmentary, but some usages in some contexts are fairly inscrutable. Nonetheless, we still have 1,624 uses antedating Paul that are fairly easy to categorize.

6. It is all well and good for Käsemann and Stuhlmacher to call attention to four, possibly six, texts in Qumran where "righteousness of God" *may* refer to God's apocalyptic power. But if there are 471 occurrences of "righteousness" (and its cognates) in the Qumran literature, and only six of those can even plausibly be construed in such a manner (though plausibly construed otherwise also), then the prevailing usage is the other 465 and it would be curious lexicography indeed to suspect that just over 1 percent of the uses had more influence on Paul's or anyone else's usage than did the other 98-plus percentage.

away the sin of the world." But such a new usage would be just that, a new usage—a usage that would have been unintelligible to his generation were he not to have made the new usage clear by some contextual means.

2.2. The Dominance of the Cremer-Käsemann Hypothesis Regarding Righteousness

Students of the New Perspectives on Paul tend to associate its beginnings with either E. P. Sanders or, to a lesser degree, Krister Stendahl. Undeniably, these two figures raised important questions that altered the status of subsequent Pauline scholarship. Somewhat overlooked, however, is the equally profound influence of Ernst Käsemann, whose pertinent contribution was itself dependent on the work of August Hermann Cremer (1834–1903).[7] Cremer is perhaps best remembered for his seminal *Biblisch-theologisches Wörterbuch der neutestamentlichen Gräzität* (1866), which appeared in numerous German editions, including a posthumous one edited by Julius Kögel. It also appeared in several English translations as *Biblical-Theological Lexicon of New Testament Greek*. For our purposes, however, Cremer's influence is more specific. As he himself was influenced by Albrecht Ritschl,[8] in his *Die Paulinische Rechtfertigungslehre Im Zusammenhange Ihrer Geschichtlichen Voraussetzungen*, he proposed that δικαιοσύνη θεοῦ in the OT was a relational concept (*Verhältnisbegriff*), that δικαιοσύνη was the attribute that sustained or upheld an existing relationship. Cremer further proposed, then, that when Paul spoke of the "righteousness of God," he was influenced by this OT concept and thus intended the same.

A generation or so later, Cremer's view was picked up and developed somewhat further by Ernst Käsemann, for whom δικαιοσύνη θεοῦ was divine power (perhaps even apocalyptic power), but divine power in service of the maintenance of a relationship:

> From the outset it will be noticed that in the field of the Old Testament and of Judaism in general, righteousness does *not convey primarily the sense of a personal, ethical quality*, but of a *relationship*; originally signifying trustworthiness in regard to the community, it came to mean the rehabilitated standing of a member of the community who had been acquitted of an offence against it. Any interpretation which begins from the general concept and its specifically *juridical* application is bound to centre on the character of righteousness as gift and, in practice, on anthropology. But the formulation which Paul has taken over speaks primarily of *God's saving activity*, which is present in his gift as a precipitate without being completely dissolved into it.[9]

Käsemann's student, Peter Stuhlmacher, continued to promote this viewpoint, especially on the basis of later Jewish writings that were almost contemporary with Paul. Despite

---

7. For the survey of Cremer's influence on Käsemann, I am especially indebted to "Chapter One: History of Interpretation of 'the Righteousness of God' in Paul," in C. Lee Irons, "ΔΙΚΑΙΟΣΥΝΗ ΘΕΟΥ: A Lexical Examination of the Covenant-Faithfulness Interpretation" (PhD diss., Fuller Theological Seminary, May 2011), 12–82.

8. Ibid., 24–26.

9. Käsemann, "The 'Righteousness of God' in Paul," 172.

the nuance and shadings, what was common to these views was the rejection of the idea that δικαιοσύνη θεοῦ was moral or forensic: It was not God's character as an upright being—and therefore an upright judge "who will by no means clear the guilty"—nor was it associated with "righteousness by faith," an imputed righteousness based upon a righteousness achieved by Christ. It was God manifesting his faithfulness to his covenant people by appearing in works of apocalyptic power. In this form, δικαιοσύνη θεοῦ also appeared in the *Interpreter's Dictionary of the Bible*, in the respective articles by Elizabeth R. and Paul J. Achtemeier, "Righteousness in the OT" and "Righteousness in the NT."[10] The chain of influence would then be something like this:

Ritschl

to

Cremer

to

Käsemann

to

Stuhlmacher, E. Achtemeier, P. Achtemeier (et al.)

to

New Perspective(s) on Paul[11]

That is, part of what has been overlooked in the discussion of the NPP is the profound influence of the Käsemann hypothesis thereon. For all the comparatively smaller differences among the various proponents of the NPP, the notion that δικαιοσύνη θεοῦ has something to do with "faithfulness to the covenant" is virtually universal—as is the corresponding notion that justification has something to do with "membership in the covenant." Note what N. T. Wright has said, almost in passing:

> That is why, in the great sweeping argument of the letter to the Romans, Paul's exposition of God's faithfulness to his covenant (in technical language, his "righteousness"), is explained in terms of the fulfilment of the promises to Abraham (3:21–4:25), and then explored in terms of the undoing of Adam's sin (5:12–21) and ultimately of the liberation of the whole creation (8:17–25).[12]

---

10. *Interpreter's Dictionary of the Bible* 4 (Nashville: Abingdon Press, 1962), 80–85, 91–99. While the influence is not always acknowledged by proponents of the NPP, portions are acknowledged on some occasions. James D. G. Dunn, for instance, acknowledged the conscious influence of the Achtemeiers (2), and acknowledged that he later recognized the influence of Cremer on the discussion (3n7) in the introductory chapter of his *The New Perspective on Paul*, rev. ed. (Tübingen: Mohr Siebeck, 2005). But in his groundbreaking Manson Memorial Lecture, there is no mention of Cremer, no mention of the Achtemeiers, and only negative statements about Käsemann, for perpetuating, with Bultmann, a "Lutheran" understanding of Paul that erroneously (in Dunn's view) "made this (Lutheran) understanding of justification their central theological principle." Cf. "The New Perspective on Paul," *Jesus, Paul and the Law: Studies in Mark and Galatians* (Louisville, KY: Westminster/John Knox, 1990), 185.

11. I don't by any means suggest that this list is exhaustive or even comprehensive. But these are representative figures whose influence has been substantial. Were I more poetically inclined I might even attempt to describe the influence in "Tinker to Evers to Chance" language.

12. *What Saint Paul Really Said: Was Paul of Tarsus the Real Founder of Christianity?* (Grand Rapids: Eerdmans, 1997), 48 (parentheses original). Also, "'The righteousness of God' would

Similarly, James D. G. Dunn has said, "People are righteous when they meet the claims which others have on them by virtue of their relationship."[13] While I am not yet willing to concede with Wright that this is "technical language" within the Hebrew Bible, the LXX, or early Judaism, it has become virtually technical language in biblical studies since the nineteenth century (and perhaps this is what Wright intended). Gottlob Schrenck, for instance, said, "A man is righteous when he meets certain claims which another has on him in virtue of relationship. Even the righteousness of God is primarily His covenantal rule in fellowship with His people."[14] Schrenck's view, self-consciously dependent on Cremer, was also that of Ernst Käsemann:

> From the outset it will be noticed that in the field of the Old Testament and of Judaism in general, righteousness does not convey primarily the sense of a personal, ethical quality, but of a relationship; originally signifying trustworthiness in regard to the community. . . . But the formulation which Paul has taken over speaks primarily of God's saving activity.[15]

Käsemann's view was then propagated by his student, Peter Stuhlmacher, who said:

> God's righteousness is praised as that absolute activity of God which creates the order of salvation and well-being. But also in the situation of judgment the righteousness of God is evidenced as salvific, since it enables those without rights to gain justice and the repentant to gain new recognition. . . . In the Old Testament and early Judaism, God's righteousness thus means the activity of God through which he creates well-being and salvation in history (specifically that of Israel), in creation, and in the situation of the earthly or eschatological judgment. . . . In the Old Testament, in the early Jewish tradition, and in the New Testament, God's righteousness thus means the salvific activity of God the creator and judge, who creates for those concerned righteousness and well-being.[16]

This view had become so common by the mid- to late twentieth century, that it appeared not only in the contested arena of academic journals, but also in mainstream reference works. Consider Elizabeth R. Achtemeier's entry on God's righteousness in the Old Testament in the *Interpreter's Dictionary of the Bible*:

> Each man is set within a multitude of relationships: king with people, judge with complainants, priests with worshipers, common man with family, tribesman with community,

---

have one obvious meaning: God's own faithfulness to his promises, to the covenant." Ibid., 96. Again, "δικαιοσύνη, I suggest, can often be translated, more or less, as 'covenant membership.'" *The Climax of the Covenant: Christ and the Law in Pauline Theology* (Philadelphia: Fortress, 1992), 203. Nor is Wright at all alone in this assessment. Cf. Sam K. Williams: "For example, most Pauline scholars now agree that in the OT and in Paul 'righteousness' designates conduct or activity appropriate to a relationship rather than an inherent quality, static attribute or absolute moral norm" (241). Williams, "The 'Righteousness of God' in Romans," *Journal of Biblical Literature* 99, no. 2 (1980): 241–90. For numerous examples of such, see Stephen Westerholm, *Perspectives Old and New on Paul: The "Lutheran" Paul and His Critics* (Grand Rapids: Eerdmans, 2004), 253–54, though Westerholm himself advocates the traditional understanding (261–96).

13. Dunn, *Romans 1–8*, Word Biblical Commentary, 38A (Waco, TX: Word, 1991), 41.

14. Schrenck, "δίκη, κτλ," *Theological Dictionary of the New Testament* 2 (citing both Eichrodt and Cremer), 195.

15. Käsemann, "'The Righteousness of God' in Paul," 173.

16. Stuhlmacher, *Paul's Letter to the Romans*, trans. Scott J. Hafemann (Louisville, KY: Westminster/John Knox Press, 1994), 30.

community with resident alien and poor, all with God. And each of these relationships brings with it specific demands, the fulfilment of which constitutes righteousness. The demands may differ from relationship to relationship; righteousness in one situation may be unrighteousness in another. Further, there is no righteousness outside of the relationship itself. When God or man fulfils the conditions imposed upon him by a relationship, he is, in OT terms, righteous.[17]

Yet this notion, so common today that Wright can refer to it as "technical language," was unheard of in the entire history of the Christian tradition from the ancient fathers until the late nineteenth century.[18] In terms of the history of interpretation, the idea is extremely new. That it is new concerns me not at all; I am, after all, proposing a new paradigm for reading Galatians in this very work. Whether the novelty reflects insufficient evidence or mistaken construal of that evidence is a matter that interests me more. What new evidence, if any, was unearthed by Cremer et al., that warranted their understanding Paul's Greek differently than did the Greek fathers (whose native tongue was Paul's), for instance? Or what new way of conceiving/perceiving that evidence afforded them a perspective that altered all ancient, medieval, reformational, and post-reformational students of Paul before them? I will address these matters below in "Observations and Working Hypothesis."

2.3. The Previous Historical Situation from the Ancient Church to the Late Nineteenth Century: The Dominance of the Ethical/Forensic Understanding

For nearly nineteen centuries, God's righteousness was consistently understood to be an expression of his moral/ethical character; that he was/is entirely upright in all that he is and therefore all that he does, as the Psalms routinely celebrate: "The LORD is righteous [צדיק] in all his ways [בכל דרכיו] and kind in all his works [בכל מעשיו]" (Ps. 145:17).[19] Further, since God was understood to be upright in all his ways, he was also understood to be upright/righteous in his judgment of his creation, accounting for the frequency of the "righteous/righteousness/justify" language in forensic or judicial contexts:

---

17. Elizabeth R. Achtemeier, "Righteousness in the OT," *The Interpreter's Dictionary of the Bible* (Nashville: Abingdon Press, 1962), 80.

18. Irons, ΔΙΚΑΙΟΣΥΝΗ ΘΕΟΥ, "History of Interpretation of Righteousness of God," 2.

19. Note that by employing "works" and "ways," this ethical character was not described as "static," as the detractors of the older position often (and gratuitously?) suggest, e.g. Sam K. Williams: "In the OT and in Paul 'righteousness' designates conduct or activity appropriate to a relationship rather than an inherent quality, static attribute or absolute moral norm" (241). Williams, "The 'Righteousness of God' in Romans," 241–90. In the ancient world (as in our own), it would have been difficult to refer to a "static attribute" as virtuous, or even meaningful. How would an attribute be known if it did not express itself in acts of virtue or piety? Could one be courageous without acting courageously, wise without acting wisely, or righteous without acting righteously? Could "the clever Ulysses" have been referred to as such had he not *acted* cleverly? When we today refer to someone as "charitable," we ordinarily imply that the individual has *acted* charitably and done so consistently.

Then hear in heaven and act and judge [ושפטת] your servants, condemning the guilty [להרשיע רשע] by bringing his conduct on his own head, and vindicating the righteous [ולהצדיק צדיק] by rewarding him according to his righteousness. (1 Kings 8:32)

In such forensic contexts, as Gottlob Schrenk noted,

> The concept of virtue is replaced by the basic question of how man is to stand before this judgment expressed in the Law as a standard. . . . It is as he satisfies the demand of God that he has right on his side and therefore a righteous cause before God.[20]

I prefer to refer to this ethical/forensic understanding as one view rather than two, because the latter is merely the expression of the former in a particular circumstance. That is, an ethically "righteous" or "upright" judge will condemn the guilty and acquit the innocent/righteous. He will vindicate the righteous, as Solomon (above) prayed, "by rewarding him according to his righteousness." Note from Solomon's prayer that there are two parties in court who can be described as "righteous": either the judge or the accused. The "righteousness" of the judge requires that he acquit the innocent; and in this declarative act of "justifying/acquitting" the innocent/righteous individual, the judge manifests his own righteousness while declaring that of another. One could also refer to this forensic or judicial usage as "declarative" usage, since the point of the tribunal/court is to make a declaration about a matter. Some of the texts, for example, that have often been referred to as "forensic" or "judicial" are not quite technically judicial, in the sense of referring literally to court actions. They are nonetheless declarative uses of the vocabulary.

2.4. The Lexical Data

There is much literature that possibly illuminates Paul's vocabulary: The LXX, the Hebrew Bible, the Apocrypha, Pseudepigrapha, and Qumran, listed roughly in order of their determinative influence on him.[21] Since Paul's citations of the OT were overwhelmingly

---

20. Schrenk, "δίκη, κτλ," 178–225, esp. 185.

21. An excursus such as this is already lengthier than most editors (or readers) desire, so I have chosen to do very little with the secular Greek background to Paul's usage. Those who have done so agree that the δικ- vocabulary there is ordinarily forensic and ethical. Throughout this excursus, I suggest that the ethical is semantically prior to the forensic, and that the forensic is a semantic extension of that: it is the particular moral uprightness manifested in public judicatory by a judge who condemns the guilty and acquits the innocent. However, it is of small consequence to my thesis whether the forensic is the original semantic domain or the ethical; it is far more consequential that they are closely related, since a court is a place where public judgment is rendered regarding upright or wicked behavior. When Socrates was on trial (BCE 393), the language surely had judicial overtones. Early in his remarks, Socrates said, "For I am more than seventy years of age, and this is the first time that I have ever appeared in a *court of law* [δικαστήριον, 17c]." Both Socrates (δικαστοῦ, 18a; δικασταί, 26d; 41c) and Meletus (οἱ δικασταί, 24d) used the δικ- language to designate the *judges* who heard the case. Yet the term is also employed ethically. In 32d, Socrates said, "And then I showed, not in words only, but in deed [οὐ λόγῳ ἀλλ᾿ ἔργῳ], that . . . I cared not a straw for death, and that my only fear was the fear of doing an *unrighteous* or unholy thing" (τοῦ δὲ μηδὲν ἄδικον μηδ᾿ ἀνόσιον ἐργάζεσθα). For a recent survey of the secular Greek usage from the sixth century BCE to the second

Septuagintal rather than free translations of the Hebrew, his vocabulary was probably more influenced by the LXX. Since the vocabulary of the LXX was itself, of course, pervasively influenced by the Hebrew behind it, these two are, perhaps, a toss-up. Of the subsequent Jewish literature and its influence on Paul, there is diversity of opinion today. Tradition-historical interpreters often regard the later Jewish literature as being more determinative of Paul's usage, since it is judged to be not only historically more proximate to him but, possibly for this reason, a greater influence on him and the audiences to whom he wrote. This is a plausible enough theory, but not without three difficulties. First, the actual allusions to and quotations from the canonical OT in Paul's writings are extensive and often preceded by some introductory formula suggestive of its special role as religiously authoritative;[22] whereas the alleged allusions to the later Jewish writings are much more tenuous and not preceded by such introductory formulas. Second, the Jewish tradition to which Paul was committed was precisely that: a tradition. That is, any tradition as aware as Paul's of its historic roots, and of its *Tanakh*, is a tradition whose language is profoundly influenced by ancient (rather than merely contemporary) sources. For such a tradition, it is entirely likely that its Holy Scripture would have a conserving influence on the ordinary processes of semantic change. Third, a scriptorium was not a library; the primary activity therein was *copying* ancient manuscripts, not reading them (at least in the library sense of the word). And this copying activity also had its own hierarchy of perceived importance;[23] ordinarily, Torah would be copied first, then the rest of *Tanakh*, and then the various other writings that were available.[24] That is to say, we may not assume Paul was

century AD, cf. Irons, "Chapter 3: Righteousness in Extra-Biblical Greek," in ΔΙΚΑΙΟΣΥΝΗ ΘΕΟΥ, 115–49. Irons surveyed 1,700 instances in the secular Greek literature. Even before the fifth century, Irons noted that δικαιοσύνη "is already understood to denote justice as a virtue and even as the sum total of all virtue" (118). Irons especially looked for some evidence of the Cremer hypothesis, that δικαιοσύνη is a relational term, but he could not find it. To the contrary, he observed, "For the Greeks, as for the Hebrews, it is just to keep one's oaths and alliances, and unjust to violate them. But it does not follow that δικαιοσύνη itself *means* keeping one's oaths and covenants, since the term is broader and can be applied to ether activities such as judging or paying back deposits" (124; emphasis original). One of Irons's conclusions for the whole of the Greek corpus antecedent to Paul was that "δικαιοσύνη comes to refer to all sorts of upright behavior in the social realm, whereas their opposites are called ἀδικία" (146).

22. Most commonly (thirty-four times), but not exclusively, γέγραπται.

23. Which is why such a large amount of the manuscript evidence for the Greek New Testament comes from the lectionaries. As the Christian church expanded geographically, at a minimum, a lectionary was needed to read the lessons for the Christian year; in some locales, for a season of time, this was all they had and only later would they acquire an entire Greek text of the New Testament. What was true in the translation of the LXX was likely true in the copying of manuscripts also: The Torah was translated first, then later the prophets, and later yet, the writings. D. A. deSilva, "Jewish Writings and Literature," in *Dictionary of New Testament Background*, ed. Craig A. Evans and Stanley E. Porter (Downers Grove, IL: InterVarsity Press, 2000), 1291. The Manual of Discipline at Qumran, for instance, may have been important to the Qumran covenanters, but we cannot assume it was equally important to (or even known by) Paul.

24. In my opinion, it remains unproven whether Paul was even familiar with the (Essene?) writings at Qumran. Since the entirety of that body of literature has only recently been made available to the scholarly community (portions were not available to the entire public until just prior to the close of the twentieth century), all speculation about Qumran's content or influence, including my own, are necessarily premature; we will have greater confidence fifty years from

familiar with literature simply because it existed in his day; nor may we assume he was equally familiar with literature he did know. His familiarity with the others must be demonstrated on a case-by-case basis.

The value, therefore, of studying the Qumran manuscripts resides in their contribution to our understanding of how *some* of Paul's contemporaries employed language; whether Paul was himself aware of or influenced by such usage would be a much more difficult proposition to prove. At the most, if a contextual argument could be made for Paul's own usage, especially where it might be distinctive from the LXX or Hebrew Bible, the sectarian literature might render such a contextual argument more plausible.

2.4.1. The Hebrew Bible: צדיק *and Its Cognates*

By my count, the root appears 196 times in its adjectival form; in its nominal form 95 times, and in its verbal form 38 times, for a total of 329 times. Whatever difficulties attend this discussion are not due to the infrequency of the lexical stock. By comparison, Paul uses the noun δικαιοσύνη 58 times, the verb δικαιόω 27 times, and the adjective δίκαιος 17 times (and also employs δικαίωμα 5 times and δικαίωσις twice). As might be expected, the semantic range of the root differs somewhat with differing parts of speech. What might be less expected, in the present moment, is that the term is overwhelmingly employed in ethical/forensic ways and rarely (if ever) employed relationally/soterically. Before examining that usage, a word or two of explanation might be in order in each case.

I often employ the "slashed" terms for both categories, rather than create four categories (or more), and I should explain that choice. First, in the history of interpretation, we note largely two approaches: the pre-Cremer approach that understood the terms ethically and forensically, and the post-Cremer approach that understands the terms relationally or soterically. Second, there is some conceptual reason for this history that explains the slashing also.

Conceptually, there is a strong relationship between the ethical and the forensic usage. If an individual is ethically upright, and if the same individual serves as a judge, he will judge rightly, upholding justice. Put in divine terms, if "the LORD is righteous [צדיק] in *all* his ways [בכל דרכיו]" (Ps. 145:17), then, of course, it will also be the case that "God is a *righteous* judge [שופט צדיק]" (Ps. 7:11). Anyone who is morally or ethically upright will uphold justice when charged with administering it. A "righteous" person, when in the office of a judge, will condemn the guilty and exonerate/acquit/

---

now than we do today. However, from what we know now, the covenanters appear to have been sectarian at a minimum and separatist at a maximum. Insofar as this is true, and insofar as they deliberately cut themselves off from the mainstream of Jerusalem Judaism, it is possible, perhaps even likely, that their literature was poorly known (if known at all) by outsiders such as Paul. We can surely say this with some confidence that the rigorous ritual demands of the Manual of Discipline are the least-Galatian writings of the period. If Paul taught Torah-free discipleship, the Qumran scrolls surely did not: "Every initiate into the Council of the Yahad is to enter the covenant in full view of all the volunteers. He shall take upon himself a binding oath to return to the Law of Moses according to all that He commanded with all his heart and with all his mind, to all that has been revealed from it to the Sons of Zadok—priests and preservers of the covenant, seekers of His will—and the majority of the men of their covenant" (1QS 5:7–9).

justify the innocent. This is why Solomon could appeal to God to "hear in heaven and act and judge [ושפטת] your servants, condemning the guilty . . . and vindicating the righteous [ולהצדיק צדיק]" (1 Kings 8:32).

The same conceptual relation exists between the ethical and the forensic on the other side of judgment. An innocent/righteous individual will be (or ought to be) acquitted in judgment, whereas the wicked/unrighteous will be condemned in judgment. Note in Solomon's prayer that he appealed not only to *God's* own uprightness, but also to the uprightness of the *innocent*: "vindicating the righteous [ולהצדיק צדיק]." Moses expected judgment to be done in a manner that those who were ethically upright/righteous would be exonerated: "If there is a dispute [ריב] between men and they come into court and the judges decide between them [ושפטום], acquitting the innocent [והצדיקו את הצדיק] and condemning the guilty" (Deut. 25:1). Such an expectation is almost common sense, and therefore it is not surprising that the prophets condemned its opposite: "Woe to those . . . who acquit the guilty [מצדיקי רשע] for a bribe, and deprive the innocent of his right!" (Isa. 5:22–23). Therefore, I reckon that while the ethical and forensic uses are conceptually distinct, they are not conceptually unrelated: A person whose ethical character/nature is righteous will act in a righteous manner if called to act *as* a judge and will be expected to be exonerated/acquitted when appearing *before* a judge. Further, I extend the meaning of "forensic" beyond the technical courtroom to any declarative context; whenever צדק is employed in a declarative sense, I call it "forensic," such as at Genesis 44:16. Joseph had by now understood that his brothers had betrayed him; and when he confronted them, Judah spoke for them all: "What shall we say [מה נאמר] to my lord? What shall we speak [מה נדבר]? Or how can we clear ourselves [ומה נצטדק]?" Note that here, at least, the hitpael of צדק is virtually interchangeable with the most common verbs of declaring, speaking, or communicating, אמר and דבר. Each of the three verbs is declarative; and in this context, none is technically forensic/juridical, since there is no courtroom in the official sense.

Similarly, there is some relationship between the relational/soteric understanding of "righteousness" among proponents of the Cremer-Käsemann theory. The relationship that Cremer et al. speak about is almost always soteric or, at a minimum, covenantal.[25] While Cremer emphasized more the relational dimension of צדק, and while Käsemann may have emphasized more the "saving power" dimension, the power of the latter was the *power* to restore the covenant people to a right relation to Yahweh and the cosmos, and the *relation* of the former was secured by the powerful activity of God to restore that relation. Käsemann himself at times affirmed both the relational and the soteric activity, and he apparently did not see them as being in any conflict or competition:

> From the outset it will be noticed that in the field of the Old Testament and of Judaism in general, righteousness does not convey primarily the sense of a personal, ethical quality, but of a relationship; originally signifying trustworthiness in regard to the community. . . . But the formulation which Paul has taken over speaks primarily of God's saving activity.[26]

---

25. Later, I will suggest that some confusion exists here, especially by many proponents of the NPP, because I will argue on two separate grounds that one could be a party to the Sinai covenant without being declared just at all and without experiencing salvation in its ordinary theological sense.

26. Käsemann, "'The Righteousness of God' in Paul," 173.

I therefore will sometimes speak of the relational/soteric uses, because so much scholarship has spoken of them interchangeably. When I actually analyze the texts, however, and submit the results of that analysis in tables at the end of the excursus, I employ only three categories—ethical, forensic, and soteric—because I do not regard the alleged "relational" category actually to exist clearly in any of the five relevant bodies of literature that antedate Paul. To be sure, as I often indicate, God is affirmed throughout the Hebrew Bible as sustaining the relationship of maker to his creation; and he therefore also sustains the relation of judge to what he has made (what intelligent creator would not use perceptive discrimination as part of the creative process itself, determining at each moment whether the created thing comports with the creator's purpose?).

I also affirm throughout that God instituted a covenant at Sinai by which he obliged Israel to himself and himself to Israel in specific ways. God is the treaty suzerain, the covenant sovereign, within that treaty; and Israel is the treaty vassal, the covenant servant. But the צדק language is no more relational than is any of the other abstract language used to describe the covenant suzerain. Each of Yahweh's attributes—his holiness, mercy, steadfast love, goodness, uprightness, glory, and so forth—is disclosed to the covenant people through the history of their interactions with him. Each of his attributes is relational/covenantal, if we mean by such that Israel *discovered* those properties within the history of the outworking of the Sinai covenant; but צדק does not *mean* that God is relational or that he is faithful to his relationships (though he may be both). In fact, as Mark A. Seifrid has pointed out, it is remarkable how *un*related "covenant" and "righteousness" are in the Hebrew Bible:

> "Covenant" (ברית) occurs 283 times, צדק-terminology some 524 times, and yet in only seven passages do the terms come into any significant contact. This lack of convergence in usage is all the more striking when we take into account that both ברית and the צדק word-group have fields of meaning having to do with relationships, and both have ethical and juridical dimensions.[27]

צדק means that God (or humans, when applied to them) is upright, that his character is consistently virtuous and praiseworthy. This, of course, *affects* all of his relationships, because an upright person relates differently to others than does an unrighteous or wicked person. The Hebrew Bible affirms that Yahweh is righteous in *all* his ways (Ps. 145:17), not merely in his "relational" or "soteric" ways.

2.4.1.1. Ethical/Forensic Uses

The overwhelming usage of the צדק vocabulary in the Hebrew Bible is moral/ethical. This is revealed especially by its synonyms and antonyms. Consider its antonyms. Interceding for Sodom, Abraham raised this question: "Will you indeed sweep away the righteous with the wicked [צדיק עם רשע]? . . . Far be it from you to do such a thing, to put the righteous to death with the wicked, so that the righteous fare as the wicked!" (Gen. 18:23–25). While Abraham was the first to pair "righteous" and "wicked," he

---

27. Mark A. Seifrid, "Righteousness Language in the Hebrew Scriptures and Early Judaism," *Justification and Variegated Nomism: A Fresh Appraisal of Paul and Second Temple Judaism*, ed. D. A. Carson, Peter O'Brien, and Mark Seifrid, 2 vols. (Grand Rapids, MI: Baker Academic, 2004), 423.

was not the last; in the Hebrew Bible, the two are paired 86 times.[28] In such paired texts, especially those in the wisdom literature, the contrast is one of virtue and vice, of moral good and moral evil; the contrast is not between those who are faithful to their relationships and those who are not, as even an abbreviated sample indicates.

> Therefore the wicked will not stand in the judgment, nor sinners in the congregation of the righteous; for the LORD knows the way of the righteous, but the way of the wicked will perish. (Ps. 1:5–6)

> The LORD tests the righteous, but his soul hates the wicked and the one who loves violence. (Ps. 11:5)

> The wicked borrows but does not pay back, but the righteous is generous and gives. (Ps. 37:21)

> For the scepter of wickedness shall not rest on the land allotted to the righteous, lest the righteous stretch out their hands to do wrong. (Ps. 125:3)

> Blessings are on the head of the righteous, but the mouth of the wicked conceals violence. (Prov. 10:6)

> The lips of the righteous know what is acceptable, but the mouth of the wicked, what is perverse. (Prov. 10:32)

> The thoughts of the righteous are just; the counsels of the wicked are deceitful. (Prov. 12:5)

> One who is righteous is a guide to his neighbor, but the way of the wicked leads them astray. (Prov. 12:26)

> The heart of the righteous ponders how to answer, but the mouth of the wicked pours out evil things. (Prov. 15:28)

> When the wicked increase, transgression increases, but the righteous will look upon their downfall. (Prov. 29:16)

Whether in thought (Prov. 12:5), word (Prov. 10:6; 15:28), or deed (Ps. 11:5; 37:21; Prov. 12:26), the contrasting pairs here are evidently ethical in nature. These texts, and many more like them, cannot easily be construed in such a manner that "righteous" means something like "faithful to a relationship," or "wicked" means unfaithful to the same.

The use of synonyms is similar to the use of antonyms. צדיק is sometimes paired with another word of general moral uprightness, such as at Deuteronomy 32:4: "The Rock, his work is perfect, for all his ways are justice. A God of faithfulness and without iniquity, just and upright [צדיק וישר] is he." This pairing is used for human virtue as well, as at Psalm 33:1: "Shout for joy in the LORD, O you righteous [צדיקים]! Praise befits the upright [לישרים]." These two terms of general moral virtue are also paired thirteen

---

28. Gen. 18:23, 25; Exod. 9:27; 23:7; Deut. 25:1; 2 Sam. 4:11; 1 Kings 8:32; Isa. 5:23; Jer. 12:1; Ezek. 13:22; 18:20, 24; 21:3–4; 33:12; Hab. 1:4, 13; Mal. 3:18; Ps. 1:5–6; 7:9; 11:5; 34:21; 37:12, 16–17, 21, 32; 58:10; 75:10; 94:21; 125:3; 129:4; Job 34:17; Prov. 3:33; 10:3, 6–7, 11, 16, 20, 24–25, 28, 30, 32; 11:8, 10, 23, 31; 12:3, 5, 7, 10, 12, 21, 26; 13:5, 9, 25; 14:19, 32; 15:6, 28–29; 17:15; 18:5; 21:12, 18; 24:15–16, 24–26; 28:1, 12, 28; 29:2, 7, 16, 27; Eccl. 3:17; 7:15; 8:14; 9:2; Neh. 9:33; 2 Chron. 6:23.

other times.[29] צדיק similarly finds itself paired with synonyms such as "innocent" (נקי, Ps. 94:21; Job 22:19; 27:17), or "blameless" (תמים, Gen. 6:9; Job 12:4). Solomon honored his father by referring to his father's virtue in a prayer: "You have shown great and steadfast love to your servant David my father, because he walked before you in faithfulness [באמת], in righteousness [ובצדקה], and in uprightness [ובישרת] of heart toward you" (1 Kings 3:6). Similarly, Yahweh testifies of himself through Jeremiah, saying, "Let him who boasts boast in this, that he understands and knows me, that I am the LORD who practices steadfast love [חסד], justice [משפט], and righteousness [וצדקה] in the earth" (Jer. 9:24). Indeed, צדק is paired with חסד on seven other occasions,[30] and it is paired with אמת eight times.[31] The pairing of צדיק with such synonyms and antonyms suggests that the LXX translators were making a wise decision to translate צדק with δίκαιος, a term ordinarily employed to indicate uprightness of a general sort.

By extension, the vocabulary that ordinarily denotes moral uprightness is frequently employed in judicial settings to describe either an upright judge or an acquitted/innocent party. A wicked judge perverts justice by condemning the innocent and acquitting the guilty, but an upright/righteous judge does just the opposite. Consider Leviticus 19:15: "You shall do no injustice [עול] in court [במשפט].[32] You shall not be partial to the poor or defer to the great, but in righteousness [בצדק] shall you judge [תשפט] your neighbor." Since courts are arenas in which cultures punish their wicked and exonerate their virtuous, the language of "righteousness" and "justice" are frequently paired in the Hebrew Bible. Note even in Abraham's intercession regarding the virtuous in Sodom how close the relationship is: "Far be it from you to do such a thing, to put the righteous to death with the wicked, so that the righteous fare as the wicked! Far be that from you! Shall not the Judge of all the earth [שפט כל הארץ] do what is just?" (Gen. 18:25). Note the close relationship between moral/ethical language (the contrasting pair of righteous/wicked) and the reference to the perfect, paradigmatic, divine "Judge of all the earth."

The frequent forensic use of the צדק language, then, is not really a second or different category from the ethical use of such language; the courtroom is precisely the place where the wicked and the virtuous are distinguished when a formal complaint is made. This is why I prefer to say that the forensic usage of this language is merely an *extension* of the moral/ethical usage. It is not so much a different *definition* of צדק, as it is a usage of that language in the particular courtroom *setting*.[33] If baseball were as common in the ancient Near East as were courts, we would find the צדק language employed to describe umpires who called strikes strikes and balls balls, because the

---

29. Isa. 26:7; Hos. 14:9; Hab. 2:4; Ps. 11:7; 32:11; 64:10; 97:11; 112:4; 119:137; 140:13; Prov. 17:26; 21:18; 29:27.

30. Ps. 33:5; 36:10; 40:10; 103:17; Prov. 14:34; 21:21; Hos. 10:12.

31. 1 Kings 3:6; Ps. 40:10; 119:142; Prov. 11:18; Isa. 48:1; 59:14; Jer. 4:2; Zech. 8:8.

32. "Injustice" (עול) is paired with צדק-language ten times and with שפט/משפט-language six times. With צדק, it appears at Lev. 19:15; Deut. 32:4; Isa. 26:10; Ezek. 3:20; 18:24, 26; 33:13, 18; Zeph. 3:5; Prov. 29:27. With שפט/משפט, it appears at Lev. 19:15, 35; Deut. 32:4; Ezek. 18:8; Zeph. 3:5; Ps. 82:2.

33. In the same way that "healthy" means one thing when serving a vegetable at the dinner table and a more specific thing when a physician uses it to describe a cancer patient at the five-year checkup.

particular virtue of an umpire is to call the game correctly. So also, the *particular* virtue of a judge is to condemn the morally wicked and exonerate the morally righteous.

This close relationship between the צדק language and the courtroom is disclosed in the frequency with which the צדק group is paired in the Hebrew Bible with the שפט group. I find at least 124 occasions where the two lexical stocks are paired.[34] The conceptual relation between ethical virtue and legal justice is profoundly close—so much so that when the prophets anticipate a restored, penitent, and faithful Israel, they are characterized both by ethical virtue and by an upright system of justice: "And I will restore your judges [שפטיך] as at the first, and your counselors as at the beginning. Afterward you shall be called the city of righteousness [עיר הצדק], the faithful city. Zion shall be redeemed by justice [במשפט], and those in her who repent, by righteousness [בצדקה]" (Isa. 1:26–27). Contextually, in a text such as this, there can be little doubt that the צדק language is being employed ethically. Consider verse 21: "How the faithful city has become a whore, she who was full of justice [משפט]! Righteousness [צדק] lodged in her, but now murderers."

2.4.1.2. Relational/Soteric Uses

Before examining the proposed relational/soteric uses of the צדק group in the Hebrew Bible, I will express my concerns about such language, in hopes that those who have more sympathy for the view will continue to sharpen the formulation and make it more attractive to me and others like me. First, "relation" and "relational" are nebulous terms, until/unless we describe what *kind* of relationship we are talking about. If צדק denotes behavior that sustains a relationship, then this may create both theological and exegetical difficulty. Proponents of the view, nonetheless, appear to wish "behavior that maintains a relationship" to be the basic or primary definition.

God always sustains the relation of Creator to his creation; for instance, he cannot un-become its maker, nor can it un-become his creature. As creation's maker, God is also its judge, because all makers *are* judges. Rembrandt cannot paint without having some idea beforehand of what he desires to paint; and throughout the process of painting, he constantly evaluates/judges what he is making, testing its conformity to his creational purpose, and judging that it either does or does not satisfy him as creator.[35] So, in itself, one could affirm that God's "righteousness" means that he has a creational (and therefore judicial) relationship to his creature that takes us right back to the notion of *forensic* righteousness and adds nothing to it. If being creation's maker

---

34. Gen. 18:19, 25; Lev. 19:15; Deut. 1:16; 4:8; 16:18–19; 25:1; 32:4; 33:21; 1 Sam. 12:7; 2 Sam. 8:15; 15:4; 1 Kings 8:32; 10:9; Isa. 1:21, 26–27; 5:7, 16; 9:7; 11:4; 16:5; 26:9; 28:17; 32:1, 16; 33:5; 43:26; 50:8; 51:5; 54:17; 56:1; 58:2; 59:4, 9, 14; Jer. 4:2; 9:24; 11:20; 12:1; 22:3, 13, 15; 23:5; 33:15; Ezek. 18:5, 9, 19, 21, 27; 23:45; 33:14, 16, 19; 45:9; Hos. 2:19; Amos 5:7, 24; 6:12; Mic. 7:9; Hab. 1:4; Zeph. 2:3; 3:5; Ps. 1:5; 7:8, 11; 9:4, 8; 19:9; 33:5; 35:24; 36:6; 37:6, 30; 50:6; 51:4; 58:1, 11; 72:1–2; 82:3; 89:14; 94:15; 96:13; 97:2; 98:9; 99:4; 103:6; 106:3; 119:7, 62, 75, 106, 121, 137, 160, 164; 143:2; Job 8:3; 9:15; 13:18; 29:14; 34:5, 17; 35:2; 37:23; 40:8; Prov. 1:3; 2:9; 8:16, 20; 12:5; 16:8; 18:5; 21:3, 15; 31:9; Eccl. 3:16–17; 5:8; 1 Chron. 18:14; 2 Chron. 6:23; 9:8.

35. A similar creative process is reflected in the creation narrative in Genesis, because in the process of creating, God pauses at each creative moment and observes/judges that what he has made "is good." Such perceptive and discriminating judgment is part of creating per se.

and judge is a relationship, then it is merely tautological to affirm that God, the maker/judge, remains the maker/judge of what he has made.

If "righteousness" means something like "faithfulness to a relationship," then one must be clear about what *kind* of relationship one is discussing. Is Yahweh "righteous" in his relation to Israel in a manner that differs from his "righteousness" in regard to the nations? Is Yahweh's relation to each the same—that of Creator to creature—or is his relationship different toward the Israelites (e.g., that of covenant Suzerain)? If Yahweh "judges the world with righteousness" (Ps. 9:8; 96:13; 98:9), does "righteousness" denote a different thing or a different kind of "relationship" than it does when he judges Israel? Yahweh also judges Israel sometimes to the point that only a remnant remains. What sort of "relationship" is conveyed when Isaiah says, "For though your people Israel be as the sand of the sea, only a remnant of them will return. *Destruction is decreed, overflowing with righteousness*" (Isa. 10:22)? Such a text suggests that the same Yahweh who judges the *world* judges his people Israel *also* (with catastrophic destruction), and in each case, in "righteousness."

Perhaps the element of truth in the common observation that "God's righteousness" is relational is due to the fact that God covenanted with Israel at Sinai, establishing a treaty that dictated the terms of a particular relationship. Within that covenant, Israel continued to learn about their covenant suzerain and learned about *many* of his attributes, all within the context of that treaty. In this sense, Yahweh's "righteousness" could never be divorced from the treaty by which Israel knew (related to) Yahweh. But this is not necessarily truer of "righteousness" than of "lovingkindness," "faithfulness," or even "wrath" or "jealousy." Consider Deuteronomy 29:20: "The LORD will not be willing to forgive him, but rather the *anger* of the LORD and his *jealousy* will smoke against that man, and the curses written in this book will settle upon him." Note that the anger and jealousy spoken of here are associated with the covenantal curses "written in the book" of the law. The wrath is the wrath due to a violated covenant; the jealousy is the jealousy of a covenant suzerain whose lordship is spurned.[36] But is "wrath" a "relational" term? Is "vengeance" a "relational" term, because it is sometimes "vengeance for the covenant"?[37]

It might be more precise, lexically speaking, to say that there is nothing "relational" about צדק at all. צדק is merely one of *many* attributes of the Yahweh who disclosed himself to the people with whom he had inaugurated a treaty (a covenantal relationship) at Sinai. It is no more "relational," in and of itself, than are Yahweh's other attributes, whether they be lovingkindness, faithfulness, jealousy, vengeance, or even wrath.

The alleged soteric uses of the צדק group are found in three books of the Hebrew Bible: Psalms, Isaiah, and Daniel.[38] There is also a possible relational/soteric use in Hosea 10:12.

> From the days of Gibeah, you have sinned, O Israel; there they have continued. Shall not the war against the unjust overtake them in Gibeah? When I please, I will discipline them,

---

36. In fact, the LXX renders "the curses written in this book" more paraphrastically, yet more expressly covenantally, as "the curses *of this covenant* which are written in the book of this law" (αἱ ἀραὶ τῆς διαθήκης ταύτης αἱ γεγραμμέναι ἐν τῷ βιβλίῳ τοῦ νόμου τούτου).

37. "And I will bring a sword upon you, that shall execute vengeance for the covenant [δίκην διαθήκης]," Lev. 26:25.

38. Ps. 40:9; 65:5; Isa. 45:8, 13, 25; 51:5; 58:8; 60:21; 62:1; Dan. 8:14; 9:24.

and nations shall be gathered against them when they are bound up for their double iniquity. Ephraim was a trained calf that loved to thresh, and I spared her fair neck; but I will put Ephraim to the yoke; Judah must plow; Jacob must harrow for himself. Sow for yourselves righteousness [לצדקה]; reap steadfast love; break up your fallow ground, for it is the time to seek the LORD, that he may come and rain righteousness [צדק] upon you. (Hos. 10:9–12)

It is plausible that the result clause "that he may come and rain righteousness upon you" is soteric—that "raining righteousness" refers to the eschatological work of the Spirit in re-creating the cosmos so that righteousness reigns, or at least reigns in Israel. But two other things are equally plausible, and perhaps even more likely. First, in light of the repeated use of agricultural imagery here ("thresh," "yoke," "plow," "harrow," "sow," "reap," "break up . . . fallow ground"), it is plausible that "rain righteousness" will be the natural fruit of spiritual repentance. That is, if Israel will change their ways and return to the law and the covenant, eventually this will be rewarded, by the terms of that covenant itself, with divine blessing ("rain righteousness"). Second, if the two uses of the צדק vocabulary here are intended to be similar, then the first is rather evidently an ethical usage, and therefore perhaps the second is also. It is possible that what God will "rain" on Israel is obedience,[39] as the reward for the *effort to* obey. That is, if we substitute "righteousness" with "upright behavior" in both cases, then the passage would make entire sense. Thus, while it is easy to concur with those who believe the text has eschatological overtones, the eschaton *itself* will be a place where uprightness reigns; therefore, one can affirm the eschatological overtone while affirming an ethical understanding of צדק. In fact, in a text that contrasts Israel's previous rebellion (and God's subsequent curse) with the future state, what would that state be if not the opposite of the rebellious, disobedient state from which Israel will be delivered? צדק, if this reading of the passage is correct, does not mean "salvation"; rather, one of the things that will characterize the eschatological state is צדק. "Salvation" is the more comprehensive term; and when the earth (or Israel) is finally saved from Adamic rebellion and its consequences, of course moral virtue will reign. The earth will then also yield abundant agricultural harvest: "For you also, O Judah, a harvest [קציר] is appointed, when I restore the fortunes of my people" (Hos. 6:11). But צדק does not mean "salvation"; it is one of the (many) things that Yahweh's soteric activity procures or provides.

PSALM 40:9–11 (AND 65:5)

I have told the glad news of deliverance [צדק] in the great congregation; behold, I have not restrained my lips, as you know, O LORD. I have not hidden your deliverance [צדקתך] within my heart; I have spoken of your faithfulness and your salvation [אמונתך ותשועתך]; I have not concealed your steadfast love and your faithfulness [חסדך ואמתך] from the great congregation. As for you, O LORD, you will not restrain your mercy [רחמיך] from me; your steadfast love and your faithfulness [חסדך ואמתך] will ever preserve me!

The translators of the ESV take the first use of צדק here as an expression of soteric power, translating צדק as "deliverance."[40] This requires of them a different translation of תשועה, which they translate as "salvation," even though "deliverance" and "salvation"

---

39. In which case what is pledged is similar to the "new covenant" pledged in Jer. 31:31–34.
40. So RSV, but KJV translates "righteousness."

are ordinarily translated as the same thing from the same root. Several nouns have the suffix "your" attached in this passage: deliverance, faithfulness, salvation, steadfast love, and mercy. It is even possible that this cluster of nouns is intended to be somewhat ambiguous. One cannot but note that some of the terms here are more expressly relational (faithfulness, steadfast love), and at least one is a more evident expression of soteric power (salvation). But does צדק mean the same thing as תשועה here? Or does it mean the same as "your steadfast love and faithfulness" (חסדך ואמתך)?

It is possible/plausible that צדק is employed in apposition to תשועה, referring to an act of deliverance. It is also possible/plausible that, in the terms of the Sinai covenant administration, Yahweh pledged to bless obedient Israel and to curse disobedient Israel, so that, when they repented and he blessed them with deliverance from their enemies, he was proving his faithfulness, his steadfast love, and his uprightness/righteousness/ צדק. That is, it is plausible that צדק is employed here differently than in its ordinary ethical/forensic sense; but the text also makes perfect sense if it is used in that ordinary sense. The so-called soteric use is not more evident, more natural, or more necessary.[41]

ISAIAH 45:8, 13, 23–25

"Shower, O heavens, from above, and let the clouds rain down righteousness [צדק]; let the earth open, that salvation and righteousness [ישע וצדקה] may bear fruit; let the earth cause them both [יחד] to sprout; I the LORD have created it. . . . I have stirred him [Cyrus] up in righteousness [בצדק], and I will make all his ways level; he shall build my city and set my exiles free, not for price or reward," says the LORD of hosts. . . . "By myself I have sworn; from my mouth has gone out in righteousness [צדקה] a word that shall not return: 'To me every knee shall bow, every tongue shall swear allegiance.' 'Only in the LORD,' it shall be said of me, 'are righteousness and strength [צדקות ועז]; to him shall come and be ashamed all who were incensed against him. In the LORD all the offspring of Israel shall be justified [יצדקו] and shall glory.'"

The six uses of the root צדק in Isaiah 45 are challenging, for a number of reasons. Literally, the section appears to be divided into five separate strophes beginning at 44:24, several of which expressly refer to Cyrus as Israel's deliverer (44:28; 45:1), and each of which begins with "Thus says the LORD" (44:24; 45:1, 11, 14, 18). While there is some unity in this sixth prophecy, each of its five strophes has its own integrity as well. It is entirely possible, therefore, that the צדק vocabulary might vary in its usage throughout the strophes. Surely here, we observe a pairing of "salvation and righteousness" (45:8), which may be the sort of pairing some interpreters judge to be a kind of parallelism, suggesting that "salvation and righteousness" is a kind of hendiadys that means something like "soteric faithfulness" or "righteous power."[42] Such a view is surely plausible. צדק here is not only paired with ישע. "Righteousness and strength" (צדקות ועז) are also paired here; they could be interpreted synonymously with the

---

41. So also with Ps. 65:5: "By awesome deeds you answer us with righteousness, O God of our salvation, the hope of all the ends of the earth and of the farthest seas." Surely there is some association of "awesome deeds," "righteousness," and "God of our salvation." But such association does not and need not mean that "righteousness" *means* "awesome deeds" or "salvation."

42. Though I think the qualifier "both" (יחד) here may suggest that each noun is conceived as acting differently from the other.

other paired expression and taken to mean "righteous power" or "soteric faithfulness." In verse 13, it is not entirely clear whether "in righteousness" is a reference to Cyrus's power or a reference (as I think more likely) to Yahweh's purposes in stirring Cyrus up. Yahweh consoles Israel in the presence of this powerful pagan by assuring them that his "stirring up" Cyrus and making him great is to achieve a righteous purpose, a purpose according with Yahweh's own plans for Israel and their rebuilt city. Here also, a soteric understanding of "righteousness" is plausible. When the text says "from my mouth has gone out in righteousness [צדקה] a word that shall not return," the meaning appears to be either that the promissory word is upright/trustworthy, or that the word is one of fidelity to God's covenant purposes for Israel, or an expression of an immutable divine decree. Here also, it is entirely possible that we encounter a usage of צדק that is unusual, which gives credence to the suggestion that sometimes "righteousness" suggests faithfulness or saving power. On the other hand, "righteousness" would also be plausible here as a reference to Yahweh's upright behavior in restoring his penitent people, and his stirring Cyrus up to act righteously could also plausibly be construed as causing Cyrus also to defend a just cause.

ISAIAH 51:5 AND 62:1

> My righteousness [צדקי] draws near, my salvation [ישע] has gone out, and my arms will judge [ישפטו] the peoples; the coastlands hope for me, and for my arm they wait. (Isa. 51:5)

> For Zion's sake I will not keep silent, and for Jerusalem's sake I will not be quiet, until her righteousness [צדקה] goes forth as brightness, and her salvation [וישועתה] as a burning torch. (Isa. 62:1)

These two texts may be usefully evaluated together, because in each case the nouns "righteousness" and "salvation" are paired (though the one pair has a first-person suffix and the second pair has a third-person suffix). Here again we see that, at a minimum, Yahweh's salvation/deliverance of his people is associated in some way with "righteousness." In the first case, however, the judicial/forensic domain is not entirely absent: "my salvation" is interpreted by the expression "my arms will judge the peoples." Indeed, the previous verse also suggests judicial overtones: "Give attention to me, my people, and give ear to me, my nation; for a law will go out from me, and I will set my justice [ומשפטי] for a light to the peoples." Again, by the terms of the Sinai covenant administration, Yahweh had pledged to bless obedient Israel and to curse disobedient Israel—and often to do so via the hand of "the nations." Thus, just as judgment/cursing often took place via the agency of the nations, so also salvation/blessing took the form of deliverance from (and judgment upon) the nations.

Similarly, the eschaton is routinely pictured as a re-creation, a new Eden, a restored order in which original creational purposes would thrive. Thus "her righteousness" in Isaiah 62:1, while paired with "her salvation," could plausibly be understood to refer to an Israel renewed in the image of their maker, living in uprightness as renewed people. This interpretation might be suggested by the following context: "The nations shall see your righteousness, and all the kings your glory, and you shall be called by a new name that the mouth of the LORD will give. You shall be a crown of beauty in the hand of the LORD, and a royal diadem in the hand of your God" (62:2–3). Israel is pictured in these verses as a glorious, beautiful nation, the envy of (and exemplar for) other nations. In such a context, "your righteousness" might very well refer to the upright character of Israel in the renewed eschatological state. If so, then even this "soteric" use does not wander far from the ordinary ethical meaning of "righteousness."

ISAIAH 58:8 AND 60:21

> Then shall your light break forth like the dawn, and your healing shall spring up speedily; your righteousness [צדקך] shall go before you; the glory of the LORD shall be your rear guard. (Isa. 58:8)

> Your people shall all be righteous [צדיקים]; they shall possess the land forever, the branch of my planting, the work of my hands, that I might be glorified. (Isa. 60:21)

These texts are similar to the ones above; "your healing" and "your righteousness" could understandably be construed as parallel terms, so that each refers to an act of God's power for which Israel is the benefactor. However, it is equally plausible that the "righteousness" spoken of here is true moral uprightness, the kind of moral uprightness routinely associated with the redeemed state. If so, while not divorced from soteric/redemptive realities, the term itself could plausibly be a reference to that moral rejuvenation that characterizes that soteric state.

2.4.1.3. Mixed Uses

By my count, twenty-seven of the usages of the צדק stock in the Hebrew Bible are mixed; that is, in twenty-seven texts, it is not easy to determine whether the language is employed ethically, judicially, or soterically—because, contextually, it appears to communicate at least two of those realities. Jeremiah 12:1 says, "Righteous [צדיק] are you, O LORD, when I complain [אריב] to you; yet I would plead my case [משפטים אדבר] before you. Why does the way of the wicked prosper? Why do all who are treacherous thrive?" In a text like this, the judicial overtones are unmistakable; the complainant brings a dispute (ריב) and sets forth a legal case. But the ethical overtones are prominent also and form part of the ריב itself: Why should the way of the wicked (an ethical term) prosper, and why should treacherous people thrive? Is it God's moral uprightness or his judicial integrity that is being appealed to in a text such as this? I suspect the answer is both.

A similar example of a blend of both forensic and ethical righteousness appears in Job 32:1. After Job completes his lengthy defense, the text says, "The words of Job are ended" (Job 31:40). But the text goes on to record, "So these three men ceased to answer Job, because he was righteous [צדיק] in his own eyes." In his own eyes, was Job ethically upright, or did Job have a valid case? Yes and yes. Precisely *because* his behavior was upright, he had a valid *case*, as the previous chapters amply illustrated.[43] Throughout his forensic/legal/judicial case, Job argued on ground after ground that his behavior was not culpable, that it was not deserving of what had happened to him. When he said, "Behold I have prepared my case [משפט]. I know that I shall be

---

43. Job replied to his several "accusers" several times, in chapters 9–10, 12–14, 16–17, 19, 21, 23–24, and 26, but then his final oration was given in 29–31.

in the right [אצדק]" (Job 13:18), he was expressing confidence that there is (or ought to be) a proper relationship between courts and conduct, between ethical and judicial uprightness.

These mixed usages also occur when the ethical and soteric senses are blended. Consider Isaiah 60:21: "Your people shall all be righteous [צדיקים]; they shall possess the land forever, the branch of my planting, the work of my hands, that I might be glorified." On the one hand, the term is employed ethically here to describe a people who are ethically upright. On the other hand, these people are upright because they are renewed/re-created, dwelling forever in the land in shalom, as the preceding context indicates:

> Violence shall no more be heard in your land, devastation or destruction within your borders; you shall call your walls Salvation, and your gates Praise. The sun shall be no more your light by day, nor for brightness shall the moon give you light; but the LORD will be your everlasting light, and your God will be your glory. Your sun shall no more go down, nor your moon withdraw itself; for the LORD will be your everlasting light, and your days of mourning shall be ended.

Is this a soteric use or an ethical use? Again, the answer is both. When the people of God reflect the holy/upright character of God, this is a sign of the eschaton, a sign that "salvation" has come.

The Cremer-Käsemann hypothesis is not without some plausible substantiation in the Hebrew Bible. There are indeed several texts where the צדק stock appears to be a manifestation of the character of God in his role as faithful covenant suzerain, who remains faithful to his covenantal commitments displayed in mighty acts of soteric deliverance. It must be noted, however, that such usages are extremely rare. Insofar as Paul's language is influenced by the Scriptures, we would expect his ordinary usage to conform to the ordinary usage of the Hebrew Bible (and/or the LXX), which is overwhelmingly ethical and forensic. Yet, due to the unusual uses of a more soteric nature in several OT texts, we remain open to considering the possibility that Paul could occasionally, like Isaiah, employ this lexical stock in an unusual manner.

The plausibility of the Käsemann hypothesis, therefore, has always had both a positive and a negative dimension. Negatively, its plausibility rests on overlooking the overwhelmingly frequent ethical and forensic usages of the צדק vocabulary in the Hebrew Bible. Positively, its plausibility also relies on the suggestion (implicit or explicit) that perhaps in the intertestamental period, something happened to change the nature of the language, so that language that once ordinarily referred to virtue came to refer to something like God's saving power. Käsemann's citation of (only several) Qumran texts became fairly important, because much (though not all) of the plausibility of his reasoning depended on a diachronic analysis of the צדק stock, suggesting that at a later moment, the stock changed its semantic range and "righteousness of God" came to mean a *different* thing than it had meant before. This is, of course, entirely possible within standard lexical and semantic theory. Words are often used in new and different ways over time (though some change less than others), and it is entirely possible, therefore, that a lexical stock that was employed preponderantly to describe ethical virtue (and, by extension, judicial uprightness) would later be employed for other uses. It is, however, less likely that this would occur in a culture so grounded in given literature, especially literature that was regarded as being sacred. That is, if there were a break-away culture from Temple Judaism that moved in a secularist direction, as much of the West moved after the Enlightenment, then it would be entirely possible that its entire language stock would take on new overtones in its new secular setting. It is far less likely that, if intertestamental Judaism still professed allegiance to *Tanakh*, it would employ terms frequently used therein in entirely distinctive ways.

Before turning to literature after the Hebrew Bible, we summarize by noting that 61 percent of the uses of the צדק group are ethical, almost 20 percent are judicial, 8 percent are mixed uses, 10 percent are indeterminate, and 1.5 percent are plausibly soteric.

2.4.2. The LXX: δικαιοσύνη and Its Cognates

Interestingly, while the δικ- group translates the Hebrew צדק group fairly consistently, the lexical stocks are not pure overlaps. The canonical LXX[44] employs the adjective 283 times (to the Hebrew, 196), the noun 240 times (to the Hebrew, 95), and the verb 41 times (close to the Hebrew, 38). Proportionally, the LXX corresponds fairly roughly to the Hebrew, with the adjective appearing most frequently, then the noun and the verb less frequently.

2.4.2.1. Ethical Uses

As with the Hebrew צדק, the LXX frequently employs the δικ- stock to denote ethical uprightness: "For the Lord is righteous [δίκαιος]; he loves righteous deeds [δικαιοσύνας ἠγάπησεν]; the upright [εὐθύτητα] shall behold his face" (Ps. 11:7). Of the 564 uses in the LXX of this vocabulary stock, I count 353 as ethical uses. This ethical use of the stock is reflected in the antonyms and synonyms with which the stock is used. With the adjective alone, on 74 occasions δίκαιος is paired with its antonym "wicked"/ἀσεβής.[45] As with the Hebrew, the first pairing appears with Abraham interceding for Sodom: "Will you indeed sweep away the righteous [δίκαιον] with the wicked [ἀσεβοῦς]?" (Gen. 18:23). Its synonyms also denote ethical uprightness; it is paired with "blameless"/ἄμεμπτος,[46] "innocent"/ἀθῷος,[47] "upright"/εὐθύς,[48] "holy"/ ὅσιος,[49] "true"/ἀληθινός,[50] and others. The ease with which "righteous" can be paired with these terms is instructive, because each of these terms of moral virtue has its own particular semantic range; yet δίκαιος comprehends uprightness so generally that it can be employed virtually synonymously with any of them.

---

44. Just to keep matters clear, the Apocryphal uses will be categorized separately.

45. Gen. 18:23, 25; Exod. 9:27; 23:7; Deut. 25:1; Ps. 1:5–6; 10:5; 57:11; Prov. 3:33; 10:3, 6–7, 11, 16, 20, 24–25, 28, 30, 32; 11:3, 7, 8, 11, 18–19, 23, 31; 12:5, 7, 10, 21, 26; 13:5, 9, 22, 25; 14:19, 32; 15: 28–29; 18:5; 21:7, 12, 26; 24:15, 16, 24, 25:26; 28: 1, 12, 28–29; 29:2, 7, 16; Eccl. 3:16–17; 7:15; 8:14; 9:2; Job 10:15; Wis. 3:10; 4:16; 10:6, 20; 12:9; Hos. 14:10; Hab. 1:4, 13; Isa. 5:23; Jer. 12:1; Ezek. 33:12.

46. Job 1:1; 9:24; 12:4; 15:14; 22:19.

47. Exod. 23:7; Ps. 94:21.

48. Ps. 31:11; 32:1; 63:10; 96:11; 111:4; 139:14; Hos. 14:9.

49. Deut. 32:4; Ps. 145:17; Prov. 17:26; 18:5; 21:15.

50. Deut. 25:15; 32:4; Job 1:1; 17:4; 27:17; Isa. 59:4.

Since the primary use of the Hebrew צדק is ethical, it is not surprising that the Septuagint translators would have represented it with a Greek term that is also primarily an ethical term. Nor is it surprising that the first usage of δίκαιος in the LXX is so manifestly ethical: "Noah was a righteous [δίκαιος] man, blameless [τέλειος] in his generation. Noah walked with God" (Gen. 6:9). This general expression of moral approval toward Noah was not forgotten; he was also referred to by this adjective in the Pseudepigrapha[51] and Apocrypha.[52]

It is also probably worth noting that other terms were available to the LXX translators. When they wanted to indicate that God was "faithful" to his people or to his covenant, they routinely employed πιστός.[53] They also employed ἔλεος or ἀλήθεια,[54] or both, as at 1 Samuel 2:6 "Now may the Lord show steadfast love [ἔλεος] and faithfulness [ἀλήθειαν] to you." They also sometimes employed a verbal clause, calling him "the one who keeps covenant" (ὁ φυλάσσων διαθήκην, Deut. 7:9; cf. Deut. 7:12; 1 Kings 8:23; 2 Chron. 6:13; Neh. 1:5; 9:32; Dan. 9:4) or the one "who shows steadfast love" [ποιῶν ἔλεος] to "thousands," and/or "to the third and fourth generation" (Exod. 20:6; 34:7; also Deut. 5:10; Jer. 32:18). Especially in contexts that indicate pangenerational trustworthiness, the LXX routinely employs ἔλεος and/or ἀλήθεια:

And Solomon said, "You have shown great and steadfast love to your servant David my father. . . . And you have kept for him this great and steadfast love [τὸ ἔλεος] and have given him a son to sit on his throne *this day*. (1 Kings 3:6; emphasis added)

As for you, O LORD, you will not restrain your mercy from me; your steadfast love and your faithfulness [τὸ ἔλεός σου καὶ ἡ ἀλήθειά σου] will ever [διὰ παντὸς] preserve me! (Ps. 40:11)

For the LORD is good; his steadfast love endures forever [εἰς τὸν αἰῶνα τὸ ἔλεος], and his faithfulness to all generations [ἕως γενεᾶς καὶ γενεᾶς ἡ ἀλήθεια αὐτοῦ]. (Ps. 100:5)

For great is his steadfast love toward us, and the faithfulness of the LORD endures forever [ἡ ἀλήθεια τοῦ κυρίου μένει εἰς τὸν αἰῶνα]. (Ps. 117:2)

Your faithfulness endures to all generations [εἰς γενεὰν καὶ γενεὰν ἡ ἀλήθειά σου]; you have established the earth, and it stands fast. (Ps. 119:90)

Who made heaven and earth, the sea, and all that is in them, who keeps faith forever [τὸν φυλάσσοντα ἀλήθειαν εἰς τὸν αἰῶνα]. (Ps. 146:6)

You will show faithfulness [ἀλήθειαν] to Jacob and steadfast love [ἔλεον] to Abraham, as you have sworn to our fathers from the days of old.[55] (Mic. 7:20)

---

51. Sybil. 1:269, 280; 4 Bar. 7:8.
52. Sir. 44:17.
53. Deut. 7:9; 32:4; Isa. 49:7.
54. Exod. 34:6; Num. 14:18.
55. There are several passages where God's "righteousness" is also referred to as having this pangenerational quality: "But the steadfast love [τὸ δὲ ἔλεος] of the Lord is from everlasting to everlasting on those who fear him, and his righteousness [ἡ δικαιοσύνη αὐτοῦ] to children's children" (Ps. 103:17; cf. also Ps. 111:3; 119:142). But "righteousness" is not any more enduring than "steadfast love," and apart from the temporal qualifier, it would not necessarily enjoy such a denotation. Since God is himself everlasting, any of his character traits can be qualified with qualifiers such

Part of the plausibility of construing δίκαιος to mean something like "God's faithfulness to his people and/or covenant" was the assumption that Greek and Hebrew were, of course, different languages, and it wasn't always easy to communicate in Greek something that was easily communicated in Hebrew.[56] But as we have seen, that view faces two serious problems in the present case. First, the Hebrew stock itself is ethical; the antonyms and synonyms demonstrate evidently that צדק is ordinarily used to denote ethical uprightness. Second, the Greek language was perfectly capable by the time of the LXX of handling the idea or concept of faithfulness to a covenant or to a people; the translators of the LXX knew this and employed τό ἔλεος and/or ἡ ἀλήθεια for this purpose. The Hebrew they were translating was an ethical (not a relational) term; and when they desired to speak of fidelity to commitments, covenants, and/or people, they found Greek terms that were better suited to the task than the δικ- stock.

2.4.2.2. Forensic Uses

The forensic use of the δικ- vocabulary is also well established in the LXX, where it accounts for 111 of the 564 uses, or almost 20 percent. Fifty-eight times in the LXX, the δικ- vocabulary is paired with κρίμα,[57] 34 times with κρίνω,[58] and 39 times with κρίσις.[59] The God who is "righteous" in all his ways is also righteous/upright when he judges. A recurring cause of praise to God in the Psalms is due to the certainty that he will judge the entire created order, and do so in perfect judicial uprightness: "And he judges the world with righteousness [ἐν δικαιοσύνῃ]; he judges the peoples with uprightness [ἐν εὐθύτητι]" (Ps. 9:8; cf. also 96:13; 98:9). Somewhat surprisingly, Yahweh's judicial uprightness is celebrated even in circumstances where his judgment falls upon his covenant people:

> "Now, therefore, our God, the great, the mighty, and the awesome God, who keeps covenant and steadfast love, let not all the hardship seem little to you that has come upon us, upon our kings, our princes, our priests, our prophets, our fathers, and all your people, since the time of the kings of Assyria until this day. Yet you have been righteous [δίκαιος] in all that

---

as "everlasting." But the very presence of such a modifier proves that the trait is not necessarily timeless otherwise (which is why most of the traits can also be associated with temporal human beings). To the critical question of which of these roots in Greek communicated the notion of faithfulness, the answer is fairly clear: ἀλήθεια and ἔλεος routinely are employed to communicate such a trait; it is not at all clear that the δίκ- vocabulary is employed in the LXX to do the same.

56. Such was the thesis of Thorleif Boman, *Hebrew Thought Compared with Greek* (New York: Norton, 1970). This thesis was subjected to fairly rigorous criticism by Barr in *The Semantics of Biblical Language*.

57. Deut. 4:8; 1 Sam. 2:10; 2 Sam. 8:15; 1 Kings 10:9; 1 Chron. 18:14; 2 Chron. 9:8; Ps. 18:10; 35:7; 36:6; 71:1; 88:15; 96:2; 118:7, 62, 75, 106, 121, 160, 164; Prov. 1:3; 2:9; 12:5; 21:15; Eccl. 5:7; Job 9:15; 13:18; 29:14; 34:5; 36:17; 40:8; Hos. 2:21; Amos 5:7, 24; 6:12; Mic. 7:9; Hab. 1:4; Zeph. 2:3; 3:5; Zech. 7:9; Isa. 5:16; 9:6; 16:5; 32:16; Jer. 9:23; 12:1; 22:13, 15; 23:5; Ezek. 18:5, 8, 27; 33:14, 16, 19; 44:24; 45:9; Dan. 13:9.

58. Gen. 18:25; Lev. 19:15; Deut. 16:18; 25:1; 1 Sam. 2:10; 1 Kings 3:9; 8:32; 2 Chron. 6:23; Ps. 7:9; 9:5, 9; 34:24; 50:6; 57:2, 12; 71:2; 81:3; 95:13; 97:9; Prov. 17:15; 30:12; 29:7; Eccl. 3:17; Job 8:3; 37:23; Zech. 7:9; Isa. 1:17; 16:5; 43:26; 50:8; Jer. 11:20; Ezek. 44:24; Dan. 9:24;13:53.

59. Gen. 18:19; 18:25; Lev. 19:15; Deut. 16:18–19; 25:1; 32:4; 33:21; 2 Sam. 15:4; Ps. 1:5; 9:5; 36:30; 71:2; 93:15; 98:4; 105:3; 118:137; 142:2; Prov. 18:5; Eccl. 3:16; Job 35:2; Isa. 1:17, 21; 5:7; 32:1; 33:5, 15; 54:17; 56:1; 58:2; 59:4, 9, 14; 63:1; Jer. 4:2; 22:3; Ezek. 44:24; Dan. 3:27; 13:53.

has come upon us, for you have dealt faithfully and we have acted wickedly [ἐξημάρτομεν].
Our kings, our princes, our priests, and our fathers have not kept your law or paid attention
to your commandments and your warnings that you gave them. Even in their own kingdom,
enjoying your great goodness that you gave them, and in the large and rich land that you
set before them, they did not serve you or turn from their wicked works. Behold, we are
slaves this day; in the land that you gave to our fathers to enjoy its fruit and its good gifts,
behold, we are slaves." (Neh. 9:32–36)

Even when it is not in the apparent self-interest of God's covenant people, the strict,
unwavering judicial righteousness of God is both celebrated and solicited. Solomon
actually requested such judgment from God:

"If a man sins against his neighbor and is made to take an oath and comes and swears his
oath before your altar in this house, then hear in heaven and act and *judge your servants,
condemning the guilty* by bringing his conduct on his own head, and vindicating the righteous [τοῦ δικαιῶσαι δίκαιον] by rewarding him according to his righteousness." (1 Kings
8:31–32; emphases added)

The sensibilities of the ancient Near East (and perhaps those of the ancient world in
general) were pre-enlightened—individuals who did not wish to cohabit with the
wicked on the earth or the wicked within the covenant community. They tired of the
insurrection against God's just rule, and they pled with him to squelch the insurrection,
rejoicing whenever he did so.

2.4.2.3. Mixed Judicial/Ethical Uses

There are some uses of the δικ- stock in the LXX that are difficult to categorize,
because they appear to be both ethical and judicial. This is nowhere more the case than
in Job, where the majority of the narrative is indeed forensic or judicial as Job pleads
his case, acting as his own attorney (as did Socrates, with nearly identical results).
Yet the precise nature of his reasoning is not to refer to obscure criminal statutes or
constitutional law; his reasoning consists of referring to his general moral uprightness. While he does not claim sinless perfection, he does claim that, compared to the
common lot of humans, his behavior has been upright. So he makes his judicial "case"
by appealing to his ethical character, and he can employ the δικ- stock either way and
possibly both ways simultaneously. Consider several examples of this:

"Behold, I have prepared my case; I know that I shall be in the right [δίκαιος ἀναφανοῦμαι]."
(Job 13:18)

So these three men ceased to answer Job, because he was righteous [δίκαιος] in his own
eyes. Then Elihu the son of Barachel the Buzite, of the family of Ram, burned with anger.
He burned with anger at Job because he justified himself [ἑαυτὸν δίκαιον] rather than
God. (Job 32:1–2)

[Elihu continues], "For Job has said, 'I am in the right [δίκαιός εἰμι], and God has taken
away my right [μου τὸ κρίμα].'" (Job 34:5)

In each of these texts, we perceive that the δικ- language is employed both in its judicial
sense, as Job seeks justice (which, from his viewpoint, means that he would be declared

righteous), and in its moral/ethical sense, as Job appeals to his own behavior as being ethically right and therefore worthy of exoneration (declared to be right by the trial).

The psalmist can make a similar statement: "The Lord judges the peoples; judge me, O Lord, according to my righteousness [κρῖνόν με κύριε κατὰ τὴν δικαιοσύνην μου] and according to the integrity [τὴν ἀκακίαν μου] that is in me" (Ps. 7:8). Here, the overall concern is clearly judicial ("judge me"), yet the argued basis for such vindication is the psalmist's own ethical virtue (τὴν δικαιοσύνην μου). This substantiates my general claim that the forensic usage is but an extension of the basic moral/ethical usage: courts (whether formal or informal) are expected to condemn the wicked and exonerate the upright. We see a similar overlapping of the ethical and forensic in Psalm 119: "I have done what is just and right [κρίμα καὶ δικαιοσύνην]; do not leave me to my oppressors [τοῖς ἀδικοῦσίν με]" (Ps. 119:121). Note that the psalmist's "oppressors" are those who charge him with wrongdoing (τοῖς ἀδικοῦσίν με). The reason their charge is oppressive is because it is unjust; it is contrary to the facts of the case, and the facts of the case here are the psalmist's own virtuous behavior (κρίμα καὶ δικαιοσύνην).

2.4.2.4. *"Soteric" Uses*

Judges 5 records the song of Deborah, and at verses 10 and 11, we find:

> Tell of it, you who ride on white donkeys, you who sit on rich carpets and you who walk by the way. To the sound of musicians at the watering places, there they repeat the righteous triumphs [δικαιοσύνην] of the LORD, the righteous triumphs [δίκαιοι] of his villagers in Israel. Then down to the gates marched the people of the LORD.

This celebration of military victory over Jabin, the king of Canaan, repeats/celebrates the "righteous triumphs" of the Lord.[60] Here, the LXX translated the Hebrew (צדקות יהוה) somewhat literally, and the English translators were compelled by the context to understand this as a somewhat unusual use of both roots. It may not appear immediately evident why a word that ordinarily means "upright" could be used here to mean something like "acts of deliverance," but the LXX followed the Hebrew fairly literally. Such a "soteric" use of the δικ- vocabulary appears again at Psalm 70:15–16 (ET 71:15–16):

> My mouth will tell of your righteous acts [τὴν δικαιοσύνην σου], of your deeds of salvation [τὴν σωτηρίαν σου] all the day, for their number is past my knowledge. With the mighty deeds of the Lord [ἐν δυναστείᾳ κυρίου] God I will come, I will remind them of your righteousness, yours alone.

Again, the LXX is fairly literal, translating צדקתך with δικαιοσύνην σου, תשועתך with τὴν σωτηρίαν σου, and בגברות with ἐν δυναστείᾳ. Contextually, this psalm evidently appears to celebrate powerful acts of deliverance and uses three different expressions to communicate essentially the same thing—powerful soteric acts of deliverance that are, in some senses, "your righteousness."[61] Yet the English translators believe the

---

60. KJV, somewhat more conservatively, translated "righteous acts"; RSV translated "the triumphs," as does NRSV.

61. So KJV, "thy righteousness."

context warrants a less literal translation, "righteous acts," since the context appears to be a recitation of salvation history.

Perhaps there is no clearer example of a soteric use of the δικ- vocabulary than that found in Isaiah 51:5–8:

> My righteousness [ἡ δικαιοσύνη μου] draws near, my salvation [τὸ σωτήριόν μου] has gone out, and my arms will judge the peoples; the coastlands hope for me, and for my arm they wait. Lift up your eyes to the heavens, and look at the earth beneath; for the heavens vanish like smoke, the earth will wear out like a garment, and they who dwell in it will die in like manner; but my salvation [τὸ δὲ σωτήριόν μου] will be forever, and my righteousness [ἡ δὲ δικαιοσύνη μου] will never be dismayed. Listen to me, you who know righteousness [κρίσιν], the people in whose heart is my law; fear not the reproach of man, nor be dismayed at their revilings. For the moth will eat them up like a garment, and the worm will eat them like wool; but my righteousness will be forever [ἡ δὲ δικαιοσύνη μου εἰς τὸν αἰῶνα], and my salvation to all generations [τὸ δὲ σωτήριόν μου εἰς γενεὰς γενεῶν].

Three times in this passage, God's "righteousness" is spoken of in parallel with his "salvation"; and twice, the paired items are referred to as having an everlasting duration. There can be little disputing the reality that in a text such as this, "my righteousness" is a reality that is, at a minimum, coterminus with "my salvation." Many are understandably persuaded that the terms are virtually interchangeable in this passage.

I have no objection to noting that passages like these (I find seven in the LXX) contain an unusual extension of the ordinary semantic range of the δικ- vocabulary. Literary language, and especially poetic language, often extends the semantic ranges of the terms it employs—and not merely by employing figures of speech. Somewhere between what we ordinarily call a figure of speech and a "literal" or ordinary use of a term is another usage, an extension of the term to do something it ordinarily does not. As an observer of grammar, I would not regard it as either exceptional or objectionable to take these passages in such a manner.

However, even extended uses of terms are meaningful only if they extend something that is still truly there. Why would the δικ- vocabulary, which is employed 564 times in the LXX in a prevailingly ethical and judicial manner, be employed seven times to appear almost synonymous with σωτήριον? Even if there are a small number of such texts, how do we account for them? I suspect the answer is this: Within the Sinai covenant administration, "salvation" itself is often juridical/judicial. If Israel obeys the covenant, then Yahweh pledges to bless them in the land and to protect them/deliver them/save them from the surrounding nations. If Israel disobeys the covenant, then Yahweh pledges to hand them over *to* the same nations, even to exile them into their midst. That is, if Yahweh is an upright judge, and if he has pledged to bless/curse Israel *via* the nations, conditioned on their obedience/disobedience, then he displays his judicial uprightness when he defends penitent Israel and judges the nations around them:

> "But if in spite of this you will not listen to me, but walk contrary to me, then I will walk contrary to you in fury, and I myself will discipline you sevenfold for your sins. . . . And I will scatter you among the nations, and I will unsheathe the sword after you, and your land shall be a desolation, and your cities shall be a waste." (Lev. 26:27–28)

"And because you listen to these rules and keep and do them, the LORD your God will keep with you the covenant and the steadfast love that he swore to your fathers. . . . If you say in your heart, 'These nations are greater than I. How can I dispossess them?' you shall not be afraid of them but you shall remember what the LORD your God did to Pharaoh and to all Egypt. . . . So will the LORD your God do to all the peoples of whom you are afraid. . . . But the LORD your God will give them over to you and throw them into great confusion, until they are destroyed. And he will give their kings into your hand, and you shall make their name perish from under heaven. No one shall be able to stand against you until you have destroyed them." (Deut. 7:12–24)

"And if you faithfully obey the voice of the LORD your God, being careful to do all his commandments that I command you today, the LORD your God will set you high above all the nations of the earth. And all these blessings shall come upon you and overtake you, if you obey the voice of the LORD your God. . . . The LORD will cause your enemies who rise against you to be defeated before you. They shall come out against you one way and flee before you seven ways. . . . And all the peoples of the earth shall see that you are called by the name of the LORD, and they shall be afraid of you. . . . But if you will not obey the voice of the LORD your God or be careful to do all his commandments and his statutes that I command you today, then all these curses shall come upon you and overtake you. . . . The LORD will cause you to be defeated before your enemies. You shall go out one way against them and flee seven ways before them. And you shall be a horror to all the kingdoms of the earth." (Deut. 28:1–25)

As we reconsider the same verses from Isaiah 55 in this light, note the emphasis (italicized below) on Yahweh's judgment of Israel's enemies:

"My righteousness [ἡ δικαιοσύνη μου] draws near, my salvation [τὸ σωτήριόν μου] has gone out, and *my arms will judge the peoples*; the coastlands hope for me, and for my arm they wait. Lift up your eyes to the heavens, and look at the earth beneath; for the heavens vanish like smoke, *the earth will wear out like a garment, and they who dwell in it will die in like manner*; but my salvation [τὸ δὲ σωτήριόν μου] will be forever, and my righteousness [ἡ δὲ δικαιοσύνη μου] will never be dismayed. Listen to me, you who know righteousness [κρίσιν], the people in whose heart is my law; fear not *the reproach of man*, nor be dismayed at *their revilings. For the moth will eat them up like a garment, and the worm will eat them like wool*; but my righteousness will be forever [ἡ δὲ δικαιοσύνη μου εἰς τὸν αἰῶνα], and my salvation to all generations [τὸ δὲ σωτήριόν μου εἰς γενεὰς γενεῶν]."

Seen from this point of view, it is perfectly natural for the Israelites to associate Yahweh's judicial uprightness with his "salvation/deliverance" of Israel from the nations. In the same way today, a person innocent of a criminal charge or a civil lawsuit longs for his "day in court," because that judicial day and judicial activity will release him from the false charges of his accusers. If he is held in jail pending trial, then what is the judicial day but the day of deliverance? What does the righteous judge do, in such a circumstance, but release/deliver the innocent? That is, there is an enormous element of truth in recognizing the parallel use of terms like δικαιοσύνη and σωτήριον in passages such as Isaiah 55. The truth, however, does not reside in the fact that δικαιοσύνη *means* σωτήριον. Rather, in a covenant administration in which Yahweh pledged to judge Israel *via* the nations if Israel disobeyed, and pledged to judge the nations *via* Israel if Israel repented, he was merely judging rightly when he "saved/delivered" penitent Israel from the surrounding nations.

2.4.2.5. Conclusions Regarding the LXX Usage of the δικ- Vocabulary

The LXX demonstrates the same range, with the δικ- stock, that the Hebrew OT did with the צדק stock. Further, it reflects similar proportion to the Hebrew Bible: 63 percent of its usage is ethical and just shy of 20 percent is judicial. The ethical and forensic usage of the vocabulary accounts for well over 80 percent of its usage. Various mixed or hybrid uses account for another 10 percent, about 8 percent are indeterminate, and slightly over 1 percent are "soteric" in the sense described above. Each of these categories is within a percentage point or two of what it is in the Hebrew Bible.

Turning our attention to Apocryphal, Pseudepigraphic, and Qumran literature, therefore, is somewhat necessary. Does the Hebrew/Aramaic intertestamental literature show a trajectory of employing the צדק language differently than it was employed in *Tanakh*, and does the Greek intertestamental literature employ the δικ- language differently than did the LXX? If so, then the Käsemann hypothesis (that such language influenced Paul's usage) is more plausible, though it would still enjoy the burden of proving that such intertestamental literature had a greater influence on Paul's vocabulary than did the vocabulary of *Tanakh*/LXX—a burden I do not recall Käsemann (or his advocates) addressing. In light of Paul's frequent citations of the Scriptures, and in light of there being no clear citation by him of intertestamental literature, I regard that burden as insurmountable. But for our purposes, that insurmountable burden is somewhat irrelevant, because in actual fact intertestamental literature does *not* diverge from the usage in *Tanakh* or the LXX. The two respective lexical stocks, Hebrew and Greek, employ the language as did the Hebrew and Greek Scriptures before; indeed, if anything, the intertestamental literature shows *less* variation from the ethical/forensic usage than did the canonical literature.[62] In each case, the lexical stock is overwhelmingly ethical and juridical, and an alleged relational or soteric use is as rare as or rarer than it was in the Hebrew Scriptures or the LXX.

2.4.3. Late (Intertestamental) Jewish Sources

There are three bodies of literature that sufficiently antedate Paul so that they could be relevant to his usage of the δικ- vocabulary: the OT Apocrypha, the Jewish Pseudepigrapha, and the Dead Sea Scrolls. We know substantially less about this literature than we might wish, and even less about their possible influence on Paul. He may have known as much as Josephus and Philo did about the community at Qumran, for instance, or he may have known less. Even Josephus and Philo appear to have known nothing about any writings there, so it is possible that Paul knew nothing more than they did on this point.[63] Similarly, how much of the Apocryphal and Pseudepigraphic material Paul may have been familiar with remains unresolved. If, however, Jewish contemporaries of Paul employed language in particular ways, then it is certainly plausible that Paul

---

62. Semantic change can go in either direction. Some terms broaden their usage; others narrow them.

63. And, of course, it is indeed possible that the scrolls found there were placed there by other Jews fleeing Roman persecution in Jerusalem, rather than by the community itself. If the low area between the site of the community and the caves had water in it at the time, then it would have been odd to put the scrolls on the other side of this body of water.

may have employed the same language in the same ways. Therefore, it is worthwhile to search relevant literature, especially to determine whether it discloses uses that may differ from that found in the Hebrew Bible or the LXX.

When we search this literature, we find that the δικ- vocabulary in the Apocrypha and Pseudepigrapha and the צדק vocabulary in the Qumran literature is quite common. My searches yielded 122 uses of the δικ- vocabulary in the Apocrypha, 343 uses in the Pseudepigrapha, and 471 uses of the צדק vocabulary at Qumran, for a total of 936, slightly more than the 893 uses in the Hebrew Bible and the LXX. What I found was neither surprising nor enlightening, because the vocabulary was used almost identically to its use in the Hebrew Bible and the LXX.

In the Apocrypha, of 122 uses of the δικ- stock, 84 (69 percent) were ethical, 27 (22 percent) were forensic, 7 were mixed, 3 were "soteric," and 1 was indeterminate. In the Pseudepigrapha, 292 (85 percent) were ethical, 27 (8 percent) were forensic, 21 (6 percent) were mixed, and 3 were indeterminate. In the Qumran literature, 230 (49 percent) were ethical, 59 (12.5 percent) were forensic, 30 (6.5 percent) were mixed, 2 were "soteric," and 128 (27 percent) were indeterminate, due to the fragmentary nature of some of the scrolls. Much of the material from Qumran was so fragmentary that it was impossible to make a responsible contextual decision. If you run the numbers again, without the large number of textually indeterminate ones, you find that 71 percent of the uses are ethical, 18 percent are forensic, 8 percent are mixed, and 1 percent is "soteric." My primary concern, in investigating this literature, was to see if the language stock had changed diachronically, resulting in a significantly different understanding of "righteousness of God" (in all its cognate forms) from what was found in the Hebrew Bible or the LXX. I found no evidence of such change.

2.4.3.1. *The Qumran Literature*

2.4.3.1.1. ETHICAL USES

One of the tests of the suggestion that the semantic range of the צדק vocabulary is relational or soteric is the antonyms and/or synonyms with which the word is used. צדק is frequently paired with other language that indicates moral/ethical uprightness:

So shall all together comprise a Yahad whose essence is truth [אמת], genuine humility [וענות טוב], love of charity [ואהבת חסד] and righteous intent [ומחשבת צדק]. (1QS 2:24)

For the Lord attends to the pious [חסידים] and calls the righteous [וצדיקים] by name. (4Q521 f2ii+4:5)

A text belonging to [the Instructor, who is to teach the Ho]ly Ones how to live [according to the book of] the Yahad Rule. . . . He is to teach them . . . to distance themselves from all evil and to hold fast to all good deeds [מעשי טוב]; to practice truth [אמת], justice [וצדקה] and righteousness [ומשפט]. (1QS 1:1–5)

Similarly, in Qumran, there are twenty-five texts where the antonym of צדיק is רשע.[64] At 1QHa 12:39 we find: "But not for man, [but for] Your [glory] You have worked, for

---

64. CD 1:19; CD 4:7; CD 11:21; 1QpHab 1:12; 1QpHab 1:13; 1QpHab 5:9; 1QHa 12:39; 1QHa 15:15; 1Q34bis f3i:2; 1Q34bis f3i:5; 4Q171 f1_2ii:12; 4Q171 f1_2ii:21; 4Q171 f1_2ii:23;

You created both the righteous [צדיק] and the wicked [ורשע]." It would be extremely difficult to construe רשע to mean "nonrelational," "dysfunctional," or anything else. The translations routinely translate "wicked" or "ungodly" as a term of general moral disapproval; and the antonym, our צדיק, is ordinarily translated "righteous."

2.4.3.1.2. FORENSIC USES

Ninety-six times in the Qumran literature, the צדק stock is found with the משפט or שפט language, indicating that the forensic usages are common here. Typical examples include these:

> For who is like You among the gods, O Lord? And who is as Your truth? And who can be justified [יצדק] before You, when he enters into judgment [בהשפט]? (1QHa 15:31)

> For no one is justified [קלא יצד] in Your jud[g]ment [במשפטכה], and no one is bl[ameless in] Your litigation. (1QHa 17:14–15)

Such passages are used just as they are in the Hebrew Bible.

2.4.3.1.3. SOTERIC USES

Ernst Käsemann brought 1QS (Manual of Discipline) 11:12 before the consideration of New Testament scholarship in his "'The Righteousness of God' in Paul."[65] Note both Käsemann's citation and his commentary on it:

> Similarly, in the Rule of Qumran 11.12: "If I stumble by reason of the wickedness of my flesh, my justification lies in the righteousness of God." The significance of this statement is for the most part not perceived; certainly, it has not had the attention it merits. The methodological implication of Paul's adoption of a ready-made formulation is that the righteousness of God, as he uses the term, is not to be subsumed under the general concept δικαιοσύνη and thus deprived of its peculiar force.[66]

Three things catch the eye about Käsemann's comments. First, he refers to the expression as a "ready-made formulation" that Paul adopted, suggesting that the term was technical; and second, he suggests that there was a "peculiar" semantic force to the term here that was/is to be distinguished from the "general" concept of δικαιοσύνη.[67] Finally, he asserts that Paul adopted this formula. That the expression was technical or formulaic is repudiated by the context in which the צדק stock is used flexibly:

> As for me, my justification [משפטי] lies with God; In His hand are the perfection of my walk and the virtue of my heart. By His righteousness [ובצדקותו] is my transgression blotted out. ... From His righteous fount [וממקור צדקתו] comes my justification [משפטי], the light of

---

4Q171 f3_10iv:7; 4Q171 f3_10iv:8; 4Q177 f9:7; 4Q253a f1i:4; 4Q266 f2i:23; 4Q266 f3i:1; 4Q271 f5i:14; 4Q424 f3:2; 4Q428 f18:5; 4Q508 f1:1; 4Q511 f63iii:4; 4Q521 f14:2.

65. Reprinted in *New Testament Questions of Today* (Philadelphia: Fortress, 1969), 168–82.
66. Käsemann, "'The Righteousness of God' in Paul," 172.
67. Barr, in *The Semantics of Biblical Language*, would almost surely also quibble with Käsemann here for confusing words and concepts and, in this case, for confusing a Hebrew/Aramaic word with a Greek one. I will express additional concerns.

my heart from His wondrous mysteries. . . . The source of righteousness [מקור צדקה], gathering of power, and abode of glory are from fleshly counsel hidden. . . . As for me, to evil humanity and the counsel of perverse flesh do I belong. My transgressions, evils, sins and corrupt heart belong to the counsel of wormy rot and them who walk in darkness. Surely a man's way is not his own; neither can any person firm his own step. Surely justification [המשפט] is of God [לאל]; by His power [ומידו] is the way made perfect. All that shall be, He foreknows, all that is, His plans establish; apart from Him is nothing done. As for me, if I stumble, God's lovingkindness [חסדי אל] forever shall save me. If through sin of the flesh I fall, my justification [משפטי] will be by the righteousness of God [בצדקת אל] which endures for all time. Though my affliction break out, He shall draw my soul back from the Pit, and firm my steps on the way. Through His love He has brought me near; by His lovingkindness [ובחסדיו] shall he provide my justification [משפטי]. By His righteous truth [בצדקת אמתו] has He justified me [שפטני]; and through His exceeding goodness shall He atone for all my sins. By His righteousness [ובצדקתו] shall He cleanse me of human defilement and the sin of mankind—to the end that I praise God for His righteousness [צדקו]. . . . Establish all of his works in righteousness [בצדק]; raise up the son of your handmaiden. . . . Surely apart from You the way cannot be perfected, nor can anything be done unless it please You. (1QS 11:2-5-6, 9–17)

We note that the expression "righteousness of God" is anything but formulaic here. It is used interchangeably with "his lovingkindness" and "his righteous truth," from which two expressions the passage also says "my justification" comes, and "his righteousness" appears interchangeable with "righteousness of God." Twice the passage attributes "my justification" generally "with God" or "of God," without referring to any specific divine attribute. In other words, whatever "my justification" (משפטי) means here, it is attributed to God generally twice, to "his righteousness" twice, to "the righteousness of God" once, to "his lovingkindness" once, and to "his righteous truth" once. Further, "his righteousness" is affirmed here not only to procure "my justification," but it also "shall cleanse me of human defilement." The expression "righteousness of God" here, at least, was anything but a "ready-made formulation." It was entirely interchangeable (for substance) with "his righteousness" and also possibly (for substance) with "his lovingkindness" and "his righteous truth." Indeed, the root צדק appears eight times in this passage, with remarkable variety.

This is surely not a "ready-made formulation." Indeed, other than in the preceding lines (1QS 10:25), the particular lexeme צדקת אל does not appear at all at Qumran, צדקות אל appears only four times,[68] and צדק אל appears only twice.[69] This was not a "ready-made formulation" at Qumran at all, if the identical lexeme appears only twice in so vast a literature (where the root צדק appears 471 times), and if its closest comparable lexemes appear only six times themselves. That is, Käsemann's thesis finds itself between a rock and a hard place: if the lexeme has "peculiar force" in this text, so that "general" considerations about its meaning do not apply, then the lexeme is entirely *too* peculiar (appearing only twice in the Qumran literature) for it likely to have been noticed by anyone, much less determinative of anyone else's usage or adoption by them. If, on the other hand, even in this text the root צדק is employed eight times with substantial flexibility, then it is not a "ready-made formulation,"

---

68. 1QS 1:21; 10:23; 4Q256 2:5; 4Q260 5:5.
69. 1QM 4:6; 4Q423 f6:4.

and the same "general" considerations that would dictate sound lexical semantics apply here also.

Käsemann's misunderstanding is somewhat understandable.[70] Probably less than half of the (nonbiblical) Dead Sea Scrolls had been published when he wrote his essay; the entirety of it was not available to the public until 1991. And machine-readable (therefore searchable) texts were not available until about the turn of the millennium. He could not possibly do, therefore, what we can easily do: run a search on a particular lexeme or its closest equivalents. He had a hunch—a plausible hunch—that could not easily be tested for its veracity. It turns out, in my judgment, that the hunch was entirely wrong. There is no reason, from the immediate context or its broader context, to assert that צדקת אל is either a "ready-made formulation" or subject to "peculiar" semantic considerations. And surely, if the formulation appears only twice (or, with its closest lexemes, eight times) in 471 uses of the germane root, then it is entirely unlikely that it could have had any influence on Paul at all. Even assuming that Paul was familiar with the Manual of Discipline, and even assuming he was familiar with this particular passage, what Paul would have noticed would have been the remarkable fluidity of the root צדק in its eight uses here in this context. The influence of Käsemann's unsubstantiated hunch, however, has been profoundly disproportional to its cogency. The hunch, we can now say with some confidence, was and is entirely unsubstantiated. But a generation of New Testament scholarship has proceeded as though the hunch were so well established that it can be referred to, as N. T. Wright has referred to it, as "technical language."[71]

"My justification" in this passage is due to "his lovingkindness," "his righteous truth," "his righteousness," or "the righteousness of God"; it can also be said to be "of God" or "with God." If, in such a context, "righteousness of God" is a soteric term because it is associated with "my justification," then "God" is a soteric term, "righteous truth" is a soteric term, and "lovingkindness" is a soteric term. Yet the Qumran literature plainly paints a picture of God that is not universally soteric; the righteous God by whom the covenanters found justification is the same righteous God by whom the wicked (and even Israel)[72] will surely be judged.[73]

The alleged "soteric" use of צדק in the Qumran literature is explicable in the same manner as the usage in the Hebrew Bible. In the covenant Yahweh made at Sinai with Israel, he pledged blessings to their obedience and curses to their disobedience. To her

---

70. But it is not entirely understandable. The flexibility with which the צדק stock was employed eight different ways in the *immediate* context suggests that any particular usage of it there was also "general," not "peculiar" or a "ready-made formulation," especially apart from any corroborating evidence elsewhere. That is, even without searching the remainder of the scrolls, the thesis faced some difficulty in its own immediate context, in which to assert that one of the eight uses of the root was "peculiar" or a "ready-made formulation" was still nothing but an unsubstantiated assertion.

71. Wright, *What Saint Paul Really Said*, 48. As I mentioned earlier, I believe Wright means that the expression has now become "technical" in NT studies; though it is possible that he embraces Käsemann's errant hypothesis that it was "technical" in Paul's time.

72. CD 20:15–17: "Now at that time God's anger will burn against Israel, as He said, 'Neither king nor prince' [Hos. 3:4] nor judge or one who exhorts to do what is right will be left."

73. 4Q88 9:4–7: "Then shall they extol the name of the Lord, [fo]r He comes to judge every wo[r]k, to make an end of the wicked from upon the earth."

obedience, Yahweh pledged protection and deliverance *from* the surrounding nations; but to their disobedience, he pledged judgment *at the hands of* the same nations (Deut. 28:33–36, 49–50). He pledged to judge them, and to judge them righteously, and he warned that he would "by no means clear the guilty" (Exod. 34:7). When, therefore, on the occasions of their penitence, God's "righteousness" delivered them from judgment and from the nations, Yahweh uprightly fulfilled the covenant pledges he had made. By the terms of the covenant, Yahweh pledged to judge Israel uprightly and either to bless or to curse them, depending on their obedience or disobedience. The Sinai covenant had this profoundly judicial character built into it; and it is this judicial character of the covenant itself that accounts for the use of the צדק (and δικαιοσύνη) language in (those rare) texts that describe Israel's deliverance/salvation from the nations surrounding them.

2.4.3.2. Apocrypha

The Apocrypha employs the δικ- vocabulary somewhat frequently; it appears 122 times. By my reckoning, 84 (68.9 percent) of these uses are ethical, 27 (22.1 percent) are forensic, and 3 (2.5 percent) would be regarded by many as soteric. This ratio is similar to what we find in the Hebrew OT and in the other portions of the LXX.

2.4.3.2.1. ETHICAL USES

In the Apocryphal books, the δικ- vocabulary reflects the same ethical nature as its use in the rest of the LXX. The term is overwhelmingly employed in an ethical manner, as its synonyms and antonyms reveal. Among the synonyms with which it is paired are ἔλεος/ἐλεημοσύνη,[74] ἀγαθός/ἀγαθωσύνη,[75] and σώφρων/σωφροσύνη,[76] εὐθύς/εὐθύτης,[77] and ὅσιος/ὁσιότης.[78] The antonyms with which the group is paired are similarly ethical antonyms, such as ἁμαρτία/ἁμαρτάνω/ἁμαρτωλός[79] or πονηρία/πονηρός. First Esdras 4:39–40 demonstrates this typically ethical understanding of the group by both the synonyms and antonyms with which it is paired, in a hymn to truth:

> With her there is no partiality or preference, but she does what is righteous [τὰ δίκαια] instead of anything that is unrighteous [ἀδίκων] or wicked [πονηρῶν]. All men approve her deeds [τοῖς ἔργοις αὐτῆς], and there is nothing unrighteous [ἄδικον] in her judgment.

2.4.3.2.2. FORENSIC USES

The Apocrypha also witnesses many forensic uses of the δικ- group, as did the LXX. Many times, the vocabulary is employed to describe whether an individual is declared innocent of a charge or not. Sirach 9:12 says, "Do not delight in what pleases the ungodly [ἀσεβῶν]; remember that they will not be held guiltless [οὐ μὴ δικαιωθῶσιν] as

---

74. Tob. 1:3; 2:14; 3:2; 4:7; 12:8; 14:7, 11; Sir. 44:10; Bar. 5:9.
75. Tob. 12:8; 1 Macc. 11:33; 4 Macc. 2:23; Wis. 1:1; Sir. 45:26.
76. 4 Macc. 1:6, 18; 2:23; 15:10; Wis. 8:7.
77. Wis. 9:3; 10:10; Dan. 3:4.
78. Wis. 9:3; 14:30.
79. Esth. 4:6; Tob. 4:5, 17; 12:9; Man. 8; Wis. 10:13; Sir. 10:23, 29; 23:28–29.

long as they live." Later (26:29), a similar sentiment appears: "A merchant can hardly keep from wrongdoing [πλημμελείας], and a tradesman will not be declared innocent [οὐ δικαιωθήσεται] of sin." Indeed, the δικ- vocabulary discloses its comfort in the forensic arena by the many times it finds itself paired with the κρίμα vocabulary and its cognates, as at 1 Maccabees 2:29: "Then many who were seeking righteousness and justice [πολλοὶ ζητοῦντες δικαιοσύνην καὶ κρίμα] went down to the wilderness to dwell there."[80]

Many of these forensic uses demonstrate the close conceptual relationship between the forensic and the ethical, as has been seen before in the Hebrew Bible and the LXX. God is celebrated as the one great paradigm judge of all, because of his moral/ethical qualities that guarantee that his judgments are always just:

> Then the high priest Simon, facing the sanctuary, bending his knees and extending his hands with calm dignity, prayed as follows: "Lord, Lord, king of the heavens, and sovereign of all creation, holy among the holy ones [ἅγιε ἐν ἁγίοις], the only ruler, almighty, give attention to us who are suffering grievously from an impious and profane man, puffed up in his audacity and power. For you, the creator of all things and the governor of all, are a just Ruler [δυνάστης δίκαιος], and you judge those who have done anything in insolence and arrogance [ὕβρει καὶ ἀγερωχίᾳ]. You destroyed those who in the past committed injustice [ἀδικίαν], among whom were even giants who trusted in their strength and boldness, whom you destroyed by bringing upon them a boundless flood. You consumed with fire and sulphur the men of Sodom who acted arrogantly [ὑπερηφανίαν], who were notorious for their vices [ταῖς κακίαις]; and you made them an example to those who should come afterward. (3 Macc. 2:1–5)

2.4.3.2.3. SOTERIC USES

The so-called soteric use of the δικ- language is comparatively rare in the Apocryphal literature. Perhaps the best example is in the fifth chapter of Baruch:

> Take off the garment of your sorrow and affliction, O Jerusalem, and put on for ever the beauty of the glory from God [τὴν εὐπρέπειαν τῆς παρὰ τοῦ θεοῦ δόξης]. Put on the robe of the righteousness from God [τὴν διπλοΐδα τῆς παρὰ τοῦ θεοῦ δικαιοσύνης]; put on your head the diadem of the glory of the Everlasting. For God will show your splendor everywhere under heaven. For your name will for ever be called by God, "Peace of righteousness [εἰρήνη δικαιοσύνης] and glory of godliness [δόξα θεοσεβείας]." Arise, O Jerusalem, stand upon the height and look toward the east, and see your children gathered from west and east, at the word of the Holy One, rejoicing that God has remembered them. For they went forth from you on foot, led away by their enemies; but God will bring them back to you, carried in glory, as on a royal throne. For God has ordered that every high mountain and the everlasting hills be made low and the valleys filled up, to make level ground, so that Israel may walk safely in the glory of God. The woods and every fragrant tree have shaded Israel at God's command. For God will lead Israel with joy, in the light of his glory, with the mercy and righteousness [ἐλεημοσύνη καὶ δικαιοσύνη] that come from him. (Bar. 5:1–9)

---

80. Also 1 Esdr. 4:39; Tob. 3:2; 1 Macc. 11:33; 2 Macc. 7:36; 9:18; 12:6; 3 Macc. 2:3, 22; Wis. 1:1; 5:18; 9:3; Sir. 42:2; 45:26.

Unmistakably, the text is eschatological, and its overall message is surely soteric. The precise question we raise, however, is whether δικαιοσύνη means something like "salvation" or "saving power" in this passage. The consequences are not terribly significant, since the ethical and forensic uses are so well established in the Apocryphal literature. However, a good case can be made for the fact that δικαιοσύνη is employed even here in its ordinary ethical sense, because the eschaton will be a place in which its inhabitants are morally renewed. To test this counter-thesis, we ask of this passage: Is each use of δικαιοσύνη soteric (as opposed to ethical or forensic) in this text, and are the other abstract expressions in the passage soteric (as opposed to ethical or forensic)?

We note that δικαιοσύνη appears three times in the text. The first usage is the most figurative, and therefore the most difficult: "Put on the robe of the righteousness from God [τὴν διπλοΐδα τῆς παρὰ τοῦ θεοῦ δικαιοσύνης]; put on your head the diadem of the glory of the Everlasting." The picture of humanity regalized is a beautiful eschatological picture, but not the easiest one to discern in terms of what "robe of righteousness" means. Since this robe is "from God," it is possible that we have here the forensic image of imputed righteousness, since such clothing language appears elsewhere. It is possible that what is emphasized is the pure soteric gift ("from God"); and it is also possible that this refers to ethical righteousness, as Adam's race, originally created to "exercise dominion over" the created order (Gen. 1:28), is now restored to its regal responsibility. The second usage appears to be somewhat more clearly ethical, even though the overall context remains eschatological. We note that "peace of righteousness" is parallel to "glory of godliness," so perhaps both "righteousness" and "godliness" here are terms of ethical approval as Israel, in the eschatological state, manifests their moral rejuvenation. The third use is also somewhat difficult; what, precisely, constitutes the "mercy and righteousness that come from" God? Are these references to God's merciful and upright character or references to eschatological/soteric gifts that are given from him to Israel? The two need not be exclusive, but we note that "mercy" here is ἐλεημοσύνη, a term ordinarily employed ethically for acts of charity or almsgiving to those who are needy.[81] Yet it is also sometimes understood as a *general* term of moral uprightness, as at Deuteronomy 6:25: "And it will be righteousness for us [ἐλεημοσύνη ἔσται ἡμῖν], if we are careful to do all this commandment before the LORD our God, as he has commanded us."[82] Yet elsewhere, it may have soteric associations, as at Psalm 103:6: "The LORD works righteousness and justice [ἐλεημοσύνας . . . καὶ κρίμα] for all who are oppressed."[83] Baruch 5 can surely be read in such a manner that "righteousness" appears to be a reference to God's saving activity in the eschaton. But it can also be read, even in that eschatological context, in a manner that refers to the moral/ethical renewal that will characterize the eschatological state.

---

81. So it is translated at Tob. 1:3, 16; 2:14; 4:7–8, 10; 12:8; 14:2, 10–11; Sir. 3:30; 7:10; 12:3; 17:22; 29:8, 12; 31:11; 35:2; 40:7, 24.

82. So also this ethical use is common in the wisdom literature, where in Proverbs "steadfast love and faithfulness [ἐλεημοσύναι δὲ καὶ πίστεις]" characterize "those who devise good [ἀγαθοῖς]" (Prov. 14:22; cf. Prov. 3:3; 20:28).

83. Though here the term may merely be forensic, almost the equivalent of κρίμα, since the "oppressed" are described as τοῖς ἀδικουμένοις, "those who have been treated unjustly."

2.4.3.3. Pseudepigraphic Literature

The δικ- language is common in the Pseudepigrapha, appearing 343 times. Of these, I regard 292 (85.1 percent) of the uses to be ethical, 27 (7.9 percent) to be forensic, and 0 to be soteric. This is the highest ratio of ethical uses in any of the five works of literature that antedate Paul. Taken together, the ethical and forensic uses account for 93 percent, not very different from the Hebrew Bible (80.6 percent) or the LXX (82.3 percent), and very similar to the Apocrypha (91 percent). Somewhat surprisingly, the Apocrypha and Pseudepigrapha are more "conservative" than the earlier literature, but a little less likely than the earlier literature to employ the language in a manner that could be construed as soteric. Semantic change can, of course, move in either direction; terms can take on newer denotations or can become more technical and restricted. Somewhat surprisingly (to me, anyway), the range here has become more restricted/technical, and yet not at all in the direction suggested by Käsemann and so many of his followers. To the contrary, the Pseudepigraphic literature displays the highest ratio of ethical usage, and the highest ratio of the combined ethical/forensic usage. In other words, far from demonstrating that the δικ- language over time was becoming more likely to be used in allegedly soteric or relational ways, the evidence is just the opposite, demonstrating a more restricted or restrained use than characterized in the Hebrew Bible or the LXX.

2.4.3.3.1. ETHICAL USES

As in the other literature, we find the δικ- group here to be prevailingly ethical. Sometimes its usage is almost a formulaic term of approval, as in the Testament of Abraham, where Abraham is routinely described honorifically as "just/righteous."[84] Its synonyms and antonyms are ordinarily ethical, and sometimes it even appears with a cluster of ethical terms, as at Testament of Abraham 4:6:

> "Master and Lord, let your power know that I am unable to remind that righteous man [τὸν δίκαιον ἄνδρα] of his death, for I have not seen upon the earth a man like him, pitiful [ἐλεήμονα], hospitable [φιλόξενον], righteous [δίκαιον], truthful [ἀληθινὸν], devout [θεοσεβῆ], refraining from every evil deed [ἀπὸ παντὸς πονηροῦ πράγματος]."

It appears with ἅγιος and its cognates 14 times, with ὅσιος (or ὁσιότης) 13 times, with εὐσέβεια (and cognates) 11 times, with ἀγαθός and its cognates 16 times, and with ἀλήθεια and its cognates 21 times. The evidence is similar for its antonyms. It is paired with ἁμαρτία and its cognates 38 times and with κακία and its cognates at least 13 times.

2.4.3.3.2. FORENSIC USES

There are forensic uses of the lexical stock in the Pseudepigrapha, just as there were in the LXX and the Apocrypha. One characteristic of ethically virtuous individuals and cultures is that they exonerate the innocent and condemn the wicked, and they are generally eager to promote civil justice in this sense. Sybil. 2:61–64 is a good example of such:

---

84. Testament of Abraham 1:5; 2:3, 6, 12; 7:8. Noah is also honored the same way: Sybil. 1:269, 280; 4 Bar. 7:8.

Render all things due [πάντα δίκαια νέμειν], and into unjust judgment do not come [μηδ᾿ εἰς κρίσιν ἄδικον ἔλθῃς]. Do not cast out the poor unrighteously [ἀδίκως], nor judge by outward show [μὴ κρῖνε προσώπῳ]. If you judge wickedly God hereafter will judge you. Avoid false testimony [μαρτυρίην ψευδῆ φεύγειν]; tell the truth [τὰ δίκαια βραβεύειν].

When upright humans clear the innocent and condemn the guilty, they imitate God, who is both morally upright and an upright judge: "Righteous [δίκαιός] is the Lord, true are his judgments [τὰ κρίματα]; with him there is no partiality [προσωποληψία]. He will judge [κρινεῖ] us consistently" (Testament of Job 43:13; cf. also Pss. Sol. 2:15). Such divine righteousness is exhibited even in God's judgments upon Israel: "We have justified [ἐδικαιώσαμεν] your name that is honored forever. For you are the God of righteousness [τῆς δικαιοσύνης], judging Israel with chastening [κρίνων τὸν Ισραηλ ἐν παιδείᾳ]" (Pss. Sol. 8:26).

I was unable to find any soteric uses of the δικ- vocabulary in the Pseudepigrapha. I do not regard this as indicating anything distinctive about this literature, since it was/ is also extremely rare in the other literature, never arising to more than 2.5 percent of the uses by the most generous accounting—and possibly not appearing at all (if, as I suggest, the eschaton will be characterized by a rejuvenated moral life, those "soteric" uses themselves may be ethical).

2.5. Observations and Working Hypothesis Regarding the Cremer-Käsemann Hypothesis

The overwhelming evidence from the Hebrew Bible, the LXX, and the late Jewish literature supports an ethical/forensic understanding. If this body of literature is averaged, then 87.26 percent of the time the language is either ethical (69.8 percent) or forensic (17.46 percent). Soteric texts appear only 1 percent of the time, far less than the mixed uses (8.4 percent) or indeterminate uses (12.6 percent). Blink, once or twice, when reading this literature, and you will miss the suggested "soteric" uses altogether. This does not mean that Paul could not have employed it soterically, because Paul could very well have simply coined a new usage anyway, a novel use that no one else had employed before him. But the almost common notion today that the δικ- vocabulary was virtually "technical" in the literature antecedent to Paul is so erroneous as to border on fraud. In 1,829 relevant texts, I could find only seventeen that could plausibly be construed as suggesting something like soteric power, and each of those texts could be equally plausibly construed otherwise.

The following table summarizes the results from each of the five relevant bodies of literature, without distinguishing adjectives from nouns from verbs. "Indeterminate" either means that the text was obscure (which is common in the Qumran literature) or that the context did not, in my judgment, sufficiently indicate how the term was used (in these cases, I thought a plausible case could be made for more than one use). "Technical" is for those expressions, such as "Teacher of Righteousness," that was so technical I did not regard it as being properly placed in any category. "Mixed" is employed for those circumstances in which the term appears to be employed in more than one way, where it is equally plausibly forensic or ethical, for instance.

Literature	Ethical	Forensic	Soteric	Mixed	Ind	Technical	Total
HMT total	200	65	5	27	32	0	329
HMT %	**60.8**	**19.8**	**1.5**	**8.2**	**9.7**	**0**	
LXX total	353	111	7	52	41	0	564
LXX %	**62.6**	**19.7**	**1.2**	**9.2**	**7.3**	**0**	
Apocrypha total	84	27	3	7	1	0	122
Apocrypha %	**68.9**	**22.1**	**2.5**	**5.7**	**0.8**	**0**	
Pseudepigrapha total	292	27	0	21	3	0	343
Pseudepigrapha %	**85.1**	**7.9**	**0**	**6.1**	**0.9**	**0**	
Qumran total	230	59	2	30	128	22	471
Qumran %	**48.8**	**12.5**	**0.4**	**6.4**	**27**	**4.7**	
Qumran % of det.	**71.4**	**17.8**	**1**	**8.4**	**12.6**	**1.4**	

If interested, readers can view my categorization and determine whether they agree with my judgments. I do not expect substantial disagreement, especially since I permitted myself the category of "Indeterminate" where I thought a case could be plausibly otherwise argued. In this table, I print as little context as is necessary to check my categorization.

If we regard the Hebrew OT and LXX as comparatively "early" Jewish writings, and the Apocrypha, Pseudepigrapha, and Qumran as comparatively "later" writings, then we have about the same amount from each of the two broad eras: 893 from the early material, 936 from the later material, which are about 900 each. Note also that the percentages are about the same. If the ethical and forensic categories are added together, then the least they constitute is 80.6 percent (HMT), and the most is 93 percent (Pseudepigrapha). Indeed, all three of the later texts are even more "conservative" than the two earlier ones. The three later texts average 91 percent ethical/forensic uses, whereas the average of the two earlier texts is almost 10 percent less, at 81.5 percent. In none of the literature is the so-called soteric use common: in the two earlier texts, it appears about 1.35 percent; and in the later texts 1.17 percent. It is especially interesting to note that possible "soteric" uses are more common in the canonical literature than the later literature. The inference, if not the overt statement, of proponents of the Käsemann/Stuhlmacher hypothesis was that the later material was more flexible than the earlier, that in the later literature the צדק (and δικαιοσύνη) language had moved away from its ethical and forensic usages to a more soteric use. But the evidence, at least as I have categorized it, is just the opposite: the HMT and LXX employ the two lexical stocks with greater flexibility (though not significantly so) than do the post-canonical writings.

Insofar as *we* know the postbiblical literature in question (apart from how well Paul knew it), it hardly adds substantially to the Cremer hypothesis (which depended on canonical OT texts). We find in the later Jewish literature what we find in the canonical OT: almost countless texts that employ the צדק/δικαιοσύνη language in an ethical or forensic manner and only a small number that even plausibly employ it in a relational/soteric manner.

Many so-called soteric texts are themselves judicial: Yahweh saves/rescues/delivers Israel *from the nations* by vindicating/delivering his covenant people and judging/vanquishing their enemies. He arbitrates the dispute (ריב) between Israel and the nations in Israel's favor, vindicating the righteous and condemning the wicked.[85] Apocalyptic power especially is judicial power, as the Creator of the world judges the wicked and acquits the righteous. Inasmuch as there is some truth in saying that divine righteousness is displayed when God "makes things right" at the close of history, Yahweh ordinarily "makes things right" for the righteous by making them very *wrong* for the wicked.

Further, in a manner that can only be introduced/encouraged/suggested in this volume, it is entirely likely that the "soteric" language is actually due to the nature of the Sinai covenant administration itself, in which, especially in the latter chapters of Deuteronomy, Yahweh pledges himself to cursing Israel when they are disobedient and to blessing them when they are obedient. Having pledged such arbitration/judgment, Yahweh would of course be "unrighteous" if he did not fulfill the pledge and "righteous" if he did fulfill it. So in those moments when, under the encouragements of Yahweh's servants the prophets, Israel did "return" and did forsake their idolatry and other misdeeds, they could and did appeal to Yahweh's righteousness—to his moral/ethical uprightness, an uprightness that would not violate the terms of a covenant he himself sovereignly administered. As we saw in our discussions of this covenant in Galatians 3, "the law is not of faith" (3:12) and therefore not of grace but of works. Its pledged blessings or cursings were conditioned on Israel's obedience, so that when they repented and returned, Yahweh would deliver them—would "save/rescue" them from the nations around her—not by his grace but by their works of repentance. That is, even the "soteric" righteousness could be covenantal righteousness (as the NPP often suggests); not some *general* covenantal righteousness, but rather the *specific* righteousness of a *specific* covenant that is "not of faith, but rather 'the one who does them shall live by them'" (Gal. 3:12).

Consider the conditional nature of the Sinai covenant administration and note how it pledges *either* blessing *or* cursing:

> "If you walk in my statutes and observe my commandments and do them, then I will give you your rains in their season, and the land shall yield its increase, and the trees of the field shall yield their fruit. . . . I will give peace in the land, and you shall lie down, and none shall make you afraid. And I will remove harmful beasts from the land, and the sword shall not go through your land. You shall chase your enemies, and they shall fall before you by the sword [μαχαίρᾳ]." (Lev. 26:3)

> "But if you will not listen to me and will not do all these commandments, . . . then I will do this to you: I will visit you with panic, with wasting disease and fever that consume the eyes and make the heart ache. And you shall sow your seed in vain, for your enemies shall eat it. I will set my face against you, and you shall be struck down before your enemies. Those

---

85. When plaintiffs appear before judgment, whether in the ancient Near East or today, "innocent" and "guilty" were and are often relative terms. The "innocent/acquitted/righteous" are not parties who live in Edenic sinless perfection; their "righteousness" is relative to the dispute or alleged wrongdoing in question. So also, the "wicked/unrighteous/guilty" are not necessarily people without some redeeming qualities; their "unrighteousness" is, again, relative to the matter brought before the court. Apocalyptic literature tends to address these distinctions between the righteous and unrighteous without ordinarily articulating such nuance.

who hate you shall rule over you, and you shall flee when none pursues you. . . . And if by this discipline you are not turned to me but walk contrary to me, then I also will walk contrary to you, and I myself will strike you sevenfold for your sins. And I will bring a sword upon you [ἐφ' ὑμᾶς μάχαιραν], that shall execute vengeance for the covenant [δίκην διαθήκης]. (Lev. 26:3–7, 14–25)

This latter expression, "vengeance of the covenant," is rare (in this specific form, only here in the LXX). But we must note its form, δίκην διαθήκης: "vengeance of the covenant," which could also be translated "punishment of the covenant" or even "righteousness/ justice of the covenant."[86]

In some of the Jewish literature, God is celebrated as "righteous" in this punitive sense; not merely in his soteric works of delivering Israel *from* their enemies, but also in his acts of judicial punishment of them *by* their enemies. Consider the first person (singular or plural) in Tobit:

Righteous art thou, O Lord [δίκαιος εἶ κύριε]; all thy deeds and all thy ways are mercy and truth, and thou dost render true and righteous judgment for ever [καὶ πάντα τὰ ἔργα σου καὶ πᾶσαι αἱ ὁδοί σου ἐλεημοσύναι καὶ ἀλήθεια καὶ κρίσιν ἀληθινὴν καὶ δικαίαν σὺ κρίνεις εἰς τὸν αἰῶνα]. Remember *me* and look favorably upon *me*; do not punish *me* [μή με ἐκδικήσῃς] for *my* sins and for *my* unwitting offences and those which *my fathers* committed before thee. For they (my fathers) disobeyed thy commandments, and thou gavest *us* over to plunder, captivity, and death; thou madest *us* a byword of reproach in all the nations among which *we* have been dispersed. And now thy many judgments are true [νῦν πολλαὶ αἱ κρίσεις σού εἰσιν ἀληθιναί] in exacting penalty *from me* for *my* sins and those of *my* fathers because *we* did not keep thy commandments. For *we* did not walk in truth before thee. (Tobit 3:2–5)

Note that God is here celebrated as being δίκαιος in *all* his deeds, including his acts of rendering true and righteous judgment (κρίσιν ἀληθινὴν καὶ δικαίαν) *against* the covenant people. Because the Lord was δίκαιος, he handed his sinful people over to the nations for exile (Tobit 1–2). It was precisely in such true judgments (αἱ κρίσεις . . . ἀληθιναὶ) *against* his own covenant people that God was disclosed to be δίκαιος. Now, one could plausibly argue that such chastisement served greater, long-range goals of preserving a covenant people from utter destruction (by encouraging their national repentance), and thus "saving" them. Nonetheless, for those compatriots of Tobit who were put to "plunder, captivity, and death" by God's righteousness, such righteousness would hardly have been construed as "soteric" in any ordinary sense. Similarly, such righteousness was only "faithfulness to a relationship" if the nature of the particular covenantal relationship was one in which God had pledged, as covenant suzerain, to reward obedience and punish disobedience. But again, if such "faithfulness to a relation-ship" entailed putting "to . . . death" (εἰς . . . θάνατον) some with whom the relationship was made, then the relationship was not an especially enviable one.[87]

---

86. In the Maccabean literature, when the modifier is not "the covenant" but "divine," the ETs often translate ἡ θεία δίκη or τὴν τοῦ θεοῦ δίκην "divine *justice*," rather than "vengeance" (2 Macc. 8:13; 4 Macc. 4:13, 21; 8:21; 9:9; 12:12; 18:22). Cf. also Esther 16:4, which refers to "the evil-hating *justice* of God" (θεοῦ μισοπόνηρον . . . δίκην).

87. I suppose an executioner has a "faithful relationship" with those he executes, because he does indeed faithfully perform his task; but I doubt those who inhabit death row take much pleasure in the executioner's "faithful relationship" to them.

In passages such as these, the "soteric" righteousness of the Cremer-Käsemann-NPP reigning paradigm is not, in fact, another category distinct from the ethical/forensic righteousness characteristic of the earlier paradigm from the early fathers until the nineteenth century; it is, rather, the expression of ethical/forensic righteousness within a specific covenantal setting conditioned on the behavior of the covenant people. If so, then Yahweh expresses his "righteousness" both *through* exile and through return *from* exile. Each is the act of a covenant suzerain who is upright; each is the act of a covenant suzerain who maintains not some general "relationship" nor a "soteric" relationship but a specific, covenantal relationship—one in which he has pledged equally to curse or to bless, to exile or to return from exile. The evidence from late Jewish sources is not significantly different[88] from the evidence of the Hebrew Bible and the LXX. There is substantial, if not overwhelming, evidence of an ethical/forensic usage, whereas the evidence of a relational/soteric usage is both infrequent and disputed.

2.6. Distinguishing Association and Definition

Have not Cremer/Käsemann/Stuhlmacher confused lexical association with definition? That there are texts in which δικαιοσύνη is associated with σωτηρία is not disputed,[89] but such association is not definition. Especially in the more eschatological texts, σωτηρία is associated with a number of good things. Consider Isaiah 52:7: "How beautiful upon the mountains are the feet of him who brings good news [εὐαγγελιζομένου], who publishes peace [εἰρήνης], who brings good news of happiness [ἀγαθά], who publishes salvation [σωτηρίαν], who says to Zion, 'Your God reigns.'" In such texts, the entirety of the present age is perceived as yielding to an ideal age, an age that reverses the curse of the present age and replaces it with blessing. But we would not ordinarily say that "good" *means* "salvation," or that "peace" *means* "salvation." Rather, we would say that the ultimate salvation of the created order will be characterized by many things, including that righteousness will reign again on earth, as hoped for in the Psalms. But this does not mean that "righteousness" *means* "salvation" or "saving power" or "saving relationships." Righteousness is one of the many things that will characterize the "salvation" that will appear in the eschaton. In its ethical sense, the eschaton will be characterized by virtue and justice; in its forensic sense, the wicked will receive their just punishment.

The association of δικαιοσύνη with σωτηρία in these five LXX texts does not mean that δικαιοσύνη *means* "salvation." In fact, there are eleven texts in the LXX that associate δικαιοσύνη with εἰρήνη,[90] but Cremer and Käsemann did not argue that δικαιοσύνη means "apocalyptic peace" or "eschatological peace" or "soteric peace." Consider Isaiah 32:17: "And the effect of righteousness [τὰ ἔργα τῆς δικαιοσύνης] will be peace [εἰρήνη], and the result of righteousness [κρατήσει ἡ δικαιοσύνη], quietness

---

88. The difference, at most, is one of proportion. Even as the amount of apocalyptic literature is greater in later Judaism than in the OT, so also warfare between the "righteous" and the "wicked" is perhaps more frequent.

89. In the LXX, there are five such passages: Ps. 50:16; 70:15; Isa. 33:6; 46:13; Odes 11:19.

90. Ps. 35:27; 72:3, 7; 85:10; Prov. 16:8; Isa. 9:7; 32:17; 39:8; 48:18; 60:17; Bar. 5:4.

[ἀνάπαυσιν, lit. "rest"] and trust [πεποιθότες] forever." Or consider Psalm 72:7: "In his [the king's] days may righteousness [δικαιοσύνη] flourish, and peace abound [πλῆθος εἰρήνης], till the moon be no more!" Baruch also celebrates the appearance of both peace and righteousness, while not implying that the one defines the other:

> Take off the garment of your sorrow and affliction, O Jerusalem, and put on for ever the beauty of the glory from God. Put on the robe of the righteousness from God [τὴν διπλοΐδα τῆς παρὰ τοῦ θεοῦ δικαιοσύνης]; put on your head the diadem of the glory of the Everlasting. For God will show your splendor everywhere under heaven. For your name will for ever be called by God, "Peace of righteousness [εἰρήνη δικαιοσύνης] and glory of godliness." (Bar. 5:1–4)

Since the eschaton is perceived as a time of rich and profound blessedness, many good traits are associated with it, and "salvation" is one of the more comprehensive of those traits. But other traits are also associated with that era and therefore with one another, without this implying that each of those abstract nouns means the same thing as any of the others. Qumran also anticipated that moment and described it richly, as at 4Q215a f1ii:5–10:

> For the time of righteousness is coming [באה עת הצדק], and the land is full of true knowledge and the praise of God in [. . .] the era of peace is coming [בא קצה שלום]. . . . Every tongue shall bless Him, and every person shall bow down to Him . . . for the dominion of Good is coming [בא ממשל הטוב] and the [holy] throne will be exalted.

What is "coming" can be described either as a "time of righteousness," an "era of peace," or "the dominion of Good." But "righteousness" is not synonymous with "peace" or "good." Though שלום, הצדק, and הטוב are associated with one another as realities characteristic of the eschaton, they retain their distinctive definitions. In any language, there are many terms frequently or commonly associated with each other, but this association does not imply synonymity. "Viola" may be frequently associated with "cello," but they are different instruments playing different parts, and the words themselves do not mean the same thing. "Judge," "prosecuting attorney," and "jury" are frequently associated, but a judge is neither a jurist nor a prosecutor.

2.7. The Particular Lexeme δικαιοσύνη θεοῦ

Is it not artificial to suggest that "righteousness of God" means something different from "your righteousness" (when addressed to "God") or "his righteousness" (when referring to God's righteousness)? Käsemann both acutely anticipated and deftly parried the obvious criticism of his viewpoint by suggesting that δικαιοσύνη θεοῦ was a technical expression, and that δικαιοσύνη meant something different when qualified by the genitive θεοῦ. This was a necessary step for him to make, because—as anyone who evaluates either the actual usages of the δικ- group or the צדק group realizes—the terms overwhelmingly are employed in ethical and forensic/judicial senses, and only rarely (and then debatably) in relational or soteric senses. Thus the plausibility of the Käsemann hypothesis rests substantially on the cogency of the idea that δικαιοσύνη, when employed *in the two-word expression* δικαιοσύνη θεοῦ, means something different from what it ordinarily means.

This notion that δικαιοσύνη might have a different meaning when qualified by a particular genitival noun such as θεοῦ is not implausible. After all, when we refer to an expression such as "the love of God," we recognize a perfection that not only is the source of all human love, but a perfection that virtually embarrasses, by comparison, all human love. We even celebrate this liturgically by singing "Love divine, all loves excelling." So it is not implausible that any abstract noun, when paired with θεοῦ, might denote a *perfection* of that quality that distinguishes it from mere creaturely expressions. Plausible, therefore, as the thesis was and is, it faces two substantial difficulties.

First, if the modifying noun θεοῦ suggests a perfection of the attribute in question, then this would be a difference of *degree*, not kind. Divine love may be greater in degree than human love, but if it were altogether different in *kind*, then we would not be able to use the same term for both human and divine love (nor could the great ethical program of *imitatio Dei* be possible anywhere). So also with righteousness; if divine righteousness were not only different in degree but also different in kind than human righteousness, then we probably would not be able to employ the same term to designate both. So the first problem with the Käsemann hypothesis is this: "faithfulness to a relationship" or "soteric power" are not different in *degree* from "moral or judicial uprightness"; they are different in *kind*, as Cremer, Käsemann, et al., were all quick to point out. The weight of what they were contending for was precisely that while δικαιοσύνη might ordinarily be a reference to moral/ethical (and therefore judicial) uprightness, when followed by θεοῦ it meant something else altogether than its ordinary Greek denotation; it meant something like "faithfulness to a relationship" or "saving power." But this is not really cogent. It would be perfectly cogent to suggest that divine righteousness is perfect in degree, whereas all human righteousness is imperfect in degree. But to suggest that it is different in kind altogether begs the question of why the LXX translators did not then simply employ a Greek word that meant what the Hebrew did. Such language, however, was available to them—and to Paul. The natural way of referring to someone as "faithful" in Greek would have been to employ πιστός. The LXX candidly ascribes to God this attribute:

> "Know therefore that the LORD your God is God, the faithful God [θεὸς πιστός, Heb. הנאמן] who keeps covenant and steadfast love with those who love him and keep his command-ments, to a thousand generations." (Deut. 7:9)

> "The Rock, his work is perfect, for all his ways are justice. A God of faithfulness [θεὸς πιστός, Heb. אמונה] and without iniquity, just and upright is he." (Deut. 32:4)

And Paul employed this language also:

> What if some were unfaithful? Does their faithlessness nullify the faithfulness of God [τὴν πίστιν τοῦ θεοῦ]? (Rom. 3:4)

> God is faithful [πιστὸς ὁ θεός], by whom you were called into the fellowship of his Son, Jesus Christ our Lord. (1 Cor. 1:9)

> No temptation has overtaken you that is not common to man. God is faithful [πιστὸς δὲ ὁ θεός], and he will not let you be tempted. (1 Cor. 10:13)

As surely as God is faithful [πιστὸς δὲ ὁ θεός], our word to you has not been Yes and No. (2 Cor. 1:18; also 1 Thess. 5:24; 2 Thess. 3:3)

God's faithfulness, either to a relationship or a covenant, is a true enough idea; but it was an idea the Greek language had a perfectly competent way of expressing, and that way was πιστός, not δικαιοσύνη.

Similarly, if the expression δικαιοσύνη θεοῦ is alleged to mean "saving power" or "soteric power," then once again there were perfectly adequate Greek terms available to the LXX translators if they wished to convey such: δύναμις, κράτος, or ἰσχύς.

But for this purpose I have raised you up, to show you my power [τὴν ἰσχύν μου], so that my name may be proclaimed in all the earth. (Exod. 9:16)

Your right hand, O Lord, glorious in power [δεδόξασται ἐν ἰσχύι], your right hand, O Lord, shatters the enemy. (Exod. 15:6)

But Moses implored the Lord his God and said, "O Lord, why does your wrath burn hot against your people, whom you have brought out of the land of Egypt with great power and with a mighty hand [ἐν ἰσχύι μεγάλῃ καὶ ἐν τῷ βραχίονί σου τῷ ὑψηλῷ]? (Exod. 32:11; cf. also Deut. 9:26, 29; 26:8; Josh. 4:24)

Yours, O Lord, is the greatness and the power [ἡ μεγαλωσύνη καὶ ἡ δύναμις] and the glory and the victory and the majesty, for all that is in the heavens and in the earth is yours. (1 Chron. 29:11)

O Lord, in your strength [ἐν τῇ δυνάμει σου] the king rejoices, and in your salvation how greatly he exults! (Ps. 21:1)

Be exalted, O Lord, in your strength [ἐν τῇ δυνάμει σου]! (Ps. 21:13)

God is our refuge and strength [δύναμις], a very present help in trouble. (Ps. 46:1; also Ps. 54:1; 58:11, etc.)

In addition to these more literal ways of referring to divine power, figurative language was employed in the antecedent literature and could have been employed by Paul. Perhaps the most common of the figurative expressions was "arm of the Lord":

"Say therefore to the people of Israel, 'I am the Lord, and I will bring you out from under the burdens of the Egyptians, and I will deliver you from slavery to them, and I will redeem you with an outstretched arm and with great acts of judgment.'" (Exod. 6:6)

"Terror and dread fall upon them; because of the greatness of your arm, they are still as a stone, till your people, O Lord, pass by, till the people pass by whom you have purchased." (Exod. 15:16)

"Or has any god ever attempted to go and take a nation for himself from the midst of another nation, by trials, by signs, by wonders, and by war, by a mighty hand and an outstretched arm, and by great deeds of terror, all of which the Lord your God did for you in Egypt before your eyes?" (Deut. 4:34)

"You shall remember that you were a slave in the land of Egypt, and the Lord your God brought you out from there with a mighty hand and an outstretched arm. Therefore the Lord your God commanded you to keep the Sabbath day." (Deut. 5:15)

"The great trials that your eyes saw, the signs, the wonders, the mighty hand, and the out-stretched arm, by which the LORD your God brought you out. So will the LORD your God do to all the peoples of whom you are afraid." (Deut. 7:19; cf. also Deut. 11:2; 26:8; 2 Kings 17:36; Ps. 98:1; Isa. 30:30; 33:2; 48:14; 51:9; 52:10; 53:1; 62:8; Jer. 32:17; Ezek. 20:33; 30:22)

Both literally and figuratively, then, the antecedent literature easily communicated the idea of God's power and did so without the need for employing the δικ- group.

A second difficulty with the idea that θεοῦ, when attached to δικαιοσύνη, alters its meaning is the fact that δικαιοσύνη is often attributed to God by qualifying pronouns such as αὐτοῦ or σου, in places where it manifestly refers to God's ethical (and therefore judicial) uprightness. If the implied antecedent of αὐτοῦ or σου is θεοῦ, then it seems highly artificial to suggest that the abstract noun alters its meaning merely because it is now "God's righteousness" rather than "thy righteousness" (when addressing God) or "his righteousness" (when referring *to* God).

Lead me, O LORD, in your righteousness [ἐν τῇ δικαιοσύνῃ σου] because of my enemies; make your way straight before me. (Ps. 5:8)

I will give to the LORD the thanks due to his righteousness [τὴν δικαιοσύνην αὐτοῦ]. (Ps. 7:17)

They shall come and proclaim his righteousness [τὴν δικαιοσύνην αὐτοῦ] to a people yet unborn, that he has done it. (Ps. 22:31)

In you, O LORD, do I take refuge; let me never be put to shame; in your righteousness [ἐν τῇ δικαιοσύνῃ σου] deliver me! (Ps. 31:1)

Vindicate me, O LORD, my God, according to your righteousness [κατὰ τὴν δικαιοσύνην σου], and let them not rejoice over me! (Ps. 35:24)

Then my tongue shall tell of your righteousness [τὴν δικαιοσύνην σου] and of your praise all the day long. (Ps. 35:28)

The heavens declare his righteousness [τὴν δικαιοσύνην αὐτοῦ], for God himself is judge! (Ps. 50:6; cf. also Ps. 97:6; 98:2; 103:17; 111:3, 9; 112:9)

I leave open the possibility that δικαιοσύνη is sufficiently flexible that it can, in some particular contexts, be construed as meaning something like "God's faithfulness" or "God's power." Language is a flexible phenomenon, and competent people (especially poets) often extend the semantic range of terms, employing them in contexts that enlarge or alter their ordinary usage. Therefore, if in a given context such consid-erations suggest that δικαιοσύνη be construed as meaning "God's faithfulness" or "God's power," then I am more than willing to consider such reasoning. But I regard it as artificial to think that the qualification of δικαιοσύνη by θεοῦ, on that ground alone, ordinarily or commonly means something different than when δικαιοσύνη is qualified by αὐτοῦ or σου when God is the evident antecedent. As we saw earlier in the immediate context of the Qumran text cited by Käsemann (1QS 11:14), "his righteousness" appears twice and "righteousness of God" once, suggesting that the root צדק itself means the same thing regardless of whether it is qualified by אל or by the third person suffix ו.

2.8. The Usage in Galatians Is, in Fact, Ethical/Forensic

The initial usage (Gal. 2:16) is manifestly forensic, citing Psalm 143:2, which is indisputably so. Paul said,

> We know that a person is not justified by works of the law [ἐξ ἔργων νόμου] but through faith in Jesus Christ, so we also have believed in Christ Jesus, in order to be justified by faith in Christ and not by works of the law, because by works of the law no one will be justified [ἐξ ἔργων νόμου οὐ δικαιωθήσεται πᾶσα σάρξ].

Commentators appear to be in agreement that Paul's causal clause here cites Psalm 143:2, "Enter not into judgment [במשפט] with your servant, for no one living is righteous before you [כי לא יצדק לפניך כל חי, ὅτι οὐ δικαιωθήσεται ἐνώπιόν σου πᾶς ζῶν]." For our purposes, it is sufficient to note that the first time the δικ- language appears in Galatians, it is a reference to a plainly judicial reality: the appearance of a human before God's judgment, before which no flesh will be justified. Apart from some contextual indication, we would assume that the language continues to be used this way in the remainder of his discussion.[91]

In his first usage of the lexical stock, Paul expressly denied that the members of the Sinai covenant were justified thereby. Despite the now common comments in biblical studies to the contrary,[92] Paul did not understand "to be justified" to mean "to be members of the covenant community." Not only did he affirm the testimony of Psalm 143 that "no flesh" (including, presumably, flesh that was party to particular covenants) would be justified before God; but he expressly added to his citation of Psalm 143 the qualifying expression ἐξ ἔργων νόμου, indicating that Torah observers (and therefore members of the Sinai covenant) were *also* in the category of the non-justified.

Shortly later (Gal. 3:10–13), Paul would expressly affirm that the members of the Sinai covenant were, in fact, under a threatened curse sanction; and Israel's history, whether recounted in the canonical OT or in the later Jewish writings, routinely observed that the members of the covenant community were quite often judged to be "unrighteous/unjustified/cursed." Indeed, one could argue that one of Paul's more important concerns throughout his letters is to indicate that the members of the Sinai covenant were no more justified than those who were not members thereof:

> There will be tribulation and distress for every human being who does evil, the Jew first and also the Greek, but glory and honor and peace for everyone who does good, the Jew first and also the Greek. For God shows no partiality. For all who have sinned without the law will also perish without the law, and all who have sinned under the law will be judged by the law. For it is not the hearers of the law who are righteous before God, but the doers of the law who will be justified. (Rom. 2:9–13)

---

91. In the antecedent literature, the verb was always employed forensically profoundly more than the noun or adjective. In the Hebrew Bible, the verb was used forensically 82 percent of the time; in the LXX, 78 percent; in the Apocrypha, 92 percent; in the Pseudepigrapha, also 92 percent; and at Qumran, 82 percent. That Paul's usage follows this trend is hardly surprising.

92. "To put it in formulae: righteousness, *dikaiosyne*, is the status of the covenant member." N. T. Wright, *Justification: God's Plan & Paul's Vision* (Downers Grove, IL: InterVarsity, 2009), 134; cf. 12, 116, 121–22.

2.9. How Did We Get Here?

The question that occurs to me, having examined over eighteen hundred uses of the pertinent lexical stock in the literature antecedent to Paul, is this: How did we arrive at the present circumstance, where so many New Testament scholars assume that "the righteousness of God" is technical language, or shorthand language for God's saving power? That is, Käsemann's plausible hunch that the expression *might* be so construed in some *particular* texts has now become the majority presumption for many texts. I could find only seventeen texts where such a construal was plausible, and each of those was also as plausibly capable of an alternative construal. Well over a thousand of the pertinent texts were unquestionably ethical and almost three hundred were indisputably forensic. How, then, did we reach the point where Sam K. Williams could accurately state, "For example, most Pauline scholars now agree that in the OT and in Paul 'righteousness' designates conduct or activity appropriate to a relationship rather than an inherent quality, static attribute or absolute moral norm."[93]

We could, of course, leave the question unanswered and simply chalk it up to another example of the Alice Dictum ("Curiouser and curiouser!"). But it may also help to provide explanation, when "most Pauline scholars" hold a view that appears to be so profoundly unwarranted by an examination of the antecedent literature. I suggest that there are three ways of accounting for the discrepancy between "most Pauline scholars" and virtually all pre-Pauline texts.

First, I believe the matter may be due in part to scholarly deference. We do not, and indeed we cannot, independently investigate every sentence that every scholar makes. By its very nature, scholarship often (and rightly) "builds" on previous results from previous studies. When the Käsemann view was promoted by a growing cluster of first-rate New Testament scholars, and when that view even appeared in standard reference works (e.g., the two Achtemeier articles in *IDB*), it is not necessarily surprising that many individuals would simply defer to Cremer-Käsemann-Stuhlmacher-Achtemeiers, and then proceed under the assumption that this cluster's evaluation of the pertinent literature was correct. Such an assumption would be neither uncharitable nor unscholarly.

Second, I believe the discrepancy between the pertinent literature and the present scholarly consensus is due, in part, to the inability to search the Qumran material until comparatively recently. The entirety of the Qumran material from all of the caves was not available photographically until the early 1990s, and it was not digitized and formatted for machine searching until about the turn of the millennium.[94] The ability to test claims made about that literature has only recently become possible. Käsemann made a plausible conjecture about the meaning of "righteousness of God" at 1QS 11:14. Whether the conjecture was anything more than conjecture, however, depended upon the ability to do two things: one, investigate the immediate context of 1QS 11:12 (in which we find seven other uses of the root צדק that were unmentioned by Käsemann);

---

93. "The 'Righteousness of God' in Romans," 241–90.

94. An informative and engaging narrative of the process of preserving, reconstructing, publishing, and digitizing the DSS is provided in ch. 4, "Technology and the Dead Sea Scrolls," in James VanderKam and Peter Flint, *The Meaning of the Dead Sea Scrolls: Their Significance for Understanding the Bible, Judaism, Jesus, and Christianity* (New York: HarperCollins, 2002), 59–81.

and two, search the Qumran material in its entirety to determine whether the usage at 1QS 11:12 was usual or unusual within that corpus. While the first of these could have (should have?) been done by Käsemann himself, it could not have been done by the many others who may not yet have had access to the material, and the second could not have been done by any of us until roughly a decade ago. Now we can easily run a search and find three pertinent things. First, that the precise lexeme צדקת אל, on which so much of Käsemann's thesis depended, appeared only twice in all 471 appearances of the relevant root at Qumran (and therefore was unlikely to have had profound influence on the use of the lexical stock). Second, that even its two closest lexemes, צדקות אל and צדק אל, appeared only six times out of the 471 uses of the צדק stock in that literature (and therefore were also unlikely to have been influential in subsequent use). Third, that the ordinary ethical and forensic usages of the lexical stock are as common in the Qumran literature as they are in the Hebrew Bible, the LXX, the Apocrypha, and the Pseudepigrapha (that is, later Jewish sources did not employ the vocabulary stock any differently than it was used in the earlier canonical sources). For roughly a half century, claims could be made based on some texts in the Qumran literature that simply could not be tested. The coming half-century will and should put such claims to a test, now that we can run searches on the entirety of the literature to determine whether readings of particular texts are representative of the body of literature as a whole or whether those readings of particular texts are idiosyncratic or unusual.

A third way of accounting for the discrepancy between the way the lexical stock is used in the literature prior to Paul, and how it is understood by many Pauline scholars, is due to the understandable confusion of *association* with *definition* (whether "power" or "relationship"). That is, the God who disclosed himself to the Israelites did so through a series of covenants, none more determinative of their corporate life than the covenant made at Sinai. This covenant/treaty did indeed establish a covenant relationship between Yahweh and Israel, a relationship even analogous in some ways to a marriage covenant. Therefore, everything Israel learned about Yahweh was colored or flavored by this treaty relationship. Yahweh's truthfulness, for example, was not mere truthfulness in its general sense but truthfulness manifested through Yahweh's role as treaty suzerain. Yahweh's mercy, as another example, was exhibited by his role as covenant suzerain. In this sense, then, *each* of Yahweh's attributes was "relational," if we mean that Israel encountered these attributes as they were displayed by their covenant suzerain. In this sense, of course, Yahweh's "righteousness" was relational. But it was not any more relational than any of the *other* attributes he disclosed in his covenantal dealings with Israel. One could argue that his "vengeance of the covenant" (Lev. 26:25) was relational also, or his "anger" (Deut. 29:20; Judges 2:20; 2 Chron. 29:10) was relational, or his jealousy, mercy, and so on. That is, if each of Yahweh's attributes is disclosed via a covenant, then each of his attributes is "relational," but *none more so than the others*. "Righteousness" per se is not a relational term, in and of itself, as the variety of ethical synonyms and antonyms with which it is used in all five categories of antecedent literature indicates.

The same kind of confusion of association with definition might account for those various statements that suggest that "righteousness" *means* "saving power." Surely, the two are associated closely in some texts (in seventeen of the 1,829 texts). Especially in apocalyptic and eschatological texts, "salvation/deliverance" and "righteousness" sometimes appear simultaneously and/or in parallelism. But this is because the eschaton itself is inaugurated by a great act of judgment: a judicial act in which the covenant suzerain acknowledges the complaint of his penitent people, decides in their favor against the oppressing nations, and delivers his people from the threat. There is an association, in the courtroom, between "righteousness" and the judgment of the wicked oppressors, which judgment constitutes simultaneously the deliverance/salvation of the oppressed. But, for this very reason, "righteousness" is only "saving power" for the oppressed; it is condemning/destructive power for the oppressors. When Isaiah anticipated a "branch" from Jesse appearing, note that Isaiah referred to him as "righteous" and that his righteous activity will be dual-sided:

> With righteousness [בצדק] he shall judge the poor, and decide with equity for the meek of the earth; and he shall *strike the earth* with the rod of his mouth, and with the breath of his lips he *shall kill the wicked*. Righteousness [צדק] shall be the belt of his waist, and faithfulness the belt of his loins. (Isa. 11:4–5)

If, as so many say today, the "righteousness of God" is revealed when he "makes things right" for the innocent and godly, then it is equally true that the "righteousness of God" is revealed when he makes things very, very *wrong* for the wicked: "Destruction is decreed, overflowing with righteousness [צדקה]" (Isa. 10:22).

Some proponents of the righteousness-as-saving-power view appear to have recognized that "saving" power for the upright was often destructive for the wicked. Elizabeth Achtemeier recognized that "righteousness" was often associated with an act of delivering the Israelites that was also an act of destruction/judgment of their enemies:

> His righteous judgments restore the right to those from whom it has been taken, but they also put down the wicked. Those judgments which bring salvation for Israel at the same time bring destruction upon her foes. . . . There are two sides to his righteousness: salvation and condemnation; deliverance and punishment.[95]

Achtemeier recognized that "righteousness" is not purely or exclusively soteric; it often includes acts of judicial destruction. If such a qualification were consistently made, then it would be mostly unobjectionable. We could say something such as this: "Righteousness" is a soteric term, but soteric in the destructive sense of the term. The problem then largely becomes one of quibbling and semantics. But not one in a hundred people thinks of "soteric" as a destructive term, and not one in a hundred thinks of "saving" power as destructive power. It is, therefore, unnecessarily misleading to suggest that "righteousness" is soteric; but it is not at all misleading to say that it is juridical, judicial, or forensic. These terms are associated with the right treatment, respectively, of *both* the wicked *and* the upright; these terms, and the concepts to which they point, routinely recognize that justice metes out different rewards for different behaviors. "Saving power," by contrast, ordinarily denotes rescue or deliverance *from* destruction or threat.

We could illustrate this from the Noahic flood. If we polled a thousand people and asked whether the Noahic flood was judicial or soteric, I would be surprised if any

---

95. "Righteousness in the Old Testament," 83.

said it was soteric. All would regard it (rightly) as an act of judgment. Peter, however, perceived the flood judgment as also having a soteric dimension: "While the ark was being prepared, in which a few, that is, eight persons, were brought safely [διεσώθησαν, KJV/RSV/NRSV 'were saved'] through water" (1 Pet. 3:20). In a technical sense, then, one could say with the apostle Peter that the Noahic flood had a soteric dimension, since Noah and seven others were "saved" from the deluge that destroyed the rest of the inhabited world. But this is a peculiar usage; and even as a peculiar usage, Peter qualifies the matter twice: first by adding the prefix διά to the verb σῴζω, and second by expressly designating the ark—not the flood waters—as the soteric instrument. Insofar as the eschatological state begins with an act of righteous judgment, and insofar as this act of righteous judgment therefore delivers/saves the innocent from the wicked, there is a strong *association* between "righteousness" and eschatological/soteric activity.

"Righteousness" is also associated with the eschaton insofar as the eschatological state is routinely perceived as a morally rejuvenated reality, where the people of God imitate God's various virtues. The same "power" that vanquishes the wicked rejuvenates the righteous and confirms them in upright behavior: "Then justice will dwell in the wilderness, and righteousness abide in the fruitful field. And the effect of righteousness will be peace, and the result of righteousness, quietness and trust forever" (Isa. 32:16–17).

"Righteousness" is therefore associated with the eschaton, when Yahweh's saving power will be expressed. But that eschaton will be a time of great judicial activity and a time of great moral renewal. "Righteousness," in these eschatological texts, does not take on a new meaning,[96] apart from its ordinary ethical and forensic meanings; rather, in the eschaton, as a perfected state, we witness *both* judicial righteousness *and* ethical righteousness in their most perfect expression. But the same eschatological power that displays "righteousness" in a previously-only-hoped-for form also enacts perfected expressions of truth, mercy, shalom, and so on. *All* ideals are perfected in the eschaton, virtually by definition, and the association of each of these ideals with the saving power that creates them does not mean that any of these ideals *means* "saving power."

When "salvation" comes, many other things will come also, including peace, righteousness, and judgment (among others; this graphic is not intended to be comprehensive). It is not surprising, therefore, that there are many texts that associate "salvation" with "peace," "righteousness," or "judgment." There is no salvation without the judgment of the wicked who resist God's reign; there is no salvation if God's people are not morally renewed in righteous behavior; there is no salvation until/unless comprehensive shalom replaces the Adamic curse in the material and social arenas. But neither "peace" nor "righteousness" nor "judgment" *means* "salvation" or "saving power."

---

96. Throughout this excursus, I suppose I have been promoting in the lexical arena what the empirical scientists promote in their arena: parsimony. A simpler explanation—provided that it does not oversimplify and therefore distort the matter—is preferable to a less simple explanation. Since the antonyms and synonyms (both in Hebrew and in Greek) for the pertinent lexical stocks routinely pair the "righteous" vocabulary with other ethical vocabulary (and, by extension, with forensic vocabulary), we need not propose another semantic realm unless the ethical/forensic understanding cannot make sense of the data. And (here the parsimony) if we *need* not propose another semantic realm, then we *should* not propose one.

EXCURSUS 3

Getting Out and Staying Out:
Israel's Dilemma at Sinai[1]

3.1. Introduction

When E. P. Sanders wrote about "comparing patterns of religion," he was concerned to find some way of evaluating religious traditions that wasn't inherently prejudiced against some of them. He thought that it is especially unhelpful to compare one religion by the standards or emphases of another.[2] This was and is all well and good as far as it goes, but even here, "patterns of religion" has its limits for understanding the Holy Scriptures, as I will attempt to make clear. Further, even Sanders's apparently neutral "getting in and staying in" has substantial inadequacies, especially for explaining the Sinai covenant. The assumption behind such language is not merely that all religions discuss getting in and staying in, but that they do so because the parties *desire* to get in and stay in—an assumption that does not comport well with the realities of the Sinai covenant.

3.2. "Religion" versus "Covenant"

The Scriptures record a series of treaties/covenants;[3] some of them are more religious, some of them less. Neither the prediluvian nor the postdiluvian treaty with Noah is particularly religious. The first prepares Noah, his family, and the animal kingdom to evade coming judgment; and the second assures the same that God will not continue to judge the earth in this manner, but that he will delay his judgment until the conclusion of history. But at least by any ordinary definition of "religion," there simply isn't much religion in either of these covenants. To understand this literature, then, we need to understand the patterns of particular treaties,[4] not "patterns of religion." Geerhardus Vos was right:

---

1. This first appeared, apart from slight modifications, in *Pittsburgh Theological Review* 3 (2011–12): 23–37.

2. E. P. Sanders, *Paul and Palestinian Judaism: A Comparison of Patterns of Religion* (Philadelphia: Fortress, 1977), esp. ch. 2, "The holistic comparison of patterns of religion," 12–32.

3. For our purposes, I employ the terms "treaty" and "covenant" interchangeably, with no intention to distinguish the one from the other. I vary them for variety only.

4. διαθήκη can also mean "testament," as it routinely does in the Testaments of the Twelve Patriarchs, for instance. But in the OT literature, its common use is to translate *berith* as "treaty."

The Bible is, as it were, conscious of its own organism; it feels, what we cannot always say of ourselves, its own anatomy. The principle of successive *Berith*-makings (Covenant-makings), as marking the introduction of new periods, plays a large role in this, and should be carefully heeded.[5]

Treaties differ. Some are advantageous to be a party to and some are not. I regard the Abrahamic covenant to have been advantageous: God simply pledged to an older, childless couple that he would give them numerous descendants, give their descendants a marvelous arable land, and one day bless all the nations of the world through one of their descendants.[6] This strikes me as advantageous in every manner. On the other hand, the covenant with Phinehas that his descendants would be priests, while religious, is not especially advantageous. Slaughtering and sacrificing animals is probably distasteful in some respects, and surely there was an occasional Levite who might have wished to pursue a career in another field. Thus "getting in" some covenants is more advantageous than others; for some, depending on their terms, it might be preferable to "get out" rather than to get in.

3.3. "Getting Out and Staying Out"

The least advantageous biblical covenant for anyone would likely be the Sinai covenant. The circumstances of its inauguration were terrifying: thunder, lightning, smoke, and a loud trumpet—phenomena that made the Israelites tremble in fear (Exod. 19:16; Deut. 5:6; Heb. 12:19). All of the available evidence suggests that the Sinai treaty might be better thought of as one where the goal is to get out and stay out, rather than to get in and stay in.[7] "Getting in" the Sinai covenant, that is, was analogous to getting in the Titanic. Israel did not desire to enter the covenant before it was inaugurated, and they did not desire to remain in it once it was inaugurated; more than once they expressed their preference to return to Egyptian bondage, and they even expressed their opinion that Yahweh delivered them from Egypt because he "hated" them (Deut. 1:27). They grumbled against the mediators of that covenant, and they persecuted and put to death the executors of its prophetic lawsuit. In most of what follows, I will simply permit the evidence to speak for itself, citing texts that indicate how frightening and/or burden-some "getting in" and "staying in" was for the people in this covenant.

---

5. Geerhardus Vos, *Biblical Theology of the Old and New Testaments* (Grand Rapids: Eerdmans, 1948), 16.

6. In the original pledge, it was unclear whether the blessings would come through Abraham's descendants in their plurality or through a particular individual descendant. This is due to the ambiguity inherent in a collective noun such as זֶרַע. Since the LXX translators had no equivalent collective noun at their disposal, they were forced to choose either a singular or plural form of σπέρμα. At Gen. 22:18, then, they elected to employ the singular (ἐν τῷ σπέρματί σου), a translation that Paul approved in Gal. 3:16 (οὐ λέγει· καὶ τοῖς σπέρμασιν, ὡς ἐπὶ πολλῶν ἀλλ᾽ ὡς ἐφ᾽ ἑνός· καὶ τῷ σπέρματί σου, ὅς ἐστιν Χριστός.).

7. I speak of Israel corporately here; below I will clarify that the individuals within the "remnant" of Israel might have had a different point of view. As a nation or a corporate group, however, Israel was justifiably terrified about entering this covenant.

3.3.1. Evidence before the Treaty

Before the Sinai covenant was instituted, there were many phenomena that the Israelites found frighteningly off-putting:

> The LORD said to Moses, "Go to the people and consecrate them today and tomorrow, and let them wash their garments and be ready for the third day. For on the third day the LORD will come down on Mount Sinai in the sight of all the people. And you shall set *limits* for the people all around, saying, 'Take care *not to go up* into the mountain or touch the edge of it. Whoever touches the mountain *shall be put to death.* . . . On the morning of the third day there were *thunders and lightnings and a thick cloud on the mountain and a very loud trumpet blast,* so that all the people in the camp *trembled.* . . . And the LORD said to him, "Go down, and come up bringing Aaron with you. But do not let the priests and the people break through to come up to the LORD, *lest he break out against them."* (Exod. 19:10–12, 16, 24; emphases added)

Verse 24 is disturbingly proleptic of Israel's subsequent future under this covenant administration, because Yahweh did indeed "break out against them" on numerous occasions.[8]

3.3.2. Evidence Immediately after the Treaty

This fear that Yahweh would break out against them was not assuaged by the inaugurating of the covenant; to the contrary, the instituting of the covenant filled the Israelites with more dread:

> Now when all the people saw the thunder and the flashes of lightning and the sound of the trumpet and the mountain smoking, the *people were afraid and trembled,* and they *stood far off* and said to Moses, "You speak to us, and we will listen; but do not let God speak to us, *lest we die."* (Exod. 20:18–19; cf. Deut. 5:25; emphases added)

3.3.3. Evidence That the Israelites Preferred Their Tenure in Egypt

Yahweh did indeed "break out against them" again and again. Charlton Heston saw more of the Promised Land than Moses did, because Yahweh judged the Israelites for their sins in the wilderness. He sent fiery serpents upon them and "they bit the people, so that many people of Israel died" (Num. 21:6). This pattern began shortly after the treaty was inaugurated. While we may tend to romanticize the Exodus, and while it surely was the central event of Israel's history, Israel did not universally regard it as a good thing. They were delivered from one severe taskmaster to serve another, whom they judged to be even more severe.

---

8. I'm a little surprised that N. T. Wright refers to Deut. 27–30 as referring to the exile. While the Babylonian exile was perhaps the supreme expression of the curse sanctions of Deut. 27–30, death by serpents, defeat by the Assyrians, and a divided kingdom were also expressions of the curse sanctions of these chapters. Perhaps that is all Wright means: that the most extreme curse sanction mentioned in those chapters is defeated and scattered by a foreign nation. *Justification: God's Plan & Paul's Vision* (Downers Grove, IL: InterVarsity, 2009), 60–61, 63, 241–42.

> But the people thirsted there for water, and the people grumbled against Moses and said, "Why did you bring us up out of Egypt, to kill us and our children and our livestock with thirst?" (Exod. 17:3)

> And all the people of Israel grumbled against Moses and Aaron. The whole congregation said to them, "Would that we had died in the land of Egypt! Or would that we had died in this wilderness!" (Num. 14:2)

> "And you murmured in your tents and said, 'Because the LORD hated us he has brought us out of the land of Egypt, to give us into the hand of the Amorites, to destroy us.'" (Deut. 1:27)

> "And say to the people, 'Consecrate yourselves for tomorrow, and you shall eat meat, for you have wept in the hearing of the LORD, saying, "Who will give us meat to eat? For it was better for us in Egypt." Therefore the LORD will give you meat, and you shall eat.'" (Num. 11:18)

> "Why is the LORD bringing us into this land, to fall by the sword? Our wives and our little ones will become a prey. Would it not be better for us to go back to Egypt?" (Num. 14:3)

Some might argue that in each case the language is merely temporary anguish or exasperation; and, if there were not a wide body of literature suggesting the contrary, I would take it to be so myself. But these texts tend to speak of the nation as a whole, whereas most of the language that celebrates the Sinai covenant is the language of the minority/remnant. For the majority of the Israelites, throughout the majority of their history, laments such as these were common and understandable. Serving as slave laborers for the Egyptians would surely have been unpleasant in many ways, but at least the Egyptians never broke out against them and never sent poisonous reptiles to bite and kill them. It would have been contrary to Egyptian national interest to destroy its own slave labor force. But apparently it was not contrary to Yahweh's interest to do this; so, at least in this regard, the Israelites were indeed better off in Egypt.

3.3.4. The Prophetic Evidence

The prophetic evidence that the Sinai covenant was no bargain is interesting. Because they were bearers of the covenant lawsuit (ריב), they spent the majority of their respective careers declaring God's judgment on the Israelites.

> "Hear the word of the LORD, O house of Jacob, and all the clans of the house of Israel. Thus says the LORD: 'What wrong did your fathers find in me that they went far from me, and went after worthlessness, and became worthless? They did not say, "Where is the LORD who brought us up from the land of Egypt, who led us in the wilderness, in a land of deserts and pits, in a land of drought and deep darkness, in a land that none passes through, where no man dwells?" And I brought you into a plentiful land to enjoy its fruits and its good things. But when you came in, you defiled my land and made my heritage an abomination. The priests did not say, "Where is the LORD?" Those who handle the law did not know me; the shepherds transgressed against me; the prophets prophesied by Baal and went after things that do not profit. Therefore I still contend [אריב] with you,' declares the LORD, 'and with your children's children I will contend [אריב].'" (Jer. 2:4–9)

The Israelites, for their part, responded to these rebukes in an interesting manner. They had a virtual "open season" on the prophets, putting them to death with remarkable consistency. This murderous treatment of the prophets is candidly recorded in both the Old and New Testament Scriptures.

[Elijah] said, "I have been very jealous for the LORD, the God of hosts. For the people of Israel have *forsaken your covenant*, thrown down your altars, and *killed your prophets* with the sword, and I, even I only, am left, and they seek my life, to take it away." (1 Kings 19:10)

"Nevertheless, they were disobedient and rebelled against you and cast your law behind their back and *killed your prophets*, who had warned them in order to turn them back to you, and they committed great blasphemies." (Neh. 9:26)

"Thus you witness against yourselves that you are sons of those who *murdered the prophets*." (Matt. 23:31)

"Woe to you! For you build the tombs of *the prophets whom your fathers killed*." (Luke 11:47)

"You stiff-necked people, uncircumcised in heart and ears, you always resist the Holy Spirit. As your fathers did, so do you. *Which of the prophets did not your fathers persecute?*[9] And *they killed those* who announced beforehand the coming of the Righteous One, whom you have now betrayed and *murdered*, you who received the law as delivered by angels and did not keep it." (Acts 7:51–53)

For you, brothers, became imitators of the churches of God in Christ Jesus that are in Judea. For you suffered the same things from your own countrymen as they did from the Jews, who *killed both the Lord Jesus and the prophets*, and drove us out. (1 Thess. 2:14–15)

Why all of this prophet-killing? Why not hunt deer, as we do in western Pennsylvania? Because Israel was trying to get *out of* the Sinai covenant, *out* from under the burden of its threatened curse sanctions, and *out* from under the prophets' condemning lawsuit against them. The consistent "pattern of religion" from the initial days to its concluding days was that the Israelites attempted to get *out* of this covenant. "Getting in" this covenant frightened them, and "staying in" it was burdensome.

3.4. The Conditional (and Often Capital) Nature of the Sinai Treaty

The reason for all of this resistance to the Sinai covenant was and is fairly evident: its only proposed benefits were conditional on the obedience of the Israelites. Six tribes stood on Mount Gerizim holding forth conditional blessings, while six tribes stood on Mount Ebal holding forth conditional cursings (Deut. 27; Josh. 8:33–34):

"Now therefore, *if you will indeed obey* my voice and keep my covenant, you shall be my treasured possession among all peoples, for all the earth is mine; and you shall be to me

---

9. Stephen's rhetorical question is one of the boldest in history. Think of how easily he could have been refuted, if his claim were false. All someone had to say was, "Well, there was So-and-so." But no one did say this, because no one could. Characteristically, the prophets were indeed put to death by the Israelites.

a kingdom of priests and a holy nation. These are the words that you shall speak to the people of Israel." (Exod. 19:5–6)

If they obeyed, then their tenure in Canaan would be blessed; but if they disobeyed, then their tenure would be cursed.[10] Of course, as the story played out, the Israelites ordinarily disobeyed and were ordinarily cursed.

These curses were not gentle slaps on the wrist. As was the case in Numbers 21, God often inflicted death as punishment. To inflict such punishment, he employed serpents, Assyrians, and Babylonians—but death it was. Furthermore, the laws that were part of that covenant were filled with capital crimes that, if committed by individuals, required their being put to death. Among those capital crimes were manslaughter (Exod. 21:12), negligent homicide (Exod. 21:29), cursing one's parents (Exod. 21:17; Lev. 20:9), striking one's parents (Exod. 21:15), adultery (Lev. 20:10), homosexuality (Lev. 20:13), bestiality (Exod. 22:19; Lev. 20:15–16), incest (Lev. 20:11–12), kidnapping (Exod. 21:16), Sabbath-breaking (Exod. 31:14–15), sacrificing children to Molech (Lev. 20:2), sorcery (Lev. 20:27; Deut. 13:5), blasphemy (Lev. 24:16–17), entering the tabernacle unlawfully (Num. 1:51), and rebellion against lawful authority (Josh. 1:18).[11]

The apostle Paul, therefore, was not employing ministerial or apostolic exaggeration when he candidly referred to this covenant administration as an administration of "death" and "condemnation" (2 Cor. 3:7, 9). It *threatened* condemnation and death, it ordinarily *brought* condemnation and death, and it required some of its members to put others of its members *to* death. This is perhaps why Paul called the Sinai covenant "Hagar," because it was a covenant that bore children "for slavery" (Gal. 4:24).[12] At an existential level, then, the typical Israelite was probably a good deal more interested in "getting *out*" and "staying *out*" than in "getting in" or "staying in."

---

10. So, e.g., Douglas J. Moo: "For, while *torah* may in its root sense mean 'instruction,' the *Mosaic torah* is instruction *with sanctions*" (emphases original). " 'Law,' 'Works of the Law,' and Legalism in Paul," *Westminster Theological Journal* 45 (1983): 83. In a footnote, Moo rightly refers favorably to Walther Zimmerli's recognition of the significance of these sanctions, and he equally (and correctly) refers unfavorably to both von Rad and Noth for failing to estimate rightly the significance of them. Indeed, the *Interpreters Dictionary of the Bible*, 4 vols. (Nashville: Abingdon, 1962), e.g., has no entry on "sanction," and its entry on "curse" makes no reference to its role in the covenant. It is as though one or two generations of scholars simply overlooked this important covenantal reality. Happily, N. T. Wright has recognized the importance of these sanctions: "All this is the language of the covenant (Daniel 9:4), more specifically, of the covenant in Deuteronomy 27–30. . . . There were the terms and the conditions; Israel broke them; and the exile—the specific covenantal curse—has come upon the people." *Justification*, 63.

11. Those who object to Israel having so many capital crimes may be semi-consoled to know that its laws also attempted to evade/avoid abuses by requiring, for instance, multiple witnesses for capital crimes (Num. 35:30; Deut. 17:6).

12. When Paul said regarding Abraham's two wives "these women are two covenants [αὗται γάρ εἰσιν δύο διαθῆκαι]. One is from Mount Sinai, bearing children for slavery; she is Hagar," there is some legitimate debate as to whether he is contrasting Sinai to the Abrahamic covenant, on the one hand, or to the new covenant, on the other. I think, in light of the five contrasts he observes between the Abrahamic and Sinai covenants in chapter 3, the more likely contrast is between Sinai and Abraham. For our purposes, however, it is enough to note that he candidly described the "covenant" itself, made on Mount Sinai (and not some later alleged Jewish perversion thereof) as the one that enslaved its children.

3.5. Proto-Conclusion

I do not suggest that it was pious, right, or obedient for the Israelites to resist getting in and staying in this covenant. Yahweh, like Godfather Vito Corleone, makes offers we cannot refuse. It was sinful and rebellious for Israel to resist the yoke of this covenant, burdensome though it was. It was indeed burdensome and neither getting into this covenant originally at Mount Horeb nor staying in it under the administration of Moses or the prophets was any bargain. Sanders's proposal that we compare religions by studying how they address the question of "getting in" and "staying in" is not really suitable for understanding the covenant administration made at Sinai, because there is actually more evidence that Israel desired to get *out* of that covenant than to stay *in* it.[13]

Sanders was and is right that Israel "got in" the Sinai covenant by divine election. But he and his followers suggest that they "stayed in" the covenant by faithful obedience. In point of fact, however, Israel could not "get out" of that covenant by their disobedience. When they obeyed, they were in the covenant; when they disobeyed, they still remained in the covenant. In the one circumstance, they received the blessings of the covenant; in the other, they received its curses. But in both circumstances, they remained in the Sinai covenant; the curses themselves were *covenant* sanctions. There was nothing they could do to get out of it; if there had been such a way to get out, they would have exercised it, which was their consistent stated desire. They were unconditionally in that covenant; nothing they did or did not do was requisite to "stay in," other than the divine election by which they "got in."[14]

So, for Israel at Sinai (and subsequent thereto), there was no difference between "getting in" and "staying in." They got in *and* stayed in by the same condition: divine election. It is misleading, therefore, to examine or compare a "pattern of religion" at Sinai by suggesting that the terms of getting in *differed* from the terms of staying in. It is even more misleading to suggest or imply that the Israelites ever *desired* to get in or stay in that covenant. The consistent testimony of the Holy Scriptures, from before the inauguration of that covenant until its conclusion, is that the Israelites wished that Yahweh had chosen someone else. To be sure, the pious within Israel loved the world's Creator/Redeemer, and they loved the revelation he gave them.[15] But the covenant was not made with the pious *within* Israel; it was made with the *entire* nation, whether

---

13. I don't believe Sanders or his followers would necessarily dispute this. They would probably say that what they *mean* by "staying in" the Sinai covenant is something like "staying in without the prophets bringing a successful suit against us, and without Yahweh sending snakes, Assyrians, and Babylonians to sanction us." But then, what is the value of "staying in" as an expression to compare patterns of religion, when there are many other religions that do not threaten such sanctions? Do Buddhists worry about serpents and Assyrians?

14. This divine election, while sovereign, is not, properly speaking, "gracious." While people commonly refer to God's "gracious" election of Israel, the people of Israel thought that by imposing this covenant on them God "hated" them. They certainly do not appear to have regarded the covenant itself or election thereto as "gracious" in any ordinary sense of the term.

15. "Oh how I love your law! It is my meditation all the day" (Ps. 119:97). Perhaps too much is made of this single declaration about loving the law by the psalmist. Only in this psalm (at vv. 113, 163, and 165 also) does anyone in the entire Bible talk about loving the law. Considering how central Torah was to Israel, I regard it as surprising that there is only one chapter, and four verses within that chapter, where anyone expresses love for Torah. Though there was remarkable

pious or impious, obedient or disobedient. The entire nation—all twelve tribes—were represented on Mounts Ebal and Gerizim; and all twelve took upon themselves the conditional cursings and blessings articulated on the two mounts, with full awareness that this covenant could have either outcome.

I do not hesitate to add here that the result would have been the same regardless of the nation/clan God covenanted with in this manner. Had he appeared to the Gordon clan in central Virginia and offered us a covenant in which he proffered either blessings or cursings in the Commonwealth of Virginia, depending upon our obedience, we would have resisted this yoke just as the Israelites did; we would have disobeyed its commands just as the Israelites did; and we would have suffered the curse sanctions just as the Israelites did. So, if my view is anti-Semitic, it is equally anti-Gordonic. Anyone who agrees with the apostle Paul that all humans, Jew or Gentile, are "under sin" (Rom. 3:9) realizes the futility of a covenant whose proffered blessings depend upon the obedience of sinners.[16]

Sanders never addressed the possibility that there would be a religion one could not get out of. For him, "staying in" was tacitly thought to be an aspect of any given religion, and that each religion would have provisions for doing so. But there were and are some treaties in which there simply is no exit (with due apologies to Jean-Paul Sartre). "Staying in," for such treaties, is a nonissue, because one party (in this case the Israelites) simply cannot get out.

3.6. E. P. Sanders's Followers

Typically, the followers of E. P. Sanders also have some difficulty dealing with a religion that is informed by a number of diverse treaties. They tend to confuse the various covenants in the Old Testament (often speaking about "the covenant," without specifying which treaty they are referring to);[17] they regard them as soteric and even, at times,

---

moral wisdom in it, that wisdom always had sanctions attached to it, and those sanctions were a frightening burden.

16. As T. L. Donaldson has put it, "Israel, the people of the law, thus functions as a kind of representative sample of the whole. Their plight is no different from the plight of the whole of humankind, but through the operation of the law in their situation that plight is thrown into sharp relief." Donaldson, "The 'Curse of the Law' and the Inclusion of the Gentiles: Galatians 3.13–14," *New Testament Studies* 32, no. 1 (January 1986): 104.

17. N. T. Wright has recently been clearer about what he means. "Here we have it: *God's single plan, through Abraham and his family, to bless the whole world.* This is what I have meant by the word *covenant* when I have used it as shorthand in writing about Paul. . . . The 'covenant,' in my shorthand, is not something other than God's determination to deal with evil once and for all and so put the whole creation (and humankind with it) right at last." Cf. *Justification*, 67, 95 (emphases original). This is much clearer, and Wright's clarification regarding his "shorthand" is much appreciated. In my judgment, Wright's "covenant" is then virtually identical with what the Reformed tradition ordinarily calls "the covenant of grace," and it is no worse or better than the common convention (except that, by employing a different convention, he misled some of us unwittingly until this recent clarification was made). I would still suggest that such a definition of "covenant" (as I have always complained about the similar "covenant of grace") uses a biblical term unbiblically, which is something Wright warns against on pp. 81–82 of the same volume. That is, biblically, a *berith* or a *diatheke* is always a historical treaty of some sort, enacted

suggest that to be "in the covenant" is the virtual equivalent of being justified. This is confusing and unhelpful. The Abrahamic covenant differs from the Sinai covenant in at least four ways.[18] The Abrahamic covenant justifies (Gal. 3:6–8); the Sinai covenant does not (Gal. 3:11–12). The Abrahamic covenant blesses (Gal. 3:8–9, 14); the Sinai covenant curses (Gal. 3:10, 13). The Abrahamic covenant is pistic (Gal. 3:6–9); the Sinai covenant is legal ("the law is not of faith," Gal. 3:10–12). The Abrahamic covenant is characterized by "promise" (Gal. 3:17); the Sinai covenant is characterized by "law" (Gal. 3:17). Sanders and his followers tend to amalgamate the series of seven (or eight) Old Testament covenants, and they refer to the hodgepodge of all seven as "the covenant," though some of these treaties are quite different from one another.

Further, when Dunn or Wright suggest that being "in the covenant" (whichever one they mean) means to be justified, or that it is somehow soteric to be "in the covenant," there is an enormous amount of explaining to do.[19] When the prophets declared God's condemnation and judgment (not justification) on the Israelites for their disobedience, they were still "in the (Sinai) covenant," and the sanctions that followed their prophetic lawsuit were precisely the sanctions of the covenant. Those sanctions, threatened in the concluding chapters of Deuteronomy, came upon them precisely because they were *in* the covenant. When Gentiles, who were not in that covenant, had the same behavior, Yahweh left them alone and visited no sanctions upon them at all. Why? Not because the Gentiles were "in the covenant," but because they were *not* "in the covenant." Since the Gentiles had no representatives at Mount Ebal threatening cursings, the Gentiles did not experience such.[20]

E. P. Sanders has rightly challenged the academic community to be careful about comparing religions by terms that favor some religions to others. He also has rightly attempted to find some "neutral" categories, as it were, by which this can be done. If we can find such categories, then by all means we should employ them. But if the categories prevent an accurate assessment of some or all of those religions (or aspects thereof), then the categories must be jettisoned. The Hebrew Scriptures record a series of treaties—treaties that work toward a common purpose but vary in some important ways from one another, and some of these treaties did not have an escape clause. Getting in and staying in were by the same means: divine election. The sons of Phinehas

---

in space and time with particular parties; it is not an eternal purpose or decree to rescue the creation or any part thereof.

18. Cf. my "Abraham and Sinai Contrasted in Galatians 3:6–14," in *The Law Is Not of Faith: Essays on Works and Grace in the Mosaic Covenant*, ed. Bryan Estelle, J. V. Fesko, and David VanDrunen (Phillipsburg, NJ: P&R, 2009), 240–58.

19. James D. G. Dunn: "God's justification is rather God's acknowledgement that someone is in the covenant." Dunn, "The New Perspective on Paul," 190. Wright: "Justification in this setting, then, is not a matter of how someone enters the community of the true people of God, but of how you tell who belongs to that community. . . . Within this context, 'justification,' as seen in 3:24–26, means that those who believe in Jesus Christ are declared to be members of the true covenant family." *What St. Paul Really Said*, 119, 129.

20. The only exception to this general principle was when the Gentile nations invaded Israel. Then, Yahweh often (but not always!) undertook the role of divine warrior and conquered the Gentiles. Ordinarily, however, the Gentiles lived unscathed by Yahweh's judgment if they just left Israel alone. If the Israelites were idolatrous, then Yahweh judged them; if the Canaanites were idolatrous, then Yahweh let them be.

may have been "worthless men" (1 Sam. 2:12), but they were not thereby exempt from God's sovereign election of them as priests. David may well have been a "man of blood" (2 Sam. 16:7–8), but his lineage could not escape God's sovereign election of them to build a permanent house in Jerusalem. Similarly, the Israelites (except for the pious "remnant") may have wished that Moses never yoked them to Yahweh at Sinai; but he did, and they were, and nothing could be done about it. Though resistant, they "got in" against their wishes. Once in, they attempted to forsake the covenant, but they could not escape its lawsuit or sanctions; they "stayed in" against their wishes. Until Jeremiah's "new covenant" rendered the previous covenant obsolete, and until an "easy" yoke was offered as an alternative (Matt. 11:30), a yoke remained on their necks "that neither our fathers nor we have been able to bear" (Acts 15:10). Existentially, then, the majority of the Israelites (except the "remnant") actually wished to "get out" of the Sinai covenant and "stay out" of it. Therefore, "getting in" and "staying in" are not descriptively helpful in explaining this treaty.

Bibliography

Bachmann, Michael. *Anti-Judaism in Galatians? Exegetical Studies on a Polemical Letter and on Paul's Theology*. Translated by Robert L. Brawley. Grand Rapids: Eerdmans, 2008.

Barrick, William D. "The New Perspective and "Works of the Law" (Gal 2:16 and Rom 3:20)." *Master's Seminary Journal* 16, no. 2 (September 1, 2005): 277–92.

Baugh, Steven M. "Galatians 3:20 and the Covenant of Redemption." *Westminster Theological Journal* 66, no. 1 (March 1, 2004): 49–70.

Beale, Gregory K. "Peace and Mercy upon the Israel of God. The Old Testament Background of Galatians 6,16b." *Biblica* 80 (1999): 204–23.

Belleville, Linda L. " 'Under law': Structural Analysis and the Pauline Concept of Law in Galatians 3:21–4:11." *Journal for the Study of the New Testament* 26 (February 1, 1986): 53–78.

Bird, Michael F., and Preston M. Sprinkle, eds. *The Faith of Jesus Christ: Exegetical, Biblical, and Theological Studies*. Colorado Springs: Paternoster, 2009.

Boer, Martinus C. de. "Paul's Use and Interpretation of a Justification Tradition in Galatians 2.15–21." *Journal for the Study of the New Testament* 28, no. 2 (December 1, 2005): 189–216.

Bonneau, Normand. "The Logic of Paul's Argument on the Curse of the Law in Galatians 3:10–14." *Novum testamentum* 39, no. 1 (January 1, 1997): 60–80.

Braswell, Joseph P. " 'The Blessing of Abraham' Versus 'the Curse of the Law': Another Look at Gal 3:10–13." *Westminster Theological Journal* 53, no. 1 (March 1, 1991): 73–91.

Brondos, David A. "The Cross and the Curse: Galatians 3.13 and Paul's Doctrine of Redemption." *Journal for the Study of the New Testament* no. 81 (March 1, 2001): 3–32.

Campbell, D. A. "The Meaning of ΠΙΣΤΙΣ and ΝΟΜΟΣ in Paul: A Linguistic and Structural Perspective." *Journal of Biblical Literature* 111, no. 1 (March 1, 1992): 91–103.

Campbell, Douglas A. "Galatians 5.11: Evidence of an Early Law-Observant Mission by Paul?" *New Testament Studies* 57, no. 3 (July 2011): 325–47.

Carson, D. A., Peter T. O'Brien, and Mark A. Seifrid, eds. *Justification and Variegated Nomism: A Fresh Appraisal of Paul and Second Temple Judaism*. 2 vols. Grand Rapids: Baker, 2004.

Chester, Stephen J. "When the Old was New: Reformation Perspectives on Galatians 2:16." *Expository Times* 119, no. 7 (April 1, 2008): 320–29.

Choi, Hung-Sik. "Pistis in Galatians 5:5–6: Neglected Evidence for the Faithfulness of Christ." *Journal of Biblical Literature* 124, no. 3 (September 1, 2005): 467–90.

Cosgrove, Charles H. "Arguing like a Mere Human Being Galatians 3.15–18 in Rhetorical Perspective." *New Testament Studies* 34 (1988): 536–49.

Das, A. Andrew. "Another Look at *ean mē* in Galatians 2:16." *Journal of Biblical Literature* 119, no. 3 (September 1, 2000): 529–39.

———. "The Irony of Galatians: Paul's Letter in First-Century Context." *Interpretation* 57, no. 3 (July 1, 2003): 328–30.

Donaldson, T. L. "The 'Curse of the Law' and the Inclusion of the Gentiles: Galatians 3:13–14." *New Testament Studies* 32 (1986): 95–99.

―――. "Israelite, Convert, Apostle to the Gentiles: The Origin of Paul's Gentile Mission." In *The Road from Damascus: The Impact of Paul's Conversion on His Life, Thought, and Ministry*, edited by Richard Longenecker, 62–83. Grand Rapids: Eerdmans, 1997.

―――. *Paul and the Gentiles: Remapping the Apostle's Convictional World.* Minneapolis: Fortress, 1997.

Dunn, James D. G. "'A Light to the Gentiles,' or 'The End of the Law'? The Significance of the Damascus Road Christophany for Paul." *Jesus, Paul, and the Law: Studies in Mark and Galatians.* Louisville: Westminster/John Knox, 1990.

―――. "The New Perspective on Paul." *Jesus, Paul, and the Law: Studies in Mark and Galatians.* Louisville, KY: Westminster/John Knox, 1990.

―――, ed. *Paul and the Mosaic Law.* Grand Rapids: Eerdmans, 2001.

―――. *The Theology of Paul the Apostle.* Grand Rapids: Eerdmans, 1998.

―――. "Works of the Law and the Curse of the Law." *Jesus, Paul, and the Law: Studies in Mark and Galatians.* Louisville, KY: Westminster/John Knox, 1990.

Garlington, Don B. "'Even We Have Believed': Galatians 2:15–16 Revisited." *Criswell Theological Review* 7, no. 1 (September 1, 2009): 3–28.

―――. "Paul's 'Partisan ἐκ' and the Question of Justification in Galatians." *Journal of Biblical Literature* 127, no. 3 (September 1, 2008): 567–89.

―――. "Role Reversal and Paul's Use of Scripture in Galatians 3.10–13." *Journal for the Study of the New Testament* 65 (March 1, 1997): 85–121.

Goddard, A. J., and Stephen Anthony Cummins. "Ill or Ill-Treated? Conflict and Persecution as the Context of Paul's Original Ministry in Galatia (Galatians 4.12–20)." *Journal for the Study of the New Testament* 52 (1993): 93–126.

Gombis, Timothy G. "The 'Transgressor' and the 'Curse of the Law': The Logic of Paul's Argument in Galatians 2–3." *New Testament Studies* 53, no. 1 (2007): 81–93.

Goodrich, John K. "Guardians, not Taskmasters: the Cultural Resonances of Paul's Metaphor in Galatians 4.1–2." *Journal for the Study of the New Testament* 32, no. 3 (March 1, 2010): 251–284.

Gordon, T. David. "Abraham and Sinai Contrasted in Galatians 3:6–14." In *The Law Is Not of Faith: Essays on Works and Grace in the Mosaic Covenant*, edited by Bryan Estelle, J. V. Fesko, and David VanDrunen, 240–58 (Phillipsburg, NJ: P&R, 2009).

―――. "A Note on ΠΑΙΔΑΓΩΓΟΣ in Gal. 3. 24–25." *New Testament Studies* 35, no. 1 (January 1989): 150–54.

―――. "Observations on N. T. Wright's Biblical Theology with Special Consideration of 'Righteousness of God.'" In *By Faith Alone*, edited by Gary L. W. Johnson and Guy P. Waters, 61–73. Wheaton: Crossway, 2007.

―――. "The Problem at Galatia." *Interpretation* 41 (January 1987): 32–43.

―――. "Why Israel Did Not Obtain Torah-Righteousness: A Translation Note on Romans 9:32." *Westminster Theological Journal* 54 (1992): 163–66.

Hafemann, Scott J. "Paul and the Exile of Israel in Galatians 3–4." In *Exile: Old Testament, Jewish, and Christian Conceptions*, edited by James M. Scott, 329–71. Leiden: E. J. Brill, 1997.

―――. *Paul, Moses, and the History of Israel: The Letter/Spirit Contrast and the Argument from Scripture in 2 Corinthians 3.* Peabody, MA: Hendrickson, 1995.

Hahn, Scott. "Covenant, Oath, and the *Aqedah: diathēkē* in Galatians 3:15–18." *Catholic Biblical Quarterly* 67, no. 1 (January 1, 2005): 79–100.

Harrisville, Roy A. "*Pistis Christou* : Witness of the Fathers." *Novum testamentum* 36, no. 3 (July 1, 1994): 233–41.

Hong, In-Gyu. "Does Paul Misrepresent the Jewish Law? Law and Covenant in Gal 3:1–14." *Novum testamentum* 36, no. 2 (April 1, 1994): 164–82.

Hübner, Hans. *Law in Paul's Thought.* Translated by James C. G. Greig. Edinburgh: T & T Clark, 1984.

Hunn, Debbie. "Christ versus the Law: Issues in Galatians 2:17–18." *Catholic Biblical Quarterly* 72, no. 3 (July 1, 2010): 537–55.

———. "*Ean mē* in Galatians 2:16: a look at Greek literature." *Novum testamentum* 49, no. 3 (January 1, 2007): 281–90.

Johnson, S. Lewis, Jr. "Paul and 'the Israel of God': an Exegetical and Eschatological Case-study." *Master's Seminary Journal* 20, no. 1 (2009): 41–55.

Kim, Seyoon. *Paul and the New Perspective: Second Thoughts on the Origin of Paul's Gospel.* Grand Rapids: Eerdmans, 2002.

Koptak, Paul E. "Rhetorical Identification in Paul's Autobiographical Narrative: Galatians 1:13–2:14." *Journal for the Study of the New Testament* 40 (October 1, 1990): 97–113.

Kuula, Kari. *The Law, the Covenant and God's Plan. 1, Paul's Polemical Treatment of the Law in Galatians.* Helsinki / Gottingen: Suomen Eksegeettinen Seura / Vandenhoeck & Ruprecht, 1999.

Longenecker, Richard, ed. *The Road from Damascus: The Impact of Paul's Conversion on His Life, Thought, and Ministry* (Grand Rapids: Eerdmans, 1997).

Lull, David John. "The Law Was Our Pedagogue": A Study in Galatians 3:19–25." *Journal of Biblical Literature* 105, no. 3 (September 1, 1986): 481–98.

Martin, Troy W. "The Covenant of Circumcision (Genesis 17:9–14) and the Situational Antithesis in Galatians 3:28." *Journal of Biblical Literature* 122, no. 1 (March 1, 2003): 111–25.

———. "Whose Flesh? What Temptation? (Galatians 4.13–14)." *Journal for the Study of the New Testament* no. 74 (June 1, 1999): 65–91.

Martyn, J. Louis. *Galatians: A New Translation with Introduction and Commentary.* The Anchor Bible. New Haven, CT: Yale University Press, 2004.

Matera, Frank J. "The Culmination of Paul's Argument to the Galatians: Gal 5:1–6:17." *Journal for the Study of the New Testament* 32 (February 1, 1988): 79–91.

———. *Galatians.* Collegeville, MN: Liturgical Press, 2007.

———. "Galatians and the Development of Paul's Teaching on Justification." *Word & World* 20, no. 3 (June 1, 2000): 239–48.

———. "Galatians in Perspective: Cutting a New Path through Old Territory." *Interpretation* 54, no. 3 (July 1, 2000): 233–45.

Matlock, R. Barry. "Detheologizing the *pistis Christou* debate: Cautionary Remarks from a Lexical Semantic Perspective." *Novum testamentum* 42, no. 1 (January 1, 2000): 1–23.

———. "The Rhetoric of *pistis* in Paul: Galatians 2:16, 3:22, Romans 3:22, and Philippians 3:9." *Journal for the Study of the New Testament* 30, no. 2 (December 1, 2007): 173–203.

———. "Sins of the Flesh and Suspicious Minds: Dunn's New Theology of Paul." *Journal for the Study of the New Testament* 72 (1998): 67–90.

Merk, Otto. "Der Beginn der Paränese im Galaterbrief." *Zeitschrift für die neutesta-mentliche Wissenschaft und die Kunde der älteren Kirche* 60 (1969): 83–104.

Moo, Douglas J. "'Law,' 'Works of the Law,' and Legalism in Paul." *Westminster Theological Journal* 45, no. 1 (March 1, 1983): 73–100.

Moore, George Foot. "Christian Writers on Judaism." *Harvard Theological Review*. Vol. 14, no. 3 (July 1921): 197–254.

Najman, Hindy. "Angels at Sinai: Exegesis, Theology and Interpretive Authority." *Dead Sea Discoveries* 7, no. 3 (January 1, 2000): 313–33.

Neusner, Jacob. "Comparing Judaisms." Review of *Paul and Palestinian Judaism: A Comparison of Patterns of Religion*, by E. P. Sanders. *History of Religions* 18, no. 2 (November 1978): 177–91.

Oakes, Peter. "The Curse of the Law and the Crisis in Galatia." *Journal for the Study of the New Testament* 30, no. 5 (January 1, 2008): 89–318.

O'Brien, Kelli S. "The Curse of the Law (Galatians 3.13): Crucifixion, Persecution, and Deuteronomy 21.22–23." *Journal for the Study of the New Testament* 29, no. 1 (September 1, 2006): 55–76.

Räisänen, Heikki. *Paul and the Law*. Philadelphia: Fortress, 1983.

Russell, Walt. "The Apostle Paul's Redemptive-Historical Argumentation in Galatians 5:13–26." *Westminster Theological Journal* 57 (1995): 333–57.

Saldarini, Anthony J. Review of *Paul and Palestinian Judaism: A Comparison of Patterns of Religion*, by E. P. Sanders. *Journal of Biblical Literature* 98, no. 2 (June 1979): 299–300, 302–3.

Sandnes, Karl Olav. *Paul—One of the Prophets?* Wissenschaftliche Untersuchungen zum Neuen Testament 2.43. Tübingen: Mohr-Siebeck, 1998.

Schreiner, Thomas R. *The Law and Its Fulfillment: A Pauline Theology of Law*. Grand Rapids: Baker, 1993.

Scott, Ian W. "Common Ground? The Role of Galatians 2.16 in Paul's Argument." *New Testament Studies* 53, no. 3 (2007): 425–35.

Scott, James M. *Adoption as Sons of God: An Exegetical Investigation into the Background of ΥΙΟΘΕΣΙΑ in the Pauline Corpus*. Wissenschaftliche Untersuchungen zum Neuen Testament 2.48. Tübingen: J. C. B. Mohr, 1992.

Seifrid, Mark A. "The Galatians Debate: Contemporary Issues in Rhetorical and Historical Interpretation." *Trinity Journal* 25, no. 2 (September 1, 2004): 267–70.

Silva, Moisés. "Abraham, Faith, and Works: Paul's Use of Scripture in Galatians 3:6–14." *Westminster Theological Journal* 63, no. 2 (September 1, 2001): 251–67.

Stendahl, Krister. "Paul and the Introspective Conscience of the West." *Harvard Theological Review* 56, no. 3 (July, 1963): 199–215. Reprinted in his *Paul among Jews and Gentiles*, 78–97. Philadelphia: Fortress, 1976.

Talbert, Charles H. "Paul on the Covenant." *Review & Expositor* 84, no. 2 (March 1, 1987): 299–313.

Taylor, Greer M. "The Function of ΠΙΣΤΙΣ ΧΡΙΣΤΟΥ in Galatians." *Journal of Biblical Literature* 85, no. 1 (March 1966): 58–76.

Udoh, Fabian E. "Paul's Views on the Law: Questions about Origin (Gal 1:6–2:21; Phil 3:2–11)." *Novum testamentum* 42, no. 3 (January 1, 2000): 214–37.

Van Voorst, Robert E. "Why Is There No Thanksgiving Period in Galatians? An Assessment of an Exegetical Commonplace." *Journal of Biblical Literature* 129, no. 1 (March 1, 2010): 153–72.

Vos, Johan S. "Paul's Argumentation in Galatians 1–2." *Harvard Theological Review* 87, no. 1 (January 1, 1994): 1–16.

Walker, William O. "Does the 'We' in Gal 2.15–17 Include Paul's Opponents?" *New Testament Studies* 49, no. 4 (October 2003): 560–65.

———. "Galatians 2:8 and the Question of Paul's Apostleship." *Journal of Biblical Literature* 123, no. 2 (June 1, 2004): 323–27.

———. "Why Paul Went to Jerusalem: The Interpretation of Galatians 2:1–5." *Catholic Biblical Quarterly* 54, no. 3 (July 1, 1992): 503–10.

Watson, Francis B. *Paul, Judaism and the Gentiles beyond the New Perspective*. Revised and expanded edition. Grand Rapids: Eerdmans, 2007.

Westerholm, Stephen. "On Fulfilling the Whole Law (Gal 5:14)." *Svensk exegetisk årsbok* 51 (January 1, 1986): 229–37.

———. *Perspectives Old and New on Paul: The "Lutheran" Paul and His Critics*. Grand Rapids: Eerdmans, 2004.

———. "The Righteousness of the Law and the Righteousness of Faith in Romans." *Interpretation* 58, no. 3 (July 1, 2004): 253–64.

Williams, Sam K. "Promise in Galatians: A Reading of Paul's Reading of Scripture." *Journal of Biblical Literature* 107, no. 4 (December 1, 1988): 709–20.

Wilson, Todd A. "The Law of Christ and the Law of Moses: Reflections on a Recent Trend in Interpretation." *Currents in Biblical Research* 5, no. 1 (October 1, 2006): 123–44.

Witherington, Ben III. *Grace in Galatia: A Commentary on Paul's Letter to the Galatians*. New York: T & T Clark, 2004.

Wright, N. T. *The Climax of the Covenant: Christ and the Law in Pauline Theology*. Philadelphia: Fortress, 1992.

———. "The Paul of History and the Apostle of Faith." *Tyndale Bulletin* 29 (January 1, 1978): 61–88.

Young, Norman H. "Who's Cursed—and Why? (Galatians 3:10–14)." *Journal of Biblical Literature* 117, no. 1 (March 1, 1998): 79–92.